ENCYCLOPEDIA
of the
HOLOCAUST

ENCYCLOPEDIA
of the
HOLOCAUST

Israel Gutman, Editor in Chief

Volume 4

Yad Vashem
The Holocaust Martyrs' and Heroes'
  Remembrance Authority
Jerusalem

Sifriat Poalim Publishing House
Tel Aviv

MACMILLAN PUBLISHING COMPANY
NEW YORK
Collier Macmillan Publishers
LONDON

Copyright © 1990 by Macmillan Publishing Company
A Division of Macmillan, Inc.
Foreword copyright © 1990 by Elirion Associates

Macmillan Publishing Company
866 Third Avenue
New York, New York 10022
Collier Macmillan Canada, Inc.
Library of Congress Catalog Card Number: 89-13466
Printed in the United States of America

printing number
2   3   4   5   6   7   8   9   10

Library of Congress Cataloging-in-Publication Data

Encyclopedia of the Holocaust / Israel Gutman, editor in chief.
p.   cm.
Includes bibliographical references.
ISBN 0–02–896090–4 (set)
Trade edition ISBN 0–02–546705–0 (set)
1. Holocaust, Jewish (1939–1945)—Dictionaries. I. Gutman,
Israel.
D804.3.E53   1990   89-13466
940.53'18'-03—dc20   CIP

Acknowledgments of sources
and permissions to use previously published materials
are made in Acknowledgments, page xix.

S

SA (Sturmabteilung; Storm Troopers), the Nazi party's main instrument for undermining democracy and facilitating Adolf HITLER's rise to power.

Early History (1923–1926). The name "Storm Troopers" was derived, like many others in the Nazi vocabulary, from the military jargon of World War I. Hitler conceived of the organization's structure, role, and social composition as being similar to those of the urban street gangs known as "shock troops" and Benito MUSSOLINI's Blackshirts. Led by Hermann GÖRING, the SA and other ultranationalist groups tried to imitate Mussolini's March on Rome. The result was the Munich Putsch (the Beer-Hall Putsch) of November 9, 1923. The attempted putsch ended in failure when members of the SA and their associates were easily dispersed by the fire of the Bavarian state police. Subsequently, the SA, together with all the other Nazi organizations, was outlawed.

After the SA was legalized once more in 1924, Hitler never again risked an open confrontation with the organs of the state, regarding the SA more as a political tool subordinated to himself as the party Führer. He developed the concept of SA terror by means of street fights between the storm troopers and their political enemies, especially the Communists. The storm troopers' terror activities were accompanied by propaganda against the Weimar Republic as "Jewish, corrupt, and a disgrace to German dignity, integrity, and greatness." The SA caused constant turmoil in Germany, but nonetheless acted more or less within the limits of the Weimar Constitution. This strategy, which required blind obedience to Hitler's tactics, did not always satisfy the impatient members or the *Oberste SA Führer* (Supreme Commander of the SA; OSAF), Reichswehr captain Ernst RÖHM, a former Freikorps leader who had taken over the northern SA during Hitler's imprisonment in the Landsberg prison in 1924. Röhm shared the attitude of many World War I veterans that the SA should revolutionize the regular army and direct it toward war against domestic and foreign enemies. Many members also developed a vague plan for far-reaching social change, designed to benefit the SA's own membership. On the whole, the SA was characterized by virulent antisemitism (partly a legacy from World War I), antidemocratic illegal military activities, the rejection of bourgeois law and order, a lower middle-class mentality, corruption, and bids for personal power.

From 1926 to 1931. When his semi-independence was rejected by Hitler, Röhm left Germany, and another army captain, Franz Felix Pfeffer von Salomon, took his place. The new SA leader followed the same line as his predecessor, but with less ability. As long as the SA membership came mainly from the army and from Freikorps veterans, Hitler had to accept Pfeffer's role as OSAF.

Toward the end of the 1920s, the traditional German Right had great difficulty in attracting the younger, half-educated urban population and peasantry. The SA benefited from this situation, focusing on recruitment in the provincial areas, while the Communists and Social Democrats concentrated their efforts on the urban proletariat. The SA "spirit" was unified not so much through a clear ideology as by the prevailing conditions of widespread unemployment and low wages, and by barroom camaraderie, romantic quasi-military outdoor drill, and campfire talk. The problems of alienation from urban life and the decline of agriculture also drew people to the SA.

Pfeffer was forced to step down in 1930, after the Berlin SA launched an aborted revolt against the party because of its desire for greater independence and its impatience with the party's tactics against the Weimar Republic. For a short while, Hitler himself assumed command of the SA, but following the Nazi electoral breakthrough of 1930, he invited Röhm to return to Germany and serve as chief of the SA High Command.

Under Röhm (1931–1934). Röhm divided Germany into twenty-one military-like SA districts, each under an SA *Obergruppenführer*. Röhm also created flying squads, the Nationalsozialistisches Kraftfahrkorps (Nazi Motor Corps), and reorganized the SA High Command, dividing it into two main departments (*Abteilungen*). Department I was placed under former general Franz Ritter von Hörauf, and was responsible for organization and planning. Department Q (Quartiermeister, or Quartermaster), under Oswald Fuchs, was the operational headquarters of the SA. Röhm himself directly controlled divisions IC (intelligence); IIA (personnel); IVA (organization and finance); PR (press service); the SA unit in charge of the party's central office; the Munich and Bavarian SA; and, nominally, Heinrich HIMMLER's SS.

Membership in the SA grew enormously between 1930 and 1932, owing in great part to the economic crisis and the unemployment that at the time was devastating the middle and working classes. But perhaps even more important was the bankruptcy of political alternatives, especially that of the right wing, and their inability to appeal to the masses of the young. In its propaganda, the SA presented itself as an alternative to the "mechanical, competitive, and alienating modern world of the liberal-conservatives or Communists," putting forward the Jew as a symbol of these menaces. SA men became part of a dynamic mob, giving them a sense of belonging to a community, whose members were promised personal rewards at the expense of the rich and the powerful. In his strategy for undermining the Weimar Republic, Hitler had to find a way to restrain the SA, while at the same time brandishing it as a threatening weapon against the upper, conservative classes and the army. He coaxed these segments of society with the argument that if they did not cooperate with the Nazi party they were risking an open SA revolution.

When the SA and the rest of the Nazi party failed to topple the Weimar Republic in the November 1932 elections, they felt they had suffered a serious setback. But ultraconservatives and army generals, thinking that Hitler could ensure mass SA support for a coalition government, made him chancellor on January 30, 1933. This opened up access to power and key positions for the SA. In particular, SA men were drafted into the auxiliary police, and as such they arrested, tortured, and terrorized political, ideological, and personal enemies in abandoned barracks or factory yards that became known as CONCENTRATION CAMPS.

After Hitler had established himself as sole ruler, or leader (Führer), of Germany, the SA perceived itself as the decisive power in the country. It appointed SA commissars to supervise the state bureaucracy and coordinate its "revolutionary change" with the party, and awaited the personal, social, and economic rewards promised to the rank and file. It also made Jews its target of attack. Hitler, however, was not interested in the social revolution envisioned by the SA. He was more concerned with the military expansion of the Third Reich as a racial entity. For this he needed upper-class expertise, army support, and time for consolidating his power. When Röhm openly expressed disappointment and gave the impression that he intended to take over the army, he and the SA leadership were massacred by Himmler's SS. The night of mass political assassinations, on June 30, 1934, called the *Nacht der langen Messer* ("Night of the Long Knives"), resulted in the SA's losing its position of predominance in the Third Reich to the SS. However, the organization was allowed to continue to exist, and Hitler used it as a potential revolutionary antisemitic threat that could be unleashed against the upper classes, the banned working-class parties, and the unions to secure their cooperation with the Nazi regime.

BIBLIOGRAPHY

Fischer, C. *Stormtroopers: A Social, Economic, and Ideological Analysis, 1929–1935.* London, 1983.

Merkl, P. H. *The Making of a Stormtrooper.* Princeton, 1980.

Reiche, E. G. *The Development of the SA in Nuremberg, 1922–1934.* Cambridge, 1986.

SHLOMO ARONSON

Jewish prisoners in the Sachsenhausen camp.

"SABBATH DELIGHT." *See* Oneg Shabbat.

SACHSENHAUSEN, concentration camp near Berlin. The Sachsenhausen camp was located in the immediate vicinity of the Inspectorate of Concentration Camps, on the outskirts of ORANIENBURG. It was built by teams of prisoners transferred to the site from small camps in the Ems area and elsewhere, beginning in July 1936. As indicated in a letter written by Heinrich HIMMLER to the minister of justice, Sachsenhausen, like BUCHENWALD, was built with a view to its use in wartime, for an expected intake of large numbers of prisoners. In November 1938, following the KRISTALLNACHT pogrom, 1,800 Jews were sent to Sachsenhausen; some 450 of them were murdered shortly after their arrival in the camp.

The figures in the table show the fluctuation of the Sachsenhausen prison population (as of the end of December of each year).

1936	1939	1942
2,000	12,168	16,577
1937	**1940**	**1943**
2,523	11,697	28,224
1938	**1941**	**1944**
8,309	11,111	47,709

The total number of persons imprisoned in Sachsenhausen was approximately 200,000. When World War II began, conditions in the camp deteriorated sharply: in 1939, more than 800 prisoners died there, and in 1940 this number increased to nearly 4,000. In 1940, 26,000 prisoners, mainly from Poland, were delivered to the camp; most of them stayed only a short while and were then transferred to other camps in the Reich. At some point, probably in August 1941, the SS set up an installation for mass executions by shooting, disguising it as a prisoners' examination room. In the following months, 13,000 to 18,000 Soviet prisoners of war, who were not even registered in the camp's lists, were murdered there. The camp also had a gas chamber, probably installed in 1943; it was added to an existing crematorium compound. The gas chamber was used on special orders only; one such occasion, presumably, was in February 1945, when the SS had several thousand physically debilitated prisoners killed on the eve of the camp's evacuation. In addition to the Soviet prisoners of war executed on arrival and those prisoners who died en route to and from the camp and during its evacuation, some 30,000 persons perished in Sachsenhausen.

In the first few years, the most important work project was a brickyard that prisoners built in the spring of 1938, on the Oder-Havel canal. Some two thousand prisoners were put to work on the project on a daily basis. In April 1941 a satellite camp was established for the brickyard work team; conditions in it were exceptionally harsh, and prisoners whose assignment to it was lengthy had little chance of surviving.

From 1943 on, the prisoners were employed primarily in various branches of the armaments industry, especially in the production of engines for aircraft, tanks, and vehicles. In 1944, seven thousand prisoners were assigned to the Heinkel Works in Oranienburg. Another large contingent was employed at the DEMAG tank plant in Falkensee, near Berlin. Special satellite camps were put up for both these plants. The brickyard was converted to the manufacture of grenades.

Sachsenhausen was liberated on April 27, 1945, by advance troops of the Soviet army. At that point the camp contained only three thousand prisoners, most of whom were not fit for marching. All the other prisoners had been evacuated by the SS.

BIBLIOGRAPHY

Szalet, T. *Experiment "E": A Report from an Extermination Laboratory.* New York, 1945.

Todeslager Sachsenhausen: Ein Dokumentarbericht vom Sachsenhausen-Prozess. Berlin, 1948.

Van Dam, H. G., and R. Giordano, eds. *KZ-Verbrechen vor deutschen Gerichten: Dokumente aus den Prozessen gegen Sommer (KZ Buchenwald); Sorge, Schubert (KZ Sachsenhausen); Unkelbach (Ghetto in Czenstochau); Der Prozess zu Ulm.* Frankfurt, 1962.

FALK PINGEL

SAFRAN, ALEXANDER (b. 1910), Chief Rabbi of ROMANIA from 1940 to 1947. A native of Bacău, Safran studied at the rabbinical seminary in Vienna, and completed his doctorate at the University of Vienna. On his return to Romania he became rabbi in his hometown. In 1940, at the age of thirty, he was elected Chief Rabbi of Romania at a most critical moment for the country's Jews, with the IRON GUARD gaining in strength and the whole country becoming fascist.

The body that elected Safran was composed of rabbis and Jewish community representatives of the Regat (Romania in its pre–World War I borders), with the chief rabbis of the other parts of the country (BESSARABIA, BUKOVINA, and TRANSYLVANIA) also supporting their choice. Within a short while Safran gained the recognition and respect of the Jewish and Romanian establishments. From April to August 1940 he was a member of the Romanian senate, the only public office still held by a Jew after the dissolution of all political parties and organizations by King Carol II in 1938. Safran cooperated with Wilhelm FILDERMAN, the veteran leader of Romanian Jewry and president of the Federatia Uniunilor de Comunitati Evreesti (Union of Jewish Communities), in efforts to persuade the Romanian government to desist from, or at least to moderate, its anti-Jewish legislation.

Even under the fascist regime of the Iron Guard (September 6, 1940, to January 24, 1941), Safran remained the representative of Romanian Jewry vis-à-vis the authorities, and as their dedicated spiritual leader he tried to keep up the Jews' morale with his sermons and by organizing relief operations. He helped the Jewish communities to establish independent Jewish educational institutions when Jewish students were excluded from the public schools, and he saw to it that the new schools were given a Jewish and Zionist complexion. Together with Filderman, Safran tried—unsuccessfully—to prevent the deportation to TRANSNISTRIA of the Jews of Bessarabia and Bukovina. In the fall of 1941 Safran lodged appeals with the country's dictator, Ion ANTONESCU; with the head of the Romanian church, Patriarch Nicodim; with the archbishop of Bukovina, Tit Simedria; and with Queen Mother Helena.

Following the dissolution of the Jewish communities by the authorities on December 17, 1941, Safran was one of the group that proposed the establishment ,of the Jewish Council, an underground leadership headed by Filderman and made up of representatives of all sectors of the Jewish population. As of the summer of 1942, Safran's home became the council's meeting place. The council was to play a role in forestalling the deportation of Romania's Jews to the extermination camps in Poland. Safran established highly important contacts with the royal court, with Romanian churchmen, and with the papal nuncio, Archbishop Andrea Cassulo, who frequently intervened on behalf of the Jews. In the summer of 1942 Safran persuaded the archbishop of Transylvania, Nicolae Balan, to intervene with Antonescu against the planned deportation of Romanian Jews to Poland. Through Cassulo, Safran transmitted to the Vatican reports on the true situation of Romanian Jewry and the threat of their ex-

Alexander Safran, Chief Rabbi of Romania, speaking at a Lag ba-Omer celebration (a Jewish semi-holiday) in Bucharest (May 5, 1942).

termination, and he also asked for the Vatican's intercession on behalf of the Jews of Hungary.

When Romania was liberated in August 1944, Safran was not prepared to cooperate with the Jewish Communists of the new Jewish Democratic Committee in the breakup of traditional Jewish organizations, since he would thereby be playing a part in bringing Jewish life in Romania to a standstill. As a result, in December 1947 he was dismissed from his post and forced to leave the country. He took up residence in Switzerland and became the rabbi of the Jewish community in Geneva. Safran's memoirs, *Resisting the Storm: Romania 1940–1947*, appeared in 1987.

BIBLIOGRAPHY

Lavi, T. *Rumanian Jewry in World War II: Fight for Survival.* Jerusalem, 1965. (In Hebrew.)

Lavi, T., ed. *Rumania*, vol. 1. In *Pinkas Hakehillot; Encyclopaedia of Jewish Communities*. Jerusalem, 1969. (In Hebrew.)

JEAN ANCEL

SAJMIŠTE, fairground in the Yugoslav town of Zemun (Ger., Semlin), on the Sava River, opposite Belgrade; site of an internment camp for Serbian Jews prior to their murder by gas van in the spring of 1942 (*see* GAS VANS).

In the fall of 1941, most of the male Jews and GYPSIES in SERBIA had been executed by Wehrmacht firing squads, as the most convenient way of simultaneously meeting the 100 to 1 reprisal quota for German soldiers killed by partisans and "solving the Jewish question." But the Wehrmacht would not shoot women and children, who were therefore interned in Sajmište until they could be deported to a "reception camp in the east." The large, unheated pavilions of the fairground were converted to barracks by constructing multistoried wooden scaffolding, through which the prisoners had to crawl on hands and knees. On December 8, 1941, the internment of all the remaining Jews and Gypsies began—mostly women and children, but also a few men.

In the spring of 1942 the Gypsy prisoners were freed, but the Jews were not deported to

SAJMIŠTE

HUNGARY

0   miles   60

0 kilometers 80

BAČKA
annexed by
Hungary,
April 1941

ROMANIA

Osijek

BANAT

Djakovo

Novi Sad

CROATIA

SAJMIŠTE • • Belgrade
• Avala

SERBIA
under German occupation
from April 1941

BOSNIA
• Sarajevo
AND
HERZEGOVINA

MONTENEGRO

© Martin Gilbert 1982

the "east," as planned earlier. The German authorities had constantly complained about a lack of assistance from Berlin in the task of removing the Serbian Jews, and in early March a gas van arrived from Germany for the Serbian authorities to use in eliminating the Jews in that area. Over a nine-week period between early March and early May, the Jews of Sajmište were loaded by groups into the gas van under the pretext of being relocated, gassed as the truck drove through Belgrade, and buried at Avala, south of the city. About 7,500 Jews perished at Sajmište —6,280 in the gas van and the rest from hunger and exposure.

After all the Jews had been killed, the Sajmište camp was filled with political prisoners. Though the German plenipotentiary to the Balkans, Herman Neubacher, complained in 1943 that the continuing existence of the camp "before the eyes of the people of Belgrade was politically intolerable for reasons of public feelings," it remained in use for detaining political prisoners throughout the German occupation, and by the end of the war, forty-seven thousand people had perished there.

BIBLIOGRAPHY

Browning, C. R. "The Final Solution in Serbia: The Semlin Judenlager—A Case Study." *Yad Vashem Studies* 15 (1983): 55–90.
Ivanović, L., and N. Vukomanović. *Dani smrti na Sajmištu.* Novi Sad, 1969.
Shelah, M. "Sajmiste, an Extermination Camp in Serbia." *Studies on the Holocaust Period* 4 (1986): 127–152. (In Hebrew.)

CHRISTOPHER R. BROWNING

SALIÈGE, JULES-GÉRARD (1870–1956), archbishop of Toulouse; an active opponent of anti-Jewish measures in France. Prior to World War I, Saliège came under the influence of innovative Catholic thinkers who advocated theological reassessment and deeper involvement in social and political issues. Saliège opposed racism as un-Christian in the 1930s and continued to do so with the advent of Vichy's antisemitic ideology in 1940. During the deportations of Jews from unoccupied France in August 1942, he composed a pastoral letter that he disseminated among all the parishes in his diocese. The letter, which had considerable impact on French public opinion and was widely reproduced, forcefully denounced the inhuman actions and demanded recognition of Jews as "brothers." Saliège's strong protest was part of the upheaval in opinion among leading Catholic figures in France on the "Jewish question," which produced widespread popular support for Jews in southern France from the summer of 1942.

BIBLIOGRAPHY

Guitton, J. *Le Cardinal Saliège.* Paris, 1957.
Marrus, M. R., and R. O. Paxton. *Vichy France and the Jews.* New York, 1981.
Wellers, G., A. Kapsi, and S. Klarsfeld, eds. *La France et la question juive (1940–1944): La politique de Vichy, l'attitude des églises et des mouvements de résistance.* Paris, 1981.

RICHARD COHEN

SALONIKA, main city and port of Macedonian GREECE. Between 1911 and 1941, the character of Salonika was transformed. In 1911 the Sephardic Jews, numbering 80,000 out of a total population of 173,000, were a dominant element. By the beginning of World War II, Salonika had become a Greek city with a large and unassimilable Judeo-Spanish-speaking minority. Jewish emigration, which increased after the turn of the century, was stimulated when waves of Anatolian Greek refugees were settled in Salonika by the Greek government after the population exchange with Turkey in 1923. From the ranks of these Greeks developed a fascist and anti-Jewish movement, the Ethniki Enosis Elladas (Greek National Union; EEE), which perpetrated attacks on the Jews (those that took place from 1931 to 1934 led to a mass exodus to Palestine of some 10,000 Jews). Anti-Jewish measures included a forced closing of stores on Sundays and increased emphasis on Greek studies in Hebrew and Ladino schools. After 1936 Ioannis Metaxas, the Greek dictator, restricted new Jewish and other minority participation in the army officer corps, but he restrained the antisemitic EEE.

On April 9, 1941, Germany conquered Salonika and its fifty thousand Jews. Within a week the Jewish council was arrested, apartments were confiscated, and the Jewish hospital was taken over for use by German troops. Three Jewish newspapers in French and Judeo-Spanish were suspended, and the antisemitic collaborationist newspapers *Nea-Evropi* and *Apoyeuma* appeared. During April and May of 1941 EINSATZSTAB ROSENBERG, assisted by WEHRMACHT units, systematically looted the five-hundred-year-old literary and cultural treasures from the dozens of private and institutional libraries and synagogues of this great center of Sephardic civilization. Most of the items were shipped to Frankfurt, where the Nazis were building up a Jewish research library.

The succeeding fourteen months were relatively calm in Salonika, with no new anti-

On July 11, 1942, 9,000 Jewish men were massed at Plateia Eleftheria (Liberty Square) in Salonika. Forced to do calisthenics in the blazing sun, the prisoners were beaten if they slowed down.

Jewish measures. The Jewish community was more concerned with the threat of starvation. During the severe winter of 1941–1942 some six hundred persons died of cold and disease. The community was thus unprepared for the developments of the next eight months, when the Jewish population was systematically ghettoized, its property liquidated or transferred to Nazi personal and state coffers, its real estate absorbed by the Greek municipality, and its members almost totally exterminated in the crematoria of AUSCHWITZ. On July 11, 1942, nine thousand Jewish males aged eighteen to forty-five were forced to gather at Plateia Eleftheria (Liberty Square), where they were humiliated in the burning sun all day. About two thousand were sent on forced labor for the German army. By October, two hundred and fifty had died. The community ransomed its young men through negotiations with Dr. Maximilian Merton, the adviser to the German military administration in German-occupied MACEDONIA. Part of the money was raised in Salonika and Athens; the rest came from the transfer of the five-hundred-year-old graveyard to the municipality, which systematically destroyed it, recycled its ancient stones for building material, and established a university in the midst of its ruins.

In December 1942, Dr. Zvi KORETZ, the chief rabbi, was made president of the newly created JUDENRAT (Jewish Council). Despite his efforts and protests and those of the Greek government and church, he was designated to represent the Jewish community in dealings with Dieter WISLICENY and Alois BRUNNER, Adolf EICHMANN's representatives, after their arrival on February 6, 1943. Beginning on February 8, Merton issued a series of edicts to implement the NUREMBERG LAWS and isolate the Jews. These were enforced by Vital Hasson, Edgar Chounio, L. Topaz, and J. Albala, who were convicted after the war for collaboration. Rabbi Koretz's role as head of the Judenrat is controversial. Historians writing in the immediate postwar years criticized his seeming lack of leadership; others have tried to revise this picture.

Beginning on February 25, deportation convoys were prepared by assembling Jews in the Baron Hirsch quarter, located near the railway station. These transports, nineteen or twenty in all and comprising at least 43,850

Jews, arrived from March 20 to August 18 at Auschwitz-Birkenau, where most of the Jews were gassed on arrival. Although 11,200 survived Selektionen (4,200 women and 7,000 men), most of these died later. Some of the women were subjects of Dr. Carl CLAUBERG's sterilization research at Auschwitz. In August, Rabbi Koretz and the Judenrat, including the Jewish police, were deported to BERGEN-BELSEN. The blocked bank accounts of Jews were taken over by the German military administration in Salonika.

Jews holding Spanish, Italian, Turkish, and some other passports were not killed, although 367 Jews granted Spanish nationality passed through Bergen-Belsen on their way to Spain. Italian efforts to protect Salonikan Jews were a source of friction with the Germans. Some individuals were helped to escape to the Italian zone, and others were given Italian citizenship. Italy was only partially successful in protecting the Salonikan diaspora in occupied Europe. An undetermined number of Salonikan Jews escaped to Palestine with partisan help.

Hundreds of Jews from Salonika survived the many labor and extermination camps. After the war they joined the Jews who had taken refuge in the mountains or those (about 500) who had fought with the partisans. In 1945 the Salonikan Jewish community numbered 1,950. Many of them suffered insults and attacks as "Communists" during the subsequent civil war in Greece. This persecution stimulated further emigration to Israel, the United States, and South America.

BIBLIOGRAPHY

Eck, N. "New Light on the Charges against the Last Chief Rabbi of Salonica." Yad Vashem Bulletin 17 (December 1965): 9–15; 19 (October 1966): 28–35.

Molho, M., and N. J. Nehama. In Memoriam. Salonika, 1973.

Roth, C. "The Last Days of Jewish Salonica: What Happened to a 450-Year-Old Civilization." Commentary 10/1 (July 1950): 49–55.

STEVEN B. BOWMAN

"SANCTIFYING LIFE." See Kiddush ha-Hayyim.

"SANCTIFYING THE NAME [OF GOD]." *See* Kiddush ha-Shem.

SARAJEVO, city in YUGOSLAVIA; capital of the republic of Bosnia and Herzegovina. Founded in the thirteenth century, Sarajevo came under Hungarian, Ottoman, and Austro-Hungarian rule, and after World War I became part of Yugoslavia. Following the German occupation of that country in April 1941, Sarajevo became part of the Independent State of CROATIA.

Jews first settled in Sarajevo in the fifteenth century, and the community became one of the important Sephardic centers in Europe. Early in 1941, Sarajevo had a Jewish population of eight thousand to nine thousand Sephardim and one thousand Ashkenazim, approximately 10 percent of the total population.

When the Germans occupied the city the local Croatian population (most of whom were Muslims) went on a rampage against the Jews and destroyed the magnificent Sephardic synagogue. Like the rest of Croatian Jewry, Sarajevo Jews suffered severely as a result of the anti-Jewish legislation, under which they were deprived of their livelihood, were required to wear the Jewish BADGE, were restricted in their freedom of movement and the area in which they could live, and were exposed to sporadic waves of arrest, physical assault, and execution in retaliation for sabotage acts carried out by the resistance movement.

On the night of September 3–4, 1941, the mass deportation of Sarajevo Jews to concentration camps was launched. Five hundred Jews were dispatched to the Kruscica camp, about 54.5 miles (88 km) northwest of Sarajevo. From there the women and children were moved to Loborgrad, about 198 miles (320 km) northwest of Sarajevo, and the men to the JASENOVAC camp. In the second wave, at the end of October, some fourteen hundred persons were deported, and in the third wave, which took place on November 17 and 18, three thousand were deported. Most of the men were taken to Jasenovac and murdered there; the women and children were put into the Djakovo camp, about 99 miles (159 km) northeast of Sarajevo. They remained there until early January 1942, when they too were taken to Jasenovac and murdered. By early 1942 the Jewish community of Sarajevo had been liquidated. The deportation operation was supervised by Sturmbannführer Alfred Heinrich, the SS representative in Sarajevo, and was carried out under the command of USTAŠA security police officer Ivan Tolj. The officials whom the authorities placed in charge of the Jews, two judges named Srecko Bujas and Branko Milaković, tried to save the Jews and relieve their plight, but all their efforts were in vain.

Some twenty-four hundred Sarajevo Jews survived, most of them by fleeing to the Italian-occupied zone of Croatia. Others escaped to the partisans and took part in the liberation of the country. When the war was over, fourteen hundred Jews returned to Sarajevo. A few years later some five hundred of them settled in Israel. In 1987 Sarajevo had a Jewish population of about eleven hundred.

BIBLIOGRAPHY

Friedenreich, H. P. *The Jews of Yugoslavia: A Quest for Community.* Philadelphia, 1979.

Loker, Z., ed. *Yugoslavia.* In *Pinkas Hakehillot; Encyclopaedia of Jewish Communities.* Jerusalem, 1988. (In Hebrew.)

Shelah, M. "The Jews of Yugoslavia: The Communities in Serbia and Croatia." *Pe'amim* 27 (1986): 31–61. (In Hebrew.)

MENACHEM SHELAH

SATU-MARE (Hung., Szatmár-Németi or Szatmár), city in northern TRANSYLVANIA that Hungary acquired from Romania in September 1940. A center of Orthodoxy and Hasidism (the home of Rabbi Joel Teitelbaum, the founder and leader of the Satmar Hasidic sect), the city had, according to the census of 1941, a population of 52,011, of whom 12,960 (24.9 percent) were Jewish. László ENDRE and the other leading "de-Judaizers" of Hungary convened in Satu-Mare on April 26, 1944, to work out the details for the liquidation of the Jews of northern Transylvania, excepting those of the Hungarian autonomous district of Székely Land, whose fate was decided two days later in TÎRGU-MUREŞ (Maros-Vásárhely).

The Jews of Satu-Mare were ordered into a

SATU-MARE

Annexations from June to September 1940: (1) Bessarabia and (2) N. Bukovina to USSR; (3) N. Transylvania to Hungary; (4) S. Dobruja to Bulgaria.

0   160 miles   1 in.

0   300 km.   3 cm.

ghetto, established in the Jewish section of the city, on May 3. At its peak, it held some 19,000 Jews, including those who were brought in from the rural communities in the Arded (Erdöd), Carei (Nagykároly), and Satu-Mare (Szatmár-Németi) districts. The internal administration of the ghetto was the responsibility of a Judenrat (Jewish Council), composed mostly of the traditional leaders of the community, including Zoltán Schwartz and József Borgida. The police officer in charge of the ghetto was Béla Sárközi, who acted in concert with other police and gendarmerie officials in pursuit of Jewish wealth. The ghetto was liquidated between May 19 and June 1 through the deportation to AUSCHWITZ of 18,863 Jews in six transports. According to the census of 1947, the city, which reverted to Romania after the war, had around 7,500 Jews. Many of them were from southern Transylvania and other parts of Romania where the Jews had survived almost intact.

BIBLIOGRAPHY

Braham, R. L. *Genocide and Retribution*. Boston, 1981. See pages 31–32, 101–112.

A szatmári zsidóság története. Tel Aviv, 1983.

RANDOLPH L. BRAHAM

SAUCKEL, FRITZ (1894–1946), Nazi plenipotentiary-general for labor mobilization from 1942 to 1945. Sauckel was born at Hassfurt am Main, to a family of minor officials. He spent the years before World War I working in the Norwegian and Swedish merchant navies. During the war he was interned in a French prisoner-of-war camp, and he later worked in a factory. An early Nazi (he joined the party in 1921), Sauckel was appointed *Gauleiter* of Thuringia in 1925 and its governor in 1933. He also held senior honorary rank in the SA (Sturmabteilung; Storm Troopers) and the SS.

When World War II broke out, Sauckel was appointed Reich defense commissioner for the Kassel military district, and in 1942, plenipotentiary-general for labor mobilization. His task was to supply the manpower required for the armaments and munitions production program. As a result, millions of workers were seized in the occupied territories to work in German industry. Sauckel di-

Fritz Sauckel in his prison cell in Nuremberg, where he was held during his trial before the International Military Tribunal. [United States Army]

rected that they were to be exploited "to the highest degree possible at the lowest conceivable degree of expenditure." This policy also accounted for the death of many thousands of Jewish workers in Poland. Sauckel was tried and convicted at Nuremberg for war crimes and crimes against humanity, and was hanged there on October 16, 1946.

BIBLIOGRAPHY

Ferencz, B. *Less than Slaves: Jewish Forced Labor and the Quest for Compensation.* Cambridge, Mass., 1979.

Homze, E. L. *Foreign Labor in Nazi Germany.* Princeton, 1967.

LIONEL KOCHAN

SCHACHT, HJALMAR (1877–1970), German economist and political figure. In his capacity as currency commissioner (1923) and president of Germany's central bank, the

Hjalmar Schacht in his prison cell in Nuremberg, during the period when he was on trial before the International Military Tribunal. [United States Army]

Reichsbank (1924–1930), Schacht assisted in halting the galloping inflation of 1923. In 1930 he resigned his post, in protest against the government's policy on the reparations that the Versailles Treaty had imposed on Germany. Schacht took an extremely active part in the rightist nationalist opposition and played a central role in the political intrigues that culminated in Adolf Hitler's appointment as chancellor in January 1933.

In March 1933 Schacht was reappointed president of the Reichsbank, and in August 1934 he also became minister of economic affairs. In May 1935 he was made *Generalbevollmächtigter für die Kriegswirtschaft* (Chief Plenipotentiary for the War Economy). It was Schacht who directed the rehabilitation of the German economy under Hitler and the reestablishment of Germany's military power. He did not, however, join the Nazi party and did not have the full confidence of the Nazi regime's leaders, his differences with them becoming sharper as time went on. In November 1937, when preparations began for putting the German economy on a war footing, Schacht resigned as minister of economic affairs, and in January 1939 he was dismissed from his post as Reichsbank president. Officially, however, he retained a post in the cabinet as minister without portfolio, up to 1943. Following the July 20, 1944, assassination attempt against Hitler, Schacht was put in a concentration camp because of his loose ties with the conservative resistance circles led by Carl Friedrich Goerdeler. Because of these circumstances, Schacht was one of the few defendants at the NUREMBERG TRIAL to be acquitted of all charges.

Schacht's positions and actions in connection with the persecution of the Jews have not yet been thoroughly researched. At the Nuremberg trial and in his books of memoirs, he claimed to have been a "protector of the Jews." Research literature also frequently contains the assessment that Schacht's "protective hand" enabled the Jews to maintain their economic activities, with hardly any interference, until his resignation as minister of economic affairs at the end of 1937. Schacht's views, even those that emerge in the books he wrote after the war, were those of a "respectable" conservative antisemite who disapproved of violence against Jews but favored legal restrictions, designed to "put the Jews in their proper place" and keep them from "instilling a foreign spirit into the host nation." Nevertheless, for pragmatic reasons Schacht wanted certain Jews to take part in Germany's economic life, and he had the courage to protest, in confidential memorandums and even in public, against the "illegal" persecution of the Jews. He denounced the November 1938 KRISTALLNACHT pogroms at a meeting of Reichsbank employees as "a crime that ought to make the face of every decent German flush with shame."

At the end of 1938, Schacht, with Hitler's permission, negotiated with George Rublee, director of the INTERGOVERNMENTAL COMMITTEE ON REFUGEES set up at the EVIAN CONFERENCE, a proposal to facilitate the emigration of the Jews of Germany with the help of an international loan to be raised by world Jewry. The representatives of Jewish organizations were divided over Schacht's proposal, which lent itself to the interpretation that world Jewry was prepared to give up to the Reich a large part of the assets of German Jewry. The negotiations continued even after Schacht's dismissal from the Reichsbank in January 1939, but no agreement was reached.

All in all, Schacht's statements and memorandums on the persecution of the Jews are evidence that the persecution and the anti-Jewish policy as a whole did not mean enough to him to impel him to an open confrontation with Hitler or other top Nazi leaders. The boycott of Jewish businesses and the elimination of Jews from the German economy proceeded throughout the time that Schacht was in office, and there is no record of any important issue on which he gave all-out support to the Jews, even in matters that were under his direct authority.

After the war, Schacht wrote two books about his years in office, published in English as *Account Settled* (1949) and *Confessions of the Old Wizard* (1955).

BIBLIOGRAPHY

Barkai, A. *The Nazi Economy: Ideology, Theory, Policy.* Tel Aviv, 1986. (In Hebrew.)

Schleunes, K. *The Twisted Road to Auschwitz: Nazi Policy toward German Jews, 1933–1939.* Urbana, Ill., 1970.
Simpson, A. E. *Hjalmar Schacht in Perspective.* The Hague, 1969.

AVRAHAM BARKAI

SCHELLENBERG, WALTER (1910–1952), head of espionage services in the Third Reich. Schellenberg was born in Saarbrücken and studied medicine and law, graduating from the University of Bonn with a degree in law. He joined the Nazi party and the SS in May 1933, and the Head Office (Hauptamt) of the SD (Sicherheitsdienst; Security Service) in 1934. Schellenberg organized the consolidation of the Sicherheitspolizei (Security Police) and the SD into the REICHSSICHERHEITSHAUPTAMT (Reich Security Main Office; RSHA). He himself assumed command, in September 1939, of its Section (Amtsgruppe) IV E, dealing with internal counterespionage in Germany and the Nazi-occupied countries. In November 1939, Schellenberg's success in kidnapping from the Netherlands two British military intelligence agents brought him promotion to the rank of *Standartenführer* in the SS. He was entrusted with security police preparations for an eventual invasion of Great Britain. When this was canceled, he became acting chief of Amt VI, dealing with foreign intelligence (with Heinrich HIMMLER's support), on June 22, 1941, the day the Germans invaded the Soviet Union. He saw his mission as the gathering and evaluation of both overt and covert information, to be used primarily for planning and achieving long-range objectives. To facilitate this, Schellenberg set up information centers under the aegis of Amt VI in all the European capitals.

In the summer of 1942, Schellenberg became involved in Operation Zeppelin, for the parachuting of retrained anti-Communist Soviet prisoners of war into Soviet territory. It was hoped that this would counter the effects of anti-Nazi partisans. Most of the parachutists were eventually caught and executed by the NKVD, the Soviet secret police. Some of the candidates for the mission, found unsuitable for it by the Nazis, were killed, with Schellenberg's knowledge and cooperation.

From August 1942, Schellenberg encouraged Himmler's attempts to extricate Germany from the war in the west. As the signs of Germany's impending defeat increased, Himmler formulated plans to contact the western Allies through the International RED CROSS and Allen Dulles, chief of the United States Office of Strategic Services (OSS) in Bern, Switzerland, and offer them a separate peace. These plans did not come to fruition, but they were instrumental in gaining the release of numerous people held prisoner by the Nazis.

In 1944, with the liquidation of the ABWEHR (the German military intelligence service), Schellenberg was made chief of the combined SS and Wehrmacht intelligence network. His authority in the SS was now surpassed only by that of Himmler.

After the war, Schellenberg was tried in the American zone of occupied Germany as a co-defendant along with Ernst von WEIZSÄCKER and others. He was acquitted of the crime of genocide, but was found guilty of complicity in the murder of Soviet prisoners of war during Operation Zeppelin, and was sentenced in 1949 to six years' imprisonment (to begin as of June 1945). Owing to ill health he was released in June 1951. Schellenberg moved to Switzerland, where he wrote his memoirs, published in English as *The Schellenberg Memoirs* (1956).

BIBLIOGRAPHY

Brissaud, A. *Histoire du service secret nazi.* Paris, 1972.

LIONEL KOCHAN

SCHINDLER, OSKAR (1908–1974), protector of Jews during the Holocaust. Schindler was born in Svitavy (Ger., Zwittau), in the Sudetenland, and came to KRAKÓW in late 1939, in the wake of the German invasion of Poland. There he took over two previously Jewish-owned firms dealing with the manufacture and wholesale distribution of enamel kitchenware products, one of which he operated as a trustee (*Treuhänder*) for the German occupation administration.

Schindler then established his own enamel works in Zablocie, outside Kraków, in which he employed mainly Jewish workers, thereby protecting them from deportations. When the liquidation of the Kraków ghetto began in early 1943, many Jews were sent to the PŁASZÓW labor camp, noted for the brutality of its commandant, Amon GOETH. Schindler used his good connections with high German officials in the Armaments Administration to set up a branch of the Płaszów camp in his factory compound for some nine hundred Jewish workers, including persons unfit and unqualified for the labor production needs. In this way he spared them from the horrors of the Płaszów camp.

In October 1944, with the approach of the Russian army, Schindler was granted permission to reestablish his now-defunct firm as an armaments production company in Brünnlitz (Brnenc, Sudetenland) and take with him the Jewish workers from Zablocie. In an operation unique in the annals of Nazi-occupied Europe, he succeeded in transferring to Brünnlitz some seven hundred to eight hundred Jewish men from the GROSS-ROSEN camp, and some three hundred Jewish women from AUSCHWITZ. In Brünnlitz, the eleven hundred Jews were given the most humane treatment possible under the circumstances: food, medical care, and religious needs. Informed that a train with evacuated Jewish detainees from the Goleszow camp was stranded at nearby Svitavy, Schindler received permission to take workers to the Svitavy railway station. There, they forced

Oskar Schindler (second from left) and a group of his Polish and Jewish employees in Kraków (1940).

the ice-sealed train doors open and removed some one hundred Jewish men and women, nearly frozen and resembling corpses, who were then swiftly taken to the Brünnlitz factory and nourished back to life, an undertaking to which Schindler's wife, Emilie, particularly devoted herself. Those whom it was too late to save were buried with proper Jewish rites.

Schindler was devoted to the humane treatment of his Jewish workers and to their physical and psychological needs. He used his good connections with the ABWEHR and with friends in high government positions, as well as his jovial and good-humored disposition, to befriend and ingratiate himself with high-ranking SS commanders in Poland. This stood him in good stead when he needed their assistance in extracting valuable and crucial favors from them, such as ameliorating conditions and mitigating punishments of Jews under his care. He was imprisoned on several occasions when the Gestapo accused him of corruption, only to be released on the intervention of his connections in Berlin ministries.

In 1962, Oskar Schindler planted a tree bearing his name in the Garden of the Righteous at YAD VASHEM, Jerusalem.

BIBLIOGRAPHY

Keneally, T. *Schindler's List*. New York, 1982.

MORDECAI PALDIEL

SCHIPER, IGNACY (Yitzhak; 1884–1943), Jewish historian and public figure. Schiper was born in Tarnów, in Eastern Galicia, and studied at the Universities of Kraków and Vienna, majoring in philosophy. In 1907 he was awarded the degree of doctor of jurisprudence, his thesis dealing with the economic situation of the Jews of Poland in the Middle Ages. In the pre–World War I period, Schiper was constantly on the move through the towns and cities of Galicia as a lecturer and propagandist on behalf of his party, the Po'alei Zion Zionist Socialists. He was elected to the Sejm (the Polish parliament) in 1919 and held his seat until 1927. He left his party over differences with its leadership and joined the General Zionists, but continued to play an important role in the Polish Zionist movement and in Jewish public affairs.

Schiper was a prolific and original historian, ranked as one of the two outstanding Jewish historians in independent Poland (the other was Meir Balaban). His studies dealt with a broad range of historical periods and processes, and he advanced innovative and bold theses, not all of which were accepted by his colleagues. He regarded himself as the historian of the people, stressing the study of economic activities and the struggle for survival of the ordinary Jew, in contrast to his predecessors, who concerned themselves with learned and prominent Jews. Schiper greatly influenced the young Jewish historians who embarked on their scholarly research in the interwar period, among them Emanuel RINGELBLUM.

When World War II broke out in September 1939, Schiper was seriously ill, but the difficulties and dangers of that fateful moment spurred him to further activity. He had been about to leave Poland for Palestine, but was prevented from doing so by the abrupt closing of the Italian Travel Agency in Poland. During the war and the existence of the WARSAW ghetto, Schiper was active in public affairs. He often appeared at public meetings, took part in Idische Kultur Organizacje (Jewish Culture Organization) activities, and lectured in the clandestine seminars held by the He-Haluts Zionist movement. He spoke out against the positions taken by the Warsaw JUDENRAT (Jewish Council) and the corruption in its ranks. For a while he served on a committee appointed to suggest ways of improving the work of the Judenrat, but its attempts proved of no avail.

Even in the ghetto, Schiper continued his scholarly work. At a closed Zionist meeting held during Passover 1942, he stated that when the time came for the Jews to face deportation from the ghetto, they should rise up and fight like the Maccabees, for the sake of their honor. In the event, however, when the deportations were launched in July 1942, Schiper opposed a policy of resistance. In a statement he made at the time, he pointed out that the Jewish people had on more than one occasion gone through difficult trials and had suffered destruction and loss of life, but by accepting partial losses they had managed to keep intact their identity as a people and had assured their continued existence.

Schiper lived through most of the deportations from the Warsaw ghetto, but after the January 1943 deportation he came to the conclusion that the fate of the Jews of Warsaw was sealed, and tried to escape to take refuge among the Poles, on their side of the city. Schiper, however, was "as poor as a church mouse" (as Ringelblum put it in a biographical sketch of him), and could not afford the cost of being smuggled over to the "Aryan" side of Warsaw and safeguarded there. He was seized during the period of the final deportation and the ghetto uprising, and was deported to MAJDANEK, where he was apparently killed in the course of the general massacre of Jews in the Lublin camps in November 1943.

BIBLIOGRAPHY

Biderman, I. M. *Mayer Balaban, Historian of Polish Jewry: His Influence on the Younger Generation of Jewish Historians.* New York, 1976. See pages 235–244.
Ringelblum, E. *Writings from the Warsaw Ghetto.* Vol. 2. *1942–1943.* Tel Aviv, 1985. (In Yiddish.)
Rosenthal, D. "Dr. Yitzhok Schipper." *Jewish Frontier* 41/4 (April 1974): 5–10.

ISRAEL GUTMAN

SCHMID, ANTON (1900–1942), German soldier who rescued Jews during the Holocaust. A sergeant in the Wehrmacht, stationed in VILNA, Schmid was responsible for collecting straggling German soldiers near the railway station and reassigning them to new units. A large group of Jews from the Vilna ghetto were assigned to different labor duties in Schmid's outfit: upholstering, tailoring, locksmithing, and shoe mending. He gained their affection and confidence. Shocked by the brutalities of the mass killings at PONARY, Schmid decided in late 1941 to do whatever he could to help Jews survive. He managed to release Jews incarcerated in the notorious Lakishki jail, rescued Jews in various ways, and surreptitiously supplied food and provisions to Jews inside the ghetto. In three

Anton Schmid.

houses in Vilna under his supervision, Jews were hidden in the cellars during Nazi-staged *Aktionen.* Schmid also became personally involved with leading figures in the Jewish underground, such as Mordecai TENENBAUM (Tamaroff), and cooperated with them. He helped some of them reach Warsaw and Białystok (to report on the mass killings at Ponary) by transporting them over long distances in his truck. Some of these underground operatives met, planned activities, and slept in his home. He sent other Jews to ghettos that were relatively more secure at that time, those of Voronovo, LIDA, and GRODNO.

The circumstances of Schmid's arrest are still shrouded in mystery. It was later learned that he was arrested in January 1942 and was sentenced to death by a military tribunal. He was executed on April 13 of that year and was buried in a Vilna cemetery. In 1964, Schmid was posthumously recognized by YAD VASHEM as a "RIGHTEOUS AMONG THE NATIONS."

BIBLIOGRAPHY

Arad, Y. *Ghetto in Flames.* Jerusalem, 1980.

MORDECAI PALDIEL

SCHOEPS GROUP. *See* Deutscher Vortrupp, Gefolgschaft Deutscher Juden.

SCHONFELD, SOLOMON (1912–1982), English rabbi, educator, and rescue activist. Schonfeld studied at Slobodka, Lithuania, and at Nitra, in Slovakia. In Nitra he became the student and lifelong friend of Rabbi Michael Dov WEISSMANDEL, who helped inspire his rescue work. At twenty-two, Schonfeld succeeded his father as rabbi of Adas Yisroel, a small Orthodox congregation in the Stamford Hill section of London; principal of the first Jewish Secondary School; and presiding rabbi of the Union of Orthodox Hebrew Congregations.

Schonfeld was the creator of the Chief Rabbi's Religious Emergency Council (CRREC), a rescue organization nominally under the auspices of Chief Rabbi Dr. Joseph Hertz, who was later to become his father-in-law. In actuality, during the CRREC's ten years of existence, Schonfeld was the prime mover behind its every act and rescue effort. The purpose of the CRREC, founded in early 1938, was to bring to England Orthodox rabbis, teachers, and other religious functionaries whom the British refugee organizations did not wish to sponsor, considering them "unproductive." In the winter of 1938, Schonfeld organized two children's transports to bring to London more than 250 Orthodox children from Vienna who were being ignored by the official Jewish community there. Until he could place them, he housed them temporarily in his emptied secondary schools and in his own home. He also established a rabbinical academy, Yeshivat Ohr Torah, to bring over 120 students who were over sixteen years of age.

Although essentially a loner and an iconoclast, Schonfeld won over British public figures and government officials to his rescue schemes. He obtained entry permits that enabled him to rescue more than thirty-seven hundred Jews before and immediately after the war.

During the war, Schonfeld tried to implement a number of rescue schemes, such as obtaining 1,000 visas to MAURITIUS for alleged "rabbis" that served as protective papers in Nazi-occupied countries. After the war he helped rehabilitate Jewish DISPLACED PERSONS in the British sector of Germany, sending in five synagogue ambulances with ritual objects, kosher food, and medicine. Schonfeld made several trips to Poland and Czechoslovakia to bring children, mostly war orphans, to England.

Rabbi Schonfeld (in uniform) with the few existing relatives, meeting a boatload of orphans he brought from Poland in 1946. [David Kranzler]

BIBLIOGRAPHY

Kranzler, D., and G. Hirschler, eds. *Solomon Schonfeld: His Page in History.* New York, 1982.

DAVID KRANZLER

SCHUTZSTAFFEL. *See* SS.

SCHWARTZ, JOSEPH J. (1899–1975), American Jewish leader; European director of the JOINT DISTRIBUTION COMMITTEE (JDC) from 1940 to 1949. Schwartz was born in the Ukraine in 1899 and was taken to the United States in 1907. He studied for the rabbinate at the Rabbi Isaac Elchanan Theological Seminary in New York City and served as rabbi of Congregation Pincus Elijah in New York from 1922 to 1925. In 1927, he received a Ph.D. from Yale University in oriental studies. He was an instructor at the American University in Cairo, Egypt, in 1930, and from 1930 to 1933 he taught at Long Island University. He then joined the Brooklyn Jewish Federation as a social worker; in 1939 he became an adjunct secretary at the JDC, working with Moses A. Leavitt.

Very soon, Schwartz was sent to serve as the committee's deputy director for Europe, under Morris C. Troper, working out of Paris. By 1940, Troper had returned to the United States, and Schwartz became "Mr. Joint" for Europe. At the time of the fall of France in 1940, Schwartz moved the JDC office to Lisbon, and from there he directed rescue and aid operations throughout the Holocaust period. He was responsible for organizing the emigration from Europe of persons who could still obtain visas to countries in the Western Hemisphere, arranging for berths on Portuguese and Spanish ships. He transmitted funds to France, where his co-workers became active in rescuing and hiding adults and, mainly, some seven thousand children after 1942. Schwartz also actively supported the armed Jewish underground, much against the JDC's policy at that time in the United States. In Switzerland he nominated Saly MAYER, president of the Federation of Swiss Jewish Communities (Schweizerischer Israelitischer Gemeindebund), as the JDC's Swiss representative. In close cooperation with Schwartz, Mayer transmitted funds to occupied Europe. Schwartz also aided "illegal" Jewish emigration to Palestine in 1940 and 1941, and established another JDC outpost in Istanbul. In conjunction with Judah L. Magnes, president of the Hebrew University, he was responsible for the upkeep of

Joseph Rosensaft (left), chairman of the displaced persons' provisional committee at Bergen-Belsen, speaking to Joseph J. Schwartz, the European director of the American Jewish Joint Distribution Committee, at the United Jewish Appeal Conference in Atlantic City on December 15, 1945.

Jewish religious institutions in Palestine and for sending many thousands of parcels to the Soviet Union from Tehran. These saved the lives of thousands of Jewish refugees in the starvation-ridden areas of Soviet Central Asia.

At the end of the war, Schwartz moved back to liberated Paris, reorganized the French JDC operation, and began sending JDC teams to the newly established DISPLACED PERSONS' camps in Germany, fighting for Allied army recognition and entry permits, which were slow in coming. Schwartz also negotiated agreements with eastern European authorities to send JDC teams to these countries. He directed his attention especially to Hungary and Romania, where relatively large Jewish communities had survived. It would be no exaggeration to say that until about 1947 or 1948 the Jews in these countries were kept alive, in part at least, by the JDC, directed by Schwartz. In Poland, too, Schwartz managed to negotiate agreements with the local government enabling the JDC to send aid in attempts at Jewish reconstruction, for instance in the newly Polish region of Silesia. Also of vital importance was Schwartz's help in facilitating the illegal movement of Jewish refugees through Europe with the BERIḤA organization, which was directed by local Zionist-oriented and Palestinian Jewish activists.

In August 1948, Schwartz met with Israeli officials and arranged for the JDC's crucial support for mass emigration to Israel. At the same time, he negotiated an agreement establishing the Malben service for the aged in Israel, which provided care for elderly refugees immigrating there. In 1950, with the closure of the displaced persons' camps in Germany, where he had supervised the JDC's activities, Schwartz became the vice-chairman of the United Jewish Appeal in the United States, raising money for the new state of Israel. From 1955 he was executive vice president of the State of Israel Bonds Organization, until his retirement in 1970.

Schwartz was one of American Jewry's outstanding leaders. Possessing an overpowering intelligence and a great store of general Jewish knowledge, a pro-Zionist sympathizer who was very careful to remain objective as one of the heads of a nonpolitical organization, he was a man of tact and a deep understanding of the human condition, a true humanitarian.

BIBLIOGRAPHY

Agar, H. *The Saving Remnant: An Account of Jewish Survival.* New York, 1960.

Bauer, Y. *American Jewry and the Holocaust: The American Jewish Joint Distribution Committee, 1939–1945.* Detroit, 1982.

Bauer, Y. *My Brother's Keeper: A History of the American Joint Distribution Committee, 1929–1939.* Philadelphia, 1974.

YEHUDA BAUER

SCHWARZBART, IGNACY ISAAC (1888–1961), Zionist politician and activist. Born in Chrzanów, Galicia, Schwarzbart became a lawyer. During World War I he moved to Vienna, served as an officer in the Austro-Hungarian army, and, in 1918, joined the Polish army.

After the war Schwarzbart resumed his legal practice and also took up journalism,

Ignacy Isaac Schwarzbart eulogizing Samuel Artur Zygelbojm, who committed suicide in London on May 12, 1943.

contributing to Zionist dailies in Yiddish and Polish. In the interwar period he was a delegate to most of the Zionist congresses, on behalf of the General Zionist movement. He was a member of the executive committee of the WORLD JEWISH CONGRESS, was active in the Kraków municipal council as a member of its Jewish faction, and was one of the leaders of the Kraków Jewish community. In November 1938 he was elected to the Sejm (the Polish parliament) as a member for the Kraków district.

In September 1939, when World War II broke out, Schwarzbart left Poland, together with the Polish government, for France (by way of Romania), where the POLISH GOVERNMENT-IN-EXILE was set up. He was appointed a member of the Polish national council-in-exile. Following France's surrender in July 1940, Schwarzbart moved to London, where the Polish government-in-exile had transferred its institutions.

At the beginning of 1940 Schwarzbart founded *Przyszłość* (The Future), a periodical for Polish Jewish affairs, publishing it first in France and then in London. In January 1940 he also established in France the Organizing Committee of the Polish Jewish Representation.

From 1940 to 1946, Schwarzbart served as a member of the National Council of the Polish Republic and as the representative of the Delegation of Polish Jewry. The important archive accumulated in his office has been preserved; it represents a rich source for the history of Polish Jewry in the Holocaust and of the relations between Jews and Poles during the war. Schwarzbart's war diary is also an important historical document.

Schwarzbart remained active in the Zionist movement and maintained his journalistic activities. From 1946 to 1961 he lived in the United States and was active in the World Jewish Congress. He published several booklets on the WARSAW GHETTO UPRISING, among them *The Story of the Warsaw Uprising: Its Meaning and Message* (1953), and memoirs on Jewish life in Kraków between the world wars, *Tzvishn Beyde Velt Milkhomes* (Between the Two World Wars; 1958).

ELISHEVA SHAUL

SCHWEIZERISCHER HILFSVEREIN FÜR JÜDISCHE FLÜCHTLINGE. *See* Switzerland.

SD (Sicherheitsdienst des Reichsführers-SS; Security Service of the SS), the Nazi party's intelligence service; a major instrument for the implementation of the "FINAL SOLUTION." In 1931 Heinrich HIMMLER established the nucleus of an intelligence service in the SS headquarters and appointed Reinhard HEYDRICH as its chief. The new section operated out of Munich, at first on a modest scale; a year later it became the Security Service of the SS. Its function was to uncover the party's enemies and keep them under surveillance; however, the relationship of the SD with similar services maintained by party organizations was not clearly defined.

In April 1934, on the eve of the Röhm purge (*see* RÖHM, ERNST), Himmler took over the Prussian Gestapo, the final link that he needed to complete his takeover of the entire political police apparatus in Germany; he appointed Heydrich as its director. Himmler and Heydrich moved to Berlin and the SD headquarters moved with them. On June 9 of that year, Rudolf HESS designated the SD as the sole party intelligence service. Whereas most of the senior Gestapo men were recruited from among the professional police officers, the SD attracted an elite of ambitious intellectuals and devoted much effort to studying and formulating the political and ideological goals of the SS. The Gestapo had the status of a national political police, but the division of labor between the two intelligence branches, the SD and the Gestapo, was not clear-cut. The fact that both organizations were headed by the same people did not mean that there was no rivalry between them.

The first attempt to define the respective responsibilities of each branch was made in the wake of the liquidation of the Röhm group. Himmler announced that the SD was an intelligence and counterintelligence service whose task it was to assist the Gestapo by identifying the enemies of the state; the Gestapo's task was to deal with these enemies once they were uncovered. Further guidelines were issued on July 1, 1937, allocating areas of responsibility to either the Gestapo or the SD, while some areas, such as the "Jewish issue," remained the joint responsibility of both organizations.

These guidelines, however, failed to resolve all the existing differences regarding the coordination of work between the Gestapo and the SD. The SD chiefs also tried their hand in espionage abroad by seeking to gain control over military intelligence. This goal was achieved in July 1944, after the attempt on Hitler's life, in which the ABWEHR (the Wehrmacht intelligence service) chiefs were found to have been involved. By means of the large organization it established, and with the help of a network of informers who submitted regular reports, the SD was able to keep track of the changing mood of the public. In this field the SD considered itself the central branch of the intelligence service, its task being to provide the political leaders with the basic data they required for the decision-making process.

On September 27, 1939, Heydrich unified his command over the Gestapo and the SD by creating the REICHSSICHERHEITSHAUPTAMT (Reich Security Main Office; RSHA). It was only after the outbreak of the war that the SD was assigned operational tasks, when it joined the EINSATZGRUPPEN that followed the invading German army into Poland. Its personnel served in command positions or in the rank and file of the Einsatzgruppen, which in the summer of 1941 launched a systematic murder campaign against Jews and other groups in the German-occupied areas of the Soviet Union. The staff organization of the civil administration centers in the German-occupied areas included officers or inspectors from the Sicherheitspolizei (Security Police) and the SD. The officer, a *Höherer SS- und Polizeiführer* (Higher SS and Police Leader), was the commander of all the SS and police units in his area. The Security Service personnel engaged in intelligence activities and in punishing and murdering the local population, chiefly the Jews.

It was only in 1935 that the Jewish Section of the SD (Section II 112) adopted a basic policy and its own independent *modus operandi*. The concept that the Jews, by their very nature, were enemies of the state and of the Nazi regime determined the SD's goal and methods. In a memorandum drawn up by the section in December 1936, the "provisional goal" it set was "to rid Germany of the Jews." From then on the SD kept the Jewish organizations and institutions under its surveillance and supervision in order to harass the Jews and exert pressure on them to leave Germany. In 1937 the section outlined the practical steps that had to be taken to achieve its goal: economic dispossession, public pressure, and terrorization.

The first director of the Jewish Section of the SD was Leopold von Mildenstein, followed in 1936 by Herbert Hagen. Adolf EICHMANN joined the section in early 1935 and was put in charge of subsection 112/3, which dealt with "Zionists." He entered upon his major role in the murder of the Jews when he was dispatched from the section to head the ZENTRALSTELLE FÜR JÜDISCHE AUSWANDERUNG (Central Office for Jewish Emigration) in Vienna. The Jewish Section of the SD had a central role in organizing and implementing the "Final Solution." In a judgment rendered on October 1, 1946, the International Military Tribunal at Nuremberg declared the SD (as well as the SS and the Gestapo) to be a criminal organization.

BIBLIOGRAPHY

Adam, U. *Judenpolitik im Dritten Reich.* Düsseldorf, 1972.
Aronsohn, S. *Heydrich und die Anfänge des SD und der Gestapo, 1931–1935.* Berlin, 1967.
Hohne, H. *The Order of the Death's Head: The Story of Hitler's SS.* London, 1969.
Krausnick, H., et al. *The Anatomy of the SS State.* London, 1967.
Ramme, A. *Der Sicherheitsdienst der SS: Zu seiner Funktion im faschistischen Machtapparat und im Besatzungsregime des sogenannten Generalgouvernements Polen.* Berlin, 1970.

YEHOYAKIM COCHAVI

SECOND WORLD WAR. *See* World War II.

SECRET STATE POLICE. *See* Gestapo.

SECURENI, transit camp for Jews from BESSARABIA who were deported to TRANSNISTRIA. The Secureni camp was set up in the town of that name, in the Khotin district of northern Bessarabia, at the end of July 1941. The town's Jewish population of four thousand, representing 73 percent of its total population, had previously been expelled to Transnistria; many of the Jews had been killed during the occupation by Romanian and German troops and by local inhabitants, mostly Ukrainians. In fact, the town became one large camp for thirty thousand Jews who were brought there from all over the district. The camp population consisted of three groups, according to their origins: the Khotin group, made up of twenty thousand persons; the Noua Sulita group of some one thousand persons; and the rest of the deportees, nine thousand in number, who came from various places in northern Bessarabia.

Each group had its own committee and several subcommittees, the latter representing the various component subgroups. Eventually a central committee was formed that maintained contact with the Romanian authorities and endeavored to obtain food and firewood and ease the living conditions in the camp. Governing the camp was the mayor of Secureni, who, after being bribed, made some improvements—enlarging the camp area so that it came to comprise practically the entire town (except for the main street), providing flour and sunflower seeds, and permitting the inmates to purchase food in the local market by selling whatever possessions they had. Most of the Jews in the camp, however, could not afford to buy the daily bread ration. The skilled workers among the Jews left the camp clandestinely and found temporary employment with local farmers. Other inmates manufactured soap and candy in the camp. The bribes also helped alleviate the lot of the persons put on forced labor, who were rotated every few weeks.

Many Jews, however, succumbed to starvation and disease, despite the presence of doctors among the deportees. They gave all the help they could, but had no medicine available and were powerless in the face of the absolute lack of hygiene and sanitation. The camp guards, Romanian gendarmes, raped the girls and women in the presence of members of their families, and many of the rape

victims committed suicide. During the high holidays, prayer houses were set up in the camp. The Union of Jewish Communities in Bucharest tried to obtain permission to send help to Secureni, but its efforts were of no avail. On October 3, 1941, all the Jews in the camp were deported to Transnistria. It is estimated that not more than five hundred survived from among the thirty thousand deportees.

BIBLIOGRAPHY

Ancel, J., and T. Lavi, eds. *Rumania*, vol. 2. In *Pinkas Hakehillot; Encyclopaedia of Jewish Communities*. Jerusalem, 1980. (In Hebrew.)

Igeret, Z., ed. *Securiani: Its Flowering and Destruction*. Tel Aviv, 1964. (In Hebrew.)

JEAN ANCEL

SECURITY SERVICE OF THE SS. *See* SD.

SEMLIN. *See* Sajmište.

SENDLER, IRENA ("Jolanta"; b. 1916), one of the most active members in the Rada Pomocy Żydom (Council for Aid to Jews), known as ZEGOTA, a Polish underground organization in the Warsaw area. From the early days of the German occupation, Sendler worked to alleviate the suffering of many of her Jewish friends and acquaintances. Employed in the Social Welfare Department of the Warsaw municipality, she received a special permit allowing her to visit the ghetto area at all times, ostensibly for the purpose of combating contagious diseases. This gave her the opportunity to provide many Jews with clothing, medicine, and money. When walking through the ghetto streets, Sendler wore an armband with the Star of David, both as a sign of solidarity with the Jewish people and so as not to call attention to herself.

At the end of the summer of 1942, Sendler was approached and asked to join the newly founded Council for Aid to Jews. She became a valuable asset to Zegota, for she had already enlisted a large group of people in her

SECURENI

Annexations from June to September 1940: (1) Bessarabia and (2) N. Bukovina to USSR; (3) N. Transylvania to Hungary; (4) S. Dobruja to Bulgaria.

Irena Sendler.

charitable work, including her companion Irena Schulz, who had a widespread network of contacts in the ghetto and on the "Aryan" side. Irena Sendler specialized in smuggling Jewish children out of the ghetto and finding secure places for them with non-Jewish families in the Warsaw region. Each of her co-workers was made responsible for several blocks of apartments where Jewish children were sheltered. She herself oversaw eight or ten apartments where Jews were hiding under her care. The sheltering families were supported by funds from Zegota.

In October 1943, Irena Sendler was arrested by the Gestapo, taken to the infamous PAWIAK PRISON, and brutally tortured to make her reveal information. Failing to elicit such information, her interrogators told her she was doomed. However, on the day set for her execution, she was freed, after her underground companions bribed one of the Gestapo agents. Officially she was listed on public bulletin boards as among those executed. Forced to stay out of sight for the remainder of the German occupation, Sendler continued working surreptitiously for Zegota. In 1965 she was recognized by YAD VASHEM as a "RIGHTEOUS AMONG THE NATIONS."

BIBLIOGRAPHY

Bartoszewski, W., and Z. Lewin, eds. *Righteous among Nations: How Poles Helped the Jews, 1939–1945.* London, 1969.

MORDECAI PALDIEL

SERBIA, one of the constituent republics of YUGOSLAVIA, in the eastern part of the country. Until the establishment of Yugoslavia, in 1919, Serbia was an independent kingdom; in the interwar period it was a province of the kingdom of Yugoslavia. It now has the status of a republic, the largest and most important of the six that together constitute present-day Yugoslavia.

Jews had been living in Serbia since Roman times, but the modern Jewish community was founded by Jews from Spain (Sephardim) who came there via Greece and Turkey. Most of them settled in BELGRADE and its vicinity and engaged in commerce or became artisans. They integrated well into the country and took part in the Serbian struggle for independence. When Yugoslavia was founded, Belgrade was one of three centers of Jewish population in the country and the seat of the Union of Yugoslav Communities. When World War II broke out, Serbia, including the Banat, had a Jewish population of about sixteen thousand, of whom eleven thousand lived in Belgrade, and the rest in Niš, Smederevo, Zrenjanin (Petrovgrad, Veliki Bečkerek), Bačka Palanka, and Šabac.

Following the occupation of Yugoslavia by the Germans in April 1941, Serbia—including the Banat—was placed under a military administration. Three German air force generals took turns during 1941 serving as the military governors of Serbia: Bernhard Danckelman, Ludwig Schröder, and Helmuth Forster. In the wake of the Serbian uprising of July 1941, the German army commander, Gen. Hermann Böhme, was given emergency powers, and up to the end of that year he was the highest authority in Serbia.

The military administration consisted of an operational military wing and an administrative civilian wing (Verwaltungsstab). The civilian wing, which was also in charge of Jewish affairs, was headed by SS-Gruppenführer

Harold Turner, who had at his disposal Einsatzgruppe Serbien. Its commanders were SS-Standartenführer Wilhelm Fuchs (to January 1942) and SS-Gruppenführer August Meiszner (from January 1942). The security police had its main office in Belgrade and maintained branches in cities and towns all over Serbia. Section IV (the Gestapo) had a subsection for Jewish affairs, headed by SS-Untersturmführer Fritz Stracke, which dealt with the implementation of German policy toward the Jews.

Others involved in determining and carrying out Jewish policy were (1) the representative of the German Foreign Ministry in Belgrade, Felix Benzler, who advocated the deportation of the Jews to the east; (2) the representative of the FOUR-YEAR PLAN in Belgrade, Hans Neuhausen, who was the official in charge of economic affairs in Serbia and as such took part in robbing the Jews of their possessions and in establishing concentration camps; and (3) the Serbian quisling puppet government, under Milan Nedić, whose police and gendarmerie assisted the Germans in rounding up the Jews.

The persecution and murder of the Jews of Serbia extended over three periods: April to August 1941 (legislation, dispossession, forced labor); August to December 1941 (imprisonment and murder of male Jews); December 1941 to May 1942 (imprisonment and murder of Jewish women and children).

April to August 1941. Between the end of April 1941 and mid-June of that year, the German administration issued numerous directives concerning Jews. These directives defined who was to be regarded as a Jew; provided for a census of the Jewish population and the wearing of distinctive badges (*see* BADGE, JEWISH); excluded Jews from certain professions or prohibited them from accepting non-Jewish clients; restricted their freedom of movement; and confined them to residence in certain areas. Plundering Jews of their possessions was institutionalized: in Belgrade alone, some nine hundred Jewish businesses were confiscated by June 1941. On three occasions collective fines were imposed on the Jewish community, and Jewish bank accounts were blocked. A postwar Yugoslav government commission estimated that the value of the assets of which the Jews were robbed was 1.5 billion dinars ($30 million), a figure that does not presume to cover the total property of which the Jews were deprived.

At the very beginning of the occupation all Jewish men aged sixteen to sixty were drafted for forced labor, mainly in order to clean up the war damage caused to Belgrade. In May 1941 Jewish workers were assigned to similar work in Smederevo, which had been partly destroyed when ammunition dumps in the city blew up in a huge explosion.

August to December 1941. The German attack on the Soviet Union led to the outbreak of a general rebellion in Serbia, in July 1941. In the first few months the insurgents, under the leadership of Communist party members, scored remarkable successes, and were in de facto control of large parts of the country. The Germans reacted with brutal and relentless terror tactics, burning down villages, destroying crops, and murdering thousands of

SERBIA

hostages. The Wehrmacht adopted a policy of retaliation under which 100 Serbians were executed for every German soldier killed, and 50 executed for every German wounded. To make up the required quota, and in order not to antagonize the local population more than they considered advisable, the Germans seized Jewish men and killed them. This was the way in which the Germans planned to exterminate the Jews of Serbia.

In August 1941 the mass imprisonment of Jewish men was launched all over Serbia. By early September most of them had been put into Topovske Šupe, a concentration camp in the midst of Belgrade. Jews from southern Serbia were imprisoned in the "Red Cross" (Crveni Krst) camp near Niš, and the "Kladovo Group" was held in a concentration camp situated in Šabac. The "Kladovo Group" consisted of refugees from Austria, Germany, and Czechoslovakia who had left for Palestine in late 1939 and for various reasons had not been able to proceed beyond the Yugoslav-Romanian border, on the lower Danube. They had stayed in Kladovo and then moved to Šabac, where they fell into German hands. In early September, at the height of the drive against the Serbians, Harold Turner, at the demand of the German military authorities, handed over Jewish hostages to fill the murder quotas. Turner's own written notes reveal that he was well aware that the Jews had nothing to do with the Serbian uprising, but, as he put it, "they had to be got rid of, anyway." Mass murders of Jews took place in Jajinci, Jabuka, Zasavica (near Šabac), and Bubanj (near Niš). By December, most of the Jewish men had been killed; the rest—a group from Niš, and several hundred men who had been put to work in the SAJMIŠTE camp, near Belgrade—were murdered in February and March 1942, respectively.

December 1941 to May 1942. A meeting was held in Belgrade on October 20, 1941, attended by Turner, security police chief Wilhelm Fuchs, Franz RADEMACHER of the German Foreign Ministry (where he was in charge of Jewish affairs), and Franz Stuschke and SS-Obersturmbannführer Friedrich Suhr, two of Adolf EICHMANN's men. At the meeting it was decided that for the time being the Jews were to be concentrated in one camp, since it was not possible to deport them to the east before the summer of 1942. Accordingly, between December 1941 and February 1942, all the Jewish women and children in Serbia—seventy-five hundred to eight thousand persons—were taken to the Sajmište camp. Conditions in the camp were very bad: the living accommodations did not shelter the inmates from the weather, sanitation was nonexistent (there was a single shower for all the prisoners, and very few toilets), and the food was bad. As a result, the mortality rate soared.

In the early spring of 1942 the German authorities in Serbia realized that they would not be able to deport the Jews as quickly as they had thought, and they asked Berlin to provide another solution. In late February a gas van (see GAS VANS) arrived in Belgrade, sent from Berlin, of the kind that had by then been tried out in Poland and in the Soviet Union. This gas van was used from March to May of 1942 to kill all the Jews imprisoned in Sajmište.

After that only a few Jews were left in Serbia. Most of them had been given refuge by Serbian friends or had escaped to the partisans. In November 1943 SS-Standartenführer Paul BLOBEL, the officer in charge of AKTION 1005, came to Belgrade in order to set up a unit that would disinter the bodies of the murder victims and burn them. The unit, consisting of fifty Sicherheitspolizei (Security Police) men and German military police, as well as 100 Jewish and Serbian prisoners, was engaged in its gruesome task of obliterating the traces of the murders up to the fall of 1944.

Approximately 14,500 Serbian Jews—90 percent of Serbia's Jewish population of 16,000—were murdered in World War II.

BIBLIOGRAPHY

Browning, C. *Fateful Months: Essays on the Emergence of the Final Solution.* New York, 1985.

Ivanović, L. "Teror nad Jevrejima u okupiranom Beogradu." *Godisnjak Grad Beograda* 13 (1966): 289–316.

Shelach, M. "Sajmiste: An Extermination Camp in Serbia." *Holocaust and Genocide Studies* 2 (1987): 243–260.

MENACHEM SHELAH

SERED, concentration and labor camp in SLO-VAKIA. Labor camps for Jews were established in Slovakia under Law 198/1941 (the Jewish Code), which provided for the drafting of Jews for forced labor. In the winter of 1941–1942 a team of Jewish craftsmen was sent to a military camp near the town of Sered to prepare the camp for Jewish labor draftees. Without waiting for the renovation and construction work to be completed, however, the Slovak authorities began using the camp for Jews being rounded up for deportation to Poland. The labor camp came into existence at the very time when the mass deportations were taking place (the spring and summer of 1942), with half-finished structures used to launch a production program. Guarding the camp were members of the HLINKA GUARD, commanded by Imrich Vasina, and a regime of terror prevailed. Five transports took 4,500 Jews from the Sered camp to Poland. The last of the five departed on the Day of Atonement, 1942; it contained 300 Jews and consisted, in part, of Jews who had been working in the labor camp and their families.

The camp regime improved considerably after the last transport. The volume of production was expanded, and the camp supplied manufactured goods both to the civilian market and to government agencies. Its sales were profitable, and in general the production of the camp factories was impressive.

Conditions in the camp became better, the food was adequate, and leave passes were available for the inmates. After the 1942 deportations, the camp population numbered some one thousand persons, and in the course of 1943 it increased to thirteen hundred. There were nurseries and elementary school classes for the children, and women from among the inmates were employed as the teachers. The camp commandant was assisted by a Jewish council. Its chairman, Alexander Pressburger, had a flair for human relations and was well qualified to ease tension and solve problems in the communal life of the camp population. Members of youth movements joined up to form two communes, one under the auspices of Maccabi ha-Tsa'ir and the other of Ha-Shomer ha-Tsa'ir. A rich program of cultural activities was developed, consisting of performances, recitals, language courses, and lectures; there was also an athletic field and a swimming pool.

In 1944 an underground was organized in the camp and weapons were smuggled in from the outside. During the SLOVAK NATIONAL UPRISING in August 1944, the camp gates were opened and many of the young people left for central Slovakia, where they joined the rebel forces. Within a few days, following the German occupation of western Slovakia, the camp was once again in operation, under a new commandant, Alois BRUN-

The Sered concentration camp in Slovakia.

NER. Between October 1944 and March 1945, 13,500 Jews were deported from Sered to AUSCHWITZ and THERESIENSTADT. On April 1, 1945, the camp was liberated by the Red Army.

BIBLIOGRAPHY

Felstiner, M. "Alois Brunner: Eichmann's Best Tool." *Simon Wiesenthal Center Annual* 3 (1986): 1–46.
Jelinek, Y. "The Role of the Jews in Slovakian Resistance." *Jahrbuch für Geschichte Osteuropas* 15/3 (September 1967): 415–422.

AKIVA NIR

SERENI, ENZO (1905–1944), Zionist emissary, pioneer, and thinker; one of the parachutists sent by the Palestinian YISHUV to occupied Europe. Sereni was born in Rome, of an old and distinguished family. As a youth he became a Zionist socialist and an activist among Jewish youth in Italy. He received a doctorate in philosophy in 1925. In 1927 he immigrated to Palestine, where he worked in the orchards. The following year he helped found Kibbutz Givat Brenner. In 1931 and 1932, Sereni was an emissary for Zionist YOUTH MOVEMENTS in Germany; he was there again in 1933 and 1934, working in the Haavara (*see* HAAVARA AGREEMENT) and the YOUTH ALIYA.

At the outbreak of World War II, Sereni enlisted in the British army and was employed in the antifascist campaign in Egypt. He was sent in 1941 to Iraq, where he helped to prepare the Jewish youth for underground activity and for immigration to Palestine. In 1943 he was appointed a liaison officer between the Palestinian parachutists (*see* PARACHUTISTS, JEWISH) and their British trainers, and despite his age and the opposition of all his acquaintances he insisted on joining them. In May 1944 he was dropped into northern Italy, where he was captured by the Germans. He was interned in DACHAU, and became a leading figure among the prisoners. Sereni was executed there in November 1944.

Sereni had a unique, multifaceted, and lively personality; he combined a broad general education and individualism with a socialist labor movement outlook and constant activity for the general interest of the community. He studied classical literature and pursued scholarly research, particularly on fascism. After his death, his widow, Ada Sereni (née Ascarelli), was one of the leaders of the "illegal" immigration movement to Palestine.

BIBLIOGRAPHY

Bondy, R. *The Emissary: The Life of Enzo Sereni.* Tel Aviv, 1973. (In Hebrew.)
Brent, P. L., and C. Urquhart. *Enzo Sereni: A Hero of Our Times.* London, 1967.
Carpi, D., A. Milano, and U. Nahon, eds. *Scritti in memoria di Enzo Sereni: Saggi sull' ebraismo romano.* Jerusalem, 1970. (In Italian and Hebrew.)

DINA PORAT

SEYSS-INQUART, ARTHUR (1892–1946), Austrian Nazi statesman. Wounded in World War I, Seyss-Inquart walked with a limp. As a lawyer in Vienna he was active in nationalist circles, and while initially not antisemitic, he became increasingly attracted to National Socialism. Seyss-Inquart was held in esteem by the Austrian chancellor, Kurt von Schuschnigg, who appointed him to the Council of State and as mediator between himself and the extreme Right. In the Nazi party in Austria, Seyss-Inquart was not considered a reliable member; he was, however, highly regarded by Adolf Hitler, who pressured Schuschnigg into appointing Seyss-Inquart Austrian minister of the interior and of public security (February 16, 1938).

Following the resignation of Schuschnigg, on Hitler's ultimatum, Seyss-Inquart was appointed chancellor (March 11, 1938); he immediately invited the German armed forces to enter Austria. In return, Hitler appointed him Reich commissioner of Ostmark, as Austria was now called; however, Seyss-Inquart's influence on the Austrian ANSCHLUSS was slight. Heinrich Himmler accorded him the rank of SS-*Obergruppenführer*. About a year later (May 1, 1939), Seyss-Inquart was appointed minister without

Arthur Seyss-Inquart (second from left) and Konrad Henlein (third from left), leader of the Nazi Sudeten party, January 30, 1939.

portfolio in the central German government. In October 1939 he was appointed deputy governor-general in Poland. There, he was responsible for examining the territory to be used for the Lublin Reservation, where the Jews deported from the Reich were to be deported (*see* NISKO AND LUBLIN PLAN).

On May 19, 1940, Hitler appointed Seyss-Inquart Reich Commissioner of the Occupied NETHERLANDS, with instructions to endeavor to create friendship between the Dutch and the Germans. Hitler hoped that the man who had helped in the annexation of Austria would succeed in the same way in the Netherlands. Indeed, in the first months Seyss-Inquart acted with restraint, creating the impression that the Germans would not make life difficult for the Dutch. However, it quickly became clear to him that apart from the small organized minority in the Dutch National Socialist movement (*see* NATIONAAL SOCIALISTISCHE BEWEGING), the Dutch rejected the efforts of the Germans to win them over. In time, the Germans began to take draconian steps against the Dutch. The acts against the Jews, which began in late 1940 and reached a peak in February 1941, contributed in particular to the anti-German climate, and in reaction the Amsterdam dockworkers went on strike. Seyss-Inquart reacted sharply to these incidents, rightly seeing in them the failure of his policy. He took an active role in the anti-Jewish legislation, the pillage of Jewish property, and the dispatch of the Jews to the extermination camps. He knew that the removal of the Jews from Europe was Hitler's supreme mission, and he wanted to be among the initiators of the campaign, rather than allowing the local SS to deal exclusively with the "FINAL SOLUTION." At a very early stage, Seyss-Inquart was aware of Hitler's intentions: in a well-attended meeting of Nazi officials on May 15, 1941, that deliberated on the confiscation of Jewish property, he indicated that the financing of a "Final Solution" was to be an objective of the expropriation.

In the power struggles between himself and the representatives of Heinrich HIMMLER and Adolf EICHMANN, Seyss-Inquart was aided by two friends who were related to him, Dr. Friedrich Wimmer, *Generalkommissar* of Administration and Justice, and Dr. Hans Fischböck, *Generalkommissar* of Finance and the

Economy. He initiated several of the harshest measures taken against the Jews in an attempt to become the person responsible for dealing with the Jews. In the last months of the war, Seyss-Inquart began negotiations with the Allied armies in an attempt to ease the suffering of the Dutch population. He was one of the war criminals indicted for crimes against humanity; at the NUREMBERG TRIAL he was sentenced to death. In all his activity Seyss-Inquart remained loyal to Hitler, and Hitler praised him highly on a number of occasions. A collection of his speeches, *Vier Jahre in den Niederlanden: Gesammelte Reden*, was published in Amsterdam in 1944.

BIBLIOGRAPHY

Michman, J., H. Beem, and D. Michman, eds. *The Netherlands*. In *Pinkas Hakehillot; Encyclopaedia of Jewish Communities*. Jerusalem, 1985. (In Hebrew.)

Newman, H. J. *Arthur Seyss-Inquart: Het leven van een Duits onderkonig in Nederland*. Utrecht, 1967.

Pauley, B. F. *Hitler and the Forgotten Nazis: A History of Austrian National Socialism*. Chapel Hill, 1981.

Rosar, W. *Deutsche Gemeinschaft: Seyss-Inquart und der Anschluss*. Vienna, 1971.

Warmbrunn, W. *The Dutch under German Occupation, 1940–1945*. Stanford, 1963.

JOZEPH MICHMAN

SHANGHAI. Before World War II, Shanghai was China's largest port and a metropolis of over four million inhabitants. These included a hundred thousand foreigners in the city's International Settlements, ruled by eleven countries, including the United States, Britain, and JAPAN. Shanghai became a haven for Jewish refugees from Germany, Austria, and Poland because it was the only place in the world where one could land without a visa or official paper of any kind. Of far greater consequence for the refugees was Japan's pro-Jewish policy, promulgated on December 6, 1938, which opened the militarily controlled harbor to the Jews despite attempts by the United States, Britain, and France to restrict their entry. After KRISTALLNACHT (November 9–10, 1938), the trickle of refugees to East Asia became a flood, reaching its height of about seventeen thousand—including one thousand Polish refugees stranded without visas in Kōbe, Japan—at the start of the war in the Pacific on December 7, 1941.

The refugees found two Jewish communities in Shanghai. The smaller community, dating from the mid-nineteenth century, consisted of four hundred to five hundred Sephardim from Baghdad, who had risen to the top of Shanghai's social and economic ladder. The more recent community of Russian Jews, numbering between three thousand and four thousand, had migrated in several waves, most arriving after the Bolshevik Revolution of 1917 and after Japan's occupation of Manchuria in 1931 and 1932. The Russian Jews never attained the economic and social success of the Sephardim, remaining primarily small traders and shopkeepers.

With the help of two local Sephardic relief committees and of subsidies from the American Jewish JOINT DISTRIBUTION COMMITTEE (known as the Joint), five large refugee camps were set up to house and feed over three thousand of the most indigent. On their own initiative, and with help from friends and relatives abroad, the remaining refugees managed to eke out a livelihood ranging from poor to good in Shanghai. A few were even able to establish successful enterprises, providing the city's "international clientele" with European-style goods and services that were unavailable from war-torn Europe.

The refugees managed to re-create some facets of their European life-style in Shanghai, as reflected in their social, religious, and cultural institutions and activities. These included a *kehillah* (congregation), with religious services ranging from Liberal to Orthodox; a thriving Zionist movement; a German-language press, including three dailies; and a high level of theatrical, radio, and musical productions. In addition, two elementary schools, trade and adult-education seminars, and even a dancing school were instituted. The small group of Polish refugees, representing the elite of the Polish Jewish intelligentsia, included writers, actors, and labor and Zionist leaders, as well as students and rabbis of the Mir Yeshiva.

With the advent of the war in the Pacific, events took a turn for the worse for the refugees when the transmission of private funds, as well as public funds from the American Joint, was forbidden by the United States government. Representatives of the Joint in Shanghai borrowed money locally for almost a year, on the Joint's postwar repayment guarantee, though many refugees were still forced to sell their last belongings to buy food. But the worst fears of the refugees were realized on February 18, 1943, when under Nazi pressure the Japanese established a ghetto, euphemistically referred to as the "restricted area." Once again pariahs, the refugees relocated to still shabbier quarters in a two-mile-square guarded sector of Hongkew. While this was not nearly as terrible as the ghettos in Europe, life there was miserable as economic restrictions reduced most to penury. Yet even at the worst, the inner world of the refugees—with its educational, social, cultural, and religious activities—managed to continue. Conditions improved considerably with the resumption of funds from the United States in December 1943, when the State and Treasury departments granted permission for the transfer of funds to enemy-occupied territories in Europe and China. The money from the Joint was transferred by Saly MAYER, the Joint representative in Switzerland, to the offices of the International RED CROSS in Shanghai.

The end of the war and the revelation of the horrors of the Holocaust in Europe found most of the refugees unable or unwilling to return "home." About half found their way to the Western Hemisphere, while the rest made use of the welcome offered by the newly created state of Israel. By the time the Maoist Communist regime took over Shanghai in 1949, most of the Jews had left. The few thousand remaining were able to leave by the mid-1950s, signaling the end of this remarkable East Asian haven for Jews.

[See also Rescue of Polish Jews via East Asia; Sugihara, Sempo; Va'ad Ha-Hatsala; Warhaftig, Zorah.]

BIBLIOGRAPHY

Dicker, H. Wanderers and Settlers in the Far East. New York, 1962.

Kranzler, D. Japanese, Nazis, and Jews: The Jewish Refugee Community of Shanghai, 1938–1945. New York, 1976.

Kranzler, D. "The Jewish Refugee Community of Shanghai, 1939–1945." Wiener Library Bulletin 26 (1972–1973): 28–37.

YIVO. Catalog of the Exhibition "Jewish Life in Shanghai." New York, 1948.

DAVID KRANZLER

SHAVLI. See Šiauliai.

SHE'ERIT HA-PELETAH. See Displaced Persons; Refugees.

SHEPTYTSKY, ANDREI (1865–1944), head of the Greek Catholic (Uniate) church in southeast Poland, and one of the leaders of the Ukrainian nationalist movement in Poland during the interwar period and the Nazi occupation of 1941 to 1944; an influential figure among the Ukrainian population. The contradiction between Sheptytsky's friendly attitude toward the Jews and the German-oriented policy he advocated made him a controversial personality.

Sheptytsky came from an aristocratic Polish family. In 1888 he adopted the Greek Catholic faith and joined the Basilian order. He was appointed bishop of Stanislav (present-day Ivano-Frankovsk) in 1899, and the following year became the metropolitan of the Uniate church. Under the Austrian regime in Eastern Galicia, Sheptytsky devoted himself to promoting church interests; in the period between 1918 and 1939 he took an active part in the struggle of the Ukrainian population in independent Poland for national rights.

During the 1930s, extremist tendencies in the Ukrainian national movement gained in strength, especially in the ORHANIZATSYIA UKRAINSKYKH NATSIONALISTIV (Organization of Ukrainian Nationalists; OUN), which had a pro-German orientation and was influenced by fascist and Nazi ideology. A sizable number of clerics were active in the OUN or were at least sympathetic to its views. Sheptytsky's own attitude toward the OUN was ambivalent; he disapproved of the movement's terrorist actions against the Polish authorities and against its own opponents in the Ukrainian community, but he did not unequivocally denounce its political orientation. He may have been motivated by the desire to maintain the unity of the Uniate church, many of whose clerics and lay adherents sympathized with the Ukrainian nationalists.

Sheptytsky's relations with the Jewish leaders of Eastern Galicia were close and of long standing. In July 1941, when LVOV came under German occupation, Sheptytsky promised Rabbi Ezekiel Lewin to restrain the Ukrainians from killing Jews. No information is available as to whether or not he tried, but the Ukrainian attacks on Jews continued and, indeed, were intensified. Rabbi Lewin himself was attacked and killed by Ukrainians on his way home from his meeting with Sheptytsky. In February 1942 Sheptytsky wrote to Heinrich HIMMLER, asking him to halt the Ukrainian police's participation in the murder of Jews. In the following months Sheptytsky, with the help of a handful of confidants, enabled several dozen Jews to take refuge in monasteries under his control; in his own residence as well he took in some Jews for varying periods of time, thereby saving their lives.

While carrying out these humanitarian acts, however, Sheptytsky maintained his pro-German orientation. In July 1941 he hailed the German army as the liberator of the Ukrainians from the Soviet enemy, and in February 1942 he was one of several Ukrainian leaders affixing their signatures to a letter they sent to Hitler, pledging support for the "New Order" in Europe under Nazi German hegemony in which, they hoped, an independent Ukraine would find its place. Sheptytsky was undoubtedly aware that a "New Order" in Europe under Hitler meant a Europe without Jews. On other occasions, Sheptytsky urged the Ukrainians to cooperate with the Germans.

In November 1942 Sheptytsky issued a pastoral letter entitled "Thou Shalt Not Murder." He may have had in mind Ukrainian participation in the murder of Jews, but his main purpose was evidently to appeal for an end to the murders being committed by members of Ukrainian nationalist groups antagonistic to one another. Sheptytsky's pro-German policy was most clearly evidenced by his support for the formation of the Ukrainian army division SS Division Galicia, in the fall of 1943. His deputy, Josyf Slipyi, officiated at a solemn mass in the Lvov cathedral to celebrate the establishment of the division, and Sheptytsky appointed Vasyl Laba, a senior cleric and one of his close aides, to serve as chief chaplain of the division.

Even in the final stages of the German occupation, Sheptytsky did nothing to reduce the Ukrainian nationalists' cooperation with Germany. His compassion for the Jews on the one hand, and his support for the course pursued by the Ukrainian nationalists on the other, formed the tragic contradiction that marked his conduct in his final years.

BIBLIOGRAPHY

Armstrong, J. *Ukrainian Nationalism, 1939–1945.* New York, 1955.

Kahana, D. *Lvov Ghetto Diary.* Jerusalem, 1978. (In Hebrew.)

Prus, E. *Władyka Switojurski: Rzecz o arcybiskupie Andrzeju Szeptyckim (1865–1944).* Warsaw, 1985.

AHARON WEISS

SHIPS. *See* Aliya Bet; Exodus 1947; St. Louis; Struma.

SHO'AH. *See* Holocaust.

ŠIAULIAI (Shavli), city in the Lithuanian SSR; the largest in the northwestern part of the country. Jews first settled in Šiauliai in the seventeenth century. On the eve of World War II it had a Jewish population of 5,360. About 1,000 of the city's Jews managed to flee into the Soviet interior in the four days prior to the German occupation on June 26, 1941. Including refugees from Poland and Jews who had come from nearby towns, Šiauliai's Jewish population at the time of its occupation was 6,500.

In the first two weeks of the occupation, 1,000 Jews were murdered by Germans and Lithuanians. From July 25 to August 31, a ghetto was established in the Kaukazas and Trakai quarters of the city. A further 1,000 Jews, who had been sent to the town of Zagare, were killed there between September and December, as were 750 Jews who had been permitted to work in nearby villages. At the same time, 1,000 Jews took refuge in the Šiauliai ghetto, having fled from their homes, which were being set on fire in the nearby towns. The ghetto population again grew, to between 4,500 and 5,000. The ghetto had a five-member JUDENRAT (Jewish Council), headed by Mendel Leibowich. There was a forty-bed hospital in the ghetto, and the 1,000 children of school age were given an education, although on an irregular basis.

Beginning in September 1941, groups of Jews from Šiauliai were put to work in the area, doing construction work at the Zokniai airfield; mining peat at Radviliškis, Baciunai, and Rekyva; working in the arms warehouses in Linkaiciai; and unloading sugarcane in Pavenciai. In 1943 such groups were sent to the brick factory in Daugialiai, the lime quarry in Akmene, and the seed-growing plant in Vidukle. In Šiauliai itself Jews worked in the tanning and linen factories, in the "Maistas" and "Gubernija" cooperatives, and in various workshops.

At the end of 1941 a nonpartisan underground organization was formed in the ghetto, named Masada, made up of members of all the Zionist YOUTH MOVEMENTS. In 1942 another organization, called Selbstschutz (Self-Defense), was set up, comprising Masada, He-Haluts, NETSAH (No'ar Tsiyyoni Halutsi, or Zionist Pioneering Youth), and the Communists. Arms were smuggled into the ghetto, but no uprising took place. The underground newspapers *Masada, Ha-Tehiyya,* and *Mi-Ma'amakim* were published.

The history of the Šiauliai ghetto can be divided into four periods. The first, from September to December 1941, was the period of the *Aktionen*; the second, which was relatively quiet, lasted until September 1943. The third period extended from September 1943 to the summer of 1944; the fourth began

A group of Jews lined up in front of the "White Prison" in Šiauliai before being taken to the nearby forest to be shot. The two bearded men are Rabbis Nochomsuky (right) and Bakesht (left).

on the eve of the ghetto's liquidation and lasted until the completion of the deportation of the surviving Jews to Germany, on July 22, 1944.

In the third period, which began in September 1943, the ghetto was put under the authority of the SS and became a concentration camp. Some of the inhabitants were moved into camps adjoining the places where they worked. On November 5, an *Aktion* took place in the Šiauliai concentration camp that led to the deportation to extermination camps of 574 children and several hundred elderly men and disabled persons. Similar *Aktionen* took place in the camps adjoining the various workplaces. In July 1944, when the Red Army was approaching, the remaining Jews of Šiauliai were taken to Germany, mostly to the STUTTHOF camp. The majority of them perished; only some 500 Šiauliai Jews lived to see the liberation.

BIBLIOGRAPHY

Arad, Y. *Ghetto in Flames: The Struggle and Destruction of the Jews in Vilna in the Holocaust.* Jerusalem, 1980.

Itsikas, S. "The Story of the Siauliai Ghetto (1941–1944)." In vol. 4 of *Lithuanian Jewry*, edited by L. Garfunkel, pp. 185–234. Tel Aviv, 1984. (In Hebrew.)

Yerushalmi, A. *The Shavli Register: A Diary from*

a Lithuanian Ghetto (1941–1944). Jerusalem, 1958. (In Hebrew.)

HAYA LIFSHITZ

SICHERHEITSDIENST. *See* SD.

SIGHET MARMAŢIEI (Hung., Máramarossziget), city in Maramureş county, northern TRANSYLVANIA, that was under Hungarian rule from 1940 to 1944; a center of Orthodoxy and Hasidism. In 1941 there were 10,144 Jews in the city, 39.1 percent of the total population. That same year, a large number of "alien" Jews were deported from Sighet to KAMENETS-PODOLSKI, where they were massacred late in August. Although the county belonged geographically to northern Transylvania, which Hungary acquired from Romania in September 1940, its Jews were liquidated together with those of Carpathian Ruthenia (the TRANSCARPATHIAN UKRAINE) and northeastern Hungary.

The Jews of Sighet were ordered to enter a ghetto in April and early May of 1944. Established in two peripheral sections of the city, which were inhabited primarily by the poorer strata of Jewry, the ghetto was extremely crowded, with approximately twenty people in almost every room. The ghetto contained close to thirteen thousand Jews, including those brought in from the rural communities in the neighboring districts of Drăgomiresti (Drágomérfalva), Ocna-Şugătag (Aknasugatag), and Vişeu de Sus (Felsöviso). It was guarded by the local police and fifty gendarmes brought in from Miskolc. The commander of the gendarmes, a Colonel Sárvári, was among those who tortured the Jews into confessing where they had hidden their valuables. Internally, the ghetto was administered by a Zsidó Tanács (Jewish Council), headed by Rabbi Samu Danzig. The ghetto was liquidated when the Jews were deported to AUSCHWITZ in four transports between May 16 and 22, 1944.

In 1947, Sighet still had 2,308 Jews, including not only survivors but also a considerable number of Jews who settled there from other parts of Romania, to which the city reverted after the war.

BIBLIOGRAPHY

Braham, R. L. *Genocide and Retribution*. Boston, 1983. See pages 40–42, 157–162.

Rosmann, S., ed. *Memorial Book for the Jews of Carpatho-Russia–Maramos*. Rehovot, Israel, 1968. (In Hebrew.)

Wiesel, E. *Night*. New York, 1960.

RANDOLPH L. BRAHAM

SIGHET MARMAŢIEI

Annexations from June to September 1940: (1) Bessarabia and (2) N. Bukovina to USSR; (3) N. Transylvania to Hungary; (4) S. Dobruja to Bulgaria.

SIKORSKI, WŁADYSŁAW EUGENIUSZ (1881–1943), Polish general and statesman. Sikorski graduated in engineering from the Lvov Technical Institute. Before World War I he was active on behalf of Polish independence, and when the war broke out he became one of the prime movers in the establishment of the Polish Legions. In the 1919–1920 Polish-Soviet war Sikorski commanded the Third and Fifth armies.

In 1921 and 1922 Sikorski served as chief of the General Staff; in 1922 and 1923 as prime minister and minister of defense; and from 1925 to 1928 as commander of the Lvov military district. He was then put at the disposal of the minister of defense, and was not appointed to any post. Sikorski was opposed to the regime of Marshal Józef Piłsudski and his successors, and in 1936 he joined in organizing the Morges Front, a political alliance of liberal democratic opposition forces. He was the author of several books and wrote hundreds of articles for the press.

In late September 1939 Sikorski went to France as head of the POLISH GOVERNMENT-IN-EXILE, located in Angers. He remained there until June 1940, when, after the French surrender, it moved to London. In November 1939 he was also appointed commander in chief of the Polish armed forces. As prime minister and chief of the General Staff from 1940 to 1943, Sikorski was engaged in drawing up the Polish war aims, planning the formation and deployment of Polish armed forces abroad, and organizing a resistance movement in occupied Poland. During this period he made three visits to the United States in his capacity as prime minister. On July 30, 1941, Sikorski signed an agreement with the USSR, and he visited Moscow in December of that year, at which time he and Stalin issued a joint Polish-Soviet declaration. In April 1943, however, the Soviets severed diplomatic relations with the Polish government-in-exile when the latter demanded that the International RED CROSS investigate the KATYN affair—the murder of thousands of Polish officers in the Katyn forest.

In official statements he made on behalf of the Polish government-in-exile on December 18, 1939, and February 24, 1942, Sikorski outlined his plans for the future, mentioning that after the war changes would have to be introduced in Poland, based on the model of the democratic parliamentary regimes of the West. Sikorski's attitude toward the Jews was not always positive, but in a series of declarations he condemned the crime of genocide that was being committed against the Jews and appealed to the English-speaking countries—in vain, as it turned out—to take determined retaliatory measures against the Germans, as a means of halting the extermination.

On July 4, 1943, returning from a visit to the Polish army units in the Middle East, Sikorski was killed in an airplane crash over Gibraltar.

King George VI and Queen Elizabeth, accompanied by Gen. Władysław Sikorski, commander in chief of the Polish armed forces. They are on an inspection tour in Scotland, where they are being shown the deployment plan of Polish soldiers in defense positions. [Imperial War Museum]

BIBLIOGRAPHY

Korpalska, W. *Władysław Eugeniusz Sikorski: Biografia polityczna*. Wrocław, 1981.
Rozek, E. J. *Allied Wartime Diplomacy: A Pattern in Poland*. New York, 1958.

EUGENIUSZ DURACZYNSKI

SILESIA, EASTERN UPPER (Ger., Ostoberschlesien), administrative district comprising the areas east of the Polish district of Silesia (Śląsk) that were incorporated into the Reich. The central part of this unit consisted of Zagłębie, the eastern section of the mining and industrial basin of southeast Poland, a densely populated urban region. On the eve of World War II Zagłębie had a Jewish population of sixty-five thousand, of whom most were concentrated in the area's two large cities, BĘDZIN and SOSNOWIEC.

The annexation of Zagłębie and the creation of Ostoberschlesien as an administrative unit of the Reich had been included in the plans for the invasion and occupation of Poland. With this step the Germans planned to bring under their control all of Poland's natural resources and its heavy industry. Even before the occupation had been completed, the Germans began seizing control of the mines and large industrial plants and, at the same time, expelling the "undesirable" population from the area, mainly the Jews. Plans for the expulsion of the Jews from the area (mostly those of Zagłębie) existed on paper from September 1939 to January 1942. However, for a variety of reasons—mainly opposition to the move on the part of the *Generalgouverneur*, Hans FRANK—these plans were not carried out. Only two small-scale transfers of Jews took place in that period: a transport of 1,500 Jews that was dispatched to the east as part of the Nisko Plan (*see* NISKO AND LUBLIN PLAN) in October 1939, and the transfer of 5,000 Jews from Polish Silesia (Katowice, Chorzów, and other places) to cities in Eastern Upper Silesia in the spring of 1940.

In the first few months of the war, many regulations and decrees were issued against the Jews: levies of gold and silver in November and December 1939; the wearing of a white armband with a Star of David on it (later replaced by the yellow Jewish BADGE); restrictions on movement and on access to information, such as the possession of radio sets. On November 17 the confiscation of Jewish property was launched in the area, by means of HAUPTTREUHANDSTELLE OST (Main Trusteeship Office East) in Katowice. Wide sectors of the Jewish population were impoverished by the confiscations, and large numbers of Jewish males were put on forced labor.

Following the consolidation of the area's administration, and especially as a result of its incorporation into the Reich, conditions of life for the Jews underwent some changes. No closed ghettos were set up in Eastern Upper Silesia before the spring of 1943, although Jews were not allowed to live in certain areas; food rations were larger than in the GENERALGOUVERNEMENT; restrictions on movement were not as severe and were introduced only gradually; a central JUDENRAT (Jewish Council) was appointed, which was put in charge of all the communities in the district. Under these circumstances the chances for survival of the Jews in the district were better than for the rest of the Jews in occupied Poland.

The central Judenrat (Zentrale der Jüdischen Ältestenräte in Ostoberschlesien, or

EASTERN UPPER SILESIA

© Martin Gilbert 1982

Central Office of the Jewish Councils of Elders in Eastern Upper Silesia) was established in early 1940 and eventually incorporated some forty-five communities with a Jewish population of 100,000. In 1940 the large Jewish populations that came under the Zentrale were those of Będzin (24,495), Sosnowiec (22,407), Chrzanów (6,807), Zawiercie (6,030), Dąbrowa Gornicza (5,663), Oświęcim (Auschwitz; 5,372), and Olkusz (2,707).

For most of its existence the central Judenrat was headed by Moshe MERIN, who had his office in Sosnowiec. Merin was regarded as a forceful Judenrat chairman, capable of exerting authority over the Jewish population. He was in favor of adopting a policy of obedience to the Germans, by means of which, he hoped, he would be able to mitigate the impact of their anti-Jewish decrees. He was also an able administrator. Merin and his colleagues in the Zentrale leadership evolved an extensive program of institutional activities, dealing with the requirements of the Jews in the district in every sphere of life—welfare, health, education, culture, legal affairs, and so on. In the spring of 1941 Merin could point to a number of impressive achievements. There was not much hunger (in relative terms) in the district; the mortality rate from natural causes had not risen; no beggars were roaming the streets; the Treuhandstelle paid out some reimbursements for the property that had been confiscated; and all the refugees—of whom there were ten thousand in April 1941, following the evacuation of Oświęcim—had a roof over their heads. For these achievements Merin gained public legitimacy for his leadership, although many Jews in the district regarded him as the Nazis' henchman.

The fortunes of the Jews of Eastern Upper Silesia were profoundly affected by the manner in which the manpower they represented was utilized by the Germans. ORGANISATION SCHMELT, an economic agency belonging to the SS, operated in the district, and through it the Germans, from October 1940, recruited young Jews for work in Upper Silesian, Lower Silesian, and Sudetenland labor camps. On April 20, 1942, Organisation Schmelt had under its control sixty-five hundred forced laborers, in forty labor camps. The young Jews in the camps were employed on infrastructure projects required for the district's economic development. At the time when a growing number of young Jews was being put into the camps, the SS also began hiring them out to factory owners and small entrepreneurs in Upper and Lower Silesia, with the wages for their work enriching the Organisation Schmelt's coffers. The Judenrat and the Jewish police played an active role in organizing the transports of young Jews to the labor camps.

The Organisation Schmelt staff also controlled the "shops" that were established in the district, as of early 1940; these were workshops that manufactured goods for the German army, mainly clothing and shoes. The largest such shop, when its operations were at their height, employed sixty-six hundred Jews. By May 1942 most of the Jewish breadwinners in Eastern Upper Silesia were employed in the camps or in the shops, working for the German war economy. The Jewish workers in the shops were fully exploited:

they had to provide their own work tools, they worked for ten to twelve hours a day, and their pay was below the minimum needed for their most basic requirements. However, for a long time the "worker" documents that the Organisation Schmelt issued to the Jews employed in the shops protected them from being sent to labor camps, and in the initial deportation operations many of the Jews of Eastern Upper Silesia were protected, as essential personnel working for the German war economy.

Youth movement activities were greatly expanded during the war years (see YOUTH MOVEMENTS). Despite bans and restrictions, the various movements rehabilitated their cells and broadened their range of activities. At their height, they had two thousand members. Serving as centers were the agricultural training center of the Dror Zionist youth movement in Będzin, the agricultural training farm in Środula, and the youth wing established in the Zentrale. These centers enabled the youth movements to maintain and develop their own culture even under the occupation. In addition to fostering their traditional values, the movements also adapted their programs to the new situations. Most of them had a mutual-aid fund; the cells also functioned as study groups; and the activists among them took part in the Judenrat's welfare, cultural, and educational programs.

In early 1942 the first groups of Jews from Eastern Upper Silesia, each consisting of several hundred persons, were deported to AUSCHWITZ. In May 1942 systematic extermination was launched. The first wave of deportations was mainly the result of a large-scale *Selektion*; the transports to Auschwitz were made up primarily of welfare cases, disabled, sick, and elderly persons, and large families. Also included in the first transports were many refugees. Between May and early July of 1942 most of the small communities in the area were liquidated, including those of Olkusz, Kłobuck, Jaworzno, Ząbkowice, Grodziec, Trzebinia, and Zator. Their Jewish population, which the Germans regarded as "unproductive," was deported to Auschwitz. Groups of young people were sent to labor camps, while the rest of the population, insofar as they were fit for work, were concentrated in ten large cities where the "shops" were in operation. Thousands of Jews from the large cities were also dispatched to Auschwitz; there were major deportations from Sosnowiec (3,600), Będzin (3,200), Chrzanów (3,000), and Zawiercie (2,000). The operation of deporting the Jews reached its climax in August 1942, when the Germans, after first misleading the Jews, carried out a *Selektion* among the 50,000 Jews of Będzin, Sosnowiec, and Dąbrowa Gornicza and deported about 25 percent of them to Auschwitz.

When this move was completed all the surviving Jews of Eastern Upper Silesia were under the authority of Organisation Schmelt, and were therefore classified as "essential workers" serving the German war economy. Thousands of women, children, and elderly people were employed as workers in the shops; in Będzin alone there were thirteen thousand in May 1943, and in Sosnowiec a similar number. The transports were suspended, and no large-scale deportations to Auschwitz took place in the area for about a year, except for Chrzanów, from which some three thousand Jews were deported in February 1943, when the Jewish community there was liquidated. The survival rate, based on the size of the Jewish population in the region's cities in early 1943, was about 50 percent (or 65 percent, if the young people in the labor camps are taken into account).

In the first wave of deportations the Judenrat institutions and the Jewish police took an active part in rounding up the persons designated for deportation, sorting them out and guarding them. Merin continued to believe that in order to save as many Jews as possible, German orders had to be carried out to the full. The resentment felt toward Merin and the Jewish police by the Jewish population because of this attitude weakened the Judenrat's standing. However, as time went on and the deportations failed to be renewed, Merin regained the ground he had lost. He ascribed the relatively high rate of survival to the policy he had followed during the deportations and to the "rescue through work" policy he had advocated when they were discontinued.

The difference in their reactions to the deportations caused a rift between Merin and the youth movements. An underground was set up, comprising all the pioneering youth movements. At first, as long as it had no arms and no contact with the partisans, the underground confined itself to organizational activities and propaganda. In the spring of 1943 the underground's couriers (who were young women) succeeded in bringing in a modest quantity of arms from Warsaw, and a program of weapons training was introduced. A workshop for homemade bombs was put in operation, bunkers were dug for defense, and plans were drawn up for setting fire to the large cities in case the deportations were resumed. In June 1943 two weapon-snatching operations were carried out against the Germans. The following month a group of twenty underground members made an attempt to link up with the partisans, but they all fell into a German trap and were killed.

Between January and June 1943 the underground also took up rescue efforts. In that period the He-Haluts (Zionist pioneering movement) office in Geneva forwarded South American passports to Zagłębie, and the underground members hoped that with their help they would be able to enter the internment camps for foreign nationals. This operation, handled by the underground, involved hundreds and perhaps even thousands of Zagłębie residents, but only about twenty were saved by it.

The preparations that the underground was making for defense and rescue became a controversial issue between it and the Judenrat. This reached a climax in the spring of 1943, when Merin handed over to the Gestapo two members of the pioneering underground and eight youngsters suspected of Communist activities; all ten were executed. Merin also made several unsuccessful attempts to interfere with the underground's passport operation.

In compliance with Heinrich HIMMLER's policy of concentrating the remaining Jews of Poland in large labor camps, ghettos were instituted in Zagłębie. It took until the spring of 1943 to complete the concentration of the Będzin Jews in the Kamionka ghetto, which was adjacent to Będzin, and of the Sosnowiec Jews in the Środula ghetto, adjacent to Sosnowiec. At that point the Germans were still planning to exploit the Jews as a labor force. Shortly afterward this policy was discarded and a decision was made to liquidate the ghettos. On June 21, 1943, Merin and several of his close aides were deported to Auschwitz; the next day masses of Jews were deported from the Będzin and Sosnowiec ghettos. That same month the communities of Czeladz, Strzemieszyce, and Modrzejów were also liquidated. On August 1 the ghettos of Będzin and Sosnowiec were liquidated and more than thirty thousand Jews were deported to Auschwitz. A force of 797 policemen and soldiers took part in the deportation, which took two and a half weeks, much longer than originally planned. The Germans ran into problems: the Jews were prepared, and many had gone into hiding in bunkers. On three occasions Jews opened fire on Germans. In a fight waged by seven members of the Dror movement from one of the bunkers (under the leadership of Baruch Graftek and Frumka PLOTNICKA), an SS man was killed and another wounded. The bunker was finally captured and all the fighters in it perished.

On August 26 the last remaining Jewish community in the district was liquidated, when 2,500 Zawiercie Jews were deported to Auschwitz (until then they had been protected by working in a factory that manufactured German air force uniforms). Several liquidation camps were set up in the district, where 1,300 Jews were employed in sorting out the possessions of the deported Jews. These Jews, too, were gradually dispatched to Auschwitz, the final deportation taking place in January 1944.

After the final liquidation, eighty members and sympathizers of the Ha-No'ar ha-Tsiyyoni Zionist youth movement managed to escape and make their way to Budapest, most by crossing the border into Slovakia by way of the Carpathian Mountains, and some by posing as Polish workers going to Germany and Austria to work there. In December 1943 another group, of twenty-five members of the Haluts underground, reached Slovakia. Dozens and perhaps hundreds of individual Jews also managed to cross the border into Slovakia and from there to make their way to Hungary.

BIBLIOGRAPHY

Geshuri, M. S. *On the Rivers of Zaglebie Dabrowskie.* Tel Aviv, 1972. (In Hebrew.)

Geshuri, M. S., ed. *The Book of Sosnowiec and Its Surroundings in Zaglebie.* 2 vols. Tel Aviv, 1973–1974. (In Hebrew.)

Jońca, K. *Polityka narodowościowa Trzeciej Rzeszy na Śląsku Opolskim 1933–1940.* Katowice, 1970.

Konieczny, A. *Pod rządami wojennego prawa karnego Trzeciej Rzeszy: Górny Śląsk 1939–1945.* Warsaw, 1972.

Rapaport, Y., ed. *Pinkas Zaglebie; Memorial Book.* Tel Aviv, 1972. (In Yiddish and English.)

Trunk, I. *Judenrat.* New York, 1972.

FREDKA MAZYA and
AVIHU RONEN

SILVER, ABBA HILLEL (1893–1963), American rabbi and communal leader. Born in Lithuania and brought to the United States in 1902, Silver was ordained at Hebrew Union College in 1915. He became the Rabbi of the Temple at Congregation Tifereth Israel, in Cleveland, Ohio, in 1917—a position he retained for the remainder of his career. As rabbi, Silver became active in a number of social causes, among which Zionism and his efforts at fostering Jewish education were paramount. Known for his skill as a public speaker, Silver considered himself a political Zionist in the Herzlian mold. His emphasis on political Zionism led Silver to support Chaim WEIZMANN in the latter's dispute with Louis Brandeis over the wisdom of continued diplomatic activity, in light of the acceptance of the British Mandate for Palestine. Considered a "radical" within American Zionism, Silver was closely identified with the Republican party, in contrast to the majority of Jewish leaders, who were Democrats.

With the rise of the Nazis, Silver returned to political activity after a hiatus of nearly a decade. His militantly anti-Nazi position catapulted him to a central role in American Jewish life. Silver was one of the organizers of the American Jewish Anti-Nazi Boycott (*see* BOYCOTTS, ANTI-NAZI), despite the advice of more moderate leaders against such "provocations." His boycott activities led him to oppose the HAAVARA AGREEMENT, which he saw as breaking the unity of the Jewish anti-Nazi front. In 1938 Silver assumed the chairmanship of the United Palestine Appeal (UPA). He did not see the UPA as a philanthropic agency, since he rejected the idea that Zionism could ever be reduced to phi-

Abba Hillel Silver. [Central Zionist Archives, Jerusalem]

lanthropism, but rather as an educational tool to unify American Jewry for its decisive political role.

During the 1930s Silver opposed acts designed to drive a wedge between the Zionist movement and Great Britain, such as efforts at illegal immigration into Palestine. Silver also opposed the Peel partition plan (1937), believing that Britain's reversal of its Palestine policy was only temporary. However, the war, the WHITE PAPER OF 1939, and the disturbing news filtering out of Nazi-occupied Europe led to a rethinking of his position, drawing Silver into the maximalist statist camp of David BEN-GURION, as opposed to the minimalist position of Stephen S. WISE and Chaim Weizmann.

Silver first articulated his statist position at the UPA annual convention of January 25–26, 1941, and the need for a Jewish state became central to all of his activities. In cooperation with Ben-Gurion, Silver organized the Extraordinary Zionist Conference, which met at the Biltmore Hotel in New York from May 9 to 11, 1942. The resulting BILTMORE RESOLUTION was seen by Silver as a declaration of the Jews' intention to establish Palestine as a Jewish commonwealth after the war. He devoted himself to turning this dream into a reality, assuming the cochairmanship, with Wise, of the AMERICAN ZIONIST EMERGENCY COUNCIL (AZEC). Silver's strategy was to arouse public opinion, thereby gaining the support of American politicians for Jewish and Zionist causes. He saw no efficacy in quiet diplomacy, which relied on the goodwill of leaders who had little or no interest in Jewish issues. Silver especially distrusted Franklin Delano ROOSEVELT, summing up his evaluation of the president by quoting the biblical verse "Put not your faith in princes."

Silver's activism met with some success, but also with a good deal of opposition. Many Zionists, Wise included, felt uncomfortable with Silver's brash tactics and maximalist demands. Instrumental in the creation of the AMERICAN JEWISH CONFERENCE (1942), Silver's rhetoric kept the commonwealth plank on the agenda, helping to win the conference's overwhelming approval. The victory was short-lived, however, since the AMERICAN JEWISH COMMITTEE rejected the idea of Jewish statehood and withdrew from the conference. Tension between Wise and Silver broke out into an open rift in 1944 when the latter worked, against the wishes of the administration, for a congressional resolution supporting the Jewish commonwealth. Silver resigned from the AZEC in December 1944, but returned as sole chairman in June 1945 when American Zionists and many non-Zionist American Jews, shocked by the horrors of the Holocaust, realized that his call for an unrelenting public campaign on behalf of Jewish interests was justified. He played a major role in the 1947 campaign of the Jewish Agency at the United Nations to approve the plan for the partition of Palestine.

Silver has been criticized for his stubborn emphasis on Palestine as the only haven for European Jewry in its hour of need. In his passionate speech at the American Jewish Conference, he stated his credo:

We cannot truly rescue the Jews of Europe unless we have free immigration into Palestine.

We cannot have free immigration into Palestine unless our political rights are recognized there. Our political rights cannot be recognized there unless our historical connection with the country is acknowledged and our right to rebuild our national home is reaffirmed. These are inseparable links in the chain. The whole chain breaks if one of the links is missing.

Silver was approached by Peter BERGSON (Hillel Kook) to head the Emergency Committee to Save the Jewish People of Europe. Seeking an establishment leader to give his organization some respectability, Bergson did not see Silver's activist policy as incompatible with his own. Silver, however, refused to cooperate, mistrusting Bergson's motives.

A respected scholar, Silver was also a gifted writer. His works include *The History of Messianic Speculation in Israel* (1927), *Where Judaism Differed* (1956), two collections of speeches: *World Crisis and Jewish Survival* (1941) and *Vision and Victory* (1941), and numerous articles.

BIBLIOGRAPHY

Berman, A. "American Zionism and the Rescue of European Jewry: An Ideological Perspective." *American Jewish History* 70/3 (March 1941): 310–330.

Ganin, Z. "Activism versus Moderation: The Controversy between Abba Hillel Silver and Stephen S. Wise during the 1940s." *Studies in Zionism* 5/1 (Spring 1984): 71–96.

Urofsky, M. *We Are One! American Jewry and Israel.* New York, 1978.

ABRAHAM J. EDELHEIT

SIMA, HORIA (b. 1906), Romanian fascist leader. Sima was born in Bucharest and was a teacher by profession. In 1927 he joined the IRON GUARD, a fascist and radical antisemitic movement. In 1938, when its leader and founder, Corneliu (Zelea) Codreanu, was executed, Sima took his place, all the other potential successors senior to himself having been imprisoned or put to death. When the Iron Guard was outlawed and King Carol II launched a vendetta against the movement's leaders, Sima fled to Yugoslavia (in 1939) and from there to Germany. In 1940 German influence in ROMANIA gained in strength, and the king, trying to save his regime, permitted Sima to return from exile and appointed him to a cabinet post. On September 6 of that year, the day after Carol II was deposed, Sima and Ion ANTONESCU set up a "National Legionary Government" (the members of the Iron Guard called themselves "Legionaries"), in which Antonescu was the prime minister and Sima his deputy.

Sima concentrated all his efforts on eliminating the Jews from the country's economy, seizing their property, and seeking revenge against the leaders of the previous regime who had opposed the Iron Guard. To achieve his ends he incited terror against the Jews and took personal charge of the confiscation of Jewish property conducted by his men. He was also personally involved in the murder of eleven Jews in Ploieşti. Whereas Antonescu preferred that the elimination of the Jews from the economy be a gradual process, so as to avoid upheavals, Sima urged that Jewish property be seized by force, without regard for the law or the potential damage to the economy. To carry out this aim Sima created a "Legionary Police," which competed with the regular state police and upset law and order in the country.

Sima's campaign against members of the former regime, and the terror against the Jews that he instigated, created friction between himself and Antonescu. Relying on support from Heinrich HIMMLER, Sima, on January 20, 1940, staged an Iron Guard uprising and tried to seize full power in the country. Antonescu, however, who had Adolf Hitler's support and was backed by the Romanian army, managed to defeat the uprising within three days. During the uprising a pogrom took place in Bucharest in which 123 Jews were murdered. In a letter to Himmler, Sima put the blame for his defeat on the Jews and claimed that Antonescu was in their pay. With Antonescu's secret approval, Sima escaped to Germany, where he was put into a special Iron Guard camp. In Romania he was tried *in absentia* and sentenced to death in 1941.

In the fall of 1942 Sima escaped to Italy, only to be sent back to Germany, at Ion Antonescu's request. The Germans used Sima and the Iron Guard as a potential threat to Antonescu, and in August 1944, when Antonescu's fascist regime was ousted, Sima became prime minister of a Legionary government-in-exile. From Vienna, where the government-in-exile had its seat, Sima kept up the cry for revenge against the Jews.

After the war Sima fled to Spain, where he was still living as of the late 1980s. He was the leader of one of the Iron Guard splinter groups in exile. Sima was again tried and sentenced to death *in absentia* in 1946.

BIBLIOGRAPHY

Lavi, T., ed. *Rumania*, vol. 1. In *Pinkas Hakehillot; Encyclopaedia of Jewish Communities.* Jerusalem, 1969. (In Hebrew.)

Pavel, P. *Why Rumania Failed.* London, 1943.

Sima, H. *Histoire du Mouvement Légionnaire.* Rio de Janeiro, 1972.

JEAN ANCEL

ŠIMAITE, ONA (1899–1970), Lithuanian librarian who helped Jews in the VILNA ghetto. A librarian at Vilna University, Šimaite was distressed at the sight of Jewish sufferings at the hands of the Germans and their Lithuanian collaborators. She later explained: "I could no longer go on with my work. I could not remain in my study. I could not eat. I was ashamed that I was not Jewish myself." Under the pretext of recovering library books loaned from the university to Jewish students, she was able to obtain permission to enter the ghetto. There she saved valuable literary and historical works entrusted to her by public institutions, such as YIVO (the Yivo Institute for Jewish Research), and private individuals, among them the Yiddish poet Abraham SUTZKEVER. She hid these materials in various places, including under the floor of her apartment.

Šimaite also negotiated the return of Jewish possessions, left in non-Jewish hands, that were needed by the ghetto dwellers to purchase necessary foodstuffs, and she recruited people to hide Jews outside the ghetto. On her daily visits to the ghetto she brought food and other provisions for needy Jews there. Befriending Tanya Sterntal, a lone Jewish girl in the ghetto, Šimaite de-

cided to rescue her. Spiriting her out under the watchful eyes of the guards at the gates, Šimaite hid her in several locations, until she was accidentally discovered.

Ona Šimaite was arrested in the summer of 1944 when she adopted a ten-year-old Jewish girl, registering her as a relative from a bombed-out town that, upon inquiry, turned out to be fictitious. She was brutally tortured to elicit information on her Jewish contacts but did not divulge names or places. Because of these tortures her spine was ruptured, causing her pain for the rest of her life.

The Nazis wanted to execute Šimaite but her friends from Lithuanian academic circles bribed the Gestapo and succeeded in mitigating her sentence to imprisonment in a concentration camp. Deported to the DACHAU camp, she was later transferred to southern France, where she was liberated in August 1944. Except for a brief spell in Israel, Ona continued living in France until her death.

Ona Šimaite consistently refused any honors for her deeds during the war, claiming that it was the suffering Jews who were the true heroes. In the words of Abba KOVNER, the poet-fighter of the Vilna ghetto: "If there are ten Righteous among the Nations [in the world], Ona Šimaite is certainly one of them." She was recognized by YAD VASHEM as a "RIGHTEOUS AMONG THE NATIONS" in 1966.

MORDECAI PALDIEL

SIMFEROPOL, city in the Crimean peninsula; capital of the Crimean Oblast (district), in the Ukrainian SSR. Simferopol was founded in the eighteenth century, and Jews lived there from its inception. On the eve of World War II the city's Jewish population was more than 20,000, out of a total population of 142,678.

Simferopol was occupied by the Germans on November 1, 1941. By then most of the Jews had left on their own accord or had been evacuated, but their place had been taken by Jewish refugees from KHERSON, DNEPROPETROVSK, and the Jewish kolkhozy (collective farms) in the Larindorf and Freidorf subdistricts. Approximately thirteen thousand Jews were in Simferopol when the

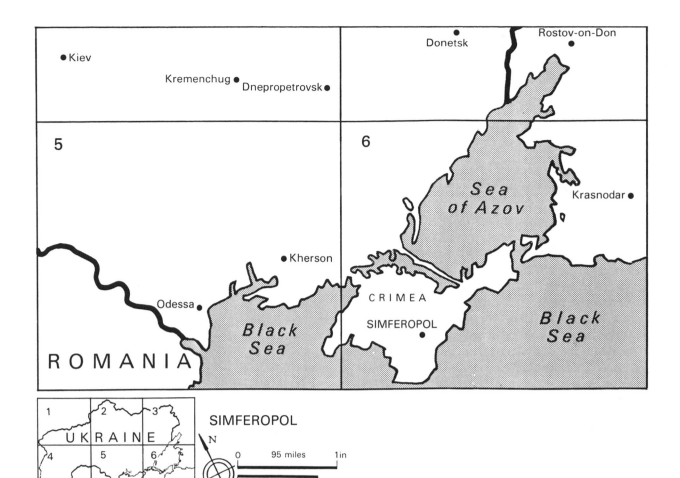

SIMFEROPOL

UKRAINE

1 2 3
4 5 6

N

0   95 miles   1in
0   120 km.   2cm.

Germans arrived, as well as fifteen hundred KRIMCHAKS, the largest community of these Jews to be found anywhere. On the day after the occupation, announcements were posted ordering the Jews to form a JUDENRAT (Jewish Council) and to report for forced labor. In the following days they were ordered to register and wear a yellow badge (*see* BADGE, JEWISH) in the form of a Star of David.

On December 9, the Krimchak Jews were rounded up and killed. From December 11 to 13 the remaining 12,500 Jews were rounded up, put on trucks, and taken out of town to be shot to death. The murder was perpetrated by the men of Sonderkommando 11b, belonging to Einsatzgruppe D, and by German police of Reserve ORDNUNGSPOLIZEI Battalion No. 3. Jews who had gone into hiding and were caught were put into the local jail, and by the middle of February 1942, 300 of them were gassed in GAS VANS.

Simferopol was liberated by the Soviets on April 13, 1944.

BIBLIOGRAPHY

Ehrenburg, I., and V. Grossman, eds. *The Black Book of Soviet Jewry*. New York, 1981.

SHMUEL SPECTOR

SIMON WIESENTHAL CENTER. *See* Museums and Memorial Institutes: Simon Wiesenthal Center.

SIXTH SLOVAK BRIGADE, Slovak army brigade in which Jews served, in special companies. Under a military law issued on January 31, 1940, Slovak Jews, together with GYPSIES and "asocial elements," were removed from the regular army units in which they were serving and transferred to labor units. Three companies in the Sixth Brigade, the Twenty-first through Twenty-third, were made up of Jews; the Twenty-second Company consisted mostly of Orthodox Jews, and it adhered to the Jewish dietary laws.

The first draftees were those born in 1919, followed by those born in 1920 and 1921. The Sixth Brigade belonged to the army labor (pioneer) units, whose commanding officer was Gen. Ladislav Bodicky. When it was set up, the brigade had a complement of about one thousand men.

The units were employed on excavations, road building, and river control; the Twenty-first Company was transferred to Poland for a time and was engaged in road repair work. The brigade was moved from eastern to northern Slovakia, where the Evangelical Christian population was sympathetic to the Jews. From there the brigade moved southwest to the Austrian border.

During the deportation of Slovak Jews to extermination camps in the spring of 1942, a large number of men serving in the brigade deserted the ranks. Some joined their families in the deportation, and others fled to Hungary or went underground with "Aryan" papers. The Ministry of the Interior pressured the army to deport the brigade to Poland, but the army and the minister of defense, Gen. František Catlos, refused; as a result, the Jewish soldiers were not deported and their lives were spared. At the time of the deportations, warrants were issued for the arrest of 250 deserters. In May 1943 the brigade was dissolved and its men were transferred to labor camps or formed into civilian work gangs and employed by building contractors.

Men of the Sixth Brigade joined in the anti-Nazi SLOVAK NATIONAL UPRISING of August 1944, and fifty-two fell in the fighting.

BIBLIOGRAPHY

Jelinek, Y. "The Role of the Jews in Slovakian Resistance." *Jahrbuch für Geschichte Osteuropas* 15/3 (September 1967): 415–422.

AKIVA NIR

SKARZYSKO-KAMIENNA (Kamienna, in German sources), forced-labor camp for Jews (*Zwangsarbeitslager-Judenlager*), adjacent to the ammunition factory in the town of that name in the Kielce district of Poland. It belonged to the German HASAG concern. SS officer Egon Dalski, the general manager of the HASAG factory in Skarżysko-Kamienna from 1939 to 1943, was also in charge of the camp; his successor in 1943 was Paul Geldmacher.

The Skarżysko-Kamienna camp was established in August 1942, in three separate localities, identified as factory camps (*Werke*) A, B, and C, respectively. It existed until August 1, 1944. The camp was under the control of the SS and Police Leader of the RADOM district, Herbert Böttcher. Most of the prisoners were from Poland, and the rest from Austria, Czechoslovakia, Germany, the Netherlands, and France; the average number of prisoners in the camp was 6,000. According to German sources, 3,241 Jews perished at Skarżysko-Kamienna between October 1, 1942, and January 31, 1943—an average of twenty-six deaths a day. On June 30, 1943, the camp population stood at 6,408. The total number of Jews who were brought there is estimated at 25,000 to 30,000, and the number who died at 18,000 to 23,000.

The three camps were situated close to the factories in which the prisoners worked, next to free Polish workers. Each department had a German manager, with Poles acting as his deputies and as supervisors. The camp security was in the hands of the Ukrainian factory police (*Werkschutz*), headed, successively, by the Germans Kurt Krause and Walter Pollmer, who were subordinate to the factory manager. Krause and his deputies—Fritz Bartenschlager, Otto Eisenschmidt, and Paul Kuhnemann—were notorious for the acts of robbery, murder, and rape for which they were responsible. The commandant of all the three camps, up to the end of 1943, was Anton Ipfling.

Factory Camp A (*Werk* A) was the largest of the three. When it was set up its commandant was Ipfling, who was later relieved by Kuhnemann. The *Lagerälteste* (camp elder) was Elias Albirt, from Kielce; a Jewish police unit, headed by Leizer Tepperman and Joseph Krzepicki, was at Albirt's disposal for the maintenance of internal order. Factory B (*Werk* B) was attached to Camp A for administration and security, but it had its own *Lagerälteste*. Among its German commandants were Leonhard Haas, Hermann Klemm, and

SKARŻYSKO-KAMIENNA

Administrative Divisions of Poland
under German Occupation, 1939–1945

1 Pomerania
2 Brandenburg
3 Saxony
4 Lower Silesia
5 Upper Silesia
6 Warthegau
7 Danzig (West Prussia)
8 East Prussia
9 Generalgouvernement
10 Białystok Region

© Polish National Publishing House, Warsaw, 1979
(Państwowe Wydawnictwo Naukowe)

■ Camp

▨ Extermination Center

Gustav Schmidtke. The prisoners from both the A and B camps worked principally in the production of ammunition for the army.

Factory Camp C (*Werk* C) belonged to the filling plant (*Füllanstalt*). Its German commandants were Paul Kiesling, Kurt Schumann, and Friedrich Schulze; the camp's internal administration was headed by Fela Markowiczowa and her brother-in-law, Heniek Eisenberg. This was the harshest and most notorious camp, on account of the deadly nature of the work there: producing underwater mines and filling them with picric acid. The acid caused the skin to turn yellow, and within three months the prisoners doing this work died of poisoning.

All the factories had two twelve-hour shifts. The prisoners were led to work by factory police and Jewish police, and were compelled to fill quotas that were beyond their strength. The camps were mixed, with men and women together, but they slept in separate huts, on bunks with two or three tiers of wooden shelves, without blankets. Sanitary conditions were intolerable. The food rations consisted of 7 ounces (200 g) of bread a day and about a pint (.5 l) of watery soup twice a day, and, occasionally, a spoonful of jam or a portion of margarine. The prisoners had to work in the same clothes week after week, and when these disintegrated—as they inevitably did, particularly in Camp C—they wrapped themselves in paper bags.

In all three camps there were epidemics of dysentery, typhus, and a disease caused by weakness, called *hasagowka* by the prisoners (after the HASAG company). Not until early 1944 did medical assistance become available in the camps. Periodic *Selektionen* took place, and the prisoners who were singled out in this way were killed by a "shock troop" (*Stosstruppe*) made up of factory police. Its members included Georg Adrianovitsch, Gerhard Sander, and two brothers, Teodor and Petro Sawczak.

Attempts to escape usually ended in the killing of those who had made the attempt. In Camps A and C, Jews caught stealing materials in the factory were hanged. During the spring of 1944, when the authorities faced a critical shortage of manpower, living conditions in the camp improved slightly, particularly the food rations, medical supplies, and clothing. Some of the prisoners had connections with the Jewish or Polish underground and received aid from these sources.

In late 1943 and early 1944 mass executions took place in Camp C. The victims were prisoners of different nationalities who had been brought in from the Gestapo jails in the Radom district. Shortly before the liquidation of the camp in the summer of 1944, a special unit of Jewish prisoners, under SS supervision, took the bodies of these victims out of the mass grave in which they had been interred in the Camp C area, in order to cremate them.

Several underground groups were active in the camp, among them a cell of the ŻYDOWSKA ORGANIZACJA BOJOWA (Jewish Fighting Organization; ŻOB), and BUND members in the camp established links with the Bund leadership in Warsaw. Jewish prisoners smuggled arms out of the factory and handed them over to Polish partisans belonging to the ARMIA KRAJOWA (Home Army). Links also existed with the Polish Communist underground, the Polska Partia Robotnicza (Polish Workers' Party).

Two days before the liquidation of Camp C a mass escape of several hundred prisoners took place. Most of them were killed during the attempt or in the surrounding forests. In late July 1944 mass *Selektionen* were carried out in all three camps, and some six hundred persons were killed on the spot. The remaining prisoners, numbering over six thousand, were transferred to the BUCHENWALD camp, to camps at CZĘSTOCHOWA and Leipzig, and to other camps in Germany.

In 1948, twenty-five German foremen from the Skarżysko-Kamienna camp were brought to trial in Leipzig. Four were sentenced to death, two to life imprisonment, and others to prison terms of varying lengths. Egon Dalski and many of his helpers were not caught.

BIBLIOGRAPHY

Bauminger, R. *Przy pikrynie i trotylu*. Kraków, 1946.
Garfinkel, M., et al. *The Yizchor Book: In Memory of the Jewish Community of Skarzysko and Its Surroundings*. Tel Aviv, 1973. (In Hebrew, Yiddish, and English.)
Kaczanowski, L. *Hitlerowskie fabryki śmierci na kielceczyznie*. Warsaw, 1984.
Strigler, M. *In the Todt Factories*. Buenos Aires, 1948. (In Yiddish.)

FELICJA KARAY

SKOBTSOVA, ELIZAVETA (Mother Maria; 1891–1945), nun in France who assisted Jews during the Holocaust. Skobtsova was born in Riga, Latvia, where her father, Juri Pilenko, was chief prosecutor for the tsarist government there. She wrote poetry in her youth, and one of her works, "Scythian Shards," was well known in literary circles in Saint Petersburg. During the Russian Revolution, Skobtsova joined the Socialist Revolutionary party. Sent to Anapa, on the Black Sea, she was arrested by the White forces. After her release, she married and bore two children. Settling in France, Skobtsova decided, after the death of her four-year-old daughter, to become a nun in the Russian Orthodox church. In 1932 she took her vows and chose the name of Maria.

Until the outbreak of World War II, Skobtsova coordinated welfare activities for Russian emigrés in France. Her church purchased for this purpose a building in Paris on Rue de Lourmel that soon became the nerve center of her extensive activities. Her immediate aide was Father Dimitri Klepinin, also a refugee from Russia.

With the onset of the persecution of Jews in France by the Germans, she decided that her Christian calling required her to come to the aid of Jews in whatever way possible. As a first step, she made the church's free kitchen available for impoverished Jews; then, she arranged temporary shelter for others. Father Klepinin issued false baptismal certificates for those needing new identities. Stunned by the German edict in June 1942 requiring Jews to wear the yellow star (*see* BADGE, JEWISH), she penned the following poem:

Israel—
Two triangles, a star
The shield of King David, our forefather,
This is election, not offense
The great path and not an evil.

Elizaveta Skobtsova.

Once more is a term fulfilled
Once more roars the trumpet of the end
And the fate of a great people
Once more is by the prophet proclaimed.

Thou art persecuted again, O Israel
But what can human ill-will mean to thee,
Thee, who has heard the thunder from Sinai?

In July 1942, Mother Maria succeeded in penetrating the Vélodrome d'Hiver sports stadium in PARIS, where thousands of Jews had been assembled on the eve of their deportation. With the connivance of garbage collectors, she smuggled out several children in garbage bins. She continued her charitable work for Jews in spite of warnings that she was being closely watched by the Gestapo. Arrested together with Klepinin on February 8, 1943, she readily admitted to the charge of helping Jews elude Nazi roundups. She was sent to the RAVENSBRÜCK concentration camp, where she died from exhaustion on March 31, 1945, days before the camp's liberation. Father Klepinin perished earlier, in February 1944, in the DORA-MITTELBAU camp.

Mother Maria and Father Klepinin were both recognized as "RIGHTEOUS AMONG THE NATIONS" by YAD VASHEM.

BIBLIOGRAPHY

Hackel, S. *Pearl of Great Price*. London, 1981.

MORDECAI PALDIEL

SLAVE LABOR. *See* Forced Labor.

SLONIM, town in Grodno Oblast (district), Belorussian SSR. Between the two world wars, Slonim was part of Poland. In September 1939 it was taken over by the Red Army. On the eve of the German invasion of the Soviet Union in June 1941, 22,000 Jews were living in the town, many of them refugees from western Poland, which was then under German rule.

On June 25, 1941, the Germans captured Slonim. In the first *Aktion*, on July 14, 1,255 Jews were executed in Petrolevits, 5 miles (7 km) from Slonim, among them intellectuals and members of the JUDENRAT (Jewish Council). In a second *Aktion*, on November 14, more than 10,000 Jews, including the second Judenrat, were murdered in Chepilovo. In December of the same year a ghetto was erected in Slonim, in the Zhabinka district. From January to March of 1942, Jews from the nearby towns of Derechin, Kholinka, Byten, Ivatsevichi, and Kossovo were concentrated there. In May, 500 Jewish men were taken from Slonim to Mogilev for forced labor. Some Jews fled to the Białystok ghetto because they heard that conditions were better there.

In the aftermath of the November 1941 *Aktion*, an antifascist committee was formed in the Slonim ghetto, comprised of young people from various political factions. The leaders of the underground included Zorach Kremen, Avraham Blumovits, Niunia Tsirinski, Aviezer Imber, Arik Stein, and Henik Malach. Members of the underground who worked for the Germans in ammunition depots managed to transfer rifles, pistols, and crates of hand grenades and bullets to the ghetto. In the debate on whether to make a

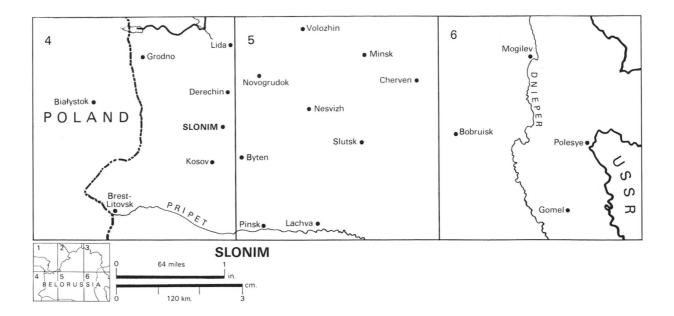

SLONIM

stand in the ghetto or to join the resistance in the forest, the underground tended to the latter view. They made contact with the partisans and transferred to them ammunition and other equipment; contacts with the Judenrat resulted in further support for the partisans. Some among the underground escaped from the ghetto to the forest.

The third *Aktion* began on June 29, 1942, and lasted until July 15. Some 10,000 Jews were killed in Petrolevits. This accelerated the flight of the Jews joining the partisans in the forest, and Jews from the Slonim ghetto were among the founders of "Schorr's 51," a partisan unit with many Jewish members and a distinguished battle record. Kremen, one of the escapees in the forest, was supplied with weapons by his comrades in the ghetto. On August 20, 1942, the Germans put 400 Slonim Jews to death, and in December they killed the remaining Jews in the town.

The Jewish partisans from the Slonim ghetto participated in the liberation of the Jews in Kossovo on October 2, 1943. At least four hundred Slonim Jews succeeded in fleeing the ghetto to the forest.

BIBLIOGRAPHY

Gilbert, M. *The Holocaust.* New York, 1985.
Lichtenstein, K., ed. *Slonim Record.* 4 vols. Tel Aviv, 1960–1978. (In Hebrew.)
Yochvedovitz-Kahane, D. *Transmigration of Bodies* [*Resurrection*]: *Through Ghettos, Forests, Borders, and Countries to Eretz Israel during World War II.* Merhavia, Israel, 1973. (In Hebrew.)

SHALOM CHOLAWSKI

SLOVAKIA, region in east central Europe. Until 1918 Slovakia was part of Hungary, and in the interwar years it was part of the Czechoslovak republic. Between March 14, 1939, and April 29, 1945, it was a satellite of Nazi Germany; since the end of World War II it has been part of Czechoslovakia. Before the war some 70 percent of the population was Roman Catholic, and the rest were Greek Catholic, Protestant, and Jewish.

The Jewish presence in Slovakia can be traced to the Roman period. During the nineteenth century the community began to grow significantly. In 1930, 135,918 Jews (4.5 percent of the population) lived in Slovakia. Most were observant (Orthodox) and lived in the eastern part of the country. As in Hungary, however, there was also a Neolog (Reform) community and a tiny Status Quo Ante community, that is, one that was neither Neolog nor Orthodox. Most Slovak Jews considered themselves to be of Jewish nationality (72,644 in the 1930 census), although a large minority (44,009 in the same census)

SLOVAKIA, October 1938

regarded themselves as Slovaks. The Zionist movement was quite strong; more than 10,000 young Jews were members of Zionist YOUTH MOVEMENTS. However, Hungarian language and culture remained important influences.

Slovak nationalists agitated for greater autonomy within the Czechoslovak republic, and they made their first major gain following the MUNICH CONFERENCE of September 1938. The Munich agreement resulted in the ceding of the Sudetenland to Germany and the establishment of the second Czechoslovak republic on October 6, with Slovakia as an autonomous region. Less than a month later, the first Vienna Award (November 2) allowed the annexation of parts of Slovakia and Ruthenia by Hungary. With this loss of territory, the Jewish population of Slovakia decreased to 88,951 (the figure in the census of December 15, 1938, did not include baptized Jews).

Following the Nazis' next incursion into Czechoslovakia, when the areas of BOHEMIA AND MORAVIA were made a protectorate of the Reich, Slovakia became a separate state, on March 14, 1939. A one-party totalitarian regime took control of Slovakia, the Hlinková Slovenská L'udová Strana (Slovak People's Party of HLINKA), more commonly known as the Ludaks. Under their leader, the Catholic priest Jozef TISO, the Ludaks advocated Christian solidarism. That ideology espoused the values of extreme nationalism, a social order purportedly based on Catholicism, the acceptance of authoritarianism, and an extreme anticommunism. The government also aligned itself with Nazi Germany, and one of its first acts was to sign the Treaty of Protection (*Schutzvertrag*) with the German foreign minister, Joachim von RIBBENTROP. In effect, the treaty allowed Germany to interfere in Slovak internal affairs and to dictate Slovak foreign policy.

From the first days of the new regime, two factions struggled for power. Tiso was made president of the Slovak state and thereby gained the upper hand. His rivals were Dr. Vojtech (Bela) TUKA, a professor and frustrated intellectual who served as prime minister, and Alexander (Saňo) MACH, head of the HLINKA GUARD and later the interior minister. The faction of Tuka and Mach was more reactionary than that of Tiso, courting Nazi Germany's favor more vociferously. Both factions favored discriminatory laws against the Jews. The Slovaks entered the war in 1941, sending soldiers against the Soviet Union shortly after the start of Operation "Barbarossa." Declarations of war against the other Allies followed.

A minority of Slovaks, mostly non–Roman Catholics, never supported the regime. Anti-Ludak partisan units came into existence in Slovakia as early as 1942, developing in the forests near Michalovce and Hummené and near the town of Banská Štiavnica. Supporters of Edvard BENEŠ and the CZECHOSLOVAK GOVERNMENT-IN-EXILE, Slovak Communists, and other opponents of the Tiso regime established the Slovenská Narodna Rada (Slovak National Council; SNR), which was dedicated to overthrowing the pro-Nazi state. Relying heavily on sympathetic officers in the Slovak army, the SNR planned an uprising under the leadership of Col. Jan Golian. As the Germans suffered increasing reversals on the field of battle, more and more Slovaks were drawn into the rebel camp. Early in the summer of 1944 Moscow sent guerrillas to Slovakia to engage in partisan activities. These forces made little effort to coordinate with the SNR. Nazi intervention to quell the partisan fighting led to a premature declaration of an uprising on August 29. The rebels at first captured much territory, making the town of BANSKÁ BYSTRICA their center. But the situation deteriorated rapidly, and on October 28, Banská Bystrica fell, heralding the end of the rebellion. After the crushing of the SLOVAK NATIONAL UPRISING, the Nazis were not ousted until April 29, 1945, when the Soviet army took Slovakia.

Antisemitism had existed in Slovakia before the region became a separate state, and it continued to thrive throughout the war years. Slovak nationalists considered the Jews in their region to be the bearers of the foreign Hungarian culture (this was true to some extent), and reviled them as "Prague oriented." Jews were also considered exploitative and overly urbanized, and traditional, religion-based stereotypes were harbored against them. With the advent of an autonomous Slovakia upon the establishment of the second Czechoslovak republic and the ceding of territory to Hungary, overt acts against the Jews began. Street attacks, the looting of property, and the forced removal of Jews (particularly those who were Hungarian citizens) to the no-man's-land between Slovakia and Hungary were carried out by the storm troops of the Hlinka Guard and the Freiwillige Schutzstaffel (voluntary defense squad; a paramilitary organization of ethnic Germans). Adolf EICHMANN, as an expert on the Jewish problem, was sent to Slovakia to organize this forced removal of Jews.

Upon the creation of the Slovak state, sporadic anti-Jewish restrictions were introduced, the first of which forbade Jews to buy and sell religious articles. At a conference in Salzburg (July 28, 1940) attended by Hitler and the Slovak leaders Tiso, Tuka, Mach, and Franz Karmasin (the leader of the local German minority, the *Karpaten-Deutsche*, or Carpathian Germans), it was decided to set up a National Socialist regime in Slovakia. This led to increased and more systematic anti-Jewish legislation. That August, Dieter WISLICENY was sent to Slovakia by the REICHS-SICHERHEITSHAUPTAMT (Reich Security Main Office; RSHA) to be an adviser on Jewish affairs. In 1941 some units of the Hlinka Guard and the Freiwillige Schutzstaffel were reorganized on the model of the SS and continued to enforce anti-Jewish measures. Around this time, Jewish males were first drafted into auxiliary labor units of the Slovak armed forces (*see* SIXTH SLOVAK BRIGADE).

The Slovaks now set up special institutions to facilitate their anti-Jewish policies. The Ústredňy Hospodarsky Urad (Central Economic Office; ÚHU), which was attached to the office of the prime minister, was established to oust the Jews from the economy and oversee the "Aryanization" (*see* ARISIERUNG) of Jewish property. Jewish assets were estimated to be worth more than 3 billion Slovak crowns (approximately $120 million), of which 44 percent was real estate, 23 percent business enterprises, and 33 percent capital. The "Aryanization" process was accomplished by the ÚHU within one year; 10,025 Jewish businesses were liquidated and 2,223 transferred to "Aryan" owners.

On September 26, 1940, a decree was promulgated establishing the ÚSTREDŇA ŽIDOV (Jewish Center; ÚŽ). The ÚŽ was to be subordinate to the ÚHU, whose orders it would transmit to the Jews. Originally modeled on the German Reichsvereinigung (Reich Association; *see* REICHSVERTRETUNG DER DEUTSCHEN JUDEN), the ÚŽ's functions initially included retraining Jews for physical work, promoting Jewish emigration from Slovakia, and administering Jewish schools and charities. The ÚŽ had a main office in BRATISLAVA (the Slovak capital) and branch offices in other Jewish population centers, such as Trnava, Nitra, and Žilina. Heinrich Schwartz, the chairman of the Orthodox Jewish community, was appointed *starosta* (head) of the ÚŽ. Following Schwartz's arrest for "noncooperation" in April 1941, Arpad Sebestyen, a more obedient *starosta*, was appointed in his stead. Sebestyen, a former Jewish school principal, served until the members of the semi-underground PRACOVNÁ SKUPINA (Working Group) managed to have him ousted in 1943 in favor of Oskar Neumann.

In the summer of 1941, when Slovak troops entered the war, anti-Jewish legislation was escalated as a complementary ideological step. Jews were now forbidden to enter certain public places and had to wear a Jewish BADGE, a yellow armband 3.9 inches (10 cm) wide with a Star of David 1 inch (2.5 cm) wide. Jewish apartments, as well as mail and other documents, also had to have a Star of David displayed on them. The legal status of the Jews was finalized with the issuance of Law No. 198/1941, known as the *Židovsky Kodex* (Jewish Code), on September 9, 1941; this law closely followed the NUREMBERG LAWS for the classification of Jews. By December of that year Jews were forbidden to congregate, and a curfew was enforced against them. A special ministerial order issued by Mach called for the removal of fifteen thousand Jews from Bratislava. By March 1942, sixty-seven hundred had been resettled in Trnava,

Nitra, and eastern Slovakia, or sent to labor camps.

The idea of deporting Slovak Jewry was enthusiastically supported by the Tiso government, the show of enthusiasm deriving in part from the intragovernmental competition for Nazi support. On May 29, 1941, the government consented to supply 120,000 workers to Germany. Basing himself on this idea, the head of the ÚHU, Augustin Moravek, proposed providing Jewish laborers to fill the quota. The exact course of events is not entirely clear; it seems that Moravek's proposal was not acted on immediately, but the same idea surfaced when the Nazis asked for the delivery of 20,000 workers toward the end of 1941. Still nothing concrete happened immediately.

At the WANNSEE CONFERENCE held in Berlin in January 1942, it was noted that Slovak cooperation in the facilitation of the "FINAL SOLUTION" seemed assured. In mid-February the German ambassador to Slovakia, Hans Ludin, asked the Slovaks for twenty thousand young Jews to "build new Jewish settlements." The Slovaks agreed, but, fearing that the German plans might leave only unproductive Jews in Slovakia, they demanded of Ludin that the entire community be deported. It is clear that at one point it was agreed to deport sixty thousand Jews, and this number was probably increased to include the entire Jewish community. On March 27, the first trainload of Jews was sent to the east from Slovakia. The Nazis demanded a fee of 500 reichsmarks for each deportee, to cover the cost of "vocational training." On June 23, the Slovaks consented to pay the fee, the equivalent of $1.8 million. They were promised that the Jews would not be returned to Slovakia and that the Germans would make no further claims on their property. From March to October 1942 about fifty-eight thousand Slovak Jews (fifty-four thousand by the end of June) were deported. Most were sent to AUSCHWITZ, MAJDANEK, and the LUBLIN area. Jewish property was sold at low prices by the Slovak authorities or distributed free to non-Jewish Slovaks as an inexpensive way to buy the goodwill of the populace.

The reaction of a segment of the Slovak Jewish leadership to the deportations and

The deportation of the Jews of Stropkov, near the Czechoslovak-Polish border, took place on May 21, 1942. A Jew is subjected to a humiliating beard trimming while waiting at the railway station to be deported.

A transport of Jews from Dobšiná, about 60 miles (96.5 km) northeast of Banská Bystrica, to Auschwitz (July 23, 1942).

Deportation of Jews from the town of Spišská, about 35 miles (56 km) northwest of Košice (1942). [Beth Hatefutsoth; courtesy of Julius Greenberg, Tel Aviv]

their rescue attempts are singular in the history of the Holocaust. The Jewish leadership was apprised of the impending deportations several weeks before they began. In an attempt to forestall them, an activist core group formed the Committee of Six, led by Gisi FLEISCHMANN. This committee later developed into the Pracovná Skupina. Their activities did not succeed in preventing the transports to the east, but the group's combined use of intervention with government and Catholic church officials, bribery, and negotiations with the Nazis contributed to the cessation of the deportations in October 1942.

From the advent of the deportations until the German occupation of Hungary in March 1944, more than ten thousand Jews escaped over the Slovak border into Hungary. Others sought protection by converting to Christianity or by obtaining false "Aryan" papers. A special group of Jews deemed "vital" to the Slovak economy were granted "certificates of exemption" from the deportations. The five companies of Jews in the Sixth Slovak Brigade and most of the Jews in the three labor camps—NOVÁKY, SERED, and VYHNE, which had been established in conjunction with the ÚŽ—were usually safeguarded from deportation. The Working Group had a hand in much of this successful rescue.

During the relatively quiet period in Slovakia between October 1942 and August 1944, the Working Group conducted negotiations with the Nazis to save the remaining Slovak Jews, as well as other Jews slated for exter-

mination. This bargaining came to be known as the EUROPA PLAN. Although the rest of European Jewry was not saved, some historians believe that the contact with the Germans may have helped maintain the remnant of the Slovak Jewish community until the outbreak of the Slovak National Uprising in late August 1944. The Slovak negotiations with the Nazis also led to a similar set of negotiations in Hungary during the Nazi occupation there (see RELIEF AND RESCUE COMMITTEE OF BUDAPEST). It must also be noted that, as in all communities, some Jews collaborated with the authorities. The man most vociferously accused was Karel Hochberg, who was said to be Dieter Wisliceny's man in the ÚŽ.

As early as the autumn of 1942, "rumors" about the fate of the Jewish deportees, based in part on information gathered by the Working Group, led elements of the Slovak body politic to clamor for an end to the deportations. On May 23, 1942, however, the Slovak parliament passed a law that permitted the expulsion of Jews from Slovakia. In an attempt to deny these "rumors," the Germans sent the journalist Fritz Fiala to meet with some Slovak inmates in Auschwitz. But certain Slovak politicians, such as the education minister, Josef Sivak, remained unsatisfied and pressed the government to demand that a Slovak delegation be allowed to visit the deportees. The Germans did not yield to these demands, but pressure from the anti-deportation faction in the government contributed to the cessation of the transports in October 1942.

The AUSCHWITZ PROTOCOLS—detailed reports by four Jewish escapees from Auschwitz who reached Slovakia in the spring of 1944—also passed through the hands of the Working Group. Rabbi Michael Dov WEISSMANDEL, a leader of the Working Group, sent the reports to the West, together with a plea to bomb the railway lines leading to Auschwitz and the camp itself (see AUSCHWITZ, BOMBING OF). Although his appeals did not lead to the bombing of the camp, the information contained in the protocols sparked increased internationally backed rescue activities in Hungary.

In the Slovak labor camps, armed cells began to form during the deportations of 1942. They did not take action at the time of the transports, but they continued to expand throughout 1943 and into 1944. By 1944 they had been incorporated into the preparations for the Slovak National Uprising. When the revolt broke out on August 28–29, 1944, over 2,000 Jewish fighters took part, and 269 were killed in action. A unit of 200 men from the Nováky camp, under the command of Jewish officers, distinguished itself at the front as the only Jewish unit of its kind to fight in the uprising. About 15 percent of the unit died in battle and another 15 percent were wounded. During the fighting, four PARACHUTISTS from Palestine—Haviva REIK, Zvi Ben-Yaakov, Rafael Reiss, and Chaim Hermesh—reached Slovakia to extend help to the Jewish remnant and to organize Jewish armed resistance. Abba Berdiczew too was sent to Slovakia, with the goal of reaching Romania. He was killed, however, on Slovak soil. The other parachutists failed to organize separate Jewish armed resistance, but their arrival did much to boost Jewish morale. In particular, they organized Jewish welfare and aid in the "liberated" rebel territory, where most of the surviving Jews had gathered. They also tried to combat the antisemitism that was rife in the rebel-held areas. Hermesh reached the partisans and remained with them until the end of the war, but Reik, Reiss, and Ben-Yaakov met their death in Slovakia.

With the collapse of the uprising, some 13,500 Jews were deported to Auschwitz, SACHSENHAUSEN, and THERESIENSTADT. Many hundreds of Jews were also killed in Slovakia itself by the German forces. About 10,000 of the post-revolt deportees survived the war, and another 4,000 to 5,000 Jews remained in hiding—in the mountains with the partisans, or in the towns and cities of Slovakia—until the end of the war. Those who hid in Bratislava were aided by the International RED CROSS representative, Georges Dunand, who arrived in Slovakia in October 1944 and worked with a Zionist youth leader, Juraj Revesz.

Including those Jews who lived in the territories that Hungary had annexed, Slovak Jewry's losses are estimated at one hundred thousand. Between twenty-five thousand and thirty thousand Slovak Jews survived the war. Upon their return to their homes, most felt unwelcome. Their requests for the return of their property were greeted with hostility by the populace and the new government. Anti-Jewish demonstrations and violence were common. After the Soviet-backed regime was established in 1948, most of the remaining Jews left Slovakia; the majority immigrated to Israel in 1949.

BIBLIOGRAPHY

Dagan, A., ed. *The Jews of Czechoslovakia*. 3 vols. Philadelphia, 1968–1984.

Dunand, G. *Ne perdez pas leur trace*. Neuchâtel, Switzerland, 1950.

Fuchs, A. *The Unheeded Cry*. New York, 1984.

Jelinek, Y. *The Lust for Power: Nationalism, Slovakia, and the Communists, 1918–1948*. Boulder, 1983.

Jelinek, Y. *The Parish Republic: Hlinka's Slovak People's Party, 1939–1945*. Boulder, 1976.

Lipscher, L. *Die Juden im slowakischen Staat, 1939–1945*. Munich, 1980.

Rothkirchen, L. *The Destruction of Slovak Jewry: A Documentary History*. Jerusalem, 1961.

YESHAYAHU JELINEK and
ROBERT ROZETT

SLOVAK JEWISH RESCUE COMMITTEE. *See* Pracovná Skupina.

SLOVAK NATIONAL UPRISING, a revolt that took place in the Slovak state, a satellite of Germany, from August 28–29 to October 27, 1944. The aims of the uprising were to oust the Hlinková Slovenská Ľudová Strana (Slovak People's Party of HLINKA; HSLS) from power and free the state from its dependence on Nazi Germany.

Planning. The uprising was planned by several groups; prominent among them were the Czechoslovak Agrarian party, the right wing of the Social Democratic party, the Communist party, estranged Slovak nationalists, and a group of army officers. In late December 1943 these groups, except for the army officers, set up the Slovenská Narodna Rada (Slovak National Council; SNR). The army officers, for their part, declared that they accepted the authority of both the SNR and the CZECHOSLOVAK GOVERNMENT-IN-EXILE.

Not all the participants in this antifascist crusade shared the same ultimate goal. Some, like the members of the Czechoslovak Communist party and the bourgeois "Flora" group (which formed around a well-known Slovak politician, Dr. Vavro Srobar), aspired to a united Czechoslovakia, believing there was a single Czechoslovak nation, as did the members of the London-based government-in-exile. However, the Slovak faction of the Communist party—particularly as represented by the future president of Czechoslovakia, Gustav Husak—advocated that Slovakia become a republic of the Soviet Union; Husak's faction failed to convince Moscow to accept their position. The Agrarian party wanted to see the emergence of a united Czechoslovak republic, but with a good deal of Slovak autonomy, since they did not believe there was a single Czechoslovak nation. These differences led to political infighting that in the end weakened the SNR.

The plans for the uprising were based on the hope that it would coincide with an advance by the Soviet army which would breach the German lines on two fronts. If the Wehrmacht were to launch a surprise invasion of Slovakia, the planners expected that their rebel forces would be able to hold out in the center of the country for as long as it would take the Soviets to arrive.

In the spring of 1944, partisan activity in the mountains of Slovakia was intense. Most of the units were under Soviet command and received their instructions from the Soviet Union. By the summer, the partisans controlled significant areas of eastern and central Slovakia. The Slovak government forces did little to prevent the partisan activity. To forestall further partisan gains, on August 28–29 the Germans invaded Slovakia without any interference from the Slovak forces loyal to the HSLS government. Some historians believe that the partisan activity that led to the invasion might have been deliberately manipulated by the Soviets to prevent local forces from liberating Slovakia.

The Revolt. The uprising encompassed an area that at its maximum was 5,366 square miles (13,900 sq km), with a population, at its maximum, of eight hundred thousand; the terrain it covered consisted primarily of alternating mountains and valleys. Pockets of resistance forces were placed in strategic locations. In this liberated area, a Czechoslovak republic was declared and a government was established. Political authority was divided between the Sbor Poverenikov (Executive Council) and the SNR. The latter had legislative and supervisory functions, and the former handled the daily affairs of the rebellion. Outstanding among the uprising's political figures were the democrat Dr. Jozef Lettrich and the Communist Husak.

For the most part, the struggle was weighted against the insurgents. First and foremost, the Germans had superior manpower and firepower. The sixty thousand rebels, of which sixteen thousand were partisans, were armed primarily with light weapons. Their heavy arsenal included only 120 cannon, fifteen tanks, and twenty-one airplanes, which had been provided by the Soviets. Moreover, the rebel Slovak army, which bore the brunt of the fighting, failed to resist with sufficient stubbornness; the partisan units had more staying power, but they lacked discipline and were untrained for frontline fighting. On the day the revolt broke out, the 178th Slovak Tatra Division in northeastern Slovakia took the town of Žilina for the rebels. Bloody battles also raged at the center of the rebellion. One such battle took place near Batovany, where a greatly outnumbered Jewish unit from the NOVÁKY labor camp fought valiantly. A group of French prisoners of war who had escaped to Slovakia also fought well at the Strecno ravine. The Second Czechoslovak Paratroop Brigade, which had been organized in the Soviet Union, distinguished itself in battle.

The Germans hoped to suppress the uprising within a few days, but the opposition proved stronger than they had expected. Late in September, SS-Obergruppenführer Gottlob Berger, the chief commander of the German forces, was replaced by the *Höherer SS- und Polizeiführer* (Higher SS and Police Leader) in Slovakia, SS-Obergruppenführer Hermann Höfle. Höfle managed to bring additional SS units into the fray to join the SS Panzergrenadier Schill Regiment, which was advancing in the direction of the Nitra valley toward BANSKÁ BYSTRICA. The SS Eighteenth Horst Wessel Division, the SS Dirlewanger Brigade, and the SS Fourteenth Grenadier Division–Galizien (Galicia) were among those that took part in the fighting. Within a matter of weeks, the German forces advanced against the rebels on three sides and crushed them. Banská Bystrica, the headquarters of the uprising, fell on October 27, 1944, thus ending the organized military struggle. Guerrilla fighting continued in the mountains until the arrival of the Soviet army.

The rebel cause was weakened not only by internal political differences, but also by Allied reluctance to support the revolt to the fullest. The Western powers regarded Slovakia as belonging to the Soviet theater of operations, and hesitated to intervene. The Soviets, for their part, were afraid of a repetition of the failed WARSAW POLISH UPRISING and were niggardly in the support they gave.

Jewish Participation. Armed underground Jewish cells existed in each of the three Slovak labor camps, Nováky, SERED, and VYHNE, long before the SNR was established. They had come into being primarily to offer resistance if deportations from Slovakia were renewed, following their cessation in the autumn of 1942. Early in 1944 contact was established between the cells in the labor camps and the SNR, chiefly through the Jewish Communist members in the SNR. From that time, the SNR included the Jewish cells in its strategy. The Jews saw this alliance in terms of possible benefit for the rescue of Slovak Jewry; an SNR victory could mean the rescue of the remaining twenty thousand Slovak Jews.

With the outbreak of fighting, the armed Jewish cells and other Jews previously not associated with the cells joined the uprising. More than 2,000 Jews fought in the uprising, 1,566 as partisans (they constituted 10 percent of the partisan forces). Five hundred Jewish fighters fell in battle—269 as partisans, which was about 17 percent of the partisans who were killed. The 200-man Nováky cell under the command of the Jewish Communist Dr. Imrich Müller (Milen), with Juraj Spitzer as its political commissar, fought as a separate unit, first within the regular army; later most of the men joined the partisan units.

During the uprising, four Jewish parachutists reached Slovakia from Palestine (*see* PARACHUTISTS, JEWISH). Three of them, Havi-va REIK, Zvi (Grunhut) Ben-Yaakov, and Rafael (Rafi) Reiss, were killed during the uprising. Only one, Chaim Hermesh, survived and continued fighting with Slovak partisans until the end of the war. Another parachutist, Abba Berdiczew, was dropped in Slovakia with the mission of reaching Romania, but he was killed in Slovakia before he could continue on his way.

As the Germans began to retake territory from the rebels, they rounded up Jews. Nearly five thousand Jews, mostly civilians, and about 19,000 partisans were captured; more than 1,500 of these Jews were killed in Kremnica, a village near Banská Bystrica. By March 1945, 13,500 Jews had been deported to AUSCHWITZ, SACHSENHAUSEN, and THERESIENSTADT. Most of them were from Sered, which had become a transit camp commanded by Alois BRUNNER. Because it was so late in the war, about 10,000 Slovak Jews survived in the camps until their liberation, and 4,000 to 5,000 remained in hiding in the cities and towns of Slovakia, or with partisan units in the mountains. Although Slovak Jews supported the national uprising, they could do little to determine its course, and their fate in the wake of its failure was part of the backlash unleashed by the Nazi victory.

BIBLIOGRAPHY

Jelinek, Y. *The Lust for Power: Nationalism, Slovakia, and the Communists, 1918–1948*. Boulder, 1983.

Lipscher, L. *Die Juden im slowakischen Staat, 1939–1945*. Munich, 1980.

Steinberg, L. *Jews against Hitler* (*Not as a Lamb*). London, 1978.

Venohr, W. *Aufstand in der Tatra: Der Kampf um die Slowakei, 1939–1944*. Königstein, West Germany, 1979.

YESHAYAHU JELINEK, AKIVA NIR,
and ROBERT ROZETT

SMOLENSK, city in the western part of the Russian Soviet Federated Socialist Republic, close to Belorussia; the administrative center of Smolensk Oblast (district) and one of the oldest Russian cities. Jews lived in Smolensk from the fifteenth century. Before World War

SMOLENSK

0   42 miles   1
                         in.

0   80 km.   3

II more than 13,000 Jews lived there, out of a total population of 156,677.

On July 16, 1941, the Germans captured the part of Smolensk on the west bank of the Dnieper, and the part on the east bank was taken on July 29. Major sections of the city and its outskirts were destroyed in the fighting. Before the occupation, however, most of the population, including the majority of the Jews, had been evacuated from the city or had left on their own.

In the first few months of the occupation, Smolensk was the headquarters of Einsatzgruppe B and was also occupied by Vorkommando (Advance Unit) Moskau, an Einsatzgruppe B detachment that was designated for entry into the Soviet capital with the German army. The German advance having been halted, the Vorkommando was kept busy in Smolensk and its environs, setting up a JUDENRAT (Jewish Council), introducing the yellow badge (*see* BADGE, JEWISH), and putting Jews on forced labor. In August a ghetto was established in the Sadki suburb in which two thousand Jews were concentrated, some ap-

parently brought there from nearby settlements. In one *Aktion* by the Vorkommando, thirty-eight Jewish intellectuals in the ghetto were murdered, having been accused of causing unrest and rebellion in the ghetto. At the beginning of December 1941, Einsatzgruppe B published statistical data on the city's population at the time, according to national origin. The total population was 24,450; the Jews are not listed among the nationalities, and it may therefore be assumed that by that time all of them had been liquidated.

Smolensk was liberated by the Soviets on September 25, 1943.

BIBLIOGRAPHY

Ehrenburg, I., and V. Grossman, eds. *The Black Book of Soviet Jewry*. New York, 1981. See pages 253–257.

SHMUEL SPECTOR

SOBIBÓR, extermination camp near the village and railway station of Sobibór, in the eastern part of the Lublin district in Poland, not far from the Chełm-Włodawa railway line. Established as part of the operation of AKTION REINHARD, the camp was built in a sparsely populated, woody, and swampy area beginning in March 1942. Local inhabitants and a group of eighty Jews from nearby ghettos were employed to construct it; Obersturmführer Richard Thomalla, a staff member of the SS construction office in Lublin, was in charge. In April 1942, SS-Obersturmführer Franz STANGL was appointed camp commandant and assumed responsibility for completion of the camp. In building Sobibór, the Germans drew on experience gained in the construction and operation of the BEŁŻEC extermination camp.

The camp staff included 20 to 30 German SS men, most of whom had previously taken part in the EUTHANASIA PROGRAM, as had Stangl. In addition, 90 to 120 Ukrainians served in the camp. Most were Soviet prisoners of war who had been trained for the job at TRAWNIKI; some were VOLKSDEUTSCHE, Soviet nationals of German origin. The German staff filled most of the command and administrative positions, while the Ukrainian unit acted as guards and security personnel, their function being, among other things, to quell any resistance offered by the Jews who were brought to the camp and to prevent their escaping. Jewish prisoners were employed as well, on various physical tasks.

The camp was in the form of a rectangle 1,312 by 1,969 feet (400 × 600 m) in area, surrounded by a barbed-wire fence 9.8 feet (3 m) high, with tree branches intertwined in it to conceal the interior. There were three camp areas, each individually fenced in: the administration area, the reception area, and the extermination area. The administration area consisted of the *Vorlager* ("forward camp"; the part of the camp closest to the railway station) and Camp I. The *Vorlager* included the railway platform, with space for twenty railway cars to be stationed, as well as the living quarters for the German and Ukrainian staff. Camp I, which was fenced off from the rest, contained housing for the Jewish prisoners and the workshops in which some of them were employed.

The reception area, also known as Camp II, was the place where Jews from the incoming transports were brought, to go through various procedures prior to their being killed in the gas chambers—removal of clothes, cutting of women's hair, and confiscation of possessions and valuables.

The extermination area, or Camp III, located in the northwestern part of the camp, was the most isolated. It contained the gas chambers, the burial trenches, and housing for the Jewish prisoners employed there. A path, 9.8 to 13 feet (3–4 m) wide and 492 feet (150 m) long, led from the reception area to the extermination area; on either side was a barbed-wire fence, and here too branches were intertwined to conceal the path from view. It was along this path that the victims were herded, naked, toward the gas chambers from the shed where they had undressed.

The gas chambers were inside a brick building. Each chamber was square, measured 172 square feet (16 sq m), and had a capacity of 160 to 180 persons. The chambers were entered from a platform at the front of the brick building; each gas chamber also had another

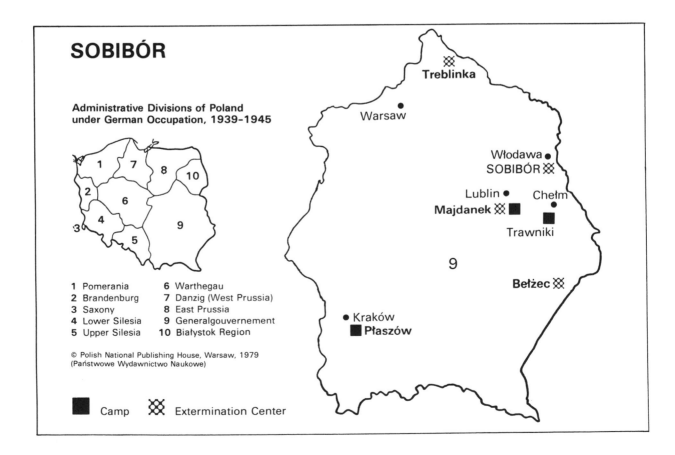

SOBIBÓR

Administrative Divisions of Poland under German Occupation, 1939-1945

1 Pomerania
2 Brandenburg
3 Saxony
4 Lower Silesia
5 Upper Silesia
6 Warthegau
7 Danzig (West Prussia)
8 East Prussia
9 Generalgouvernement
10 Białystok Region

© Polish National Publishing House, Warsaw, 1979
(Państwowe Wydawnictwo Naukowe)

■ Camp   ⊠ Extermination Center

Treblinka ⊠
Warsaw ●
Włodawa ●
SOBIBÓR ⊠
Lublin ●   Chełm ●
Majdanek ⊠ ■
Trawniki ■
9
● Kraków
■ Płaszów
Bełżec ⊠

opening, through which the bodies were removed. The gas, carbon monoxide, was produced by a 200-horsepower engine in a nearby shed, from which it was piped into the gas chambers. The burial trenches were nearby, each 164 to 197 feet (50–60 m) long, 33 to 49 feet (10–15 m) wide, and 16.4 to 23 feet (5–7 m) deep. From the railway platform to the burial trenches ran a narrow-gauge railway, used to transport persons too weak to make their way to the gas chambers on their own, as well as the bodies of those who had died en route to Sobibór. When the camp was nearing completion, in mid-April 1942, a test was made to ascertain whether the gas chambers were functioning properly. Two hundred and fifty Jews, most of them women, were brought in from the nearby labor camp at Krychów and put to death in the chambers. All the SS men of the camp were present at this experiment.

Several hundred able-bodied Jews were chosen from among the first few transports to form work teams. Some were employed in the workshops as tailors, cobblers, carpenters, and so on, to serve the needs of the German and Ukrainian camp staff; all the other work assignments related to the processing of the victims along the route that led from the railway platform to the burial trenches. A total of about 1,000 prisoners, 150 of them women, were eventually put into these teams. One group, numbering several dozen, worked on the railway platform. Its job was to remove from the cars those who were incapable of getting off on their own; to remove the bodies of those who had died en route; and to clean out of the cars the dirt that had accumulated and the articles left behind. The purpose was to ensure that when the train left the camp, it would contain no trace of the human cargo it had transported. Other work teams were assigned to the reception area, to handle the clothing and luggage left there by the victims on their way to the gas chambers. These groups had to sort out the clothing and prepare it to be sent on to a destination outside the camp; to search for money and other valuables that might have been left behind; and to remove the yellow patches from the clothing and any other signs that could have identified the clothes as having been worn by Jews. Yet another group in this

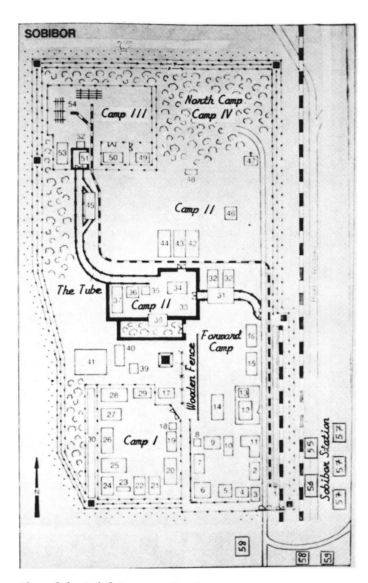

Plan of the Sobibór extermination camp.

area, the barbers, had to cut off the women's hair, package it, and prepare it for onward dispatch.

In the extermination area, two hundred to three hundred Jewish prisoners were kept, whose task was to remove the bodies of the murdered victims from the gas chambers, take them to the burial ground, and then clean up the chambers. A special team of prisoners, nicknamed "the dentists," was charged with extracting gold teeth from the mouths of the victims before their bodies were put into the trenches. Toward the end of 1942, in an effort to erase the traces of the mass killings, the bodies were exhumed and cremated; this task too was carried out by a special team of prisoners.

Nearly every day there were *Selektionen* among the Jewish prisoners, with the weak and the sick selected and sent to the gas chambers. Their place was taken by new arrivals. Any transgression by a prisoner—such as the theft of food, money, or valuables found in the luggage left behind by the victims—carried the death penalty. Only a few prisoners survived for more than a few months.

Transports: First Stage. The procedure for the reception of incoming transports was based entirely on misleading the victims and concealing from them the fate that was in store for them. When a train arrived, the deportees on board were ordered to disembark and were told that they had arrived at a transit camp from which they would be sent to labor camps; before leaving for the labor camps, they were to take showers, and at the same time their clothes would be disinfected. Following this announcement, the men and women were separated (children were as-

Railway siding at Sobibór.

signed to the women), on the pretext that the sexes had to be separated for their showers. The victims were ordered to take off their clothes and hand over any money or valuables in their possession; anyone who was caught trying to conceal any item was shot. There followed the march to the gas chambers, which had been made to resemble shower rooms. Some 450 to 550 persons entered the chambers at a time. Everything was done on the run, accompanied by shouts, beatings, and warning shots. The victims were in a state of shock and did not grasp what was happening to them. When the gas chambers were jammed full of people, they were closed and sealed and the gas was piped in. Within twenty to thirty minutes, everyone inside was dead.

The bodies were then removed from the gas chambers and buried, after the gold teeth had been extracted from their mouths. The whole procedure, from the arrival of the train to the burial of the victims, took two to three hours. In the meantime the railway cars were cleaned up, the train departed, and another twenty cars, with their human load destined for extermination, entered the camp.

The first stage of the extermination operation went on for three months, from the beginning of May to the end of July 1942. The Jews who were brought to Sobibór during this period came from the Lublin district in Poland, and from Czechoslovakia, Germany, and Austria. The latter—those from countries outside Poland—had first been taken to ghettos in the Lublin district, and from there were deported to Sobibór. Some 10,000 Jews were brought from Germany and Austria, 6,000 from THERESIENSTADT, and many thousands from Slovakia; all in all, between 90,000 and 100,000 Jews were murdered at Sobibór in this first stage. The transports came to a temporary halt at the end of July, to enable the Lublin-Chełm railway line to undergo repairs.

In Sobibór's first three months of operation, the Germans found that the gas chambers, which had a total capacity of fewer than six hundred persons, created a bottleneck in the murder program. The halt in camp operations during August and September of 1942 was therefore used to construct three more gas chambers. These were put up next to the existing chambers under the same roof, with a hallway separating the old chambers from the new. With a new capacity of twelve hundred persons, the rate of extermination could be doubled. At the end of August 1942, Stangl, the commandant of Sobibór, was transferred to the TREBLINKA extermination camp, and his place was taken by SS-Obersturmführer Franz Reichsleitner.

Second Stage. By the beginning of October 1942, work on the railway line was completed and the transports to Sobibór could be renewed. Until early November, the arriving transports brought more Jews from towns in the Lublin district; in the winter, following the closing of the Bełżec camp, and in the spring and summer of 1943, Sobibór also received transports from Eastern Galicia. The winter transports arrived bearing people who had frozen to death on the way. Some of the transports consisted of people who had been stripped naked in order to make it more difficult for them to escape from the train. One train carried 5,000 Jewish prisoners from the MAJDANEK camp. From October 1942 to June 1943, a total of 70,000 to 80,000 Jews from Lublin and the Eastern Galicia districts were brought to Sobibór; the number of victims from the GENERALGOUVERNEMENT was between 145,000 and 155,000.

By the end of October 1942, 25,000 Jews from Slovakia had been killed at Sobibór. In the second half of February 1943, Heinrich HIMMLER paid a visit to the camp. While he was there, a special transport arrived with several hundred Jewish girls from a labor camp in the Lublin district. Himmler watched the entire extermination procedure. In March of that year, four transports from France brought 4,000 people, all of whom were killed. Nineteen transports arrived from the Netherlands between March and July 1943, carrying 35,000 Jews. The Dutch Jews came in regular passenger trains, were given a polite welcome, and asked to send letters to their relatives in the Netherlands to let them know they had arrived at a labor camp. After they had written these letters, they were given the same treatment that was meted out to all the other transports. Within a few hours they all perished.

The last transports to arrive at Sobibór came from the Vilna, Minsk, and Lida ghettos, in the REICHSKOMMISSARIAT OSTLAND; 14,000 Jews came on these transports in the second half of September 1943, following the liquidation of the ghettos in these cities. This brought the total number of Jews killed at Sobibór throughout the period of the camp's operation to approximately 250,000.

At the end of the summer of 1942, the burial trenches were opened and the process of burning the victims' bodies was begun. The corpses were put into huge piles and set on fire. The bodies of victims who arrived in subsequent transports were cremated immediately after gassing and were not buried.

Resistance and Escape. On July 5, 1943, Himmler ordered the closing of Sobibór as an extermination camp and its transformation into a concentration camp. On a piece of land added to the camp area and designated as Camp IV, warehouses were built to store captured Soviet ammunition, which the prospective camp prisoners were scheduled to handle.

Throughout the camp's existence, attempts were made to escape from it; some of them were successful. In retaliation for these attempts, the Germans executed many dozens of prisoners. During the summer of 1943, in order to prevent escapes, and also as a safety measure against attacks by partisans, the Germans planted mines along the entire circumference of the camp. In July and August of that year, an underground group was organized among the Jewish prisoners in Sobibór under the leadership of Leon Feldhendler, who had been chairman of the JUDENRAT (Jewish Council) in Zółkiew, a town in Eastern Galicia. The group's aim was to organize an uprising and a mass escape from the camp. In the second half of September, Soviet Jewish PRISONERS OF WAR were brought to the camp from Minsk; one of them was Lt. Aleksandr PECHERSKY. The underground recruited him into its ranks and put him in command, with Feldhendler as his deputy. The plan was for the prisoners to kill the SS men, acquire weapons, and fight their way out of the camp. The uprising broke out on October 14, 1943, and in its course eleven SS men and several Ukrainians were killed. Some three hundred prisoners managed to escape, but most of them were killed by their pursuers. Those who had not joined the escape for various reasons and had remained in the camp were all killed as well. At the end of the war, about fifty Jews survived of those who had escaped during the uprising.

In the wake of the uprising the Germans decided to liquidate Sobibór, abandoning the idea of turning it into a concentration camp. By the end of 1943 no trace was left; the camp area was plowed under, and crops were planted in its soil. A farm was put up in its place, and one of the Ukrainian camp guards settled there. In the summer of 1944 the area was liberated by the Soviet army and troops of the Polish People's Army (see GWARDIA LUDOWA).

Eleven of the SS men who had served at Sobibór were brought to trial. The proceedings took place in Hagen, West Germany, from September 6, 1965, to December 20, 1966. One of the accused committed suicide; one was sentenced to life imprisonment; five were given sentences ranging from three to eight years; and four were acquitted. The camp area was designated by the Polish government as a national shrine and a memorial was erected on the site.

BIBLIOGRAPHY

Arad, Y. *Operation Reinhard Death Camps: Belzec, Sobibor, Treblinka.* Bloomington, 1987.

Novitch, M., ed. *Sobibor—Martyrdom and Revolt: Documents and Testimonies.* New York, 1980.

Rashke, R. *Escape from Sobibor.* Boston, 1982.

YITZHAK ARAD

SOLIDARITÉ. *See* Union des Juifs pour la Résistance et l'Entr'aide.

SONDERKOMMANDO (Special Commando).
1. A German unit, mainly of the SS, for special duties or assignments. The Sonderkommandos took part in the "FINAL SOLUTION" of the "Jewish question" in Europe. Along with the EINSATZGRUPPEN that operated in the occupied Soviet territories, there were about ten Sonderkommandos. One of them, first known as the Lange Kommando and later as Sonderkommando Bothmann, carried out the extermination operation at the Chełmno camp. The designation "Sonderkommando 1005" was given to the units whose task it was to obliterate the traces of mass slaughter by opening the burial pits and burning the corpses they contained (see AKTION 1005).

2. The designation of Sonderkommando was also given to units made up of Jewish prisoners, mainly those assigned to the death installations—the gas chambers and crematoria. Such Sonderkommandos worked at AUSCHWITZ-Birkenau; they were relieved every few months and put to death themselves. One of these Sonderkommandos staged an uprising in the Birkenau camp in 1944.

3. There was also a Jewish Sonderkommando in the Łódź ghetto. It dealt with criminal offenses and functioned as part of the JÜDISCHER ORDNUNGSDIENST (Jewish ghetto police).

SHMUEL SPECTOR

SONDERKOMMANDO 1005. *See* Aktion 1005.

SOSNOWIEC (also Sosnowice), city in southwest Poland. From the late nineteenth century Sosnowiec developed rapidly, owing to increasing exploitation of the coal mines and iron ore in the region (Zagłębie Dąbrowskie) and its location as a major railway junction. On the eve of World War II the city's population was 130,000, including 28,000 Jews.

On September 4, 1939, the Germans occupied Sosnowiec, attacking the population and especially the Jewish residents. On Saturday, September 9, they burned the Great Synagogue. In addition to the physical attacks and the personal restrictions, economic decrees were issued against the Jews, ordering, among other things, the expropriation of their money, their property, and their businesses.

In the first days of the occupation, Moshe MERIN was appointed head of the JUDENRAT (Jewish Council). Early in 1940 the Zentrale der Jüdischen Ältestenräte in Oberschlesien (Central Office of the Jewish Councils of Elders in Upper Silesia) was created in Sosnowiec, representing about forty-five commu-

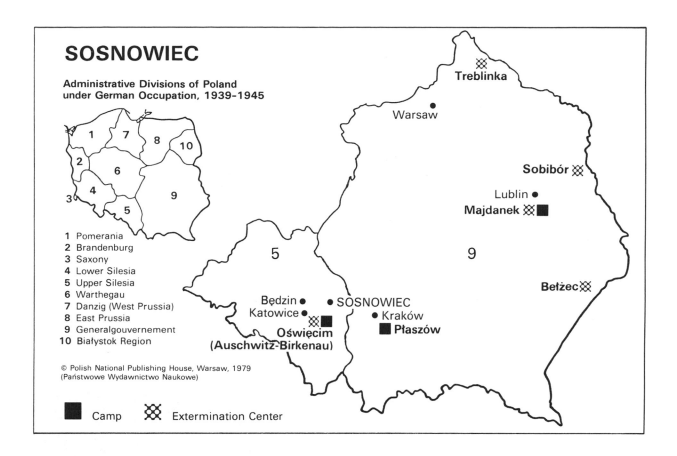

SOSNOWIEC

**Administrative Divisions of Poland
under German Occupation, 1939–1945**

1 Pomerania
2 Brandenburg
3 Saxony
4 Lower Silesia
5 Upper Silesia
6 Warthegau
7 Danzig (West Prussia)
8 East Prussia
9 Generalgouvernement
10 Białystok Region

© Polish National Publishing House, Warsaw, 1979
(Państwowe Wydawnictwo Naukowe)

■ Camp   ⊠ Extermination Center

nities and headed by Merin. It was in charge of all Jewish affairs in the area and operated with the help of the Jewish police. In the spring of 1940 the Jews of Katowice and of other towns in Polish Silesia were deported to cities in which the Zentrale operated.

One of the harsh edicts issued concerning the Jews in the area involved forced labor and the sending of Jews to forced-labor camps. This edict was implemented by Heinrich HIMMLER's *Sonderbeauftragter des Reichsführers-SS für Fremdvölkischen Arbeitseinsatz in Oberschlesien* (Special Representative of the *Reichsführer-SS* for the Employment of Foreign Labor in Upper Silesia), who administered ORGANISATION SCHMELT, the system of forced labor for the Jews of Eastern Upper SILESIA. The Judenrat was responsible for organizing the sending of forced-labor workers to the camps. It was also involved in setting up German-owned workshops to employ Jews. This activity, as the heads of the Judenrat explained, was designed to help in what they saw as "rescue through work," since the workers in the

shops received work cards exempting them from being sent to the forced-labor camps.

The Zionist YOUTH MOVEMENTS, which renewed their educational activity when the schools failed to open, also began to teach the children. They engaged in vocational training of the youth and in aid to the needy through the youth branch created by the Zentrale. On the outskirts of the city, agricultural plots were created that became a focus for the activities of the youth movements.

From May 10 to 12, 1942, about 1,500 Jews were sent to the AUSCHWITZ extermination camp in the first deportation. In the second deportation, in June, about 2,000 Jews were sent to Auschwitz. On August 12 all the Jews remaining in Sosnowiec and in the other towns in the area were ordered to report to the large central square, allegedly to have their papers signed. After a *Selektion* lasting until August 18, 8,000 of them were sent to be exterminated at Auschwitz.

The youth movements and their leaders, among them Zvi Dunski, conducted a propaganda campaign urging the Jews to disobey the instruction of the Judenrat and not to report for the deportations. They also began to organize underground resistance cells, but met with difficulties, since the conditions in the area were not suitable for effective self-defense. Their efforts to make contact with Polish underground movements also proved unsuccessful. In the underground, opinions were divided between those in favor of resistance and defense inside the ghetto, and those who thought that instead they should escape.

In the spring of 1943 the remaining Jews in Sosnowiec were transferred to the ghetto established in the Środula suburb. It was located near Kamionka, where a ghetto for the Jews of BĘDZIN was established. The two sites became a single ghetto. With great effort, the members of the youth movements and even several Jews in the ghetto acquired a few weapons, and many others began to prepare

bunkers in order to hide at the time of deportation and defend their lives.

On August 1, 1943, the general deportation and liquidation of the ghetto began. A Ha-No'ar ha-Tsiyyoni group began to take some of its members out of the ghetto, but met with difficulties after the head of the group, Józek (Azriel) Kożuch, was killed at the beginning of the deportation. A few members of the youth movements together with a small number of adults defended themselves, employing the few weapons that they possessed.

The deportation action lasted about two weeks, instead of the few days anticipated by the Germans. About a thousand Jews remained in the locality, and at the end of the year they too were sent to Auschwitz. Scores of members of the youth movements managed to escape to Slovakia and to Hungary, and from there they immigrated to Palestine.

After the war dozens of Jews settled in Sos-

Deportation of Jews from Sosnowiec.

nowiec; in 1946 they numbered about four hundred, but subsequently they too left the area.

BIBLIOGRAPHY

Geshuri, M. S., ed. *Sosnowiec and Its Environs in Zaglembie.* 2 vols. Tel Aviv, 1973–1974. (In Hebrew.)

Mazia, F. *Comrades in the Storm: The Struggle of Zionist Youth against the Nazis.* Jerusalem, 1964. (In Hebrew.)

Rappaport, R., ed. *Pinkas Zaglembie [Zaglembie Record]: Memorial Book.* Tel Aviv, 1972. (In Hebrew.)

SHLOMO NETZER

SOUSA MENDES, ARISTIDES DE (1885–1954), Portuguese career diplomat. Sousa Mendes was consul general in Bordeaux, France, in May 1940, when the Anglo-French front collapsed in the north. A wave of refugees, among them thousands of Jews, hastened to the south of France in the hope of crossing into Spain and proceeding to Portugal, from where they hoped to escape from Europe by ship. In order to cross the Spanish frontier, the refugees needed a Portuguese entry or transit visa. However, on May 10, 1940, the Portuguese government banned the further passage of refugees through its territory and instructed its consular representatives in France not to issue visas to most persons who had no final entry goal and who were seeking temporary shelter in Portugal; no visas at all were to be issued to Jews.

The sudden halt of entry into Portugal via Spain created a congestion of refugees in Bordeaux, the last major French city close to the Spanish frontier. Some ten thousand Jews were left stranded. Rabbi Haim Kruger, a refugee from Belgium, visited the Portuguese legation, where he pleaded and convinced Sousa Mendes to grant transit visas for all refugees, in spite of the Portuguese government's instructions to the contrary. Sousa Mendes then devoted all his time to issuing transit visas—close to ten thousand, according to some reports—before the arrival of the Germans.

Upon learning of Sousa Mendes's insubordination, the Portuguese government ordered his immediate recall and dispatched two emissaries from Lisbon to accompany him home. On their way to the Spanish border with Sousa Mendes, they stopped in Bayonne, a city that came under the jurisdiction of the Bordeaux consulate. Visiting at the local Portuguese legation, Sousa Mendes, still the formal superior of the Bayonne consul, ordered him to issue special visas to the Jewish refugees waiting outside. These visas were unique documents: slips of paper with the consulate seal and the inscription "The Portuguese government requests of the Spanish government the courtesy of allowing the bearer to pass freely through Spain. He is a refugee from the European conflict en route to Portugal."

Upon his return to Lisbon, the government, fuming at Sousa Mendes's disobedience, had him summarily dismissed from the Ministry of Foreign Affairs, with all his retirement and severance pensions suspended. Sousa Mendes countered by appealing directly to the government and the National Assembly to be reinstated, but to no avail. Burdened with the task of feeding a family that included thirteen children, and with no other means at his disposal, Sousa Mendes sank into poverty. He died in 1954, forgotten, heartbroken,

Aristides de Sousa Mendes.

and impoverished. (His wife had died earlier, in 1948.) In 1966, through the efforts of his daughter Joana in the United States, he was posthumously honored by YAD VASHEM as a "RIGHTEOUS AMONG THE NATIONS."

Sousa Mendes explained the motivation of his actions as follows: "If thousands of Jews can suffer because of one Catholic [i.e., Hitler], then surely it is permitted for one Catholic to suffer for so many Jews." On another occasion, he had stated: "My desire is to be with God against man, rather than with man against God."

In 1985 an international committee for the perpetuation of Sousa Mendes's memory was set up. Bending to foreign pressure, in 1988 the Portuguese National Assembly agreed to award him a full rehabilitation.

BIBLIOGRAPHY

Bauer, Y. *American Jewry and the Holocaust.* Detroit, 1981.

MORDECAI PALDIEL

SOUTH AFRICA. Adolf Hitler's ascent to power in 1933 coincided with the coalition and subsequent fusion of South Africa's two major white political parties, Jan Christiaan Smuts's South African Party and James Barry Munnik Hertzog's National Party. The new United South African National Party (the United Party), led by Hertzog, witnessed defections to the Left and Right; those to the Right formed the Purified Nationalist Party, under Dr. Daniel François Malan. The Purified Nationalists increasingly articulated the interests and concerns of anti-Jewish extraparliamentary groups such as the GREYSHIRTS and, after 1938, the Ossewa Brandwag (Ox-Wagon Sentinel). The arrival in 1936 of the *Stuttgart*, a chartered ship with 537 German Jewish refugees on board, provoked a wave of antisemitic sentiment. The newcomers were part of an increasing flow of refugees who had found a loophole in the 1930 Quota Act, which limited eastern European (mainly Jewish) immigration.

Confronted with a burgeoning "Jewish problem," the United Party introduced the Aliens Act in 1937, effectively curtailing German Jewish immigration on grounds of "unassimilability." Whereas 3,615 German Jewish refugees had entered South Africa between 1933 and 1936, fewer than 1,900 entered between 1937 and 1940. Jews were excluded from membership in the National Party, whose 1937 platform urged the complete prohibition of Jewish immigration and the introduction of quotas restricting Jewish participation in economic life.

The United Party maintained cordial relations with the Third Reich, while remaining firmly committed to the British Commonwealth. State contracts were accorded to the German transport industry, notwithstanding British opposition. Germany, in turn, viewed favorably the growth of antisemitic movements in South Africa. With war clouds looming in 1938, Hertzog gained cabinet approval for a policy of neutrality in the event of war; the Axis powers were not perceived as a direct threat to South Africa. When Britain and France declared war on Germany in 1939, Hertzog assumed that his neutral stand would be maintained. However, the cabinet was divided and the parliament favored, by 80 votes to 67, Smuts's argument to support the Commonwealth and resist Germany. The governor-general, Sir Patrick Duncan, asked Smuts to form a government. On September 6, 1939, South Africa proclaimed a state of war between itself and Germany.

South African Jewry fully supported Smuts and played a substantial role in the war effort. More than 10 percent of the entire Jewish population (90,465 in 1936) served in the Union Defense Force and other Allied forces. Of these 357 were killed, 327 were wounded or injured, 143 were mentioned in dispatches, and 94 received awards for distinguished service. On the home front, the South African Jewish Board of Deputies and the South African Zionist Federation established organizations to raise funds for refugees and for the relief of European Jewry. The Jewish War Appeal, in particular, assisted Jewish war victims and South African Jewish soldiers and their dependents. This organization worked in conjunction with international agencies such as the American JOINT DISTRIBUTION COMMITTEE and the South African RED CROSS. In the latter stages of the war, the Aliens and Refugees Committee raised funds to assist relief operations, and Jewish personnel from South Africa aided with relief work in Europe.

In addition to fund-raising and relief work, the South African Jewish Board of Deputies coordinated official Days of Mourning for European Jewry in 1942, 1943, and 1945. On each occasion, Jewish businesses closed early and special synagogue services were held. Mass meetings followed, addressed by prominent Jewish and non-Jewish personalities. The Board of Deputies also lobbied the government to permit the entry of more Jewish refugees, since Jewish immigration had virtually ceased with the advent of the war. Smuts, however, feared that this would lead to food shortages, pressure on shipping, and right-wing antisemitism. Many Afrikaner nationalists opposed the war and sympathized with Germany, supporting Hitler's racial policies. Some even resorted to antigovernment violence during the war years.

In the immediate postwar period, Smuts again opposed large-scale Jewish immigration. He planned a new immigration policy for Western and northern Europeans and feared that the arrival of Jewish refugees from Eastern Europe would jeopardize this initiative. Palestine was the preferred solution for DISPLACED PERSONS. As a result of the rigid application of immigration rules, only 1,512 Jews entered South Africa between 1946 and 1948.

BIBLIOGRAPHY

Shimoni, G. *Jews and Zionism: The South African Experience (1910–1967).* Cape Town, 1980.
South African Jewish Board of Deputies. *South African Jews in World War II.* Johannesburg, 1950.

MILTON SHAIN

SOVIET UNION. Before World War II, the Soviet Union had a Jewish population of 3,020,000 to 3,050,000. In 1939 and 1940, the Soviet Union annexed eastern POLAND, the Baltic states, BESSARABIA, and BUKOVINA, territories with a Jewish population of 1,880,000 to 1,900,000; in addition, 250,000 to 300,000 Jewish refugees were living there who had fled from German-occupied Poland after the outbreak of the war. In June 1941, when the Germans invaded the Soviet Union, 5,150,000 to 5,250,000 Jews were under its rule, more than half the total number of Jews in Europe.

The three categories of Jews—those who had been living in the Soviet Union before 1939, those living in the territories that the Soviet Union annexed, and the refugees— differed from one another in their social makeup, their way of life, and their Jewish consciousness and identification. The original Soviet Jewish population may be divided into three groups.

One group, numbering from 1,250,000 to 1,500,000, lived in the areas that had been opened up to Jewish immigration comparatively recently, that is, outside the Pale of Settlement of tsarist times in which Russia's Jews had been confined, most of them in large cities. The average age of this group was lower than that of the Jews in the rest of the USSR, and a considerable number were integrated into the Soviet establishment in administrative and scientific fields. This group was undergoing an overall process of acculturation, and manifested clear signs of assimilation. The ties of these Jews to the shtetl (pl., shtetlach; a small town with a large Jewish population), from which most of them originated, were tenuous, and they saw the shtetl as the symbol of a world whose time had long since passed. Their attitude toward the Yiddish language and culture and toward religion was marked by disrespect and scorn. The rate of mixed marriages among them and the percentage of Communist party members were high, even when compared with those of the Jews living in the large cities of what had been the Pale of Settlement.

A second group, numbering from 750,000 to 1,000,000 Jews, lived in the large cities in the areas that had historically been the centers of Jewish population. In average age and education they were not very different from the first group. The areas they inhabited, however, were far less industrialized, and the population was heterogeneous (consisting of Ukrainians, Belorussians, Russians, and Poles), a factor that to some degree had slowed their rate of acculturation to the Russian way of life. Residence in shtetlach and in

Jewish sections of cities had left its imprint on these Jews, many of whom still spoke Yiddish and spent much of their leisure time with other Jews.

A third group, numbering from 500,000 to 1,000,000, were still living in the Jewish towns and in the Jewish agricultural areas that had been established and encouraged by the Soviet regime in the 1920s and 1930s. This meant that on the eve of World War II, dozens of villages in the southern Ukraine and the Crimea were either exclusively Jewish or had a Jewish majority. Most of the Jews in this group belonged to a higher age group, and their formal education was far below the general standard prevailing among Soviet Jews. This group had a relatively large sector made up of artisans, tradesmen, and so on. Although these Jews, like the rest of the Jewish population of the Soviet Union, had no organizations of their own, they spent their life among other Jews, both at work and in their leisure time. The historical continuity of Jewish life in the area had also had its effect on daily life; the Yiddish language,

Jewish jokes, and the use of Jewish metaphors were prevalent among this group, more than among any other sector of Soviet Jewry.

In the annexed territories, the Soviet security services introduced a policy of forced Sovietization between 1939 and 1941. The Jewish organizations were disbanded, the Hebrew schools closed, independent Jewish newspapers were no longer published, and political parties were outlawed. Masses of Jews were arrested and exiled, the Soviet authorities classifying them as "politically hostile elements" or as "dangerous" because of their social background.

The refugees, most of them Jews, posed a particularly difficult problem. For the most part they had no place to live and no employment, and had left their relatives behind in German-occupied Poland. The Soviet authorities tried to deal with the problem by recruiting them for work in the interior of the USSR on a voluntary basis, but this attempt failed. The refugees, numbering hundreds of thousands, were given the option of accept-

SOVIET UNION

ing Soviet citizenship or returning to their homes in German-occupied Poland. If they became Soviet citizens they would be under certain restrictions, such as not being allowed to live within 62 miles (100 km) of the border or in the large cities. Most of the refugees opted for returning to Poland. The Soviets took this as a mark of disloyalty to their regime, and in June and July of 1940 exiled the refugees to the Soviet interior.

On June 22, 1941, the Germans launched Operation "Barbarossa," the invasion of the Soviet Union on a huge military scale, with the objective of ending the war by that winter. Initially, the Wehrmacht made rapid progress. The Red Army's lack of preparedness, the loss of numerous commanders during the Stalinist purges, the breakdown of communications, and the reluctance of the Soviet command to act on its own, without approval at the political level, brought the Soviet military position to the brink of disaster. The civilian administration was in complete disarray, with many members of the establishment seeking above all to save themselves and their families.

Evacuation. A few days after the German invasion, the Supreme Evacuation Council was set up. Its task was to organize the orderly withdrawal to the interior of entire factories, together with their employees and the employees' families, as well as administrative officials and the staff of essential institutions. Authority to transfer factories and civilians to the rear was vested in the military commands, and local authorities participated as well. In the absence of an overall evacuation plan, however, the frequent changes in the battle zone and the multiplicity of evacuation authorities caused conflicts and delay. In the first few months, the result, most of the time, was a headlong flight, rather than an evacuation. Many of those who escaped were young people, highly mobile, belonging to Soviet officialdom or employed in factories and plants. An important factor in the evacuation was the accessibility of a railway station or other means of transportation. Generally speaking, more avenues for flight were available in the large cities than in the towns.

As time went on the pace of the German advance slackened, experience was gained, and a proper procedure was established for assembling the civilians to be evacuated and providing the required means of transportation. As a result, the evacuation gradually became a planned operation. It was only in late July 1941 that the authorities considered the requests for evacuation of the general population and no longer confined themselves to the personnel of war-essential industrial plants. The chances of escaping from places occupied by the Germans early in the invasion were poor; the chances of getting away from larger population centers, and from places occupied at a later date—either on one's own or in a more or less organized manner—were better. For Jews, escaping into the interior of the USSR meant a chance of avoiding extermination.

When the Germans invaded the Soviet Union, the Soviet government called up for active service fourteen age groups, consisting of those born from 1905 to 1918, adding them to the four age groups, of those born from 1919 to 1922, who had been on active service from the beginning of the war. During the early months of the fighting, especially in the areas close to the front, the draft was carried out under chaotic conditions. In the annexed territories hardly any draft took place at all, because of the rapidity of the German occupation there, and in the areas west of the 1939 Soviet border, the draft was only partial, at best. The chances for a Jew to survive and fight in the Red Army depended, in large measure, on his place of residence and the timing of the Nazi occupation of that place. Since the Soviet Union was the sole country in Europe that was only partially occupied by the Germans throughout the war, its Jews, at least up to early 1943, were split into two groups—one group under Nazi occupation rule and the other under the Soviet regime.

Occupation and Extermination. The Germans divided the territories they occupied in the Soviet Union into four administrative units, whose borders underwent changes resulting from developments at the front. In formal terms, two of these units were under civilian administration: (1) REICHSKOMMISSARIAT OSTLAND, consisting of the Baltic states and western BELORUSSIA, including the MINSK district; and (2) REICHSKOMMISSARIAT UKRAINE (not including Eastern Galicia, which was incorporated into the GENERAL-GOUVERNEMENT), in which were located the regions of Volhynia, ZHITOMIR, Kiev, Nikolayev, Tauria, and DNEPROPETROVSK. Most of the occupied part of the Russian republic and part of the occupied UKRAINE were under a military administration. The area lying between the Dniester and Bug rivers, in which ODESSA was located, was renamed TRANSNISTRIA and handed over to Romanian rule (see below). To the Jewish population, this administrative division of the German-occupied area made little difference, since it was mainly the SS and the EINSATZGRUPPEN that dealt with the Jews.

During the preparations for Operation "Barbarossa," orders were issued to exterminate all the Jews, this being an element of the ideology motivating Adolf Hitler in his war against the Soviet Union. In the German-occupied areas there, two patterns for the murder of Jews emerged. One pattern, followed in the areas that had been annexed by the Soviet Union in 1939 and 1940, was, by and large (once the Einsatzgruppen's mass-murder drive was over), similar to the course followed in the Generalgouvernement in Poland: harassment, establishment of ghettos, starvation, and, finally, deportation to the extermination camps. In these areas, the total extermination of the Jews was completed within twelve to eighteen months after the occupation.

The other, and very different, pattern was applied in the Nazi-occupied areas within the Soviet Union's pre-1939 borders. Here, the extermination of the Jews was based on the belief that they were the main support of the Soviet regime (which had allegedly been created by Jews), and on a policy that called for the eradication of all representatives of Bolshevism. The Nazis acted on orders—mostly oral—to liquidate the Jews and on the basis of the KOMMISSARBEFEHL, and the killing of Jews was seen as an integral element in the military operations. The total murder of the Jews in these areas took a few weeks—two to three months, at most—from the day they were occupied.

To exterminate the Jews in the occupied localities in the Soviet Union, the Germans generally used one of four methods and, in some cases, a combination of these methods.

1. The German occupation authorities appointed a three- or four-member JUDENRAT (Jewish Council). Its members were mostly prominent figures of the Jewish community who had remained in their towns and had not been involved in political activities under the Soviet rule; they included elderly and highly respected persons, doctors, engineers, and the like. A few days later an announcement was made ordering the Jews to register with the Judenrat, on pain of death. After a few more days—or weeks, at the most—the Jews were ordered to report at a certain spot in the town, from which they were going to be sent to a labor camp or "moved to Palestine." These announcements usually included a threat that any Jew who failed to report, and any person who helped Jews to hide, would be executed. The Jews were told to take along only a few items, and no food at all, since it would be provided for them by the authorities. The assembled Jews were escorted by Germans and locally recruited armed units who beat them, harassed them, and shot anyone who lagged behind or voiced any kind of protest. The Jews then proceeded—usually on foot but sometimes by truck—to nearby antitank ditches, quarries, or ravines, where they were to be killed. Just before reaching the spot, they were split up into groups of 10 or 100 and ordered to undress. The slaughter site was surrounded by Germans armed with machine guns; the Jews were forced into the ditch, ravine, or quarry and fired at, from all directions. When one group was finished off, the next was brought in, to be killed in the same way. The same site also served for shooting Jews who had been caught hiding after the mass slaughter was over, and frequently also for the murder of non-Jewish Communists and partisans.

2. In some of the localities, especially in villages and towns with a small number of Jews who were known to all the inhabitants, the Germans did not appoint a Judenrat or register the Jews but proceeded immediately to round up and kill them.

3. In still other places, the extermination of the Jews began by concentrating them in a certain city quarter. They were ordered to move into the designated area (usually one in which a relatively high percentage of Jews were already living); the non-Jewish residents were ordered to leave and move into apartments that had become available in other quarters. The result was a ghetto of sorts, into which nearly all the Jewish population was packed, under terrible conditions. The ghetto was rarely fenced in and was only loosely guarded. Its inhabitants were ordered to wear a distinctive sign, either a white armband or a badge (*see* BADGE, JEWISH) with a Star of David on it. Some of the Jews—usually the young and the skilled workers—were put to work outside the ghetto, where they also suffered from brutal mistreatment. Ghettos of this kind in the old Soviet borders lasted no longer than a few weeks or months (except for that of Minsk). The Jews were taken from the ghetto, either all together or in groups, at short intervals, and shot to death at a nearby site, in the manner described above.

4. The fourth method was to crowd the Jews into a makeshift concentration camp, in the buildings of an old factory or, as sometimes happened, in an open field. The area was fenced in and put under guard. Here too, the Jews had to wear a distinctive sign, a white armband or a Star of David. From time to time they were removed from the camp, by the thousands, and taken to slaughter sites nearby to be killed.

Under a German-Romanian agreement that was signed at Tiraspol, a city northwest of Odessa, on August 30, 1941, the Germans handed over to Romania an area of 10,000 square miles (25,000 sq km), known as Transnistria. On the eve of World War II, hundreds of thousands of Jews were living there. When the Germans captured the area, they mass-murdered Jews, but after the transferral to Romania most of the surviving Jews in the region were under Romanian rule, with the Romanians benefiting from German aid and advice. The Romanians put the Jews in concentration camps, where they suffered from hunger, cold, and epidemic diseases. The Jews were also put on hard labor, accompanied by brutal mistreatment. From time to time a few Jews were murdered by the Romanians, as a warning to the rest. The Romanian army, including the personnel that dealt with the Jews, was not as efficient and disciplined as the Germans, and a few loopholes were left in the concentration camps, through which the Jews were able to obtain some food and other items. Jews from the German-occupied area did, in fact, try to escape to Transnistria, but only a few succeeded. Although hundreds of Jews died daily in the Romanian camps, when the area was liberated the number of survivors in Transnistria was much higher than in the German-occupied parts of the Soviet Union.

Following the mass murder of the Jews in the latter areas, in which the greater part of the Jewish population in every inhabited place was exterminated, the hunt for the few who had managed to escape or to hide continued unabated. The fact that every resident had a Soviet internal passport showing the bearer's nationality made it easier for the Germans and their helpers to ferret out the Jews. The regime introduced by the Germans in the Soviet areas under their control was extremely harsh, and public executions were common. As a result, very few non-Jews risked their lives to hide Jews, and only a small number of Jews were saved in this way. A part of the population, among them Soviet officials in low and intermediate ranks, collaborated with the Germans and played an active role in the murder of Jews. The majority of the population who saw the Jews being killed before their very eyes looked away; some manifested outward indifference but in fact sympathized with the Jews, while others gloated over what was happening to them.

Resistance. There was no organized physical resistance by the Jews in the Soviet Union, during or after the extermination campaign. This was caused by several factors: the lack of any Jewish organization whatsoever in the Soviet Union (it had been forbidden by the authorities); the speed with which the mass murders took place after the conquest; the absence from the scene of most of the Jewish men, who had been drafted into the Soviet army, and of the more active sector of the Jewish population, who had fled or had been evacuated; and the indifference, and often the hostility, of the local population. However, in many instances individual Jews resisted spontaneously, with acts ranging from spitting in a German's face to snatching his gun away and killing him. The only way of effective resistance open to Jews was to flee to the forest and join the partisan units (*see* PARTISANS).

The forests and other remote areas became rallying points for Soviet army officers and political commissars whose units had disintegrated, for a few Communist officials who had not managed to escape, and for Jews who had fled from their homes when they found out about German harassment and murder. The forest areas also became places of refuge for entire Jewish families running for their lives, which is how the FAMILY CAMPS IN THE FORESTS came into being. The emergence of partisan groups was a spontaneous phenomenon and it was natural for some of the units to be made up largely of Jewish fighters. Within a few months these partisan units succeeded in making contact with Soviet authorities behind the front, and special emissaries were sent to them, requesting them to put their movement on an organized basis. When this was done and the partisan groups became military combat formations, many of the units lost their distinctly Jewish character, and the Jewish officers were replaced by non-Jews. The overall Soviet partisan movement took few meaningful steps to save Jews, concentrating on attacking the enemy with such acts as cutting his lines of communication. The more brutal the German treatment of the general population, the greater was the influx of new members into the partisan movement, a development accompanied by increasing manifestations of antisemitism. The Jewish partisan often had to bear the brunt of derision and contempt, and always had to prove that he was willing to sacrifice himself and was not the coward his comrades thought him to be.

Jews in the Soviet Army. The Jews who lived under the Soviets during the Holocaust may be divided into two categories: the hundreds of thousands, mostly men, who were serving in the Red Army; and two million civilians. In the course of the war, most of the Jewish men were drafted into the Soviet army, as were the men from the rest of the population. In addition, thousands of Jews who were not conscripted volunteered for military service, and the percentage of Jews in the army was higher than their percentage in the overall population. Jews served in every branch of the service, but since they were, on the average, more educated, relatively more served in the specialized branches, such as the air force, the armored corps, the engineering corps, the artillery, and the medical corps. Many Jews served as generals in senior command positions of the Soviet army. Close to 161,000 military awards were earned by Jews for distinguishing themselves on the battlefield, and in this respect they were in fifth place among the Russian nationalities, whereas in number they were (on the eve of the war) in seventh place. The highest award for distinguished service in battle, that of Hero of the Soviet Union, was granted to 11,612 officers and men of other ranks in the Soviet army; of them, 150 were Jews, with 52 falling in battle and 36 receiving the award for the courage and resourcefulness they displayed in the bloody fighting that marked the crossing of the Dnieper. Of the others, 36 were in the artillery, 24 in the air force, 21 in the armored corps, 8 in the navy, 7 in the engineering corps, and 6 in other branches. As these figures indicate, Jewish fighters took part in formidable combat operations, in which they showed great daring and resourcefulness. The spirit of self-sacrifice manifested by the Jewish soldiers in the Soviet army was inspired by their devotion to the country and their desire to avenge, as best they could, the murder of their families and their people.

Soviet Jewry during and after the War. In the interior of the Soviet Union, the Jewish population shared the suffering, the hunger, and the diseases experienced by the rest of the country's population. The Jewish women, like other Soviet women, took the place of men in strenuous jobs in the factories, in industry, and in agriculture. Unlike the rest of the population, however, the Jews were often exposed to insults, mockery, and even physical assaults from the general population, especially from disabled war veterans back from the front who were voicing the antisemitic views that Nazi propaganda had spread among them. The Soviet authorities took no effective steps against this wave of antisemitism, and did not counter it with any propaganda of their own. For political reasons, however, mainly in the interests of Soviet foreign-policy aims, the JEWISH ANTIFASCIST COMMITTEE was set up, which under the force of circumstances became a kind of representative body of Soviet Jewry. Its chairman was the Yiddish actor Shlomo Mikhoels, and during the war he became the symbol of Jewish leadership in the Soviet Union.

Under the impact of their experience in the Holocaust, which had shaken their faith in the "brotherhood of the Soviet peoples" and had shown that the Jews of diverse countries, despite the different regimes under which they lived, shared a common fate, Soviet Jews became acutely aware of their Jewish national feelings and of the broad historical context of the Jewish tragedy. A Soviet policy that permitted ethnic solidarity to be expressed in public facilitated the emergence among Soviet Jews of a Yiddish Holocaust literature (*see* LITERATURE ON THE HOLO-CAUST: YIDDISH LITERATURE), which articulated the Jews' unique suffering at this time and ranked it among the Jewish people's martyrdom over thousands of years. A number of Jewish writers who wrote in Russian, including Ilya EHRENBURG, Vasily Grossman, Pavel Antokolski, Margarita Aliger, and Naum Korzhavin, sought to come to grips with the broad implications of the Holocaust in their works, expressing the feelings and thoughts of a broad section of Soviet Jewry who had seen at close range the atrocities suffered by their families and their people.

Beginning in 1944, and even earlier, when most of the occupied areas of the Soviet Union were liberated, the Jews who had fled or had been evacuated on the eve of the German occupation began to return. They faced a terrible situation, realizing that their Jewish community had been destroyed and that the territories that had been under German control had become one huge burial ground for Jews. Every city and town had its mass graves, bearing witness, despite the Germans' efforts to obliterate them, to what had happened. From non-Jews and from the few Jewish survivors, the returning Jews learned that a considerable number of their neighbors had helped the Germans, either directly in the murders, or by seizing Jewish property. Many of those who had collaborated with the Germans were now reinstated in the Soviet administration, in lower and intermediate ranks. Jewish appeals to the authorities to take action against the collaborators met

with evasion. The population, having absorbed Nazi propaganda, gave vent to their antisemitic feelings. The apartments in which the Jews had lived—those that the war had spared—were occupied, and many Jews had to resort to long and exhausting litigation to get them back. Despite the general shortage of experienced manpower, the authorities preferred not to reinstate Jews in some of the positions and posts they had held before the war.

A wide gulf opened between the expectations of the Soviet Jews and this reality. They had hoped that, in view of the Holocaust that Soviet Jewry had experienced and the loyalty and devotion they had shown in the war, the Soviet regime would launch a broad campaign to eradicate antisemitism; that a Jewish republic would be established in the Crimea, whose Tatar population had been exiled, or in the Volga region, from which the ethnic Germans had been removed; that Jewish cultural life would be encouraged and supported; and that the Jewish Antifascist Committee would expand its range and would operate as a representative Jewish organization within the Soviet Union. Many Jews had hoped that the infrastructure established during the war, of contacts and collaboration with Jewish communities outside the Soviet Union, would be permitted to broaden further. What did happen was very different.

As early as 1946 and 1947, sharp official criticism was voiced of nationalist manifestations that were finding their way into Soviet Yiddish literature, and of the alleged exaggerated attention it was devoting to the Holocaust and to Jewish suffering. Attempts to commemorate victims of the Holocaust, by putting up memorial tablets at murder sites or by issuing publications on the subject, met with growing resistance; and one obstacle after another was put in the way of a renewal of Yiddish activities in the country. There were clear indications that an antisemitic policy was being adopted by the Soviet establishment, and in early 1948, with the murder of Shlomo Mikhoels, the chairman of the Jewish Antifascist Committee, such a policy gained an almost official status.

In a single decade, from 1939 to 1948, the Jews of the Soviet Union underwent far-reaching change and upheaval. The Jewish population was halved; the Jewish shtetl ceased to exist; the greater part of the Yiddish-speaking population was annihilated; the belief in the brotherhood of the Soviet peoples was shaken to the core; the possibility of assimilation with the general population was put in doubt; and popular antisemitism again revived.

Since 1948, Soviet Jewry has experienced a number of further changes. During his last years Stalin became increasingly paranoid in his antisemitism, as demonstrated by the so-called Doctors' Plot; however, he died before his plans could be put into operation. The post-Stalinist thaw initially promised a revision, but this turned out to be premature. Reform of the Soviet government proved stillborn, while the loosening of the police state envisioned by Nikita Khrushchev collapsed with his downfall in 1964.

The Holocaust has been a major factor in the reorientation of Soviet Jewry since 1948. The Holocaust and the rise of the state of Israel have played a crucial role in the awakening of Jewish religious and national consciousness among Soviet Jewry. Despite efforts by the government to disguise the Jewishness of the victims of the Nazis and their helpers, memory of those terrible years has not been erased. Under Mikhail Gorbachev, the fate of the Jews has been described with much greater openness.

[See also Black Book of Soviet Jewry, The; Hilfswillige; Russkaya Osvoboditelnaya Armiya.]

BIBLIOGRAPHY

Ainsztein, R. "Soviet Jewry in the Second World War." In *The Jews in Soviet Russia since 1917*, edited by L. Kochan, pp. 269–287. New York, 1972.

Dallin, A. *German Rule in Russia, 1941–1945.* London, 1957.

Ehrenburg, I., and V. Grossman, eds. *The Black Book of Soviet Jewry.* New York, 1980.

Guri, M. "Jews in the Red Army during the Second World War." In *Jewish Soldiers in the Armies of Europe*, pp. 135–148. Tel Aviv, 1967. (In Hebrew.)

Shapiro, G., ed. *Under Fire: The Stories of Jewish Heroes of the Soviet Union.* Jerusalem, 1989.

Shvarts, S. *Evrei v Sovetskom Soiuze s nachala Vtoroi mirovoi voiny 1939–1965.* New York, 1966.

West, B., ed. *The Pangs of Destruction: The Jews of Russia in the Nazi Holocaust, 1941–1943.* Tel Aviv, 1963. (In Hebrew.)

MORDECHAI ALTSHULER

SPAIN. [*The first article in this entry focuses on the fate of Jewish refugees in Spain during the Holocaust period and the situation of the Spanish Jews in occupied Europe. The second article is an inquiry into the relation between Spanish fascism and the Jews of Spain.*]

General Survey

The Jews of Spain were expelled in 1492 and began to return in the nineteenth century. At the time of the Nazi rise to power in 1933, Spain had a republican regime (the Second Spanish Republic), and its constitution provided equal rights to non-Catholics. This made it possible for Jews from Germany to find refuge there. By early 1935 some three thousand Jews had entered Spain, and when the Spanish Civil War broke out in July 1936, the total Jewish population of Spain was estimated at six thousand. The HICEM society provided aid to the refugees through Ezra (aid) committees that had been set up in Barcelona and Madrid, and in 1935, on the basis of a study conducted by the Jewish Colonization Association, HICEM arranged for the settlement of sixty skilled Jewish craftsmen in Spain.

In the course of the Civil War (July 17, 1936, to April 1, 1939) most of the Jews left Spain; HICEM dealt with the exit from the country of 394 Jewish refugees. An estimated 8,000 Jews, however, went to Spain during that period as volunteers in the International Brigades; Jews accounted for 30 percent of the total number of men who volunteered to fight in the war against the Nationalists, led by Gen. Francisco Franco. They all regarded the war as part of the struggle against Fascism and Nazism, the movements then in power in the two countries (Italy and Germany) that were Franco's allies and gave him active support. In November 1938 the republican government of Spain agreed to the removal of the International Brigades from the country, and thereafter apparently not a single one of these Jews remained on Spanish soil.

After the fall of the republic, its troops and loyalists fled the country en masse, for France; the number of these refugees was estimated at the time as 400,000 to 500,000. The French authorities interned many of them in Rivesaltes, GURS, and other concentration camps, places that in the summer of 1940 were to be used as concentration camps for Jews. After the Nationalist victory, no Jewish organization was allowed to function in Spain. Jewish community life, however, was left undisturbed in the Spanish-protected part of Morocco (whose Jewish population in 1940 was 14,734) and in Tangier (8,000 Jews in 1941), which Spain had seized in 1940. The status of the Jews in these two areas was determined by the laws of the sultanate of Morocco, rather than by the laws of Spain.

Jewish Refugees in Spain. After the fall of France in the summer of 1940, tens of thousands of refugees streamed to the Spanish border, trying to reach the Iberian ports from which they hoped to sail to a safe refuge. Spanish consuls issued transit visas to persons who possessed entry visas to Portugal or other countries. Despite the stricter regulations introduced in 1940 and 1941, tens of thousands of refugees were able to cross the border even without a visa to a final destination. Refugees whose departure from Spain was held up because their ships had left before they reached the ports, or whose visas had lapsed, or who had crossed into Spain with no visa at all, were interned in the Miranda de Ebro concentration camp or expelled to France. The close ties between the Spanish security police and the Gestapo resulted in the delivery of refugees by the Spanish police to the Germans when the latter asked for them. (This practice had been in force even before Heinrich HIMMLER's visit to Madrid in October 1940, but it was greatly reinforced by that visit.) Regular emigration of Jews from Germany traveling by train via Spain continued, however, until the Germans put a total stop to the exit of Jews from the Reich, in October 1941. In the first half of World War II a total of twenty thousand to thirty thousand Jews were given permission to pass through Spain. At that point three hundred to five hundred Jews unable to find another destination were being held in Spain. More than four thousand Spanish-protected Jews in various European countries (see below) were granted special privileges (that is, compared to the rest of the Jewish population in those countries) as a result of Spanish intervention in their behalf.

In the summer of 1942, when the Nazis began deporting Jews from France and the Low Countries to extermination camps, a wave of Jewish refugees crossed the Spanish border illegally. Those who were caught were arrested, and the Spanish authorities planned to turn them back to France. In the wake of the successful landings by Allied forces in North Africa (on November 8, 1942, in Operation "Torch"), the Germans extended their occupation of France over the entire country. Hundreds of Frenchmen fled across the Spanish border in the hope that from Spain they would be able to make their way to the liberated parts of French North Africa. Again giving in to German pressure, the Spanish authorities planned to expel these new refugees and hand them over to the Germans, and they began to execute this decision. The fate of the refugees in Spain became a major issue in the determination of Allied policy on Spain. Under pressure by the Allies, with Winston CHURCHILL personally involved, Spain announced, in April 1943, that refugees arriving at the Spanish border would not be turned back, provided they were looked after while in Spain and would leave the country for another destination without delay. The Allies promptly launched an aid program on behalf of persons whom they recognized as their citizens and who were being held in Miranda de Ebro or in police stations in various parts of Spain, and arranged for their departure from the country.

The care of stateless persons—most of whom were Jewish—was at first in the hands of the unofficial representative of the JOINT DISTRIBUTION COMMITTEE in Spain, Dr. Samuel Sequerra, who operated out of Barcelona, posing as a representative of the Portuguese Red Cross. On April 10, 1943, the Spanish security police gave its approval to the establishment of the Representation in Spain of the American Relief Organizations, under the patronage of the United States embassy, headed by David Blickenstaff, an officer on the staff of the Quakers' relief organization. Most of the financing of the "representation" was provided by the Joint. It gave assistance to the refugees who had crossed the border into Spain and also helped the Jewish Agency representative select candidates for immigration to Palestine from among the refugees, as part of its efforts to get the stateless persons out of Spain. Except for one operation —smuggling a small number of children across the border from France to Spain— the unofficial representatives of the Jewish organizations in Spain and Portugal did not take any initiatives of their own to bring Jews out of German-occupied France into Spain. In most instances the refugees arranged for their own escape. As of November 1943 the ARMÉE JUIVE, the Jewish resistance movement in France, undertook this task.

The number of Jews who fled to Spain and found temporary refuge there between the summer of 1942 and the fall of 1944 is estimated at a maximum of seventy-five hundred. During this period there were occasions when refugees were forced back across the border, but this does not seem to have been part of a systematic policy, and, more importantly, it was not part of an effort to discriminate against the Jewish refugees. Despite German influence and the hostility of the ruling party toward the Jews, the Jewish refugees were not singled out for persecution. Indeed, as many refugees have reported, their being Jewish did not seem to detract from the sympathy that the average Spaniard had for them and their plight. The authorities treated the Jewish refugees as they did other fugitives, and they permitted the Jews, like the other refugees, to stay in small towns, or even in Madrid and Barcelona, until their departure from Spain—on condition that they report regularly to the police and that the Jewish relief organization cover all their expenses.

Spanish Jews in Occupied Europe. More than 4,000 Jews of Spanish origin living in German-occupied countries were under Spanish protection. Most of them had been accorded that status before World War I, when Spain took under its protection small groups of Jews residing in the Ottoman em-

pire. When the Capitulations (special privileges held by foreign governments in the Ottoman empire) were abolished, in the early 1920s, the Spanish government introduced a procedure that enabled protected persons to obtain Spanish citizenship without having to settle in Spain. At the outbreak of World War II, Jews registered in the list of protected persons held by the Spanish missions numbered 640 in Greece, 107 in Romania, fewer than 50 in Hungary, and 25 in Yugoslavia. The largest number of Jews under Spanish protection lived in France, where many Jews from the Balkans had immigrated, and of these, 2,000 lived in the German-occupied zone. Spanish passports and protective documents were also held by a few Jews in Germany, Belgium, and the Netherlands. All of these Jews were recognized by the Germans as foreign nationals entitled to Spanish protection. An unknown number of Jews who were natives of Spanish Morocco were living in French Morocco; Spain demanded that the French authorities recognize the Spanish-protective status of these Jews and exempt them from anti-Jewish measures—an issue involving the then-existing differences between the two countries over the control of Moroccan territory.

In the early part of the war, it seemed that Spanish-protected Jews might also be under the threat of "Aryanization" (*see* ARISIERUNG) of property and restrictions with regard to occupation and freedom of movement. At that time, Spain informed the German occupation authorities in France and the government of Romania that the laws of Spain did not permit discrimination on grounds of race or religion, and that therefore no such discrimination could be applied to its citizens. Spanish representatives abroad were instructed to report to Madrid on all instances of Spanish citizens being subjected to mistreatment, and to intervene with the authorities in such cases. As long as there was no violation of Spanish sovereignty, however, the representatives were not to insist on the exemption of Spanish citizens from the application of general local laws. The highly ambiguous nature of this policy—of which the Germans were well aware—placed most of the onus of protecting Spanish citizens abroad on the respective diplomatic representatives, and much depended on their goodwill and their personal attitude to those under their protection. In occupied France, for example, the property of Spanish citizens living in the country was registered with the Spanish consulate in Paris, in lieu of its "Aryanization"; but despite determined efforts, Consul General Bernardo Rolland was unable to obtain the release of fourteen Spanish citizens from the DRANCY camp, where they had been imprisoned in August 1941.

On January 21, 1943, the German embassy in Madrid advised the Spanish government that it had until March 31 to take all its Jewish citizens out of the western European countries; subsequent announcements applied the deadline to other German-occupied areas as well. In interoffice exchanges on the issue between Adolf EICHMANN and the German Foreign Ministry it was agreed that "all Jews who were in possession of a foreign nationality prior to the date on which we asked the respective governments to repatriate

them, would be permitted to leave." This gave Spain the opportunity to save the lives of the four thousand Spanish citizens—all of them Jews—who were in German-occupied areas. The Spanish government vacillated, and was inclined to bar the entry into Spain of all the protected persons. Finally, the Spanish foreign minister, Francisco Gómez Jordana y Sousa, told the Spanish consul in Paris that "entry visas to Spain would be issued to Spanish Jews who were able to prove, by producing appropriate and complete documentation, their own Spanish citizenship and that of each member of their family who is to accompany them." The demand for "complete documentation" meant that the number of prospective candidates for rescue was severely cut. At the same time, according to another instruction, received by the Spanish ambassador in Berlin, Spanish missions were to maintain supervision of the property even of those protected persons who had not qualified for entry into Spain, since

A Spanish protective document issued in Budapest on November 1, 1944. The Hungarian text reads: "I confirm that Miklós Gelléri, born in 1902 and a resident of Budapest, has applied through his relatives in Spain for Spanish nationality. The Spanish embassy has been authorized to grant him a visa before his nationality application is officially approved. The Spanish Embassy requests all the relevant authorities to take this fact into consideration and to release him from forced labor. Signed: The deputy at the Spanish Embassy."

such property was to be regarded as "national property" of Spain. On March 18 the Spanish foreign minister advised the United States embassy in Madrid that he had the possibility of rescuing Spanish Jews, but he required guarantees that the Jews who were rescued and taken to Spain would depart from the country shortly after their arrival. In order to ensure that this condition was observed, the Spanish government, in inter-office exchanges of correspondence as well as in its contacts with the Americans, stipulated that only after one group of "repatriated" Spanish Jews had left Spain would the next group be admitted to the country. In practice, the Spanish government insisted that this condition be meticulously observed.

As a result of these restrictions and conditions, only 800 Spanish citizens, at the most, were enabled to enter Spain in the period that followed, up to the end of the war. The largest single group consisted of 365 SALONIKA Jews who were held back in the BERGEN-BELSEN concentration camp for six months, pending the departure from Spain of the group that preceded it—79 Jews from France. The next group, 155 Jews from Athens, was in turn detained in Bergen-Belsen, waiting for the Salonika group to leave Spain; this group never made it.

Spanish protection did save the 107 Spanish Jews in Romania, even without "repatriation," and the same applied to Bulgaria. In Athens, the Spanish consul, Sebastian Romero Radigales, because of the determined stand that he took in protecting the Spanish Jews, was able to save 235 of them. In the summer and fall of 1944 the Spanish representative in Hungary joined the papal nuncio and other representatives of neutral countries in their efforts to save Jews. According to his reports, the Spanish representative issued 45 passports to Jews who had originally been registered as Spanish citizens, another 352 "special passports," and 1,898 "protective documents," which certified that the bearer was about to emigrate to Spain and was therefore under Spanish protection. To this figure might be added another 500, whose emigration to Spanish-controlled Tangier was being negotiated.

Spain's role in the rescue of Jews became an important subject in the country's propaganda after the war, especially when Israel, on May 16, 1949, joined the United Nations members opposing the cancellation of the diplomatic boycott of the Franco regime imposed by the United Nations in 1945. This propaganda also found its way into Spanish historiography. The major claim of Spanish propaganda was that Franco had protected "all the Spanish Jews"; this legend gained general acceptance and was sometimes associated with Franco's alleged Jewish origin (on his mother's side). The truth about the regime's real attitude, even toward those Jews who had long been under Spanish protection and who could have been saved, was withheld from the Spanish public. This had been the real test of the Spanish regime's attitude, since it concerned Jews specifically, and not refugees of various nationalities. The contribution that Spain did make to the rescue of Jews consisted primarily in the fact that when Spain formulated its general policy on the treatment of refugees, no attempt was made to discriminate against the Jews.

BIBLIOGRAPHY

Avni, H. *Spain, the Jews, and Franco.* Philadelphia, 1981.

Leshem, P. "Rescue Efforts in the Iberian Peninsula." *Leo Baeck Institute Year Book* 14 (1969): 231–256.

HAIM AVNI

Spanish Fascism and the Jews

After the forced expulsion or conversion of the entire Jewish community in 1492, there was for a long period no formal Jewish presence in Spain. Though traditional Spanish religion might sometimes invoke themes of Jewish guilt, this no longer had practical consequences in a Spanish society bereft of Jews. Modern nationalism was slow to develop in Spain, and even in the early twentieth century it failed to achieve the strength common in most other countries of southern, central, and eastern Europe.

Fascist doctrine was officially introduced to Spain by Ernesto Giménez Caballero, a leading figure of the literary avant-garde, in the late 1920s. Giménez Caballero was influenced exclusively by Italian Fascism, which was not commonly characterized by overt antisemitism. Moreover, he had earlier seen military duty in the Spanish protectorate of northern Morocco and had been greatly impressed by the preservation of the Spanish language and some aspects of Spanish culture among the Sephardic community there. At one point he obtained a fellowship to study the culture of Sephardic communities throughout the Mediterranean, and as a result he tended to think positively of Spanish Jews as rather heroic perpetuators of Spanish culture. (Somewhat the same positive impression was formed by certain Spanish army officers in Morocco, possibly including Gen. Francisco Franco himself.)

When an actual fascist movement, the Juntas de Ofensiva Nacional Sindicalista, was first founded in Spain in 1931, it too drew its major inspiration from Italy, though some of its sectors paid increasing attention to National Socialism in Germany. The movement's propaganda included references to "Jewish speculation" and "Jewish capitalism," but antisemitic themes were never prominent, if only because they could have little point of reference in Spanish society.

The chief figure of independent Spanish FASCISM, José Antonio Primo de Rivera (who founded the Falange movement in 1933), rejected antisemitism, and no specific anti-Jewish remarks are to be found in his speeches and writings. On one occasion, when a follower shouted "Down with the Jews!" at a meeting, Primo de Rivera rejected negative slogans of any kind, insisting that party propaganda must emphasize positive slogans about Spain. Though antisemitic references were sometimes found in the publications of Spanish fascism before the Civil War (1936–1939), anti-Jewish doctrines could play little role in a society almost without any Jewish community, and in which the main fascist leaders had no interest in antisemitism.

The other main force of nationalism in Spain was the Catholic Right, and in the more extreme right-wing Catholic circles there was, if anything, more rhetorical hostility to Jews than among the overt fascists. But such feelings, when expressed, remained little more than a rhetorical posture, and were not translated into concrete political gestures.

There does not seem to have been strong aversion in Spain to people of Jewish origin.

A descendant of a leading Sephardic family of Tangier, who had evidently renounced Judaism personally, played a significant role in the Falange of Seville at the beginning of the Civil War, just as Franco's Spanish Nationalist movement was pleased to receive financial contributions from affluent Jews in northern Morocco.

BIBLIOGRAPHY

Avni, H. *Spain, the Jews, and Franco.* Philadelphia, 1981.

Payne, S. G. *The Franco Regime, 1936–1975.* Madison, Wis., 1987.

Robinson, N. *The Spain of Franco and Its Policies towards the Jews.* New York, 1944.

STANLEY G. PAYNE

SPECIAL COMMANDO. *See* Sonderkommando.

SPECIAL OPERATIONS GROUPS. *See* Einsatzgruppen.

SPEER, ALBERT (1905–1981), Hitler's architect; German minister of armaments from 1942 to 1945. Born in Mannheim, Speer was the son of a wealthy architect. In 1930, while still an architect's assistant, he heard Hitler speak for the first time and was overwhelmed by the Nazi leader's power of persuasion. In January 1931 he joined the National Socialist party.

Shortly after the Nazis' rise to power, Speer was awarded his first large party contracts, redesigning Joseph GOEBBELS's official residence and planning the May 1 celebrations in Berlin. His work on these two projects attracted Hitler's attention; in the Goebbels job Speer demonstrated organizational skill, and in the May 1 pageant he produced for the first time the basic elements of the overwhelming spectacle that was to become the model for all subsequent party conventions and celebrations.

Hitler personally gave Speer assignments, and while working together the two developed close ties of friendship. Apparently seeing in the talented young man the incarnation of the unfulfilled dreams of his own youth, Hitler admitted Speer to his inner circle, opened up intoxicating new fields of action for him, and in the course of time allowed him a measure of freedom that no other member of Hitler's entourage ever enjoyed. Speer, in turn, gave Hitler outstanding service and complete loyalty.

In 1934, Speer succeeded Paul Ludwig Troost, who had died early that year, as Hitler's architect. He was given two tasks to perform: to draw up a plan for Berlin, and to create a permanent installation for party conventions and party pageantry in Nuremberg. On both of these projects, Hitler and Speer jointly developed megalomanic building plans that were to express the might and durability of the Reich and its regime.

In 1937, Speer was officially appointed inspector general of construction of the Reich's capital. This meant, among other things, that his department took charge of the apartments from which Berlin Jews were evicted in 1939. The apartments were put at the disposal of non-Jewish residents of buildings that were to be demolished to make room for Speer's construction programs and, at a later stage, of those whose dwellings were destroyed by air attacks. After deportations of Berlin's Jews to the east began in the fall of 1941, Speer's office had more apartments to allocate.

When Fritz Todt was killed in an air accident in February 1942, Speer was appointed to succeed him as minister of armaments, and in September 1943 he was named minister of armaments and war production. In this capacity he was able, by using millions of forced laborers, to raise armaments production to a remarkable degree, at the very time that Allied air attacks were growing in intensity. Hitler's backing also helped Speer in his struggles with old-time party members and in the jungle of ill-defined spheres of authority that characterized the Nazi elite.

Toward the end of the war Speer's relations with Hitler deteriorated, but it was only in the final weeks that a real change took place. In violation of an explicit order by Hitler, Speer did not permit the destruction of industry and essential installations in the areas of Germany that were about to fall into Allied hands. He later claimed that he also planned Hitler's assassination, but it is unlikely that he really meant to carry it out.

After the war, Speer was put on trial for war crimes by the International Military Tribunal at Nuremberg, charged with employing forced laborers and concentration camp prisoners. Unusual in the trial was his admission of responsibility for the actions of the Nazi regime, includings actions of which he claimed he had had no knowledge. He was found guilty on two counts, war crimes and crimes against humanity, and was sentenced to twenty years' imprisonment.

Following his release, Speer published his memoirs, *Inside the Third Reich* (1970), which gained a great deal of attention. In his book, Speer describes himself as an apolitical technician, but he again accepts responsibility for the actions of the regime and expresses repentance for his role, even for those actions of which he was not aware. He also repeats his earlier statement that his greatest guilt was for his acquiescence in the murder of the Jews.

Many scholars dealing with the Nazi era have accepted the authenticity of this self-portrait. Some, like Hugh R. Trevor-Roper, have seen in Speer, the man who ignored the political implications of the regime and served it with absolute loyalty, "the real criminal of the Nazi regime." Others believe he was far more involved in the regime's actions than he admitted.

BIBLIOGRAPHY

Goldhagen, E. "Albert Speer, Himmler, and the Secrecy of the Final Solution." *Midstream* 17/8 (October 1971): 43–50.

Reif, A. *Albert Speer: Kontroversen um ein deutsches Phänomen.* Munich, 1978.

Schmidt, M. *Albert Speer: The End of a Myth.* New York, 1984.

YEHOYAKIM COCHAVI

SPIEGEL, ISAIAH (b. 1906), writer, poet, and critic of Yiddish literature. Spiegel grew up in ŁÓDŹ, received a traditional education, and went on to study in a public school. He taught Yiddish and Yiddish literature in the Central Yiddish Schools Organization of the BUND. Spiegel remained in the Łódź ghetto throughout its existence, from May 1940 until its liquidation in August 1944, and was employed by the JUDENRAT (Jewish Council) in various departments. In August 1944 he was deported to AUSCHWITZ-Birkenau and spent the rest of the war in several labor camps.

Spiegel first published Yiddish poems in 1922. In 1930 his first book of poetry appeared in print, *Mitn Punim tsu der Zun* (Facing the Sun). On the eve of World War II he had another book of poems ready for publication, as well as a collection of stories about the Jewish weavers in the slum quarter in which he had grown up, and a Yiddish translation of Byron's poem "Cain." All these manuscripts were lost in the war.

While in the ghetto, Spiegel wrote many short stories and poems. He was one of the most prolific and important writers among the sixty or so in the Łódź ghetto. When the ghetto was liquidated in August 1944, Spiegel hid some of his writings in a cellar and took the rest with him to Auschwitz, only to have them taken away on his arrival. After the liberation he returned to Łódź and found the manuscripts of sixteen of the stories he had hidden there; he reconstructed the rest of them from memory and published them. He also published a collection of poems that included those he had composed during the war.

Spiegel's works that were saved in manuscript form all date from the early period of the ghetto, prior to the first great deportation of January to May 1942; they refer to events that occurred no later than the spring of 1941. The original manuscript differs from the published version, the many dissimilarities and revisions reflecting the changes in the author's view as a result of the Holocaust experience that had taken place in the interval.

Spiegel's ghetto writings reflect the prevailing circumstances: the lack of contact with the world outside and the absence of an armed resistance movement in the ghetto. His stories deal with the inner life of the people imprisoned in the ghetto and the human relationships between them. No mention is made of the Judenrat chairman, Mordechai Chaim RUMKOWSKI, of the JÜDISCHER ORDNUNGSDIENST (Jewish ghetto police) chiefs, or of the Germans who were in charge of the ghetto administration. The famous story *Geto Malkhes* (The Ghetto Kingdom) does not refer to "King" Rumkowski, but to "King" Hunger. Other stories depict simple people whose lot is hunger, cold, and death. Spiegel also describes instances of alienation between individuals, Jews who were unable to stand up under the terrible pressure of life in the ghetto. In all the stories there is contrast and dramatic tension between the author's muted and moderate style and the horror that pervades the subject matter. Spiegel's talent for shocking people was notably demonstrated when one of his poems was recited at a theater performance attended by Rumkowski: the Judenrat chairman's first reaction was to state that the poem's author had to be driven out of the ghetto at once.

From 1945 to 1948 Spiegel lived in Łódź and once again taught school. He lived in Warsaw from 1948 to 1950 and was secretary of the Polish Yiddish Writers' Association. Spiegel then settled in Israel, where he writes literary criticism and composes stories dealing with Israeli themes.

BIBLIOGRAPHY

Portrait of an Author—Yeshayahu Spiegel: Selected Sources about the Author and His Works. Tel Aviv, 1985. (In Hebrew.)
Yeshayahu Spiegel Jubilee Book. 2 vols. Tel Aviv, 1986. (In Yiddish.)

YEHIEL SZEINTUCH

SPORRENBERG, JACOB (1902–1952), SS officer. Born in Düsseldorf, Sporrenberg, a Catholic, studied at a vocational school. He volunteered for the border guard and for the army (the Reichswehr). In 1923 the French occupation authorities sentenced him to two years' imprisonment on a charge of underground activity for the Nazi party in the Ruhr region, but he was released on bail.

In 1925 Sporrenberg joined the Nazi party, in 1929 the SA (Sturmabteilung; Storm Troopers), and in 1930 the SS. He was a delegate to the Reichstag (parliament) in 1933. From 1933 to 1936 Sporrenberg was SS commander in the Schleswig-Holstein sector, and from 1936 to 1939, regional commander in East Prussia. Subsequently he occupied various posts in Wiesbaden and Königsberg. In 1940 he served in the SS Germany Brigade on the western front, where he was appointed *Gruppenführer*. He was sent in August 1941 to conduct the struggle against the partisans in the east and was appointed *SS- und Polizeiführer* (SS and Police Leader) in Minsk, Belorussia. Later he served in the Second Police Regiment in the fight against the partisans.

In August 1943 Sporrenberg became SS and Police Leader in the Lublin district. That November he organized Aktion "ERNTEFEST" (Operation "Harvest Festival") there, consisting of the slaughter of forty-two thousand to forty-three thousand Jews interned in the camps of MAJDANEK, TRAWNIKI, and PONIATOWA.

After the German retreat from the Lublin area in July 1943, Sporrenberg was sent to organize the defense fortifications on the Vistula-Nida line in the Radom district. In November he was sent to Norway. On May 11, 1945, several days after the German surrender, Sporrenberg was arrested by the Allies. The British extradited him to Poland, where he stood trial on a charge of collective punishment, imposition of a rule of terror by mass murders, and organization of Aktion "Erntefest." Sporrenberg was sentenced to death and hanged.

BIBLIOGRAPHY

Hilberg, R. *The Destruction of the European Jews.* 3 vols. New York, 1985.

ZYGMUNT MANKOWSKI

SPRACHREGELUNG (lit., "language regulation"), term coined by the Nazis, referring to the use of language for the purposes of the regime. Idioms coined by the Nazis served as an official language and a language of propaganda and camouflage. It was in this language that Joseph GOEBBELS, the propaganda minister, transmitted his instructions to the press. An example is the use of the word *Gleichschaltung* (coordination), which in actuality meant the elimination of political opponents and Nazi control of the German state agencies and public organizations.

This linguistic technique was employed particularly in the implementation of anti-Jewish policy, and here it was designed to fill a variety of roles. Words and expressions with a generally neutral or positive meaning were used to designate acts of terror and destruction. The intention was to hide the nature of those acts from the world and even from the German public, and also to mislead the Jews, who, failing to understand what awaited them, would take no preventive actions. Thus an apparently normal situation was created in which those who issued an order had an exact knowledge of its true content but were not obliged to call it by name. This psychological tactic helped to remove possible obstructions. Evidently, it was gradually abandoned as acts of murder became routine and were explained in writing, until Hitler saw the need to issue a special order on July 11, 1943. The order instructed that official SS reports use only the term "FINAL SOLUTION" of the Jewish problem, and not the term "destruction."

The expression "Final Solution," which was accepted as a term by all those dealing in the Holocaust, is one of the outstanding and typical examples of *Sprachregelung*. In many contexts the Nazis used the term "solution" or even "final solution" to note a way or means to overcome a difficulty. This was also true of the prefix "special" (*sonder-*), which designated exceptional cases or actions. The first to use the term "special treatment" (*Sonderbehandlung*) with regard to the Jews was apparently, and most ironically, the German president, Paul von HINDENBURG. He asked Hitler not to apply the discriminatory laws of April 1933 to Jewish civil servants (and other civil servants considered undesirable by the Nazis) who had been wounded as soldiers in World War I or who had a family member wounded in that war—excepting those persons for whom there was a "reason for special treatment." In the language of the Nazis, "special treatment" meant execution. On more than one occasion, with overt cynicism, they employed reasoning borrowed from acts for the general good. For instance, they justified shutting Jews in ghettos by the assertion that in this way they were preventing the spread of typhus; and they claimed that Jews were sent to forced-labor camps for "work education." (When they first rose to power in Germany, the Nazis had declared that the concentration camps were set up for "reeducation.")

Deportations and transfers were camouflaged by a number of special expressions. The word *Abwanderung* ("leaving [a place]") originally indicated internal migration, as a move of villagers to the town; in other words, it expressed free population movement. The Nazis used this word to indicate emigration of Jews and forced migration. The deportations of the Jews and Poles from the WARTHE-GAU to the GENERALGOUVERNEMENT were called *Umsiedlung* ("change of residence"). To indicate deportation, two expressions were used. *Aussiedlung* ("evacuation") was supposed to arouse the delusion that the Jews deported to the extermination camps were being sent to a place of resettlement. In contrast, the term *Abschiebung* ("removal") denoted that they were being removed from the place of their abode, without indicating the destination to which they were being sent. This term was for internal use only.

The expression *Verjudung* ("Judaization") was in common usage among many anti-semites, for whom it indicated the destructive influence, as it were, of the Jews on the peoples among whom they lived. The counteraction was called "removal of the Jews" or "purification from Jews" (*Entjudung*). This term was used by the Nazis to indicate the removal of Jews from the German economy, and it appears in different combinations in the relevant legislation. In euphemistic language the ghetto was called the "Jewish residential area" (*jüdischer Wohnbezirk*), and deportation to the THERESIENSTADT ghetto was described as "transfer of residence" (*Wohnsitzverlegung*). One of the most widely used words, absorbed by the Jews in the ghetto, was *Aktion* ("action"), meaning organized hostile action against the Jewish populace such as disturbances, arrests, property confiscations, deportations, and concentration in the ghetto for killing in the locality or for sending to extermination camps. This expression and many others characterized the Nazi acts of oppression and annihilation of the Jews.

BIBLIOGRAPHY

Bein, A. "The Jewish Parasite: Notes on the Semantics of the Jewish Problem, with Special Reference to Germany." *Leo Baeck Institute Year Book* 9 (1964): 3–40.

Berning, C. *Vom Abstammungsnachweis zum Zuchtwart*. Berlin, 1964.

Blumental, N. "Action." *Yad Vashem Studies* 4 (1960): 57–96.

Esh, S. *Studies in the Holocaust and Contemporary Jewry*. Jerusalem, 1973. (In Hebrew.)

Esh, S. "Words and Their Meaning: Twenty-Five Examples of Nazi Idiom." *Yad Vashem Studies* 5 (1961): 133–167.

LENI YAHIL

SS (Schutzstaffel; Protection Squad), Hitler's bodyguard, Nazi party police, and, later, the most "racially pure" elite guard of the Third Reich as well as its main tool of terror, "Germanization," and destruction.

Early History. As Adolf HITLER's personal bodyguard, recruited from the SA (Sturmabteilung; Storm Troopers) in March 1923 by Julius Schreck, a personal crony of Hitler and his future chauffeur, the SS was distinguished by a black cap with a death's-head emblem, and later by their entirely black uniforms. The two dozen bodyguards participated in Hitler's unsuccessful Beer-Hall Putsch of November 1923 in Munich. They were outlawed, as was the rest of the Nazi party, following the failed coup. When the party was legalized again at the end of 1924, Hitler reestablished the unit under Schreck and created several more such "commandos." In contrast to the SA, which tended to consider itself a semi-independent, paramilitary mass organization, the SS and its new commandos were an exclusive elite, subject directly to Hitler's authority.

In November 1925, Schreck was succeeded by Joseph Berchtold, a member of the original unit. He promised Hitler "loyalty to death," and thereafter such loyalty became fundamental to the SS ideology. At this time some two hundred men belonged to the SS.

Heinrich Himmler, *Reichsführer-SS* (front row, fourth from left), with a group of SS leaders in the Munich Braunes Haus (Brown House), the headquarters of the Nazi party, probably in 1932. In the front row, third from left, is Kurt Daluege, the commander of SS Group East; at the far right is Julius Schreck (d. May 16, 1936), one of the *Alte Kämpfer* (Old Fighters) and Hitler's chauffeur. In the third row from the bottom, second from right, is Reinhard Heydrich.

In November 1926, the Oberste SA-Führung (SA High Command) was created, and in spite of Berchtold's protests, it took over the SS headquarters. This move threatened the special status of the fledgling SS. However, the original concept of a highly loyal guard, totally attached to Hitler's person and exercising control inside the larger party and the SA, was retained by Erhard Heiden, who headed the SS from March 1927. He instituted military discipline and emphasized the gathering of information about political opponents, Freemasons, Jewish leaders, and the SA itself. This trend was institutionalized when Heinrich HIMMLER became *Reichsführer-SS* (Reich Leader of the SS; RF-SS) on January 6, 1929.

Between 1929 and 1933, the SS grew and was entrusted with the security of party headquarters and the personal security of most of the party leaders, especially at Hitler's public appearances. An embryonic secret intelligence, the SD (Sicherheitsdienst; Security Service), under Reinhard HEYDRICH, was founded, as was a bureau responsible for the racial purity of the SS and the eventual settlement of colonists in conquered eastern territories, the SS RASSE- UND SIEDLUNGS-

HAUPTAMT (Race and Resettlement Main Office; RuSHA), under Richard Walther DARRÉ.

The officer corps was recruited in the early but decisive stage from various opposition groups who came into conflict with the Weimar Republic and its institutions, either because of right-wing tendencies or lack of adjustment at a time of cultural, political, and social upheaval. They included noblemen who lent the SS social respectability; Freikorps men, members of the paramilitary organizations that had sprung up during the tumultuous period after World War I; political gangsters, who were capable of exceptional cruelty but had organizational ability; peripheral characters who had turned against society; ambitious young academics, especially lawyers, who felt that they needed to circumvent the law and change traditional bureaucratic rules; and former imperial noncommissioned officers and relatively successful managerial types, who would carefully execute the orders of the ambitious power-seekers. This last group grew faster after 1933. It helped Himmler establish his *Freundeskreis des RF-SS* (Friendship Circle) among industrialists and bankers, and served as a link to the conservatives.

Himmler demanded complete obedience from both the officers and the rank and file, copying—with due changes—from the order of the Jesuits. He emphasized unconditional loyalty to the "supreme master," Hitler, and to himself. No chief of staff was ever appointed, the most important departments remained under Himmler's direct control, and his title was featured at the top of their letterheads. This personal control also reflected the Nazi FÜHRERPRINZIP (leadership principle), combined with a large-scale bureaucratization.

Racial ideology and mythology was institutionalized in the SS. SS officers had to prove their own and their wives' "racial purity" back to the year 1700, and membership was conditional on "Aryan" appearance. Traditional symbols and pre-Christian myths were combined with an aura of fearlessness to create an SS mystique. This mystique was reflected in the wearing of the black uniform, black cap, death's-head emblem, death's-head "ring of honor" (the death's head was a popular army unit's emblem in World War I),

and officer's dagger bearing the SS motto, "Meine Ehre heisst Treue" ("Loyalty Is My Honor"). Later, pagan ceremonies were practiced and pilgrimages were made to ancient Teutonic "sacred sites." The regional organization also bore traditional titles and was first divided into squads (*Schar, Trupp*), platoons (*Sturm*), companies (*Sturmbann*), and battalions (*Standarte*), which in late 1932 were put together into county SS sections (*Abschnitte*), under regional command. The regional commanders were directly responsible to Himmler and were often rotated to avoid grass-roots power-base building, which characterized the SA.

In contrast to the vague and yet far-reaching goals of the SA, Himmler aimed after Hitler's rise to power to gain control over the political police (GESTAPO) while establishing the CONCENTRATION CAMPS of the SS. The first model of that kind was DACHAU, built early in March 1933. Himmler managed to maintain exclusive control over Dachau, as a result of his dual function as *Reichsführer-SS* and chief of the Bavarian political police, and also owing to his use of SS and SD agents within the traditional bureaucracy. After his appointment as political police chief in all the German states (1934), Himmler developed a combined strategy of recruiting key persons to the SS as *Ehrenführer* (honorary leaders) and co-opting low-grade policemen, while enjoying Hitler's support in all crucial phases.

By mid-1934 the SS, after decisively helping to crush the SA on June 30, took over all the political police and concentration camps. The Dachau commandant, Theodor EICKE, was made inspector of the concentration camps and SS guard formations on July 4, 1934. The states' political police were unified as the Gestapo and fully amalgamated with the SS in 1936. At the same time, Himmler, as chief of the German police, unified all the police functions that were formally under the Reich Ministry of the Interior, as follows. The Sicherheitspolizei (Security Police; Sipo), under Heydrich, was divided into the Gestapo, under Heydrich himself, and later under Heinrich MÜLLER, as executive director; and the KRIMINALPOLIZEI (Criminal Police; Kripo), under Arthur NEBE. The ORDNUNGS-POLIZEI (Order Police; Orpo), under Kurt DA-

LUEGE, was amalgamated with the SS as a separate SS outfit. Sipo and Orpo remained under the nominal control of the Reich Ministry of the Interior, but they had no real authority apart from Himmler's. Heydrich retained his pure SS function as SD chief, encouraging bureaucratic competition between the Gestapo and SD, and displaying ideological zeal.

Himmler maintained the concentration camp system separately as a totally SS branch under Eicke, in which guards were trained in a savage killer outfit called the SS Wach- und TOTENKOPFVERBÄNDE (Guard and Death's-Head Units). This was the source of the militarized SS units later known as the Waffen-SS, who were trained for civil war duties, and later were transferred as SS frontline units fighting under the army's operational control. *Junkerschulen* (young officers' schools) were established to train and indoctrinate young cadets, some already the products of the Nazi youth movement, the HITLERJUGEND, as the new fighting and pitiless racial elite in the forthcoming war for LEBENSRAUM. Special SS police units, the EINSATZGRUPPEN, were established to enter ceded or invaded territories. The regional SS was reorganized under *Höhere SS- und Polizeiführer* (Higher SS and Police Leaders), who acted as Himmler's personal representatives in each military district from the outset of World War II. The RuSHA was expanded to enforce the "Germanization" of the occupied territories.

Special institutions were created in cooperation between Himmler's personal office and the RuSHA. These included Lebensborn (Fountain of Life)—a system of SS stud farms that were the brainchild of Himmler's program for the propagation of a pure Aryan race—and AHNENERBE (Ancestral Heritage). The official functions of the latter were to adopt "suitable" children for childless SS families, to succor "racially sound" pregnant women and their offspring, and to conduct "racial research" that eventually culminated in MEDICAL EXPERIMENTS with the "racially inferior," mainly Jews, in concentration camps. This was done in cooperation with the chief SS physician and his own bureaucracy, which also played a major role in the EUTHANASIA PROGRAM. The creation in 1939 of spe-

cial SS courts outside the regular courts only legalized the established procedure of the SS in circumventing the law.

The SS in World War II. The war led to an enormous growth in the SS as a whole and made possible a murderous radicalization of its activities. The invasion of Poland was accompanied by special Sipo and SD units, the Einsatzgruppen, ordered by Heydrich on September 21, 1939, to prepare "a final solution to the Jewish question." They and the local SS branches were instrumental in the ghettoization of the Jews, the imposition of the Jewish BADGE, the creation of Judenräte (Jewish councils; *see* JUDENRAT), mass starvation, and the conscripting of Jews to perform hard labor. Whether the initial purpose of this policy, before the decision was made to kill all the Jews of Europe, was to use the Jews under Hitler's control as hostages (for possible blackmail of the western Allies) while decimating the ghetto inhabitants by starvation and disease, or whether there were other aims under discussion, is an unresolved matter among historians.

The SS gradually became more complex, because in vast areas Himmler's semifeudal system collapsed into uncontrollable fiefs of semi-independent camp commandants, local Gestapo despots, and individual mass killers competing with the civilian occupation administration—although all of them functioned within the general anti-Jewish policy. The cruel, inhuman regime of the SS was encouraged from above. Sipo commanders in the occupied territories competed with SS head offices in implementing and radicalizing official policies. This initiative, which in some cases came from SS middle echelons or higher ranks, is called by certain historians the "functionalist" road to the "Final Solution," in contrast to the "intentional" policy supposed to be based on Hitler's decision. The SS headquarters itself was reorganized in 1939, together with the establishment of the REICHSSICHERHEITSHAUPTAMT (Reich Security Main Office; RSHA), and again in 1942, when eleven main offices emerged.

During the war, the Waffen-SS grew into Hitler's personal multinational brigade. In June 1941, it numbered about 165,000, and by April 1945, some 800,000 men, in forty divisions. Hitler regarded them as his military guarantee against unrest and mutiny at home and abroad. Himmler saw them as an assurance of SS domination in the Nazi postwar order.

In 1941 the first implementation of the "Final Solution," during the invasion of the Soviet Union, was carried out primarily by the Einsatzgruppen, which conducted mass killings by firing squads and, later, mobile GAS VANS as well. The men of the Einsatzgruppen had been recruited from the Gestapo and the SS and had undergone special training. Their operations were made possible by a formal agreement between the SS, represented by Heydrich, and the Wehrmacht High Command that was concluded in the spring of 1941, together with the final preparations for the invasion of the Soviet Union. The SS was aided in the killings by various police units, Wehrmacht forces, and numerous local collaborators.

In the occupied countries of western and southeastern Europe, the SS, in cooperation with the SD, Gestapo, local police, and local officials, organized the mass extermination of the Jews in camps in the east from 1942 to 1944. A special terminology (see SPRACHREGELUNG) was perfected to mislead the victims. Tactics were devised to hoodwink them into surrendering themselves to resettlement or deportation, to dehumanize them, to use their leaders as hostages, and to coerce them into taking part in the *Selektionen*. The process of killing by gas in the extermination camps, as well as the camps' structure and management, was organized and overseen by SS officers, most of whom had been trained by Eicke in Dachau.

The SS WIRTSCHAFTS-VERWALTUNGSHAUPTAMT (Economic-Administrative Main Office), later known as the WVHA, planned to use the concentration camps as sources of slave labor that would also serve the enterprises of the SS under Oswald POHL. Since Pohl was entrusted at the same time with the factory-like destruction of the Jews in the extermination camps, his role, like this phase of SS policy, was inherently contradictory. Nonetheless, special procedures were invoked in the camps to select Jews for immediate mass killings or for slave labor (which usually resulted in death anyway). In 1943, Himmler undertook to expand his power by grounding

the SS in an autonomous economic enterprise called Osti (OSTINDUSTRIE GBMH), which used Jewish slave labor. Because of the lack of resources and the ongoing systematic killing operations, which vied with Osti for the Jews and depleted the ranks of the laborers, the scheme failed and had to be abandoned a year later.

When Nazi Germany's final collapse became inevitable, Himmler ordered the termination of the "Final Solution," apparently hoping to use the remnants of European Jewry as trump cards in negotiations with the West against the Soviets. The survivors of the now-evacuated camps outside the Reich were driven by the SS in pointless marches to Germany. Many perished on these DEATH MARCHES or died at the hands of the SS guards, until the latter fled from the approaching armies of the Allies.

In the charter of the International Military Tribunal at Nuremberg, the SS was viewed as a criminal organization. Thus, members of the Gestapo, the SD, the Allgemeine-SS, Waffen-SS, Totenkopfverbände, and WVHA were to be considered war criminals who had been involved in "the persecution and extermination of Jews, brutalities and killings in concentration camps, excesses under the administration of occupied territories, the administration of the slave labor program, and the mistreatment and murder of prisoners of war" (*Nazi Conspiracy and Aggression: Opinion and Judgment*, 1947; pp. 101–102).

To the very end, the SS remained the backbone of the Nazi regime. It involved hundreds of thousands of Germans in its crimes: Gestapo policemen; uniformed police, who were used as firing-squad killers or helped carry out deportations; private firms, which supplied equipment to extermination camps and used SS forced labor; and Wehrmacht units, which provided the military framework of occupation and control necessary for the SS massacres, and which themselves took part in the murders. Both during and after the war, many Germans and others used the SS as an excuse, seeking thereby to absolve the German people as a whole of the guilt associated with the attempted extermination of European Jewry.

[*See also the biographies of specific SS figures.*]

BIBLIOGRAPHY

Hohne, H. *The Order of the Death's Head: The Story of Hitler's SS.* New York, 1969.

Koehl, R. *The Black Corps.* Madison, Wis., 1983.

Krausnick, H., et al. *The Anatomy of the SS State.* New York, 1968.

Reitlinger, G. *The SS: Alibi of a Nation, 1922–1945.* Englewood Cliffs, N.J., 1981.

Sydnor, C. W. *Soldiers of Destruction: The SS Death's Head Division, 1933–1945.* Princeton, 1977.

SHLOMO ARONSON

"STAB-IN-THE-BACK" MYTH. *See* Dolchstosslegende.

STAHL, HEINRICH (1868–1942), president of the Berlin Jewish community under the Nazis. A liberal Jew and a leading member of the insurance industry, Stahl became the dominant personality in the Berlin community in June 1933. He also had a prominent role in the foundation of the REICHSVERTRE-TUNG DER DEUTSCHEN JUDEN (Reich Representation of German Jews) and was one of the signatories to its first proclamation, in September 1933. By virtue of the numerical strength and influence of Berlin's Jewish community, Stahl sought to secure for Berlin Jewry a greater role in the Reichsvertretung. This brought him into conflict with its leaders, Leo BAECK and Otto HIRSCH. The only concessions secured by Stahl were the promise of an important role in the Reichsvertretung and the assurance that the organization would be permanently located in Berlin. Stahl was deported to THERESIENSTADT in 1942, where, shortly before his death, he became deputy chairman of the camp's Ältestenrat (Council of Elders).

BIBLIOGRAPHY

Benz, W., ed. *Die Juden in Deutschland, 1933–1945.* Munich, 1988.

Boas, J. "German Jewish Internal Politics under Hitler, 1933–1938." *Leo Baeck Institute Year Book* 29 (1984): 3–25.

LIONEL KOCHAN

STAHLECKER, FRANZ WALTER (1900–1942), SS officer; commander of an Einsatzgruppe (*see* EINSATZGRUPPEN). Born in Sternenfels, Stahlecker joined the Nazi party in 1932, served in the police, and in 1934 was appointed police chief of the Württemberg region. He was then assigned to the SD (Sicherheitsdienst; Security Service) main office, and in 1938 became the SD chief of the Danube district (Vienna), retaining this post even when he was promoted to the rank of *Standartenführer* and became the Higher SS and Police Leader (*Höherer SS- und Polizeiführer*) of the Protectorate of BOHEMIA AND MORAVIA. In 1940 Stahlecker was sent to Norway, where he held the same position, and was promoted to *SS-Oberführer*. In June 1941 he became a *Brigadeführer* in the SS and a major general of police, and was appointed the commanding officer of Einsatzgruppe A, which operated in the Northern Command (the Baltic states and the area west of Leningrad), massacring Jews and other Soviet nationals. At the end of November 1941, Stahlecker was also made Higher SS and Police Leader of REICHSKOMMISSARIAT OSTLAND, which extended over Estonia, Latvia, Lithuania, and Belorussia. He was killed on March 23, 1942, in a clash with Soviet partisans.

BIBLIOGRAPHY

Krausnick, H., and H.-H. Wilhelm. *Die Truppe des Weltanschauungskriegs: Die Einsatzgruppen der Sicherheitspolizei und des SD, 1938–1942.* Stuttgart, 1981.

SHMUEL SPECTOR

STALIN, JOSEPH VISSARIONOVICH (1879–1953), Soviet ruler. Stalin was born in the town of Gori, near Tiflis (now Tbilisi), into the family of a poor Georgian shoemaker. In 1894 he was accepted to the Tiflis ecclesiastical seminary, then a hotbed of militant Georgian nationalism and revolutionary radicalism. He left the seminary in 1899 and soon joined the revolutionary movement. After the split in the ranks of the Russian Social Democrats he joined the Bolsheviks.

Stalin became a member of the Bolshevik Central Party Committee in 1912. That year he visited Vienna, where he wrote a pamphlet on the nationality problem, attacking the Austrian Marxists and the BUND. This gained him recognition as the principal Bolshevik expert on the nationality problem.

In 1913 Stalin was arrested and exiled to Siberia. After the February revolution of 1917 he returned to Petrograd and became a member of the leadership of the Bolshevik party and of the Politburo. In the first Bolshevik government he was named People's Commissar for Nationalities and later also People's Commissar of the Working Peasant Inspection. He took active part in the civil war as a political commissar in the Red Army.

Stalin soon emerged as a principal Bolshevik leader and as Leon Trotsky's main rival. In 1921 Stalin was appointed party secretary-general, and he succeeded in transforming this secondary role into the main party position. Lenin, who had promoted Stalin in order to balance Trotsky, became alarmed and requested Stalin's removal from the position of secretary-general, but his wish was disregarded. After Lenin's death in 1924 Stalin triumphed in the succession struggle, making and breaking coalitions as he

pleased, and often using assassinations for political purposes. In 1928 he emerged as the undisputed national leader.

That year Stalin launched a second revolution, this time to industrialize the Soviet Union as quickly as possible and to impose collectivization on the peasantry. The campaign was based on a combination of utopian concepts and brutality, and during it millions of peasants perished. At the same time, a cultural revolution against all religions was initiated. The industrialization was not unsuccessful, but its price was costly.

As early as 1929, when he gained control over the secret police, Stalin ruled through total terror. Show trials became a regular part of life in the country. The unlimited cult of Stalin, his brutality and criminal behavior, his efforts to change history, and his self-portrayal as the main personality of the revolution and the civil war along with Lenin —all provoked the unanimous hatred of the old party elite, who were forced, however, to pay him lip service.

From 1935 a series of show trials were held in which former leaders were tried for alleged conspiracy, and many were executed.

Joseph Stalin (right) meets with German foreign minister Joachim von Ribbentrop (center) in Moscow during the signing of the Nazi-Soviet Pact on August 23, 1939.

In a massive purge during the second half of the 1930s, many millions of human lives were taken, including most of the party elite and most of the foreign Communists who lived in the Soviet Union. A new generation, largely of peasant origin, came to power, and antisemitism became a secret ideology of the ruling class. In August 1939, Stalin concluded an alliance with Nazi Germany (*see* NAZI-SOVIET PACT). He became chairman of the Council of People's Commissars in May 1941, and at the same time, almost all the Jews who had remained in the Central Committee were fired.

In spite of Stalin's long list of mistakes, facilitating the German invasion in June 1941 and leading to military disasters in 1941 and 1942, he succeeded during the war in emerging as not only the political but also the military leader of the Soviet Union, becoming supreme commander in chief, with the unique rank of *Generalissimo*. He mobilized the country for war, and eventually the tide turned against the German invaders. Between 1943 and 1945 Stalin met with Western leaders in Tehran, Yalta, and Potsdam, where the future map of Europe was outlined.

The Soviet army invaded Manchuria and Korea in August 1945, meeting no resistance from Japan, which had just been atombombed by America. Many European and Asian states were now Soviet satellites, and the Soviet Union became an empire. All the Soviet resources were mobilized, not for the economic recovery of the population but for a new arms race and preparations for a war with the West.

In 1947 Stalin decided to support the establishment of a Jewish state in Israel, apparently in the hope that it would become a full-fledged Soviet satellite. However, Soviet attitudes toward Israel began to change at the end of 1948 when this expectation was not borne out, and at least from 1948, antisemitism was manifested as an operative ideology of the Soviet Union. All Jewish organizations were closed down, and surviving Jewish writers and activists were arrested and later executed. Stalin now regarded the Jews as a harmful national group whose alleged strong ties with American Jewry endangered the political stability of his empire.

In 1952 he convened a party congress to introduce the new young leadership that was to replace the old one after the new purge that he was preparing. The first steps in a fresh anti-Jewish purge were taken in Prague at the end of that year with the show trial of Rudolf Slánský, former general secretary of the Czechoslovak Communist party, and in 1953 with the so-called Doctors' Plot, in which a number of doctors were accused of planning to poison Stalin. In both these cases the majority of the defendants were Jewish, and preparations actually began for the deportation of Russia's Jews. However, Stalin's death in March 1953 ended the threat of a mass catastrophe.

Stalin personified not only the Communist ideology but also an oriental dictatorship. His main objective was personal power, and he manipulated ideology in order to strengthen his own power, although he certainly incorporated many elements of European radicalism, including a strong historical optimism and the belief that concentrated human efforts can create the new man and a new world.

BIBLIOGRAPHY

Agursky, M. *The Third Rome: National Bolshevism in the USSR.* Boulder, 1987.

Allilueva, S. *Twenty Letters to a Friend.* London, 1967.

Deutscher, I. *Stalin: A Political Biography.* London, 1966.

Djilas, M. *Conversations with Stalin.* New York, 1962.

Khrushchev Remembers. Boston, 1970.

Medvedev, R. *Let History Judge: The Origins and Consequences of Stalinism.* New York, 1972.

Medvedev, R. *On Stalin and Stalinism.* Oxford, 1979.

Smith, E. E. *The Young Stalin.* London, 1967.

Tucker, R. *Stalin as Revolutionary.* New York, 1973.

MIKHAIL AGURSKY

STALINGRAD (since 1961, Volgograd), city in the SOVIET UNION situated on the Volga; the scene of one of the decisive battles of WORLD

WAR II. In the summer of 1942, two German army groups—Army Group A, under Gen. Fedor von Bock, with seventy-one divisions, and Army Group B, under Field Marshal Wilhelm List, with forty-three divisions —launched a massive offensive in the direction of the Volga River. Their objective was to prepare the way for the conquest of the Caucasus and the Baku oil fields and a breakthrough to the Middle East. The capture of Stalingrad was essential for the success of the attack. Under heavy German pressure the Red Army was forced to retreat, and on September 12, 1942, elements of the German Sixth Army and Fourth Panzer Army reached the suburbs of Stalingrad. These German forces consisted of eighteen divisions and six hundred tanks, supported by some five hundred aircraft of the Fourth Corps of the German air force. Thus the battle for Stalingrad began; it was to last until February 2, 1943.

The Red Army command decided to defend the city at any cost, in order to block the German plans for the offensive. The task of defending the city was assigned to the Sixty-second Army, under Gen. Vasily Chuikov, and the Sixty-fourth Army, under Gen. Mikhail Shumilov. The Soviet divisions suffered tremendous casualties, but they succeeded in stopping the attackers.

By the middle of November 1942 the Germans, at a heavy price, had occupied most of the city and in three places had reached the banks of the Volga, but the Soviet defense had not been broken. Their success in blocking the Germans enabled the Soviets to assemble large forces for a counteroffensive, which began on November 19. The Russian objective was to encircle the German forces. Three fronts (army groups) of the Red Army launched the counteroffensive; the Southwest Front, under Gen. Nikolai Vatutin; the Don Front, under Gen. Konstantin Rokossovski; and the Stalingrad Front, under Gen. Andrei Yeremenko. The Soviets employed fifteen armies, equipped with 1,400 tanks and 17,000 pieces of artillary, supported by 1,250 aircraft. As early as November 23 they succeeded in encircling the German Sixth Army and part of the Fourth Panzer Army—a total of twenty-two divisions with 350,000 men. The next stage was to destroy the trapped

German forces; this battle lasted until February 2, 1943, when the last remnants of these forces surrendered. Some 91,000 German troops were taken prisoner, including twenty generals, one of them the commanding officer of the Sixth Army, Gen. Friedrich von Paulus, whom Hitler had made a field marshal a few days earlier.

The defeat came as a serious blow to Nazi Germany, where three days of official mourning were observed. The Soviet victory at Stalingrad put an end to the German campaign of conquest in the east and inaugurated the German retreat westward that was to end with Nazi Germany's surrender. The victory was a major boost to the morale of the Soviet troops and a tremendous source of encouragement to resistance movements in the German-occupied countries.

BIBLIOGRAPHY

Chuikov, V. I. *The Battle for Stalingrad.* New York, 1964.

Jukes, G. *Stalingrad: The Turning Point.* New York, 1968.

Kerr, W. *The Secret of Stalingrad.* New York, 1978.

Werth, A. *The Year of Stalingrad.* New York, 1947.

Ziemke, E. F. *Stalingrad to Berlin: The German Defeat in the East.* Washington, D.C., 1968.

SHMUEL KRAKOWSKI

STANGL, FRANZ (1908–1971), Nazi police officer. Stangl was born in Altmünster, Austria, the son of a former soldier in the dragoons, who brutalized him throughout his childhood. Initially a master weaver, Stangl joined the Austrian police in 1931. His talent for organization soon became evident, and he was shortly appointed *Kriminalbeamter* (criminal investigation officer) in the political division, which at that time was charged with investigating antigovernmental activities of the Right and Left.

In November 1940, Stangl became police superintendent of the Euthanasia Institute at the Hartheim castle, near Linz. In March 1942 he became commandant of the SOBIBÓR extermination camp in Poland, and from early September 1942 to August 1943 he was the commandant of TREBLINKA. In less than a year there, he supervised the mass killing of at least 900,000 Jews.

In September 1943, after the inmates' revolt in Treblinka, Stangl and most of his staff were transferred to Trieste. There, aside from a brief stint at the dreaded San Sabba concentration camp, he was largely employed in organizing antipartisan measures for Odilo GLOBOCNIK, the *Höherer SS- und Polizeiführer* (Higher SS and Police Leader) of the Adriatic seaboard area.

At the end of the war Stangl made his way back to Austria, where he was eventually interned by the Americans for belonging to the SS, although they knew nothing of his association with the extermination program. In the late summer of 1947 the Austrians, while investigating the EUTHANASIA PROGRAM at the Hartheim castle, learned of Stangl's presence in an American prisoner-of-war camp, and he was transferred to an open civilian prison in Linz. In May 1948, about to be charged, he escaped and made his way to Rome.

With assistance from Bishop Alois Hudal, rector of Santa Maria del Anima, Stangl obtained a RED CROSS *laissez-passer* (pass), money, and a job as an engineer in Damascus, Syria, where he was soon joined by his family. In 1951 the family moved on to Brazil, where, registering under their own names at the Austrian consulate, they were soon established in the city of São Bernardo do Campo, near São Paulo, where Stangl worked at the Volkswagen factory.

Sixteen years later, Stangl's presence in Brazil became known. He was arrested on February 28, 1967, and extradited to Germany that June. His trial in Düsseldorf lasted one year; in December 1970 he was sentenced to life imprisonment for joint responsibility in the murder of 900,000 people during his tenure as commandant of Treblinka. He died in prison on June 28, 1971.

BIBLIOGRAPHY

Sereny, G. *Franz Stangl: Bekenntnisse eines Biedermannes.* Hamburg, 1971.
Sereny, G. *Into That Darkness: From Mercy Killing to Mass Murder.* New York, 1983.

GITTA SERENY

STANISŁAWÓW (present-day Ivano-Frankovsk), city in the Ukrainian SSR. During the interwar period Stanisławów was a district capital in the Polish province of Eastern Galicia. In 1931, the city had a Jewish population of 24,823. It was annexed to the USSR in September 1939, and until 1942 a large number of Jewish refugees from German-occupied western and central Poland settled there.

On July 2, 1941, ten days after the German invasion of the Soviet Union, Stanisławów was occupied by Hungarian troops, Hungary being then an ally of Germany. Local Ukrainians attacked the Jews, but this was stopped by the Hungarians. Several thousand Jews from the TRANSCARPATHIAN UKRAINE, then in Hungarian hands, were exiled by the Hungarians to Stanisławów.

At the end of July the Germans took over the administration of the city, whose Jewish population had grown to forty thousand. On August 2, the Jewish professionals were ordered to report to the Gestapo. They were arrested and a few days later more than five hundred of them were taken out of town and killed. In August and September various anti-Jewish measures were enacted: Jews were

required to wear a BADGE, to perform forced labor, to pay fines, and so on. Jewish-owned assets were seized and Jewish apartments confiscated.

On October 12 a massacre took place. The Germans rounded up ten thousand Jews, brought them to the New Cemetery, took their valuables and ordered them to undress, and shot them as they stood at the edge of huge pits.

A ghetto was established in Stanisławów, and the Jews were given two weeks, from December 1 to 15, to move in. Many died in the ghetto of starvation and disease. The JUDENRAT (Jewish Council), which had been set up in the early days of the occupation, opened soup kitchens, tried to care for the elderly and for orphaned children, and ran two hospitals, but could not do much to alleviate the situation.

Another *Aktion* took place on March 31, 1942; German and Ukrainian police seized Jews in the street and in their homes and gathered them in one of the city squares, where the *Selektion* took place. Only those in possession of employment certificates were freed; all the rest, some five thousand persons, were sent to their death in the BEŁŻEC extermination camp. In the course of the *Aktion*, several hundred were killed in the streets and courtyards of the ghetto. Following this *Aktion* the ghetto area was reduced and its inhabitants were divided into three categories: category A, Jews employed as experts in factories essential to the German economy; category B, those employed in less important places; and category C, those unfit for work.

In July 1942, one thousand Jews were killed in the ghetto, on the pretext that a Ukrainian policeman had been beaten up by a Jew. Some members of the Judenrat and some Jewish policemen were also hanged on this occasion. Another *Aktion* took place on September 12; this left about a thousand corpses lying in the streets of the ghetto, while another five thousand Jews were sent to Bełżec.

That fall and the ensuing winter, hundreds of Jews were put into camps set up near essential factories and other important places of work, and as a result it was feared that the nonworking Jews would soon be put to death. Increasingly desperate attempts were made by the Jews to save themselves; some pinned their hopes on the acquisition of Aryan papers, while others sought refuge with Christian friends or tried to cross the border into Romania.

The final liquidation of the ghetto began in January 1943 and lasted until the end of February, with the German and Ukrainian police clearing the ghetto of its surviving Jews, street by street and house by house. On a single day, January 26, a thousand Jews were murdered. By March only a few hundred Jews were left in the labor camps adjoining the factories, but these too were murdered by the Germans and their Ukrainian collaborators in the course of the year.

Stanisławów was liberated by the Soviet army on July 27, 1944. Of its original Jewish population, only fifteen hundred survived the war, most of them having fled to the Soviet Union; of those who had stayed in Stanisławów, only about a hundred were kept alive in their hiding places, mostly with the help of Poles.

BIBLIOGRAPHY

"Stanisławów." In vol. 5 of *Jewish Mother-Cities*, edited by D. Sadan and M. Gelehrter. Jerusalem, 1952. (In Hebrew.)

Weitz, A. *About Your Destruction, Stanisławów: Testimonies to the Annihilation of the Stanisławów Community and Its Surroundings according to Witnesses and Documents.* Tel Aviv, 1947. (In Hebrew.)

AHARON WEISS

STARACHOWICE, labor camp in POLAND. Before World War II, Starachowice, a town in the KIELCE subdistrict of Poland, was the site of armament factories and an iron-ore mine. Under the Nazi occupation these enterprises, renamed the Hermann Göring Werke (Hermann Göring Works), employed Jews on forced labor.

Starachowice was occupied on September 9, 1939. Jewish males from the ages of seventeen to sixty were put to work in the town's factories at a low rate of pay, 55 groszy an hour, plus a bowl of soup during working hours. In February 1941 an open ghetto was established that also took in Jews from Płock and ŁÓDŹ. On October 27, the Starachowice ghetto was liquidated; some two hundred Jews were shot to death on the spot. The physically fit were separated from, the rest and moved to a nearby camp that had been prepared in advance (Julag I; from *Judenlager*, "Jewish camp") and the rest were deported to the TREBLINKA extermination camp. The Jews working in the munitions factories were also moved to Julag I.

Some eight thousand Jews passed through the camp; 9 percent died in typhus epidemics or were shot to death following a *Selektion*. The camp population averaged five thousand; from time to time the camp was replenished with prisoners from MAJDANEK, PŁASZÓW, and other places. In the summer of 1943 the prisoners employed in the factories were moved to another camp, Julag II, through which five thousand prisoners passed; 7 percent of them died of typhus or were killed. The average number of prisoners in Julag II was three thousand.

In July 1944, steps were taken to liquidate

STARACHOWICE

Administrative Divisions of Poland under German Occupation, 1939–1945

1 Pomerania
2 Brandenburg
3 Saxony
4 Lower Silesia
5 Upper Silesia
6 Warthegau
7 Danzig (West Prussia)
8 East Prussia
9 Generalgouvernement
10 Białystok Region

© Polish National Publishing House, Warsaw, 1979
(Państwowe Wydawnictwo Naukowe)

■ Camp

✖ Extermination Center

Białystok

Treblinka

Płock

Zbąszyń

Warsaw

Chełmno

Łódź

Sobibór

Lublin

Majdanek ■

STARACHOWICE

Bełchatów

Kielce

Bełżec

Oświęcim
(Auschwitz-Birkenau)

Kraków
Płaszów

the camp. When the prisoners became aware of what was happening they began destroying the camp's installations and fence, and tried to escape. The Ukrainians guarding the camp opened fire and threw hand grenades at the prisoners, killing three hundred of them on the spot. Those who escaped were captured and murdered, and the rest, fifteen hundred in number, were deported to AUSCHWITZ-Birkenau.

SHMUEL SPECTOR

STATE DEPARTMENT. *See* United States Department of State.

STATUT DES JUIFS (Jewish Law), anti-Jewish laws passed by the Vichy government in October 1940 and June 1941. Both of these laws were meant to apply to all of FRANCE despite the fact that at the time the Germans occupied only the northern three-fifths of the country. Vichy's first comprehensive anti-Jewish statute, of October 3, 1940, defined a Jew as a person with three grandparents "of the Jewish race," or with two Jewish grandparents if the spouse was also Jewish. In the latter provision, and in its explicit reference to race, the Vichy definition was both more harsh and more inclusive than that set by the Germans in the occupied zone of France and elsewhere. The law went on to provide the basis for drastically reducing the role of Jews in French society. It excluded Jews from top positions in the French civil service, the officer corps of the army, the ranks of noncommissioned officers, and professions that influence public opinion—teaching, the press, radio, film, and theater. Jews could hold menial public-service positions, provided they had served in the armed forces between 1914 and 1918 or had distinguished themselves in the campaign of 1939 and 1940. The statute also stated that a quota system would be devised to limit the presence of Jews in the liberal professions (the law, medicine, and so on). Formulated purely on French initiative, the law was hastily prepared in the Justice Ministry of Raphaël Alibert, a militant anti-

semite, friend of the monarchist ACTION FRANÇAISE movement, and the formulator of the Vichy motto "Travail, Famille, Patrie" (Work, Family, Fatherland).

Vichy's efforts to improve upon the application of this statute and to tighten up some of its provisions led to a second *Statut des Juifs*, on June 2, 1941. It emerged from Xavier VALLAT's COMMISSARIAT GÉNÉRAL AUX QUESTIONS JUIVES (General Office for Jewish Affairs; CGQJ), and was carefully drafted in a series of cabinet meetings and consultations with Justice Minister Joseph Barthélemy. After tightening the definition of who was a Jew, and tinkering with the provisions for the purging of Jews from public posts, the law opened the way for a massive removal of Jews from the liberal professions, commerce, and industry. Only a handful of well-established French Jews could benefit from the exemptions provided by the statute. Even Jewish prisoners of war, if returned from captivity, would face the rigors of the anti-Jewish law.

Keenly attentive to detail, Vallat was driven to close every loophole, to ensure that no Jew escaped the jurisdiction of the anti-Jewish program. Never fully satisfied with the handiwork of the CGQJ, the coordinator of the antisemitic legislation worked on a new *Statut des Juifs* during the fall and winter of 1941, but this law never saw the light of day. Through successive drafts, however, one can see a continuing effort to tighten the definition and to ease the task of legal determination—as, for example, in the case of the children of foreigners whose grandparents' racial makeup could not be determined. Mean-spirited and beset with contradictions on the matter of race and religion, the statutory core of Vichy's policy toward the Jews reflected the legalistic approach of the regime and the animus against all Jews, whether or not they were French citizens.

[*See also* Anti-Jewish Legislation.]

BIBLIOGRAPHY

Lubetzki, J. *La condition des Juifs en France sous l'occupation allemande, 1940–1945: La législation raciale.* Paris, 1945.
Marrus, M. R., and R. O. Paxton. *Vichy France and the Jews.* New York, 1981.

MICHAEL R. MARRUS

STERILIZATION. *See* Euthanasia Program; Medical Experiments; Physicians, Nazi.

STERN GROUP. *See* Lohamei Herut Israel.

STERN, SAMU (1874–1947), Hungarian Jewish community leader. Born in Jánosháza, Stern was a banker and served as counselor of the Hungarian royal court. For many years before the German occupation of Hungary on March 19, 1944, he was president of the Jewish community of Pest (Pesti Izraelita Hitközség), the country's largest community, and of the National Bureau of the Jews of Hungary (Magyarországi Izraeliták Országos Irodája), the central organization of Hungary's Neolog (Conservative) congregations. A very successful businessman, Stern had excellent relations with the aristocratic-conservative elements of Hungarian society, including the ruling classes. As a "Magyar of the Israelite faith," he was both highly patriotic and anti-Zionist.

After Germany occupied Hungary, Stern became head of the Központi Zsidó Tanács–JUDENRAT (Jewish Council), a position he held until late October of 1944, when he went into hiding. Although devoted to support of Jewish causes, he maintained a conservative position vis-à-vis the occupation, and he was legalistic and formalistic in his dealings with the Germans and their Hungarian accomplices. Stern later wrote and published his memoirs.

BIBLIOGRAPHY

Braham, R. L. "The Official Jewish Leadership of Wartime Hungary." In *Patterns of Jewish Leadership in Nazi Europe, 1933–1945*. Proceedings of the Third Yad Vashem International Historical Conference, edited by Y. Gutman and C. J. Haft, pp. 267–285. Jerusalem, 1979.
Stern, S. "A Race with Time: A Statement." In vol. 3 of *Hungarian Jewish Studies*, edited by R. L. Braham, pp. 1–47. New York, 1973.

RANDOLPH L. BRAHAM

STERNBUCH, ISAAC. *See* Sternbuch, Recha.

STERNBUCH, RECHA (1905–1971). Recha Sternbuch and her husband, Isaac, were Swiss representatives of the VA'AD HA-HATSALA rescue committee of the Orthodox rabbis in the United States. Initially active in assisting Jewish refugees coming to Switzerland as well as Jews entering there illegally from France, the Sternbuchs headed the Hilfsverein für Jüdische Flüchtlinge in Shanghai (Relief Organization for Jewish Refugees in Shanghai), established in 1941 to provide aid for rabbis and yeshiva students stranded in Shanghai. They later expanded their rescue activities, changing the name of their organization to the Hilfsverein für Jüdische Flüchtlinge im Ausland (Relief Organization for Jewish Refugees Abroad) and initiating numerous projects: sending parcels to Jews in Poland and Czechoslovakia, rescuing Jews by using Latin American passports, maintaining contact with Jewish leaders in Slovakia and Hungary, and monitoring developments throughout Nazi-occupied Europe. On September 2, 1942, the Sternbuchs informed Jewish leaders in the United States of the large-scale deportations taking place from the WARSAW ghetto and urged them to enlist the aid of American leaders. The Sternbuchs took part in negotiations that resulted in the rescue from the THERESIENSTADT ghetto of 1,200 Jews, who arrived in Switzerland on February 6, 1945. After World War II, Recha Sternbuch played a very active role in recovering Jewish children from non-Jewish homes, orphanages, and convents.

BIBLIOGRAPHY

Friedenson, J., and D. Kranzler. *Heroine of Rescue.* New York, 1984.
Kranzler, D. *Thy Brother's Blood: The Orthodox Jewish Response during the Holocaust.* New York, 1987.

EFRAIM ZUROFF

ST. LOUIS, German ship that in 1939 carried Jewish refugees whose landing permits to Havana were invalidated by the Cuban government and their entry denied.

When the *St. Louis*, owned by the Hamburg-America Line, departed from Hamburg for Cuba on May 13, 1939, it carried 936 pas-

Jewish refugees disembark from the *St. Louis* at Antwerp on June 17, 1939. [JDC Archives, New York]

sengers, of whom 930 were Jews bearing landing certificates for Havana. These certificates had been arranged by the Cuban director general of immigration, Manuel Benitez González, in lieu of the usual immigration visas. Although according to Cuban law such certificates required no fee, González sold them for personal gain, for as much as $160. The jealousies of Cuban government officials concerning González's illicit wealth, combined with local sentiment against the influx of additional Jewish refugees and the government's pro-fascist leanings, led the Cuban government, on May 5, 1939, to invalidate the landing certificates and curtail the director general's authority. The government decreed that the certificates would be honored only until May 6. Apparently, both the Hamburg-America Line and its passengers were aware of the decree, but they believed that the certificates, which were bought well before the decree, would be honored. Only twenty-two of the Jewish refugee passengers actually met Cuba's new visa requirements.

When the *St. Louis* reached Havana on May 27, its passengers were denied entry. The American Jewish JOINT DISTRIBUTION COMMITTEE (JDC) dispatched Lawrence Berenson to Havana to negotiate the disembarkation of the refugees. Berenson arrived in Havana on May 30, but Cuban president Federico Laredo Bru insisted that the ship leave the Havana harbor. He claimed that because the shipping line and the JDC had both known in advance that the certificates were invalid, they should

be taught a lesson about respect for Cuban law. The *St. Louis* left Havana on June 2, its captain, Gustav Schroeder, steering it in circles in the areas off Florida and Cuba while the negotiations continued.

American immigration officials announced that the refugees would not be allowed to enter the United States, but on June 5 an agreement was reached to allow them to land in Cuba for a $453,000 bond ($500 per refugee), to be deposited by the following day. The JDC could not meet the deadline, and the ship sailed for Europe on June 6. Twenty-nine passengers had been permitted to land, of whom twenty-two were Jews with valid Cuban visas; one, Max Loewe (a Jew without a valid visa), was hospitalized after a suicide attempt; and six were not Jewish.

While the *St. Louis* was en route to Europe, Great Britain, Belgium, France, and the Netherlands agreed to take in the refugees; 287 entered Britain, 214 Belgium, 224 France, and 181 the Netherlands, after the ship reached Antwerp on June 17. Most of the passengers who received temporary refuge in European countries were later victims of the "FINAL SOLUTION."

BIBLIOGRAPHY

Gellman, F. "The *St. Louis* Tragedy." *American Jewish Historical Quarterly* 61/2 (December 1971): 144–156.

Thomas, G., and M. M. Wittes. *Voyage of the Damned*. New York, 1974.

DAVID SILBERKLANG

STORM TROOPERS. *See* SA.

STRASSHOF, concentration camp near Vienna to which nearly twenty-one thousand Jews from the southern parts of Trianon Hungary were deported during the second half of June 1944. Most of these Jews, including children and the elderly, survived the war. Their transfer was based on an agreement between the leaders of the RELIEF AND RESCUE COMMITTEE OF BUDAPEST, especially Rezső (Rudolf) KASZTNER, and Adolf EICHMANN, head of the Sonderkommando (Special Commando) in Hungary.

The agreement, which involved the payment of 5 million Swiss francs, was based on the offer made by Eichmann on June 14, 1944, to allow 30,000 Hungarian Jews to be "put on ice" in Austria as a token of his goodwill with regard to Joel BRAND's "Blood for Goods" mission in Istanbul. The offer was authorized by the REICHSSICHERHEITSHAUPTAMT (Reich Security Main Office; RSHA) in response to the request for forced laborers made by SS-Brigadeführer Karl Blaschke, the mayor of Vienna. The Jews, who were transferred from the ghetto centers of Baja (5,640), DEBRECEN (6,841), SZEGED (5,739), and Szolnok (2,567), were employed in industrial and agricultural enterprises in eastern Austria. There they were under the control of a central administrative office in Vienna, headed by SS-Obersturmbannführer Hermann KRUMEY.

BIBLIOGRAPHY

Braham, R. L. *The Politics of Genocide: The Holocaust in Hungary*. New York, 1981. See pages 649–653.

RANDOLPH L. BRAHAM

STREICHER, JULIUS (1885–1946), Nazi politician specializing in antisemitic incitement. Born in Augsburg, Bavaria, Streicher became an elementary school teacher. In World War I he was awarded several medals for distinguished service. Streicher was one of the founders of the German Socialist party in 1919, but shortly thereafter he merged it with the Nazi party. From 1928 to 1940 he was the *Gauleiter* of Franconia; he was a member of the Bavarian provincial legisla-

On November 9, 1934, Julius Streicher (foreground, at the right), together with Adolf Hitler (fourth from right), Hermann Göring (to the right of Hitler), and other "old comrades," retraces the historic march of the Munich (Beer-Hall) Putsch of November 9, 1923.

ture from 1924 to 1932, and then became a member of the Reichstag. He also held the rank of *Obergruppenführer* (general) in the SA (Sturmabteilung; Storm Troopers).

Streicher was one of the most rabid antisemites in the Nazi party. He founded the newspaper *Der* STÜRMER (The Attacker) in Nuremberg in 1923, becoming its editor and, as of 1935, its owner as well. It was he who gave the newspaper its special antisemitic-pornographic character. The Nazi authorities had to dissociate themselves at times from the articles it published and even closed it down in Nuremberg, Streicher's stronghold. Streicher used his influence to bar Jews from restaurants and cafés, and he tried to persuade all the municipalities in Franconia to establish ghettos. Shortly after the Nazi rise to power, he was appointed chairman of the Zentralkomitee zur Abwehr der Jüdischen Greuel- und Boykotthetze (Central Defense Committee against Jewish Atrocity and Boycott Propaganda); he was also the organizer of the anti-Jewish BOYCOTT of April 1, 1933. Streicher was one of the instigators and authors of the NUREMBERG LAWS, and as early as 1938, in an article entitled "War against the World Enemy," he called for the total destruction of the Jewish people.

In March 1940 Streicher was suspended from his post as *Gauleiter* of Franconia, following an investigation by the supreme court of the Nazi party concerning his involvement in bribery related to the "Aryanization" of plants and enterprises. Even so, Streicher remained one of the leading protagonists of militant antisemitism.

When the war ended, Streicher tried to hide under a different identity. Disguised as a house painter, he was recognized and taken prisoner by American soldiers on May 23, 1945. He was among the major Nazi criminals tried by the International Military Tribunal at Nuremberg. In its judgment, the tribunal said of Streicher: "For twenty-five years he incited to hatred of the Jews, in speeches and in writing, and became widely known as the 'Number 1 enemy of the Jews.'" In an article from his own pen that he published on December 25, 1941, Streicher stated: "If one really wants to put an end to the continued prospering of this curse from heaven that is the Jewish blood, there is only one way to do it: to eradicate this people, this Satan's son, root and branch." The tribunal sentenced Streicher to death; he was executed by hanging, on October 16, 1946.

BIBLIOGRAPHY

Bytwerk, R. L. *Julius Streicher*. New York, 1983.

HANS-HEINRICH WILHELM

STROOP, JÜRGEN (1895–1951), SS and police chief who crushed the WARSAW GHETTO UPRISING and destroyed the WARSAW ghetto. Josef Stroop (he changed his first name to the more "Aryan"-sounding Jürgen in 1941) was born in Detmold, in central Germany, into the family of a Catholic policeman from the lower middle class. He was educated in a nationalist and militarist spirit. Volunteering for the army in World War I, he was wounded three times, and in 1918 was promoted to the rank of captain. After the war Stroop was employed in the Detmold municipal administration. In 1932 he joined the Nazi party and the SS, because of both his nationalist views and his attraction to the uniforms. He quickly rose in the ranks of the SS and by 1939 was an SS-*Oberführer* and commander of a police unit.

Upon the outbreak of war between Germany and the Soviet Union in June 1941, Stroop was sent, at his own request, to the front. After being wounded he was transferred to police functions in the occupied Soviet territories, where he specialized in persecuting the population and harassing local partisans. On April 17, 1943, on the eve of the liquidation of the Warsaw ghetto, he was summoned by the *Höherer SS- und Polizeiführer* (Higher SS and Police Leader) of the GENERALGOUVERNEMENT, Friedrich Wilhelm KRÜGER. The SS and police chiefs apparently rushed Stroop to Warsaw, doubting the ability of the local police commander, Ferdinand Sammern-Frankenegg, to carry out the liquidation of the ghetto. With the commencement of this action and the outbreak of the ghetto uprising on April 19, 1943, when Sammern-Frankenegg's helplessness became apparent, Stroop assumed command.

Stroop conducted the action against the insurgent ghetto as a military campaign; the methods he employed consisted of unrestrained and indiscriminate killing and destruction. He had under his command about two thousand men from different units, equipped like frontline troops. Stroop sent daily reports on the campaign in the ghetto to Kraków, the capital of the Generalgouvernement. His concluding report at the end of the campaign, which he called the "Great Operation" (*Grossaktion*), included the following statements:

After the first days it was clear that the Jews would not think of being deported of their own free will, but had definitely decided to defend themselves in all possible ways and with the arms in their possession. . . . The number of Jews taken from their homes in the first days and captured was relatively small. The Jews were apparently hiding in the sewers and in specially prepared bunkers. . . . Twenty- to thirty-member combat units, made up of Jewish youths eighteen to twenty-five years old, with a

Jürgen Stroop during his trial in Warsaw (1951).

certain number of women, spread the revolt and renewed it periodically. These combat units had been ordered to defend themselves with arms to the end, and when necessary to commit suicide rather than be taken alive. . . . In this armed revolt there were women in the combat units, armed like men, some of them members of the He-Haluts movement. The women often fired from guns in both hands. . . . The Jewish opposition and rebels could be broken only by the energetic and constant use of strike forces day and night. On April 23, 1943, the order was given by the SS-*Reichsführer* [Heinrich Himmler], through Wilhelm Krüger, to effect the evacuation of the Warsaw ghetto with the greatest rigor and unrelenting diligence. . . . The Great Operation terminated on May 16, 1943, at 8:15 p.m., with the blowing up of the Warsaw synagogue. There is no longer any activity in the former Jewish residential quarter . . . all the buildings and everything else have been destroyed; only the Dzielna [Pawiak] security prison was spared.

In his last daily report, dated April 16, Stroop reported that out of 56,065 Jews caught, 13,929 were exterminated and about 5,000 to 6,000 were killed in the shelling and burning.

After putting down the uprising, Stroop continued to serve as SS and Police Leader in the Warsaw district. In September 1943 he was appointed Higher SS and Police Leader in Greece, with promotion to the rank of SS-*Gruppenführer*. That November, Stroop was transferred to serve in the same capacity in the Twelfth Army District in the Reich, which included the areas of Wiesbaden, Darmstadt, and Luxembourg. He remained in this post until the end of the war.

Soon afterward, Stroop was discovered, while attempting to change his identity, in the Wiesbaden area, which was in the hands of the United States army. In a search conducted in his home, an elegantly organized album was found, containing his reports from the Warsaw ghetto campaign and a series of photographs taken by the Germans during the uprising. In January 1947 Stroop was tried by the American military court in Dachau (Trial No. 12-3188, *United States* v. *Stroop*) and charged with responsibility for war crimes perpetrated in the Twelfth Army District. Out of the twenty-two accused in this trial, which concluded in

March, thirteen were sentenced to death, including Stroop. The verdict was not carried out, and Stroop was extradited to Poland as a war criminal wanted in the Polish People's Republic.

The photographs, together with parts of Stroop's reports, were presented by the prosecution at the NUREMBERG TRIAL of the principal Nazi criminals, and constituted one of the most shocking and condemning documents in the entire trial. During his interrogation in a Polish prison, Stroop provided clarifications and supplementary information to the reports he had written during the Warsaw ghetto uprising in April and May 1943. He was held in prison in Warsaw with a member of the Polish underground ARMIA KRAJOWA (Home Army), Kazimierz Moczarski, and held lengthy conversations with him. These conversations were later the subject of the book *Gespräche mit dem Henker* (Conversations with the Hangman).

In July 1951 Stroop was tried at the Warsaw district court. He was executed by hanging that September in Warsaw.

BIBLIOGRAPHY

Moczarski, K. *Conversations with a Hangman.* Englewood Cliffs, N.J., 1981.
The Stroop Report: The Jewish Quarter of Warsaw Is No More! New York, 1979.

ISRAEL GUTMAN

STRUMA, boat used to bring Jews to Palestine in defiance of British immigration restrictions. In December 1941, 769 Jews boarded the old 180-ton cattle boat *Struma* in the port of Constanţa, Romania; their destination was Palestine. The boat was unsafe, heavily overcrowded, and without sanitary facilities. Six months had passed since the massacre of the Jews of BUKOVINA and BESSARABIA, and Romanian Jewry was searching for a way to cope with the new situation that had been created. The passengers' plan was to sail to Istanbul and there to obtain immigration visas for Palestine. From the outset the boat's engine scarcely worked, and the *Struma* reached Istanbul, its first scheduled stop, with difficulty. There, it turned out that the organizers of the trip—private individuals and former members of the Zionist Revisionist party immigration office—had misled the passengers and, contrary to what they had been assured, no visas were available to them.

For ten weeks the passengers were confined to the boat, at anchor in the quarantine section of the port. The situation deteriorated rapidly. Efforts to make the vessel seaworthy for the continuation of the voyage met with great difficulties. The many pleas from various quarters to the British to permit the entry of the Jews into Palestine on the basis of the existing modest legal immigration quota were to no avail. The Turkish authorities, for their part, were adamant in refusing permission to transfer the would-be immigrants to a transit camp on land until the resumption of their voyage could be arranged, even though the camp was maintained by Jewish organizations at their own expense.

On February 23, 1942, the Turkish police, despite the immigrants' resistance, towed the boat into the open sea, although it had no water, food, or fuel on board. Within a few hours it was sunk, struck by a torpedo apparently fired in error from a Soviet submarine. Only a single passenger was saved.

The sinking of the *Struma* touched off a wave of protests and denunciations of British policy, and put a further strain on the relations between the Jewish Agency and the High Commissioner for Palestine, Sir Harold MacMichael, who had taken the lead in opposing the granting of immigration visas to the boat's passengers. Subsequently, the British, worried about a possible repetition of the *Struma* tragedy, revised their policy of expelling persons who had entered Palestine "illegally." They set free refugees detained in the Athlit detention camp awaiting deportation from the country, subtracting their number from the immigration quota.

BIBLIOGRAPHY

Avneri, A. L. *From Velos to Taurus: The First Decade of Jewish Illegal Immigration to Mandatory Palestine (Eretz Yisrael), 1934–1944.* Tel Aviv, 1985. (In Hebrew.)
Kuperstein, L. *The Struma Scroll.* Tel Aviv, 1982. (In Hebrew.)
Ofer, D. *Illegal Immigration during the Holocaust.* Jerusalem, 1988. (In Hebrew.)

Zweig, R. W. *Britain and Palestine during the Second World War.* London, 1986. See pages 118–134.

DALIA OFER

STRUTHOF. *See* Natzweiler-Struthof.

STRY (Pol., Stryj), city in Lvov Oblast (district), in the west of the Ukrainian SSR. From 1772 to 1918 Stry was part of Austrian-ruled Eastern Galicia, and during the interwar period it belonged to Poland. In September 1939 it was occupied by the Soviets. Stry had had a Jewish population since the sixteenth century; on the eve of World War II, twelve thousand Jews lived in the city.

A few days after the German invasion of the Soviet Union on June 22, 1941, the Soviet authorities began to evacuate Stry; three hundred Jews were among the evacuees. The Germans took the city on July 2. This was the sign for anti-Jewish riots in which Ukrainian nationalists took part, as well as a Polish mob and Wehrmacht soldiers. Several dozen Jews were killed in the riots, many were wounded, and much Jewish property was looted. By the middle of August the Germans had introduced a variety of anti-Jewish decrees: Jews had to wear a white badge with a blue Star of David (*see* BADGE, JEWISH) on it; they had to surrender their valuables and furnishings; their freedom of movement was restricted; they were barred from buying food in the city market; Jewish apartments were confiscated; and Jews were put on forced labor. The implementation of some of these measures was the responsibility of the JUDENRAT (Jewish Council), which had been set up in July 1941. Jews on forced labor were assigned to work at municipal institutions, military camps, and privately owned German factories; as well as on road paving and repairing war-damaged bridges.

In early September 1941, the Germans and their Ukrainian helpers drove a thousand Jews out of their homes and took them to the Ukrainian police station, where they were beaten. The Jews were then brought to the Holobutów Forest, near the village of Rylow,

and were killed. At the end of 1941 Jews were forced to vacate certain streets in Stry and to move into an area that came to be designated as "the Jewish quarter." At first the quarter was not fenced in, but by the end of 1942 it was declared a closed ghetto.

In the winter of 1941 and the spring of 1942, groups of Jewish youths were seized and put into labor camps that had been established in the Stry area. Soon many of them died from the physical abuse to which they were exposed, or from hunger and disease; many others were killed. In May 1942 several hundred Jews were dispatched to the BEŁŻEC extermination camp. On September 13 a mass *Aktion* was launched, as a result of which five thousand Jews were taken to Bełżec. After the *Aktion* the Jews made desperate efforts to find employment in factories that performed essential work for the German economy; they also prepared hiding places and made attempts to escape to Hungary. Before long, there was another *Aktion*. On October 17 and 18 the Germans raided the ghetto alleys and houses, seized two thousand persons, and sent them to Bełżec. The area of the Jewish quarter was then reduced further, and exit from it was prohibited. The

Jews who were employed in essential enterprises wore a badge with the letter "W" on it, while all the rest were declared unfit for work. In yet another *Aktion*, from February 28 to March 2, 1943, a thousand Jews were murdered in the ghetto and its vicinity; in another mass slaughter, which began on May 22 and lasted for several days, more than a thousand were killed in the local cemetery.

Some of the survivors of the community, mainly skilled artisans, were moved into labor camps that had been set up near the factories in Stry. At the beginning of June the ghetto was liquidated, and with it the Judenrat. In July of 1943 the Jews in the labor camps were gradually liquidated, and by the end of August the city was declared *judenrein* ("cleansed of Jews"). During the months that followed, the Germans and their Ukrainian helpers continued the hunt for Jews who had gone into hiding, and whoever was discovered was killed on the spot.

Stry was liberated on August 8, 1944. Several dozen Jews had saved themselves by hiding inside the city or in nearby forests. At the end of 1944 and over the course of 1945, small groups of Stry Jews returned to the city, having survived in German labor camps or in the Soviet interior. Most of them left after a short stay and made their way through Poland to the West or to Palestine.

BIBLIOGRAPHY

Kudish, N., S. Rosenberg, and A. Rothfeld, eds. *Stryj Record*. Tel Aviv, 1962. (In Hebrew.)

AHARON WEISS

tions, but his career revived with the Nazi seizure of power in January 1933. He became, successively, state secretary in the Prussian Ministry of Culture, Education, and Church Affairs (June 1933), a member of the Prussian State Council (September 1933), and secretary of state in the Reich Ministry of the Interior (March 1935).

Stuckart headed the department for constitutional and legislative matters, and in this capacity was instrumental in helping to draft the Nuremberg Laws (1935). He joined the SS in 1936. Together with Hans GLOBKE, he edited a commentary on German racial legislation in 1936; he also published a number of works on Nazi legal theory. In 1942 he participated in the WANNSEE CONFERENCE, at which he warmly endorsed the plans for the "FINAL SOLUTION," the compulsory sterilization of all "non-Aryans," and the dissolution of mixed marriages. In racial matters Stuckart was even more extreme than Reinhard HEYDRICH.

Arrested in 1945, Stuckart was sentenced to four years' imprisonment by the International Military Tribunal at Nuremberg. He claimed to be ignorant of the extermination camps. He was released in 1949 and died near Hannover in an automobile accident that was rumored to have been the work of a group taking revenge on Nazi war criminals.

BIBLIOGRAPHY

Schleunes, K. A. *The Twisted Road to Auschwitz: Nazi Policy toward German Jews, 1933–1939*. Urbana, 1970.

LIONEL KOCHAN

STUCKART, WILHELM (1902–1953), Nazi politician and jurist responsible for the drafting of the NUREMBERG LAWS and their subsequent implementation ordinances. Stuckart was born in Wiesbaden and studied law in Frankfurt am Main and Munich. He joined a Freikorps group in the aftermath of World War I and was twice imprisoned by the French for his oppositionist activities. Already a right-wing extremist, Stuckart joined the Nazi party in 1922, became its legal adviser in 1926, and a judge in 1930. He had to resign in 1932 because of his political affilia-

STÜLPNAGEL, KARL HEINRICH VON (1886–1944), German general prominent in the resistance to Adolf Hitler in 1944. Born in Darmstadt, Stülpnagel came from a military family and joined the army in 1904. By 1935 he had reached the rank of *Generalmajor*, and at the outbreak of World War II he was a *General* of infantry. In May 1940 he commanded the Second Army Corps. After the defeat of France, he presided over the German-French armistice commission in Wiesbaden.

In February 1941, in preparation for the

German invasion of Russia, Stülpnagel took over command of the Seventeenth Army, which he led in the Russian campaign until November 1941. In February 1942 he succeeded his cousin Otto Stülpnagel as military governor of France. Stülpnagel imposed a harsh occupation regime and sought to repress the French Résistance, shooting hostages and executing their relatives. However, he had never wholly accepted the Nazi system, and as early as 1939 had taken part in plans for an anti-Hitler putsch.

In 1944 Stülpnagel emerged as a leading member of the military resistance to the Nazis, hoping to overthrow their rule before the impending Allied invasion of Europe. On July 20, in concert with the bomb plot against Hitler, he had about twelve hundred of the foremost members of the Gestapo, SD (Sicherheitsdienst; Security Service), and SS in Paris arrested, before news of the failure of the plot reached him. He was at once relieved of his post and recalled to Berlin. Stülpnagel tried to commit suicide near Verdun but succeeded only in inflicting severe facial wounds and blinding himself. He was brought to Berlin, where he was condemned to death by the People's Court (*Volksgerichtshof*) and hanged on August 30, 1944.

BIBLIOGRAPHY

Hoffmann, P. *The History of the German Resistance, 1933–1945.* Cambridge, Mass., 1977.

LIONEL KOCHAN

STURMABTEILUNG. *See* SA.

STÜRMER, DER (The Attacker), Nazi weekly newspaper with a wide circulation that addressed itself to man's basest and most primitive instincts. Founded by Julius STREICHER, *Der Stürmer* was first published in the spring of 1923. Its initial targets were Streicher's local party enemies in Nuremberg. The mainstay of the paper during the Weimar period was scandal, at first chiefly sensational political journalism, sex, and crime. Throughout this time, its antisemitic tone increased.

Front page of Julius Streicher's antisemitic weekly, *Der Stürmer*, April 1929. The cartoon, titled "Awakening of Spring in the Nuremberg Zoo," shows an "Aryan" woman comparing the Jews to the monkeys. The slogan at the foot of the page reads: "The Jews are our misfortune!" [Yad Vashem Archives, Jerusalem]

When Hitler took power in 1933, *Der Stürmer* was already one of the most popular Nazi publications, selling about twenty-five thousand copies weekly. By then its antisemitic campaign was in full swing. It sought by means of unrestrained propaganda and demagoguery to promote the idea that the Jews were the chief enemy of the Germans, and of all mankind. With the slogan "Die Juden sind unser Unglück" ("The Jews are our misfortune"), the weekly reached a circulation of about half a million copies by 1938. The actual readership was larger than the circulation figures suggest, owing to marketing and promotional techniques. *Der Stürmer* was initially sold by street vendors and small newsdealers; eventually, it was advertised by means of showcase displays put up in places where people naturally congregated—bus stops, busy streets, parks, and factory canteens. The displays were changed weekly, and were protected against vandals by "Stürmer guards." These showcases became part of everyday life in the Third Reich.

The style of the paper was crude, aggressive, and easily comprehensible; the articles were composed of simple, clear sentences, blunt and repetitive. The most striking element was the antisemitic cartoons, which became the paper's highlight after the work of Philipp Rupprecht ("Fips") first appeared on the front page on December 19, 1925. "Fips," a master caricaturist, sought to make the subjects of his cartoons contemptible through ridicule. His drawings were vivid and revolting. The essential characteristics of "Fips"'s Jews were ugly faces with huge hooked noses, bulging eyes, large ears, swollen lips, and unshaven beards; long hairy arms and hands; and short crooked legs. They were also portrayed as sexually perverted. "Fips" was a master at drawing sensuous female figures as well, which contributed significantly to Der Stürmer's appeal.

After 1933, nine special editions were published, often timed to appear at the annual Nuremberg rally, focusing on themes such as ritual murder by Jews, Jewish criminality, the world Jewish conspiracy, and Jewish sexual crimes. Circulation dropped sharply after 1940, owing partly to wartime paper shortages, although Hitler assured Der Stürmer enough paper to continue publication. However, the major reason for the reduced circulation (it dropped to under 200,000), was the disappearance of Jews from everyday life in Germany. The final issue appeared on February 1, 1945, denouncing the invading Allies as tools of the international Jewish conspiracy.

[See also Propaganda, Nazi.]

BIBLIOGRAPHY

Showalter, D. E. Little Man, What Now? Der Stürmer in the Weimar Republic. Hamden, Conn., 1982.

JACQUELINE ROKHSAR

STUTTHOF, concentration camp 22 miles (36 km) east of Danzig (Gdańsk), at the mouth of the Vistula River. It was first designated as a "camp for civilian war prisoners" and officially became a concentration camp on January 8, 1942.

The camp remained in existence from September 2, 1939, to May 9, 1945. About 115,000 prisoners passed through Stutthof; of these, 65,000 perished and 22,000 were moved to other concentration camps. In the early period of its existence, several thousand prisoners were released from Stutthof. At the end of the war a few hundred survivors were set free when Stutthof and its satellite camps were liberated by Soviet and Polish forces.

Stutthof had several dozen satellite camps, spread over what is now northern Poland and the Kaliningrad district of Soviet Russia. The largest of the satellite camps were at Thorn (Pol., Toruń) and Elbing (Pol., Elbląg); each had five thousand Jewish women prisoners. The camp staff consisted of SS men and a group of Ukrainian auxiliary police (see UKRAINISCHE HILFSPOLIZEI). The total number of SS men stationed at Stutthof during the years of its existence was three thousand. Initially, the prison population was made up of Poles from Danzig and Pomerania; they were joined later by Poles from all parts of northern Poland and from Warsaw. The camp also contained a considerable number of Soviet prisoners, as well as large groups of Norwegians, Danes, and others. In the early stage the number of Jewish prisoners was quite small.

At first, Stutthof was in effect an "extermination" camp because of the hard labor and the accompanying harsh conditions there, which caused the death of many prisoners. In 1943 conditions improved slightly, as far as the non-Jewish prisoners were concerned. The prisoners were put to work in various plants and arms factories. They were accommodated, at the beginning, in the camp's old wooden barracks; in 1943 barracks made of concrete were put up in the new camp. Relatively few attempts were made to escape. Executions took place quite frequently; the victims were for the most part activists in the resistance movement. In 1944 large transports of Jews, mostly women, were brought to the camp from the Baltic countries and AUSCHWITZ. They

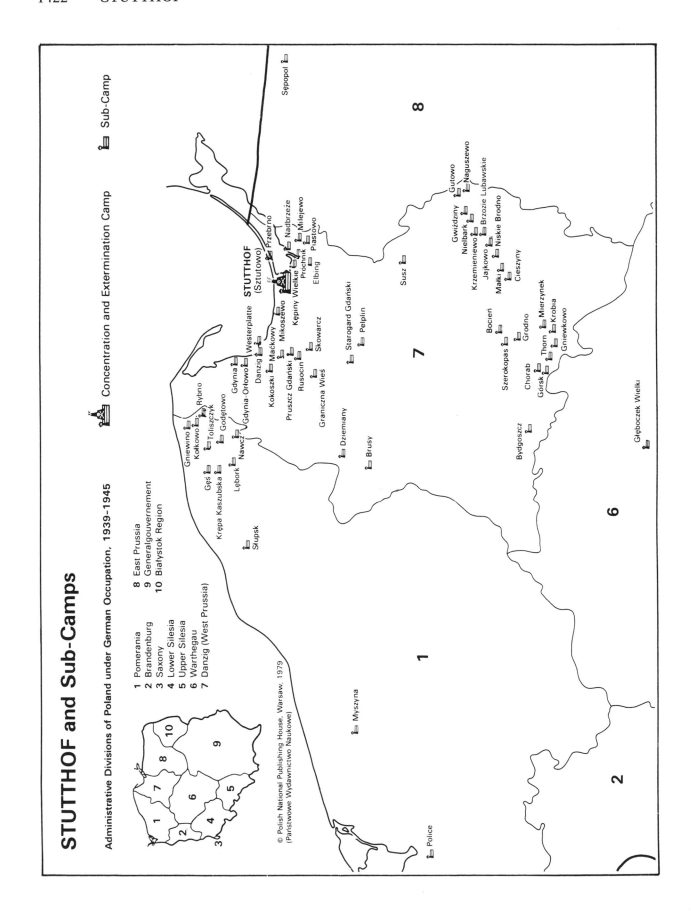

STUTTHOF and Sub-Camps

Administrative Divisions of Poland under German Occupation, 1939–1945

1 Pomerania
2 Brandenburg
3 Saxony
4 Lower Silesia
5 Upper Silesia
6 Warthegau
7 Danzig (West Prussia)
8 East Prussia
9 Generalgouvernement
10 Białystok Region

Concentration and Extermination Camp

Sub-Camp

© Polish National Publishing House, Warsaw, 1979
(Państwowe Wydawnictwo Naukowe)

were put through a *Selektion* and some were sent to the camp's gas chambers. Of the fifty thousand Jews who were brought to Stutthof, nearly all died. In January 1945, the prisoners in most of the satellite camps and the main camp itself were evacuated westward toward the vicinity of Lębork, in dreadful winter conditions. Tens of thousands perished in these DEATH MARCHES. Some groups of prisoners were evacuated by sea in small boats; many of these prisoners drowned. Stutthof was liberated on May 9, 1945.

BIBLIOGRAPHY

Dunin-Wasowicz, K. *Oboz koncentracyjny Stutthof.* Gdańsk, 1966.

Dunin-Wasowicz, K. "Żydowscy wiezniowie KL Stutthof." *Biuletyn Żydowskiego Instytuta Historycznego* 63 (1967): 3–37.

Gutman, Y., and A. Saf, eds. *The Nazi Concentration Camps: Structure and Aims; the Image of the Prisoner; the Jews in the Camps.* Proceedings of the Fourth Yad Vashem International Historical Conference. Jerusalem, 1984.

Lukaszkiewicz, Z. "Stutthof Concentration Camp." In vol. 2 of *German Crimes in Poland*, Central Commission for Investigation of Nazi Crimes in Poland, pp. 107–124. New York, 1982.

Pickholz-Barnitsch, O. "The Evacuation of the Stutthof Concentration Camp, January–April 1945." *Yad Vashem Bulletin* 17 (December 1965): 34–49.

KRZYSZTOF DUNIN-WASOWICZ

SUBSEQUENT BRITISH TRIALS. *See* Trials of War Criminals: Subsequent British Trials.

SUBSEQUENT NUREMBERG PROCEEDINGS. *See* Trials of War Criminals: Subsequent Nuremberg Proceedings.

SUGIHARA, SEMPO (1900–1986), Japanese consul general in KOVNO, Lithuania, who actively assisted Jewish refugees in 1940. In early August of that year, three weeks before the Soviet authorities intended to remove all foreign consular representatives from Kovno, Sugihara was approached by Dr. Zorah WARHAFTIG, a leader of the Mizraḥi religious

Sempo Sugihara.

Zionist movement and a representative of the Jewish Agency Palestine Office in Lithuania. Warhaftig asked Sugihara to grant Japanese transit visas to Polish Jewish refugees stranded in Kovno, as a means for them to obtain Soviet visas. He outlined to Sugihara a plan under which the refugees would travel to the Dutch-controlled island of Curaçao in the Caribbean, where no entry permit was necessary, by way of the USSR and JAPAN. The Soviets had made their approval of the plan conditional on the refugees' obtaining transit visas from Japan.

Though his government rejected the proposal, Sugihara decided to grant such visas to any Jewish refugees who requested them. During the remaining weeks before he was scheduled to leave Kovno, on August 31, Sugihara devoted most of his time to this matter. Many rabbinical students, such as those of the famed MIR academy, availed themselves of this opportunity to leave Lithuania; after spending time in China and other countries, they eventually reached the United States and Israel. In all, it appears that at least sixteen hundred visas were issued

(Sugihara estimated the figure at some thirty-five hundred).

Sugihara was reassigned to other Japanese legations in Europe. Upon his return to Tokyo in 1947, he was asked to submit his resignation for his insubordination seven years earlier. In 1984, YAD VASHEM awarded him the title of "RIGHTEOUS AMONG THE NATIONS."

Years later, recalling the dramatic and tense days of August 1940, Sugihara explained his predicament: "I really had a hard time, and was unable to sleep for two nights. I thought as follows: 'I can issue transit visas . . . by virtue of my authority as consul. I cannot allow these people to die, people who had come to me for help with death staring them in the eyes. Whatever punishment may be imposed upon me, I know I should follow my conscience'" (Ryusuke Kajiyama, in *Sankei Shinbun Yukan Tokuho*, January 24, 1985).

BIBLIOGRAPHY

Warhaftig, Z. *Refugee and Survivor: Rescue Efforts during the Holocaust.* Jerusalem, 1988.

MORDECAI PALDIEL

SUPERIOR ORDERS. Anticipating the exculpatory pleas of "act of State" and "superior orders" by the defendants in the post–World War II war crimes trials, the August 8, 1945, Charter of the Nuremberg International Military Tribunal (IMT) for the trial of twenty-four major Nazi war criminals (Hermann GÖRING and others) specifically excluded both pleas (*see* NUREMBERG TRIAL). With respect to the former, the tribunal referred to article 7 of the charter, declaring: "The principle of international law, which under certain circumstances protects the representatives of a state, cannot be applied to acts which are condemned as criminal by international law." It stated further: "The very essence of the Charter is that individuals have international duties which transcend the national obligations of obedience imposed by the individual state. He who violates the laws of war cannot obtain immunity while acting in pursuance of the authority of the State if the State in authorizing action moves outside its competence under international law."

The Supreme Court of the state of Israel, in the EICHMANN TRIAL (*Attorney General of the Government of Israel* v. *Adolf Eichmann*), on May 19, 1962, declared that the murderous acts of "that evil State" (that is, Nazi Germany) "are not laws in the contemplation of international law and can in no manner render the terrible crimes valid or absolve those who participated in committing them from the personal responsibility they bear." The court rejected the plea of "act of State," saying: "The very contention that the systematic extermination of masses of helpless human beings by a government or regime could constitute 'an act of State' appears to be an insult to reason and a mockery of law and justice."

With regard to the plea of the defendants that "in doing what they did they were acting under the orders of Adolf Hitler, and therefore cannot be held responsible for acts committed by them in carrying out these orders," the IMT quoted article 8 of its charter and declared: "The provisions of this article are in conformity with the law of all nations. That a soldier was ordered to kill or torture in violation of the international law of war has never been recognized as a defense to such acts of brutality, though, as the Charter here provides, the order may be urged in mitigation of the punishment."

After the IMT trial, the United States conducted several trials established pursuant to Control Council Law No. 10, which had been enacted by the four Allied governments in occupied Germany (*see* SUBSEQUENT NUREMBERG PROCEEDINGS). In The *Einsatzgruppen* Case, *U.S.A.* v. *Otto Ohlendorf et al.* (*see* OHLENDORF, OTTO), the defendants admitted that they had participated in the mass killings but pleaded that "they were under military orders and, therefore, had no will of their own. As intent is the basic prerequisite to responsibility for crimes, they argue that they are innocent of criminality since they performed the admitted executions under duress, that is to say, superior orders."

The court quoted with approval the statement of the IMT that the true test of superior orders is not the existence of the order but "whether moral choice was in fact possible"; it declared that "to plead superior orders one must show an excusable ignorance of their illegality" and that duress "imminent, real, and inevitable" was needed. It concluded: "The test to be applied is whether the subordinate acted under coercion or whether he himself approved of the principle involved in the order. If the second proposition is true, the plea of superior orders fails. . . . When the will of the doer merges with the will of the superior in the execution of the illegal act, the doer may not plead duress under superior orders." The court found that Ohlendorf could have refused cooperation and would have been relieved of his assignment.

Summarizing the development of legal principles relating to "superior orders," the Report of the Deputy Judge Advocate for War Crimes, European Command, June 1944 to July 1948, states:

> The principle followed was that compliance with superior orders does not constitute a defense to the charge of having committed a war crime although it may, under certain circumstances, be considered in mitigation of punishment. An accused . . . assumes the burden of establishing (a) that he received an order from a superior to commit the wrongful act; (b) that he did not know . . . that the act which he was directed to perform was illegal or contrary to universally accepted standards of human conduct; or (c) that he acted, at least to some extent, under immediate compulsion. Having satisfactorily established these elements, the amount to which the sentence should be mitigated depends upon the character and extent of the immediate compulsion under which he acted.

In dealing with the plea of superior orders in the Eichmann case, both the District Court of Jerusalem in its judgment of December 12, 1961, and the Israeli Supreme Court in its judgment of May 29, 1962, relied partly on Israeli law and partly on international law. In the application of international law, both courts quoted with approval the relevant findings of the IMT and of the American tribunal in the Einsatzgruppen case. The Supreme Court rejected the plea of superior orders simply on the ground that "in point of fact the appellant did not receive orders

'from above' at all; he was the high and mighty one, the commander of all that pertained to Jewish affairs. He ordered and commanded, not only without orders from his superiors in the hierarchy of the service, but also at times completely contrary to such orders."

Furthermore, following the judgment of the American military tribunal in the Ohlendorf case, the Supreme Court considered the element of compulsion or "necessity" and found that "had the appellant exhibited at any stage the slightest displeasure or heart-searching or even mere lack of enthusiasm for the implementation of the 'Final Solution,' his superior would willingly have relieved him of his part and replaced him by some other person more 'qualified' than he."

Finally, the District Court declared that "the rejection of the defense of 'superior orders' as exempting completely from criminal responsibility has now become general in all civilized countries. This rule has also been acknowledged by the General Assembly of the United Nations, being one of the principles of the London Charter and of the judgment in the *Trial of the Major War Criminals* (Resolution of the Plenary Session, No. 55, dated 11 December 1946)."

In view of the widespread criticism of the establishment of the IMT for the trial of the major war criminals, the United Nations General Assembly, acting on a proposal of the United States, adopted Resolution 95(II) on December 11, 1946, in which it "*affirms* the principles of international law recognized by the Charter of the Nuremberg Tribunal." In the same resolution the assembly directed the committee on the codification of international law to "treat as a matter of primary importance plans for the formulation, in the context of a general codification of offences against the peace and security of mankind, or of an International Criminal Code, of the principles recognized in the Charter of the Nuremberg Tribunal and in the judgment of the tribunal."

The committee on codification was superseded by the International Law Commission, which in 1950 adopted and submitted to the General Assembly its formulation of the Principles of International Law Recognized in the

Charter of the Nuremberg Tribunal and in the Judgment of the Tribunal. Principles III and IV deal with the exculpatory pleas of "act of State" and "superior orders." Principle III, relating to "act of State," is based on article 7 of the Charter of the Nuremberg Tribunal. However, "the last phrase of Article 7 of the charter, 'or mitigating punishment,' has not been retained in the formulation of Principle III. The commission considers that the question of mitigating punishment is a matter for the competent court to decide."

Principle IV, relating to superior orders, is based on article 8 of the Charter of the Nuremberg Tribunal and its judgment. The commission quoted with approval the statement of the court relating to article 8 and included the words "provided a moral choice was in fact possible to him" in the formulation of Principle IV. It did not include that part of article 8 relating to "mitigating punishment" for the reason stated in connection with Principle III.

The General Assembly took no action with respect to this formulation of the Nuremberg Principles, but in Resolution 488(V) of December 12, 1950, it invited comments from member states and requested the International Law Commission to take them into account in preparing the draft code of offenses against the peace and security of mankind (*see* CRIMES AGAINST HUMANITY). Thus the project for the formulation of the Nuremberg Principles was merged with and submerged in the still-ongoing effort of the commission to draft a comprehensive code of offenses against the peace and security of mankind.

BIBLIOGRAPHY

Tutorow, N. E., comp. and ed. *War Crimes, War Criminals, and War Crimes Trials: An Annotated Bibliography and Source Book.* Westport, Conn., 1986.

LEO GROSS

SURVIVORS, PSYCHOLOGY OF. [*This entry consists of four articles. The* General Survey *reviews the aftereffects of Nazi atrocities on survivors.* Survivors of Ghettos and Camps *and* Survivors in Israel *deal with elements in the psychological makeup of survivors, such as guilt and recurring trauma.* Children of Survivors *discusses the impact of the Holocaust on the families of survivors.*]

General Survey

The Holocaust was a trauma for all mankind and a monstrous enigma. To a considerable extent, it destroyed optimistic views of mankind, as well as the myth of civilization and progress in human relationships and in relations among peoples. How the idea of systematically exterminating human beings made its appearance in the twentieth century remains a mystery; all the research conducted so far in psychology, sociology, and psychiatry has given only a partial answer.

Yet paradoxically, the Holocaust, with all its trauma, has also given rise to sparks of hope for the victory of life over death and destruction. This has become evident from research on later effects among survivors in Europe, Israel, and the United States, and from studies on the relationships of survivors with their families, and particularly with their children.

The first concepts of the psychology of survivors were proposed by Paul Friedmann (1947), E. Minkovski (1946), and Leo Eitinger (1964), and are the results of early observations of injured survivors. But it is not possible to comprehend the full impact of the Holocaust by studying only the individual survivor; it is also necessary to observe survivors in relation to their families. In addition, the diverse experiences of survivors both during and after the Holocaust must be taken into account.

Numerous and contrasting opinions have been published about the victims and survivors of the Holocaust, based on the writers' differing cultural backgrounds, personal experiences, intellectual traditions, and scholarly disciplines. Thus, for example, two widely divergent opinions are expressed in the works of Bruno Bettelheim and Terence Des Pres. Bettelheim's approach to human behavior and survival in the concentration camps has influenced and shaped thinking about Holocaust survivors in Nazi-occupied Europe.

Bettelheim's crucial point, as expressed in the chapter "Self-Determination" of his book *The Informed Heart*, is the existence of the ideal of assertion of personal autonomy, which, in his view, he himself attained while imprisoned in the DACHAU concentration camp in 1938. Apparently, Bettelheim felt the need for illusion and a belief that even in the psychotic world of the concentration camps, the individual was left with a certain freedom of action and thought. In contrast to that description of himself, Bettelheim describes other survivors collectively as a regressed, submissive group, whose survival was attained at the cost of inner autonomy, humanity, and self-assertion; their later lives continued to bear the stigma of that psychosocial regression.

Des Pres approaches the survivor from a different discipline. He doubts the relevance of the psychoanalytic theory for understanding the Holocaust and describes the very human quality of the survivors' Holocaust experiences in their most humiliating and sublime aspects. However, he does not make connections to the personal past of the survivor prior to the Holocaust, to his family, or to his personality.

Neither approach allows for the past existence of the survivors and its psychological effect on them, both as individuals and as a group; a past with special, precious sets of values and traditions. The traditional defenses of Jews, transmitted from one generation to another, which remained viable during the Holocaust experience and were later utilized in adapting to life as survivors, are overlooked by both authors.

The Nazi racial ideology and practice of persecution related not only to the individual and the community of the persecuted minority, but also, and mainly, to the specific culture that was a part of each individual. Because the traumatization was both individual and collective, most individuals made great efforts to create a "new family" to replace the nuclear family that had been lost. Small groups of friends acted together during the years of the Holocaust, sharing all basic necessities. The common experiences of the members of such groups, shared stories about the past, fantasies of the future, and joint prayers, as well as poetry and expressions of personal and general human aspirations for hope and love, were methods used by the victims to resist dehumanization and regression, and to find support.

Some of the defenses were traditional. They encompassed black humor or sharp irony directed at the victims themselves and at the aggressor; identification with martyrs of the past; identification with ideologies, religious as well as political, such as those opting for universal socialism; the formation of mutually supportive systems with a special character; and the creation of fantasy. Imagination was an important means of liberation from the frustrating reality, by opening an outlet for the formulation of plans for the distant future, and by spurring to immediate action. Fantasies also made possible a transformation of the self-image from victim to hero. Ignoring these elements impairs one's ability to understand the survivors, as does ignoring the individual survivor's personality and his phase of development at the time of the trauma.

The history of the Jewish survivors, from the beginning of the Nazi occupation until the liquidation of the ghettos, reveals that there were often common features and similar psychophysiological patterns in their responses to the persecutions. The survivors often experienced several phases of psychosocial response, including attempts to actively master the traumatic situation, cohesive affiliative actions with intense emotional links, and, finally, passive compliance with the persecutors. These phases may be understood as trial periods, involving adaptation and the development of special mechanisms to cope with the tensions and dangers of the surrounding horrifying reality of the Holocaust.

It has now become clear that a uniform picture, according to which the Holocaust survivors are depicted as having suffered from a static concentration camp syndrome (as it was described in the first decade after liberation), is not valid. The aim of this research, which was conducted immediately after liberation, was to establish the results of the experiences undergone by the survivors in the light of the concentration camp syndrome, as a recognized psychopathological pattern in survivors. Consequently, clinical and theoretical research focused more on psychopathology than on the question of coping and the development of specific adaptive mechanisms during the Holocaust and after. The descriptions of the survivors' syndrome in the late 1950s and 1960s created a new means of diagnosis in psychology and the behavioral sciences, and has become a model that has since served as a focal concept in examining the results of catastrophic stress situations.

Later research showed that the adaptation and coping mechanisms of the survivors were molded specifically by their childhood experiences, developmental histories, family constellations, and emotional family bonds. From work with survivors, specific questions have been derived related to these differences: What was the duration of the traumatization? During the Holocaust was the victim alone or with family and friends? Was he in a camp or in hiding? Did he use false "Aryan" papers? Was he a witness to mass murder in the ghetto or the camp? What were his support systems—family and friends—and what social bonds did he have? Studies showed that the experiences of those who were able to actively resist the oppressor, whether in the underground or among the partisans, were different in every respect from the experiences of those who were victims in extermination camps.

The integration of the survivors into the society where they settled after the war was made more difficult by the fact that they often aroused ambivalent feelings of fear, avoidance, guilt, pity, and anxiety. Decades after the Holocaust, however, it seems that most survivors managed to rehabilitate their ego capacities and rejoin the paths their lives might have taken prior to the Holocaust. This is particularly true for those who were adolescents or young adults during the Holocaust. These survivors' families developed a life with a highly crystallized structure and a special attitude toward psychobiological continuity, fears of separation, and fear of a prolonged sickness and death. Contacts between the generations were sometimes characterized by intensive interdependency, expressed by overinvolvement, difficulties with separation, demands for socioeconomic achievement, and compliance with external values and internal standards. Research has shown

that psychopathology was not passed from one generation to another; rather, common motifs, mythologies, issues, and sensitivities are transmitted within the families and between the generations of survivors.

The experience of the Holocaust teaches that human beings can undergo extreme traumatic experiences without suffering from a total regression and without losing their ability to rehabilitate their ego strength. In the process of adaptation, the survivors discovered the powers within them, which came to expression during the different phases of their lives after the war, whether in the DISPLACED PERSONS' camps, during their emigration, or in the course of shaping their lives in their new homes.

BIBLIOGRAPHY

Bettelheim, B. *The Informed Heart*. Glencoe, Ill., 1960.

Davidson, S. "Massive Psychic Traumatization and Social Support." *Journal of Psychosomatic Research* 23 (1979): 395–402.

Des Pres, T. *The Survivor: An Anatomy of Life in the Death Camps*. New York, 1976.

Eitinger, L. *Concentration Camp Survivors in Norway and Israel*. London, 1964.

Krystal, H. "Trauma and Effect." *Psychoanalytic Study of the Child* 33 (1978): 81–116.

Krystal, H., ed. *Massive Psychic Trauma*. New York, 1968.

Niederland, W. G. "The Problem of the Survivor." *Journal of the Hillside Hospital* 10 (1961): 233–247.

HILLEL KLEIN

Survivors of Ghettos and Camps

The Jews arrested and brought to concentration camps during World War II were under sentence of death, not only the 80 percent to 90 percent who were murdered immediately after their arrival, but also those who were kept alive to work. Their chances of surviving the war were minimal. Personal qualities, qualifications, and attitudes meant nothing—there was no appeal to higher justice. Even using the most forceful psychic mechanisms of denial and repression, Jewish prisoners could hardly avoid being influenced by this fact, and by their brutal treatment on the part of the camp guards and even by some of their fellow prisoners. The Jews' death rate was higher than that of all other categories of prisoners.

Ghettos and Camps. The months or years already spent in ghettos, with continuous persecution and arbitrary selections, had brought some to a chronic state of insecurity and anxiety and others to apathy and hopelessness, even though passive or active resistance had also occurred. This depressing mental situation was complicated by overcrowding, infectious diseases, lack of facilities for basic hygiene, and continuous starvation—all contributory factors affecting the total state of health.

Evacuation of the ghettos, transport, and entry to the camps were carried out with total disregard for human feelings and family relationships. The extreme brutality used augmented the helplessness and confusion felt by prisoners who were isolated from their loved ones and fearful for their fate.

The fear of death that dominated all Jewish prisoners was very real. It was usually clear that the camp was the last stop in the prisoner's life; the farewells that took place on the train ramps were forever. The sentence of death by labor took somewhat longer for a camp inmate than the gas chamber, but it was equally effective.

Indescribable living conditions, filth and lack of hygiene, innumerable diseases and extreme nutritional insufficiency, continuous harassment and physical ill-treatment, perpetual psychic stress caused by the recurrent macabre deaths—all combined to influence deeply the attitudes and mental health of camp inmates. Yet observations and descriptions by former prisoners, some of whom were physicians and psychologists, differ considerably. Whereas some describe mainly resignation, curtailment of emotional and normal feelings, weakening of social standards, regression to primitive reactions, and, finally, "relapse to the animal state," others observed comradeship, community spirit, a persistent humanity, and extreme altruism—even moral development and religious revelation.

The vast numbers of prisoners—about a million at any one time—of various nationalities and religions in the camps made such differences inevitable. Any attempt to generalize psychological reactions for so large and varied a population without making and evaluating a broad range of individual observations should be treated with caution.

Extreme deprivation of food, over extended periods, itself causes typical changes, the most common being impaired memory, reduced initiative, fatigue, drowsiness, and irritability, succeeded by indifference, dullness, and almost total apathy. The final characteristic phase produced by hunger in the camps was that known as the MUSELMANN state, in which all mental processes were retarded and normal reactions ceased. All these were found in concentration camp inmates.

Liberation and After. When liberation came, most of the Jewish camp inmates were too weak to move or be aware of what was happening. Prisoners were not immediately restored to health by liberation; three weeks later, in BERGEN-BELSEN, the daily death toll was still some two hundred, down from the five hundred deaths taking place per day immediately after the liberation. Only after six weeks could most of the remaining prisoners be considered saved.

Awakening from the nightmare was for many perhaps even more painful than captivity. After the first physical improvement, the ability to feel and think returned and many realized the completeness of their isolation. They could no longer repress what had actually happened, and the reality was agonizing. Studies of survivors living in Israel show that 80 percent to 90 percent had lost most of their closest relatives, and three out of four had lost their entire family. Studies in Norway show that of nearly seven hundred Norwegian-born Jews deported, only eleven survived; six of these were sole survivors of their immediate families, and all had lost at least two close relatives.

These overwhelming personal losses, whose impact is beyond intellectual or emotional comprehension, together with the total disintegration of Jewish communities, necessarily resulted in radical changes in the survivors' feelings about themselves and their surroundings. An extreme sense of insecurity resulted in the need to search for someone, somewhere, who might by a miracle still be alive. Many tried to return to their home-towns to seek out surviving relatives. Of these, 90 percent fled westward again when the search proved hopeless.

The survivors also clung to the hope of finding some family member still alive in the new DISPLACED PERSONS' camps that were now set up. Many of those admitted to these camps had lost all sense of initiative. International organizations such as the UNITED NATIONS RELIEF AND REHABILITATION ADMINISTRATION, the JOINT DISTRIBUTION COMMITTEE, and the International Refugee Organization cared for them and tried to put new meaning into their lives. Their efforts should not be belittled, but in the working of these organizations the individual was of very little consequence. The ex-prisoner, now a "displaced person," was brought before boards set up by different countries, which decided on his or her "worthiness" to be received by that country.

Most of the survivors preferred to be independent of the decisions of others. They were eager to leave the countries that had become places of persecution and destruction and tried to make their way to Palestine, seeing immigration there as the solution to their problems. After the state of Israel was founded, they integrated quickly into the new society. The struggle for the young country, and the tasks of building it up, required the survivors to suppress their own problems. The majority adapted adequately to their changed life, in newly founded families, jobs, and kibbutzim. Many, however, still suffered from chronic anxiety, sleep disturbances, nightmares, emotional instability, and depressive states.

More difficult was the situation of the survivors who went to the United States, Canada, and Australia, some of them with extreme psychological traumatizations. They had to adjust to strange new surroundings, learn a new language, and adapt to new laws, in addition to building new lives.

When the survivors became entitled to compensation from the West German government for damage suffered during Hitler's regime, many were examined intensively by specialists in internal and neurological medicine. In most cases no ill-effects directly attributable to detainment in the camps were found. This was because the repeated selections of Jewish victims for extermination—in

the ghettos, on arrival at the camps, again at the frequent medical examinations, in the sick bays, and at every transfer—meant that all those showing signs of physical disease had already been eliminated and exterminated.

As the Reich neared its end, the camp prisoners—mainly Jewish—were sent on the long, infamous DEATH MARCHES, which took a horrifyin⸗ toll of lives. The weak, sick, or lame were shot on the spot. Those Jews who survived both the camps and the marches, against all the odds, to be examined later by doctors in America or Australia, were an extremely select group. Their main problems were emotional, which the German authorities did not consider as entitling them to restitution.

Many survivors described themselves as incapable of living life to the full, often barely able to perform basic tasks, in an existence without joy. They felt that the war had changed them; they had lost the essential spark of life. (According to Frederick Hocking, an Australian psychiatrist, virtually all those who were in the ghettos and/or concentration camps for more than a few months were characterized by apathy and depression, and could almost invariably be identified among waiting-room patients.) It took many years, following the extreme traumatization, before self-confidence and a sense of personal value returned, and before adjustment to the life of their communities was achieved; then, however, the recovery was often better than might be expected.

Nevertheless, rigorous investigation shows that the extreme traumatization of the camps inflicted deep wounds that have healed very slowly, and that more than forty years later the scars are present. They still hurt and sometimes bleed. For example, there are clear differences between former camp victims and statistically comparable Canadian Jews: the survivors show long-term consequences of the Holocaust in the form of psychological stress, associated with heightened sensitivity to antisemitism and persecution.

The survivors, normal people before the Holocaust, were exposed to situations of extreme stress and to psychic traumatization. Their reactions to such inhuman treatment were "normal"—because not to react to treatment of this previously unheard-of kind would be abnormal.

[*See also* United States Army and Survivors in Germany and Austria.]

BIBLIOGRAPHY

Bergman, M., and M. Jucovy. *Generations of the Holocaust*. New York, 1982.
Dimsdale, J. E., ed. *Survivors, Victims, and Perpetrators: Essays on the Nazi Holocaust*. New York, 1980.
Eitinger, L. *Concentration Camp Survivors in Norway and Israel*. London, 1964.
Holocaust Survivors: Psychological and Social Sequelae. New York, 1980.

LEO SHUA EITINGER

Survivors in Israel

In the first years after the Holocaust, few studies were made in Israel of the psychological effects of Nazi persecution, although the number of Holocaust survivors was proportionally high. As time has passed, however, research has increased significantly. In 1964 a comparison was made between Holocaust survivors now in Israel and non-Jewish Norwegians who returned to Norway after being deported to camps. The results showed that the Jewish survivors suffered more from the total isolation in the camps, from the danger of death, which was greater for the Jews, and from "survivor guilt," than did the Norwegians. The study also showed that most Israeli survivors were suffering from symptoms of the so-called survivor syndrome, but were nevertheless active and efficient, and often held important and responsible jobs and social positions.

Another study, of Israeli Holocaust survivors in kibbutzim (collective settlements), revealed that survivors who could not mourn their losses immediately after the war began mourning and working through their grief when they adjusted to life in the kibbutz. The study also indicated that many Holocaust survivors had a low threshold for emotional stress. This became apparent during stressful situations that reminded them of the Holocaust—notably during the EICHMANN TRIAL, when they had to testify against Nazi criminals, and during the 1973 Yom Kippur War. At such times, they suffered periods of depression and tension.

Surveys made in Israel more than thirty years after World War II did not show significant differences in the extent of psychological damage between people who were in hiding during Nazi occupation and former concentration camp inmates. The only difference found was that the latter experienced more pronounced emotional distress than those who survived the occupation outside the camps.

Research on elderly Holocaust survivors in Israel indicated that they encountered particular difficulties of absorption because of the serious problems they had to overcome (loss of family and of the social and cultural background they had known before the Holocaust). The community in Israel tried to provide them with personal and professional care. Nevertheless, for survivors who immigrated to Israel when elderly it was more difficult to adjust than for the younger survivors.

A controlled study carried out in a university psychiatric hospital in Jerusalem forty years after liberation revealed a difference between hospitalized depressive patients who had been inmates of Nazi concentration camps and a matched group of patients who had not been persecuted. The concentration camp survivors were more belligerent, demanding, and regressive than the control group, and this behavior may, in fact, have helped them in their survival. In a survey made in an outpatient clinic for the elderly at the same hospital, it was found that between 1983 and 1986, 25 percent of the new admissions were Holocaust survivors.

Despite the many difficulties faced by survivors in Israel, their general adjustment has been satisfactory, both vocationally and socially. For the most part, it has been more successful than that of Holocaust survivors in other countries.

BIBLIOGRAPHY

Eitinger, L. *Concentration Camp Survivors in Norway and Israel*. London, 1964.
Klein, H., and S. Reinharz. "Adaptation in the Kibbutz of Holocaust Survivors and Their Families." In *Mental Health and Rapid Social Change*, edited by L. Miller. Jerusalem, 1972.

Lifton, R. J. "The Concept of the Survivor." In *Survivors, Victims, and Perpetrators: Essays on the Nazi Holocaust*, edited by J. E. Dimsdale, pp. 106–125. New York, 1980.

Nathan, T., L. Eitinger, and H. Z. Winnik. "A Psychiatric Study of Survivors of the Nazi Holocaust: A Study in Hospitalized Patients." *Israel Annals of Psychiatry* 2/1 (1964): 47–80.

Winnik, H. Z. "Psychiatric Disturbances of Holocaust ('Shoa') Survivors." *Israel Annals of Psychiatry* 5/1 (1967): 91–100.

SHALOM ROBINSON

Children of Survivors

Most of the available information about psychological problems among survivors' children born after the Holocaust consists of clinical reports by members of the helping professions, who encountered the latter in their practice and came to realize that these patients bore a legacy of the Holocaust in their psychological makeup. Even before such awareness of the impact of the Holocaust on the second generation developed, children of survivors may have approached professionals, who were unaware of the link between these patients' problems and the Holocaust experience of their parents.

The Second Generation. Much of the published research on the second generation's problems consists of in-depth studies of individual cases. Some of the literature, however, focuses on the whole family, and there are also surveys of entire clinical series of Holocaust survivor families. Canadian researchers, including Axel Russell and John Sigal, who had gained long experience in family therapy, have applied that experience to the study of the problems of survivor families. In other countries, too—the United States, Israel, the Netherlands, France, and even Eastern Europe—there has been a growing interest in the psychosocial problems of the second generation, as documented in a survey of research done worldwide on the subject, conducted by Tikva Nathan in 1981. This study discloses that some children of survivors suffer from psychological problems, which have their roots in the atmosphere of anxiety, bereavement, and loss prevailing in their homes.

Contrary to the almost uniform pattern of reactions among the parents, in the first generation of survivors, one finds a relatively large variety of psychological phenomena among members of the second generation. These include problems of communication with the parents and problems of adaptation to the social environment. The latter express themselves in a paucity of social contacts; loneliness or strong dependency needs; a search for affection; difficulties in impulse control; and outbursts of aggression. Some of these young people suffer from neurotic disorders such as nightmares, bed-wetting, anxiety, tension, examination phobias, and low tolerance for frustration or failure. In the area of learning ability, some researchers detected a tendency toward overachievement, while others found just the opposite.

Not all of these investigations have been controlled, but the validity of the clinical findings is supported by the fact that most were conducted independently, in places far removed from one another, and with no contact between the respective research teams. Yet most of their findings are in agreement, especially with regard to the child-parent relationship in the survivor family and the family dynamics, which are characterized by fear of separation, overprotectiveness, ongoing bereavement reactions, and mutual guilt feelings in both parents and children.

The findings are also confirmed by the fact that they are largely in agreement with the descriptions that members of the second generation give of themselves, especially when they have themselves become professionals in the field. Their experiences have been documented in academic journals, in news reports, at conferences, and even in works of art.

It must be borne in mind, however, that these findings are based on research conducted in clinical settings, in patient populations, and are not applicable to the general population of survivors' children. Only a few studies have been carried out on the psychological and social adjustment of the latter group. These also include surveys of the second generation's attitudes toward the Holocaust legacy in their family, and toward their parents. Some of these studies confirm the existing clinical data on the learning achievement and even overachievement among the offspring of Holocaust survivors. Opinions diverge, however, on the subject of attitudes. Surveys conducted outside of Israel report the existence of feelings of shame and embarrassment experienced by the second generation with regard to their survivor parents, whereas among the children of Holocaust survivors growing up in Israel, only empathy and identification with their parents were demonstrated. However, the few studies that have been made within the general population of second-generation members have not definitively confirmed the earlier clinical findings (Leon et al., 1981; Sigal and Weinfeld, 1985).

The information revealed by the research shows that the relationship between survivor parents and their children bears distinctive characteristics stemming from the Holocaust experience and contains unique psychodynamic phenomena; but there is no evidence of the existence of a psychopathological syndrome, or of pathological patterns of adjustment. On the contrary, a study conducted by Tikva Nathan in 1988 among secondary school students in Israel shows that the offspring of Holocaust survivors are just as healthy mentally as their peers in school, and that they are successfully coping both in school and in social performance. This new evidence indicates that in spite of their individual vulnerabilities, such children even manifest a certain resilience to stressful life events. Thus, the Holocaust legacy may act not only as a risk factor but also as a source of strength and immunity for the children of survivors.

Parent-Child Relations in Survivor Families. The increasing awareness of the problems of Holocaust survivors as parents has found expression in numerous psychological investigations conducted since the 1960s.

The function of parenthood lends itself particularly well to demonstrating the level of integration of the adult personality necessary for mature adjustment. In survivors who were juvenile victims of the Holocaust, such maturation processes may have been affected more than in others, as shown by Keilson (1979) and Kestenberg (1972). Some younger survivors have been reported to be more anxious, while the older ones tend to be more depressed, preoccupied, and irritable. In certain cases the crucial problems of the survivor are revealed more by parenthood than by any other aspect of functioning. Since the parent-child relationship is a most intimate and sensitive channel of expression, it has proved to be an area of focus for detecting the depth of the impact of the Holocaust experience.

There is a fair degree of accord among investigators throughout the world as to the typical patterns of parent-child relations in survivor families, which are often characterized by anxiety, depression, prolonged mourning, and guilt feelings. Overprotection and separation difficulties have been typically observed. Other common manifestations are related to excessive parental expectations of achievement and of solace. It is often difficult for the children to comply with these demands. The sense of obligation they may develop toward their parents, along with feelings of guilt at not being able to oblige at all times, may alternate with outbursts of aggression and sorrow.

The children sometimes have to fulfill the difficult role of compensating their parents for all the losses and suffering sustained by the latter in the past. This special position of a child in survivor families has been noted by John J. Sigal, who calls such a child "the princeling," and by Tikva Nathan, who uses the term "the precious child." In the words of Judith S. Kestenberg, the birth of a child to a survivor constitutes "the undoing of genocide."

BIBLIOGRAPHY

Bergman, M. S., and M. Jucovy. *Generations of the Holocaust.* New York, 1982.

Keilson, H. *Sequentielle Traumatisierung bei Kindern.* Stuttgart, 1979.

Kestenberg, J. S. "Psychoanalytic Contributions to the Problem of Children of Survivors from Nazi Persecution." *Israel Annals of Psychiatry* 10/4 (1972): 311–325.

Leon, G., et al. "Survivors of the Holocaust and Their Children: Current Status and Adjustment." *Journal of Personality and Social Psychology* 41/3 (1981): 503–516.

Nathan, T. "The Second Generation of Holocaust Survivors in Psychosocial Research." *Studies on the Holocaust Period* 2 (1981): 13–26. (In Hebrew.)

Russell, A. "Late Effects: Influence on the Children of the Concentration Camp Survivors." In *Survivors, Victims, and Perpetrators: Essays on the Nazi Holocaust*, edited by J. E. Dimsdale, pp. 125–204. New York, 1980.

Sigal, J. J., and M. Weinfeld. "Control of Aggression in Adult Children of Survivors of the Nazi Persecution." *Journal of Abnormal Psychology* 94/4 (1985): 556–564.

TIKVA S. NATHAN

SURVIVORS, SECOND GENERATION OF.

Beginning in the 1980s, young adults whose parents survived Nazi persecution have come to realize a collective identity. Despite their heterogeneity as a sociological group, they share the common bond of a shattered family heritage. Those born after the 1945 liberation have diverse religious backgrounds, political attitudes, and socioeconomic and educational levels. Although the circumstances of their parents' survival varied, the parents all suffered immeasurable loss of community, family, and identity. Whether survivors talked about their dehumanization and grief or remained silent, these factors were nevertheless reflected in the socialization of their children.

The emergence of a second-generation consciousness, and the resulting development of an identifiable group, has its origin in the "roots" movement in the United States during the mid-1970s and in the more manifest antisemitism in Europe during the early and mid-1980s.

It was at the time of the social, religious, and political activism in the late 1960s and early 1970s that a number of Jewish graduate students in the United States began exploring what it meant to be children of survivors. They shared with one another their relationships with their parents, their world view as children of survivors, and the ways in which their perceptions differed from those of their American Jewish peers. These early discussions appeared in the Jewish periodical *Response*, a forum for alternative Jewish views. They inspired the psychiatric social worker Bella Savran and the writer Eva Fogelman to develop awareness groups for the children of Holocaust survivors. Independently, members of the Warsaw Ghetto Resistance Organization in the United States persuaded their children to meet and form a second-generation organization. Mental-health professionals in New York organized the Group for the Psychoanalytic Study of the Effects on the Second Generation. These heretofore small and invisible group efforts received national visibility in Helen Epstein's *New York Times Magazine* article "Heirs to the Holocaust" (June 19, 1977).

Several grass-roots efforts have helped children of survivors to meet one another, thereby reducing their sense of isolation and giving them a stronger voice in carrying out their political, educational, psychological, commemorative, and creative goals. Later events include the First Conference on Children of Holocaust Survivors, held in November 1979 under the auspices of Zachor, the Holocaust Resource Center of the National Jewish Center for Learning and Leadership. More than six hundred children of survivors attended, and the conference resulted in the formation of groups throughout the United States. Hundreds joined their parents in Jerusalem in 1981 at the World Gathering of Holocaust Survivors and took a pledge to commemorate, educate, and work toward preventing future genocides. The International Network for Children of Survivors was founded for the purpose of realizing these goals. Since 1981 second-generation members have joined survivors at several gatherings and have held a number of international conferences.

Members of the second generation have contributed to historical research on the destroyed Jewish life of prewar Europe and on the Holocaust itself; to the revival of Yiddish music, literature, and theater; to educating the post-Holocaust generations; to examining the impact of the Holocaust on survivors and their families by conducting sociopsychological research and by creating films, art, theater, fiction, and poetry; in political action, as by prosecuting Nazis, fighting for human rights, lobbying for Holocaust curricula in high schools, and aiding oppressed Jews in the Soviet Union, Ethiopia, and the Arab countries; and to fighting racism, persecution, antisemitism, and Holocaust revisionism.

Second-generation identity and activity have also emerged in Europe and Israel. In Europe, however, the lack of communal strength has impeded the progression from denial to open expression of feelings.

While some elements of survivor family dynamics transcend national borders, growing up in different countries yields different effects. Those who lived in Israel usually did not feel isolated and alienated from their peers, as did many children of survivors in Europe and in the United States. Thus, Israeli children of survivors do not necessarily experience the same Jewish identity conflicts as those who live in the diaspora. For Israeli children of survivors, identification with the suffering and losses of their parents may distance them from their society, while in the United States and Europe it may facilitate reducing isolation and improving self-esteem.

In freeing many survivors from an inability to explore their memories, the second generation has itself been freed to identify with its parents and with the destruction of European Jewry. It is now able to channel this identification into activity and programming that is societally constructive and that perpetuates Jewish continuity.

[*See also* Survivors, Psychology of.]

BIBLIOGRAPHY

Epstein, H. *Children of the Holocaust: Conversations with the Sons and Daughters of Survivors.* New York, 1980.

Steinitz, L., and D. Szonyi, eds. *Living after the Holocaust.* New York, 1976.

EVA FOGELMAN

SUTZKEVER, ABRAHAM (b. 1913), Yiddish poet and partisan fighter. Sutzkever was born in Smorgon, Belorussia. During World War I his family fled to Siberia, and in 1922 settled in VILNA, where Sutzkever attended school. In 1930 he joined the Yiddishist scout movement Bin. He wrote poetry from the age of fourteen, but it was not until 1934 that a poem of his appeared in print, in a literary magazine. In the period from 1934 to 1941 Sutzkever's poetic work grew into a unique contribution to Yiddish literature. Beginning in 1935 he was a regular contributor to *Yung-Vilne*, the organ of the modernist writers in Vilna, and to major literary journals in Warsaw and in the United States. Two volumes of poetry that he published before the Holocaust contain the poems he wrote before 1939. From June 1941 to September 1943, Sutzkever lived under the Nazi occupation in Vilna and in the Vilna ghetto. On September 12 of that year he escaped to the forest, together with his wife and Shmaryahu KACZERGINSKI, and joined the partisans.

Under the Nazi occupation Sutzkever composed over eighty poems. A substantial number of the manuscripts of these poems, or copies of them, were saved by the poet himself. It was only many years later, however, that he published, on the basis of these manuscripts, a small collection of poems from the time he spent in the Vilna ghetto and in the forest, in *Di Ershte Nacht in Geto* (The First Night in the Ghetto; Tel Aviv, 1979).

Sutzkever's ghetto poems are often written around events that he himself experienced. His life in the ghetto and the poetry he wrote there were linked to the cultural and communal life of the ghetto: some poems, for example, were devoted to theatrical performances in the ghetto; others were read in public, as a poem on the opening of an exhibition on May 1, 1943, or a eulogy for a ghetto teacher.

Sutzkever aided in selecting the material to be presented in the ghetto theater and conducted a literary youth circle in the Yugent Klub (Youth Club). While on forced labor, he had to sort for the Germans the collections of books and manuscripts in the library of the Yiddish Institute (YIVO), which was outside the ghetto. Together with Kaczerginski and others, he used the opportunity to acquire weapons and smuggle them into the ghetto. He also smuggled books, manuscripts, and works of art into the ghetto. During the time that he spent in the YIVO building he composed many of his poems, which he then read to this friends in the ghetto and to the members of the Writers' Association that had been formed there. For the dramatic chronicle *Dos Kever-Kind* (Child of the Tomb), which he read to the Writers' Association in May 1942, Sutzkever in July was awarded that year's literary prize. *Kol Nidre*, the great poem that he wrote in February 1943, is the only literary creation to describe a German *Aktion* (the liquidation of Vilna's "small ghetto" on Yom Kippur, the Day of Atonement, October 1, 1941). The dates on the manuscripts of the poems reveal that as the end of the ghetto approached Sutzkever wrote at an increasingly rapid pace. On September 12, 1943, he left the Vilna ghetto clandestinely, with a group of partisans. While serving with the Voroshilov Brigade in the Naroch Forest, Sutzkever also recorded testimonies on the crimes committed by the Nazis and on the struggle with the Nazis, and he kept a record of the partisan movement's history in the area.

On March 12, 1944, Sutzkever was flown from the Naroch Forest to Moscow. He stayed in the Soviet Union until his appearance as a witness for the Soviet prosecution in the NUREMBERG TRIAL, in February 1946. (His appearance was the result of the JEWISH ANTIFASCIST COMMITTEE's intervention with the chairman of the Lithuanian Supreme Soviet.) In 1947, Sutzkever settled in Israel. He continued to write poetry and prose, and became the editor of *Di Goldene Keyt* (The Golden Chain), a Yiddish literary and cultural quarterly that was founded in 1949.

Since 1947, the Holocaust and Israel have been the themes of Sutzkever's literary creations. English translations of some of his poems are in *Burnt Pearls: Ghetto Poems of Abraham Sutzkever* (Oakville, Ontario, 1981) and "Green Aquarium," in *Prooftexts: A Journal of Jewish Literary History* 2/1 (January 1982), pp. 95–121.

BIBLIOGRAPHY

Roskies, D. G. "The Burden of Memory." In *Against the Apocalypse: Responses to Catastrophe in Modern Jewish Culture*, pp. 225–257. Cambridge, Mass., 1984.
Wisse, R. R. "The Ghetto Poems of Abraham Sutzkever." *Jewish Book Annual* 36 (1978–1979): 26–36.

YEHIEL SZEINTUCH

SWEDEN. A handful of Jews were living in Sweden in the seventeenth century, but only in 1718 was official permission given for Jews to settle there. They were restricted at first to provincial towns and only later allowed to live in the large cities. During the course of the nineteenth century, restrictions on the Jews were abolished. In 1930 seven thousand Jews lived in Sweden, over half of them in the capital, Stockholm, and the rest mainly in Göteborg and Malmö.

Neutrality. Sweden pursued a policy of political neutrality from the mid-nineteenth century onward. It remained neutral during World War I and wanted to maintain a strictly neutral position during World War II. Guided by Prime Minister Per Albin Hansson, Sweden did manage to prevent itself from being dragged into the war. Under the impact of the war's changing events, however, there were changes in the tone of this neutrality that provide part of the background for understanding Swedish attitudes toward aid to Jews.

During the first years of the war, Swedish neutrality was tipped in the direction of Germany. Following the outbreak of the Winter War between the Soviet Union and FINLAND

SWEDEN

(1939–1940), and the German invasions of NORWAY and DENMARK in April 1940, Sweden was virtually surrounded by the Germans. The ensuing British sea blockade caused the circle around Sweden to tighten further. As a result, Sweden had to rely on Germany for imports of coal, coke, steel products, chemical products, and heavy and light machinery, while providing Germany with iron ore, indispensable for its war industry.

Thus, throughout 1940 Sweden allowed the Germans to use its railways and coastal waters to transport men and war matériel to Norway and later to Finland. In return, Germany did not attempt to directly influence Swedish policies. By the spring of 1941 Germany allowed less and less latitude to Sweden, primarily because of the planned invasion of the Soviet Union. With the outbreak of this new phase of the war, Sweden submitted to additional German demands regarding the transport of men and goods through Sweden to Finland, a German ally.

The defeats suffered by the Germans in North Africa at the end of 1942 and at Stalingrad in the winter of 1942–1943 enabled Sweden to take a harder line toward Germany and evince a more favorable policy toward the western Allies. In May 1943, Sweden succeeded in reestablishing trade relations with the Allies. On July 29 of that year, the Swedes declared that Germany could no longer transfer soldiers or war matériel across Sweden. The Germans, now interested in keeping Sweden from joining the Allies, acceded to this demand. By 1944 Swedish policy favored the Allies, without, however, interrupting the trade with Germany.

Aid and Rescue. During the refugee crisis in the 1930s, Sweden did not freely open its gates to those fleeing Nazism. When the pressure of refugees trying to enter Sweden mounted, the authorities reacted by further limiting immigration through a law that went into effect on January 1, 1938. The increased pressure from Jewish refugees and from student protests and demonstrations after both the ANSCHLUSS and KRISTALLNACHT did not substantially alter the Swedish position, which was entrenched because of fear of competition from refugees who practiced the free professions (medicine, the law, engineer-

ing, and so on). The only time the policy was waived was when 500 Jewish children from Germany were allowed to enter Sweden without their parents. This concession resulted from the urging of Swedish women's organizations. When the Reich authorities began to mark Jewish passports with a capital *J* in the fall of 1938, the Swedish authorities used this mark to discriminate against potential Jewish immigrants. In Sweden, as in most European countries, a distinction was made between political refugees and "others"—the others, for all practical purposes, being Jews. Political refugees encountered few problems in obtaining residence permits for Sweden, whereas in the case of Jews, the Swedish authorities preferred giving them transit visas only. Moreover, Jews who arrived in Sweden from Germany without a visa were turned back and forced to return to Germany. The data in Table 1 show the number of Jews among "foreign" (non-Scandinavian) refugees in Sweden between 1939 and 1943 (from figures published by the Swedish authorities); in the spring of 1944, the number of Jews who found refuge in Sweden was estimated at 12,000.

The Jews of Sweden began to extend help to Jewish refugees during the refugee crisis of the 1930s, and they established several refugee relief committees, some in cooperation with non-Jews. During the Hitler period, Swedish immigration policies presented a very serious problem for Swedish Jewry, especially the Stockholm community. Thousands of Jewish refugees applied for permission to immigrate or for temporary residence pending their emigration to another destination. Decisions on these applications were made by the Ministry of Justice and the Ministry of Social Affairs (during the war this authority was transferred to the Foreign Ministry). It was to these ministries that the Stockholm Jewish community submitted the applications for entry into Sweden. Most of them were turned down, and in many instances the Jewish community did not even submit them, knowing in advance that they would not be approved.

Owing largely to traditionally strong ties among the Scandinavian nations, Sweden tried to help its neighbors, within the confines of its neutrality. Accordingly, tens of

TABLE 1. *Jewish Refugees in Sweden between 1939 and 1943*

Date	Jewish Refugees	Political Refugees	Jews among Politicals	Total Registered Refugees	Total Actual Refugees (Estimated)
July 1, 1939	3,063	518	?	3,581	4,300–4,800
January 1, 1940	2,831	885	?	3,716	4,200
July 1, 1940	2,731	723	?	3,454	4,200
January 1, 1941	3,034	1,012	165	4,046	
July 1, 1941	2,826	964	152	3,790	
January 1, 1942	2,618	915	150	3,533	
January 1, 1943	2,946	828	138	3,289	
July 1, 1943	3,287	1,073	111	4,360	

thousands of Norwegians and Finns, among them twenty thousand Finnish children, were taken in by Swedish families. While the Nazi deportations from Norway were under way in the early winter of 1942, nine hundred Norwegian Jews (over half of the Jewish community) managed to escape to Sweden, where they were given refuge. At this time the Swedish Foreign Ministry also broadly applied a regulation that entitled the relatives of Swedish nationals to Swedish nationality. On this basis, many Swedish Jews applied to the ministry on behalf of their relatives in Norway, Denmark, and occasionally other European countries. Because of the determination displayed by the Swedish consul in Oslo, Claes Adolf Hjalmar Westring, in February 1943 about fifty Norwegian Jews were able to leave for Sweden with an official permit. Few Jews from other countries, however, benefited from this regulation.

In the spring of 1943, the Jewish Agency tried to convince Sweden to do more to rescue Jews. With the agreement of the British Foreign Office, Salomon Adler-Rudel of the Central British Fund was sent from London to Stockholm for this purpose. He proposed that the Swedish government approach the Germans with a plan to bring twenty thousand Jewish children from German-occupied countries to Sweden. The Swedish government agreed in principle, but it never presented the proposal to the Germans because of the deterioration in their relations in the summer of 1943.

That fall, when the Germans were about to deport the Jews of Denmark, Georg DUCKWITZ, a member of the German legation in Copenhagen, met in Stockholm with Swedish Prime Minister Hansson to solicit Swedish help in saving the Danish Jews. As a result the Swedish minister in Berlin, Arvid Richert, submitted a proposal to the Germans that called for the placement of Danish Jews in camps in Sweden. The Germans never responded to the suggestion, and the Swedish government reacted by publicly announcing its readiness to accept all Danish Jewish refugees. This announcement served as a kind of official authorization for the rescue effort launched by the Danes in which nearly eight thousand Jews were saved and brought to Sweden. The Swedish Jewish community also played a significant role in this rescue. Several Jewish leaders cooperated with the Danish underground, among them Ivar Philipson, a Jewish lawyer, who acted as liaison between the Danish underground and the Swedish authorities. Following this successful rescue operation, some nine thousand Danish Christians also reached Sweden, as did about one hundred Finnish Jews who the Finnish government thought were in particular danger.

With the change in Sweden's political situation and the creation in the United States of the WAR REFUGEE BOARD, which pressured neutral nations to do more to help Jews in Nazi-dominated lands, the Swedish government took decisive measures to help rescue the Jews of HUNGARY, whose deportation began in May 1944. At the end of June, King Gustav V of Sweden sent a firm message to the Hungarian regent, Miklós HORTHY, deploring the deportation of Hungarian Jewry. This note, along with earlier protests by the

The Red Cross repatriates Polish concentration camp prisoners via Sweden in 1945. [CICR Archives]

British and American governments, contributed to Horthy's decision to end the deportations in July.

In the meantime, the best-known Swedish rescue effort was getting under way. Resulting from a joint initiative by the War Refugee Board representative in Stockholm, Iver Olsen, and local members of the WORLD JEWISH CONGRESS, Raoul WALLENBERG was assigned as an attaché to the Swedish legation in Budapest. His task was to rescue Jews. Wallenberg's efforts—along with those of other members of the Swedish legation (Per Anger, Lars Berg, Göte Carlsson, and the foreign minister, Ivar Danielsson), Swedish Red Cross members (Asta Nilsson and Valdemar Langlet), other neutral diplomats in Budapest, and local Jews—contributed to the rescue of tens of thousands of Hungarian Jews from deportations and from the hands of the rampaging ARROW CROSS PARTY men.

As the war drew to an end, the Swedes launched an operation for the rescue of Scandinavian nationals, primarily Norwegians and Danes, who were imprisoned in concentration camps in the Reich. They succeeded in having these prisoners handed over to the Swedish Red Cross. The initiative and organization for this operation, however, were largely the work of Norwegians and Danes. Among those rescued were several hundred Danish Jews who had been interned in THERESIENSTADT. At the same time, Swedish members of the World Jewish Congress engaged in a special rescue operation. Under the leadership of the chairman of the Swedish branch of the congress, Hillel Storch (himself a refugee from Latvia), food parcels were sent to Jews in concentration camps. With the help of the War Refugee Board, a large storehouse for the parcels was set up in Göteborg. From there, through the Swedish Red Cross, the food was sent out, mostly to BERGEN-BELSEN. The Germans, however, distributed only a small portion of the consignments, storing the bulk of the food in the camp, where it was discovered by liberating British forces.

In 1945, Felix Kersten, the Finnish masseur who had helped Heinrich HIMMLER overcome severe stomach pains, was in Sweden. Kersten served as liaison between the World Jewish Congress and Himmler, who made some efforts toward the end of the war to alleviate the situation of the Jews. His aim in doing this was to gain the trust of the Allies

Count Folke Bernadotte (right), vice president of the Swedish Red Cross, supervising the transfer to Sweden of survivors of the Ravensbrück camp in April 1945.

and make it possible for him to save Germany from total defeat. With this purpose in mind, Himmler agreed to meet with a representative of the congress to discuss the release of Jews still in Nazi camps. Through preliminary negotiations with Kersten, a meeting between Himmler and Norbert Mazor of the World Jewish Congress took place on April 21, 1945, at Kersten's estate near Berlin. The next day, Himmler met Count Folke BERNADOTTE of the Swedish Red Cross and an agreement was made to transfer the remaining women in the RAVENSBRÜCK camp to Sweden. Among the fourteen thousand women who were saved in this manner were at least two thousand Jews.

When the war ended, the Swedes took in thousands of survivors of the Nazi camps and did everything possible to rehabilitate them. To help fund this work, the Jewish community in Sweden had already levied a tax on its members before the end of the war. The community founded fifteen special schools for the refugees, and in 1946 more than seven hundred refugees were enrolled in them. Money stemming from the JOINT DISTRIBUTION COMMITTEE, the Swedish government,

and (later) the Conference on Jewish Material Claims was also addressed to refugee aid. By the late 1950s, about half of the Jewish refugees had become integrated into the Swedish Jewish community. The rest of them emigrated, mainly to the United States, Canada, and Israel.

BIBLIOGRAPHY

Adler-Rudel, S. "A Chronicle of Rescue Efforts." *Leo Baeck Institute Year Book* 11 (1966): 213–241.

Bernadotte, F. *The Fall of the Curtain.* London, 1945.

Carlgren, W. M. *Swedish Foreign Policy during the Second World War.* London, 1977.

Lindberg, H. *Svensk flyktingspolitik under internationelt tryck, 1936–1941.* Stockholm, 1973.

Valentin, H. "Rescue and Relief Activities in Behalf of Jewish Victims of Nazism in Scandinavia." *YIVO Annual* 8 (1953): 224–251.

Yahil, L. "Raoul Wallenberg: His Mission and His Activities in Hungary." *Yad Vashem Studies* 15 (1983): 7–53.

Yahil, L. "Scandinavian Countries to the Rescue of Concentration Camp Prisoners." *Yad Vashem Studies* 6 (1967): 181–220.

LENI YAHIL

SWISS AID SOCIETY FOR JEWISH REFU-GEES. *See* Switzerland.

SWITZERLAND. Jews settled in Switzerland in the Middle Ages and have been living there ever since. Their emancipation process was lengthy; it began in 1798 and was not completed until 1874. On the eve of World War II, Switzerland's Jewish population numbered 18,000 (0.4 percent of the total). The Jewish communities are organized into the Federation of Swiss Jewish Communities (Schweizerischer Israelitischer Gemeindebund; in French, the Fédération Suisse des Communautés Israélites).

In 1933 that organization took legal steps against two Nazis for distributing the PROTOCOLS OF THE ELDERS OF ZION in Switzerland; one of the witnesses in the trial was Chaim WEIZMANN. The trial had little practical effect, but it attracted much attention. In 1936 a Jewish student, David FRANKFURTER, assassinated a Swiss Nazi party member, Wilhelm GUSTLOFF. Frankfurter was sentenced to prison, but after the war he was pardoned.

Since the time of the Congress of Vienna (1814–1815), Switzerland has been recognized as a permanently neutral country, and the Swiss have always carefully avoided being involved in any confrontation with other states. At the same time, however, Switzerland has had a long tradition of offering asylum to persons being persecuted in their own countries for their political views or their actions against the existing regime.

From the moment the Nazis came to power in Germany in January 1933, Switzerland was confronted with thousands of Jews seeking refuge. In determining its policy on the refugee problem, the Swiss federal council (Bundesrat) felt that it had to take into account the political, military, economic, and social effects of an influx of refugees. The government decided to differentiate among several categories of refugees: (1) political refugees, who were granted asylum, as had always been the practice; (2) immigrants, who were granted temporary residence for a limited period, on the assumption that they would proceed from Switzerland to their ultimate destination elsewhere; and (3) refugees who were put under special surveillance and whom the government tried to force to leave the country at the earliest possible moment. During the war, non-Jewish refugees too flocked to Switzerland from all the occupied countries, from the Netherlands in the north to Italy in the south, as well as military personnel belonging to the Allied armies. A total of 300,000 foreigners passed through Switzerland during the Nazi period (1933–1945), and 30,000 of them were Jews.

The situation of the Jewish refugees and the conditions under which they lived in Switzerland were affected by the changes that took place in Germany and Austria and, during the war, by the vicissitudes of the battlefronts. In the early years of the Nazi regime several thousand Jews went to Switzerland. For the most part, they were able to take care of themselves and eventually also to leave for other destinations. Following the annexation of Austria to Germany in March 1938 (*see* ANSCHLUSS), the situation altered. Thousands of Jews, in headlong flight, tried to enter Switzerland. The Swiss authorities and the country's population were far from welcoming them; they were, in fact, totally opposed to the idea of allowing a great stream of refugees to enter the country. Switzerland did not want to be identified with the refugee problem—so much so that it refused to host the conference that President Franklin D. ROOSEVELT called in the summer of 1938 to discuss the issue. The representatives of the thirty-two countries that took part in the EVIAN CONFERENCE had to meet on the French shore of the Lake of Geneva, in the French resort town of Evian-les-Bains.

Of special significance was the initiative undertaken by the Swiss authorities, as directed by Chief of Police Heinrich Rothmund, to distinguish the passports of German and Austrian Jews with a special mark so that they could not enter Switzerland as German tourists (the latter did not require a visa). In the fall of 1938 Switzerland and Germany reached an agreement on this issue, and on October 5 of that year the Reich Ministry of the Interior published a decree ordering every Jew of German or Austrian nationality to hand in his passport so that it could be stamped with a capital *J* (for *Jude*, or "Jew") in red. It was therefore as a result of a Swiss initiative that the Nazis introduced this discriminatory practice, which they applied to all the Jews of Germany, and which also enabled other countries to single out Jews among those seeking entry and bar them from entering. After the war broke out, further restrictions were imposed on immigration into Switzerland.

During the war Switzerland, like other neutral countries, sought to remain strictly neutral and to avoid offending Germany, on which its economy depended. While the government tried to restrain the Nazi propagandists active in the country, antisemitism did grow to some extent. At the same time, Swiss churches and other circles called on the government to abide by the traditional Swiss policy of offering refuge to the persecuted. As early as October 1939, however, the Swiss authorities imposed new restrictions on the entry of foreigners, especially Jews, into the country. Conditions for residence in Switzerland were tightened, in particular for refugees, and the police were empowered to expel

anyone who did not follow their orders. A further deterioration took place in 1940, in the wake of the German conquests in northern and western Europe. The refugees in Switzerland were put into camps, and in 1942 several dozen refugees were sent to labor camps in order "to contribute their share of the effort necessitated by the war." The entry of refugees from France was banned altogether, and persons caught trying to sneak in were expelled on the spot.

In 1941 the Swiss authorities were relatively lenient with regard to refugees from the Netherlands and Belgium, a policy from which several hundred Jews also benefited. After the German occupation of southern France, however, in November 1942, entry regulations were once again made more stringent. Except for a few special categories—unaccompanied children under sixteen, pregnant women, the ill, and the elderly (those over sixty-five)—anyone caught trying to enter Switzerland illegally was

A camp in Switzerland for Jewish refugees from Germany (1940). It was established, funded, and operated by the Joint Distribution Committee. [JDC Archives, New York]

Three hundred women prisoners from the Ravensbrück concentration camp were evacuated by the Red Cross and brought to the Swiss town of Kreuzlingen on April 9, 1945. There they were billeted in a school gymnasium whose floor had been covered with straw. [CICR Archives]

turned back and abandoned to his fate at the hands of the Nazis. Still, several thousand persons did succeed in making a "black" (illegal) entry, especially in 1943. A new problem arose when the Germans occupied central and northern Italy in September 1943. The twenty thousand Italians who crossed the Swiss border (ten thousand of them partisans) included several thousand Jews.

Altogether, tens of thousands of refugees entered Switzerland between 1940 and 1945; in February 1945 their number stood at 115,000, about half of them military personnel. In addition to those Jewish refugees entering on an individual basis, some came in special transports: in 1944, 1,684 Hungarian Jews arrived from BERGEN-BELSEN, and in 1945, 1,200 Jews came from THERESIENSTADT. These releases were the result of negotiations with Heinrich HIMMLER's representatives that took place in the final stage of the war; included among them were Hungarian Jews who were set free and transferred to Bergen-Belsen in the "Kasztner train" (*see* KASZTNER, REZSŐ).

Like the Jewish communities in other coun-

tries, the Jews of Switzerland rallied to help the refugees. Jewish aid committees joined in an umbrella organization, the Schweizerischer Hilfsverein für Jüdische Flüchtlinge (Swiss Aid Society for Jewish Refugees), which looked after the refugees' accommodation and board, tried to find them employment, arranged retraining courses, and provided financial help. The large sums required for this effort were provided by contributions from campaigns held for this purpose, as well as by the JOINT DISTRIBUTION COMMITTEE and HICEM. The central government and the Swiss cantons contributed only a relatively small share of the total expenditures, which amounted to over 16 million Swiss francs.

In World War II Switzerland, as the base of many representatives of international organizations, was a center of information from Germany, German-occupied Europe, and the satellite states. The major international Jewish organizations as well set up branches in Geneva. Jewish groups and individuals (some of the latter were themselves refugees), the He-Haluts office, and the YOUTH MOVEMENTS all helped in caring for the refugees, especially the young. The Jewish centers in

Switzerland gathered information on the fate of the Jews in the Nazi-ruled and Nazi-influenced countries. Reports on the mass extermination of Jews reached Switzerland first, and from there were passed on to the free countries in the West. In August 1942 Gerhart Riegner, the WORLD JEWISH CONGRESS representative in Geneva, received a report on the planned extermination of the European Jews by means of poison gas, among other methods. (In actuality, gassings in GAS VANS had been taking place since September 1941.) He immediately transmitted this information to the West, through the British consul in Geneva. In the West, however, the report met with disbelief (*see* RIEGNER CABLE). From Geneva efforts were also made to provide aid to Jews under Nazi domination and to rescue Jews by assuring them of immigration permits to Palestine or by obtaining for them passports from Latin American countries. Attempts to negotiate the release of Jews with the Germans were also supported by local and foreign Jews in Switzerland. In Hungary the Swiss consul, Carl LUTZ, joined forces with Raoul WALLENBERG, diplomats of neutral countries, and the Zionist youth underground in saving tens of thousands of Jews in BUDAPEST.

BIBLIOGRAPHY

Bonjour, E. *Geschichte der schweizerischen Neutralität*. Vols. 1–9. Basel, 1970–1976.

Hässler, A. H. *The Lifeboat Is Full: Switzerland and the Refugees, 1933–1945*. New York, 1969.

Ludwig, K. *Die Flüchtlingspolitik der Schweiz in den Jahren 1933 bis 1945*. Bern, 1957.

Rings, W. *Schweiz im Krieg, 1933–1945*. Zurich, 1974.

LENI YAHIL

SYRIA AND LEBANON. Before receiving its independence in 1946, Lebanon was part of Syria. According to references in the Bible, Jews lived in the Syria-Lebanon area as early as the First Temple period (955 B.C. to 586 B.C.); during the Second Temple period (520 B.C. to A.D. 70) they already formed a large community.

French domination in Syria-Lebanon was the result of the partition of the Middle East by Britain and FRANCE after the dissolution of the Ottoman empire at the end of World War I. According to the agreements at the San Remo Conference of 1920, the League of Nations assigned to France a mandate over Syria-Lebanon, and to Great Britain a mandate over Palestine, Transjordan (now Jordan), and Iraq.

In the early 1930s the Jewish population of Syria-Lebanon numbered about thirty-five thousand, with the greater part living in a few large communities: Aleppo (seventeen thousand), Damascus (eleven thousand), Beirut (fifty-five hundred), and Kamishli (one thousand). A small number of Jews lived in Tripoli, Sidon, and Bahamdoun. Although Jews were well integrated into Arab society economically, linguistically, and culturally, relations between them and the local Arab population were complicated by the general problem of minority communities in Syria. These relations deteriorated sharply in the early 1930s owing to the growth of the Syrian national movement, the disturbances in Palestine, and the spread of Nazi propaganda, which led to the persecution of Jews accused of being Zionists. The nationalist trend was reinforced by the 1936 Syrian-French treaty, which provided for Syrian independence; however, the French government never ratified the treaty.

In 1937, HITLERJUGEND (Hitler Youth) leader Baldur von Schirach, together with a fifteen-man delegation, visited Syria, where Nazi slogans fell on receptive ears, especially among the fascist-type organizations such as Antun Saadah's Syrian National Party and the Lebanese Najadah. However, the Lebanese Maronite patriarch, Antoine Pierre Arida, denounced the Nazi propaganda and the persecution of the Jews.

In 1938, attacks on Jews increased in number and severity. Several Jews were stabbed to death by Muslim nationalists; the police failed to intervene even when the attacks took place under their very eyes. In Damascus and Aleppo, posters were distributed demanding a boycott of Syrian Jews. The Jews were called upon to demonstrate their loyalty to Syria by using only Arabic at all official functions.

Vichy authorities controlled Syria-Lebanon from December 29, 1940, when the Vichy-appointed High Commissioner, Gen. Henri Dentz, took up his post in Beirut, until July

14, 1941, when British and Free French forces occupied the area. Dentz's predecessor, Gabriel Puaux, was not inclined to apply Vichy's anti-Jewish legislation, and continued to follow the policy and regulations that were in force prior to the fall of France (June 1940). The fact that Syria-Lebanon was a mandated territory, unlike the French colonies or protected states in North Africa, restricted Vichy's freedom of action. The French position in Syria-Lebanon was tenuous because the area was geographically surrounded by British forces, economically dominated by the British system, and subject to the pressure of growing Syrian nationalist aspirations.

In addition, Dentz had to deal with a split in the ranks of the French personnel in his administration, between those who supported Vichy and those who sympathized with the Free French. From August 1940, Axis interests in the Levant (the area on the eastern shores of the Mediterranean) were represented by the Italian Armistice Commission. Even when a representative of the political section of the German Foreign Ministry arrived in Syria, Dentz insisted that all contacts involving military coordination in the area should continue to be handled by the Italian liaison channels, rather than by the German ones. Nevertheless, as a result of an understanding reached by Germany and Vichy France, Dentz allowed the German air force to use Syrian airfields for the operation of supplying arms and ammunition to the Rashid Ali revolt in IRAQ, in May 1941.

Under the Vichy regime, censorship came to be more strictly applied, and the Jewish journal in the Levant, *Al-Alam al-Israili*, was forced to pay lip service to the regime. Some Jewish officials were dismissed from their posts, and many Jews were arrested; one of them was Tuvia Arazi, head of the Hagana (the underground Jewish army) intelligence network, who operated within the structure of British intelligence. According to one report, Dentz agreed to the establishment of a concentration camp in Syria, but he did not have enough time for its implementation.

The economic depression that followed the closing of the borders between Syria and its neighbors (December 29, 1940) also affected the Jews of the Levant. The shortage of basic supplies—such as gas, sugar, and bread —and the rising cost of living led to mass demonstrations against the French authorities, and in the ensuing riots dozens of people were killed. In early March 1941 the price of bread rose by 50 percent.

Reports of the persecution of the Jews in Europe were first received in Beirut, when in the early war years shiploads of Jewish refugees from Bulgaria and Greece reached that port. Abraham Almaliah, principal of the Talmud Torah (religious school) in Beirut, gave them considerable assistance and smuggled them across the border to Palestine. Between 1938 and 1941, Jewish refugees from Europe also came to Aleppo by way of Turkey. Mentally and physically exhausted after the trip, they were cared for by the local Jews and helped to reach Palestine.

Throughout the six months of Vichy rule, the Jews lived in fear of the application of anti-Jewish legislation. The authorities intended, first of all, to put into effect in the Levant the Vichy law of October 3, 1940, on "the status of foreign nationals of 'Jewish' race," which barred Jews from holding positions in the public service and managerial and other prominent posts in the private sector. A delegation of the Beirut Jewish community, headed by Joseph Farhi and Eliyahu Almaliah, met with High Commissioner Puaux (who was still in office) and argued that these Vichy laws should not be applied in the Levant, where Jews had been living "since before Jesus' time." Puaux, however, was replaced, and under his successor, Dentz, the Vichy laws were issued (on March 26 and on April 19 and 23, 1941). But there was not enough time left to implement them, because in June, British Commonwealth and Free French forces invaded Syria-Lebanon. The Vichy forces were defeated, an armistice agreement was signed on July 14, and British and Free French forces occupied Syria. Owing to concern over a hostile reaction from the Arab population, however, many months passed before the French annulled these laws officially.

The major threat facing the Jews of the Levant during World War II was that of the Arab nationalists, inspired by fascist propaganda, who worked hand in hand with the mufti of Jerusalem, Hajj Amin al-HUSSEINI. Their operational plans were to begin with an uprising in Syria. The atmosphere of anti-

Jewish incitement in Syria and the reports of the pogrom that had taken place in Iraq led to the emigration of Jews, especially young people from Syria, even before the war was over, and to clandestine immigration to Palestine.

BIBLIOGRAPHY

Abramski-Bligh, I. "The Jews of Syria and Lebanon under Vichy Rule." *Pe'amim* 28 (1986): 131–157. (In Hebrew.)

Ben-Zvi, R. Y. *Mission to Lebanon and Syria (1943)*. Tel Aviv, 1979. (In Hebrew.)

Hirszowicz, L. *The Third Reich and the Arab East*. London, 1966.

Hourani, A. *Syria and Lebanon*. Oxford, 1946.

Landshut, S. *The Jewish Communities in the Muslim Countries of the Middle East*. Westport, Conn., 1976.

IRIT ABRAMSKI-BLIGH

SZÁLASI, FERENC (1897–1946), a leading figure of Hungarian Nazism. Szálasi served on the General Staff, and after 1930, when he joined the Hungarian Life League (Magyar Élet Szövetség), the secret "race-protecting" ultrarightist organization, he emerged as one of the country's chief ideologues. Motivated by Great Magyar imperialist designs, he wrote a number of pamphlets that incorporated a blend of Italian Fascism and German National Socialism. He was the leader of the extremist ARROW CROSS PARTY and played a guiding role in many other Nazi-type parties, including the Nation's Will Party (A Nemzet Akaratának Pártja), the Hungarian National Socialist Party (A Magyar Nemzeti Szocialista Párt), and the National Socialist Hungarian Party–Hungarist Movement (Nemzeti Szocialista Magyar Párt–Hungarista Mozgalom).

Szálasi was personally erratic, and because of his political radicalism he was distrusted by the Hungarian conservative-aristocratic establishment. On October 15, 1944, when Miklós HORTHY, the regent of Hungary, failed in his attempt to extricate Hungary from the Axis alliance, Szálasi, with the aid of the Germans, emerged as the new head of state. Under his regime, the Jews of BUDAPEST suffered a reign of terror that lasted until the liberation of the city in February 1945. Szálasi fled with the retreating Nazi forces but was captured by the Americans, who extradited him to Hungary in October 1945. Found guilty

Ferenc Szálasi (seated, center) and members of his cabinet, formed in October 1944. Seated second from the right is Károly Beregffy, the minister of war, and standing second from the left is Fidel Palffy, minister of agriculture.

by a People's Tribunal of war crimes and crimes against the people, he was executed on March 12, 1946.

BIBLIOGRAPHY

Karsai, E. *Szálasi naplója: A nyilasmozgalom a II. világháború idején.* Budapest, 1978.
Macartney, C. A. *October Fifteenth: A History of Hungary, 1929–1945.* New York, 1957.

RANDOLPH L. BRAHAM

SZATMÁR-NÉMETY. *See* Satu-Mare.

SZEGED, city in southern HUNGARY. Jews lived in Szeged from 1781. In 1905, the Neolog (Conservative) community erected the Great Synagogue, which remains a Hungarian national landmark to the present day.

In March of 1944, at the beginning of the Nazi occupation, 4,161 Jews lived in the city and thousands more in the surrounding smaller communities. The Nazis used the six gendarmerie districts of Hungary as an organizational structure to facilitate the systematic deportation of the country's Jews to AUSCHWITZ. The Szeged area was one of these districts. In May 1944, the Szeged Jews were concentrated in pigsties on Dorozsma Street. Bishop Endre Hamvas protested this measure, and as a result, a ghetto was set up in the Jewish part of the city. It encompassed the synagogue and Margit, Korona, and Bus Peter streets. A local Zsidó Tanács (Jewish Council) was established under the leadership of Dr. Robert Papp, and also a forty-man ghetto police unit, led by Sándor Gerle.

On June 16 and 17, the ghetto was liquidated, and the Jews of Szeged joined those from some of the neighboring communities who had been transferred to the nearby Rokus sports field and brickyards. Hungarian police herded a total of 8,612 Jews into these areas, where they suffered terrible conditions. Between June 25 and 28, freight cars overloaded with Jews left the Rokus station destined for Auschwitz. Among the victims was the chief Neolog rabbi of Szeged, Emmanuel Loew, aged ninety. The authorities deported 41,449 Jews from the Szeged district by June 30,

The Szeged synagogue, which was located in the ghetto, was used as a warehouse.

when they deemed the district cleared of Jews.

Five thousand seven hundred forty Jews from the Szeged area were among the 20,782 sent to the STRASSHOF concentration camp near Vienna, Austria. Used mostly as agricultural laborers in eastern Austria, 70 percent of these Jews remained alive until the end of the fighting. Of the original Szeged Jewish population, over half (2,124) survived the war.

BIBLIOGRAPHY

Braham, R. *The Politics of Genocide.* New York, 1981. See pages 645–652.
Lavi, T., ed. *Hungary.* In *Pinkas Hakehillot; Encyclopaedia of Jewish Communities.* Jerusalem, 1976. See pages 393–399. (In Hebrew.)

ROBERT ROZETT

SZENES, HANNAH (1921–1944), poet; one of the group of Palestinian Jews who parachuted into Nazi-occupied Europe (*see* PARACHUTISTS, JEWISH). Szenes was born into an assimilated Budapest Jewish family that produced a number of Hungary's poets, writers, and musicians. Hannah, too, at an early age displayed remarkable talent, keeping a diary and composing poems—first in Hungarian, and later, when she became an ardent Zionist, also in Hebrew. In 1939, at the age of nineteen, she immigrated to Palestine and two years later joined Kibbutz Sedot Yam, near Caesarea.

Hannah Szenes.

Hannah Szenes volunteered in 1943 to parachute into occupied Europe in order to aid Jews under Nazi oppression, and she underwent training in Egypt. In March 1944, about a week before the German occupation of Hungary, Szenes was dropped into Yugoslavia, where, together with fellow parachutists from Palestine, she spent three months with TITO's partisans. She was hoping that with the partisans' help she would be able to get into Hungary. She was convinced that even if she and her comrades did not succeed in rescuing Jews, their personal sacrifice would be a symbol and inspiration to the Jews of Europe. A chance meeting with a Jewish woman partisan inspired her to compose a poem, "Ashrei ha-Gafrur" (Blessed Is the Match), the text of which she deposited with Reuven Dafni, a fellow parachutist.

At the beginning of June 1944 Szenes crossed the border into Hungary and was immediately captured, with a radio transmitter in her possession. She was taken to Szombathely, put into prison, and tortured; but no torture, and not even the threat that her mother's life was at stake, could extract from her the code for the transmitter with which she had been equipped. After five months in jail she was brought to trial, at which she forcefully and proudly defended herself. She was convicted of treason against Hungary, and shot by a firing squad.

Hannah Szenes has been the subject of novels, plays, and a motion picture; she has become a symbol of courage, steadfastness, and moral strength. Her writings have been published in many editions. In 1950 her remains were brought to Israel and interred on Mount Herzl in Jerusalem. A village, Yad Hannah, commemorates her name.

BIBLIOGRAPHY

Breslavski, M., ed. *Hannah Szenes: Her Life, Mission, and Death.* Tel Aviv, 1966. (In Hebrew.)

Hay, M. *Ordinary Heroes: Chana Szenes and the Dream of Zion.* New York, 1986.

Masters, A. *The Summer That Bled: The Biography of Hanna Senesh.* London, 1972.

Palgi, Y. *And Behold, a Great Wind Came.* Tel Aviv, 1977. (In Hebrew.)

Syrkin, M. *Blessed Is the Match: The Story of Jewish Resistance.* Philadelphia, 1947.

DINA PORAT

SZLENGEL, WŁADYSŁAW (d. April 1943), Jewish poet and songwriter who wrote in Polish. Many of Szlengel's poems were composed in the WARSAW ghetto; they deal with the distressed situation there and with the resistance offered by the Jews in the final months of the ghetto's existence.

Before the war Szlengel wrote poems and lyrics, including satiric poems for the press and stage. In the ghetto, he composed works of prose and poetry for Sztuka (Art), one of the clubs for the emerging elite and the few people of means in the ghetto. Szlengel succeeded in conveying in his writings of that period his views on the occupiers and his misgivings about the running of the ghetto's institutions. Emanuel RINGELBLUM reported that Szlengel's poems "were highly popular in the ghetto and reflected its moods." They passed from hand to hand and were recited at meetings.

When the deportations from the Warsaw ghetto were launched, Szlengel's mood changed. From then on his works emphasized the terror felt in the ghetto and the bitter settling of accounts between men and God (one of his poems is entitled "A Reckoning with God"). In the poem "Telephone," Szlengel complains that no one is left whom he can call in the Polish side of the city. In his last poems, which he wrote when he was working in a broom workshop, Szlengel records the decline of the ghetto and its final days. One poem titled is "The Small Station of Treblinka," and another, "A Page from the Diary of the *Aktion*." Szlengel was apparently a ghetto policeman for a time, but he resigned since he was incapable of taking part in the roundups of ghetto inhabitants conducted by the ghetto police during the deportations. Even in the final stages of that period, Szlengel continued to recite his poems before small groups in clandestine gatherings. In these poems, Szlengel bids farewell to life (as in "Five Minutes to Twelve"), expresses his admiration for those offering resistance with weapons in their hands, and calls for revenge:

> Hear, O God of the Germans,
> the Jews praying amid the barbarians,
> an iron rod or a grenade in their hands.
> Give us, O God, a bloody fight
> and let us die a swift death!

Szlengel was killed in April 1943. He is known to have been in a bunker during the WARSAW GHETTO UPRISING, but the circumstances and the exact date of his death are not known. Only a part of his poetry and prose writings has been preserved. A collection of his writings in Polish was published under the title *Co czytałem umarłym* (What I Read to the Dead), the name of one of his prose compositions.

BIBLIOGRAPHY

Szlengel, W. *Rufe aus dem Ghetto, aus dem Abgrund—Die Stimme der Toten aus dem Ghetto zu Warschau: Gedichte von Wladyslaw Szlengel und andern.* Wilhelmshaven, West Germany, 1960. (Translated from Polish.)

ISRAEL GUTMAN

SZTEHLO, GÁBOR (1909–1974), Evangelical minister in BUDAPEST, Hungary, who saved many Jewish children during the Holocaust. Sztehlo represented the Protestant Good Shepherd (Jo Pasztor) Committee before international welfare and rescue organizations. Originally established as an association of Jews converted to Protestantism, this committee, under Sztehlo's leadership, dedicated itself during the second half of 1944 to the rescue of abandoned Jewish children, in coordination with the International RED CROSS. In November of that year, with the increase of anti-Jewish terror in the streets of Budapest, Sztehlo decided to expand his aid services to save Jewish children. Other welcome guests included young Jewish conscripts of the Hungarian labor battalions who had deserted their units and sought shelter.

With the intensification of the Russian siege in December 1944, Sztehlo's institutions were damaged by artillery shells, and many were no longer suitable for shelter. Sztehlo then transferred thirty-three children with forged

Gábor Sztehlo.

documents to the cellars of his own home. There he hid with his family for twenty feverish days, with shells exploding above them as the Germans on the upper floors of the building exchanged fire with the Russians, a block away. When Budapest was liberated, Sztehlo assembled the children and brought them to new quarters, caring for them until Jewish organizations or families came to claim them. Sensitive to the religious needs of the children, he facilitated their attendance at services in reconstituted synagogues. Survivors credit him with the rescue of hundreds of Jewish children.

In 1972 Gábor Sztehlo was recognized by YAD VASHEM as a "RIGHTEOUS AMONG THE NATIONS."

BIBLIOGRAPHY

Braham, R. L. *The Politics of Genocide: The Holocaust in Hungary.* New York, 1981.

MORDECAI PALDIEL

SZTÓJAY, DÖME (1883–1946), Hungarian pro-Nazi military figure. Sztójay, also surnamed Sztójakovics, took part in the counterrevolutionary movement of the 1920s, and from 1925 to 1933 served as a military attaché in Berlin. Following a stint in the Ministry of Defense, he was appointed Hungarian minister in Berlin in 1935. He headed the quisling government appointed three days after the German occupation of HUNGARY on March 19, 1944. As prime minister (he also doubled as foreign minister), Sztójay presided over a government that adopted the anti-Jewish decrees providing the "legal" basis for the separation, plundering, ghettoization, and deportation of the Jews of Hungary. By July 1944, when he was compelled (because of illness) to yield his position to Lajos

Döme Sztójay.

Reményi-Schneller, only the Jews of Budapest remained in the country. Sztójay fled Hungary with the retreating Nazi forces, but he was captured by the Americans, who extradited him to Hungary in October 1945. On March 22, 1946, a People's Tribunal in Budapest found him guilty of war crimes and crimes against the people, and he was shot shortly thereafter.

BIBLIOGRAPHY

Macartney, C. A. *October Fifteenth: A History of Hungary, 1929–1945.* New York, 1957.

RANDOLPH L. BRAHAM

T

TALLINN (Russ., Revel), Baltic port in the southwestern part of the Gulf of Finland; capital of the Estonian SSR. In 1919 Tallinn became the capital of independent ESTONIA. On the eve of World War II, its population was nearly 150,000.

The Jewish community of Tallinn was established in the middle of the nineteenth century by discharged cantonists (soldiers drafted as youngsters into the Russian army) who had retained their Jewish identity during their years of military service. In 1939, twenty-three hundred Jews were living there, constituting about half of the total Jewish population of Estonia. Besides its local Jewish organizations, Tallinn was also the site of the central institutions of Estonian Jewry. In 1940 and 1941, when Estonia was incorporated into the Soviet Union, most of these institutions were abolished. Several hundred Jews were among the Tallinn residents who were arrested by the Soviets and exiled to distant parts of the USSR.

When the Germans invaded the Soviet Union on June 22, 1941, many Jews volunteered for the local defense units. In the evacuation of the city organized by the Soviet authorities, about half of the Jewish population was able to escape from Tallinn, despite the siege and the heavy shelling to which the city was exposed.

The Germans occupied Tallinn on July 25. Immediately thereafter, Jews were ordered to wear a yellow badge (*see* BADGE, JEWISH) and were subjected to severe restrictions. Some of the women and children were put on forced labor, such as the extraction of peat; most of the men were confined in the city jail, and during September and October of 1941 they were murdered at Kabarneeme, at the killing site of Kalevi-Liiva. The killing was done primarily by Estonian Nazi collaborators, the members of the Omakaitse organization, under the command of Sonderkommando 1a personnel. According to German records dated December 19, 1941, 610 Jews had been killed by that date; the remaining Jews of Tallinn were murdered in early 1942.

On September 22, 1944, Tallinn was liberated by the Red Army. Only five Jews had survived in the city, but after a time about a thousand of the Jews who had been exiled by the Soviets or evacuated returned there.

BIBLIOGRAPHY

Dworzecki, M. "Patterns in the Extermination of Estonian Jewry." *Yalkut Moreshet* 11 (November 1967): 135–147. (In Hebrew.)

Levin, D. "The Jews of Estonia in the First Year of the Soviet Regime (1940–1941)." *Behinot: Studies on the Jews in the USSR and Eastern Europe* 7 (1976): 73–84. (In Hebrew.)

DOV LEVIN

TARNOPOL. *See* Ternopol.

TARNÓW, city in southern POLAND, east of Kraków; one of the oldest cities in the country. The presence of Jews in Tarnów was first recorded in the mid-fifteenth century. Under

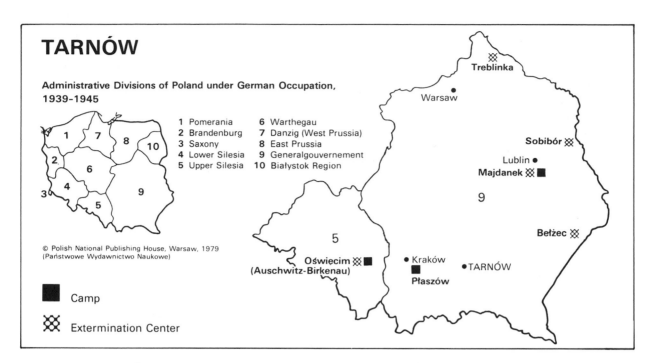

TARNÓW

Administrative Divisions of Poland under German Occupation,
1939-1945

1 Pomerania	6 Warthegau
2 Brandenburg	7 Danzig (West Prussia)
3 Saxony	8 East Prussia
4 Lower Silesia	9 Generalgouvernement
5 Upper Silesia	10 Białystok Region

© Polish National Publishing House, Warsaw, 1979
(Państwowe Wydawnictwo Naukowe)

■ Camp

▨ Extermination Center

Austrian rule (1772–1918), it became an important trade center, in which the Jews played the leading role. In independent Poland during the interwar period, Tarnów Jewry was impoverished as a result of the government's discriminatory policy, but there was much educational and cultural activity in the community. On the eve of World War II, twenty-five thousand Jews were living in Tarnów, representing 55 percent of the city's total population.

After World War II broke out in September 1939, thousands of Jewish refugees from western Poland converged on Tarnów, but as

A Jew in a prayer shawl in Tarnów is humiliated by German soldiers.

A memorial in Tarnów commemorating the Jews killed in the cemetery during the *Aktion* of June 11, 1942. The texts, in Hebrew, Yiddish, and Polish, read: "Here lie 800 of our children, brutally killed by the German murderers in the month of Tammuz 5702 [June 1942]. May the Lord avenge their blood."

the Germans advanced eastward, the Jews of Tarnów itself fled to the east. The Germans occupied the city on September 8. From the first day of the occupation, Wehrmacht troops harassed the Jews, seizing them for forced labor and robbing them of their belongings. On September 9, most of the city's synagogues were set on fire. In early November a JUDENRAT (Jewish Council) was established. At first its members, while carrying out the German orders, sought also to provide relief to the community, by organizing economic support for the needy, attempting to have hostages set free, and offering medical aid. The Judenrat also helped the Jewish refugees in the city find places to stay. On Passover of 1940, several Judenrat members were arrested for their devoted services to the community. They were replaced by persons of lesser standing, whose behavior came

to be sharply criticized by members of the community.

In the spring of 1940 the Jews of Tarnów were subjected to increasingly harsher decrees: a collective fine of half a million zlotys was imposed; Jews were apprehended on the street for forced labor; valuables in Jewish possession had to be handed in; and apartments in designated streets had to be evacuated. During the first half of 1941, the Gestapo seized Jewish refugees whose presence in the city was "illegal" and killed them. That December, following the outbreak of war between Germany and the United States, more than one hundred Jews were arrested and many of them were put to death.

In an *Aktion* that took place on June 11, 1942, thirty-five hundred Jews were deported to BEŁŻEC, and several hundred others were murdered in the streets of the city or in the

Jewish cemetery. On June 15 the Germans resumed the *Aktion*, and within three days another ten thousand persons were deported to Bełżec. Many others were murdered in the cemetery or in huge pits that had been prepared near the city.

On June 19 a ghetto was established, with sporadic killings taking place within its walls. On September 10 all the ghetto inhabitants had to assemble in a city square and were subjected to a *Selektion*. Persons possessing a document that showed them to be working at jobs of importance to the German economy were separated out, while the rest, some eight thousand in all, were taken to Bełżec to be killed there. In October, Jews from neighboring localities were imprisoned in the Tarnów ghetto, whose population increased to fifteen thousand. The wave of deportations to the extermination camps continued, and in mid-November another train left for Bełżec, carrying twenty-five hundred Jews.

Against the background of this liquidation process, a Jewish underground was organized in Tarnów in the fall of 1942. Among those who took the lead were members of the Zionist youth movement Ha-Shomer ha-Tsa'ir, later joined by members of other political movements. Some members of the JÜDISCHER ORDNUNGSDIENST (Jewish ghetto police) also took part, and helped the underground acquire weapons. One group of underground members left the ghetto for the forests in order to take part in armed struggle against the Germans, but most of them fell in battle against SS units. Others remained active in the ghetto and concentrated on trying to arrange border crossings into Hungary, where they hoped they would find refuge; only a few, however, managed to escape in that way.

During the course of 1943 more killings took place in the ghetto, and the final liquidation was launched on September 2. Approximately seven thousand Jews were deported to AUSCHWITZ, and three thousand to PŁASZÓW; three hundred were left behind in Tarnów to sort out the belongings of the deported Jews. They too were deported to Płaszów in late 1943, when Tarnów was declared *judenrein* ("cleansed of Jews").

BIBLIOGRAPHY

Tarnow: The Life and Destruction of a Jewish City. Tel Aviv, 1954. (In Yiddish.)
Tarnow Remembrance Book. Vol. 2. Tel Aviv, 1968. (In Hebrew.)

AHARON WEISS

"TEHRAN CHILDREN," group of about one thousand Jewish children who reached Palestine through Iran in February 1943.

At the outbreak of World War II, about three hundred thousand Jews fled eastward from Poland, into the Soviet Union. Some migrated to Siberia; others reached the Soviet republics in Central Asia. Starving, ill, and in need, they stayed in different camps along their way. On this long march, with all its hardships, thousands of children lost their parents.

In 1942 an agreement was signed between the POLISH GOVERNMENT-IN-EXILE and the Soviet government according to which Polish refugees who had chanced into Soviet territory would be enlisted in the Polish army (Anders Army). The emigration of twenty-four thousand Polish soldiers and refugees was authorized, and from April until August of 1942 they were taken via the Caspian Sea to Tehran. Among them were about one thousand Jewish children and eight hundred Jewish adults. Most of the children were orphans; a minority arrived with one parent and some with both. A number had parents who had remained in the Soviet Union and had handed the children over, as a last hope of keeping them alive, to Polish orphanages directed by priests and nuns; some of these children also reached Tehran. In Tehran the Jewish adult refugees created an orphanage with the active aid of the Jewish community.

Two Jewish Agency emissaries, Reuven Shefer and Avraham Zilberberg, were sent from Palestine as soon as the news of the arrival of the Jewish children reached the country, and they opened a Palestine Office. In October 1942, Zipporah Shertok, wife of the head of the Jewish Agency's Political Department, Moshe Shertok (later Sharett), went to Tehran to direct the orphanage, Beit

The "Tehran Children" in a temporary camp (1942).

ha-Yeled ha-Yehudi (Jewish Child's Home), together with a group of Zionist pioneers who had arrived with the refugees. No more entry visas to Iran were accorded to the Palestinian emissaries. There were severe shortages at the orphanage, principally of food, which was in short supply throughout Iran. An unceasing effort was made to bring more children out of the Polish orphanages.

In January 1943, after immigration permits had been obtained from the Mandatory authorities and a ship from the British authorities in Iran, the children and their escorts sailed to Karachi in India (now Pakistan). From there they went to Suez, and on February 18, 1943, they reached Palestine by train. They were 1,230 in number, 369 adults and 861 children; 719 of the children were without parents and the other 142 with one or both parents. From the time of their departure from Tehran, their journey was followed with strong emotion in the YISHUV (the organized Jewish community in Palestine), and throughout their train journey to Athlit, thousands welcomed them with great enthusiasm. YOUTH ALIYA activists, headed by Henrietta Szold and Dr. Hans Beyth, made all-out efforts to absorb them, initially in

Athlit and subsequently in eleven transit camps, where they recuperated and regained strength after their three years of suffering.

BIBLIOGRAPHY

Tomer, B. Z., ed. *Red, White, and the Smell of Oranges: The "Tehran Children."* Jerusalem, 1971. (In Hebrew.)

DINA PORAT

TEMESVÁR. *See* Timişoara.

TENENBAUM, MORDECHAI (1916–1943), one of the leaders of the VILNA, WARSAW, and BIAŁYSTOK undergrounds (in the last he was also in command of the uprising). Born in Warsaw, Mordechai Tenenbaum (Tamaroff) was the seventh child in a family of moderate means. He went to a Tarbut, a secular school in which Hebrew was the language of instruction. In 1936, he was accepted as a student in the Warsaw Oriental Institute; the knowledge of Semitic languages that he acquired there was to help him later in circulating in occupied Poland by posing as a Tatar. Erudite in literature, history, and philosophy, Tenenbaum was self-taught.

For a short time Tenenbaum was a member of the Ha-Shomer ha-Le'ummi (national guard) movement; in 1937 he joined the Freiheit youth organization (which was renamed Dror). He engaged in training for kibbutz life in Baranovichi and attended a course for Hebrew tutors in Vilna and a military training course organized by his movement in Zielonka. At the end of 1938, Tenenbaum was called to Warsaw to join the staff of the He-Haluts head office. He was a regular contributor to the movement's periodicals, and his ideological articles, which were to guide the movement and its *hakhshara* (agricultural training program), were remarkable for their revolutionary content and the passionate zeal that inspired them.

In September 1939, before the fall of Warsaw, Tenenbaum and his comrades in the He-Haluts head office left the city and made their way to Kovel and Vilna, their purpose being to evade the Germans and reach Palestine. The number of available immigration "certificates" to Palestine was negligible, and Tenenbaum provided his comrades with forged immigration documents; he, however, chose to stay behind in Vilna and see the struggle through.

In June 1941, Vilna was taken by the Germans, who lost no time in launching *Aktionen*. Tenenbaum tried to help his fellow members by providing them with forged work permits, but many were caught. During the lull in the *Aktionen*, Tenenbaum sent his girlfriend, Tama Schneiderman, on a mission to Warsaw. In accordance with a joint decision made by the He-Haluts leaders, he moved the survivors of the He-Haluts kibbutz from Vilna to the Białystok ghetto, which was still relatively quiet. He accomplished this thanks to the help he received from Anton SCHMID, an anti-Nazi Austrian sergeant (*Feldwebel*) in the German army.

Tenenbaum took part on January 1, 1942, in a meeting of He-Haluts youth in the ghetto, who issued a call to the Jews not to permit themselves "to be led like sheep to the slaughter," to refuse to cooperate, and to resist deportation by all available means. A copy of this appeal, to which he had added a

Mordechai Tenenbaum.

comment of his own, was hidden away by Tenenbaum and was found in the ghetto after the city was liberated. Tenenbaum left Vilna with forged documents identifying him as a Tatar by the name of Yussuf Tamaroff, and went by train to the GRODNO and Białystok ghettos. Together with Zvi Mersik, he arranged a meeting of He-Haluts members in the area and conducted a regional seminar of the movement.

In March of that year, Tenenbaum returned to Warsaw and rejoined his colleagues from the He-Haluts head office. At a meeting attended by representatives of all political parties, he gave a report on the situation in Vilna and the other ghettos he had visited, trying to convince his audience that events in Vilna provided evidence that it was the Germans' policy to exterminate all the Jews under their control. Some of those present did not agree with Tenenbaum's assessment. Shortly thereafter, reports came in of the mass murder of Jews in Lublin and its vicinity and of the gassing of Jews in the

CHEŁMNO extermination camp, which the Germans had put into operation in December 1941.

The various movements decided to unite and operate as undergrounds, and Tenenbaum became one of the founders of the Antifascist Bloc (Blok Antyfaszystowski) and one of the editors of its organ, *Der Ruf* (The Call). He visited branches of the movement in the Kraków, Częstochowa, and Będzin ghettos, gathering information and guiding and encouraging the underground activities. Together with Yitzhak ZUCKERMAN, Tenenbaum edited *Yediot*, the underground organ of the Dror movement in the Warsaw ghetto, writing the paper's editorials and contributing articles, thereby reinforcing the fighting spirit of Jewish youth and their determination to resist the Germans. By hiding copies of the paper in safe places, Tenenbaum preserved them for posterity. Tenenbaum was one of the founders of the ŻYDOWSKA ORGANIZACJA BOJOWA (Jewish Fighting Organization; ŻOB) in July 1942, and was active in acquiring arms from outside the ghetto and training the movement's members in their use. In November 1942, by decision of the ŻOB and the Żydowski Komitet Narodowy (Jewish National Committee), Tenenbaum left for Białystok in order to organize and lead a resistance movement there. When he arrived, he found the ghetto sealed and surrounded by Germans to prevent the entry of Jews from neighboring communities that were being liquidated. Tenenbaum attempted to reach Grodno, but was stopped on the way by Germans, who discovered that his papers were false. Though shot in the leg, he escaped, and after many vicissitudes managed to reach the one Grodno ghetto that was still in existence (the other having been destroyed).

After recovering from his wounds, Tenenbaum traveled to Białystok, the only other ghetto in the area that was still intact. He sought to unify all the underground movements in the ghetto, to acquire arms, and to manufacture explosive devices. He succeeded in gaining the support of the JUDENRAT (Jewish Council) chairman, Efraim BARASZ, and through him obtained the money needed for his operations. Tenenbaum then assumed yet another task, the establishment of an underground archive. He collected German documents; evidence concerning Białystok, Grodno, and other towns in the area; the minutes of Judenrat meetings and copies of the announcements it had made; and folklore items and songs composed in the ghetto. He also kept a diary and urged others to do so, and wrote articles, letters, and manifestos. All this he preserved as a memorial to the Jews, their sufferings, and their struggle against their murderers, and as a means to indict the Germans before history for their unspeakable crimes. He made a firm demand to the Polish underground to supply the ghetto fighters with weapons, and turned with a last-minute appeal to the civilized world to save the remnants of Polish Jewry. His writings are marked by honesty and human warmth as well as by accuracy and clear analysis, and they represent an extraordinary testimony of the era, unparalleled among underground leaders. Only Emanuel RINGELBLUM's archive can be compared with the record that Tenenbaum bequeathed to posterity.

In January 1943 Tenenbaum sent Tama Shneiderman, his friend and liaison officer, to the Warsaw ghetto, and Bronka Winicki, a young girl from Grodno, to the "Aryan" part of Białystok. Schneiderman took money and reports with her to deliver to the ŻOB. She failed to return from her mission, and her disappearance during the first Warsaw ghetto uprising, which took place that month, ended the contact between Białystok and Warsaw.

At the beginning of February 1943, the Germans began the deportation of the Jews of Białystok. Because of the scarcity of weapons in the underground's possession, Tenenbaum decided to keep his forces intact and hold back, but to intensify efforts to obtain more arms and train his men. He also sent emissaries into the forests to make contact with the partisans and to search for arms. The Jews employed in German factories were instructed to sabotage the products on which they were working. Weapons were stolen from the Germans, food was stockpiled, and, in the large bunker that the Dror underground had built at 7 Chmielna Street, its members listened to foreign broadcasts. Tenenbaum drew up a call for resistance: "Let us fall as heroes, and though we die, yet we shall live." He moderated a heated discussion in Kibbutz Dror in which the issue was whether to fight in the ghetto or to join the partisans in the forest; his position, which prevailed, was that the underground should first fight in the ghetto and only then continue the struggle in the forest. The minutes of that historic meeting have been preserved in the underground's archive. In July 1943, Tenenbaum succeeded in unifying all the underground movements in the ghetto—only a few weeks before the ghetto's liquidation. He became commander of the Białystok ghetto united underground, with Daniel Moszkowicz, a Communist, as his deputy.

On August 16, 1943, anticipating the liquidation of the ghetto by the Germans, Tenenbaum gave the signal for the uprising. His plan was to break the German blockade of the ghetto and thereby to enable many of its inhabitants to escape to the forests and continue the fighting from there. But the German forces surrounding the ghetto were too strong; masses of Jews, who were crowded into a single street, were seized with panic and despair and did not join the fight that the underground had launched. The wooden houses in the ghetto failed to provide any cover for the fighters. Nevertheless, some groups of fighters held out for a month and even harassed the German forces at night; some small groups that had been caught jumped from the trains that were rushing them to their death or fought their way through the German lines and joined the partisans.

On the day of the uprising, Tenenbaum displayed superb self-control and leadership. All trace of him was lost during the fight, and it is not known when or where he fell. Rumor had it that he and his deputy committed suicide. After the liberation the Polish government gave Tenenbaum, posthumously, the award of Virtuti Militari. Most of Tenenbaum's archive is kept by YAD VASHEM; a small part is preserved by the ŻYDOWSKI INSTYTUT HISTORYCZNY (Jewish Historical Institute) in Warsaw, and another part by BET LOḤAMEI HA-GETTA'OT.

BIBLIOGRAPHY

Jewish Resistance during the Holocaust. Proceedings of the Conference on Manifestations of Jewish Resistance. Jerusalem, 1971.

Tenenbaum-Becker, N. *A Man and Fighter.* Jerusalem, 1974. (In Hebrew.)

Tenenbaum-Tamaroff, M. *Pages from Fire.* Jerusalem, 1985. (In Hebrew.)

BRONIA KLIBANSKI

TEREZÍN. *See* Theresienstadt.

TERNOPOL (Pol., Tarnopol), city in the Ukrainian SSR; it was founded by Poles in 1540. During the period from 1772 to 1918 the city was in the province of Galicia, then under Austrian rule; between the two world wars it was part of Poland. In 1939 it was annexed by the USSR. Jews lived there from the time of its foundation and for a long period constituted a majority. In 1939 there were eighteen thousand Jews living in Ternopol.

On July 2, 1941, the city was conquered by the Germans. Two days later a pogrom was begun that lasted over a week (July 4–11). Both Germans and Ukrainians participated, and some five thousand Jews were murdered. In July and August of that year, decrees were issued against the Jews: their movement inside and outside the city was restricted; they were forbidden to change their places of residence; many of their homes and valuables were confiscated; and hundreds were taken out daily for forced labor. In September, an order was issued to set up a ghetto. The concentration of the Jews in the ghetto and the fencing of its area continued until the beginning of December. The JUDENRAT (Jewish Council) allocated the houses in the ghetto, conducted a census, and supplied forced laborers. In the fall and winter of 1941–1942, the Judenrat was compelled to send groups of young people to the labor camps set up in the area, among them Kamionka, Hluboczek Wielki, and Borki Wielkie. At the beginning of 1942 the Germans dismissed the chairman of the Judenrat, Gustav Fischer, claiming that he was not sufficiently compliant in executing their orders, and replaced him with Jakob Lipe.

On March 23, 1942, an *Aktion* was carried out, ending with the killing of seven hundred

Jews in the Yanovka Forest. That spring the Judenrat opened several workshops in the ghetto to ensure jobs vital to the German economy, in the hope of gaining a certain immunity in the event of further *Aktionen*. In July the sporadic killings increased, and from August 27 to 30, another *Aktion* was carried out. After a *Selektion*, more than three thousand persons, most of them aged and sick, were deported to the BEŁŻEC extermination camp. A few hundred men were sent to the labor camp in the area. At the beginning of September, the Germans reduced the area of the ghetto and living conditions deteriorated.

Another *Aktion* came on September 30, 1942. The Judenrat was ordered to gather one thousand Jews, but since it was unsuccessful in assembling that number, the Germans conducted their own manhunt, and eight hundred Jews were put onto a train destined for Bełżec. During the first half of November there were two further *Aktionen* in Ternopol, and an additional twenty-five hundred Jews were sent to Bełżec.

At the beginning of 1943, a labor camp was established in the area of the ghetto in which Jews classified as "useful" were assembled and employed in factories vital to the Ger-

man economy. Jews from other parts of the ghetto attempted to infiltrate the camp in the belief that its inmates would remain unharmed. In the *Aktion* of April 8 and 9, 1943, one thousand persons were removed from the ghetto and killed in pits adjacent to the city.

In April and May 1943, the murders in the ghetto continued, culminating in the final *Aktion* on June 20. The sick and the aged were killed on the spot, while the others were murdered in fields in the vicinity of the city. The labor camp was closed on July 22, when all its inmates were put to death, with the exception of a group of workers who were kept alive for another two weeks to sort out the belongings of the victims. At the beginning of August they too were killed. The Germans and the Ukrainians continued to hunt Jews hiding in the city and the neighboring forests; many fell into their hands up to the last days of the German occupation.

BIBLIOGRAPHY

Korngrün, P., ed. *Encyclopedia of the Jewish Diaspora: Tarnopol Volume.* Jerusalem, 1955. (In Hebrew, Yiddish, and English.)

AHARON WEISS

T4 OPERATION. *See* Euthanasia Program.

THADDEN, EBERHARD VON (1909–1964), German Foreign Office official in charge of Jewish affairs and liaison with the SS from April 1943 to the end of World War II. Thadden joined the Nazi party in May 1933 and the SS in September 1936. Accused of being the great-great-grandson of a Jew, Thadden was judged to be a "full Aryan" when Hermann GÖRING, an old friend of the Thadden family, testified that Thadden's great-grandfather was in fact the illegitimate son of a Russian nobleman.

Thadden entered the Foreign Office in 1937. He then joined the Waffen-SS and was wounded on the eastern front. He returned to Foreign Office duty in Greece in 1942, and succeeded Franz RADEMACHER as head of the Jewish desk (renamed Inland II A) in April 1943. Thereafter he was involved in the ongoing Jewish deportations throughout Europe, and especially the massive deportations of Hungarian Jews between May and July 1944. He was indicted by German judicial authorities in 1950, but the charges were dropped. An investigation was resumed in 1958, but Thadden was killed in an automobile accident in 1964 before he could be brought to trial.

BIBLIOGRAPHY

Braham, R. L. *The Politics of Genocide: The Holocaust in Hungary.* New York, 1981.
Hilberg, R. *The Destruction of the European Jews.* New York, 1985.

CHRISTOPHER R. BROWNING

THERESIENSTADT (Czech, Terezín), ghetto established in northwestern Czechoslovakia. Theresienstadt was founded as a garrison town in the late eighteenth century during the reign of Emperor Joseph II and named after his mother, Empress Maria Theresa. In World War II, the town served as a ghetto to which the Nazis expelled 140,000 Jews, mostly from the Protectorate of BOHEMIA AND MORAVIA, but also from central and western Europe. Control of the ghetto was in the hands of the Zentralamt für die Regelung der Judenfrage in Böhmen und Mähren (Central Office for the Solution of the Jewish Question in Bohemia and Moravia), which came under the REICHSSICHERHEITSHAUPTAMT (Reich Security Main Office; RSHA). It was run by the SS and commanded, in turn, by Siegfried Seidl (November 1941–July 1943), Anton Burger (July 1943–February 1944), and Karl Rahm (February 1944–May 1945). Czech gendarmes served as the ghetto guards, and with their help the Jews in the ghetto were able to maintain contact with the outside world. The "small fortress," which was near the ghetto, was used as an internment camp for political prisoners, non-Jews and Jews, mainly from the Protectorate.

The Nazi plan to establish a ghetto in Theresienstadt is first mentioned in a document dated October 10, 1941. The plan was (1) to concentrate in Theresienstadt most of the Jews of the Protectorate as well as certain categories of Jews from Germany and western European countries: prominent persons, persons of special merit, and old people; (2) to transfer the Jews gradually from Theresienstadt to extermination camps; and (3) to

A main street of the Theresienstadt ghetto.

camouflage the extermination of European Jews from world opinion by presenting Theresienstadt as a "model Jewish settlement." The leaders of Czechoslovak Jewry supported the plan in the hope that it would mean that the Jews would not be deported to the east and would stay in their country throughout the war.

The first group of Jews, from Prague, came to Theresienstadt at the end of November 1941, and by the end of May 1942, 28,887 Jews had been deported to the ghetto, one-third of the Jewish population of the Protectorate. In the first few months, conditions in Theresienstadt were similar to those in the Nazi concentration camps, and it did not take long to dispel the hope that Theresienstadt would save Jews from deportation to the east; the first such deportation, of 2,000 Jews to Riga, took place in January 1942. From then on, for as long as the ghetto existed, deportation and the threat of deportation cast a pall of fear and terror over the ghetto population.

Living conditions in the ghetto itself actually improved as time went on. When the removal of the non-Jewish population was completed (July 1942), Theresienstadt, within the walls of the ghetto, in some respects took on the character of a "free" town. It was in that summer, too, that thousands of Jews from Germany and Austria were brought in, most of them old people and some of them persons of special merit who had distinguished themselves in World War I or in some other way.

In September 1942 the ghetto population reached its peak, 53,004 people, living in an area of 125,770 square yards (115,004 sq m). In that month, 18,639 persons arrived in Theresienstadt, and 13,004 were deported to the extermination camps; 3,941 died in the ghetto. Deportations to Theresienstadt came to an end in the first half of 1943, by which time some 90 percent of the Jews of the Protectorate and nearly all the Jews left in Germany and Austria had been brought into the ghetto. In 1943 and 1944 the remaining Jews of the Netherlands and Denmark were also taken to Theresienstadt. Deportations to the east—to ghettos in Poland and the Baltic states and, as of October 1942, to the TRE-BLINKA and AUSCHWITZ extermination camps

Jewish children in the Theresienstadt ghetto, photographed by members of the International Red Cross investigation committee when they visited the ghetto on July 23, 1944. [IRC Geneva]

—were continued (with intervals from time to time). The final phase began in the fall of 1944 and continued for as long as the gas chambers in the east were still in operation. By then, only 11,068 people remained in the ghetto.

The composition of the Theresienstadt ghetto population reflected that of central and western European Jewry. The majority were assimilated Jews, but there were also groups of Orthodox Jews and Zionists. There were a few groups of Protestants and Catholics who under the racial laws were classified as Jews. The Zionists, especially the members of the Zionist youth movements, made efforts to carry on educational and cultural activities, and represented the most active, enterprising, and influential element in the population.

The internal affairs of the ghetto were run by an Ältestenrat (Council of Elders), to which Jewish leaders from among the prisoners were appointed. Heading the council was Jacob EDELSTEIN, who was succeeded, in turn, by the sociologist Paul EPPSTEIN and Rabbi Benjamin Murmelstein of Vienna. Rabbi Leo BAECK was also imprisoned in Theresienstadt. The Jewish leadership had the terrible task of making up the lists of those to be deported. It was also responsible for allocating the work to be done in the ghetto, distributing the food, providing housing for new arrivals, and overseeing sanitation and health services, the care of the old and the young, cultural activities, and the maintenance of public order. In all the areas of which it was in charge, the council also exercised judicial authority. Its substantial achievements helped ease the prisoners' lot.

Education, which was the Jewish leadership's chief concern, was for the most part in the hands of youth counselors who had been members of YOUTH MOVEMENTS. The atmosphere in the youth hostels (*Jugendheime*), which housed a substantial part of the children of school age (up to the age of sixteen), was almost totally divorced from the harsh reality of the ghetto. Although schooling was prohibited, regular classes were held, clandestinely; indeed, the educational effort made in Theresienstadt was an outstanding example of moral resistance to the Nazi regime.

Thanks to the large number of artists, writers, and scholars in the ghetto, there was an intensive program of cultural activities, with several orchestras, an opera, a theater troupe, and both light and satiric cabarets. Lectures and seminars were held, and a sixty-thousand-volume library was established, with special emphasis on Jewish subjects. For many, this library provided their first opportunity to gain an understanding of their Jewish identity. Every week there were dozens of performances and lectures. Religious observance had to contend with difficult conditions, but it was not officially banned.

The Nazis used the multifaceted activities

Examples of currency produced by the Nazis as part of their effort to deceive the world into believing that Theresienstadt was an autonomous Jewish city. In reality, it was a ghetto and a transit station for Auschwitz and other places. [A Living Memorial to the Holocaust—Museum of Jewish Heritage, New York]

in the Theresienstadt ghetto for their own purposes; they even printed special currency for use there. At the end of 1943, when word spread in the outside world of what was happening in the extermination camps, the Nazis decided to allow an International RED CROSS investigation committee to visit Theresienstadt. In preparation for the visit, more prisoners were deported to Auschwitz, so as to reduce the ghetto population of its congestion. Dummy stores were put up, as well as a café, a bank, kindergartens, a school, and flower gardens—all the trappings of a place in which human beings lead normal lives. The Red Cross committee's visit took place on July 23, 1944; the meetings of the committee members with the prisoners had all been prepared in advance, down to the last detail. In the wake of the "inspection" the Nazis made a propaganda film showing how the Jews were leading a new life under the benevolent protection of the Third Reich. When the filming was completed, most of its "cast," including all the members of the internal leadership group and nearly all the children, were deported to the gas chambers in Auschwitz.

As a result of the intolerable conditions in the ghetto—overcrowding, a total lack of sanitation facilities, and appalling nutritional shortages—diseases and epidemics broke out and took a fearful toll. In 1942, 15,891 persons died in Theresienstadt, equal to 50.4 percent of the average total population. By the end of 1943 the ghetto health department had managed to set up a network of hospitals, with 2,163 beds, and a beginning was made in regular medical checkups and inoculations against contagious diseases. That year the mortality rate dropped to 29.4 percent, and the following year, 1944, to 17.2 percent.

In the last six months of the ghetto's existence, more Jews were added to its population; 1,447 from Slovakia, 1,150 from Hungary, and 5,932 (persons of "mixed blood") from the Protectorate, Germany, and Austria. Before the war came to an end, the International Red Cross, which took an interest in the fate of the Jews in Theresienstadt, succeeded in transferring some of them to neutral countries: 1,200 Jews to Switzerland on February 5, 1945, and 413 Danish Jews to Sweden on April 15 of that year. At the end of April the ghetto experienced its final shock, when the Germans brought in thousands of prisoners who had been evacuated from concentration camps. As a result there was a new outbreak of epidemics in Theresienstadt, from which many died, among both the recent arrivals and the veteran prisoners. On May 3, five days before the ghetto was liberated by the Red Army, the Nazis handed Theresienstadt over to a Red Cross representative, putting him in charge of the ghetto and its prisoner population. The last Jew left Theresienstadt on August 17, 1945.

According to a number of statistical sources (which differ slightly), between November 24, 1941, and April 20, 1945, 140,000 Jews had been expelled from their homes and taken to Theresienstadt. Of these, 33,000 died there, 88,000 were deported to extermination camps, and 19,000 were alive (either in Theresienstadt or among the two groups that had been transferred to Switzerland and Sweden) when the ghetto was liberated; 3,000 of those deported survived the extermination camps. By national origin, the people who had been taken to Theresienstadt came from Czechoslovakia (75,500), Germany (42,000), Austria (15,000), the Netherlands (5,000), Poland (1,000), Hungary (1,150), and Denmark (500).

After the war, two of the commandants of Theresienstadt, Siegfried Seidl and Karl Rahm, were sentenced to death by a Czechoslovak court and were hanged; Anton Burger escaped and was sentenced to death *in absentia*.

BIBLIOGRAPHY

Adler, H. G. *Theresienstadt, 1941–1945: Das Antlitz einer Zwangsgemeinschaft.* Tübingen, 1960.

Adler, H. G., ed. *Die verheimlichte Wahrheit: Theresienstädter Dokumente.* Tübingen, 1958.

Bondy, R. *"Elder of the Jews": Jakob Edelstein of Theresienstadt.* New York, 1989.

Lederer, Z. *Ghetto Theresienstadt.* London, 1953.

Schwertfeger, R. *Women of Theresienstadt.* New York, 1989.

Volavkova, H., ed. *I Never Saw Another Butterfly: Children's Drawings and Poems from Terezin Concentration Camp, 1942–1944.* New York, 1962.

OTTO DOV KULKA

THESSALONIKI. *See* Salonika.

THIERACK, OTTO (1889–1946), president of the People's Court (*Volksgerichtshof*) and later Reich minister of justice. Thierack was born in Wurzen, Saxony, and studied law and political science at the Universities of Marburg and Leipzig. He served as a volunteer in World War I and then practiced as a lawyer in Leipzig. In 1921 he was appointed public prosecutor in Leipzig, and in 1926, in Dresden. He joined the Nazi party in 1932 and took a leading part in the Nazi administration of justice as vice president of the Reich court in Leipzig (1935) and as president of the People's Court in Berlin (1936). The latter court dealt out summary justice *in camera* and without right of appeal to all those accused of crimes against the Third Reich.

In 1942, Hitler appointed Thierack Reich minister of justice. He occupied this office until 1945, combining it with the presidency of the Academy for German Law and the high rank of *Brigadeführer* in the SS. In his judicial capacity Thierack perverted the law into an instrument of Nazi rule and made the judges a direct support of the conduct of the state. He legalized the proposal of Joseph GOEBBELS that certain categories of foreigners imprisoned or conscripted by the Third Reich should be transferred to concentration camps and subjected to "extermination through work" (*Vernichtung durch Arbeit*). Thus, in September 1942, Thierack reached agreement with Heinrich HIMMLER concerning "the transfer of asocials for the execution of their sentences." This agreement affected Jews, GYPSIES, and also all workers conscripted from the east, especially Russians and Ukrainians. It was intended to make the eastern territories suitable for German colonization. Thierack advised that "in the future, Jews, Poles, Gypsies, Russians, and Ukrainians are not to be sentenced by the regular courts but administered by the *Reichsführer*, in view of the leadership's plans for settling the eastern problem."

Thierack was arrested and interned at the end of the war, but hanged himself at the Neumünster camp before he could be brought to trial at Nuremberg.

BIBLIOGRAPHY

Boberach, H., ed. *Richterbriefe: Dokumente zur Beeinflussung der deutschen Rechtsprechung, 1942–1944*. Boppard am Rhein, West Germany, 1975.

LIONEL KOCHAN

THIRD REICH (Drittes Reich), Nazi designation of Germany and its regime during the period from 1933 to 1945. The German term *Reich* (kingdom, realm) is the equivalent of the Latin word *imperium* (empire). The name "Third Reich" was coined in 1923 by the writer Arthur Moeller van den Bruck in a book titled *Das Dritte Reich*. The term encompasses two meanings. In its secular and historical meaning, it is based on the assumption that the medieval Holy Roman Empire of the German People, which officially lasted until 1806, was the First Reich; the German Empire, extending from 1871 to 1918, was the Second Reich; and the Third Reich was the state that the Nazis hoped to establish. The "spiritual" meaning of the term is taken from Christian religious mysticism, the millenarian vision (the "thousand-year kingdom") of Joachim of Fiore, a twelfth-century mystic (d. 1202). According to that vision, the history of mankind is divided into three kingdoms: the "kingdom of the Father," the "kingdom of the Son," and, finally, the "third kingdom" (interpreted by the Nazis as the Third Reich), the "kingdom of the Holy Spirit"—the end of days, when mankind will achieve longed-for perfection. Despite its pagan ideological roots, Nazism accepted the millenarian meaning of the Third Reich, leading Hitler to forecast that it would last for "a thousand years."

BIBLIOGRAPHY

Grünberger, R. *A Social History of the Third Reich*. London, 1971.
Hildebrand, K. *The Third Reich*. London, 1984.

Moeller van den Bruck, A. *Germany's Third Empire*. New York, 1971.

ISRAEL GUTMAN

THRACE, region in the east of the Balkan Peninsula. The Jewish communities of Thrace were primarily of Sephardic origin and engaged in the wholesale and retail trade, particularly in fabrics and tobacco. In 1941 Thrace was annexed to BULGARIA, except for areas bordering on Turkey that were under German control. On March 4, 1943, nearly all the Jews of Bulgarian Thrace were arrested, confined in tobacco warehouses, deported to Bulgarian concentration points at Gorna Dzhumaya and Dupnitsa, and released to the Germans. The latter shipped them to TREBLINKA, where they were all killed on arrival. Some reports claim that Jews were put on gunboats and drowned in the Danube. Bulgarian statistics list 4,058 deportees from eleven towns, among them Serrai, Dráma, Kavalla, Xánthi, and Komotinē. The Germans removed nearly all the Jews of Dhidhimótikhon (970), Souflion (32), and Orestiás

(160) to SALONIKA on May 8 and shipped them to AUSCHWITZ the following day. About 200 Jews survived in Thrace among the partisans or hidden by their Christian neighbors, as well as 42 young men who were in Bulgarian labor camps. An undetermined number also escaped to the Italian zone in 1941 and 1942. The local population showed considerable sympathy for the Jews during the deportations.

BIBLIOGRAPHY

Chary, F. *The Bulgarian Jews and the Final Solution, 1940–1944*. Pittsburgh, 1972.
Matkovski, A. *A History of the Jews in Macedonia*. Skopje, 1982.

STEVEN B. BOWMAN

TIMIȘOARA (Hung., Temesvár), city in southwestern ROMANIA in the area of Transylvania, near the Yugoslav border. Timișoara was under Hungarian rule until 1918 and thereafter under Romanian rule. Jews first established a community there in 1739. During the nineteenth century they initiated the industrial-

THRACE

© Martin Gilbert 1982

TIMIŞOARA

Annexations from June to September 1940: (1) Bessarabia and (2) N. Bukovina to USSR; (3) N. Transylvania to Hungary; (4) S. Dobruja to Bulgaria.

0   160 miles   1 in.
0   300 km.   3 cm.

ization of the city. In 1930, 9,368 Jews lived in Timişoara, comprising about 10 percent of the city's population. After World War I, antisemitism increased there, especially in the second half of the 1930s. In 1936 members of the IRON GUARD threw a bomb into an audience during a Jewish theater performance, killing two. Ritual slaughter was outlawed in 1938, and in 1939 some 1,000 Jews were deprived of their Romanian citizenship. In July 1941 the Jews throughout southern TRANSYLVANIA were moved from small villages to larger cities. Thousands of Jews, lacking almost everything, reached Timişoara, swelling the Jewish population to 11,788. On August 4, all the Jewish males between the ages of eighteen and fifty were taken to forced-labor camps. The Jewish community obtained provisions for them and also worked to have men released. Many were let go or were at least sent to work near Timişoara. During 1941 and 1942 most of the buildings owned by the Jewish community were confiscated by the Romanian authorities.

In the summer of 1942 it became known to the leaders of the Jewish community that plans had been made to deport the Jews from southern Transylvania. The leader of the Timişoara Jewish community, Shmuel

Ligeti, contacted Jewish leaders in BUCHAREST. They intervened with government officials to avert the move, and the deportation order was rescinded. During 1944 local Germans (VOLKSDEUTSCHE) tried to intensify anti-Jewish activity in Timişoara, but with little success.

Beginning in 1943, many Jews from Hungary who had fled to Romania reached Timişoara. This flight reached its peak in the spring and summer of 1944, with Timişoara as one of the main crossing points on the Hungarian-Romanian frontier. When Romania withdrew from the Axis on August 23, the flow of refugees virtually ceased.

About 100 Jews from Timişoara were deported to TRANSNISTRIA and met their death there, and among the draftees to labor camps some also died. Most of the community, however, lived to see the Soviet army enter the city in September 1944. In 1947, 13,600 Jews were living in Timişoara, but by 1971 only 3,000 remained, many having emigrated to Israel or moved to other Jewish centers in Romania.

BIBLIOGRAPHY

Lavi, T., ed. *Rumania*, vol. 1. In *Pinkas Hakehillot; Encyclopaedia of Jewish Communities*. Jerusalem, 1969. (In Hebrew.)

ROBERT ROZETT

TÎRGU-MUREŞ (Hung., Maros-Vásárhely), capital of the former Hungarian autonomous district known as the Székely Land, in northern TRANSYLVANIA, which Hungary acquired from Romania in September 1940. According to the census of 1941, the city had a population of 44,933, of whom 5,693 (12.7 percent) were Jewish. Most of the Jews belonged to the Orthodox community, which was under the leadership of Samu Abrahám. It was in Tîrgu-Mureş that László ENDRE and the other Hungarian leaders involved in the "FINAL SOLUTION" program discussed the details for the liquidation of the Jews of the Székely Land on April 28, 1944.

The Jews of Tîrgu-Mureş were ordered into a ghetto on May 3, 1944. Established in a dilapidated brickyard on the outskirts of the

TÎRGU-MUREŞ

Annexations from June to September 1940: (1) Bessarabia and (2) N. Bukovina to USSR; (3) N. Transylvania to Hungary; (4) S. Dobruja to Bulgaria.

city, it contained 7,380 Jews, including those brought in from the neighboring communities. Among the latter were the Sabbatarians of Bezidul Nuo (Bözödújfalú), adjacent to Tîrgu-Mureş, the descendants of the Székelys (members of the Transylvania branch of the Magyars) who had converted to Judaism in the early days of the Transylvanian principality. Many of the ghetto inhabitants, who found no shelter in the brick-drying barns, had to live under the open sky. Like all the other ghettos in Hungary, that of Tîrgu-Mureş had a "mint," a special building used by the gendarmes for torturing Jews in an effort to obtain their wealth. Responsibility for the selection of the ghetto site and for the inhuman conditions that prevailed there has been attributed to the mayor, Ferenc Májay, and to the local gendarmerie and police officials, including Geza Bedö, who served as the commander of the ghetto. The Hungarians were assisted by SS advisers, including a Major Schröder. The JUDENRAT (Jewish Council), which included Samu (Shimon) Abrahám, Máyer Csengeri, and Mór Darvas, did its best to alleviate the lot of the Jews, but was basically helpless. The Jews were deported to AUSCHWITZ in three transports, between May 27 and June 8.

In 1947, Tîrgu-Mureş had 2,420 Jewish in-

habitants, consisting of local survivors and Jews who came to live there from other parts of Romania, to which the city reverted after the war.

BIBLIOGRAPHY

Braham, R. L. *Genocide and Retribution.* Boston, 1983. See pages 37–38, 143–150.
Perri (Friedmann), J. *A Marosvásárhely zsidóság története.* 2 vols. Tel Aviv, 1977. (In Hungarian and Hebrew.)

RANDOLPH L. BRAHAM

TISO, JOZEF (1887–1947), Slovak priest and politician who ruled SLOVAKIA from 1939 to 1945. Born into a lower-middle-class family, Tiso was trained as a Catholic priest. He excelled in his studies, and earned the degree of doctor of theology in 1910. Following the establishment of Czechoslovakia in 1918, Tiso became a Slovak nationalist. In 1925 he was elected to the Czechoslovak parliament, and he served as minister of health from 1927 to 1929. His extremism led to his detention and to his loss of the title of Monsignor. In the Slovak People's Party (the party of Andrej HLINKA), Tiso belonged to the clerical wing, his views having been influenced by Othmar Spann, an Austrian philosopher who advocated an authoritarian and corporate Catholic style of government. After Hlinka's death in 1938, Tiso won the struggle for leadership of the party. A few weeks later, in the wake of the MUNICH CONFERENCE of September 29–30, 1938, Slovakia became an autonomous entity, with Tiso as its prime minister.

In March 1939, prompted by Adolf Hitler, Tiso declared Slovakia's independence and brought the country into the Nazi camp. His regime contained elements of authoritarianism, Christian solidarity, and democracy. In October of that year he became president of Slovakia and was also elected *vôdca* (leader) of the state. He opposed the radicals of the HLINKA GUARD and prevailed against them, since Berlin was aware that there was no viable alternative to Tiso's clerical camp. Even after the anti-Nazi SLOVAK NATIONAL UPRISING of 1944, he remained loyal to the Reich, and Slovakia became a de facto protec-

Jozef Tiso (left), Slovak priest and political leader who ruled Slovakia from 1939 to 1945, and Andrej Hlinka (center), founder and leader of the Slovak People's Party.

torate and satellite of the Reich. Time and again his policy was condemned by the Vatican, and he was included in the list of war criminals compiled by the Allies during the war.

Tiso hated the Jews, but did not thirst for their blood. According to the Neo-Thomist doctrine, to which he adhered (in his interpretation), it was advisable to accept a minor evil in order to prevent a great evil. This led him to surrender the Slovak Jews and thereby avoid a Nazi-inspired radical regime from taking over and the Reich from taking revenge. Even when the Vatican warned him that the Jews who were deported were facing extermination, Tiso failed to intervene, and kept up his anti-Jewish propaganda. Under the existing regulations he had the power to grant exemptions from deportation, and he issued some eleven hundred certificates to this effect,

mainly to baptized and wealthy Jews. In March 1943 the deportations from Slovakia were halted, only to be renewed after the 1944 uprising. Tiso's sympathizers claim that he had no choice in the matter and that in 1943 and 1944 he made efforts to save the surviving Jews of Slovakia, but extant documentation does not bear this out.

In April 1945 Tiso fled to Austria, where he was apprehended. He was extradited to Czechoslovakia, brought to trial and sentenced to death, and executed. Many believed that the trial, and particularly his execution, was motivated by political considerations. To this day, his partisans believe that Tiso was a victim of the Slovak people's aspiration for self-determination.

BIBLIOGRAPHY

Jelinek, Y. "Dr. Jozef Tiso and His Biographers." *East Central Europe* 6/1 (1979): 76–84.
Southerland, A. X. *Dr. Jozef Tiso and Modern Slovakia*. Cleveland, 1978.

YESHAYAHU JELINEK

TITO (Josip Broz; 1892–1980), Yugoslav leader, statesman, and marshal. Tito was born in Kumrovec, Croatia. In his youth he was active in the metalworkers' union. While serving in the Austro-Hungarian army in World War I, he was captured by the Russians, and in 1917 he joined the Red Army. He returned to YUGOSLAVIA in 1920; from 1928 to 1934 he was imprisoned for Communist activities, and following his release he became active in the Comintern (Communist International). In 1937 he was elected secretary-general of the Yugoslav Communist party, which had been illegal since 1920.

Early in July 1941, shortly after the Germans invaded the Soviet Union and three months after they occupied Yugoslavia, there was a popular uprising against the conquerors in Serbia. Within a short while the Communists, under Tito's leadership, managed to place themselves in the vanguard of the rebellion. Gradually the revolt spread to all parts of the country. Despite the very difficult conditions under which they operated, Tito

President Tito (right) greets Albert Bajs, president of the Yugoslav Jewish Federation, in February 1950. On this occasion Frederick White, the representative of the Joint Distribution Committee, was awarded the medal for excellence of the Yugoslav Order of the Flag. [Beth Hatefutsoth]

and his men succeeded in creating a great fighting force of 200,000 to 300,000 men, known as the PARTISANS, that at the height of the struggle, in 1943, kept some twenty German divisions occupied.

During the conflict with the Germans, Tito instructed his men to provide every assistance to Jews who were trying to escape the Germans and their collaborators. In those years and in the postwar era, Tito displayed sympathy toward the Jews of his country as well as with the struggle to establish the state of Israel.

In the course of World War II and during the long years of his leadership that followed, Tito was one of the world's foremost statesmen. He became premier of Yugoslavia in 1945 and its president in 1953. In 1961 he wrote a book about his military exploits, *Vojna djela* (published in English as *Military Works*).

BIBLIOGRAPHY

Auty, P. *Tito*. London, 1974.
Djilas, M. *Wartime*. New York, 1977.

MENACHEM SHELAH

TODT ORGANIZATION. *See* Organization Todt.

TOTENKOPFVERBÄNDE (officially, SS-Totenkopfverbände; SS Death's-Head Units), units of the SS (Schutzstaffel; the elite guard of the Nazi party), originally formed to guard CONCENTRATION CAMPS. The Totenkopfverbände developed from the Wachtruppe Oberbayern der Allgemeinen SS (Upper Bavarian Guard Troop of the General SS), the Dachau guard unit (*see* DACHAU). They were molded from 1934 onward by Theodor EICKE, the *Inspekteur der Konzentrationslager und Führer der SS-Wachverbände* (Inspector of Concentration Camps and Commander of SS Guard Formations). Eicke instituted the wearing, on the right collar of the guards' uniforms, of the *Totenkopf* (death's head) symbol, from which the Totenkopfverbände later took their name. The procedures established by Eicke (who was killed on the eastern front in 1943) did not change radically throughout its history, that is, until the end of the Nazi regime. These procedures called for stringent discipline within the ranks of the guards, and later of the Totenkopfverbände; strict distance between the guards and the inmate victims; training of the guards to view the inmates as enemies of the state who should be destroyed if possible; and a system of extremely cruel punishment for inmates to be enforced by the guards. Eicke wanted the Totenkopfverbände to be an elite unit within the elite SS.

In March 1935 the Dachau unit and the guard units of the concentration camps were reorganized into six units under Eicke:

1. Oberbayern (Upper Bavaria), at Dachau
2. Ostfriesland (East Friesland), at Esterwegen
3. Sturmbann Elbe (Elbe Company), at Lichtenburg
4. Sachsen (Saxony), at Sachsenburg

5. Brandenburg, at ORANIENBURG and COLUMBIA HAUS
6. Hansa, at Fehlsbüttel

At the Nuremberg PARTEITAGE ("Party Days") rally in September 1935, Adolf HITLER publicly recognized the Totenkopfverbände units as party formations, making the Reich assume the cost of their operation, and thereby allowing for their expansion. In March 1936, Heinrich HIMMLER authorized an expansion from 1,800 to 3,500 men, and on March 29 the formations were officially designated as a separate SS unit named Totenkopfverbände, removed from the authority of the Allgemeine SS (General SS), and given distinctive dark brown uniforms. Originally recruited from the same class of men as the SA (Sturmabteilung; Storm Troopers) rowdies, the candidates for the expanded Totenkopfverbände were supposed to be at least 5 feet 10 inches tall (1.78 m), healthy, of "racially pure stock," and between the ages of seventeen and twenty-two. In reality they often fell short of these requirements.

In September 1937 the Totenkopfverbände were reorganized again to coincide with the consolidation of the concentration camps in Germany. This time three SS-Totenkopfstandarten (SS Death's-Head Regiments) were established:

1. Oberbayern (Upper Bavaria), at Dachau
2. Brandenburg, at SACHSENHAUSEN
3. Thüringen, at BUCHENWALD

Following the ANSCHLUSS (annexation) of Austria in March 1938, a fourth regiment, Ostmark (Austria), was set up for the MAUTHAUSEN camp.

On August 17, 1938, Hitler declared that in order to fulfill special domestic tasks of a political nature, the Totenkopfverbände; the recently created reserve units, the SS-Verfügungstruppen (SS Special Service Troops); and the SS-Junkerschulen (SS Cadet Schools) were to be armed, trained, and organized as military units, outside the structure of both the army and the police. In the event of mobilization, the Totenkopfverbände would be transferred to the Verfügungstruppen. Later, Himmler ordered that in case of such a mobilization, Allgemeine SS men over the

age of forty would be called up to replace the Totenkopfverbände men as concentration camp guards. This opened the way for a further expansion of the formations and for the creation of eight new Totenkopfstandarten. By the outbreak of World War II the Totenkopfverbände and their reserves numbered some twenty-four thousand men. Nine days after German forces invaded Poland, the three original Totenkopfstandarten, followed by some of the newer regiments, were sent there. Acting with a cruelty consonant with their training, they perpetrated horrors that were typical of the era of terror in Nazi-occupied Europe.

In October 1939 Hitler agreed to set up the SS field divisions that would later form the Waffen-SS. Among them was to be the Totenkopfdivision ("Totenkopf" Division), which Eicke was charged with establishing. His jobs as inspector of the concentration camps and commander of the Totenkopfverbände were now divided between Richard GLÜCKS, who took over the former, and SS-Oberführer Alfred Schweden, who assumed the latter post, now renamed *Inspekteur der Totenkopfverbände*. To set up his division, Eicke drew upon the three original Totenkopfstandarten as well as newer Totenkopfverbände, other arms of the SS, and new recruits. About one-half of the original complement of 15,000 men in the Totenkopfdivision came from the Totenkopfverbände. Himmler also designated certain units of the latter as replacement/training battalions for the Totenkopfdivision. At the same time, the Totenkopfverbände in the camps were reinforced by an influx of men and women (for the RAVENSBRÜCK women's camp). When the theater of war shifted to western Europe, Eicke's division went with it, fighting with extreme abandon during attacks, offering suicidal defenses, and committing brutal barbarities when frustrated in their objectives—all of these actions bearing the mark and style of the original Totenkopfverbände.

On August 15, 1940, as part of Himmler's ongoing drive to decrease Eicke's power, the Totenkopfverbände that had been designated as reserves for the Totenkopfdivision were transferred to the Kommandoamt der Waffen-SS (Command Office of the Waffen-SS). This office was soon to evolve into the

SS-Führungshauptampt, or SS Operational Main Office, under SS-Brigadeführer Hans Jüttner. All sixteen existing reserve Totenkopfstandarten, two Totenkopf cavalry regiments, and the motor and motorcycle regiments that had been created by Eicke were included in the transfer. In September, Jüttner disbanded some of the reserve Totenkopfverbände and consolidated the rest. At the same time, the office of Inspector of the Totenkopfverbände was abolished. In April 1941, in the course of preparations for the campaign against the Soviet Union, the remaining Totenkopfverbände officially became part of the Waffen-SS, completing their transition into the German army and closing the chapter of the autonomous Totenkopfverbände.

In this new context the Totenkopfverbände continued to expand. Typically, Himmler's own personal bodyguard, the Begleitungsbataillon des Reichsführers-SS (Bodyguard Regiment of the Reich Leader of the SS), was composed of a Totenkopf unit when it was established on May 15, 1941. The battalion was stationed in the Soviet Union with the Kommandostab Reichsführer-SS (Command Staff of the Reich Leader of the SS). The Kommandostab had been created in May 1941 as part of the SS-Führungshauptamt, but it was soon to come under Himmler's personal command as a private army. In that capacity both the Kommandostab and the Begleitungsbataillon were charged with killing Jews. The Totenkopfdivision also took part in atrocities, chiefly against partisans and enemy soldiers. Moreover, several "graduates" of the latter and of the Totenkopfverbände, as well as transferees to the units, played significant roles in the killing of Jews. The Totenkopfdivision, however, was primarily a fighting outfit. In northern Russia and later in the Ukraine it earned a reputation for waging fanatically tenacious battles in which it suffered staggering losses. Inculcated by Eicke and his staff with a most rabid racism, its fighters generally preferred death to being defeated and taken prisoner by their "racial inferiors."

Owing mainly to the high casualty rate in the Totenkopfdivision, there was a great deal of movement of personnel between it and other branches of the SS. Many Totenkopfverbände men from the concentration camps were brought to the Totenkopfdivision as replacements, especially after the latter sustained many dead and wounded in the winter of 1941–1942. Similarly, wounded men from the division were sent to the Totenkopfverbände in the camps after they had recuperated. The number of men in the Totenkopfverbände grew constantly; according to official SS figures, there were 40,000 men and women in its units on January 15, 1945, guarding 714,211 camp inmates.

The following summary outlines the development of the Totenkopfverbände from 1934 to 1941:

July 1934. Theodor Eicke institutes the Death's Head (*Totenkopf*) insignia for the Wachtruppe Oberbayern der Allgemeinen SS (Upper Bavarian Guard Troop of the General SS) in Dachau.

March 1935. Under Eicke the Guard Troop is reorganized into six units, all remaining under the General SS. The units are posted as guards at concentration camps.

March 1936. The six units under Eicke are officially designated as SS-Totenkopfverbände, and they are independent of the General SS.

September 1937. Still under Eicke, the Totenkopfverbände are reorganized into three *Standarten* (regiments).

August 1938. The Totenkopfverbände begin their expansion. By September 1939, eight new regiments are established and the number of men, including reserves, reaches twenty-four thousand.

October 1939. (1) Eicke establishes and commands the Totenkopfdivision, a part of the new Waffen-SS. The division includes the original three Totenkopf *Standarten*. (2) SS-Oberführer Alfred Schweden takes command of the remaining Totenkopfverbände. There is a flow of men between the Totenkopfverbände and the Totenkopfdivision.

April 1941. The Totenkopfverbände are completely incorporated into the Waffen-SS and lose their autonomy. Near the end of the war, they number about forty thousand.

BIBLIOGRAPHY

Hohne, H. *The Order of the Death's Head: The Story of Hitler's SS.* New York, 1971.

Sydnor, C. W. *Soldiers of Destruction: The SS Death's Head Division, 1933–1945.* Princeton, 1977.

YEHUDA BAUER

TOTUL PENTRU ȚARĂ. *See* Iron Guard.

TRANSCARPATHIAN UKRAINE (Zakarpatskaya Oblast [district]; formerly known also as Podkarpatská Rus, Carpathian Ruthenia, and Ruthenia), region in the Carpathian Mountains that now forms part of the Ukrainian SSR; it covers an area of 4,900 square miles (12,700 sq km) and in 1939 had a population of one-half million. That population was multinational: about half were Ruthenians, a branch of the Ukrainian people; about one-third were Hungarians; and 15.4 percent were Jews. The Transcarpathian Ukraine experienced many vicissitudes in the twentieth century. Prior to World War I it was part of Hungary, and after the war it was incorporated into Czechoslovakia. In March 1939, following an abortive attempt at establishing independence, it reverted to Hungary. After World War II, the Transcarpathian Ukraine was annexed by the Soviet Union and incorporated into the Ukrainian SSR.

There is evidence of the presence of Jews in the region from the fifteenth century, but the number of Jews before the eighteenth century was rather small. In the nineteenth century, the Transcarpathian Ukraine witnessed a large influx of Jews from Russia, Romania, and Poland. This, together with the high birthrate, which was the highest among European Jews, resulted in the rise of the Jewish population. The Jews of the region were known for their strict piety; the larger part (56 percent in 1930) lived in rural areas, and 18 percent of them were farmers, the highest percentage among Jewish populations in the world. They were also very poor. Nevertheless, a network of Jewish and Hebrew educational institutions was established, including Hebrew secondary schools. The schools remained in operation almost up to the time in 1944 when the region's Jews were deported to extermination camps.

The Transcarpathian Ukraine had the only

TRANSCARPATHIAN UKRAINE

© Martin Gilbert 1982

legally functioning schools in Nazi-ruled Europe in which Hebrew was the medium of instruction. It was also the scene of lively Zionist activity, despite the opposition of the Hasidic rabbis in the region, who were known as the world leaders of Hasidic opposition to Zionism.

During the Czechoslovak period, the Jews were able to develop an independent Jewish life, and they were highly appreciative of the attitude displayed toward them by the Czechoslovak authorities. The strengthening of Jewish consciousness among the Jews reduced their attachment to Hungary and to the Hungarian language. When the region was seized by Hungary in 1939, these Jews, who were known for their pro-Czechoslovak sympathies, were among the first victims of the antisemitic new regime.

For the five months that preceded the Hungarian occupation of the Transcarpathian Ukraine, it was an autonomous region within the Czechoslovak state. The local administration contained strong Nazi elements who sought to vent their spite on the Jews. Generally speaking, the Ruthenian population did not support the anti-Jewish policy pursued by the local government; nevertheless, when the pro-Nazi elements were removed and the region was annexed to Hungary, the Jews felt some relief.

Transcarpathian Jewry now had to renew its previous ties with the Jewish leadership in BUDAPEST. After some hesitation, the latter took the new community under its wing.

Still, the gap between the Jews of the great metropolis and those of the distant border region was not entirely bridged. Until the German occupation of Hungary in March 1944, the Jews of the Transcarpathian Ukraine, to a large degree, managed to hold on to their way of life, and even to provide refuge and aid to Jews from Slovakia and Poland who had fled to the region to escape deportation and death. Businesses, which had ostensibly been handed over to non-Jews, in fact remained in the hands of their original owners, and the Jews continued to play an active role in the local economy. One exception to this relatively tranquil state of affairs was the expulsion of "Jewish foreign nationals" from the region, in July and August 1941. A very large number of Jews whose families had been living in the Transcarpathian Ukraine for generations were expelled as "foreign nationals," and in some instances entire communities were expelled. As many as eighteen thousand Jews were affected, and most of them were murdered by the SS, in KAMENETS-PODOLSKI and KOLOMYIA, in German-occupied Eastern Galicia.

When reports of the massacre reached Budapest, the Jews there intervened with the central Hungarian authorities, and the deportations were discontinued. Seven transports that were en route to the border were sent back, and the passengers on these trains were released and permitted to return to their homes. The drafting of local Jews into the Hungarian army's MUNKASZOLGÁLAT (Labor Service System) also exacted a heavy toll, and many of the young Jews from the Transcarpathian Ukraine perished in the service. When Hungary was occupied by the Germans, on March 19, 1944, the new masters imposed the payment of heavy tributes on some of the Jewish communities. In UZHGOROD the Greek Catholic Church, whose local bishop had been known for his humanitarian attitude toward the Jews, helped them find the sum required for the ransom.

The plan for the total deportation of Hungarian Jewry, which the Nazis put into effect in 1944, was begun in the Transcarpathian Ukraine. A rapid process of ghettoization was launched; the Jews from the small localities and provincial towns were rounded up and taken to district centers, and from there were deported to the east. The entire process of deportation from the region was under way by mid-May 1944; for the most part it was the Hungarian police and gendarmerie who did the job, with a few German units and some Jewish collaborators also taking part. The local Hungarian population showed less sympathy toward the Jews than did the Ruthenians.

A small number of Jews escaped to the mountains or took refuge in prepared hiding places. Only 20 percent of Transcarpathian Jewry survived the war, and when the area was annexed by the Soviet Union, most of the survivors chose to leave. After a short stay in the Sudeten region, in Bohemia, most of these Jews emigrated to Israel or to other countries.

BIBLIOGRAPHY

Braham, R. L. *The Politics of Genocide: The Holocaust in Hungary.* New York, 1981.
Dinur, D. *Chapters in the History of the Jews of Carpathian Russia from the Earliest Settlement to the Holocaust (1493–1943).* Tel Aviv, 1983. (In Hebrew.)
Dinur, D. *The Holocaust of the Jews of Carpathian Russia.* Tel Aviv, 1983. (In Hebrew.)

YESHAYAHU JELINEK

TRANSFER AGREEMENT. *See* Haavara Agreement.

TRANSNISTRIA, region in the western Ukraine, between the Bug River in the east, the Dniester in the west, the Black Sea in the south, and a line beyond Mogilev in the north. The designation "Transnistria" is an artificial geographic term, created in World War II; it refers to the part of the UKRAINE conquered by German and Romanian forces in the summer of 1941, which Hitler handed to ROMANIA as a reward for its participation in the war against the Soviet Union.

Before the war this area had a Jewish population of 300,000. Tens of thousands of them were slaughtered by Einsatzgruppe D, commanded by Otto OHLENDORF, and by German and Romanian forces. When Transnistria was occupied it was used for the concentration of

TRANSNISTRIA

the Jews of BESSARABIA, BUKOVINA, and northern Moldavia who were expelled from their homes on the direct order of the Romanian dictator, Ion ANTONESCU. The deportations began on September 15, 1941, and continued, with some interruptions, until the fall of 1942. Most of the Jews who survived the mass killings carried out in Bessarabia and Bukovina were deported to Transnistria by the end of 1941. According to the records kept by the Romanian gendarmerie and army, 118,847 Jews were deported in that first phase. The deportations were resumed in the summer of 1942, with 5,000 Jews, mostly from CHERNOVTSY, forced across the Dniester River.

Also deported to Transnistria, by the hundreds, were political prisoners—Jews and non-Jews—who were suspected Communist sympathizers, and Jews who had evaded the existing regulations on forced labor; some of these were expelled together with their families. The total number of deportees was apparently 150,000, although German sources put the figure at 185,000. In the fall of 1942 the Romanian army general staff proposed that another 12,000 Jews be deported, for failing to report for forced labor or to comply with all the relevant regulations. This proposal, however, was not implemented, because in the meantime the Romanian government had changed its policy and refused to go along with the German plan for deporting all the Jews of Romania to the BEŁŻEC extermination camp. On October 13, 1942, the Romanians called a halt to the deportations to Transnistria.

The status of the deportees and of the local

Ukrainian Jews in Transnistria was laid down in Decree No. 23 of November 11, 1941, signed by Antonescu. The Jews were deprived of their freedom of movement and were not permitted to choose their place of residence; they were confined to ghettos and camps and were all put on forced labor, "for the public good." They were promised a daily wage, but in practice received no pay at all for their work. The ghettos and camps were in the hands of the gendarmerie headquarters and the Romanian administrative authorities in Transnistria. In late November 1941 most of the Jews from Bessarabia and Bukovina were herded into ghettos and camps in northern and central Transnistria. Following the Antonescu-ordered slaughter of the Jews of ODESSA, in which 25,000 Jews were massacred, the Romanian occupation authorities, in coordination with the Germans, deported the surviving Jews of Odessa and its environs to extermination camps in the Golta district: 54,000 to the BOGDANOVKA camp, 18,000 to the Akhmetchetka camp, and 8,000 to the DOMANEVKA camp. In Bogdanovka all the Jews were shot to death, with the Romanian gendarmerie, the Ukrainian police, and Sonderkommando R, made up of VOLKS-DEUTSCHE (ethnic Germans), taking part.

In January and February 1942, 12,000 Ukrainian Jews were murdered in the two other camps. Another 28,000 Jews, mostly from the Ukraine, were killed by the SS and German police, with the help of local German inhabitants of villages in southern Transnistria. By March 1943 no more than 485 Ukrainian Jews were left in all of southern Transnistria. A total of 185,000 Ukrainian Jews were murdered by Romanian and German army units.

The Romanians had no plans for the resettlement of tens of thousands of deportees from Romania, concentrated for the most part in northern and central Transnistria, and their sole aim was to drive the Jews further east and north. No provisions were made for the most basic necessities of life—lodging, food, medical care, and so forth. Ukrainian Jews, in places where they had survived, received their Romanian brethren with warm hospitality and tried in every possible way to find housing for them. In turn, Ukrainian Jews who had managed to escape from the areas where the German ex-termination drive was raging were given shelter by the Romanian Jews in the ghettos.

The winter of 1941–1942 was severe, with tens of thousands of deportees perishing from starvation, the cold, typhus, and dysentery. The deported Romanian Jews organized on their own, and the communal leaders among them, who had been deported with the other members of their respective communities, tried to establish mutual aid in order to ensure their survival. However, in that first winter these efforts had meager results. In some ghettos soup kitchens, hospitals, orphanages, and bakeries were set up, and cooperative societies of tradesmen were formed. The doctors among the deportees tried to combat the further spread of contagious diseases although they lacked the necessary equipment and disinfectants, and many doctors were among those who perished from the intolerable conditions. The situation improved as the winter of 1942–1943 drew near, when the first shipments of aid from the Jewish communities in the Regat (Romania in its pre–World War I borders) and in southern Transylvania reached the Jews in Transnistria. On December 17, 1941, Wilhelm FILDERMAN, president of the UNIUNEA EVREILOR ROMÂNI (Union of Romanian Jews), obtained Antonescu's consent for aid to be sent to Transnistria; but the authorities placed all sorts of obstacles in the way, and only part of the aid reached the deportees.

As soon as the Zionist movement in Romania and the Comisia Autonoma de Asistenta (Autonomous Committee for Assistance) received reports of the dreadful conditions prevailing in Transnistria, they organized aid shipments to the area, with the help of other volunteer groups. These first reports told only part of the story, because the Romanian authorities prohibited the exchange of mail between the deportees and the Jews in Romania. Even after official permission had been granted for aiding the deportees, the authorities interfered by means of fiscal and administrative measures, such as the imposition of an unrealistic rate of exchange for Romanian currency (as against the occupation mark), high customs tariffs, and delays in sending the shipments. Despite all these difficulties, however, the aid consignments that Romanian Jewry sent to Transnistria, beginning in the second winter spent by the deportees there (1942–1943), played an important role in helping at least some to survive.

The determined efforts made by the Jewish organizations, together with the second thoughts that the Romanian leaders were having about their policy, paved the way for representatives of the Autonomous Committee being permitted to visit the area. The first such visit, by a delegation headed by Fred Saraga, took place in early January 1943. Although the governor of Transnistria, Gheorghe Alexianu, barred the delegation from establishing direct contact with the Jewish leaders in the ghettos and camps, it was able to gain a clear picture of the situation of the deportees and their needs. The delegation's report on its visit was translated into several languages and copies were forwarded to Jewish organizations in other countries, in order to enlist their support for the help needed by the Jews in Transnistria.

Toward the end of 1943, aid for the deported Jews in Transnistria was being sent there by the American Jewish JOINT DISTRIBUTION COMMITTEE (known as the Joint), the RESCUE COMMITTEE OF THE JEWISH AGENCY IN TURKEY, the WORLD JEWISH CONGRESS, and the OEUVRE DE SECOURS AUX ENFANTS (OSE). In February 1943 Pope PIUS XII made a nominal contribution to the aid effort, to symbolize his interest, and in April the papal nuncio in Bucharest, Archbishop Andrea Cassulo, visited Transnistria. However, the Consiliul Evreesc (Jewish Council) focused its struggle on the repatriation of the deportees and on the release of some of them to go to Palestine. Also in April 1943, the council, with the help of the CENTRALA EVREILOR (Jewish Center), whose agreement was needed for every relief and repatriation operation, obtained Antonescu's permission for the return to Romania of 5,000 orphans and other Jews who had been deported "by mistake." The 5,000 were not repatriated, owing to German opposition, the technical and bureaucratic obstructions put in the way by the governor of Transnistria, and the intervention of the mufti of Jerusalem, Hajj Amin al-HUSSEINI, with the German Foreign Office. Filderman, who in May 1943 was himself expelled to Transnistria and kept there for a while, upon his release and return to Romania that August called upon the Romanian government to enable all the Jews who had been deported to return to Romania.

Finally, with the Soviet army closing in on Transnistria, permission was given for the Jews to come back, and in mid-December 1943 the first group of survivors—1,500 Jews from DOROHOI—returned to their former homes in Romania. In March 1944 a group of 1,841 orphans, out of 4,500 still alive at the time, came back. On March 15, the Soviet army launched the liberation of Transnistria. At this point a Jewish committee that had come to Transnistria from Bucharest succeeded in repatriating another group, consisting of 2,518 deportees. Of the Jews who had been deported to Transnistria—a total of 145,000 to 150,000—some 90,000 perished there. Many of the remaining survivors were allowed to return to Romania in 1945 and 1946.

BIBLIOGRAPHY

Fisher, J. S. *Transnistria: The Forgotten Cemetery.* New York, 1969.

Lavi, T., ed. *Rumania,* vol. 1. In *Pinkas Hakehillot; Encyclopaedia of Jewish Communities.* Jerusalem, 1969. See pages 349–388. (In Hebrew.)

Porat, D. "The Transnistria Affair and the Rescue Policy of the Zionist Leadership in Palestine, 1942–1943." *Studies in Zionism* 6/1 (1985): 27–52.

JEAN ANCEL

TRANSYLVANIA, NORTHERN, the area transferred (together with the so-called Székely Land in southeastern Transylvania) from Romania to HUNGARY under the terms of the Vienna Award imposed on Romania by Germany and Italy on August 30, 1940. Northern Transylvania encompassed 16,830 square miles (43,591 sq km) and had a population of approximately 2.5 million, of whom almost 165,000 were Jews. They represented four-fifths of the 200,000 Jews who lived in all of Transylvania. The Jews of the region were mostly Orthodox, and many belonged to Hasidic sects. Among the major centers of Jewish population and Jewish learning were DEJ (Dés), CLUJ (Kolozsvár), SIGHET MARMA-

ŢIEI (Máramarossziget), TÎRGU-MUREŞ (Maros-Vásárhely), ORADEA (Nagyvárad), and SATU-MARE (Szatmár-Németi). When the area was incorporated into Hungary, the Jews were subjected to the anti-Jewish measures in effect in that country. They were discriminated against in the socioeconomic sphere and were deprived of their basic civic rights. Jewish men of military age (twenty to forty-eight) were compelled to enlist in the labor service system (MUNKASZOLGÁLAT) of special forced-labor units.

After the German occupation of Hungary on March 19, 1944, the Jews of northern Transylvania were among the first to be the victims of the "FINAL SOLUTION" program. During the first phase of the occupation they were, like the other Jews of Hungary, subjected to a series of anti-Jewish decrees, including the compulsory wearing of a yellow badge (*see* BADGE, JEWISH). With the restriction of communication and travel, each community was virtually sealed off from the others. The primary channel of communication was the central Zsidó Tanács (Jewish Council) of Budapest, which for the most part merely transferred the instructions of the German and Hungarian authorities.

The region was divided into two gendarmerie districts and identified for purposes of the anti-Jewish drive as Operational Zone II. The expropriation, ghettoization, and deportation of the Jews were implemented according to the plans worked out by the relevant German and Hungarian officials at Satu-Mare on April 26, 1944, and at Tîrgu-Mureş two days later. Late on May 2, the eve of the ghettoization, the mayors issued special instructions to the Jews and had them posted in all the areas under their jurisdiction. From that time on, the Jews were prohibited from leaving their homes (except for one hour early in the morning in order to shop), and were called upon to surrender all their valuables. The ghettoization began the following day at the crack of dawn and was completed within ten days. It was carried out smoothly, without major incidents of resistance on the part of either Jews or Christians. Some of the Jews, unaware of the realities of the "Final Solution," went to the ghettos resigned to their fate. Others believed a rumor that they were being resettled at Kenyérmező, where they would be employed on agricultural projects. Still others sustained their hope in the expected quick victory of the Allies. The Christians, even those friendly to the Jews, were mostly passive. Many cooperated with the authorities on ideological grounds or in the expectation of quick material rewards.

The ghettoization and deportation were carried out by the gendarmerie and the local police and mayoral authorities under the overall command of Gendarmerie Col. Tibor Paksy-Kiss. Guidance in implementing these measures was provided by Lt.-Col. László FERENCZY, the officer in charge of the drive to oust the Jews in the country as a whole, and by special SS advisers. The procedures used in the anti-Jewish operations were in accord with those detailed in Decree No. 6163/1944, which was issued under the signature of László BAKY, one of the leading antisemites of Hungary, on April 7, 1944.

In the villages and smaller towns, the Jews were assembled in their synagogues and community buildings, where they were deprived of their valuables. After a few days they were transferred to the larger cities, usually the county seats, where they were quartered in the ghettos that had been established for the local Jewish population. In some cities, among them Bistriţa (Besztercze), Sighet Marmaţiei, Oradea, and Satu-Mare, the ghetto was established in the Jewish quarter. In others, including Cluj, Tîrgu-Mureş, and Şimleul-Silvaniei (Szilagysomlyo), local brickyards were used for that purpose. In Dej, the Jews were concentrated in a forest, where most of them lived under the open sky. Each ghetto had its Jewish Council, which was usually composed of the traditional leaders of the local Jewish community. The councils acted in accordance with the instructions received from the central Jewish Council and the local Hungarian or German authorities. In each ghetto there was a special building, the "mint," in which the gendarmes and local police authorities extracted confessions from the Jews about their valuables. The Jews, especially those perceived to be wealthy, were subjected to barbaric tortures. Spouses were often tortured in front of each other, or children in front of their parents.

The ghettos were short-lived, for the Jews of northern Transylvania were among the first to be entrained. Before their entrainment, which took place under horrible circumstances, they were subjected to another hunt for hidden valuables. The Jews were crowded into small freight cars, 80 to 100 per car, and were supplied only with two buckets, one with water and another for excrement. The deportations to Auschwitz took place along the rail lines leading to Kassa (Košice), where the freight trains were taken over by the Germans. The first transport left from Sighet Marmaţiei on May 16 and the forty-fifth from Oradea Mare on June 27, 1944.

With the deportation of 131,641 Jews, northern Transylvania became *judenrein* ("cleansed of Jews"), except for the Jews in the labor service units and the pitifully few exempted ones.

RANDOLPH L. BRAHAM

TRANSYLVANIA, SOUTHERN, the part of Transylvania that under the second Vienna Award (August 30, 1940) was retained by RO-

TRANSYLVANIA, August 1940

1. Annexed by the USSR, June 27, 1940

2. Annexed by Hungary, August 30, 1940

GREATER GERMANY

SLOVAKIA

HUNGARY

BUKOVINA

MOLDAVIA

Satu-Mare
Sighet Marmaţiei

Şimleul Silvaniei

2

Oradea
Dej
Bistriţa

Cojocna
Cluj   Sărmaş

Turda
Tîrgu-Mureş

Luduş

TRANSYLVANIA

Arad
Brad
Alba-Iulia

Deva

Braşov

BANAT

OLTENI

WALACHIA

MANIA; the other part, northern Transylvania, was awarded to HUNGARY. In the fall of 1944, northern Transylvania was liberated by the Soviet army, with the help of Romanian forces, and in August 1945 it was restored to Romania. According to the 1930 census, 192,833 Jews lived in Transylvania, the majority in the areas that in 1940 were ceded to Hungary. The 1941 census showed that southern Transylvania had a Jewish population of 40,937. The Jews of northern Transylvania suffered the same fate as the Jews of Hungary proper; most were deported to the extermination camps.

The Jews of southern Transylvania shared the overall fate of the rest of the Jews of Romania but with some differences, deriving in part from the central governmental authorities' hostility to them (most were Hungarian-speaking), and in part from the more humane attitude displayed by the local authorities.

Initially, in the first few months of the National Legionary Government (September to December 1940), the Jews of southern Transylvania were subjected to terror by the local authorities (then composed mostly of IRON GUARD men) and to the organized pillage of their property, through forced expropriation of Jewish-owned stores and workshops, forced sales, and eviction from their apartments and houses. Hundreds of Jews were brutally tortured, to force them to agree to "sell" their property to the guardsmen.

After the fall of the Legionary regime in January 1941, the laws on forced labor were applied with greater severity in southern Transylvania. Thousands of Jews were put to work on the Boj-Cojocna railway line in the vicinity of Brad, as well as on a variety of other public works. For the most part, the men were not removed from southern Transylvania, which made it possible to alleviate their conditions in the forced-labor battalions. The number of southern Transylvanian Jews sent to serve in labor battalions in TRANSNISTRIA was also relatively small, as was the number deported there on political grounds.

In the summer of 1941, after the outbreak of the war with the Soviet Union, the order of Ion ANTONESCU, the dictator of Romania, to expel the Jews from villages and towns was also applied in southern Transylvania. It was carried out there in a haphazard and disorganized manner, and caused much suffering to the Jews. During the expulsion operation, Turda, Alba-Iulia, Deva, and other urban centers proved unsuitable for absorbing the Jews who were expelled from their homes. As a result, in late 1941 and early 1942 the authorities set up makeshift ghettos, once again dispersing the Jews who had already been concentrated in the towns. Most of the Jews in the towns were also ejected from their homes, and Jews in some districts were concentrated in the villages rather than in the major district city. After being forced out of their homes the Jews became destitute overnight and turned into welfare cases, their neighbors—Romanians, Hungarians, and Germans—robbing them of their belongings.

In the summer of 1942 the threat of deportation hung over the heads of southern Transylvania's Jews. The German extermination plan drawn up by Gustav RICHTER, adviser on Jewish affairs in the German legation in Bucharest, provided for the region's Jews to be the first ones deported to the extermination camps in Poland, for technical reasons. The Romanian plan, drawn up by Radu LECCA, the official "in charge of the solution of the Jewish problem," also called for the immediate and total expulsion of the Jews of southern Transylvania. Jewish leaders in the area lost no time in trying to forestall these plans. Most active in the efforts was Franz Neumann, from the city of Arad, a convert to Christianity who used his close ties with Iuliu Maniu, leader of the opposition (a native of Transylvania), to persuade him to lodge a protest with Antonescu. Neumann also bribed Veturia Goga (the widow of the antisemitic leader Octavian GOGA), who had much influence on Antonescu, by contributing 400 million lei to the Armaments Ministry, which she headed. The leaders of southern Transylvanian Jewry, including Dr. Shmuel Ligeti and Istvan Antal, went to Bucharest, where they enlisted the help of Dr. Wilhelm FILDERMAN and arranged for Chief Rabbi Alexander SAFRAN to meet with Archbishop Nicolae Balan and gain his support for their cause.

These efforts made by the local leadership bore fruit and played a role in foiling the deportation plans. In the summer of 1943, the situation of southern Transylvania's Jews improved somewhat. The housing problem was alleviated to a degree, and most of the Jews found a place to live with the help of the local Jewish communities, in abandoned buildings, factory courtyards, and the apartments of Jews who had escaped expulsion. The Jewish community boards, the leaders of the illegal Zionist movement, and the aid organizations that had been formed in Bucharest all joined in helping to improve the situation. For their part, the Jews of southern Transylvania were the principal source of aid to their brethren in northern Transylvania and Hungary when Hungarian Jews were being rounded up for deportation to the extermination camps. At seven secret border crossing points, thousands of escaping Jews were brought to a safe haven in Romania and provided with forged documents and financial assistance. Most of the Romanian authorities manifested goodwill and facilitated the escapes, thereby helping to save the Jews' lives.

In early September 1944, shortly after the surrender of the Romanian army to the Soviet forces, the Hungarian army crossed the frontier and occupied a strip along the northern border of southern Transylvania. Most of the Jews in that area fled, but the Hungarians showed no mercy in murdering the Jews whom they were able to seize in Luduş and Arad, as well as 126 others in the villages of Sărmaş and Sărmăşel.

The Hungarian military authorities forced the Jews to wear a yellow badge (*see* BADGE, JEWISH) and made preparations to introduce the racial laws that were in force in Hungary. During the few weeks that the Hungarians occupied the strip, arrests, murders, and executions were the order of the day. That month the area was liberated, and when the Romanian army reoccupied most of northern Transylvania at the end of October, it was empty of Jews.

The Romanian regime, which was regarded as antisemitic, actually saved the Jews of southern Transylvania from extermination; Hungary, with whose culture and heritage the Jews of southern Transylvania identified, was responsible for the destruction of the largest community in the region.

BIBLIOGRAPHY

Ancel, J. "Plans for Deportation of Romanian Jews and Their Discontinuation in Light of Documentary Evidence." *Yad Vashem Studies* 16 (1984): 381–420.

Lavi, T. *Rumania*, vol. 1. In *Pinkas Hakehillot; Encyclopaedia of Jewish Communities.* Jerusalem, 1969. (In Hebrew.)

JEAN ANCEL

TRAWNIKI, labor camp established in the fall of 1941 in Trawniki, southeast of Lublin, Poland, in what had once been a sugar factory; it was used to house Soviet prisoners of war and Polish Jews. Trawniki belonged to the network of camps under the control of Odilo GLOBOCNIK, the *Höherer SS- und Polizeiführer* (Higher SS and Police Leader) in the Lublin district. In the spring of 1942, Jews from Germany, Austria, and Czechoslovakia were brought to Trawniki. Many of them died of starvation and disease, were deported to the BEŁŻEC extermination camp, or were shot in the nearby forest.

Late in 1942, a brush factory that had been in operation in the Międzyrzec Podlaski ghetto was transferred, together with its crew, to Trawniki. After the liquidation of the WARSAW ghetto in the wake of the ghetto revolt in 1943, the Fritz Schulz Works in Warsaw was moved to Trawniki with ten thousand workers; it consisted of workshops for tailors, furriers, and broom makers. Among the arrivals from Warsaw were Dr. Emanuel RINGELBLUM and thirty-three members of the ŻYDOWSKA ORGANIZACJA BOJOWA (Jewish Fighting Organization; ŻOB). The latter set up an underground in the camp, acquired a few arms, and made plans for an uprising. In May 1943, Jews from the Netherlands and from Białystok, Minsk, and Smolensk were brought to Trawniki, as were factories working for the Wehrmacht. That July, OSTINDUSTRIE GMBH (Osti), which belonged to the SS, requested that the Trawniki camp be enlarged because of the importance to the Wehrmacht of the goods (army uniforms and so on) that were being manufactured there. In October the Wehrmacht factories were transferred to Osti. The Jewish prisoners in Trawniki were also employed in peat mining

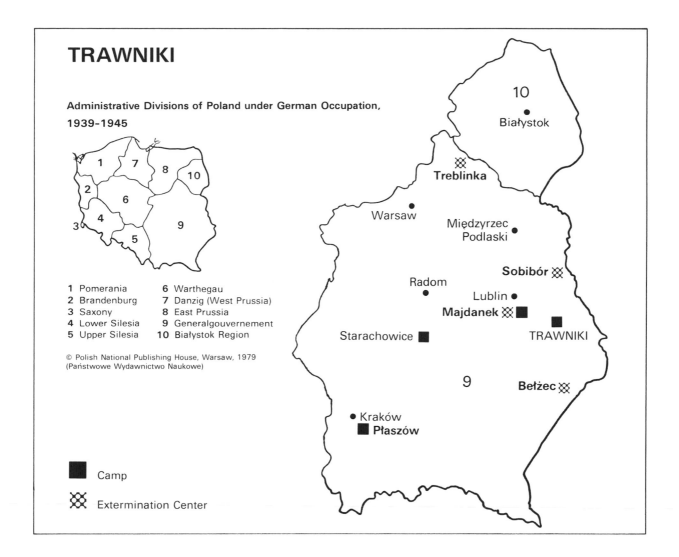

TRAWNIKI

Administrative Divisions of Poland under German Occupation, 1939–1945

10 Białystok

XX
Treblinka

Warsaw

Międzyrzec Podlaski

Sobibór XX

Radom

Lublin ●
Majdanek XX ■

Starachowice ■

TRAWNIKI ■

9   **Bełżec** XX

● Kraków
■ **Płaszów**

1 Pomerania   6 Warthegau
2 Brandenburg   7 Danzig (West Prussia)
3 Saxony   8 East Prussia
4 Lower Silesia   9 Generalgouvernement
5 Upper Silesia   10 Białystok Region

© Polish National Publishing House, Warsaw, 1979
(Państwowe Wydawnictwo Naukowe)

■ Camp

XX Extermination Center

and in earth-moving operations outside the camp.

As a result of the uprising that took place in the SOBIBÓR camp on October 14, 1943, the Nazis became alarmed about the possibility of more such rebellions breaking out, and Heinrich HIMMLER ordered the *Höherer SS-und Polizeiführer* in the Lublin district to liquidate all the Jewish camps. This order led to the "ERNTEFEST" *Aktion* of early November 1943, in which forty-three thousand Jews were killed. The turn of Trawniki came on November 5: ten thousand Jews were taken out of the camp, brought to pits that had been prepared in advance, and killed. The Jewish underground members were taken by surprise, but they resisted, and all fell in battle. In the spring of 1944 the remaining prisoners in the camp were transferred to the Stara-chowice camp, in the Radom district. Some twenty thousand Jewish prisoners passed through Trawniki in the period of its existence.

BIBLIOGRAPHY

Arad, Y. *Belzec, Sobibor, Treblinka: The Operation Reinhard Death Camps*. Bloomington, 1987.
Rutkowski, A. "L'opération 'Erntefest,' Fête de la Moisson." *Le Monde Juif* 29/72 (October–December 1973): 12–33.

SHMUEL SPECTOR

TREBLINKA, extermination camp in the northeastern part of the GENERALGOUVERNE-MENT. It was situated in a sparsely populated

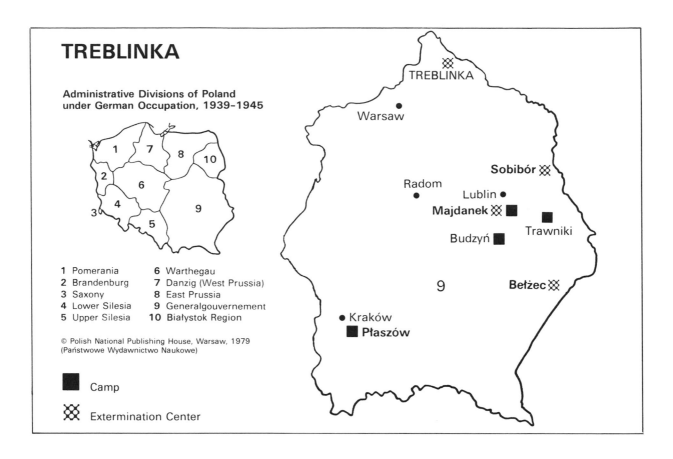

TREBLINKA

**Administrative Divisions of Poland
under German Occupation, 1939–1945**

1 Pomerania
2 Brandenburg
3 Saxony
4 Lower Silesia
5 Upper Silesia
6 Warthegau
7 Danzig (West Prussia)
8 East Prussia
9 Generalgouvernement
10 Białystok Region

© Polish National Publishing House, Warsaw, 1979
(Państwowe Wydawnictwo Naukowe)

■ Camp

▧ Extermination Center

area near Malkinia, a railway station on the main Warsaw-Białystok line; the camp's precise location was 2.5 miles (4 km) northwest of the village and railway stop of Treblinka. The site selected was heavily wooded and well hidden from view. A penal camp, known as Treblinka I, had been set up nearby in 1941; Poles and Jews were imprisoned there, working in quarries from which they extracted materials used in the construction of fortifications on the German-Soviet border. The extermination camp was established as part of AKTION REINHARD; work on it began in late May and early June of 1942 and was completed on July 22 of that year. The project was carried out by German firms, using inmates of Treblinka I and Jews brought in from neighboring towns. In addition to the camp structures and gas chambers, a branch railway track, leading from the camp to the nearby railway station, was constructed. Huge pits were dug within the camp grounds to be used as mass graves.

The camp was laid out in a rectangle 1,312 feet wide by 1,968 feet long (400 × 600 m),

resembling the SOBIBÓR camp, which had already been built. Two barbed-wire fences surrounded the camp; the inner one had tree branches, periodically replenished, entwined in the wire to block any view of the camp and its activities. Watchtowers 26 feet (8 m) high were placed along the fence and at each of the four corners. The camp was divided into three parts: the living area, the reception area, and the extermination area.

The living area contained housing for the Germans and Ukrainians who worked there, as well as the camp offices, the clinic, storerooms, and workshops. One section, demarcated by its own fence, contained the barracks housing the Jewish prisoners who worked in the camp and the workshops in which they were employed as tailors, shoemakers, and carpenters.

In the reception area, the deportees on incoming transports were taken off the train and subjected to a variety of procedures before being forced into the gas chambers. In addition to the railway siding and platform, this area contained the "deportation square," a fenced-in section with two barracks in which the new arrivals had to remove their clothes. On another lot near the railway platform were two large storerooms where the personal possessions taken from the victims were sorted and stored.

The extermination area, called the "upper camp" by the Germans, was in the southeastern part. Covering an area of 656 by 820 feet (200 × 250 m), it was completely fenced in and separated from the rest of the camp. In this area was a brick building containing three gas chambers, each measuring 13 by 13 feet (4 × 4 m). An adjoining shed housed a diesel engine that produced the carbon monoxide for the chambers. The gas was introduced by way of pipes attached to the ceilings of the gas chambers that ended in what looked like shower heads, to create the impression that the chambers were merely bathhouses. In the building a hallway led to each of the three gas chambers; inside each, facing the entrance, was a second door through which the dead bodies were removed. At a distance of

Kurt Franz, deputy commandant of Treblinka from September 1942.

492 to 656 feet (150–200 m) from the gas chambers, to the east of the building, lay the huge trenches in which the bodies were interred. A narrow path, fenced in on each side and camouflaged with tree branches, led from the reception area to the extermination area. It was along this path, nicknamed the "pipe," or "tube" (*Schlauch*), that the Jews, now naked, were driven to the gas chambers.

The camp's first commander was SS-Obersturmführer Imfried Eberl. In August 1942 he was replaced by SS-Obersturmführer Franz STANGL, the former commander of So-bibór. The German staff, numbering between 20 and 30 SS men, all of whom had taken part in the EUTHANASIA PROGRAM, held the command and administrative positions in the camp. A Ukrainian company consisting of 90 to 120 men served as camp guards and security personnel. They had the tasks of ensuring that no Jews would escape and of quashing any attempt at resistance. Some of the Ukrainians were given other duties, including the operation of the gas chambers. Most of them were Soviet prisoners of war who had volunteered to serve the Germans and had been enlisted and trained for their duties at the TRAWNIKI camp. Some of the Soviet prisoners of war were of German extraction (VOLKS-DEUTSCHE), and the majority of these were appointed platoon or squad commanders. There were also between 700 and 1,000 Jewish prisoners in the camp, who performed all the manual labor, including work that was part of the extermination process. In addition, they attended to the personal needs of the German and Ukrainian staff.

Groups of Jewish prisoners were employed on construction work as well, which proceeded even while the extermination process was in operation. They were also kept busy cutting tree branches in the adjoining woods and using them for camouflage, as well as on other jobs. These prisoners were taken from the incoming transports, put to work for a few days or weeks at the most, and then selected out and killed, their places taken by new arrivals. In September 1942 the camp commanders decided to introduce more efficient methods and thereby to reduce the time required for the killing of each transport. The plan was to establish a permanent staff of Jewish prisoners (rather than one that was continually replaced), the members of which would each specialize in one particular phase of the process. Though such a permanent staff did come into being, under the prevailing conditions its "permanence" was of short duration: the frequent *Selektionen*; the death penalty meted out for the slightest offense; illness; epidemics; and suicides all took their toll. Among the Jewish prisoners were fifty women used for auxiliary help in the laundry and the kitchen; some women were also put to work in the extermination area.

Railway Transports. The Treblinka extermination process was based on experience the Germans had gained in the BEŁŻEC and Sobibór camps. An incoming train, generally consisting of fifty to sixty cars (containing a total of six thousand to seven thousand persons), first came to a stop in the Treblinka village railway station. Twenty of the cars were brought into the camp, while the rest waited behind in the station. As each part of a transport was due to enter the camp, reinforced Ukrainian guard detachments took up position on the camp railway platform and in the reception area. When the cars came to a stop, the doors were opened and SS men ordered the Jews to get out.

A camp officer then announced to the arrivals that they had come to a transit camp from which they were going to be dispersed to various labor camps; for hygienic reasons, they would now take showers and have their clothes disinfected. Any money and valuables in their possession were to be handed over for safekeeping and would be returned to them after they had been to the showers. Following this announcement, the Jews were ordered into the "deportation square."

At the entrance to the square, the men were ordered into a barrack on the right and the women and children to the left. This had to be done on the run, with the guards shouting at them, driving them on, and beating them. The women and children were made to enter a barrack on the left side of the square, where they had to undress. Beginning in the fall of 1942, the women's hair was shorn at this point, behind a partition that was put up for this purpose. From the barrack, they entered, naked, the "pipe" that led to the gas chambers. Women and children were gassed first, while the men were kept in the deportation square, standing naked and waiting until their turn came to enter the "pipe." Once the victims were locked inside the gas chambers, which had the appearance of shower rooms, the diesel engine was started and the carbon monoxide poured in. In less than thirty minutes, all had died of asphyxiation. Their bodies were removed and taken to the trenches for burial. In the initial stage it took from three to four hours for all the people in the twenty railway cars to be liquidated, but with time the Germans gained expertise and reduced the duration of the killing process to no more than an hour or two.

While the killing was going on, the railway cars that had brought the victims were being cleared of the corpses of those who had died en route and of the articles and the dirt that had been left behind. This work was done by a team of some fifty male prisoners. The twenty-car segment of the train then pulled out to make room for another twenty cars, with their human load, to enter the camp from the station where they had been kept waiting. At this time another team of prisoners, also numbering some fifty men, went into action to collect the clothes and other articles that had been left in the deportation square barracks and transfer them to the sorting area. Here a team of one hundred prisoners searched the clothing and articles for any money or valuables. They also removed the yellow badges from the clothing and any other sign that might have identified the clothes, destroyed all passports and identity cards, and prepared the items for forwarding from the camp. A group of two hundred to three hundred, kept apart from the other Jewish prisoners, was employed in the extermination area, on such tasks as removing the corpses from the gas chambers, cleaning the chambers, extracting the victims' gold teeth, and burying their bodies. When the practice of cremating the bodies was introduced in the spring of 1943, with the aim of removing all traces of the mass murder that had been committed in Treblinka, this group of prisoners was charged with the task.

The Germans soon realized—as they previously had at Bełżec and Sobibór—that the bottleneck in the extermination process at Treblinka was the limited capacity of the gas chambers, which covered an area of no more than 57 square yards (48 sq m). It was therefore decided to increase the number of gas chambers, and ten more were built between the end of August and the beginning of October 1942, with a total area of 383 square yards (320 sq m). They were inside a brick building that had a hallway down the center and five doors on each side, each door leading to a gas chamber. A second door in each chamber could be opened only from the outside and was used to remove the corpses. The capacity of the new gas chambers was more than sufficient for the entire human load of twenty railway cars at one time.

Another improvement in the extermination process was the introduction of what was called the *Lazarett* (infirmary). When a transport arrived, those too weak to reach the gas chambers on their own were told they would be put into the sick bay. They were taken to a closed-in, camouflaged area with a Red Cross flag flying over it. Inside was a large ditch where SS men and Ukrainians were waiting for the sick Jews and killed them on the spot.

Extermination Program. The mass extermination program at Treblinka went into effect on July 23, 1942, and the first transports to reach the camp were made up of Jews from the Warsaw ghetto. Between that date and September 21, 254,000 Jews from Warsaw and 112,000 from other places in the Warsaw district were murdered at Treblinka, making a total of 366,000 from the district. From the Radom district 337,000 Jews were murdered, and from the Lublin district 35,000, most of them before the winter of 1942–1943. The total number of victims who had been residents of the Generalgouvernement was

ADMINISTRATION AND STAFF LIVING AREA

1. Entrance to the camp and Seidel street
2. Guard's room near the entrance
3. SS living quarters
4. Arms storeroom
5. Gasoline pump and storeroom
6. Garage
7. Entrance gate to Station square
8. Camp Command and Stangl's living quarters
9. Services for SS — barber, sick bay, dentist
10. Living quarters of Domestic Staff (Polish and Ukrainian girls)
11. Bakery
12. Foodstore and supply storeroom
13. The barrack in which "Gold Jews" worked
14. Ukrainian living quarters and latrines — "Max Bialas barracks"
15. Zoo
16. Stables, chicken coop, pig pen
17. Living quarters for Capos, women, tailor shop, shoe-repairs, carpentry shop and sickroom
18. Prisoners' kitchen
19. Living quarters for men prisoners, prisoners' laundry and tool room
20. Locksmithy and smithy
21. Latrine
22. Roll-call square

RECEPTION AREA

23. Station platform (ramp) and square
24. Storeroom for belongings taken from victims — disguised as a station
25. Deportation square
26. Barrack in which the women undressed and relinquished their valuables
27. Room in which women's hair was cut
28. Barrack in which men undressed, also used as a storeroom
29. Reception square
30. "*Lazarett*" — execution site
31. "The Tube" — the approach to the gas chambers

EXTERMINATION AREA

32. New gas chambers (10 chambers)
33. Old gas chambers (3 chambers)
34. Burial pits
35. "The Roasts" for burning bodies
36. Prisoners' living quarters, kitchen, and latrines

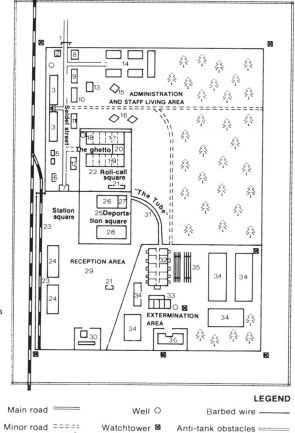

LEGEND

Main road ═══	Well O	Barbed wire ———
Minor road ═════	Watchtower ⊠	Anti-tank obstacles ═════
Woods	Railway	Earth wall

Plan of the Treblinka extermination camp (Spring 1943).

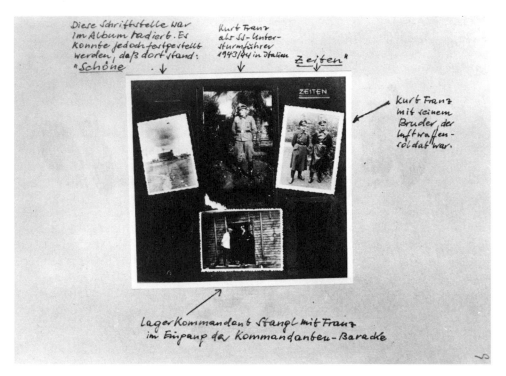

A page from Kurt Franz's photo album, "Schöne Zeiten" (Happy Days), about life in Treblinka. The handwritten descriptive text was prepared by the prosecution for the first Treblinka trial (October 12, 1964, to August 24, 1965).

738,000. From the Białystok district, over 107,000 Jews were taken to Treblinka to be killed, most of them between November 1942 and January 1943.

Jews from outside Poland were also killed at Treblinka. From Slovakia, 7,000 Jews who had first been deported to ghettos in the Generalgouvernement were murdered in the summer and fall of 1942; from THERESIENSTADT, five transports brought 8,000 Jews in the period from October 5 to October 25, 1942. From GREECE, over 4,000 Jews who had first been deported from their homes in THRACE to Bulgaria came in the latter half of March 1943; and from MACEDONIA, the part of Yugoslavia that Bulgaria had annexed, 7,000 Jews were murdered in Treblinka at the end of March and the beginning of April 1943. From Salonika, at least one transport of 2,800 Jews came at the end of March 1943.

A total of 29,000 Jews from countries other than Poland were murdered at Treblinka. Two thousand GYPSIES as well were among the victims there. The mass extermination program continued until April 1943, after which only a few isolated transports arrived; the camp had fulfilled its function.

In late February and early March of 1943, Heinrich HIMMLER visited Treblinka; following this visit, in accordance with his orders, an operation was launched to burn the bodies of the victims. The mass graves were opened and the corpses were taken out, to be consumed by the flames of huge pyres (the "roasts"). The bones were crushed and, together with the ashes, were reburied in the same graves. This burning of corpses in an effort to obliterate traces of the killings was continued until the end of July 1943. On its completion, the camp was shut down, in the fall of 1943. A total of 870,000 people had been murdered there.

Escape and Resistance. Hundreds of attempts to escape were made from the trains that were on their way to the camp. Some of those who tried to escape were killed by their jump or were shot to death by the transport escorts. Others were caught by railway guards or were handed over to the police by local inhabitants who found them. Some of the escapees managed to reach ghettos that were still in existence at the time, only to be sent to their death when it was the turn of the Jews in those ghettos to be deported. There were also many attempts to escape from the camp itself, especially in the first few months of its existence, when order and security had not been fully established. As a rule, the attempts were made at night, and involved getting through the fence or hiding in the railway cars that had been loaded with the victims' clothing and valuables (often by the would-be escapees themselves) and were about to leave the camp. Another method was to dig an underground passage leading to a point beyond the camp perimeter, but all those who tried this means of escape were caught. Everyone caught in an escape attempt was hanged. Even of those who did make good their escape from the train on the way to the camp or from the camp itself, not many survived. As time went by, more stringent security measures were taken in the camp, and for every prisoner who escaped, ten of those left behind were executed. Measures of this kind deterred escape attempts.

Several efforts at resistance were made in Treblinka, both by individuals and by entire transports, in which SS men and Ukrainians were killed or wounded. At the beginning of 1943, a resistance group was formed among the inmates. It was led by persons who held the senior posts entrusted to prisoners; one of them was Dr. Julian Chorazycki, who was the SS men's physician. At a latter stage the chief KAPO, Marceli Galewski, and other Kapos and work-team leaders also joined. Efforts were made to obtain weapons with the help of the Ukrainians, but these efforts failed and led to Dr. Chorazycki's death. Prisoners from both parts of the camp, the main camp and the extermination area, belonged to the underground resistance group. In the extermination area, the resistance was led by a Jewish officer from the Czech army, Zelo Bloch. The group's plan, which took form in April 1943, was based on taking weapons from the SS armory and then seizing control of the camp, destroying it, and fleeing to the forests to join the partisans. Fifty to seventy men were members of the resistance, but it was expected that all the prisoners would join in an

uprising if it were to break out.

When the burning of the bodies was nearing completion and it was clear that both the camp and the prisoners were about to be liquidated, the leaders of the underground resolved that the uprising must not be postponed any longer. A date and time were fixed: the afternoon of August 2, 1943. Initially the uprising went according to plan; with the help of a copied key, the armory was opened and weapons taken out and handed to the resistance members. At this point, the resistance men began to suspect that one of the SS officers, Kurt Küttner, had noticed unusual activities going on and was about to alarm the camp guard; the man was shot at once. This shot alarmed the guards and put an end to the removal and distribution of weapons from the armory, and the plan to seize control of the camp was abandoned. Instead, those resistance members who had arms in their hands opened fire at the SS men and set some of the camp buildings on fire. Masses of prisoners now tried to storm the fence and escape from the camp; they were fired at from all the watchtowers and most of them were hit, falling in or near the fence area. Those who succeeded in getting out of the camp were apprehended and shot by additional German security forces who had been alerted to the scene and, pursuing the escaped prisoners, combed the surrounding area. Of the approximately seven hundred and fifty prisoners who had tried to make their escape, seventy survived to see liberation.

Most of the camp structures, except for the gas chambers, were made of wood and went up in flames. Of the prisoners who were left, some were killed on the spot, while the rest were made to demolish the remaining structures and fences and obliterate the traces of the activities that had taken place at the camp. When this work was over, these prisoners too were shot. The grounds were plowed under and trees were planted; the camp was turned into a farm, and a Ukrainian peasant family was settled there.

Two trials were held in the Federal Republic of Germany, both in Düsseldorf, of SS men who had served in Treblinka. In the first trial, lasting from October 12, 1964, to August 24, 1965, there were ten defendants, including the deputy camp commandant, Kurt FRANZ. Of the ten, one was acquitted, five were sentenced to prison terms ranging from three to twelve years, and four were given life sentences. The second trial was that of Franz Stangl, the Treblinka camp commandant, who had escaped to Brazil but was extradited to Germany. His trial, conducted from May 13 to December 22, 1970, resulted in a sentence of life imprisonment.

During the period from 1959 to 1964, the area of the Treblinka camp was made into a Polish national monument, in the form of a cemetery. Hundreds of stones were set in the ground, inscribed with the names of the countries and places from which the victims had originated.

BIBLIOGRAPHY

Arad, Y. *Operation Reinhard Death Camps: Belzec, Sobibor, Treblinka.* Bloomington, 1987.
Donat, A., ed. *The Death Camp Treblinka.* New York, 1979.
Sereny, G. *Into That Darkness—From Mercy Killing to Mass Murder.* London, 1974.
Wiernik, Y. *A Year in Treblinka.* New York, 1945.

YITZHAK ARAD

TRIALS OF WAR CRIMINALS. [*This entry consists of fourteen articles on the search for justice after World War II:*

General Survey
Krasnodar Trial
Nuremberg Trial
Subsequent British Trials
Bergen-Belsen Trial
Zyklon B Trial
Subsequent Nuremberg Proceedings
West Germany
Postwar Dispensation of Justice in Germany
Hungary
The Netherlands
Norway
Poland
Romania

Other trials of war criminals are dealt with in Barbie Trial; Demjanjuk Trial; *and* Eichmann Trial. *For discussion of related issues, see* Crimes against Humanity; Extradition of War Criminals; *and* Laws Punishing Nazis and Nazi Collaborators; *see in addition the entries listed under* War Crimes *and* War Criminals.]

General Survey

At the end of World War II, German and Japanese nationals accused of war crimes against Allied citizens stood trial in a variety of courts. "Major" war criminals were those military or political leaders whose crimes had no particular geographical location. They were brought to Nuremberg or Tokyo, where they were tried before *ad hoc* courts established by Allied international agreement. Numerically, and in spite of the wide publicity they received, these trials were a small part of a very large picture. The overwhelming majority of post-1945 war crimes trials were those of "minor" war criminals. They were civilians or former members of enemy armed forces whose crimes were committed in specific locales, as in a concentration camp. Minor war crimes trials were conducted by military courts in the British, American, French, and Soviet zones of occupied Germany; in Italy and Austria; and by courts established for that purpose in Allied countries. The new governments installed in the former occupied and satellite countries also tried war criminals, and after the creation of the Federal Republic of Germany, German courts began prosecuting war criminals on their own. Two war criminals, Adolf Eichmann and John (Iwan) Demjanjuk, were brought to Israel, where they were tried for their crimes in 1961–1962 and 1988–1989, respectively (*see* EICHMANN TRIAL *and* DEMJANJUK TRIAL).

The term "Nuremberg trials" is often used to describe four different criminal proceedings. The first was the trial of twenty-four indicted "major" German and Austrian war criminals, conducted by the International Military Tribunal (IMT) from October 18, 1945, until October 1, 1946. Only twenty-two of them were actually tried: Robert Ley committed suicide, and Gustav Krupp von Bohlen was too ill to stand trial. Judges from Great Britain, France, the Soviet Union, and the United States presided over the IMT, which tried defendants on charges of conspiracy, crimes against peace, war crimes, and crimes against humanity. Nuremberg was also the site of twelve ensuing trials of 177 members of organizations and groups alleged to have been of a criminal character (*see* SUBSEQUENT NUREMBERG PROCEEDINGS). Former members of the Gestapo and the SS, as well as civil servants and industrialists, were among those tried. American lawyers served as judges in these proceedings. The third type of "Nuremberg trial" was held in Tokyo. A multinational panel of eleven judges, who comprised the IMT in East Asia, presided over the trials of Japanese military and political leaders. The trials of "minor" war criminals conducted by military and national courts were the fourth type of Nuremberg proceeding. These trials were held in the zones of former Axis territory occupied by the victorious powers, or in the liberated territories, at or near the scenes of the crimes.

BIBLIOGRAPHY

Conot, R. E. *Justice at Nuremberg.* New York, 1983.
Mushkat, M. "The Concept of 'Crime against the Jewish People' in the Light of International Law." *Yad Vashem Studies* 5 (1961): 237–254.
Rückerl, A. *The Investigation of Nazi Crimes, 1945–1978: A Documentation.* Hamden, Conn., 1980.
Woetzel, R. *The Nuremberg Trials in International Law.* New York, 1960.

PRISCILLA DALE JONES

Krasnodar Trial

The first trial of Nazi criminals was held in the city of KRASNODAR from July 14 to 17, 1943, before the Soviet military tribunal of the North Caucasian Front. The trial dealt with the crimes committed by the Nazis in the city, involving seven thousand acts of murder.

Thirteen Soviet citizens were brought to trial; all had served in the auxiliary unit of Sonderkommando 10a (from Einsatzgruppe D), under the command of Dr. Kurt Christmann. They were charged with participating in murders committed by that unit, which was responsible for annihilating all the patients in the Krasnodar municipal hospital, in the Berezhanka convalescent home, and in the regional children's hospital. In their testimony, the accused described the setup and action of the GAS VANS used for these murders.

In the four days of the trial twenty-two witnesses from the locality appeared, including Ivan Kotov, who survived the gas van by breathing through a piece of material soaked in urine. On July 17, 1943, eight of the accused were sentenced to death by hanging, and three others to twenty years' imprisonment with forced labor. This was the first trial in which the mass murders of the EINSATZGRUPPEN and the use of gas vans were made known to the world. Recorded sessions of the trial appeared in newspapers in the Soviet Union and the West, and later were collected in booklets that were published in several languages.

BIBLIOGRAPHY

The People's Verdict: A Full Report of the Proceedings at the Krasnodar and Kharkov German Atrocity Trials. London, 1944.
Prozess in der Strafsache gegen die faschistischen deutscher Okkupanten und ihre Helfershelfer wegen ihre Bestialitäten im Gebiet der Stadt Krasnodar und des Krasnodarer Gaus während der zeitweiligen Besatzung dieses Gebietes: Verhandelt am 14–17 juli 1943. Moscow, 1943.

SHMUEL SPECTOR

Nuremberg Trial

The original intention of the International Military Tribunal (IMT) had been to hold the trial of the major Nazi war criminals in Berlin, and the opening session, on October 18, 1945, did indeed take place there. But for lack of adequate accommodation in the ruins of the German capital, the trial was moved to Nuremberg—selected, among other reasons, because of what it symbolized as a Nazi stronghold that had gained infamy for the racist laws named after it (*see* NUREMBERG LAWS).

During the war itself, it was primarily declarations by the Allied powers that put the world—and the criminals—on notice that the Allies were determined to punish the perpetrators of war crimes. The major declarations on the punishment of war crimes, including those that specifically mention the criminals responsible for the Holocaust, were the St. James Palace Declaration of January 13, 1942; the Moscow Declaration by the Three Powers of November 1, 1943; the decision to establish the UNITED NATIONS WAR CRIMES COMMISSION; and, especially, the London Agreement of August 8, 1945. The London Agreement established the charter of the IMT, which came to be held at Nuremberg.

The designation of the Nuremberg court as a "military tribunal" was not meant to imply that the court had any military or political objectives of judging the vanquished countries or their populations. It meant rather that the court's purpose was to sit in judgment on the men and women who were guilty of crimes against humanity and peace, by planning, executing, and organizing such crimes, or by ordering others to do so during World War II. The term "international" was included in the tribunal's official designation to underline the universal validity of its judgment and its importance for the entire world.

The IMT tried twenty-two of Nazi Germany's political, military, and economic leaders: Hermann GÖRING, Rudolf HESS, Joachim von RIBBENTROP, Wilhelm KEITEL, Ernst KALTENBRUNNER, Alfred ROSENBERG, Hans FRANK, Wilhelm FRICK, Julius STREICHER, Fritz SAUCKEL, Alfred JODL, Martin BORMANN, Franz von PAPEN, Arthur SEYSS-INQUART, Albert SPEER, Konstantin Freiherr von NEURATH, Hjalmar SCHACHT, Walther FUNK, Karl Dönitz (the commander of the navy, whom Adolf HITLER, on the eve of his suicide, appointed as his successor); Erich Raeder (the commander of the navy prior to 1943); Baldur von Schirach (leader of the HITLERJUGEND and *Gauleiter* of Vienna); and Hans Fritzsche (in charge of radio propaganda).

The individual defendants were indicted under Article 6 of the charter, as follows:

Article 6. The Tribunal established by the Agreement referred to in Article 1 hereof for the trial and punishment of the major war criminals of the European Axis countries shall have the power to try and punish persons who, acting in the interests of the European Axis countries, whether as individuals or as members of organizations, committed any of the following crimes:

The following acts, or any of them, are crimes coming within the jurisdiction of the Tribunal for which there shall be individual responsibility:

(a) Crimes against Peace: namely, planning, preparation, initiation or waging of a war of aggression, or a war in violation of international treaties, agreements or assurances, or participation in a common plan or conspiracy for the accomplishment of any of the foregoing;

(b) War Crimes: namely, violations of the laws or customs of war. Such violations shall include, but not be limited to, murder, ill-treatment or deportation to slave labor or for any other purpose of civilian population of or in occupied territory, murder or ill-treatment of prisoners of war or persons on the seas, killing of hostages, plunder of public or private property, wanton destruction of cities, towns or villages, or devastation not justified by military necessity;

(c) Crimes against Humanity: namely, murder, extermination, enslavement, deportation, and other inhumane acts committed against any civilian population, before or during the war, or persecutions on political, racial or religious grounds in execution of or in connection with any crime within the jurisdiction of the Tribunal, whether or not in violation of the domestic law of the country where perpetrated.

Leaders, organizers, instigators and accomplices participating in the formulation or execution of a common plan or conspiracy to commit any of the foregoing crimes are responsible for all acts performed by any person in execution of such plan.

The judgment, which was delivered on September 30 and October 1, 1946, sentenced twelve of the defendants to death: Göring, Ribbentrop, Keitel, Kaltenbrunner, Rosenberg, Frank, Streicher, Sauckel, Jodl, Bor-

Brig. Gen. Telford Taylor, a member of the United States prosecution panel at the Nuremberg Trial. [United States Army]

The first session of the International Military Tribunal, on November 20, 1945. Sidney S. Alderman (standing), of the United States prosecution panel, reads the indictment. The tribunal, from left to right: Lt. Col. A. F. Volchkov, Soviet alternate member; Maj. Gen. I. T. Nikichenko, Soviet member; Justice Norman Birkett, British alternate member; Justice Geoffrey Lawrence, president; Francis Biddle, United States member; Judge John J. Parker, United States alternate member; Professor Henri Donnedieu de Vabres, Frenchmember; Robert Falco, French alternate member. [United States Army]

mann, and Seyss-Inquart. Bormann, who was not captured, was sentenced *in absentia*, and Göring committed suicide; the other ten were hanged, on October 16, 1946. Hess, Funk, and Raeder were sentenced to life imprisonment; Speer, Neurath, Dönitz, and Schirach were given sentences ranging from ten to twenty years; and von Papen, Schacht, and Fritzsche were acquitted (*see* Appendix, Volume 4).

The Nuremberg Trial was the first of its kind in history. It was a trial designed to punish the leaders of a regime, a government, and an army who were responsible for crimes committed in the framework of their policy and its implementation by means of an independent court of law of an international character. This court would try them in accordance with the principles of justice and the rules of law, with the accused having every opportunity to defend themselves.

The judges appointed to the tribunal were urged to follow the law and their conscience, notwithstanding the fact that they were nationals of the countries that had won the war—the United States, the Soviet Union, Great Britain, and France—and that it was the governments of these countries which had appointed them. These governments also set up an investigation and prosecution team that was subject to the provisions of the tribunal's charter. Cooperating with this team, in addition to the four major powers, were representatives of countries that had been occupied by Nazi Germany, such as Poland, Norway, and Belgium, and of nongovernmental international organizations, the latter in the status of *amici curiae* (friends of the court). This was also the status accorded to the WORLD JEWISH CONGRESS, in its role as the representative of the Jewish people.

Both the indictment and the judgment of the IMT stressed the legal definition of a war of aggression. A formal state of war exists as soon as such a state is declared, but this is not always accompanied by an act of aggression. On the other hand, aggression, in the form of an armed attack, can be carried out without being preceded by a declaration or announcement, and without the victim putting up any resistance or being able to defend himself. This was the case in Austria and Czechoslovakia, which the IMT cited as ex-

amples of states victimized by Nazi planning and preparing for wars of aggression.

The IMT determined that wars of aggression, in any form, are prohibited under a great number of international treaties; it also stressed that such wars violate the dictates of conscience and of humanity, which have long been officially recognized as sources for the law of war. The tribunal, however, disregarded the charges in the indictment against the defendants of conspiracies to commit war crimes, and dealt only with the defendants' common plan to prepare and conduct a war of aggression; the tribunal considered that all the other crimes were derived from the crimes against peace. It left no doubt, however, that under its charter all the leaders, organizers, inciters, and accessories to a criminal act who participated in the decision or implementation of a common plan or a conspiracy to commit crimes were guilty not only of their own acts but also of the crimes carried out by any other person in the execution of the common plan or conspir-

Hermann Göring and other defendants at the Nuremberg Trial. Göring is seated in the first row of the defendants' box, at the far left. [Library of Congress]

acy. This crime—participation in a criminal organization—was included in the IMT charter so that this category of criminals would not escape justice even when their responsibility for any specific criminal act could not be proved. In adopting the rule that participation in a criminal organization was a crime, the IMT had in mind the members of several Nazi frameworks classified by its charter as criminal organizations, and it planned to indict them, unless they could prove that despite their membership in such criminal organization or conspiracy they bore no personal responsibility for the criminal acts. The basis of this decision was the fact that these were voluntary organizations whose members had joined them in full knowledge of their criminal aims and methods.

The tribunal refused to accept the prosecution's demand to include the Reich government, the German General Staff, and the high command of the German armed forces among the organizations that it declared as criminal. The Soviet member of the tribunal, Lt. Gen. Roman A. Rudenko, submitted a minority opinion on this issue. The tribunal did declare as criminal the NAZI PARTY leadership, the SS, the GESTAPO, and the SA. The prosecution itself excluded certain categories from the charge of criminal participation in criminal organizations—persons holding strictly administrative posts in the police and members of certain party or official bodies—so as to remove the slightest suspicion of trying anyone under the principle of collective responsibility.

The IMT, like the courts of many countries, also held to the principle that persons committing a criminal violation of international law are individually responsible for violation, on the grounds that crimes of this nature are the result of their own acts and not of the "state" as an abstract body, and that the official position of such criminals does not absolve them from punishment. Control Council Law No. 10 also laid down that a person being investigated or tried for any of the acts defined as criminal by the IMT charter would not be permitted to claim that the statute of limitation applied to his crime, insofar as the entire period of the Nazi regime, January 30, 1933, to July 1, 1945, was con-

cerned. The charter also provided that any immunity, pardon, or amnesty granted by the Nazi regime would not be regarded as an impediment to the trial and punishment of persons accused of war crimes, in their various forms.

In addition, the tribunal took a clear stand on the issue of responsibility for crimes carried out on orders from above, since many of the crimes had been committed in accordance with Reich policy and the decrees of its leaders, and by the official authority of those concerned. It declared that the following of SUPERIOR ORDERS was not an excuse for the perpetration of a crime.

The portion of the IMT judgment dealing with war crimes and crimes against humanity committed by the defendants in the trial and by the criminal organizations concerns, in large measure, the persecution and murder of the Jewish people. In its analysis of these crimes, the IMT found it appropriate to single out the persecution of the Jews as a manifestation of consistent and systematic inhumanity on a huge scale.

The testimony given at the Nuremberg Trial, the documents presented by the prosecution, and the entire record of its proceedings constitute an incomparable source for the study of the Holocaust, and for the determination of the measures that must be taken to prevent its recurrence in any form, with regard to any social or national group, and especially to prevent the recrudescence of antisemitism and of discrimination against foreigners.

The conclusions arrived at by the IMT were also applied to the drafting of (1) the international convention for the prevention of the crimes of GENOCIDE (the Genocide Convention), adopted by the United Nations on December 9, 1948; (2) the Human Rights Declaration of December 10, 1948; (3) the Convention on the Abolition of the Statute of Limitations on War Crimes and Crimes against Humanity of November 26, 1968; and (4) the Geneva Convention on the Laws and Customs of War of 1949, and its supplementary protocols of 1977.

The principle that the only legal wars are wars in self-defense or against aggression—a fundamental rule of present-day international law—also derives from the United Nations Charter, the IMT charter, and the IMT judgment.

BIBLIOGRAPHY

Conot, R. E. *Justice at Nuremberg*. New York, 1983.
Davidson, E. *The Trial of the Germans: An Account of Twenty-Two Defendants before the International Military Tribunal at Nuremberg*. New York, 1967.
International Military Tribunal. *The Trial of the Major War Criminals before the International Military Tribunal, Blue Series*. 42 vols. Nuremberg, 1947–1949.
Smith, B. F. *The Road to Nuremberg*. New York, 1981.
Tusa, A., and J. Tusa. *The Nuremberg Trial*. London, 1984.

MARIAN MUSHKAT

Subsequent British Trials

The Royal Warrant of June 14, 1945, provided the basis for jurisdiction of the British military courts for the trial of "minor" German and Japanese war criminals. Based on the Royal Prerogative, the Royal Warrant made "provision for the trial and punishment of violations of the laws and usages of war committed during any war in which . . . [His Majesty's Government] have been or may be engaged at any time after the second day of September, nineteen hundred and thirty-nine." The Regulations attached to the warrant governed the custody, trial, and punishment of persons charged with such violation of the laws and usages of war.

All German and Japanese atrocities committed before the outbreak of World War II, and all acts that were not violations of the rules and customs of warfare—war crimes in a strict sense—were, therefore, beyond the scope of British war crimes courts. Consequently, the jurisdiction of these courts was narrower than that of the International Military Tribunal (IMT). A suspected war criminal within the command area of a British court's convening officer came under the jurisdiction of that court, whether or not his or her offense had been committed before or after the promulgation of the Royal Warrant, or "within or without" the command area.

The rules of procedure applicable in a regular court-martial were to apply, with certain modifications. Regulation 8 of the Royal Warrant introduced a relaxation of the rules of evidence otherwise applied in British courts. Under this provision, affidavits or statutory declarations, which normally would not be received as evidence in a British court, were admissible in evidence before British military courts. Further, hearsay testimony was admissible as evidence in certain situations. Given the special character of the war crimes trials and the nature of Nazi criminality—crimes that left few survivors—the admission of hearsay was perhaps the most important provision in the Royal Warrant. The courts were left to judge the weight to be attached to this type of evidence.

Those found guilty of war crimes could be sentenced to (1) death by hanging or shooting; (2) imprisonment for life or any other term; (3) confiscation of their property; or (4) payment of a fine. British military courts trying German war criminals awarded the first two penalties only. Decisions of the court could not be appealed. The accused could, however, petition the confirming officer against the finding and/or the sentence. Every sentence had to be confirmed. The secretary of state for war, or any officer not below the rank of major general authorized by him, could mitigate or remit a confirmed sentence, provided that this office held a command or rank superior to that of the confirming officer.

Two to eight military courts functioned concurrently under the Royal Warrant in the British zone of occupation in Germany. War crimes trials in this zone were initially held where crimes had been committed. Later, these trials were held in Hamburg, where three courts were established, and at Brunswick, where another court was established.

Under the Royal Warrant, two classes of criminals were to be tried: those who had committed breaches of the rules of war against British subjects, especially soldiers; and those who had committed war crimes against Allied nationals in British zones. The first class of criminals were those accused of shooting parachute troops or maltreating prisoners of war (POWs). The second class of criminals were concentration camp commandants and guards. The British tried those criminals in the second class who could not be delivered to the Allies owing to multiple jurisdictional claims.

When Germans had committed crimes against a non-British subject in the British zone, the British commander could order trial by a British military court or deliver the accused to the Allied authority whose national had been the victim of the crime. Most war crimes in the British zone were classified as: (1) crimes by concentration camp guards and other personnel whose victims were of various nationalities; (2) crimes against British subjects; and (3) crimes in the British zone of occupation against a specific and small number of nationals of an Allied power.

German crimes against European Jews played no part in any of the trials of Nazi war criminals conducted by British military courts, unless the Jewish victims were also Allied nationals. German crimes against German Jews were considered acts of violence other than war crimes, and for this reason, such crimes could not be tried in British military courts. The only British trial in which Allied Jewish victims were specifically mentioned as Jews was that of Generalfeldmarschall Fritz Erich von Lewinski (called von MANSTEIN), who was tried in late 1949.

British Policy toward German War Crimes Trials. From the outbreak of the war in September 1939 until the release of the last war criminal in British custody in June 1957, most British Foreign Office officials were skeptical of the very idea of prosecuting and sentencing Nazi war criminals for atrocities committed during the war. Officials of Allied governments-in-exile did not share this skepticism. Against the early victims of Nazi aggression, such as Poland or Czechoslovakia, Nazi Germany was waging a cruel and savage battle, ignoring the established laws of warfare, and violating various international conventions to which Germany had given its signature concerning the rights of victors toward inhabitants of occupied territories. Allied governments such as Great Britain and the United States, which did not experience German occupation, were less inclined to view Nazi misconduct as considerably worse than that of aggressors in past wars. British and American skepticism as to the accuracy of reports of German atrocities only reinforced these doubts; moreover, the British and American governments were uncertain what, if anything, should be done in response. The British Foreign Office was, at first, reluctant to make any public statement regarding German atrocities. Foreign Office officials wished particularly to avoid commenting on German crimes against German nationals. Later, as pressure from the Polish, Czech, and other Allied governments mounted for a statement from the British government, Foreign Office officials carefully distinguished between atrocities committed against German nationals and crimes committed in occupied countries.

While publicly expressing sympathy for the victims and condemnation of the perpetrators, the Foreign Office remembered the disastrous experience of German war crimes trials after World War I. Conducted at Leipzig by German courts, these trials resulted in such inadequate sentences that the whole process became known as the "Leipzig fiasco." Hoping to prevent a repetition of that disaster, the Foreign Office tried to avoid any statement that might later be construed as an obligation to prosecute Nazi war criminals. Consequently, the Foreign Office was often one step behind the Polish, Czech, and other Allied governments, which were pressing for a British commitment to exact retribution. The Foreign Office also lagged behind Winston CHURCHILL, who made public pronouncements on German atrocities and on the need to punish Nazi war criminals.

Foreign Office efforts to maintain a detached attitude toward Nazi war crimes began to crumble with the St. James's Palace Declaration of January 13, 1942. In this document, the eight signatory Allied governments, and the French National Committee, condemned Nazi atrocities in the occupied territories. They also declared that the trial and punishment of Nazi war criminals would be one of their principal war aims. A direct result of the St. James's Declaration was that, for the first time, government officials outside the Foreign Office expressed an interest in formulating a positive policy on war crimes. Attorney General Sir Donald Somervell and Solicitor General Sir David Maxwell Fyfe sought permission to investigate British war crimes policy, in order to assist the British government in the formulation of that policy. British adherence to the St. James's Declaration was advocated publicly, in Parliament and, on several occasions, by representatives of the Allied governments. Reports of atrocities coming from German-occupied Europe throughout 1942 and news of Japanese brutalities against POWs aroused British public opinion and, eventually, began to erode Foreign Office skepticism. Allegations of Japanese atrocities, particularly against British subjects in occupied British territory, also undermined the noncommittal attitude of the Foreign Office.

By October 1942, the detached attitude of the Foreign Office was under fire on every front. Faced with intensifying pressure from Parliament, the public, and the Allies—including the Soviets, who openly declared that those guilty of war crimes should be put on trial—many Foreign Office officials had come to believe that a policy statement on Nazi war criminals would soon be necessary. That statement was the Anglo-American-Soviet declaration of December 17, 1942. These three governments, and nine other Allied governments, condemned the Nazis' "bestial policy of cold-blooded extermination" of European Jewry, and reaffirmed their resolution to ensure that those responsible for these crimes should not escape retribution.

Churchill's involvement in the making of war crimes policy grew as news of Nazi atrocities continued to reach London. In October 1943, the Cabinet approved his recommendation that the foreign ministers of Great Britain, the United States, and the Soviet Union issue a new declaration. The American president, Franklin D. ROOSEVELT, and the Soviet leader, Joseph STALIN, accepted Churchill's draft, which came to be known as the Moscow Declaration of November 1, 1943. This document pledged that those responsible for German atrocities should be returned to the countries where their crimes were committed, and then judged and punished "on the spot by the peoples whom they have outraged." The Moscow Declaration added that "most assuredly the three Allied powers will pursue [war criminals] . . . to the uttermost ends of the earth and will de-

liver them to their accusers in order that justice may be done" (Foreign Office document 371 34378 C13682/31/62). The prosecution of war criminals where they committed their crimes meant that Great Britain would not bear exclusive responsibility for their trial. Churchill feared that Britain would not be capable of executing criminals over an extended period, since Britain had not suffered like the subjugated countries. In November 1944, the Cabinet decided that military courts, established in Germany or wherever appropriate, should adjudicate war crimes against British subjects or in British territory.

Foreign Secretary Anthony EDEN and Lord Chancellor Viscount Simon were convinced of the desirability of carrying out war crimes trials as quickly as possible after the cessation of hostilities. They held that the speed of military tribunals was of great advantage both in ensuring justice and in returning Europe to peace.

By the end of the war, the unprecedented nature and extent of Nazi criminality had become clear. It was also apparent that the number of German war criminals would be in the millions. Most official British and American declarations condemning German atrocities had promised to punish instigators and perpetrators. However, by late 1944, doubts as to the practicality of large-scale retribution were being voiced.

By 1946, criticism was increasingly heard in Parliament that British trials of Nazi war criminals had not yet ended. Moreover, successive British military governors in Germany, and many British officials at home, hoped for a return to normalcy in the British zone of Germany. This pressure eventually led to the cessation of British war crimes trials. It also made more difficult the extradition of war criminals, traitors, and collaborators, especially to Eastern European countries.

Perhaps the most fundamental question raised by war crimes trials was that of responsibility: to what extent were perpetrators of Nazi war crimes, acting under SUPERIOR ORDERS, responsible for their deeds? Were they more or less culpable than their instigators? This dilemma provoked considerable controversy when death sentences passed on perpetrators were commuted because their instigators had, for a variety of procedural reasons, received less severe sentences.

The Trials. The trial of the commandant and staff of the BERGEN-BELSEN camp, which lasted from September 17 to November 17, 1945, was the first British trial of German war criminals (*see* TRIALS OF WAR CRIMINALS: BERGEN-BELSEN TRIAL). The last British trial of a Nazi war criminal was that of Gen. Erich von Manstein, which began on August 23 and ended on December 19, 1949. The British conducted 357 trials of German, Italian, and Austrian nationals. Three hundred and fourteen of these trials involved 989 German nationals or those in German employ.

The British held trials for crimes against Allied civilians, including concentration camp internees, and against Allied military personnel. Some German officers were tried for both kinds of offenses. Many trials for crimes against Allied civilians involved commandants, guards, and other staff of concentration camps, including Bergen-Belsen and AUSCHWITZ, GROSS-ROSEN, Lahde-Weser, Neugraben-Tiefstak, NEUENGAMME, RAVENSBRÜCK, Sasel, Stocken and Ahlen, and NATZWEILER-STRUTHOF. In addition, the British tried those responsible for FORCED LABOR by civilians in work connected with military operations, for the deportation of civilians for slave labor, and for the killing of civilians as a reprisal for partisan activities. Dr. Bruno Tesch, in the ZYKLON B case (*see* TRIALS OF WAR CRIMINALS: ZYKLON B TRIAL), and the staff of the Velpke Children's Home, were also tried (*see* Appendix, Volume 4).

Among the high-ranking German officers tried by British military courts were Senior General Eberhard von Mackensen; Lieutenant Generals Kurt Maeltzer and Kurt Wolff; Generals Günther von Blumentritt, Curt Gallenkamp, Max Simon, Kurt Student, and Nikolaus von Falkenhorst; and Field Marshals Albert Kesselring and Erich von Manstein. The British also tried cases involving war crimes at sea, including the illegal scuttling of U-boats and firing at life rafts carrying survivors of torpedoed ships.

As for crimes against Allied POWs, the British prosecuted German military personnel who had served in POW camps. Other cases involved the employment of POWs on prohibited and dangerous work or as human screens in the face of fire; summary executions of escapees; and the issuing of illegal orders that denied Allied POWs protection by German escorts if attacked by the local populace. The British also prosecuted cases on behalf of airmen and POWs from Great Britain, the United States, Australia, New Zealand, and Poland, as well as of civilians from France, Denmark, the Netherlands, Poland, Greece, Yugoslavia, and the Soviet Union.

British Clemency for War Criminals. In addition to establishing a number of clemency boards to review sentences of individual German war criminals, the British instituted a number of general clemency measures. The first was the September 1949 decision to allow one-third remission of sentence for good conduct in jail; the second was the February 1950 decision to commute all life sentences to twenty-one years' imprisonment; the third was the December 1951 decision to allow credit for pretrial custody; and the fourth was the April 1955 decision to reduce all twenty-one-year sentences to twenty years' imprisonment.

The Wade Review, held in 1949, was the first general review of sentences of war criminals in British custody in Germany. Secretary of State for War Emanuel Shinwell, who was then responsible for the exercise of clemency, authorized that review. In 1950, Shinwell transferred the clemency authority to Foreign Secretary Ernest Bevin, who, in turn, delegated that authority to Gen. Brian Robertson, Britain's high commissioner in Germany. The Wade Review Board reduced 66 sentences out of a total of 372 considered. The Wade committee did not question the judgment; it tried instead to introduce uniformity of sentence by instituting a sentence of fifteen years for all those who were accessories in the first degree to the murder of Allied POWs, and ten years for all those guilty in the second degree.

Sir Ivone Kirkpatrick, Robertson's successor as high commissioner, conducted a general review of sentences between 1951 and 1953. In reviewing sentences, the high commissioner exercised authority delegated to him by the foreign secretary. However, in June 1951 the Cabinet withdrew the delegation of clemency authority from the high commissioner, and directed that, in the future, the monarch would grant clemency on the advice of the foreign secretary.

At the same time, Foreign Office officials were growing increasingly eager to divest themselves of all responsibility for clemency and custody of war criminals. By November 1951, the Foreign Office had recommended that the three occupying powers propose the following solution of the clemency and custody problem to the West Germans: (1) the Federal Republic should accept responsibility for the custody of war criminals; (2) West Germany should be invited to appoint representatives to an advisory clemency tribunal, which would advise the three powers on clemency concerning all war criminals imprisoned in the Federal Republic; and (3) this tribunal, whose unanimous decisions would be binding upon the convicting power, should be authorized to take into account all relevant circumstances, including uniformity of sentences, without, however, being competent to question the correctness of the conviction. This proposed tribunal, known as the Mixed Board, began its work in August 1955.

In the interim, however, clemency boards were set up in each of the three zones of Germany. In the British zone, the Mixed Consultative Board (MCB), under the chairmanship of Sir Alexander Maxwell, began work in the fall of 1953. This Anglo-German clemency board, composed of three British and two German members, carried out the third general review of sentences of war criminals passed by British military courts. When the MCB considered clemency advisable, such was recommended. Final decision lay with the secretary of state, who, if he agreed with the case for clemency, would make a submission for the approval of the monarch. Superior orders, and the degree of the accused's personal responsibility, as well as his or her age, health, rank, and mental capacity, were among the factors the Maxwell board considered in its deliberations. By March 1954, the British held only sixty-nine war criminals in the Werl prison, who were believed to be among the very worst of the Nazi war criminals.

The MCB often recommended clemency on the ground that the accused co-defendants had received much lighter sentences. Although the Foreign Office maintained that this should not be a reason for clemency, they were disinclined to challenge MCB recommendations. However, Foreign Office officials, notably Eden, did on occasion reject MCB recommendations.

By the end of October 1954, the MCB had virtually finished its work. When the board began its work in the fall of 1953, the British held eighty-one war criminals in custody; by October 1954, that number had dropped to forty-one. The release rate during these twelve months was nearly double what it had been during the previous twelve months.

For some years, the Foreign Office had been under pressure from Germans of every political persuasion to release the "honorable" German soldiers among those held in Werl. By the fall of 1954, Chancellor Konrad Adenauer had begun to speak on behalf of the remainder. Noting the approaching end of the occupation, the establishment of West German sovereignty, and closer German cooperation with the West, Adenauer renewed his government's request for additional generous clemency measures, pointing out that the majority of those detained had been held for nearly ten years.

The Mixed Board for War Criminals (MBWC) carried out the fourth and final set of sentence reviews of "minor" German war criminals in British custody. The MBWC was composed of three German members and a British, an American, and a French member. It began its work on August 11, 1955, and disposed of the last cases subject to its jurisdiction on June 4, 1958.

When the MBWC began to function in August 1955, 19 war criminals were in French custody, 26 in British custody, and 49 in American custody. In addition, 253 war criminals in American custody who had been released on parole were still subject to the jurisdiction of the MBWC.

From mid-August 1955 until the fall of 1957, the MBWC considered and acted upon petitions for clemency submitted in behalf of all the prisoners detained in British or French custody. During this period, the

MBWC also dealt with some of the American cases. By early August 1956, the MBWC had reviewed at least once the sentences of all twenty-six war criminals in British custody in the Werl prison. For various reasons unconnected with the MBWC, such as expiration of sentences, sixteen were released at that time. Toward the end of September 1956, Foreign Secretary Selwyn Lloyd directed that the nine remaining prisoners in Werl should be released by June 30, 1957, and that, if possible, these releases should be justified on grounds of health.

During the 1950s, the West German government criticized the Foreign Office for not granting a general amnesty to all war criminals. Parliament and British public opinion found fault with the Foreign Office for being too lenient in the exercise of clemency. In the face of such criticism, the Foreign Office strove to balance the Allied demand to honor the original findings and sentences of the courts, and the German wish not to acknowledge the correctness of those convictions. Here there was a noteworthy difference between the German and Japanese postwar experiences. In the Japanese peace treaty, Japan had been obliged to recognize the validity of sentences passed at trials of Japanese war criminals. In contrast, West Germany never recognized the validity of sentences passed at Allied trials of Nazi war criminals.

BIBLIOGRAPHY

Best, G. *Humanity in Warfare: The Modern History of the International Law of Armed Conflicts.* London, 1983.
United Nations War Crimes Commission. *History of the United Nations War Crimes Commission and the Development of the Laws of War.* London, 1948.
United Nations War Crimes Commission. *Law Reports of Trials of War Criminals.* Vol. 1. London, 1947.
Webb, A. M. *The Natzweiler Trial.* London, 1949.

PRISCILLA DALE JONES

Bergen-Belsen Trial

The trial of the BERGEN-BELSEN camp staff was held from September 17 to November 17, 1945, before a British military tribunal at Lüneburg, Germany. The accused were on trial for crimes committed in the AUSCHWITZ and Bergen-Belsen camps. The charge sheet referred to the role of the accused in planning and conspiring to torture and murder prisoners, in committing acts of murder, and in meting out inhuman treatment and punishment with their own hands. Most of the victims were Jews, although British, Italian, and French prisoners were killed as well.

Among the accused were Josef KRAMER, who had been a commandant of concentration camps from 1943 on and before his arrival in Bergen-Belsen had been on the staff of the Auschwitz-Birkenau camp; Dr. Fritz Klein, who took an active part in making *Selektionen* and sending people to their death; and prisoners who collaborated with the Nazis and were given the status of agents of the camp administration, such as Stanisława Staroska, a Polish woman known as "Stana the Flogger." Forty-five persons stood trial, twenty-one of them women (*see* Appendix, Volume 4).

When the British liberated Bergen-Belsen in April 1945, they found hundreds of rotting corpses on the ground and in the barracks. Among the survivors, many were too weak to move unassisted. Hundreds of prisoners had been beaten, tortured, or starved to death, or had died of diseases such as typhus. The housing for the prisoners was intolerable; barracks that could hardly hold one hundred persons had over one thousand piled in. Hundreds of deaths were caused by the dreadful sanitary conditions, the victims having been left for many days lying in the bunks in filth and excrement.

Kramer, Klein, and nine others—among them two women, Irma Grese and Elisabeth Volkenrath, who were charged with torturing and assaulting prisoners—were sentenced to death by hanging. Erich Zoddel, the camp's *Lagerälteste* (chief KAPO), was sentenced to life imprisonment, Staroska to ten years, and others to periods of one to three years. Fourteen of the accused were acquitted.

BIBLIOGRAPHY

Belsen. Tel Aviv, 1957. (In Hebrew.)
Phillips, R., ed. *Trial of Josef Kramer and Forty-Four*

The Bergen-Belsen trial, held in Lüneburg by a British military tribunal from September 17 to November 17, 1945. In the first row of the defendants' box, at the far left, is Josef Kramer, former commandant of Bergen-Belsen.

Others (*The Belsen Trial*). London, 1949.
United Nations War Crimes Commission. *Law Reports of Trials of War Criminals*. Vol. 2. London, 1947. See pages 1–156.

MARIAN MUSHKAT

Zyklon B Trial

In March 1946 the trial of Bruno Tesch, Joachim Drösihn, and Karl Weinbacher was held before a British military tribunal in Hamburg. The accused were owners and executives of a Hamburg factory that from January 1, 1941, to March 31, 1945, manufactured poison gas used to kill concentration camp prisoners. The gas, called ZYKLON B, was manufactured by the Tesch and Stabenow Company. It was used by the SS TOTENKOPFVERBÄNDE (Death's-Head Units) stationed in AUSCHWITZ and the other extermination camps.

The defendants in the trial claimed that they did not know to what use their product was put, a claim that was rebutted by Tesch's official company reports of his trips to Auschwitz. Tesch and Weinbacher (the executive manager of the "factory for means of death") were sentenced to death and executed; Drösihn, an employee of the factory, was acquitted.

The trial was conducted on the basis of Military Order 81/45, which derived its authority from a British law of June 14, 1945, that laid down the principles of the NUREMBERG TRIAL. The Zyklon B Trial established for the first time that the manufacture of gas for killing prisoners was a war crime.

BIBLIOGRAPHY

Barrington, J. H., ed. *The Zyklon B Trial: Trial of Bruno Tesch and Two Others.* London, 1948.
United Nations War Crimes Commission. *Law Reports of Trials of War Criminals.* Vol. 1. London, 1947. See pages 93–104.

MARIAN MUSHKAT

Subsequent Nuremberg Proceedings

On December 20, 1945, four weeks after the opening of the trial of the major war criminals by the International Military Tribunal, the Allied Control Council promulgated its Law No. 10. This law empowered the commanding officers of the four zones of occupation to conduct criminal trials on charges of aggression, war crimes, crimes against humanity, and membership in an organization aiming at such crimes. Under the charge of CRIMES AGAINST HUMANITY, the persecution of nationals of belligerent and nonbelligerent countries on political, religious, and racial grounds was declared punishable under the principles of international law. Pursuant to Law No. 10, the Office of the United States Government for Germany (OMGUS) established six military tribunals, composed of civilian judges recruited, for the most part, from among state supreme court judges in the United States. In 1,200 sessions of twelve trials (the Subsequent Nuremberg Proceedings), held between December 1946 and April 1949, they tried 177 persons. The prosecution consisted of 100 attorneys, at most, with 1,600 assistants. The defense was handled by 200 attorneys, chiefly German lawyers. On trial in these cases were representatives of the leadership of the Reich ministries, the Wehrmacht, industrial concerns, the German legal and medical establishment, and the SS.

The destruction of Jews was not classified as a separate criminal offense at Nuremberg, a fact that has since often been deplored. In legal terms, this offense was one of the several atrocities summarized as "crimes against humanity." All the judgments rendered at Nuremberg claimed to enforce statutory law or international common law, and widespread petitions to administer retroactive and *ad hoc* special law were rejected by the courts. As a result, the "FINAL SOLU-TION" was classified among the conventional crimes—murder, maltreatment, abduction, enslavement, and robbery—committed on racial grounds. Since it was the tribunals' task to prove the criminal nature of many of the activities carried out by the pillars of the German state (the administration, the armed forces, the judiciary, and industry), each of the twelve cases dealt with a specific sphere. The destruction of the Jews had not been confined to a specific sphere and was largely in the hands of the regular state institutions and industrial companies. It therefore appears in the Nuremberg Proceedings not as a single entity but split up into detailed component parts, next to and in conjunction with other criminal pursuits.

Chronologically, the succeeding stages of the persecution of the Jews are distributed among the Subsequent Nuremberg Proceedings in the following pattern:

1. *Preparation of the Nuremberg Laws* and their decrees of implementation. These were dealt with in count 5 of Trial 11, The Ministries Case, as a component part of the extermination program. The defendant Wilhelm STUCKART, former state secretary (*Staatssekretär*) of the Reich Ministry of the Interior, was found guilty of this and other crimes, for which he was sentenced to forty-six months' imprisonment.

2. *Application of the Law for the Protection of German Blood and Honor by Rassenschande (race defilement) tribunals* occurred in Trial 3, The Justice Case, in which two "special judges" (*Sonderrichter*) were found guilty of judicial murder and sentenced to life imprisonment.

3. *Forced "Aryanization" of Jewish-owned capital.* This was one of the counts in Trial 5, The Flick Case. Friedrich Flick, a coal and steel producer, and his associates were acquitted on this count, on formal as well as factual grounds. The court considered outside its jurisdiction crimes committed before the outbreak of the war, and also did not consider forced "Aryanization" a form of racial persecution.

4. *Forced "Aryanization" of agricultural property.* This charge came up in count 5 of Trial 11, The Ministries Case, against Richard Walther DARRÉ, the former minister of agriculture. It was one of the charges of which he was found guilty and sentenced to seven years in prison.

5. *Abduction and mass shooting of Jews* in concentration camps maintained by the Wehrmacht in Serbia, in retaliation for partisan attacks. In Trial 7, The Hostage Case, this was one of the counts with which the generals of the southeast front were charged. Generals Wilhelm List and Walter Kuntze were found guilty of this and other charges and were sentenced to life imprisonment and a fifteen-year term, respectively.

6. *The extermination campaign by the Einsatzgruppen* in the war against the Soviet Union. This was the subject of Trial 9, The *Einsatzgruppen* Case, which led to fourteen death sentences and prison terms ranging from three years to life.

7. *Logistic support for the Einsatzgruppen,* direct orders to them, and responsibility for their actions under the law of war. These charges against the army and army group commanders invested with executive power on the eastern front were heard in Trial 12, The High Command Case. Another count in this case was that of issuing orders for the so-called special treatment (*Sonderbehandlung*) of Jewish prisoners of war in the Soviet army in or near prisoner-of-war camps maintained by the Wehrmacht. Generals Georg Karl Friedrich Wilhelm von Küchler, Hermann Hoth, Hans Reinhardt, Hans von Salmuth, Karl von Roques, Hermann Reinecke, and Otto Wöhler were found guilty of these charges and sentenced to prison terms ranging from eight years to life.

8. *The deportation of Jews* from western Europe came up in Trial 8, The RuSHA Case (RASSE- UND SIEDLUNGSHAUPTAMT; Race and Resettlement Main Office). That agency, through its Ahnentafelamt (Genealogical Office), had drawn up the family trees of all Jews and descendants of Jews in the German Reich, the Netherlands, Belgium, Norway, and France, in order to determine the fate of MISCHLINGE (partial Jews). These family trees were used to compose the lists for the transports of Jews. Eight defendants were found guilty of these charges, among others, and sentenced to prison terms ranging from thirty-four months to life.

9. *Events relating to the deportations from Denmark, Slovakia, Croatia, Serbia, France, Italy, and Hungary* were investigated in The Ministries Case, to determine the role played by German Foreign Office diplomatic personnel in these events. Ernst von WEIZSÄCKER, Gustav Adolf Steengracht von Moyland, Ernst Wörmann, and Edmund VEESENMAYER were found guilty and sentenced to prison terms of seven to twenty years.

10. *Deportations from Greece.* Evidence presented by the prosecution in The Hostage Case inculpated generals Wilhelm Speidel, Hubert Lanz, and Helmuth Felmy in this crime. The generals were found guilty, but their role in the deportations was not included in the judgment.

11. *Antisemitic indoctrination* of the population and dulling of their conscience during the extermination process was one of the charges proven in The Ministries Case against Otto Dietrich, chief of the Reich press section (among other offenses). He was sentenced to seven years in prison.

12. *Pillage of the property left behind by the Jews who were abducted from Germany,* which had been assigned to the financial offices, was one of the charges heard in The Ministries Case against Lutz Schwerin von Krosigk, former Reich minister of finance, who was sentenced to ten years in prison.

13. *Administration of concentration camps and the Vernichtung durch Arbeit (annihilation through work) system* in the SS-run companies OSTINDUSTRIE GBMH (Osti) and Deutsche Erd- und Steinwerke (German Earth and Stone Works; DEST) were among the counts heard in Trial 4, The Pohl Case, against Oswald POHL and the managers of the SS WIRTSCHAFTS-VERWALTUNGSHAUPTAMT (Economic-Administrative Main Office; WVHA). This case ended in three acquittals, eleven sentences of prison terms ranging from ten years to life, and three death sentences.

14. *The enslavement of Jews* by private industry, through forcing them to work under conditions like those in concentration camps, was investigated in Trial 10, The Krupp Case, against Alfred Krupp and eleven directors of his company. The tribunals found that Krupp and ten members of his staff were implicated in the German government's forced-labor program and sentenced them to prison terms of two to twelve years. Included in the findings of the tribunals was that of maltreatment of prisoners engaged in the construction of a munitions factory at AUSCHWITZ.

The Nuremberg Military Tribunals. Trial 12, The High Command Case, November 28, 1947, to October 28, 1948. Left to right are Judge Winfield B. Hale, of the Tennessee Court of Appeals; Presiding Judge John C. Young, of the Colorado Supreme Court; and Judge Justin W. Harding, assistant attorney general of Ohio. [United States Army]

15. *The government-sponsored slave economy* figured in Trial 2, The Milch Case, against Field Marshal Erhard Milch, a member of the Main Planning Office, who was sentenced to life imprisonment. His sentence was later reduced to fifteen years, and he was released in 1954.

16. *Sale of* ZYKLON B (*prussic acid*) *to the SS and construction of industrial plants in Auschwitz* were among the charges heard in Trial 6, The I.G. FARBEN Case, in which twenty-four directors and engineers of the concern were on trial. The tribunal acquitted the defendants of the Zyklon B charge because it was not proved that they had known to what use it was to be put (*see also* ZYKLON B TRIAL).

17. *Medical experiments on human beings in concentration camps,* including sterilization experiments for future application to *Mischlinge,* were dealt with in Trial 1, The Medical Case. One of the defendants in this case was Wolfram Sievers, managing director of

AHNENERBE (the Ancestral Heritage Society), who was charged with establishing a collection of skeletons and skulls of Jews for anthropological research at the Reich University in Strasbourg. Seven defendants were acquitted, nine others were sentenced to prison terms ranging from ten years to life, and Sievers and six doctors and medical officials were sentenced to death.

18. *Hoarding of dental gold from Auschwitz* in the coffers of the Reichsbank was a charge in The Ministries Case against Reichsbank vice-chairman Emil Johann Puhl, for which he was sentenced to five years' imprisonment.

With the exception of the Reichsbahn (the national railway system) and the REICHS-SICHERHEITSHAUPTAMT (Reich Security Main Office; RSHA), the Subsequent Nuremberg Proceedings systematically exposed the principal agencies involved in the extermination of the Jews, determined the culpability of their personnel, and passed sentences on a few of their leading figures. But their achievement of laying bare the structure of the crimes committed by the bureaucracy did not play any role in later criminal trials; a precedent was not established. Both in Germany and in other countries, the courts now turned their attention predominantly to the personnel who had been directly engaged in carrying out the liquidation process in the extermination camps and the killing squads. Thus the conventional image of the barbaric Holocaust agent emerged.

Contrary to the expectations of their originator, OMGUS, the Subsequent Nuremberg Proceedings had no influence on the way the German people viewed their recent history. The Germans, for the most part, felt that the sentences meted out were arbitrary decisions made by the victorious powers, and they exerted constant organized pressure on United States High Commissioner John J. McCloy to suspend the sentences. Such demands benefited from the growing interests of the United States in founding the North Atlantic military alliance, interests that included the indispensable territory and forces of western Germany. By 1951, primarily at the urging of the German churches and political parties, a hurried pardoning policy was introduced that led to the commutation to prison terms of twelve of the twenty-five death sentences and to the release of the last of the prisoners by 1958. These ex-convicts resumed their interrupted careers or retired, usually keeping entitlements to pensions for their official services. According to Article 7.1 of the Transition Agreement, one of the 1955 Paris Agreements under which the Federal Republic of Germany regained sovereignty from the Western powers, all the judgments passed in war crimes trials were established as having the effectiveness of law. Later, the German federal government arrived at a different interpretation of this agreement. In its opinion, and under the federal supreme court opinion of January 9, 1959, the Nuremberg judgments lacked the power of law.

[See also Appendix, Volume 4.]

BIBLIOGRAPHY

Taylor, T. *Final Report to the Secretary of the Army on the Nuremberg War Crimes Trials under Control Council Law No. 10.* Washington, D.C., 1949. *Trials of War Criminals before the Nuremberg Military Tribunals under Control Council Law No. 10,* vols. 1–15. Washington, D.C., 1949–1952.

JÖRG FRIEDRICH

West Germany

As early as 1943, the Allies in the war against Germany agreed that they would punish officials of the Nazi regime who were responsible for its crimes. On the basis of that agreement, Allied military tribunals after the war convicted and sentenced, according to a reliable estimate, some sixty thousand Germans and Austrians of war crimes and CRIMES AGAINST HUMANITY. Military tribunals of the western Allies alone passed more than eight hundred death sentences (no precise information is available on the number of death sentences passed on Germans and Austrians by the Communist countries).

Laws 4 and 10 (passed in 1945) of the Allied Control Council (consisting of the four powers—the United States, the USSR, Britain, and France—who were in charge of the zones of occupation in Germany) laid down that German courts which had been rehabilitated after the war were empowered to try only those Nazi crimes that had been committed by Germans against Germans, or against stateless persons, and then only with the agreement of the military administration of the respective zone of occupation. This meant that the great majority of Nazi crimes—against citizens of Poland, the USSR, Yugoslavia, France, and the Netherlands, and nationals of other Allied countries—were excluded from the jurisdiction of the German judicial institutions.

Until late 1950, the crimes related to the Nazi regime that were tried by German courts in the Federal Republic of Germany dealt mainly with relatively minor transgressions, such as denunciations, physical injury, deprivation of liberty, and coercion in various degrees and at various times. Some grave crimes, however, were also within the competence of German courts in that period, such as crimes committed in the concentration camps, murders during the course of the EUTHANASIA PROGRAM, and the so-called final-phase crimes, or the murder of those German soldiers and civilians who in the last few days of the war resisted the continuation of meaningless warlike action. Almost all these criminal trials resulted from charges brought by the victims or their heirs against participants in the crimes who were known or who had been discovered by chance.

In 1950, shortly after the establishment of the Federal Republic of Germany in the three Western zones of occupation, the restrictions imposed by the Allies at the end of the war on the jurisdiction of German courts were removed, as far as the Federal Republic was concerned. This meant that the public prosecutors were now free to embark upon a systematic investigation of all Nazi crimes and to prosecute the criminals involved in them. It did not, however, work out this way, owing partly to a lack of personnel and adequate material resources, and partly to the inadequacy of the lines of communication among the prosecuting attorneys, on a higher rather than the local level. However, the main reason was that the Germans at the time were preoccupied with the rehabilitation of the country and the restoration of its economic strength, lost as a result of the war.

The experience gained in the DENAZIFICATION process, which had been quite discouraging, created a situation in which very few people were interested in a renewed confrontation with the Nazi crimes and in dealing with the crimes by means of criminal proceedings. German politicians in positions of responsibility were aware that a new and stronger drive for the prosecution of Nazi crimes would not be popular with the electorate. In addition, the growing tension between East and West put pressure, on both sides, to embark on the rearmament of Germany; this in turn diminished the Allies' interest in pursuing the punishment of Nazi crimes. This tendency was clearly demonstrated by the pardons granted to Nazi criminals who in the first few postwar years had been given severe sentences by the Allied military tribunals.

According to the statute of limitations of May 8, 1950, the operative date for Nazi crimes, as distinguished from other crimes, was the day the war ended, rather than the date on which the crime was committed, since prosecution of these crimes had not been possible during the Nazi regime. The statute thus made it possible to inaugurate a series of trials for crimes committed in the AUSCHWITZ and TREBLINKA extermination camps, in the BUCHENWALD, NEUENGAMME, GROSS-ROSEN, FLOSSENBÜRG, and SACHSENHAUSEN concentration camps, in the THERESIENSTADT camp, and in the SAJMIŠTE (Semlin) detention camp.

However, from 1951 to 1955 the number of proceedings conducted in the courts of the Federal Republic was sharply reduced, because by the time the statute was issued, five years after the end of the war, offenses that bore a maximum sentence of five years could no longer be prosecuted. In most of these cases, too, criminal proceedings were instituted on the basis of complaints submitted by victims of the crimes or their heirs, and, sometimes, against suspects of Nazi crimes who had been discovered by chance. There was still no attempt to launch a systematic effort for the investigation and prosecution of all crimes committed under the Nazi regime against Jews, GYPSIES, and real or imagined political opponents.

On May 8, 1955, the statute of limitations was to go into effect for Nazi-related crimes with a maximum sentence of ten years. As far as the prosecution of Nazi crimes was concerned, this meant, for all practical purposes, that henceforth only acts of premeditated murder could be prosecuted. At about the same time, on May 3, 1955, the *Überleitungsvertrag* (transition agreement) between Germany and the United States, Britain, and France went into effect, containing the following provision:

> Persons who have been tried for a crime by the American, British, or French authorities in their respective zones of occupation and the proceedings against them [having] terminated, will not be tried again for the same crime by the German public prosecution, regardless of the outcome of the trial under the Allied occupation authorities—conviction, acquittal, or dismissal of the case because of lack of evidence; this provision also applies to cases in which new evidence has come to light against persons who have been either acquitted or have had their case dismissed.

Nevertheless, 1955 was the year that marked the beginning of a change in the prosecution of Nazi crimes.

It began with an investigation instituted on the basis of a complaint concerning the murder of Jews in the German-Lithuanian border region by members of an Einsatzkommando (mobile killing sub-unit). In this case, contrary to the previous practice, the prosecution did not confine itself to the specific facts mentioned in the complaint. For the first time, the prosecution pursued all leads that came to light during the investigation of other crimes committed by EINSATZGRUPPEN and Einsatzkommandos, and added these criminal charges to the initial complaint. The mass of information gathered by this process made it clear that apart from a few proceedings by Allied military tribunals against top Nazi officials, some of the worst crimes committed by the Nazi regime had yet to be prosecuted.

In the fall of 1958 the ministers of justice of all the *Länder* (states) of the Federal Republic decided to establish the LUDWIGSBURGER ZEN-TRALSTELLE (Central Office of the Judicial Administrations of the *Länder* for Investigation of Nazi Crimes), in Ludwigsburg. The new office was given the assignment of discovering all available sources of information on Nazi crimes and instituting criminal proceedings against the persons reponsible for these crimes.

The results of the decision soon made themselves felt. In the first twelve months of its existence, the Ludwigsburger Zentralstelle initiated four hundred extensive investigations. The most important among these concerned, in part, the crimes committed by Einsatzgruppen and Einsatzkommandos in the Soviet Union and Poland; by the Sicherheitspolizei (Security Police), ORDNUNGSPOLIZEI ("order" police), and the so-called Volksdeutscher Selbstschutz (Ethnic Germans' Self-Defense Force) in the occupied territories; and in the Auschwitz, BEŁŻEC, SOBIBÓR, Treblinka, and CHEŁMNO extermination camps.

On May 8, 1960, fifteen years after the war had ended, the statute of limitations on the crimes of manslaughter, deliberate physical injury leading to death, and deprivation of liberty with lethal results, committed under the Nazi regime, went into effect. Political figures active in the Social Democratic party of the Federal Republic of Germany had attempted to introduce a law that would block

the statute of limitations from going into effect, but the majority of the Bundestag (the German parliament) were in favor of the statute being applied. Henceforth, only murder could still be prosecuted by the courts.

Even the charge of murder, according to the law existing at the time, would be subject to a statute of limitations on May 8, 1965, unless criminal proceedings were instituted against suspects before that date. Accordingly, the Ludwigsburger Zentralstelle, together with the prosecuting attorneys in the various German states, made efforts to collect all available evidence as quickly as possible and use it in time to institute criminal proceedings against persons known to be, or suspected of being, participants in a crime of murder under the Nazi regime.

Since most of the available documentary evidence at that time was to be found in archives of countries outside Germany, the Ludwigsburger Zentralstelle applied to the competent authorities in Western countries for their assistance in this effort. These official authorities, especially in the United States, as a rule gave the Zentralstelle broad access to the material held in their archives, and on request supplied it with copies of documents. Most of the relevant documents, however, were held by the Communist countries of Eastern Europe. Among these countries, Poland was the first to indicate that it was ready to cooperate with the German prosecution in providing evidence of Nazi crimes, and this was followed, in the early 1960s, by the Soviet Union making similar hints. For political reasons, however, the government of the Federal Republic would not approve of the Ludwigsburger Zentralstelle's establishing contact with the appropriate official organs in Eastern European countries—most of which were still without diplomatic relations with the Federal Republic (the only exception being the Soviet Union).

In late 1964, it became clear that despite all the efforts being made, the majority of Nazi acts of murder would benefit from the statute of limitations when it went into effect the following May 8, because the necessary investigations could not be made in time. At this point, the government of the Federal Republic of Germany decided to request all foreign governments to put at its disposal all evidence in their possession on Nazi war crimes. The government also instructed the Ludwigsburger Zentralstelle to seek to utilize the relevant archival material held by the Communist-bloc countries. As a result of such efforts, these countries—primarily Poland, the Soviet Union, and Czechoslovakia —as of 1965 enabled German prosecuting attorneys and Zentrale Stelle officials in many instances to examine the contents of their archives and, on request, provided them with copies of hundreds of thousands of documents and protocols of interrogations and investigations.

In the meantime the Bundestag, in March 1965, after an extremely sharp floor debate, passed a law that postponed the date for the statute of limitations on Nazi acts of murder to December 31, 1969. It was hoped that by then, by putting additional staff on the job, it would be possible to advance the investigation of Nazi crimes to a point at which judicial proceedings could commence in all known cases and, as far as anyone could judge, there would be no more Nazi crimes left to be revealed.

After 1965 the Zentralstelle's staff was increased to a total of 121, including 48 prosecuting attorneys and judges. In addition, the public prosecutors and courts in the Federal Republic for a number of years had 200 prosecuting attorneys and examining magistrates dealing exclusively with the investigation of Nazi crimes, with the assistance of over 200 criminal-investigation officers. There were also the judges sitting in the main trials by jury of Nazi crimes that went on at any given time. In many foreign countries, German consular officials were busy taking evidence from witnesses to Nazi crimes. In the Soviet Union and Czechoslovakia, but primarily in Poland and Israel, the local authorities, at the request of German prosecuting attorneys, took evidence, in thousands of cases, from witnesses who had been among the victims.

Despite all the greatly increased efforts, it soon became obvious that the task of completing the investigation of all Nazi crimes and instituting criminal proceedings, where this was indicated, could not be carried out by the end of 1969. The Bundestag therefore—not without pressure from abroad— extended the statute of limitations for Nazi

murder acts by another ten years, up to December 31, 1979.

In the 1970s the influx of documentary evidence was kept up, especially from Poland, albeit on a reduced scale. In 1978, the issue of the statute of limitations was revived all over the world. Foreign countries and multinational organizations and institutions—including the European Parliament in Strasbourg—pressed for the total abolition of the statute of limitations as far as war crimes and crimes against humanity were concerned.

In early 1979, the American television series "Holocaust" was broadcast in the Federal Republic and had the effect of reviving German interest, especially among young people, in the relentless prosecution of Nazi crimes. Under the impact of these developments, the Bundestag in July 1979 decided to abolish the statute of limitations for the crime of murder in general, thus enabling Nazi killers to be brought to trial without the particular impediment of the statute of limitations.

From its inception in December 1958 until the summer of 1986, the Ludwigsburger Zentralstelle launched investigation of over five thousand cases, involving thousands of suspects, and on their completion submitted its findings to the respective prosecutors in the Federal Republic. This led to the instituting of a total of 4,853 official criminal trials, which covered the entire spectrum of Nazi violence in all its forms. Many proceedings involved crimes in the concentration camps, including satellite camps and Aussenkommandos (detachments); the murders by the Einsatzgruppen and Einsatzkommandos, by the mobile units of the Ordnungspolizei, and by the local police and the Gestapo offices, especially in connection with the forced *Umsiedlung* ("resettlement"; actually deportation) of the Jews—their expulsion from their homes and deportation to the ghettos and extermination camps; the murder of hospital patients and inmates of mental institutions in the Euthanasia Program; and the murder of Poles and Jews by members of the Volksdeutscher Selbstschutz. In addition to these spectacular mass-murder actions, the trials also involved thousands of cases of violence against individual victims or small groups.

In the majority of the cases, however, the proceedings ended without convictions being made. In many instances the participants in the crime could not be found, despite determined efforts; quite frequently, the evidence in hand was not enough to prove with certainty the guilt of the surviving suspects who were being interrogated and tried. The persons presumed to have taken part in the crimes benefited from the legal principles developed by the German courts and the federal supreme court, according to which an accused could not be convicted on the basis of membership in a unit or organization that took part in a crime. For such a person to be convicted, his actual participation in the criminal act carried out by the unit or organization had to be proved. In view of the contradictions contained in testimonies given by different witnesses, and their diminishing ability to remember events that had taken place so long before, the courts and the prosecution often found it impossible to determine individual guilt, even when the crime itself was revealed down to the last detail. In the cases that did end in a conviction, but in which the accused had not acted on their own initiative and had merely followed the orders of their superiors, the courts as a rule concluded that the accused had been accessories to the crime and not the actual perpetrators. This finding enabled the courts to refrain from imposing the sentence of life imprisonment that was mandatory for murder, and instead to sentence the convicted criminal to a prison term of limited duration. Considering the immense number of victims and the enormous cruelty of the murderous deeds, such leniency seemed uncalled for, even in the eyes of unbiased observers.

From the end of the war up to January 1986, German courts in the Federal Republic tried 90,921 persons indicted for taking part in Nazi crimes; 6,479 persons were given substantial sentences, 12 being sentenced to death (as long as the death penalty was still in force) and 160 to life imprisonment. Another 1,300 suspects, at least, were still under investigation by the public prosecution on January 1, 1986, while the Ludwigsburger Zentralstelle was conducting preliminary probes of another 101 cases, in which the number of suspects had yet to be determined.

For the German Democratic Republic (DDR), no detailed official information has been made available regarding its efforts to bring Nazi criminals to justice. What is certain, however, is that no systematic attempt was made to prosecute Nazi crimes. When a person's participation in Nazi crimes did come to light on the basis of a complaint or by chance, a stiff sentence was imposed, as a rule. According to the DDR prosecutor general, a total of 12,861 persons had been convicted of "fascist war crimes and crimes against humanity" by the end of 1976.

BIBLIOGRAPHY

Friedrich, J. *Die kalte Amnestie: NS-Täter in der Bundesrepublik.* Frankfurt, 1984.
Hellendall, F. "Nazi Crimes before German Courts: The Immediate Post-War Era." *Wiener Library Bulletin* 24/3 (Summer 1970): 14–20.
Henkys, R. *Die nationalsozialistischen Gewaltverbrechen.* Stuttgart, 1965.
Jäger, H. *Verbrechen unter totalitärer Herrschaft.* Freiburg, 1967.
Lichtenstein, H. *In Namen des Volkes?* Cologne, 1984.
Rückerl, A. *The Investigation of Nazi Crimes 1945–1978: A Documentation.* Hamden, Conn., 1980.
Rückerl, A. *NS-Verbrechen vor Gericht.* Heidelberg, 1982.

ADALBERT RÜCKERL

Postwar Dispensation of Justice in Germany

In 1955 the Federal Republic of Germany added to its criminal code a paragraph (220a) adapting the provisions of the 1948 United Nations Genocide Convention and making a life sentence mandatory for murder with the intention of destroying a national group. However, because GENOCIDE did not appear as a crime in the criminal code that was in force when the Nazis were in power, the Federal Republic does not apply paragraph 220a against Nazis found guilty of that crime. The indictments and judgments are based on the statutes that were in force when the crime was committed. Murder, physical injury, and deprivation of liberty had been illegal in the Third Reich throughout its existence. Such criminal acts, though, were not subject to prosecution in Nazi Germany when committed on official orders. After the war the courts claimed that at the time the criminal acts were committed, they had been under duress and unable to try the offenders, but that this by no means implied that the acts in question had been legal or that the state's power to prosecute them had lapsed; and the courts in the newly created Federal Republic were empowered to try the offenders. Doubt also remained as to whether the legal officers who had served under the Nazi regime were capable of dispensing justice.

In 1949, in the course of consultations on the draft constitution of the Federal Republic, concern had been expressed over the possibility that Heinrich HIMMLER's police and Nazi judges would be reinstated in the civil service. This in fact did take place. On the basis of the constitutional entitlement of former government officials to be maintained by the state (article 131), nearly all the police, judges, and public prosecutors who had served under the Nazis were reinstated in their posts. Consequently, attempts to convict Nazi judges of judicial murder all failed. During the Hitler period, judges had obeyed Nazi laws and had been blind to the illegality of their actions; this blindness carried over into the new postwar period, and proceedings instituted against these judges regularly ended in an acquittal. In turn, the issues of obedience to official orders and awareness of the illegality of such orders assumed roles of central importance in the Federal Republic trials of Nazi criminals. This had not been the case in proceedings conducted by the occupying powers (*see* SUPERIOR ORDERS).

Most of the persons brought to trial in the courts of the Federal Republic had either killed with their own hands or had been in charge of killings. The higher the rank of those accused, the farther removed they had been from the actual scene of the crime, and, consequently, the more successful were their eventual efforts to invoke the protection of the popular excuse of not having been aware of the end goal, that is, extermination. On the other hand, those whose awareness of the end goal was not in doubt—the actual killers—only in rare cases had acted on their own, and they thus found legal refuge in claiming that they had only been following superior orders. The courts therefore spent much time trying to establish whether the acts of murder carried out by the defendants were indeed to be regarded as murders they had committed on their own. In this way, the judges managed to perpetuate a system in which it could not be proved that the so-called desk criminals had been aware of the killing, or that the executioners had killed with intent or on their own initiative. The courts of the Federal Republic found no solution to this dilemma.

It was not until a new generation had come to maturity in the late 1950s, which had not witnessed or supported Nazi crimes, or taken part in them, that this situation changed. Although the majority of the German population still called for an end to the prosecution of Nazi crimes, a minority vehemently insisted on the prosecution of the crimes involving mass extermination.

This new drive primarily affected the lowest ranks in the chain of command, the subordinate echelons of the police and the SS who were charged with the physical destruction of the masses of victims delivered into their hands—the EINSATZGRUPPEN and the personnel in the concentration camps. Prosecution of the Einsatzgruppen murders, which the Nuremberg Military Tribunals had documented as having been a joint effort of the Wehrmacht and the SS, was now confined to the SS only. In concentration camp trials, the accused were primarily camp guards and the camp commandants. Efforts to have the deportations from German cities classified as participation in murder were of no avail. This was also the outcome of efforts to convict Gerhard Peters, the managing director of DEGESCH (Deutsche Gesellschaft für Schädlingsbekämpfung mbH, or German Vermin-combating Corporation), the sole supplier of ZYKLON B hydrogen cyanide to the SS; the top officials of the Reichsbahn (the German RAILWAYS); and the participants in the WANNSEE CONFERENCE.

In the German courts the chain of command leading to the "FINAL SOLUTION" was confined to the originators: Adolf HITLER, Hermann GÖRING, and Reinhard HEYDRICH, at the top level, and to the actual murder personnel at the lowest level. The responsibility of the intermediate level—the bureaucratic-military-industrial elites, which the Nuremberg Military Tribunals had exposed —was not recognized by the West German courts. Unlike the Nuremberg courts, which considered certain state organs to be criminal, the West German courts tended not to consider them as such. They based their reasoning on the idea that most Nazi crimes had resulted from the direct and conspiratorial delegation of orders from Hitler (*Führerbefehle*) to the actual murderers.

In contrast to the Nuremberg judgments, the German courts' dispensation of justice to Nazi criminals gained a degree of acceptance among the German population. The guilt of the concentration camp killers and SS firing squads was not in doubt. Yet they were given every consideration by the courts, which felt that although the accused had engaged in a mass murder operation, they were not "murderous types." The view of the courts was that since the Holocaust was carried out in obedience to orders, the executioners, for the most part, were not impelled by any murder motive of their own. Under German law a murder motive is the intent to murder in a particularly reprehensible, compulsive, malicious, and bestial fashion, and this was not seen as fitting the discipline and speed required by the extermination operation. In the view of the judges the extermination personnel became the "murderous type" only if they were imbued with Hitlerian racist hatred, or if they performed the killing in an excessively cruel manner.

Another factor inhibiting the courts was the time that had elapsed between the crimes and the trials. By the time the trials were held, decades had passed since the criminal acts had been committed, and only in a few cases was it possible to arrive at precise findings. When it came to examining the executioners' motivation, the courts, as a rule, accepted the perpetrators' own testimony of having acted in obedience to orders. Counterarguments could not be put forth easily, because the external details of the extermination operation could not be reconstructed conclusively on the evidence given by the victims. Moreover, in West German courts, the fact that a person had been a member of a murder squad or an extermination camp staff was not considered as incriminating; it

had to be proved that the suspect had personally taken part in killing or in giving orders to kill. Few witnesses had survived, and those who had survived did not always remember with sufficient accuracy such particulars as dates, times of day, places, faces, and ranks. It was therefore rarely possible to give a verdict of guilty, which had to be based on many small details.

The defense, for its part, diligently and skillfully tracked down inaccuracies in the evidence submitted by the survivors. The victims' memories often retained the overall situation, but not the minutiae of the crime. The factory-like procedure of killing had left the memory blurred.

In general, the German courts decided that the crimes they were asked to judge did not meet the criteria of murder as required by law. If the defendants were shown to have killed, they were also generally shown to have acted as tools of the Nazi machine. This meant that they were at most guilty of being accessories to murder, an offense punishable by terms in prison ranging from three years to life (as of 1975, from three to fifteen years). In most cases the judges' evaluation of the seriousness of the crimes committed in the extermination operation restricted the punishment they dealt out to the minimum required by law. The accused also benefited from the fact that they were no longer considered to represent a threat to the community.

The full force of the law was applied only in the rather rare cases of excessively cruel and sadistic criminals. Inflicting more pain and physical or mental torture "than was necessary" was shown to be in violation of orders the defendants had received. Federal German criminal courts regarded such behavior as indication of murderous intent, and in these cases they could therefore pass sentences of life imprisonment.

BIBLIOGRAPHY

Friedrich, J. *Die kalte Amnestie: NS-Täter in der Bundesrepublik.* Frankfurt, 1984.
Lichtenstein, H. *In Namen des Volkes?* Cologne, 1984.
Rückerl, A. *The Investigation of Nazi Crimes, 1945–1978: A Documentation.* Hamden, Conn., 1980.

Rückerl, A. *NS-Verbrechen vor Gericht*. Heidelberg, 1982.

JÖRG FRIEDRICH

Hungary

Since the end of World War II nearly forty thousand suspected war criminals have been investigated and tried in HUNGARY, and more than nineteen thousand have been found guilty. As early as December 1944, the Hungarian provisional government in Debrecen began to take measures toward prosecuting suspected war criminals, and special courts for that purpose, called people's tribunals, began to try cases as soon as the war ended. By the end of 1946 most of the leading Hungarian politicians who had cooperated with Nazi Germany or had created the circumstances for Hungary's collaboration with the Nazis had been tried and punished.

Among the first of the major cases was that of former premier László Bárdossy (1941–1942), whose trial began on October 29, 1945. Bárdossy was accused of having violated the Hungarian constitution. Among the more specific charges against him was that of complicity in the murder of Hungarian Jews at KAMENETS-PODOLSKI and Novi Sad. Bárdossy was found guilty and was hanged on January 10, 1946.

Former premier Béla Imrédy (1938–1939) was brought to trial on November 14, 1945. He was accused, in part, of having prepared for the later persecution of the Jews by drafting the First Anti-Jewish Law in his capacity as a government minister and by signing the Second Anti-Jewish Law while serving as premier. On March 1, 1946, he was executed.

The notorious antisemites Andor Jaross (former minister of the interior) and his undersecretaries, László BAKY and László ENDRE, were tried between the end of December 1945 and early January 1946. All three were accused of war crimes and of having played major roles in the plundering and deportation of Hungarian Jewry. On March 26, 1946, Endre and Baky were hanged; on April 11, 1946, Jaross was shot.

In the series of trials held between December 1945 and March 1946, most of the other members of the governments of Döme SZTÓJAY and Ferenc SZÁLASI were tried, including the former prime ministers themselves. Most of the former ministers were executed.

Other significant trials also resulted in death sentences. Márton Zöldi and József Grassy were tried for their role in the Novi Sad massacre. A court convicted them, but a subsequent appeal led to an overturning of the verdict. Later they were extradited to Yugoslavia, the scene of the massacre, where a court again convicted them and sentenced them to death; both were executed. Emil Kovacz, an ARROW CROSS PARTY leader who was instrumental in deporting Jews from Budapest during the Szálasi regime, was also sentenced to death and executed, as were Péter Hain (Regent Miklós HORTHY's personal detective, chief of the Hungarian secret police, and a German agent) and László FERENCZY of the gendarmerie. Both Hain and Ferenczy had been instrumental in the deportation of Hungarian Jewry. In 1967, former Arrow Cross men from the organization's headquarters in the Budapest suburb of Zugló were put on trial. Three of the defendants, Vilmos Kroszl, Lajos Nemeth, and Alijos Sándor, were executed. Sixteen others were sentenced to long terms of hard labor.

BIBLIOGRAPHY

Levai, E. "The War Crimes Trials relating to Hungary." *Hungarian Jewish Studies* 2 (1969): 252–296.

Levai, E. "The War Crimes Trials relating to Hungary: A Follow-Up." *Hungarian Jewish Studies* 3 (1973): 251–290.

ROBERT ROZETT

The Netherlands

In late 1943 the government-in-exile of the Netherlands, which had its seat in London, enacted four laws providing for the prosecution of war criminals in the Netherlands and of Dutch collaborators with the German enemy. These laws and their eventual application represented significant departures from the Netherlands' legal tradition in this area:

1. The offenses and crimes that were classed as such by the new laws were not included in the prewar code of criminal law, the retroactive force of the laws being justified by the argument that before the war the

legislator had not been aware that such crimes existed.

2. A special juridical authority (including its own court of appeals) was established for war criminals and collaborators.

3. Contrary to accepted practice, these special tribunals, in addition to three professional judges, included two military men.

The special tribunals were activated in the Netherlands in late 1945 and ceased to operate in 1950. In 1944 and 1945, as the Netherlands was being liberated, regular and irregular Dutch forces arrested 450,000 suspects (some 5 percent of the country's population), of whom, however, only 200,532 had their files forwarded to the prosecution. Before long the Dutch government freed the majority of the suspects, and by the end of 1945 the number in detention was down to 90,000.

A total of 14,562 persons were convicted and sentenced in the Netherlands, the punishment pronounced by the courts decreasing in severity as time elapsed and the impact of liberation declined. This development was a result of both the indifference manifested by the public and the policy of reconciliation with the past that was adopted by successive ministers of justice (who were all from the Catholic party). They not only based their policy on humane considerations, but also took political interests into account (most of the criminals were Catholics). One hundred and nine death sentences were passed, but only thirty-nine were carried out, among them those of five Germans and one Jewish woman. All the other death sentences were commuted to life imprisonment. In the course of time, all prison sentences passed by the special tribunals were reduced. As a result, by early 1960 only forty-nine persons were still in prison, and these were also set free, with the exception of four who were accomplices in the murders of Jews. Attempts were made by members of parliament and cabinet ministers to have these four set free as well, but such attempts were long foiled by the violent reaction among the Dutch public. One of the four (Willi Lages) was set free for health reasons in 1966 (he died in 1971); one died in prison; and in 1989 the last two criminals, Ferdinand aus der Fünten and Franz Fischer, were amnestied, a decision that caused angry demonstrations in many parts of the country.

Among the collaborators whom the prosecution sought to bring to trial were two heads of the JOODSE RAAD (Jewish Council), Abraham ASSCHER and Professor David COHEN. They were arrested in 1947, but a month later the minister of justice ordered their release, in the face of widespread public indignation and legal opinions which argued that their arrest had no legal foundation. The minister of justice decided (in 1950) to close the files on Asscher and Cohen, on grounds of public interest, but without giving his decision the character of a rehabilitation. Another affair that agitated public opinion in the Netherlands over many years was the conviction of Friedrich Weinreb, a Jew who during the war had pretended that owing to his ties with German army officers he could arrange for many Jews to emigrate. In 1948 Weinreb was tried and sentenced to six years' imprisonment, on a charge of collaboration with the enemy. In the mid-1960s it was claimed that his conviction had been a miscarriage of justice; the government appointed an inquiry commission, which found that Weinreb was guilty of informing on people and that such informing had led to the arrest and subsequent death of dozens of persons. The first report of the inquiry commission was submitted in 1976, and a supplementary report, in 1981. No retrial was held, since Weinreb had in the meantime fled to Switzerland.

Another famous case was that of Pieter Menten, a wealthy businessman with close connections in the Dutch administration. Habib Kenaan, an Israeli journalist, proved that Menten had been responsible for the murder of Kenaan's family and of many other Jews in Galicia, and that he had robbed them of their possessions, which he had transferred to the Netherlands. He had also managed to conceal from the Dutch authorities the fact that he had served with the German administration in Poland. In 1980 Menten was brought to trial, and was sentenced to ten years in prison and a fine of 100,000 gulden.

Judicial proceedings in the Netherlands against war criminals and collaborators were treated with indifference by the Dutch public in the immediate postwar period, a fact that enabled certain government circles to intervene, discreetly, in behalf of influential suspects. The growing interest in the events of World War II in the 1960s, together with the findings of the inquiry commissions and the great number of research studies published, brought home to the Dutch public that grave errors had been made in the way the prosecution of Nazi criminals and their helpers had been handled.

BIBLIOGRAPHY

Belinfante, A. D. *In plaats van Bijltjesdag.* Assen, Netherlands, 1978.

Groen, K. *Landverraad wat deden we met ze?* Weesp, Netherlands, 1974.

Leeuw, A. J. van der. "The Emigration Lists of Friedrich Weinreb." In *Patterns of Jewish Leadership in Nazi Europe 1933–1945.* Proceedings of the Third Yad Vashem International Historical Conference, edited by Y. Gutman and C. J. Haft, pp. 259–265. Jerusalem, 1981.

Mason, H. L. *The Purge of Dutch Quislings: Emergency Justice in the Netherlands.* The Hague, 1952.

Veth, D. G., and A. J. van der Leeuw. *Rapport uitgebracht door het Rijksinstituut voor Oorlogsdocumentatie inzake de activiteiten van Drs. F. Weinreb gedurende de jaren 1940–1945.* 2 vols. The Hague, 1976.

JOZEPH MICHMAN

Norway

The government of Vidkun QUISLING could not prevent the emergence of a Norwegian movement of resistance to the Nazis and of aid to and rescue of their victims. Members of the resistance movement—and those Jews who had not managed to escape to Sweden—who fell into the hands of the occupation authorities were brutally tortured and murdered. It was therefore natural for the Norwegian government-in-exile in London to join in the warnings and declarations issued by the Allies concerning their determination to punish the Nazi criminals.

The trials in Norway were based on a decree issued on May 5, 1945, and a special law (Law No. 14) passed on December 13, 1946 (the text of the latter was influenced by the NUREMBERG TRIAL). According to this legislation, punishment for crimes that had been accepted as crimes either formally or by international consensus before World War II could be enforced retroactively. Punishment for other categories of crimes, as spelled out in Law No. 14, could not be applied retroactively to World War II. The courts that tried the Nazis also based themselves on a resolution that the Norwegian parliament had adopted on April 9, 1940.

Apart from the Quisling trial, some of the most important trials of Nazis held in Norway dealt with the following war criminals:

1. Karl-Hans Klinge, a German police officer notorious for the inhuman torture of prisoners;
2. Police officer Richard Wilhelm Bruns and other police officers charged with cruel mistreatment and murder;
3. SS-Obersturmbannführer Gerhard Flesch, who, as superior officer to the commandant of the Falstad concentration camp, ordered the commandant to have shot three Jews whom Flesch had encountered by chance;
4. Hans Paul Helmut Latza, president of the Nazi Court, who bore responsibility for numerous acts of murder;
5. Hauptsturmführer Oskar Hans, charged with the murder of 312 persons, among them Jews of Norwegian and other nationalities.

In these trials, all of the accused were sentenced to death.

BIBLIOGRAPHY

Anderaes, J., et al. *Norway and the Second World War.* Lillehammer, Norway, 1983.

United Nations War Crimes Commission. *Law Reports of Trials of War Criminals.* Vols. 3, 5, 6. London, 1947–1949.

MARIAN MUSHKAT

Poland

In view of the enormous crimes committed by the Nazis in Poland, the Polish authorities in the liberated areas of the country regarded the capture and punishment of the criminals as one of their most urgent tasks. The Polski Komitet Wyzwolenia Narodowego (Polish

Trial held in Lublin between November 27 and December 2, 1944, of six SS guards from Majdanek. They were accused of killing, torturing, and beating prisoners of war and civilians, and of raping women in the camp. They were found guilty and were executed.

Committee of National Liberation), established in liberated Lublin on July 21, 1944, issued an order on August 31 of that year on the punishment of Nazi criminals found guilty of the murder and persecution of civilians and prisoners of war; and of Polish traitors.

The order established strict criminal responsibility for all kinds of war crimes and CRIMES AGAINST HUMANITY, in the same manner in which these terms were later defined in article 6 of the Charter of the International Military Tribunal at Nuremberg (*see* NUREMBERG TRIAL). By an order dated September 12, 1944, special courts were established for the trial of Nazi criminals, with the participation of lay judges. The proceedings were of a summary nature and there was no appeal.

In 1949 the special courts were abolished and subsequent trials of war crimes came before regular courts, with selected judges conducting the trials according to the general rules of procedure. On January 22, 1946, the Najwyzszy Trybunal Narodowy (Supreme National Court) was created, to deal with trials of special significance.

The special courts established in September 1944 lost no time in tackling their task. The first trial of war criminals in Poland was held from November 27 to December 2, 1944 (when fighting was still in full swing); the accused were staff members of the MAJDANEK camp who had fallen into Polish hands. The total number of Nazi war criminals tried after the war was 5,450—a tiny fraction of the total, since most of the criminals had fled with the retreating German forces. The attempts made after the war to extradite war criminals to Poland were only partially successful; the total number extradited was 1,803. In 1947 and 1948 difficulties were encountered in extraditing Nazi war criminals to Poland from the western zones of occupation in Germany, and from 1950 on, no more extraditions were granted. This meant that another 5,600 Nazis listed as war criminals by the UNITED NATIONS WAR CRIMES COMMISSION were not extradited. Poland's request for them was disregarded.

A mass of documentation, on a variety of subjects, was accumulated in the numerous trials of Nazi war criminals by Polish courts: on the almost total extermination of the Jewish population; the selective killing of other parts of the Polish population; terror actions and persecution on grounds of ethnic origin, religion, and race; the network of extermination camps, concentration camps, and labor camps; the actions designed to restrict the natural growth of the native populations of the occupied countries; the forced-labor organization that involved moving people, by force, out of the borders of their own country; the destruction and theft of art works and antiquities; the forced assimilation into the German nation of select groups of children and youngsters; the ruin of the economy of the occupied countries; the destruction and theft of private property; the destruction of WARSAW in 1944; and other war crimes and crimes against humanity.

The trials before the Supreme National Court were of special importance. The first such trial (June 7 to 21, 1946) was that of Arthur GREISER, the *Gauleiter* (district leader) of the WARTHEGAU. Among the charges against him were those of taking part in preparing a war of aggression against Poland, organizing the killing actions against the Polish population, and participating in the creation of ghettos and in the murder of the Jewish population in the places where they lived and in the gas chambers of the CHEŁMNO camp. Next to be tried (August 27 to September 5, 1946) was Amon GOETH, who had been the commandant of the PŁASZÓW camp. He was charged with the murder of civilian prisoners in the camp and the final liquidation of the KRAKÓW and TARNÓW ghettos.

In the trial of Ludwig FISCHER, who had been governor of the Warsaw district, and in that of Ludwig Leist, the former governor of Warsaw, and of two Higher SS and Police Leaders, Josef Meisinger and Max Daum (December 17, 1946, to late February 1947), all the accused were found guilty of crimes against the population of Warsaw and its vicinity, including the abominable treatment of the population after the suppression of the 1944 WARSAW POLISH UPRISING. Fischer was also convicted on the charge of setting up the Warsaw ghetto and the TREBLINKA extermination camp.

The trial of Rudolf HÖSS, the man who set up the AUSCHWITZ-Birkenau extermination camp and was its commandant until October 1943, was held March 11 to 29, 1947. This trial reconstructed, with great precision, the teams that had established and operated Auschwitz, making it a major element in the Nazi GENOCIDE system. These were the men who were responsible for the fate of the 300,000 prisoners whose names were listed in the camp rolls (most of them from Poland, but also including people from other German-occupied countries, and Soviet prisoners of war); and of over 1 million other prisoners, brought from various parts of Europe, who were not even registered in the camp and, on their arrival in Auschwitz,

The first Auschwitz trial, held in Kraków, Poland, from March 11 to 29, 1947.

were taken straight to the gas chambers.

The decisive majority of the people murdered in Auschwitz were Jews. The first Auschwitz trial was followed by the trial of Arthur LIEBEHENSCHEL (November 24 to December 16, 1947), who succeeded Höss as the commandant of Auschwitz, and thirty-nine other defendants, many of whom had held responsible posts in the camp. In the trial held from April 5 to 27, 1948, the accused was Albert FORSTER, who had been *Gauleiter* of DANZIG and then of Danzig–East Prussia. The charges against him included participation in preparations for a war of aggression, in the murder of Jewish and Polish populations, and in the persecution and deportation of a great number of Poles.

In the last trial before the Supreme National Court (April 17 to June 5, 1948), the man in the dock was Josef Bühler, who had been deputy governor of the GENERAL-GOUVERNEMENT (that is, the deputy of Hans FRANK, who was tried at the Nuremberg Trial). Bühler was charged for his share in directing the mass murder campaign against the Generalgouvernement population, which included Jews of Polish nationality, and for other crimes against "the Polish state and Polish citizens." The Nazi criminals who were tried by the Supreme National Court were all sentenced to death and executed, with the exception of Leist and some of the Auschwitz camp staff.

Of the thousands of trials held before the special courts and, later, the regular courts, the most important were those of the following persons:

1. Erich KOCH (1959), who had been governor of East Prussia, which had parts of northern Poland annexed to it.
2. Jürgen STROOP (1951), who in 1943, as an SS-*Gruppenführer*, was in charge of suppressing the WARSAW GHETTO UPRISING.
3. Franz Konrad (1951), an SS officer charged with committing multiple murders in the Warsaw ghetto and assisting in the suppression of the ghetto uprising.
4. Herbert Buttcher (1949), SS and Police Leader in the Radom district, who was charged, in part, with the extermination of the Jews of Ostrowiec, CZĘSTOCHOWA, and PIOTRKÓW TRYBUNALSKI.
5. Hans BIEBOW (1947), chief of the ŁÓDŹ ghetto administration.
6. Jacob SPORRENBERG (1950), SS and Police Leader in the LUBLIN district, charged with, among other crimes, the mass murder of Jews, mainly in Aktion "ERNTE-FEST."
7. Paul Otto Geibel (1954), SS and Police Leader in Warsaw, charged with the role he played in the destruction of the Polish capital in 1944, among other crimes.

Also brought to trial were several dozen persons who had served on the staffs of the Auschwitz, Majdanek, and STUTTHOF camps.

The Polish courts regarded the administrative institutions of the concentration camps—the camp command, administrative officers, and personnel—as criminal organizations, under the definition of that term by the Nuremberg International Military Tribunal. Also declared to be criminal organizations were the Generalgouvernement administration; the paramilitary Selbstschutz, a self-defense organization made up of VOLKS-DEUTSCHE (ethnic Germans) in Poland; and the UKRAINSKA POVSTANSKA ARMYIA (Ukrainian Insurgent Army).

The trials of Nazi criminals in Poland were conducted in accordance with established legal procedure, with the accused having the rights of defense. The accused were tried for acts and crimes in violation not only of state law, but also of international law, mainly the Fourth Hague Convention.

BIBLIOGRAPHY

Central Committee for the Investigation of German Crimes in Poland. *German Crimes in Poland*. Warsaw, 1947.
Cyprian, T., and J. Sawicki. *Processy wielkich zbrodniarzy wojennych w Polsce*. Łódź, 1949.
Kubicki, L. *Zbrodnie wojenne w świetle prawa polskiego*. Warsaw, 1963.
Muszkat, M. *Polish Charges against War Criminals*. Warsaw, 1948.

LESZEK KUBICKI

Romania

Punishment of Romanian war criminals was not universally accepted, and was carried out against the background of the severe political struggle in Romania between the Communist party, supported by the Soviet occupying force, and the traditional forces, which included the parties in opposition to the regime of Ion ANTONESCU and to the king and his followers. The trials of Nazi war criminals can be divided into three periods: (1) from the overthrow of the Antonescu regime on August 23, 1944, until the rise of a majority Communist government on March 6, 1945; (2) the transitional period, from the establishment of a partially Communist regime on March 6, 1945, until the establishment of a completely Communist regime on December 30, 1947; and (3) from December 30, 1947, to 1955.

In the first period, Romania had to fulfill the conditions of the cease-fire agreement signed in Moscow on September 12, 1944, according to which it had undertaken to arrest war criminals, to immediately dissolve pro-Nazi organizations, and to prevent the establishment of such organizations in the future. The Romanian government also undertook to imprison German and Hungarian citizens and to extradite them to the Soviet Union. These conditions were met; Antonescu did not have an existing fascist party apparatus, and he himself dissolved the pro-Nazi IRON GUARD. Until March 6, 1945, the various Romanian governments were very slow in dealing with legislation against war criminals. Only on January 20, 1945, were the first laws concerning legal steps against Nazi criminals passed, and since these regulations were prepared by the Ministry of the Interior, the organizations of Nazi war victims could do little to influence their wording. The committee that prepared the regulations was acutely split on how to define the term "war criminal" in a way that would satisfy all the political forces in the government. The two veteran Romanian parties, the National Liberal Party (Partidul National-Liberal) and the National Peasants' Party (Partidul National-Taranesc), wanted to reduce the negative responsibility, while the Communists and the Social Democrats wanted to expand it.

The compromise arrived at satisfied the Jewish public only partially. The regulations did not recognize the right of the victims to be represented in the courts, and no Jewish organization was included in the judiciary bodies or in the prosecution that prepared the trials. At the same time, certain judges presiding in these trials had, under Antonescu, condemned Jews to long terms of imprisonment or had decreed death penalties for transgressions against the racial laws of the Antonescu regime. In this first period the Communist party supported the punishing of war criminals as part of their power struggle and out of a desire to remove members of the "old" political powers from key positions.

By the second period, beginning in March 1945, some of the most important Nazi criminals involved in the extermination of the Jews of BESSARABIA and BUKOVINA and of the Jewish deportees in TRANSNISTRIA were brought to trial. To strike a "balance," some of the Jewish deportees who had collaborated with the Romanian authorities in those regions were also tried. Under Soviet pressure, the first pro-Communist government, under Petru Groza, which was established on March 6, 1945, began to speed up punishment of the Nazi criminals. The Soviet Union sought to bring to a conclusion the trials of perpetrators of crimes on its territory and on the territories it had annexed from Romania—Bessarabia and northern Bukovina.

During the second period a new law was issued to purge the public administration, and another law was issued to bring to trial those responsible for the national disaster and for war crimes and to punish them. This law authorized the continuation of the local war trials, originally restricted to a period of six months, and expanded the range of criminal responsibility. In this period the heads of the fascist regime were sentenced, and five, including Ion Antonescu, were executed, in June 1946. In the course of 1946, with the approach of the general elections (November 19, 1946), Petru Groza's government reneged on its declarations, and ceased bringing war criminals to trial in order to prove to its opponents that it was not pro-Jewish and not influenced by the Jews.

The peace treaty between the Allies and Romania, signed in Paris in 1947, again stipulated that Romania must bring war criminals to trial, but even after that time not all the war criminals known to the Jews were punished. The organizers and perpetrators of the IAŞI pogroms of June 29, 1941, were brought to trial only in May 1948. This delay constituted part of the effort of Romanian foreign policy to conceal the war crimes committed by Romanian soldiers and citizens against Jews with Romanian citizenship.

The third period, 1947 to 1955, witnessed the arrest and imprisonment of tens of thousands of opponents of the regime who had previously belonged to the now dissolved old Romanian parties or to the Iron Guard; among those arrested were thousands of war criminals. The aim was not to sentence the criminals who had oppressed, plundered, violated, and murdered the Jews, but to liquidate all opposition to the Communist regime. Nevertheless, in these trials a large proportion of the war criminals were sentenced. Many, however, evaded punishment or fled Romania.

In 1955 the punishment laws were repealed, effectively ending any further possibility of trying and sentencing Nazi war criminals. This was perhaps the reason for the nonintervention of Romanian jurists in the international debate on the law of limitation for Nazi war crimes. Romanian legal and historical studies tend to lay stress on Hungarian crimes against the Romanians in northern Transylvania, and they omit practically any mention of Romanian war criminals. The 1955 repeal of the punishment laws also granted a general pardon to a large number of war criminals already serving prison sentences. All the criminals sentenced to terms of up to ten years were released, and the prison sentences of the rest were greatly reduced.

JEAN ANCEL

TUCHIN (Pol., Tuczyn), small town in Rovno Oblast (district), Ukrainian SSR. Between the two world wars Tuchin was under Polish rule, and in September 1939 it was included in the area annexed by the Soviet Union. On the eve of World War II about three thousand Jews lived there.

On July 6, 1941, the Germans occupied Tuchin, and local Ukrainians, with the help of the Germans, immediately carried out a pogrom, leaving seventy Jews dead, many others injured, and much property pillaged. On the following day, a unit from Sonderkommando 4a arrived in the town and, using lists prepared by the Ukrainians, arrested and executed thirty Jews. That same month the Jews were ordered to wear the Jewish BADGE (a white armband with a yellow Star of David), to pay a ransom in gold, and to work as forced laborers in agriculture, in the tanneries, and so on. A JUDENRAT (Jewish Council) was created, headed by Gecel Schwarzman, one of the prominent businessmen of the town during the Polish rule, and the leader of the Jewish community. Through bribing the Germans, the Jews were able to delay being shut up in a ghetto until early September of 1942.

Following the destruction of the Jews of neighboring ROVNO in mid-July 1942, refugees reached Tuchin and related what had happened in their town. The heads of the Tuchin community decided to resist; among the principal organizers of the resistance were the chairman of the Judenrat, Gecel Schwarzman, and his deputy, Meir Himmelfarb. A program of action was prepared that took into account the structure of the ghetto—about sixty single-story houses, dispersed along a single road. The plan was to set fire to the houses, to begin shooting in order to sow panic among the Germans, and immediately to begin a mass flight to the nearby forests. With Judenrat funds, kerosene was purchased and distributed. Four fighting groups were organized, and five rifles and twenty-five revolvers and hand grenades were acquired. A group of Jews whose work consisted of felling trees in the forests tried, without success, to make contact with Col. Dmitri Medvedev's unit of Soviet partisans. When the Jews of the ghetto gathered for prayer on Yom Kippur (September 21, 1942), the chief organizers of resistance presented the program of revolt to them and instructed them on how to act.

On Wednesday evening, September 23, the Germans placed a blockade around the ghetto. The heads of the insurrection decreed a state of full alert, and the fighting groups took up their positions: two by the two gates of the ghetto, one at the exit of the main street, and the fourth as a reserve at the Judenrat building. On the following day (September 24)

1

BELORUSSIA

TUCHIN Zhitomir
Rovno

1   2   3   TUCHIN
UKRAINE   N
4   5   6

0   95 miles   1 in
0   120 km.   2 cm.

at dawn, the Germans and the Ukrainian auxiliary police moved past the boundaries of the ghetto. In accordance with a prearranged signal, the resisters within set fire to the houses of the ghetto and the German warehouses bordering it. The fighting groups began shooting, the enclosure of the ghetto was broken, and the Jews were signaled to flee. Under cover of the smoke and fire, about two thousand Jews escaped to the forest; this accounted for approximately two-thirds of the ghetto residents, including women with children and elderly people. The fire and shooting continued all that day and the next day (Friday, September 25). Several Germans and Ukrainian auxiliary policemen were killed; the number of their wounded is not known. About a third of the Jews of the ghetto fell, including almost all the fighters. The insurrection ended on Saturday, September 26, when the heads of the revolt, Schwarzman and Himmelfarb, surrendered to the German commander. They were shot and buried in the Jewish cemetery.

The fate of those who fled was harsh. Within three days half of them were caught and killed. About three hundred women with babes in arms could not tolerate the conditions of the forest, returned to the town, and

were shot. Of the remainder, many died, and others were handed over or killed by peasants. After a time, some of the youths joined Soviet partisan units, and fell in combat. When Tuchin was liberated, on January 16, 1944, about twenty of its Jews were left in the region.

BIBLIOGRAPHY

Ayalon, B. H., ed. *Tutchin-Krippe (Wolyn). In Memory of the Jewish Community.* Tel Aviv, 1967. (In Hebrew.)

Spector, S. *The Holocaust of Volhynian Jews, 1941–1944.* Jerusalem, 1986. (In Hebrew.)

Spector, S. "The Jews of Volhynia and Their Reaction to Extermination." *Yad Vashem Studies* 15 (1983): 159–186.

SHMUEL SPECTOR

TUKA, VOJTECH (1880–1946), prime minister of SLOVAKIA during World War II and the moving spirit behind the deportation of Slovak Jews. A professor of law at Pécs and later at Bratislava University, Tuka served as secretary of the separatist Slovak People's Party and editor of its organ, *Slovak.* After World War I, he collaborated with the Hungarian Irredenta movement and pursued an anti-Czech policy. In 1923 he established the fascist Home Guard (Rodobrana). He was condemned by a Czechoslovak court in 1929 for high treason. During the pre-Munich period, prior to the autumn of 1938, Tuka became the ideologist and advocate of an "independent Slovakia," representing the pro-German radical wing of the HLINKA People's Party. As chief negotiator of the 1942 deportations, he adamantly rejected intervention against the expulsion of Slovak Jews. After the war, Tuka was condemned to death by the National Tribunal at Bratislava, but he died while in prison.

BIBLIOGRAPHY

Dagan, A., ed. *The Jews of Czechoslovakia: Historical Studies and Surveys.* Vol. 3. Philadelphia, 1984.

Lipscher, L. *Die Juden im slowakischen Staat, 1939–1945.* Munich, 1980.

Prime Minister Vojtech Tuka (front left). Behind him is Alexander Mach (in uniform), commander of the Hlinka Guard, head of the secret police, and minister of internal affairs.

Neuman, Y. *In the Shadow of Death: The Fight for the Rescue of Slovak Jewry*. Tel Aviv, 1958. (In Hebrew.)

Stanek, I. *Zrada a pád*. Prague, 1958.

LIVIA ROTHKIRCHEN

TUNISIA, republic in North Africa, bordering on Algeria to the west and on Libya to the east. Jews have lived in Tunisia for at least two thousand years. A small number of Spanish exiles settled in Tunisia after the expulsion of the Jews from Spain in 1492, and at a later stage were joined by Italian Jews, mainly from Leghorn. Tunisian Jewry consisted of two main social elements: the Leghorn community, called "Grana," whose cultural affinity was with Italy and who were considered to be under Italian protection; and the "Touansa" (that is, Tunisians), who were in the majority and were subjects of the bey (the ruler). This division did not disappear even when Tunisia became a French protectorate in 1881, despite the organizational and political changes effected by the French.

The French authorities refused to grant Tunisian Jews French nationality as they had done in Algeria, despite the pressure exerted by French Jewry. Shortly before World War I, however, this attitude was modified, and French nationality was awarded, on a selective basis, to thousands of Tunisian Jews serving in the army or the French administration.

On the eve of World War II, Tunisia's Jewish population numbered eighty-five thousand, representing 2.7 percent of the total. Unlike the other Jewish communities of North Africa, the Tunisian Jews were concentrated in only a few places, and over half lived in Tunis, the capital. This was one reason why the modernization process of Tunisian Jewry went much deeper and was more comprehensive than that of other North African Jewish communities. The process affected every sphere of life and was accompanied by a lively political and intellectual ferment in which Jews of all political orientations took part—Zionists, Socialists, and Communists. The numbers of the last two categories grew with the arrival of anti-

TUNISIA

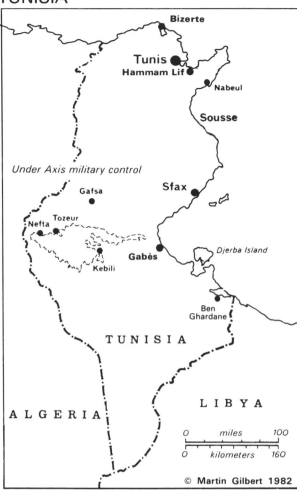

Fascist activists fleeing from Benito MUSSO-LINI's Italy, who found refuge in Tunisia.

The fate of Tunisian Jews during World War II differed from that of Jews in the other countries of North Africa; they were the only ones who experienced direct German occupation, which began in November 1942. Until then, their situation was essentially the same as that of the Jews of MOROCCO, since most were Tunisian subjects and only a few thousand were citizens of France or Italy.

In the first few weeks of the war, and also after the fall of France in June 1940, anti-Jewish incitement increased greatly, with the participation of the Muslim population. In Tunis, Hammam Lif, Nabeul, Gafsa, and many other places, Jewish houses and stores were attacked. The French authorities ascribed these events to the influence of the local European press, but an important fac-

tor was the new situation created by the downfall of France: at the time when the Vichy regime was taking its first steps, France appeared to the Muslims as a giant torn to shreds by the Nazis. The defeat suffered by the colonial power strengthened the local population's longing for independence, and their first blows were aimed at the colonial order's weakest link—the Jews.

The perceived preferment of Jews had been one of the most hateful aspects of the colonial regime in the eyes of the native population. Like the Jews of Algeria and Morocco, Tunisian Jewry was seized with a genuine wave of pro-French patriotism when France entered the war. The "solidarity with liberal, peace-loving France," the "protector of the weak and oppressed"—as the Chief Rabbi of Tunis, Haim Bellaiche, put it—was authentic. The chief rabbi called on the Jews to buy French government bonds, and in all the cities of Tunisia the Jews organized ongoing fasts and prayers for the victory of France and its allies.

Tunisian Jews suffered a bitter disappointment when, like the other Jews of North Africa under the Vichy regime, they were subjected to a long series of racist laws. The extent to which these laws were applied depended on the goodwill of the governor-general, Vice Adm. Jean-Pierre Estéva, and the cooperation of the officials working under him in the administration. In this respect Tunisian Jews were lucky, and the French race laws were applied only in part. As a devout Christian, Estéva was not inclined to put the anti-Jewish decrees into practice, and until March 1942 he held up the implementation of the major decrees relating to the STATUT DES JUIFS (Jewish Law). From October 1940, Estéva gave concrete expression to his sympathy for the Jewish community by such acts as distributing gifts to needy Jews and paying an official visit to the ancient synagogue in Djerba.

In addition to the governor-general's sympathetic attitude—and, in some degree, to the pro-Jewish attitude of Bey Sidi Mohammed al-Mounsaf—the Italians also, in practice, interfered with the application of the anti-Jewish laws. The Italian representatives in Tunisia were particularly incensed by the Vichy authorities' plan, in 1942, to confiscate

Jewish property, in accordance with the decrees on the "Aryanization" (*see* ARISIERUNG) of the economy. The Italians demanded that the French abstain from confiscating the property of the five thousand Jews in Tunisia who were Italian nationals; their assumption was that this was only a pretext of the French to enable them to seize all the large assets held by Italian nationals, and thereby to impair Italy's standing in Tunisia. When the controversy with the French on this issue was at its height, the Italians asked the Germans to intervene. The Germans gave their support to the Italian stand, and as a result the French were forced to relinquish the whole idea of "Aryanization." They did not want to apply it to Tunisian subjects only, because they felt that if they did so, the Tunisian Jews would hand their property over to the Italian nationals among the Jews, a process that would inflict further damage on the Tunisian economy.

On November 9, 1942, German and Italian forces entered Tunisia, in reaction to the Allied invasion of Algeria and Morocco. Until early December, their military situation was precarious and they were subject to incessant air attacks by the Allies, which nearly forced them out of Tunisia on November 24. On the political level, German policy was full of contradictions. For example, the Germans permitted the Tunisian national movement, Neo-Destour, under Habib Bourguiba, to operate freely—but they did not withdraw recognition of French sovereignty and did not touch the basic structure of the French protectorate regime. The Italians did not like this ambivalent German policy, having hoped that in Tunisia they would be recompensed, to some degree, for the loss of Libya. The Muslims were also unhappy, since they had expected that the Germans would drive the French out and recognize Tunisia's independence. As time went on, the growing number of contradictions in German policy and the increasing evidence of their military failure made the Tunisians less and less inclined to cooperate with them. Only a few Tunisians joined the Arab units created by the Wehrmacht (by means of the Deutsch-Arabische Lehrabteilung, or German-Arab Training Unit) or the ranks of the African Phalanges established by French officers under German auspices.

This situation forced restraint on the Germans, and it was only on November 23, 1942, that they took the first step against the Jews, when they arrested four leaders of the Jewish community, among them its president, Moïse Borgel. A few days later, however, the four were released, on the intervention of the French governor-general, the Muslim mayor of Tunis, and the Italian consul. On December 6 the Germans announced the dissolution of the Jewish Community Board and ordered Borgel to form a new, nine-member board, which within one day had to recruit 2,000 Jews for forced labor. On the intervention of the French authorities the new board was given another twenty-four hours to deliver the conscripts, but despite its efforts it was unable to produce more than 120 men.

The German reaction was to seize several dozen Jewish community leaders as hostages, to make mass arrests in the Jewish quarter, and to threaten to blow up Tunis's central synagogue. Several board members, who felt that they had no choice and were afraid of worse to come, asked for a further extension so that they could organize properly to fulfill the demand. Walther RAUFF, SS commander in Tunis, granted their request, and the board, headed by Paul Ghez, embarked on its task. To recruit the requisite number of forced laborers, the board had to take immediate charge of the whole range of community affairs in order to set up teams to gather and classify candidates for forced labor, as well as to arrange for their transfer to the camps (as the Germans had ordered), their subsistence, and the care of the families they left behind. The new board gradually became the intermediary between the Jews and the Germans, the latter having preempted from the French authorities jurisdiction over the affairs of the Jewish community.

Altogether, five thousand Jews were put on forced labor. They were dispersed over thirty locations and camps, along the front line. The largest camp, and the one with the harshest conditions, was at Bizerte. In the first few weeks, the board leaders tried to ensure that the enlistment for forced labor was applied equally to all sectors of the Jewish population. But as time went on the impression grew that forced labor was mainly for the poorer sectors, and that the sons of bourgeois families were being exempted for health reasons—not always fairly. As the military situation of the Germans deteriorated, more and more prisoners escaped from the camps. The board was increasingly lax in its recruiting effort, and from March 1943 the number of new recruits was much lower than the number of escapees. At the time of the German collapse and surrender, in early May, only sixteen hundred Jews were employed on forced labor.

Forced labor was also introduced in other places, but not on as large a scale as in Tunis. In Sfax the SS demanded a permanent force of one hundred Jews to unload military trucks and construct air raid shelters. The forced laborers received their pay from the Jewish community. Several weeks after they first came to Sfax, the Germans planned to imprison in a camp all the Jews who were fit for work, but they gave up the idea when they realized that this might lead to epidemics. In Sousse all Jews in the eighteen-to-fifty age bracket were called up for forced labor. Every morning the Jewish laborers were taken to the port to repair the damage caused by the Allied air raids. In Sousse, too, the Germans wanted to put all the Jews in the area into a single large concentration camp, and to require them to wear a yellow badge; neither of these intentions, however, was carried out.

Most of the labor camps where the Jews were held were situated on isolated farms or in the open fields, and were generally devoid of the installations required for a camp. Only in Bizerte was there a real camp. At first it housed five hundred men on forced labor. The prisoners were divided into work teams, headed by Jewish personnel appointed by the Germans or by the board. The camp was guarded by German, Italian, or French troops—not by the SS, which was restricted to Tunis and the other cities. The Bizerte camp had a brutal regimen, the prisoners working fourteen hours a day on arduous assignments, and being punished for even the slightest transgression. In the Italian-controlled camps the prisoners received much better treatment.

Forced labor was only one of the anti-Jewish aspects of the German occupation of Tunisia. Twenty Jewish political activists were seized by the Nazis and deported to extermination camps in Europe, where they all perished. The Germans also confiscated a considerable amount of Jewish property, and from time to time imposed heavy fines on the Jews. On February 13, 1943, the Jews of Djerba were ordered to pay a fine of 10 million francs, within two weeks; since they did not have that sum in cash, the Germans agreed to accept fifty kilograms of gold instead. Enormous sums were also extracted by the Germans from the Jews of Tunis and Gafsa.

The situation of Tunisian Jewry would undoubtedly have become even worse had the Germans stayed on. Their army, with few SS men in it but with many remnants of the forces of Gen. Erwin Rommel, whom the British had defeated in Libya, suffered from lack of discipline and self-confidence. Hemmed in on all sides, with no escape route open for an orderly withdrawal, and with little help from the local population, the Germans' sole concern was to survive. Tunis and Bizerte were liberated by the Allies on May 7, 1943. Six days later, the battle for Tunisia was over. But this was not the end of the troubles of the Tunisian Jews. As soon as the French came back, dozens of Jews holding Italian nationality were arrested, on charges of "collaborating" with the enemy. They were put into the same camps that were being emptied of the forced laborers imprisoned by the Nazis, and several weeks went by before they were released.

BIBLIOGRAPHY

Abitbol, M. *North African Jewry during World War II.* Detroit, 1989.

Bessis, J. *La Méditerranée fasciste: L'Italie mussolinienne et la Tunisie.* Paris, 1981.

Borgel, R. *Etoile jaune et Croix gammée: Récit d'une servitude.* Tunis, 1944.

Carpi, D. "The Italian Government and the Jews of Tunisia in the Second World War (June 1940–May 1943)." *Zion* 52/1 (1987): 57–106. (In Hebrew.)

Ghez, P. *Six mois sous la botte.* Tunis, 1943.

Sabille, J. *Les Juifs de Tunisie sous Vichy et l'occupation.* Paris, 1954.

MICHEL ABITBOL

TURKEY. *See* Rescue Committee of the Jewish Agency in Turkey.

U

UGIF. *See* Union Général des Israélites de France.

UJRE. *See* Union des Juifs pour la Résistance et l'Entr'aide.

UKRAINE, Soviet republic in the southwestern USSR. The Ukraine has its origin in Kievan Russia, which existed from the ninth to the thirteenth century. Beginning in 1238, what is now the Ukraine came first under Tatar rule and then under Lithuanian, Polish, and even Turkish rule; it was eventually incorporated into the Russian empire, except for its western part—Galicia and BUKOVINA —which was ruled by the Habsburgs.

Jews lived in Kievan Russia; the Jewish population increased rapidly in the last third of the sixteenth century, by the end of which the Ukraine contained 45 percent of the entire Jewish population of the Polish kingdom. The Jews were artisans and engaged in trade. They also leased estates, villages, and the right to collect taxes from the Polish nobility in the Ukraine, which put them between the oppressing nobility and their subjects, the peasants. This added an economic and social dimension to the existing religious animosity against the Jews. Hatred of the Jews erupted with great force during the Khmelnytsky rebellions (1648–1649) and the Haidamack massacres in the eighteenth century, when tens of thousands of Jews were murdered and entire communities were destroyed.

In the late eighteenth century the Frankist and Hasidic movements developed in the southeastern Ukraine, and they later spread throughout the Ukraine. Most of the Jewish population was then concentrated in the Pale of Settlement in the western Ukraine, living in towns where Jews constituted 50 percent, or even the majority, of the inhabitants. About 3 percent of the Jews were engaged in agriculture. In the second half of the nineteenth century, the Haskalah (Enlightenment) movement made great strides in the Ukraine, as did Ḥibbat Zion (Love of Zion), the forerunner of the Zionist movement. The 1905 revolution stimulated and excited the Jewish community, and many Jews flocked to the revolutionary political parties. The reaction that followed the revolution, however, led to a rise in antisemitism. In World War I it was the Jews of Eastern Galicia who first bore the brunt of the suffering, when the Russian army conquered the area and its Cossack units ran wild against the Jews. In the late summer of 1915 it was the turn of the Jews of the western Ukraine to suffer, when that region became the scene of battles and tens of thousands of Jews fled to the central and eastern Ukraine, or were forced out of their former homes. The February 1917 revolution gave equal rights to the Jews, and in July 1917 national minorities were recognized as having the right to national autonomy. In September 1917 a Ministry for Jewish Affairs was established.

In the civil war that broke out in the spring of 1918, most of the Ukraine was seized by

the Germans, but after their surrender and withdrawal in November of that year a new government, the so-called Directory, was established, headed by Simon Petliura. By the end of 1919, following the war with Poland, the Bolsheviks gained control of the larger part of the Ukraine; in the 1920 peace treaty the Ukraine became a Soviet republic and part of the USSR, although portions were annexed to Poland (Volhynia and Eastern Galicia) and Romania (Bukovina). The remnants of Petliura's defeated army settled in Poland and western European countries, and by the late 1920s they had organized into paramilitary nationalist groups. The latter engendered the ORHANIZATSYIA UKRAINSKYKH NATSIONALISTIV (Organization of Ukrainian Nationalists), which in the 1930s attracted to its ranks the young generation of Ukrainians in western Europe and in Poland. In the Soviet Ukraine, the forced collectivization of agriculture and the ensuing starvation led to the deaths of millions of people. This was followed by the Stalinist purges, from which the Ukrainian intelligentsia suffered the most. All these events led to strong hatred of the Soviet regime among the Ukrainian population. In September 1939 the western Ukraine (Volhynia and Eastern Galicia) was incorporated into the Soviet Ukraine, followed in June 1940 by Bukovina and BESSARABIA. In 1954 the Soviet Ukraine had an area of 232,000 square miles (600,000 sq km) and a population of forty-two million.

During the civil war, one hundred thousand Jews were murdered in pogroms staged by the Directory units, the White Army under Gen. Anton Denikin, the Poles, and a variety of armed gangs. Many Jews were disabled for life, Jewish property was pillaged and destroyed, and many of the towns and villages in which Jews had lived were totally abandoned.

Under the Bolshevik regime (beginning in the summer of 1918), the Jewish leftist political parties were incorporated into the Communist party as separate factions. After a while, however, the factions were abolished and the Communist party created its own Jewish department, the Yevsektsiya, which helped liquidate the existing Jewish institutions and organizations.

Most of the Jewish breadwinners in the Ukraine during the 1930s were skilled workers, technically trained members of the intelligentsia, professionals, or office workers. Side by side with a rapid process of assimilation among the Jews, many fell victim to the purges or were thrown out of the party, the diplomatic service, and other fields of employment. The Jews living in the western Ukraine, under Polish rule, and in Romanian-held Bukovina suffered from political and economic discrimination, and from frequent antisemitic outbreaks, which sometimes came close to pogroms. Nevertheless, the Jews in these areas led an intense community life in the cultural and political spheres, with the national Jewish movements and political parties predominating in the latter. In September 1939, the western Ukraine was incorporated into the Soviet Union; before long, its Jewish institutions and organizations were abolished, thousands of Jewish leaders and activists were exiled, and the Jewish economy was completely Sovietized. With its new borders, the Ukraine had a Jewish population of 2.4 million (early 1941).

On June 22, 1941, Germany attacked the Soviet Union, its forces advancing rapidly, and by that October it had conquered the entire Ukrainian republic, except for the Lugansk district. The invading German army was accompanied by Ukrainian nationalist military units (*see* NACHTIGALL BATTALION). Leading public figures in the western Ukraine—including the head of the Uniate church, Archbishop Andrei SHEPTYTSKY, and the heads of the Autocephalous Orthodox Church of the Ukraine—welcomed the Germans as liberators, in the hope of being granted independence. In the eastern Ukraine the Germans were also received warmly. Some of the Soviet prisoners of war who were Ukrainians, as well as young Ukrainian civilians, volunteered for service in auxiliary units of the German army, police, and SS. In late 1943, a Ukrainian SS division was formed as part of the Waffen-SS, made up of volunteers from Eastern Galicia.

EINSATZGRUPPEN C and D, marching in with the German army, installed a regime of terror and mass murder in the Ukraine, executing hundreds of thousands of Jews and tens of thousands of other citizens whom they suspected of being Communists or Soviet officials. Instead of granting independence to the Ukraine, as the Ukrainian nationalists had hoped, the Germans turned the larger part of the region over to the REICHSKOMMISSARIAT UKRAINE civil administration, and put the rest of the eastern Ukraine under a military administration. Eastern Galicia was annexed as a district to the GENERALGOUVERNEMENT. Despite earlier promises, the Germans did not abolish the kolkhozy (collective farms), and extracted tremendous quantities of grain and other foodstuffs and raw materials from the Ukraine, letting the local population starve, especially in the cities. Millions of people were sent on forced labor to the Reich. A large partisan movement was formed under Communist leadership, which operated mostly in the northern, heavily wooded part of the republic. It was in this area that partisan formations saw action, under the command of Sidor KOVPAK, Aleksandr Saburov, Aleksei Fyodorov, Mikhail Naumov, Andrei Melnyk, and others.

In the western Ukraine and in Bukovina, the local population, assisted by the UKRAINISCHE HILFSPOLIZEI (Ukrainian Auxiliary Police), staged pogroms in which thousands of Jews were murdered and much property was pillaged and destroyed; in LVOV, 5,000 Jews were murdered in two of these pogroms. The Einsatzgruppen carried out mass *Aktionen* in such places as LUTSK (where they murdered 2,000 Jews), Ostrog (3,000), and TERNOPOL (5,000).

On the eastern side of the old Polish-Soviet border, the Einsatzgruppen embarked upon the total liquidation of the Jews, with the exception of those in KAMENETS-PODOLSKI (which was incorporated into Generalbezirk Volhynia-Podolia). The extermination proceeded at a rapid pace, following a regular pattern. Immediately after occupation, the German military administration issued a series of decrees, ordering the Jews to wear distinctive badges (*see* BADGE, JEWISH) and to register, setting up Jewish committees (a form of JUDENRAT), confining the Jews to specific streets, and putting them on forced labor. After a few months the Jews were rounded up and taken to ravines, abandoned quarries, or antitank ditches, where they were killed. The job of rounding up, guarding, and transporting the Jews was in the hands of German and Ukrainian police and, at times, also of rear-echelon German army units, while the killing itself was carried out by the Einsatzgruppen or the SD (Sicherheitsdienst; Security Service). The escorts also murdered Jews who tried to escape en route or who could not keep up with the rest. Also used for the systematic murder were eight GAS VANS; the Jews were crowded into the vans, which were hermetically sealed, the exhaust fumes were piped in, and the victims choked to death while the vans were on the road to the burial pits.

The Jews of ZHITOMIR were the first victims of the systematic murder process; by September 19, 1941, the entire Jewish population of the city, numbering ten thousand, had been killed. On September 29 and 30, two weeks after Kiev was occupied, the city's Jews were brought to the ravine of BABI YAR and murdered there. On October 13, fifteen thousand Jews from DNEPROPETROVSK were murdered. The Jews of KHARKOV were rounded up in mid-December, detained in the sheds of a tractor plant, and from there taken to the Drobitski Yar ravine in early January 1942, to be murdered there. In TRANSNISTRIA, then under Romanian rule, some of the Jews from places that had escaped Einsatzgruppe D were able to survive, as were some of the Jews from Bessarabia

Forced to lie down, a group of Jewish women, children, and babies from the Volhynian village of Mizoch, 23 miles (37.5 km) southwest of Rovno in the Ukrainian SSR, are shot at close range.

and Bukovina, who had been expelled to Transnistria. The Jews of ODESSA, however—some eighty thousand of them—were all killed. Most of the Jews of Volhynia, Kamenets-Podolski, and Eastern Galicia were murdered during 1942 and 1943.

There were many instances of resistance during the liquidation process; tens of thousands of Jews tried to escape, there were uprisings in a number of ghettos (TUCHIN, Lutsk), and armed resistance based in fortified bunkers (BRODY, Vinniki, Yaktorov, Busk, Yavorov, Kuroviche, and ROGATIN). Many of the young people who managed to escape established Jewish fighting units, such as those led by Moshe GILDENMAN (from Korets) and the Lvov poet Jacob Schudrych. Others joined the Soviet partisan movement and fought in the catacombs of Odessa, in the Dnepropetrovsk and Kiev areas, and in the partisan formations led by Kovpak, Saburov, Fyodorov, and others. During the government-organized evacuation of the Ukraine on the eve of the German occupation, 800,000 of the eastern Ukraine's 1.5 million Jews (within the 1939 borders) were evacuated or escaped, as compared with no more than 50,000 Jews from among the 900,000 living in the western Ukraine and Bukovina. The Jews of the TRANSCARPATHIAN UKRAINE, which during the war was under Hungarian rule, were deported to AUSCHWITZ in the summer of 1944, and most of them perished there.

The German defeat at STALINGRAD in early 1943 marked the start of the Ukraine's liberation, which was completed in late August 1944, when the western Ukraine was set free. The Transcarpathian Ukraine and the Crimean peninsula were incorporated into the Ukraine in 1945 and 1954, respectively.

Following the liberation of the Ukraine, many Jews wanted to return to their homes there, but they encountered fierce antisemitism, which in Kiev assumed the dimensions of a pogrom. Many of the survivors therefore chose to settle elsewhere. The surviving remnants of the Jews of the western Ukraine and Bukovina availed themselves of the right of repatriation to Poland or Romania, and soon joined the BERIḤA (organized exodus). Many made their way to Israel between 1945 and 1948.

A memorial erected in 1970 by a local Jewish committee in memory of the Jews killed by the Germans during the Holocaust in the town of Pechera, in Vinnitsa Oblast (district). The Hebrew text reads: "Memorial Stone. Here lie the Jewish dead, brutally killed by the fascist murderers, whose hands are full of blood. Thousands of men, women, and children died for *kiddush ha-Shem* from 1941 to 1945 in the town of Pechera. May the Lord look kindly upon them and avenge the blood of His servants." The Russian text reads: "Reflect, O Man! Thousands of these miserable people did not live to see the victory over the German fascist hangmen and their helpers, who bestially cut short the breath, voice, thoughts, and life of women, children, and old men. Words cannot describe their death. They were your mother, your father, your brothers and sisters. They perished so that you could live in happiness. Do not suffer but fill yourself with hatred, and swear that you will never again allow this to happen. Perpetuate a living memory of them through your descendants. Do Not Forget! This Is Their Testament."

TABLE 1. *Jewish Population in the Ukraine, End of Sixteenth Century to 1959*

YEAR	SIZE	REMARKS
End of sixteenth century	45,000	
1648 census	150,000	On the eve of the 1648–1649 massacres there were actually over 300,000, but many evaded the census
1764 census	258,000	
1847 census	600,000	The real figure was 900,000, but again many evaded the census; also, Eastern Galicia and Bukovina were then under Habsburg rule and their Jewish population was not included
1897 census	1,927,268	Excluding Eastern Galicia and Bukovina
1926 census	1,574,391	Excluding Volhynia and Eastern Galicia (which belonged to Poland) and Bukovina (Romania)
1939 census	1,532,827	As above
Early 1941	2,400,000	Excluding Transcarpathian Ukraine and the Crimea
1959 census	840,314	

The Jewish population in the Ukraine between the end of the sixteenth century and 1959 is shown in Table 1.

BIBLIOGRAPHY

Armstrong, J. A. *Ukrainian Nationalism, 1939–1945.* New York, 1955.
Kubijovyc, V., ed. *Ukraine: A Concise Encyclopedia.* 2 vols. Toronto, 1963, 1971.
Spector, S. *The Holocaust of Volhynian Jews, 1941–1944.* Jerusalem, 1986. (In Hebrew.)

SHMUEL SPECTOR

UKRAINIAN INSURGENT ARMY. *See* Ukrainska Povstanska Armyia.

UKRAINISCHE HILFSPOLIZEI (Ukrainian Auxiliary Police). Ukrainian militia units were set up in the earliest days of the German invasion of the Soviet Union and the occupation of Ukrainian-inhabited areas. The initiative for this step came from the Ukrainian nationalists who accompanied the German forces on their entry into the Ukraine. These units were recruited either as mobile groups (*pokhidni grupy*) or at the initiative of local nationalist activists—in all cases with the full encouragement of the military governors.

As soon as the SD (Sicherheitsdienst; Security Service) had established its offices in the occupied area, it instituted a check on the political reliability of the Ukrainian militia personnel, especially the officers. On July 27, 1941, on Heinrich HIMMLER's orders, the formation of the mobile Ukrainian Auxiliary Police was launched, under the jurisdiction of the SS and German police commanders in the various Kommissariate (subdivisions of the German civil administration). The battalions were housed in police barracks in key places, and were deployed in major police operations such as the drive against the partisans. After the civil administration had been installed in August 1941 in the Galicia district and, throughout September, in the other parts of the German-occupied Ukraine, the militia units were renamed the Ukrainische Hilfspolizei Schutzmannschaft (Ukrainian Auxiliary Police Constabulary), and the individual policeman was generally referred to as a *Schutzmann* (constable). The units were subordinate to the German police and gendarmerie.

The Ukrainian Auxiliary Police were equipped with captured Soviet light weapons and wore black uniforms. On some occasions a collective fine was imposed upon the Jews in order to defray the costs of providing the police with uniforms and boots. The senior commanders of these units were Germans. In the first few days of the occupation, Ukrainian police, as an organized group or on an individual basis, participated in pogroms against the Jews, in Lvov, in the cities of Eastern Galicia, and in Volhynia. Later, when Ukrainian police escorted groups of Jews to places of work or were on guard duty in the ghettos, they extorted money from the Jews, harassed them, and frequently shot Jews merely for the sake of killing. When the ghettos were being liquidated, units of the Ukrainian Auxiliary Police took part in *Aktionen*: blockading the ghettos, searching for Jews who had gone into hiding, and hunting those who had escaped. They escorted Jews to their execution in pits and served as the guards surrounding the murder sites, barring access to them. They were known for their brutality and killed many thousands of Jews who could not keep up on the way to the execution sites. or who tried to escape.

In the spring of 1943, Ukrainian police in large numbers deserted with their arms and joined the UKRAINSKA POVSTANSKA ARMYIA (Ukrainian Insurgent Army). Others, especially those who served in the mobile battalions, retreated westward with the German forces, and in the final stage of the war were incorporated into the OSTBATAILLONE or into divisions of the Ukrainian National Army.

SHMUEL SPECTOR

UKRAINSKA POVSTANSKA ARMYIA

(Ukrainian Insurgent Army; UPA), military arm of the BANDERA wing of the ORHANIZATSYIA UKRAINSKYKH NATSIONALISTIV (Organization of Ukrainian Nationalists; OUN). In the late summer of 1942, OUN emissaries, headed by Vasyl Sidor, went to Volhynia to organize armed independent Ukrainian formations in the area and found resistance groups that had already sprung up. Among them were the Poliska Sich (Unit of Polesye) units, commanded by Maksim Borovets, whose code name was Taras Bulba. The emissaries sought to unite the groups and consolidate them into a Ukrainian national army; the first unit came into being on Octo-

ber 14, 1942, the date on which the UPA is regarded as having been established. On December 1, 1942, when the Ukrainisches Legion (Ukrainian Legion), which included the NACHTIGALL and Roland units, was disbanded, a group of Ukrainian officers escaped to join the UPA. One of them was Roman Shukhevych, who was appointed commander of the UPA, with the code name Taras Chuprynka. In March 1943, six thousand men of the UKRAINISCHE HILFSPOLIZEI (Ukrainian Auxiliary Police) deserted from their unit in Volhynia, taking their arms with them, and joined the UPA, adding to its strength and speeding up its consolidation. In mid-1943, UPA units began to form in Eastern Galicia, Bukovina, and Ruthenia as well.

In September 1943, the UPA's organization was changed: the military staff of the OUN became the headquarters of the UPA, and Lieutenant Colonel Shukhevych ("General Chuprynka") was appointed its commander. UPA operations were split up into four areas: (a) North: Volhynia and Polesye; (b) West: Eastern Galicia, Bukovina, Ruthenia, and the San River area; (c) and (d) South and East: parts of the Soviet Ukraine in its 1939 borders. Areas (c) and (d) existed as such for a short time only, and were abolished when the Soviet army recaptured the region. UPA units were reorganized in order to improve their tactical and military flexibility and to enable them to operate as an underground. The basic unit was the battalion (*kuren*), consisting of four hundred to eight hundred fighters, which was subdivided into companies (*sotnia*), platoons (*choten*), and squads (*roy*).

Throughout 1943, the UPA fought mostly against the Soviet partisan movement. This reached a climax in the summer of that year, when the Soviet partisan corps, commanded by Gen. Sidor KOVPAK, campaigned in the Carpathian Mountains. In the course of the fighting, UPA units murdered Jews who had taken refuge in the forests and in villages. In March the UPA also embarked upon the mass murder of Poles, first in Volhynia and later in Eastern Galicia. The number of victims among the Poles is estimated at forty thousand.

In the second half of 1944 the UPA began to attack the German army, seizing equipment and capturing soldiers in the rear of German combat units. The Germans reacted by launching large-scale raids. On June 15, 1944, a council was established, the Ukrainska Holovna Vyzvolna Rada (Supreme Ukrainian Council of Liberation; UHVR), to serve the UPA as its political and public framework. Stefan Bandera's supporters were in the majority in the UHVR, and at the end of July it signed an agreement with the Germans on a joint struggle against the Soviet Union. The agreement ended the clashes between UPA and German forces, and that August the Germans began supplying the UPA with arms and ammunition, equipment, and training materials. Prior to the German retreat in mid-1944, the UPA controlled central and southern Volhynia and wide areas of Eastern Galicia, such as the Bobrka, Przemyśl, Berezhany, and Rogatin subdistricts.

When the Red Army liberated the western Ukraine (between July 22 and October 3, 1944), the UPA entered into a bitter struggle with the Soviet authorities. At the beginning of 1945, it began an armed conflict with the Polish authorities in the southern part of the Lublin district and in the San River area. Both the Soviets and the Poles had to divert large security forces, as well as military units, to deal with the UPA. UPA forces ambushed and killed Soviet general Nikolai Vatutin, the officer commanding the First Ukrainian Front (March 2, 1944), and Polish general Karol Swierczewski, one of the commanders of the Polish army (March 28, 1947), as well as large numbers of officers, policemen, and civilian officials.

It was not until some time after the end of the war, in the summer of 1947, that the Soviets, Poles, and Czechs coordinated their operations against the UPA and dealt it the decisive blow, in which General Chuprynka (Shukhevych) was killed. By the beginning of 1948, the organization was totally liquidated; most of its men fell in battle, and only a few groups, each numbering several dozen, were able to make their way through Czechoslovakia to the American zone in Germany. The Soviets exiled tens of thousands of Ukrainians and emptied entire villages of their inhabitants; the Poles transferred all the Ukrainians from the San River area and the southern Lublin district into the German areas that it had annexed in the west.

BIBLIOGRAPHY

Kubijovyc, V., ed. *Ukraine: A Concise Encyclopedia.* 2 vols. Toronto, 1963, 1971.

Szota, W. "Zarys rozwoju Organizacji Ukrainskich Nacjonalistów i Ukrainskiej Powstanczej Armii." *Wojskowy Przegląd Historyczny* 8/1 (1963): 163–202.

Torzecki, R. *Kwestia Ukrainska w polityce III Rzeszy (1933–1945).* Warsaw, 1972.

SHMUEL SPECTOR

UMSCHLAGPLATZ (transfer point), the area separating the WARSAW ghetto from the Polish part of the city, on the corner of Zamenhof and Niska streets. From this location, hundreds of thousands of Jews were deported to extermination camps and concentration camps—mostly to TREBLINKA—from the Warsaw ghetto between July and September 1942 and January and May 1943.

The Warsaw *Umschlagplatz* (or *Umschlag*, as many referred to it) was, until the mass deportation in the summer of 1942, the only official transit point for the transfer of manufactured goods and commodities to and from the ghetto. It had a railway siding and a special 120-man Transferstelle (Transfer Office), run by the Germans, supervising the movement of individuals and goods through the junction.

When the deportations were launched on July 22, 1942, the place ceased to function as a link between the ghetto and the outside world and became the *Umschlag*, the spot where the deportees from the ghetto were assembled for deportation. SS-Obergruppenführer Karl WOLFF, of Heinrich HIMMLER's staff, was charged with providing a daily train for the deportations from Warsaw. In a letter dated July 28, 1942, Theodor GANZENMÜLLER, the *Staatssekretär* (director general) of the Reich Ministry of Transportation, stated: "Since July 22, a freight train with five thousand Jews has been making its way daily from Warsaw to Treblinka via Malkinia." Next to the *Umschlag* was a courtyard surrounded by a high fence, and in its center was a vacant building that had once served as a hospital. The Jews designated for deportation were rounded up in the streets of the ghetto and marched under guard to the *Umschlag*, where they were kept sitting on the

Jews huddled on the ground at the *Umschlagplatz*, awaiting deportation.

A memorial, dedicated in April 1988, at the site of the *Umschlagplatz* in the Warsaw ghetto. [Geoffrey Wigoder]

ground in the courtyard or on the floor inside the building, pending the arrival of the daily train. When it came they were packed in, one hundred to one hundred and twenty in each freight car. SS men, Ukrainian and Baltic forces, the Polish auxiliary police, and the JÜDISCHER ORDNUNGSDIENST were on guard during the process.

In the spring of 1988 a monument was unveiled at the *Umschlagplatz* to mark the place where some three hundred thousand Warsaw Jews were sent to their death.

ISRAEL GUTMAN

UMWANDERERZENTRALSTELLE (Central Resettlement Office), German agency that during World War II handled the expulsion of Poles from the Polish territories that were incorporated into the Reich and from the ZAMOŚĆ province in the GENERALGOUVERNEMENT. It also dealt with the administration of the transit camps in which those who had been expelled were held, and with their racial classification.

The Umwandererzentralstelle was preceded by the Sonderstab für Umsiedlung von Polen und Juden (Special Staff for the Resettlement of Poles and Jews), which had been set up in Posen on November 11, 1939, and before long became the Amt für Umsiedlung der Polen und Juden beim Höheren SS- und Polizeiführer (Office of the Higher SS and Police Leader for the Resettlement of Poles and Jews). This in turn was renamed the Umwanderungsstelle (Transfer Office) in the spring of 1940, and the Umwanderungszentralstelle (Central Transfer Office) a few weeks later.

In 1942, with the expulsions from the Zamość province, a branch office of the Umwandererzentralstelle was opened in LUBLIN, and a sub-office in Zamość. A population transfer office for the Danzig–West Prussia region had also been established in Danzig in 1940, and in 1943 it was temporarily moved to Potulic. Following the Germanization of masses of Poles by Albert FORSTER, Reich Governor of Danzig, the expulsions from the Danzig region were discontinued and the Danzig office was closed down.

These two offices had thirty branches in the various district seats and were under the authority of the Higher SS and Police Leader in their respective regions, as well as under Section IV of the REICHSSICHERHEITSHAUPTAMT (Reich Security Main Office; RSHA).

A total of 920,000 Poles and Jews were expelled by the two offices from the Polish territories incorporated into the Reich to the Generalgouvernement, and 116,000 Poles from the Zamość province of the Generalgouvernement.

BIBLIOGRAPHY

Jastrzebski, W. *Hitlerowskie wysiedlenia z ziem polskich wcielonych do Rzeszy 1939–1945.* Poznań, 1968.

Koehl, R. L. *RKFDV—German Resettlement and Population Policy, 1939–1945: A History of the Reich Commission for the Strengthening of Germandom.* Cambridge, Mass., 1957.

CZESŁAW LUCZAK

UNDERGROUND, JEWISH. *See* Resistance, Jewish.

UNGVÁR. *See* Uzhgorod.

UNION DES JUIFS POUR LA RÉSISTANCE ET L'ENTR'AIDE (Union of Jews for Resistance and Mutual Aid; UJRE), clandestine organization formed by Jewish Communists in PARIS in August 1940; until mid-1943 it was called Solidarité. Pursuing a united policy, Solidarité tried to join AMELOT, but its conditions were rejected. It refused, however, to join the Comité de Coordination des Oeuvres Israélites de Bienfaisance (Coordinating Committee of Jewish Welfare Societies) in January 1941, anticipating Gestapo controls. In May 1941 the internment of almost four thousand Jews in Paris found Solidarité, like all similar organizations, unprepared. Following the German invasion of the Soviet Union in June 1941, the French Communist party began organizing the armed struggle, and Solidarité launched industrial sabotage. Arrests of Jews in several districts of Paris that August and the appeal by David Bergelson of the JEWISH ANTIFASCIST COMMITTEE in the USSR led to temporary reconciliation with some of Amelot's organizations. Solidarité opposed the UNION GÉNÉRALE DES ISRAÉLITES DE FRANCE (General Council of French Jews; UGIF) when it began operating in January 1942, attacking it as a collaborationist organization. That same month, Solidarité, hoping for non-Jewish aid, created the Mouvement National contre le Racisme (National Movement against Racism). On the eve of the July 1942 mass deportations, it formed the "second detachment" of partisans. After these deportations, the organization appealed to the Jews to hide, not to work for German industry, and to join the anti-Nazi struggle. Its clandestine press was the first to reveal the Nazi program of extermination by gas.

By the summer of 1943, decimated by the Gestapo and faced with a declining Jewish population, Solidarité reassessed its policy and formed the Union des Juifs pour la Résistance et l'Entr'aide. Its organizations in the south of France and their fighting groups became its spearhead. In August 1943, its broader program and the news of the WARSAW GHETTO UPRISING contributed to the unification of the immigrant organizations in the Comité Général de Défense (General Defense Committee; CGD). The UJRE played a major role within the CGD, early in 1944, in bringing about unity with the CONSISTOIRE CENTRAL DES ISRAÉLITES DE FRANCE (Central Consistory of French Jews) and in forming the CONSEIL REPRÉSENTATIF DES JUIFS DE FRANCE (Representative Council of the Jews of France). When France was liberated, the UJRE could claim to have saved nine hundred children, but it had paid a heavy price: 120 of its partisans had been killed and 400 of its members had been deported to their death.

BIBLIOGRAPHY

Adler, J. *The Jews of Paris and the Final Solution: Communal Response and Internal Conflicts, 1940–1944.* New York, 1987.

Diamant, D. *Les Juifs dans la Résistance française, 1940–1944: Avec armes ou sans armes.* Paris, 1971.

Latour, A. *The Jewish Resistance in France (1940–1944).* New York, 1981.

Ravine, J. *La résistance organisée des Juifs en France (1940–1944).* Paris, 1973.

JACQUES ADLER

UNION GÉNÉRALE DES ISRAÉLITES DE FRANCE (UGIF), French Jewish council established on November 29, 1941. Following the German occupation of northern FRANCE in the spring of 1940, Theodor DANNECKER, the German expert on Jewish affairs, was sent by Adolf EICHMANN to plan the Jewish policy in France. One of his first tasks was to organize the Jewish community, appointing responsible Jewish leaders, in line with SD (Sicherheitsdienst; Security Service) policy in the Reich and the conquered countries. However, it took Dannecker several months before he was able to announce, in January 1941, the establishment of the Comité de Coordination, an amalgam of almost all the Jewish welfare societies in Paris, immigrant and native. Yet the suspicion of certain Jewish leaders and their reluctance to join the Comité persisted, and after Dannecker brought two unknown Jews from Vienna to direct the Comité's affairs, opposition grew. By May 1941 all the major immigrant organizations had resigned, leaving the group in the hands of native Jews. Having failed to receive the support of the Jewish community, the Comité was far from being the centralized organization that Dannecker had envisaged.

By the summmmer of 1941, Dannecker was already looking for an alternative, and after procuring the needed support from the various German agencies in Paris, he initiated a new compulsory organization that was to disband all other Jewish organizations. The implementation was placed in the hands of Vichy's COMMISSARIAT GÉNÉRAL AUX QUESTIONS JUIVES (General Office for Jewish Affairs), headed by Xavier VALLAT, who in turn proposed to establish an analogous organization in the unoccupied zone (southern France) to protect French sovereignty over the new creation. Three months passed before Vallat put the final touches to the law establishing the UGIF. During that period, leaders of the Jewish community in the unoccupied zone engaged in marathon discussions over the legitimacy of such an organization and whether they should participate in a racially defined body. The leadership of the CONSISTOIRE CENTRAL DES ISRAÉLITES DE FRANCE (Central Consistory of French Jews) and the Chief Rabbi of France strongly opposed the union, and counseled further deliberations with the French authorities. On January 9, 1942, the names of the eighteen council members were published in the *Journal Officiel*, nine for each zone. Albert Lévy was appointed its president and André BAUR, of the north, its vice president; although the two councils were seen as an integral part of one body, they acted autonomously throughout most of the war and had very little contact with each other.

UGIF-North (UGIF-N). Established in the wake of an intensification of anti-Jewish measures, including the imposition of a billion-franc fine on the community, UGIF-N proceeded to fulfill the welfare and relief functions previously undertaken by the Comité. Under the leadership of Baur and Marcel Stora, UGIF-N developed a wide network of social services for this purpose and operated legally. Its leaders had placed their trust in certain French officials, but, as they learned in times of crisis, this was not warranted. Thus, from April 1942, UGIF-N was forced to undertake functions beyond its original charter, such as supplying large quantities of goods to the Germans, ostensibly for the Jews deported to AUSCHWITZ. Similarly, when faced with the mass arrests of Jews in Paris in mid-July 1942, the UGIF council abided strictly by its legalistic perspective, fulfilling the responsibilities handed out to it by the German and French authorities. These ranged from providing sanitary supplies for the trains to caring for children whose parents had been sent to DRANCY, the internment center near Paris from which Jews were sent to the extermination camps in the east. The council also granted assistance to the Jews herded into the large sports arena in Paris, the Vélodrome d'Hiver, in July 1942. But, though indications of this roundup had reached the UGIF offices the previous week, no special measures were taken to alert the community.

Following the deportations, the UGIF was severely criticized by immigrant organizations, but it persisted along its original path.

It increased its financial aid and its social services to the community, succeeded in gaining a limited number of releases from Drancy, continued to care for hundreds of children in "official" homes, yet constantly cautioned against illegal measures. Nevertheless, within the council itself, certain individuals (such as Juliette Stern and Fernand Musnik) carried on contacts with elements in the resistance movement while they themselves maintained an official position in the council. This dualistic character also existed in several UGIF services.

Faced with the growing pauperization of the Jews in the occupied zone, UGIF-N tried to increase its budget (based largely on funds received from expropriated Jewish property) by uniting the two councils. This move, initiated by Baur, was thwarted for many months by the southern council, which feared the consequences for its autonomous existence. The two councils also failed to present a united stand on the issue of the forced dismissal of their immigrant employees by the authorities, resulting in very different outcomes for each zone. More employees were retained in the north, but part of that council's dismissed staff was deported in mid-March 1943. Though the councils continued to operate from different premises, their fates became more unified in the summer of 1943. First affected was UGIF-N, with the radicalization of German policy in Drancy, part of a renewed effort to increase the number of deported Jews. The UGIF was expected to take over the upkeep of Drancy and also to encourage Jews to voluntarily join their relatives in the camp. Upon their refusal to pursue the second scheme, since they viewed actions of a police nature as beyond their scope, several UGIF leaders were arrested and deported to Drancy. The direct German intervention persisted throughout the summer, resulting in further arrests and a weakened organization, but no significant change in the UGIF's orientation was effected.

From September 1943 until the liberation in August 1944, the UGIF was under the leadership of Georges Edinger, who, with the advice of his council, followed the former policy. The upkeep of Drancy now became a major part of the UGIF's budget, but other forms of welfare were still attended to. Moreover, the council continued to uphold its open-door policy, to the growing opposition of immigrant organizations, which constantly advocated the disbanding of the UGIF children's homes. The advice was not taken, and though certain measures were implemented to decrease the number of children in UGIF homes, almost five hundred remained in the UGIF's custody in July 1944. On July 21, SS-Hauptsturmführer Alois BRUNNER ordered his troops to seize the UGIF children's homes. Within four days, about three hundred children and personnel were arrested and rushed to Drancy to join the last major convoy from France to Auschwitz; it contained thirteen hundred Jews, three hundred of whom were children under eighteen. The UGIF's cautiousness had backfired. On July 25, the remaining council members decided to close all but two of the UGIF's clinics and to drastically reduce personnel, but they also resolved to continue to offer welfare for needy Jews.

UGIF-South (UGIF-S). Although formally established in January 1942, UGIF-S did not really begin to function until May 1942. The organization was divided into seven departments, constituting the major welfare societies and subordinate to a general directorship; each of the departments was given a wide range of autonomy and the council rarely dictated an overall policy. Like its northern counterpart, UGIF-S saw as its prime mission the offering of aid to the community, and reserved for the Consistoire the responsibility of representing the Jews in the unoccupied zone. Until August 1943, the UGIF's council was under the influence of its general director, Raymond-Raoul LAMBERT, who was the architect of the organization's federative structure.

Shortly after UGIF-S began to operate, it faced the grave events of the summer of 1942. The deportation of foreign Jews from the unoccupied zone had been agreed to by the Vichy government in its deliberations with the German authorities in early July; UGIF-S was unaware of the impending tragedy until late that month. During the month of deportations, UGIF-S operated in several directions: it alerted Christian relief agencies and encouraged them to intervene with Vichy, set up welfare teams in the various internment

camps, and intervened with different levels of French administrators to avoid the deportation of certain categories of Jews. On a different plane, representatives of Jewish welfare societies (OEUVRE DE SECOURS AUX ENFANTS [OSE], FÉDÉRATION DES SOCIÉTÉS JUIVES DE FRANCE) and the scout movement (ECLAIREURS ISRAÉLITES DE FRANCE; EIF), functioning within the structure of the UGIF and with its authorization, succeeded in illegally evacuating children and adults from the camps. Here then began, in the midst of the August deportations, the UGIF's dual world: the council and the departments functioned officially while certain UGIF departments began illegal work, at times with the knowledge and participation of a council member. This situation persisted until the fall of 1943.

Although the UGIF's interventions were generally unsuccessful and the deportations proceeded as planned, the council was not deterred from expending energies to help coordinate a legal immigration of Jewish children to the United States in the fall of 1942. However, this major effort fell through, because the French authorities procrastinated long enough for the project to be jettisoned by the German occupation of most of southern France in early November 1942.

The German occupation, and the Italian occupation of eight French departments east of the Rhône, presented a new situation to the UGIF. Vichy's "protection" was now severely limited, while the Italian zone quickly loomed as a haven for Jewish refugees where antisemitic measures were not implemented. Elements within the UGIF seized the opportunity and encouraged Jews to flee to that area. By August 1943, almost thirty thousand Jews were living in the region. Yet the council was less direct in promoting dispersion. Even after two major German raids in Marseilles and Lyons, the council rejected proposals to close its offices and disperse the Jewish population. It continued to negotiate on every anti-Jewish measure, to maintain a wide-ranging welfare service, and to uphold the autonomous nature of the departments' existence. These efforts enabled the services to continue their activities—the OSE, the Fédération, and the EIF both legally and illegally, and the Comité d'Assistance aux

Réfugiés, Oeuvre d'Entr'aide Française Isra-élite, and HICEM (an emigration agency) legally.

This equilibrium began to be shattered in the summer of 1943. First came Lambert's arrest after his intervention with Prime Minister Pierre LAVAL regarding German measures against Parisian Jewry, and then the German occupation of the Italian zone in September 1943, which turned the haven for Jews into a den of lions. With the active assistance of the French militia, German forces combed the region for Jews and rounded up and deported thousands. The UGIF's council and departments were in total disarray, but the major fissure within the organization was still to come. In late October, Gaston Kahn, Lambert's successor, faced a German ultimatum: either surrender a UGIF children's home near Marseilles or subject the Jews of Marseilles to a mass deportation. Rejecting a proposal to hide the children, Kahn yielded, and the children and their guardians were deported. For certain UGIF departments, this was the last straw; they resolved to terminate all outstanding legal contacts with the UGIF and to function illegally.

Nevertheless, the hardships of the summer and fall did not put an end to UGIF-S. From December 1943, the council was coordinated by Raymond Geissmann, who had been active in the UGIF from the outset and had helped solidify relations with the Consistoire Central. As part of the reorganized UGIF, in which the presidency was moved to Paris, the southern council maintained its open-door policy throughout the first half of 1944, according to the northern directive. Welfare and various forms of assistance continued to be dispatched until the UGIF disbanded in August 1944.

BIBLIOGRAPHY

Adler, J. *The Jews of Paris and the Final Solution: Communal Response and Internal Conflicts, 1940–1944.* New York, 1987.

Cohen, R. I. *The Burden of Conscience: French Jewish Leadership during the Holocaust.* Bloomington, 1987.

Haft, C. J. *The Bargain and the Bridle: The General Union of the Israelites of France, 1941–1944.* Chicago, 1983.

Rajfus, M. *Des Juifs dans la Collaboration: L'U.G.I.F. (1941–1944).* Paris, 1980.

RICHARD COHEN

UNION OF JEWS FOR RESISTANCE AND MUTUAL AID. *See* Union des Juifs pour la Résistance et l'Entr'aide.

UNION OF ROMANIAN JEWS. *See* Uniunea Evreilor Români.

UNITED KINGDOM. *See* Great Britain.

UNITED NATIONS RELIEF AND REHABILITATION ADMINISTRATION (UNRRA), organization for aiding REFUGEES and the nationals of Allies in the liberated countries of Europe and the Far East. UNRRA was officially founded on November 9, 1943, at a ceremony in the White House, with the participation of forty-four representatives of the United Nations (the official designation of the Allied powers in World War II). UNRRA's major concern was to provide aid to countries in economic distress that were unable to finance the import of basic commodities, and it also dealt with DISPLACED PERSONS (DPs) by helping millions of them to be repatriated.

UNRRA policy was determined by a council made up of one representative from each of the member states. The council met six times a year, and in the intervals between one meeting and the next, the authority to make emergency decisions was in the hands of its Central Committee, consisting of the representatives of the United States, Britain, the Soviet Union, and China. These four countries were also to provide 75 percent of UNRRA's budget. At a later stage the Central Committee was enlarged by the addition of representatives of France, Canada, Australia, Brazil, and Yugoslavia. The committee, for all practical purposes, set the agency's policy. Wide powers were given to UNRRA's director general, chosen by the council after unanimous approval by the Central Committee. This principal executive post was allotted to the United States, which had assumed

Fiorello H. La Guardia, former mayor of New York City (fourth from left), was the director general of UNRRA from March 29, 1946, to January 1, 1947. He is shown visiting the Bergen-Belsen displaced persons' camp in the summer of 1946.

responsibility for 40 percent of the agency's budget. The first director general of UNRRA was Herbert H. Lehman, former governor of New York; his deputy was Sir Arthur Salter. Lehman was followed, on March 29, 1946, by Fiorello La Guardia, former mayor of New York City, who in turn was replaced, on January 1, 1947, by Maj. Gen. Lowell Ward Rooks, who was to be the last director general.

At its first meeting, held in Atlantic City the day after the White House ceremony, the UNRRA council established several advisory committees, made up of representatives of member states: regional committees for Europe and East Asia, and committees for supply and financial control, agriculture, displaced persons, health, industrial recovery, and welfare.

While the war was in progress, UNRRA's operations were quite limited in scope. The agency was subject to the authority of the Supreme Headquarters of the Allied Expeditionary Forces (SHAEF), and it had to have the approval of the military authorities before it could operate in liberated territories of enemy or former enemy states. Beginning on May 1, 1944, UNRRA teams joined the administration of refugee camps in Egypt, Palestine, and Syria, which were populated by thirty-seven thousand refugees from Yugoslavia, Greece, Albania, and Italy. By the end of that year, UNRRA had assumed responsibility for seventy-four thousand refugees spread over various camps along the Mediterranean shore, in the Middle East, and in Africa. In Italy, UNRRA personnel were put in charge of four camps housing six thousand refugees, and two hospitals in the south of the country.

When the war ended, UNRRA was not yet prepared to cope with the enormous tasks that confronted it: caring for millions of DPs and refugees and arranging for their repatriation. It took the agency several months to recruit the trained personnel required. Even so, the staff that was hired had no preparation or training for dealing with the survivor communities. Especially in the initial period, UNRRA had problems in trying to carry out its assignment in the DP camps. As a result, in this most critical time—the first few months after the war had ended—UNRRA was unable to provide aid to the extent and in the quality that the situation called for. Later, when the agency had completed its organizational requirements, its personnel gave considerable assistance in repatriation operations from Germany, Austria, Italy, the Middle East, and China. Under agreements signed in the winter of 1945–1946 with the British, American, and French occupation authorities, UNRRA was subordinate to the respective military command in each zone of occupation. The military authorities were responsible for the maintenance of law and order, for the procurement and distribution of basic supplies, and for housing; UNRRA's job was to administer the camps, to provide health and welfare services, entertainment, and vocational training, and to complement the basic commodities supplied by the military. By the end of 1945, UNRRA was operating two-thirds of the assembly centers and camps in West Germany, which contained 75 percent of all the DPs.

UNRRA at this time also provided aid to various countries and regions, such as Albania, Greece, Yugoslavia, Czechoslovakia, Poland, Italy, China, Belorussia, the Ukraine, Austria, and the Dodecanese islands (which at that time had not yet been reincorporated into Greece). Other recipients of UNRRA aid, on a limited scale, were Finland, Hungary, Ethiopia, and the Philippines. The aid took the form of food, clothing, medicines, agricultural machinery, raw materials, and so on. By September 30, 1946, UNRRA was estimated to have expended $3.67 billion. The United States contribution to this sum was $2.7 billion; Britain contributed $642,650,000; and Canada $139 million. The sum total of contributions to UNRRA during its existence is estimated at $3.873 billion.

UNRRA was also in charge of the operations of twenty-three volunteer welfare organizations. Among these were several delegations from Jewish organizations, such as the American Jewish JOINT DISTRIBUTION COMMITTEE (the Joint), the Jewish Committee for Relief Abroad, ORT (the organization for vocational education), and HIAS (see HICEM). In April 1945, a Jewish delegation from Palestine arrived in Greece. This was followed, in December, by a twenty-person delegation to the American zone in Germany, headed by Chaim Hoffman (later Yahil), that within five months grew to seventy members.

The Joint was operating in Germany as early as mid-August 1945, and was the major Jewish welfare agency there. UNRRA's supervision of the activities of the volunteer organizations was, in large measure, a mere formality. This situation was well exploited by the BERIḤA and ALIYA BET ("illegal" immigration to Palestine) organizers. Most of the Jews who had fled from the Communist-bloc countries after the war were living in UNRRA camps in Germany and Austria. It was from these camps that many of the refugees made their way to ports in neighboring countries, in order to leave from there for "illegal" immigration into Palestine. UNRRA camps in Italy served as departure bases for the many Aliya Bet immigrants, who, in the ports of that country, boarded the ships that were to take them to their destination.

During the first half of 1947, UNRRA transferred a large part of its operations to various other international organizations and closed down most of its offices in Europe. On July 1, 1947, the Preparatory Commission for the International Refugee Organization took over from UNRRA responsibility for the 643,000 DPs with whom UNRRA had been dealing in Europe. In the course of 1948 the remaining UNRRA offices in Europe, as well as in East Asia, Central and South America, India, and Australia, were closed down. The director general, Major General Rooks, left office on September 30, 1948, and Harry Howell was appointed to supervise the operations for winding down the organization.

BIBLIOGRAPHY

Marrus, M. R. *The Unwanted European Refugees in the Twentieth Century.* New York, 1985.

Proudfoot, M. J. *European Refugees: 1939–1945.* Evanston, Ill., 1956.

Wilson, F. M. *Aftermath.* London, 1947.

Woodbridge, G. *UNRRA: The History of the United Nations Relief and Rehabilitation Administration.* 3 vols. New York, 1950.

ARIEH JOSEPH KOCHAVI

UNITED NATIONS WAR CRIMES COMMISSION (UNWCC). On December 17, 1942, a joint declaration was issued simultaneously by the British, American, and Soviet governments and signed by all the other Allied governments, warning that when the war ended, Nazi war criminals would be punished. The emerging policy of the Allied powers to punish war criminals was in large measure the result of the pressure of public opinion in countries that had been occupied by the Germans, of repeated demands raised by the governments-in-exile in London, and of the St. James Declaration of January 13, 1943, issued jointly by the representatives of all the Allied powers, which specifically addressed the issue. In a debate in the House of Lords on October 7, 1943, a proposal was raised to form a special commission, on behalf of the Allies, to investigate war crimes. This was followed, on October 20, by a conference of Allied representatives that decided on the creation of the United Nations War Crimes Commission. Its first chairman was the British representative, Sir Cecil Hurst, who was elected to the post in January 1944. He was followed, in January 1945, by the Australian representative, Lord Quincy Wright, who held the office until 1948, when the commission concluded its work.

The UNWCC and its subcommittees were charged with the following tasks: to investigate Nazi crimes, record them, and assist in the preparation of the indictments; to take the necessary steps to ensure that the war criminals were apprehended and interrogated and that the facts justifying their punishment were exposed; to determine the legal basis and principles for the punishment of these criminals and their extradition; and to define the acts of aggression and the various atrocities involved—those acts that were subsequently to be described as crimes against peace and CRIMES AGAINST HUMANITY, including the crime of GENOCIDE.

The UNWCC took part in the establishment of the Central Registry of War Criminals and Security Suspects, set up in Paris in the spring of 1945. The commission's impact can also be discerned in Allied Control Council Law No. 10, which lays down the procedure for the punishment of war criminals. It provides, among other things, that the selection of the country to which a war criminal should be extradited would be made by the Allied commander of the respective zone of occupation (of Germany), and that all persons registered by the UNWCC as suspected

of war crimes would be regarded as extraditable.

The commission also prepared draft proposals of prescriptions on the punishment of war criminals, to be included in subsequent armistice agreements and peace treaties. It dealt with the formulation of acts that constitute medical crimes, and with the activation of German courts; published the protocols of the trials of exceptionally grave war crimes; and reported on its own relations with the various national offices established for the investigation of war crimes and with the headquarters of the occupation forces in Germany, including the Supreme Headquarters of the Allied Expeditionary Forces in Europe.

Participating in the UNWCC were representatives of Australia, Belgium, Canada, China, Czechoslovakia, France, Greece, India, Luxembourg, the Netherlands, New Zealand, Norway, Poland, South Africa, the United Kingdom, the United States, Yugoslavia, and, for a period, Ethiopia. The Soviet Union did not take part in the commission's work (see below), but it undertook to act in the spirit of the commission.

Special committees—in effect, subcommittees—were appointed by the UNWCC for specific aspects of its work: a committee for the interrogation of criminals, one to advise on matters of law and jurisdiction, and another whose task was to keep the UNWCC informed on the positions taken by member governments on issues of general and specific interest.

In response to the UNWCC's deliberations and recommendations, various military headquarters in Germany established Centers of Documentation of Nazi War Crimes. This facilitated research by representatives of countries that were concerned with the investigation of war criminals and their extradition, and that wanted to obtain the relevant documentary materials. Such centers were set up in Bad Oeynhausen and Hamburg in the British zone of occupation; in Berlin, Oberursel, Pachenheim, Freuding, Heidelberg, and Bremen in the American zone; in Klagenfurt in the British zone of Austria; and in Linz in the American zone of that country. A joint documentation center was established by the western Allies in Kassel, with the regional centers remaining in operation. The

French established their documentation and investigation center in Baden-Baden, and the Soviets had theirs in East Berlin.

The UNWCC assisted in sorting out and filing the documentation gathered, and made sure that it was properly stored and preserved; the result was the formation of a highly valuable collection of documents on war crimes. In the legal sphere, the commission's contribution consisted, in part, of the draft of the London Agreement of August 8, 1945, which provided for the creation of the International Military Tribunal at Nuremberg (*see* NUREMBERG TRIAL) and a tribunal along similar lines in Tokyo. The London Agreement also served as the legal basis for the national war crimes tribunals, especially the tribunals in the zones of occupation in Germany, and first and foremost the one appointed by the American military headquarters. A major contribution made by the UNWCC to the punishment of Nazi criminals was the registers it compiled of war criminals. A total of 8,178 files, relating to more than thirty-six thousand individual criminals and criminal organizations, were compiled by the UNWCC between 1944 and 1948 (listing 34,270 Germans, 1,286 Italians, 422 Bulgarians, 69 Hungarians, 4 Romanians, and others).

In these files, 24,453 persons were listed as war criminals (Type A, accused), 9,250 as suspects (Type S), and 2,556 as witnesses (Type W). France provided the committee with the largest list of war criminals (12,546), followed by Poland (7,805), Belgium (4,592), the Netherlands (2,423), Yugoslavia (1,926), British Commonwealth countries (1,709), and Czechoslovakia (1,543). Members of the committee included experts on international law, particularly on the laws of customs of war, such as Lord Wright, René Cassin from France, Czechoslovak general Bohuslav Ecer, American professor Lawrence Preuss, Danish professor Stefan Hurwitz, and professors Tadeusz Cyprian and Marian Mushkat of Poland.

The files on war crimes and war criminals and the other material collected by the committee represent a highly important source for the documentation of the Holocaust. All the material was handed over to the United Nations archives in New York for safekeeping. As a rule, the files were classified, and it was only in 1987, in connection with the Kurt WALDHEIM affair and demands made by Israel and other countries, that access to the material was gradually facilitated.

In February 1948, with the cold war gaining in strength, UNWCC operations came to an end, when various countries failed to comply with their obligation to extradite persons who had been listed by the UNWCC as war criminals. Among the criminals who were not extradited for trial were the German officers responsible for the destruction of the WARSAW ghetto and the suppression of the WARSAW POLISH UPRISING in 1944: SS-Gruppenführer Heinz Reinefahrt, Gen. Nicholas von Vormann, Gen. Smilo von Luttwitz, and SS-Brigadeführer and General of the Waffen-SS Ernst Rode.

The Soviet Union refused to participate in the committee's work because the majority of the committee members rejected its demand that representatives of all the Baltic states, the Karelian republic, and Moldavia be included, in addition to those from the Ukraine and Belorussia. In several instances the East Berlin office dealing with war crimes supplied material to UNWCC members investigating accusations against persons suspected of war crimes. That Soviet office, however, did not deal with extradition requests, since most of the war criminals who fell into Soviet hands were put into camps without any judicial proceedings; at most, their imprisonment was preceded by no more than a cursory investigation.

[*See also* Trials of War Criminals.]

BIBLIOGRAPHY

History of the United Nations War Crimes Commission. London, 1948.
Lande, A. *The Legal Basis of the Nürnberg Trial.* New York, 1945.
Smith, B. F. *Reaching Judgment at Nuremberg.* New York, 1977.

MARIAN MUSHKAT

UNITED PARTISAN ORGANIZATION. *See* Fareynegte Partizaner Organizatsye.

UNITED STATES ARMY AND SURVIVORS IN GERMANY AND AUSTRIA. At the end of World War II, one of the problems facing the Allied powers was that of seven million DIS-PLACED PERSONS (DPs) in Germany and Austria. In an extensive operation, the Allies succeeded in repatriating over six million of these DPs, but a million refused or were unable to return to their countries of origin. They included nationals of the Baltic countries (Latvia, Lithuania, and Estonia), annexed by the Soviet Union in 1940, and Poles, Ukrainians, and Yugoslavs who resisted repatriation either because of their opposition to the Communist regime or because they were afraid of being put on trial for collaborating with the Nazis. When the cold war intensified, the United States no longer sought to exert pressure on the nationals of Communist countries to go back to their former homes. This situation compelled the Allied forces to take care of masses of people, belonging to fifty-two different nationalities and housed in nine hundred DP assembly centers. The administration of these camps was to have been the responsibility of the UNITED NATIONS RELIEF AND REHABILITATION ADMINISTRATION (UNRRA), but for a variety of reasons—lack of trained personnel, absence of a clear policy, poor planning and management—the international agency was unable to fulfill its role properly. The private relief organizations that were gradually permitted to operate in the camps could at best provide only partial aid. Consequently, the United States Army, with a shrinking budget and inexperienced personnel, had to assume the major responsibility for the DPs.

It was difficult to comply with the demands made by the diverse national groups and religious denominations, each of which demanded recognition of its own problems. In order to avoid charges of discrimination, the American army adopted a policy of evenhandedness toward all the DPs. This policy had an adverse effect on the Jewish DPs, who were housed in the same camps with Poles, Baltic nationals, and Ukrainians, where the Jews—who for years had suffered from starvation and cruel treatment in the concentration camps—remained exposed to antisemitic discrimination. The army authorities refused to grant preferential treatment to the Jews, on the ground that this would be a confirmation of the Nazi racial doctrine, which differentiated between Jews and others. The Jews were therefore dealt with according to their country of origin; Jews from Germany, for example, were classified as "enemy aliens," like the Nazis. The concentration camp survivors, with their mistrust, hypersensitivity, and habits acquired in the camps, did not compare favorably with the "clean" and "civilized" German and Austrian population, and this influenced the American soldiers' attitude toward the Jewish DPs. In addition, the Americans' contacts with antisemitic Germans often revived prejudices held earlier in the United States. Some of the American commanders also suspected that the DPs from eastern Europe included Soviet agents.

Moreover, the army's attitude toward the Jewish DPs was determined, in large measure, by a perception that through their mere presence the DPs were impeding the implementation of the American administration's long-range policy—the rehabilitation of Germany. The Jewish population in the American zone in Germany and Austria grew from 30,000 in 1945 to 250,000 in the summer of 1947, as a result of large-scale infiltration into the zone of Jews from eastern Europe (see BERIḤA). Most of these Jews had no homes and no families to return to. The only solution for them was emigration, but the gates of all the countries in the world, including the United States and Palestine, were closed to them. As time went on and the number of Jewish DPs grew, while the military budget was being reduced, opposition to the Jews became stronger, even among the senior American officers. The American policy of transferring authority to the Germans, both on a local and on a national level, conflicted with the DPs' refusal to accept and submit to German authority.

In June 1945, as a result of pressure by American Jewry, Earl G. Harrison, dean of the law faculty at the University of Pennsylvania, was sent by President Harry S. Truman on a mission to Europe to investigate the DPs' situation. His recommendations were to establish separate camps for the Jews and to give them preferential treatment in terms of food, housing, and clothing. The sympathetic attitude of the American people, Jews and

Earl G. Harrison speaking at a United Jewish Appeal conference in Atlantic City on December 19, 1945. Harrison was appointed by President Harry S. Truman on June 22, 1945, "to inquire into the conditions and needs of displaced persons in Germany who may be stateless or nonrepatriable, particularly Jews."

non-Jews alike, toward the survivors of concentration camps, together with Harrison's report, led to a decisive change for the better in the conditions of the Holocaust survivors. The commander in chief of the American forces in the European theater, Gen. Dwight D. EISENHOWER, appointed to his staff an adviser on Jewish affairs, who acted as liaison officer between the army and the DPs and made sure that problems affecting the Jews were dealt with speedily and efficiently at the highest level.

In the wake of the KIELCE pogrom in July 1946, in which forty-two Jews were killed, one hundred thousand Jewish survivors from Poland left that country and entered the American zones of Germany and Austria, causing great overcrowding in the camps and further overburdening the army's budget. On two occasions, in December 1945 and again in July 1946, the administration in Washington de-cided to close the borders between the American zones and the east, but after Jewish lobbying in Washington they were soon reopened. An order was issued by Gen. Lucius Clay, commander of the American forces in Germany, on April 19, 1947, barring the entry of infiltrators into the camps and denying them United Nations aid, but this did not prevent a further influx of twelve thousand Jews from Romania and Hungary that year. In the final analysis, the infiltration of great numbers of Jews into the American zones in Germany and Austria would not have been possible without the humanitarian approach of the American army, which more often than not closed its eyes to the immigration.

As time went on, with no solution in sight for the resettlement of the DPs, confrontations between them and the army became more frequent. Some of the Jews conducted black marketeering, a universal practice at that time, and the army reacted with raids and searches, occasionally leading to violent clashes with the DPs. The army's humanitarian approach came to be replaced by a more severe attitude, and the DPs were considered a burden.

With the establishment of the state of Israel in May 1948 and the passage of a DP bill by Congress in June of that year (the Wiley-Revercomb Displaced Persons' bill, which provided for the admission of 100,000 DPs to the United States in 1949 and 1950), the DP problem underwent a drastic transformation. Large-scale emigration to Israel and the United States now emptied the camps, diminished the black-market operations, and improved the army's attitude toward the remaining DPs.

Views differ concerning the overall relations between the American army and the Jewish DPs. Leonard Dinnerstein has stressed the negative aspects and criticized the army for its harsh attitude; Abraham Hyman, on the other hand, considered its approach to the Jews to have been "one of the brightest chapters in the history of the U.S. army." All in all, despite occasional friction, especially between the DPs and American soldiers of lower echelons, the American army deserves credit for its massive help to the Jewish DPs.

[*See also* Survivors, Psychology of.]

BIBLIOGRAPHY

Bauer, Y. *Flight and Rescue: Brichah.* New York, 1970.

Dinnerstein, L. *America and the Survivors of the Holocaust.* New York, 1982.

Genizi, H. "Philip S. Bernstein: Adviser on Jewish Affairs, May 1946–August 1947." *Simon Wiesenthal Center Annual* 3 (1986): 139–176.

Grobman, A. "American Jewish Chaplains and the Sheerit Hapletah, April–June 1945." *Simon Wiesenthal Center Annual* 1 (1984): 89–111.

Hyman, A. S. "Displaced Persons." *American Jewish Year Book* 50 (1948/1949): 455–473.

HAIM GENIZI

UNITED STATES DEPARTMENT OF STATE, the United States governmental body most directly responsible for dealing with the fate of European Jewry during the interwar period and, to a certain extent, during the war, through its powers to grant visas, formulate refugee policy, and deal with foreign governments and international agencies. It has come under severe criticism for its lack of response to the destruction of European Jewry.

The State Department's career officers were traditionally part of an upper-class elite and were insensitive, and often antagonistic, to non-"Anglo-Saxon" immigrants. This helped shape their response to the events of the Holocaust, at a time when much of the department's policy formulation was in their hands.

After Hitler's accession to power in 1933, as the plight of German Jewry grew increasingly difficult, American consuls in Germany often added to the already stringent United States visa regulations, creating extreme difficulties for German Jews trying to obtain United States entry visas. In this, and in its opposition to increasing the number of REFUGEES permitted to enter the United States, the State Department reflected the prevalent public view on relaxing the immigration restrictions.

The State Department's attitude toward the plight of the refugees hardened when, in January 1940, Breckinridge Long, a political associate of President Franklin D. ROOSEVELT, was appointed assistant secretary of state, with authority over the Visa Division and responsibility for formulating United States refugee policy. Out of fear of spies and saboteurs infiltrating among the refugees, and out of a desire to prevent the United States from being inundated by elements (both ethnic and political) perceived as undesirable, Long raised further the barriers to refugees from Europe.

In the summer of 1942, the State Department attempted to prevent news of the Holocaust, transmitted through its channels, from reaching American Jewish leadership (*see* RIEGNER CABLE). In February 1943, the State Department gave specific instructions to its representative in Switzerland not to transmit such information. When President Roosevelt acquiesced to the Jewish leadership's request to allow the transfer of funds to the Jews of Romania, the State Department delayed the transaction. Throughout the war it opposed any serious rescue or relief efforts for the Jews of Europe.

The apparent apathy of State Department officers toward the fate of the European Jews led top officials of the Treasury Department to accuse them, in a report to the president, of deliberate acquiescence in the murder of the Jews of Europe. This report was the major factor in Roosevelt's decision to create the WAR REFUGEE BOARD, which subsequently made the main decisions regarding relief and rescue attempts.

BIBLIOGRAPHY

Feingold, H. L. *The Politics of Rescue: The Roosevelt Administration and the Holocaust, 1938–1945.* New York, 1982.

Friedman, S. *No Haven for the Oppressed: United States Policy towards Jewish Refugees.* Detroit, 1973.

Morse, A. D. *While Six Million Died: A Chronicle of American Apathy.* New York, 1968.

Wyman, D. S. *The Abandonment of the Jews: America and the Holocaust, 1941–1945.* New York, 1984.

Wyman, D. S. *Paper Walls: America and the Refugee Crisis, 1938–1941.* Amherst, Mass., 1968.

ARIEL HURWITZ

UNITED STATES HOLOCAUST MEMORIAL MUSEUM. *See* Museums and Memorial Institutes: United States Holocaust Memorial Museum.

UNITED STATES OF AMERICA. The United States government response to the antisemitic policy of the National Socialist regime in Germany is best viewed in the context of the long-range contours of American foreign policy and the stringencies of the domestic economic crisis of the 1930s. During the refugee phase of the crisis (1933–1941), there was a reluctance to accept Jewish REFUGEES. Only in 1939, after the EVIAN CONFERENCE, were the existing quotas fully utilized. As the crisis developed, there was some response. Hugh R. Wilson, the United States ambassador to Germany, was "recalled for consultation" after KRISTALLNACHT, and after the ANSCHLUSS (annexation of Austria) the German and Austrian immigration quotas were unified in order not to lose the latter. In 1937 a "special care" directive was issued to American consulates at the direction of President Franklin D. ROOSEVELT. But a bill to admit ten thousand Jewish refugee children outside the quota (the Wagner-Rogers Bill), introduced in 1939 and again in 1940, did not emerge from committee. During World War II, the "Jewish question" maintained the low priority it had had before the war.

The initial context of the United States relationship to Germany was its policy of isolationism, which meant in practice a rejection of all the responsibilities of being a world power while not eschewing commercial relations. Disillusionment with America's entry into World War I was of primary importance in this consideration. Strong isolationist sentiment prevented the Roosevelt administration from assuming an effective interventionist posture. In effect it buttressed the appeasement policy of France and Great Britain, and in some respects triggered that policy. Isolationist legislation, such as the Hoover-Stimson Doctrine (1931), the Ludlow Amendment (1934–1936), and the Neutrality Laws of 1936, 1937, and 1939, undoubtedly served as a "green light" for aggression in Berlin and Tokyo.

More difficult to appraise is the direct link between isolationism and antisemitism. Whereas in Berlin the "Jewish question" was ideologically tied to all public policy, in the United States the link was indirect and minor. The Jewish community, because of its close ties to the Roosevelt administration, acted as a magnet for anti–New Deal sentiment. That was especially true in the foreign-policy area, where Jewish leaders had taken a strong interventionist position. They earned thereby the staunch opposition of isolationist spokesmen like Charles Lindbergh, who, in a speech in Des Moines in September 1941, warned the nations that Anglophiles and Jews were trying to bring the United States into the war. More outspoken antisemites, such as Charles E. Coughlin, Gerald L. K. Smith, and the National Socialist Fritz Kuhn, had long before forged a rhetorical link between the movement to "stop Hitler" and the Jews.

During the 1930s antisemitism was a sentiment that stemmed primarily from the right wing of the political spectrum. The political culture of American Jewry placed it to the Left. Jews gave strong support to the resurgence of organized labor and the organization of the CIO (Congress of Industrial Organizations). They were the nation's staunchest supporters of the welfare-state program, which dovetailed with their own social democratic proclivities. A disproportionate number of the volunteers for the International Brigade to fight Franco's forces in Spain came from the Jewish community. Some New Deal antagonists, critical of the increasing number of Jews in high positions in the administration, had taken to calling the New Deal the "Jew Deal." The possibilities of forming the necessary coalitions to shape rescue policy were thus limited to the liberal side of the political spectrum, which, given the reluctance of the liberal Roosevelt administration to act to rescue Jews, was not sufficiently broad to influence public policy. Moreover, the fear that the stream of refugees would increase unemployment was one of the main arguments of antirescue policy.

The "great debate" in American foreign policy was resolved by the Japanese attack on Pearl Harbor, but that hardly stilled the strident antisemitism which persisted in sectors of the American populace. Antirefugee and antirescue sentiment was now buttressed by a new fear that Germany would infiltrate spies into the refugee stream. It was an awareness of these popular passions which convinced Roosevelt that the war must never be allowed to be depicted in terms of a war to save the Jews. While Berlin spoke endlessly of the demonic Jews and dubbed Roosevelt himself a Jew, the American government, on those rare occasions when it addressed itself to the Jewish question at all, referred merely to "political refugees."

The existing indifference to the refugees extended, after Pearl Harbor, to the question of rescuing those in camps. Even when it became clear that Berlin had actually embarked on the "FINAL SOLUTION," the State Department tried for a time to suppress confirmation of the news, which emanated from Leland Harrison, its own consul in Bern, Switzerland. Instead, a fruitless search was undertaken for areas where masses of Jews might be resettled. Jews themselves were not anxious to pioneer outside Palestine, and the administration had "frozen" the Palestine problem, which was considered a British affair, until after the war. Only the Dominican Republic Settlement Association, a small-scale venture whose genesis can be traced to the Evian Conference, got off the ground. Efforts to rescue Jews by means of refugee ships failed; in one example, the ST. LOUIS, destined in 1939 for Cuba with a cargo of hapless refugees, was rejected by Cuba and compelled to return to Europe, where death awaited many of the passengers.

Most of the steps taken by the Roosevelt administration were intended more as gestures than as a consistent policy to ameliorate the plight of the victims. The Evian Conference, called at Roosevelt's behest in mid-1938 to bring order into the chaotic refugee situation, was foredoomed to failure since the American delegation was instructed that no tampering with the immigration laws would be countenanced. Unable to make a significant contribution to the solution of the problem, other receiving nations such as Britain and France could hardly be expected to outdo a reluctant America. Similarly, the resettlement policy, on which so much was staked, was in practice an ignominious failure. Receiving nations wanted to rid themselves of Jews rather than offer haven to them.

Between 1942 and the end of the war in Europe in 1945, the Allies gave no priority in their war aims to the rescue of Jews. Repeated suggestions for retribution, negotiations, or ameliorating the situation, such as sending food packages to camps or changing the designation of their inmates to that of prisoners of war, were rejected because it was felt that such steps would interfere with the prosecution of the war. The processed murder of the Jews was not mentioned at any of the Allied war conferences held at Tehran, Casablanca, and Yalta. As news continued to reach the West and the public at large between May and December 1942, the British government was subjected to growing pressure to do something to help the Jews. The Jewish community of Great Britain, representatives of the YISHUV (the organized Jewish community in Palestine), segments of the press, the POLISH GOVERNMENT-IN-EXILE, dignitaries of the church, and politicians (notably Eleanor Rathbone, a member of Parliament) all pressed the government on this point. Apparently, a Polish government-in-exile demand on December 9 finally persuaded it to do something. When told of the British desire to make some sort of gesture, the United States responded by favoring the issuing of a declaration rather than taking concrete action. A statement drafted by the British Foreign Office and edited by the United States State Department was issued on December 17, 1942. It was issued in the names of Belgium, Czechoslovakia, Greece, Luxembourg, the Netherlands, Norway, Poland, the USSR, Great Britain, the United States, and the French National Committee. Clearly condemning the "bestial policy of cold-blooded extermination," the declaration noted that hundreds of thousands had been killed. In the British Parliament, Anthony Eden prefaced his reading of the declaration by saying that it was about the sad fate of the Jews. The declaration, however, did not appease all those who clamored for aid to the Jews. The BERMUDA CONFERENCE was the next "gesture" made by the British and Americans to advocates of rescue. Only in 1943 were Jews mentioned in statements about retribution and war crimes.

Demonstration of Jews in New York City against the British policy in Palestine (July 1947). [Alexander Archer, Zionist Archives, New York]

As details of the fate of the Jews filtered out of Nazi-occupied Europe after October 1942, a strong movement for action developed among rescue advocates. In London and Washington the response was to convene a second refugee conference, in Bermuda, in April 1943. It soon became apparent that the purpose of this conference was to assuage public opinion without taking concrete rescue steps. Most recommendations for rescue were rejected. Especially bitter was the rejection of a recommendation that ships with empty holds returning to the American arsenal might be used to transport refugees to safe havens, thereby improving the flow of refugees from Spain and Portugal. Negotiating with Berlin for the release of the Jews and a halt to the slaughter was also rejected. Instead, the conference disinterred the INTER-

GOVERNMENTAL COMMITTEE ON REFUGEES, a defunct international refugee agency that had been created after the Evian Conference. There were also some tentative plans to establish a refugee camp in North Africa.

So meager were the results of the Bermuda conference that it was decided not to make the results public, and rescue advocates dubbed the conference a "cruel mockery." It was held at the same historical moment as the WARSAW GHETTO UPRISING, so that the connection between the martyrdom of the Jews and the indifference of the Allies was startlingly apparent. But the Bermuda Conference stratagem did not work. By the fall of 1943, rescue advocates had mounted a campaign to bring into existence a government agency for the rescue of European Jewry. Congressional hearings held in November

1943 on a rescue resolution led to the removal of Breckinridge Long, the assistant secretary of state most responsible for the potpourri of programs that made up the administration's rescue program and its hard line on the quota policy.

Predictably, firm action on the rescue question came from the Treasury Department, headed by Henry MORGENTHAU, Jr., the closest Jew to Roosevelt, rather than from the State Department. Josiah E. DuBois, Jr., an official in the Treasury Department, discovered evidence that the State Department had tried to suppress hard news of the implementation of the "Final Solution" and had otherwise sought to undermine all efforts at rescue. That information, incorporated into a secret report, was delivered to the Oval Office on January 16, 1944, together with a plan to create an interdepartmental rescue agency. Subsequently Roosevelt created the WAR REFUGEE BOARD (WRB), headed by John Pehle, a Treasury official, and staffed largely with personnel from Jewish agencies knowledgeable on rescue matters. Its financing was provided by the American Jewish JOINT DISTRIBUTION COMMITTEE.

Almost immediately, the WRB was faced with a crisis in HUNGARY. Berlin was anxious to get rid of this Jewish community before its own demise. The WRB made a broadcast to the Hungarian people, urging them not to cooperate with the scheduled deportations. Appeals were sent to all nations maintaining diplomatic contact with Hungary to increase the size of their legations so that the deportations could be monitored. In Sweden the WRB agent, Iver Olsen, recruited Raoul WALLENBERG, who went on to demonstrate what could be achieved on the rescue front where there was a will to save lives. Money was provided to underground Zionist youth groups to enable them to open up escape routes through Yugoslavia, Slovakia, and Romania. A special executive order issued by Roosevelt in April 1944 ordered that a temporary haven for rescue be established by the Army Relocation Authority in FORT ONTARIO, near Oswego, New York. The heretofore immutable immigration laws, which were a major rescue roadblock, were thus circumvented. The camp at Oswego served as a model for other potential receiving nations, including Palestine, to accept more victims of the Holocaust. Pressure was put on various neutral countries, especially in Latin America, to accept refugees. Switzerland was also prevailed upon to help Hungarian Jews, as was the International RED CROSS, represented in Hungary by Friedrich Born.

Yet despite the increase in activity by the Roosevelt administration, the rescue of the surviving Jews proved to be very difficult. In Hungary, Adolf EICHMANN encountered little difficulty in deporting the Jews who lived outside BUDAPEST. The Allies still lacked control of the physical scene of the deportations. Bombing the camps and the railways leading to them, which had been suggested by rescue advocates as early as the spring of 1943, might have served as a substitute for such on-the-ground control. But in both Britain and the United States the military high command rejected the bombing idea as needlessly interfering with the major "win-the-war" priority, and it was viewed as being of "doubtful efficacy." The American, British, and Soviet governments opposed the proposed ransom arrangement in the case of the rescue of Hungarian Jews. The breakthrough on the rescue front represented by the creation of the WRB came too late and was too weakly implemented to save the surviving Jews of Europe.

[See also American Jewry and the Holocaust; American Press and the Holocaust; Rescue of Children, United States.]

BIBLIOGRAPHY

Divine, R. A. The Reluctant Belligerent: American Entry into World War II. New York, 1965.

Feingold, H. L. The Politics of Rescue: The Roosevelt Administration and the Holocaust, 1938–1945. New York, 1982.

Smith, G. American Diplomacy during the Second World War, 1941–1945. New York, 1965.

Wyman, D. S. The Abandonment of the Jews: America and the Holocaust, 1941–1945. New York, 1984.

Wyman, D. S. Paper Walls: America and the Refugee Crisis, 1938–1941. Amherst, Mass., 1968.

HENRY L. FEINGOLD

UNITED ZION ORGANIZATION. See Irgun Berit Zion.

UNIUNEA EVREILOR ROMÂNI (Union of Romanian Jews; UER), the oldest and best-known Jewish organization in ROMANIA; the successor of the first such organization, the Union of Native Romanian Jews (Pamanteni). Until 1938, when King Carol II disbanded all the political organizations in Romania, the union excelled in defending Jewish interests, obtaining and maintaining civil rights for Jews, abolishing discrimination, combating official and concealed antisemitism, and incorporating Jews into various sectors of the country's life.

The UER was headed by Dr. Wilhelm FILDERMAN, an authoritative and well-known Jewish political figure who for many years was considered by world Jewish organizations and many Romanian statesmen as the leading Jew of Romania. His ties with the traditional Romanian establishment, and even with the government of Ion ANTONESCU, were greatly instrumental in defending the Jews under fascist rule. Filderman succeeded in mobilizing these circles in the struggle to prevent the deportation of the Jews of Old Romania (the Regat, that is, Romania in its pre–World War I borders) and of southern TRANSYLVANIA to the extermination camps in Poland.

After the liberation, the UER renewed its activity, and was considered by Filderman and his helpers as a kind of league for defending the human rights of the Romanian Jews. The Jewish Communists viewed the organization as a threat to their status, and its leader as an obstacle to their programs among the Jews. They succeeded in splitting the union and forming a new parallel, "democratic" organization, with the help of several of Filderman's close aides, including Seltzer-Sarateanu and Dadu Rosenkranz.

Late in 1947 the UER's activities were terminated. In the short period between the autumn of 1944 and the liquidation, the union made every effort to reintegrate the Holocaust survivors into Romania's economic life, and in particular to restore plundered property to the Jews. In this it met with some success, in contrast to the position of the Communist party and the Jewish Communists, who did not want to harm the hundreds of thousands of Romanians who had benefited from the pillage of the Jews.

BIBLIOGRAPHY

Ancel, J., and T. Lavi, eds. *Rumania*. 2 vols. In *Pinkas Hakehillot; Encyclopaedia of Jewish Communities*. Jerusalem, 1969, 1980. (In Hebrew.)

Safran, A. *Resisting the Storm—Romania, 1940–1945: Memoirs*. Jerusalem, 1987.

JEAN ANCEL

UNRRA. *See* United Nations Relief and Rehabilitation Administration.

UNWCC. *See* United Nations War Crimes Commission.

UPA. *See* Ukrainska Povstanska Armyia.

UPPER SILESIA. *See* Silesia, Eastern Upper.

U.S. HOLOCAUST MEMORIAL COUNCIL. The U.S. Holocaust Memorial Council, established in 1980 by a unanimous vote of Congress, represents the commitment of the American people and the government of the United States to remember one of the darkest chapters in human history—the Holocaust.

The council was charged with the responsibility of fostering remembrance in two important ways: through the annual national civic commemoration of Days of Remembrance of the Victims of the Holocaust, and by planning, raising funds for, and constructing the UNITED STATES HOLOCAUST MEMORIAL MUSEUM. The private fund-raising efforts for the museum, as well as its construction, are carried out under the auspices of the council.

The council consists of fifty-five members of various faiths and backgrounds, appointed by the president of the United States, in addition to five senators and five members of the House of Representatives. Its creation resulted from the efforts of the President's Commission on the Holocaust, established by President Jimmy Carter in 1978. The commission's report to the president on September 27, 1979, recommended the creation of an appropriate American memorial to remember the victims and to educate Americans about the Holocaust.

The council's Days of Remembrance activities include local commemorations as well as the national civic ceremony held annually in the United States Capitol Rotunda. The council works with all fifty state governors and several hundred mayors, as well as with libraries, schools, religious leaders, and military personnel, to ensure that this solemn day is commemorated throughout the United States.

The council has sponsored three international conferences in Washington: the International Liberators Conference (1981), Faith in Humankind: Rescuers of Jews during the Holocaust (1984), and Other Victims: Non-Jews Persecuted and Murdered by the Nazis (1987). The council also sponsors annual conferences for Holocaust scholars and high school teachers, conducts an annual national writing contest for junior high and high school students, publishes a directory of United States Holocaust institutions, and sponsors Holocaust exhibitions. In addition, it awards the Eisenhower Liberation Medal annually to individuals and military units that played a role in the liberation of Nazi concentration camps.

Nobel Peace laureate Elie WIESEL served as the council's founding chairman. He was succeeded as chairman in 1987 by Harvey M. Meyerhoff of Baltimore, Maryland.

SARA BLOOMFIELD

USSR. *See* Soviet Union.

USTAŠA ("insurgent"; pl., Ustaše), Croatian nationalist separatist terrorist organization. The Ustaše movement was created in 1930 against a background of tension among the peoples of Yugoslavia in the interwar period, and principally between the Croats and the Serbs. The Croats, the second largest people in YUGOSLAVIA, wanted a federal state (*see* CROATIA) where they would have extensive autonomy, whereas the Serbs, who were the largest national group and ruled the country, wanted a centralist government in which they would continue to maintain their hegemony.

The confrontation between the Serbs and the Croats reached a climax after the murder of Croat delegates in parliament (late 1928) and the establishment of the dictatorship of King Alexander (early 1929). The heads of the Farmers' party, the largest party in Croatia, did not despair of a solution in the form of a Yugoslav state, but the extremists reached the general conclusion that the only solution was the creation of an independent Croatian state. Groups of the extremists, under Ante PAVELIĆ, a member of parliament, created the Ustaše movement.

The movement worked underground, and was constantly persecuted by the authorities. In the years of its underground activity the number of its members was small, only a few thousand, and yet its ideas, and principally the vision of an independent Croatian state, found support in wide sectors of the Croatian public—among students, thinkers, and the clergy.

The Ustaše professed violent struggle as the one and only way of achieving their objectives. In 1923 Pavelić declared that "knife, revolver, and explosives are the instruments with which the [Croatian] peasant will regain the fruit of his labor, the worker his piece of bread, and the Croat his freedom. . . . They are the musical instruments on which the Croatian people will play the requiem mass of the foreign [Serbian] rule." The Ustaše carried out the words of their leader. They assailed many of their opponents, attacked government installations, sabotaged railway tracks, laid explosives in public places, and in 1932 even attempted to create a popular uprising in a remote area, Lika. Their most impressive success was the murder, in cooperation with the Macedonian terror organization Vatreshna Makedonska-Revolutsionna Organizatsiya (Internal Macedonian Revolutionary Organization), of King Alexander during his state visit to France in October 1934.

The Ustaše engaged mainly in terrorist activity and straightforward propaganda, but several ideological components were evident in their thinking, which greatly resembled that of the radical rightist movements in eastern and southeastern Europe (the ARROW CROSS PARTY in Hungary, the IRON GUARD in Romania, the HLINKA GUARD in Slovakia): an eclectic mixture of Italian Fascist ideas, eastern European agrarian popularism, and Catholic reactionism. The central place in the Ustaše ideology was occupied by the principle of the political sovereignty of Croatia, which meant opposition to the principle of the Yugoslav state. On this basis a bitter hatred of the Serbs was nourished, which in the late 1930s was expressed in Nazi racial terms. The Ustaše movement's ideology also included the classical opposition to liberal democracy, to communism, and to what was known as the "capitalist plutocracy."

The independent Croatian state that was to arise was to be corporative, in the style of Fascist Italy, and all public and private activity was to be subordinated to the state. Its ideology extolled the farmer as the central pillar and source of vitality of the Croatian people; the family as the basic cell to be fostered; and Catholicism as the source of spiritual authority. Emphasis on the religious foundation stemmed from the attachment of most of the Croatian public to the Catholic church and from political reasons, against the background of the serious discord between the Orthodoxy of the Serbs and the Catholicism of the Croats. The Ustaše professed the leadership principle of the Fascists, by which the leader was not elected and was under no supervision. He appointed and dismissed, and determined policy and its implementation. This was the line of the movement that would guide the future state.

Throughout their existence, from their foundation until their removal from power in May 1945, the Ustaše looked for strong political patrons, and in any case were a tool in the hands of foreign forces. Until April 1941 the Ustaše were under the protection of Italy. The Italians gave refuge to the exiled Ustaše, trained the terrorists, and gave an organizational structure, means of fighting, and political cover to the movement. In exchange, the Ustaše members became an auxiliary arm in furthering Benito MUSSOLINI's policy in the Balkans and the Middle East. When the Italians were interested in unrest in Yugoslavia, they dispatched Ustaše terrorists, and when they wanted quiet, they shut them in camps and placed obstacles in their way.

In the mid-1930s the heads of the Ustaše made contact with the Germans, but the Germans dissociated themselves until the eve of their invasion of Yugoslavia in April 1941. Pavelić did not give up, and courted the Germans by adapting parts of the Nazi ideology, principally with regard to the Jews. In his first memorandum to Berlin in the summer of 1936, Pavelić described the Jews of Yugoslavia as fosterers of the Serbian dictatorship and supporters of the Versailles Treaty. In the same memorandum, the Jews of Yugoslavia were described as dominating the economy and the media; as Communist leaders; and as heading the FREEMASONS. Manifestations of antisemitism by the Ustaše increased from that time, and at the outbreak of World War II, the Ustaše's hatred of the Jews rivaled their hatred of the Serbs.

Hitler's decision in April 1941 to create a Croatian satellite state in part of Yugoslavia and to govern it through members of the Ustaše brought the movement to power. In the four years of their rule they carried out a policy of genocide with regard to the Serbs: over half a million were murdered, about a quarter of a million were expelled from the country, and another quarter of a million were forced to convert to Catholicism. The members of the Ustaše killed most of the Jews of Croatia, about twenty thousand Gypsies, and many thousands of their own political opponents. The ruler (poglavnik) was Pavelić, and among his principal aides were Dr. Andrija Artuković, minister of the interior; the author Mile Budak, Pavelić's deputy; Slavko Kvaternik, minister of war; and the latter's son Eugen Dido Kvaternik, head of the security services.

After the war most of the Ustaše leaders managed to escape to South America and to Spain. They attempted to reform their movement, but without real success, although in some places (principally in West Germany, among workers of Croatian origin) they continued to issue publications. The Ustaše have been responsible for terrorist attacks on Yugoslav institutions abroad.

BIBLIOGRAPHY

Hory, L., and M. Broszat. *Der kroatische Ustascha Staat 1941–1945*. Stuttgart, 1964.

Jelić Butić, F. *Ustaše i N.D.H.* Zagreb, 1977.

Krizman, B. *Pavelić i Ustaše*. Zagreb, 1978.

Krizman, B. *Ustaše i Treci Reich*. Zagreb, 1983.

Wuescht, J. *Jugoslawien und das Dritte Reich: Eine dokumentierte Geschichte der deutsch-jugoslawischen Beziehungen von 1933–1945*. Stuttgart, 1969.

MENACHEM SHELAH

ÚSTREDŇA ŽIDOV (Jewish Center; ÚŽ), Jewish institution established by the Slovak authorities to administer Jewish life. At the time of the first Czechoslovak republic, Slovak Jewry was divided among the Orthodox, the Neolog (Conservative), and the Status Quo Ante communities. It had four prominent public organizations: the Jewish party, Orthodox Jewry's Provincial Office, the non-Orthodox Union of Jewish Communities, and the Zionist Organization. The Orthodox community did not cooperate with Zionist-oriented bodies.

When SLOVAKIA was granted autonomy in October 1938, its Jews felt the need to close their ranks. The Orthodox office did not join these efforts, but the non-Orthodox organizations, in November 1938, set up the Central Jewish Office for Slovakia (Židovska Ústredňa Uradovna pre Slovensko).

Permission to establish the office was given on October 18, 1938, at a meeting of the representatives of the non-Orthodox Jews with Prime Minister Jozef TISO. The office engaged in social, economic, cultural, and religious activities. On January 22, 1939, in Žilina, representatives from all the Jewish communities and organizations that recognized the new office met. They conferred and decided which institutions should be included in it. The *Židovske Noviny* (Jewish News) became its official organ. The Orthodox office kept up its traditional functions, and its representatives were able to establish channels to the new regime. Persons close to the Orthodox office, together with Revisionist (Zionist) activists, took a leading part in organizing "illegal" immigration (*see* ALIYA BET) to Palestine, on boats that sailed down the Danube.

These two bodies maintained their ac-

The dining hall of the Nováky forced-labor camp. The camp was established at the instigation of the Ústredňa Židov, the Jewish Center in Slovakia, in the hope that the inmates' work would save them from deportation.

tivities—and their mutual competition—even when Slovakia was declared an independent state, on March 14, 1939. At the end of July 1940, when Hitler intervened in Slovakia's affairs, the situation of the Jews took a sharp turn for the worse. This development again served to underline the need for cooperation; leaders from each side eventually claimed that their organization had originated the initiative for unity. A new joint representative body was established, headed by Heinrich Schwartz (representing the Orthodox), with Arpad Kondor (Neolog) as his deputy; representatives of the Zionist movement also joined the united body, as part of the Neolog faction.

The new united representation remained in existence until September 26, 1940, when all Jewish organizations were abolished. Their assets were confiscated and transferred to a newly established body, the Jewish Center (Ústredňa Židov). Through the Central Office for Economy (Ústredňy Hospodarsky Urad; ÚHU), the authorities organized the Jewish Center along authoritarian lines. It was headed by a *starosta* (elder), who was assisted by a consultative body. This body, however, had no voting rights, and the *starosta* came under the authority of the ÚHU and was responsible to it. Schwartz was appointed *starosta*, and he in turn appointed department heads from the consultative council's members, among whom the Orthodox Jews occupied a prominent place. Jewish activists from that period do not agree on the role played by the leaders of Orthodox Jewry in the establishment of the Jewish Center—whether or not these leaders had had advance knowledge that such a body was being planned, or had even negotiated its establishment. At any rate, the Zionist movement was being harassed by the authorities, apparently on the principle of "divide and rule"; in this, however, they failed, owing to Schwartz, who was a wise and courageous man. He promised to help the Zionist movement keep up its activities, and appointed several of its representatives to the center.

The Zionist movement held searching discussions on the nature of the center and on whether it was wise and proper to join. One of the participants in these discussions was Jacob EDELSTEIN, who went twice to Brati-

slava from Prague and gave an account of Czech Jewry's bitter experience.

After Passover of 1941, Schwartz and several other activists were arrested. Schwartz escaped to Hungary, and the Central Office for Economy appointed Arpad Sebestyen, the principal of a Bratislava Jewish elementary school, to take his place as *starosta*. During Sebestyen's term in office, several more Zionists joined the center, among them Gisi FLEISCHMANN, who headed the emigration department, and Oskar Yirmiyahu Neumann, who was in charge of the vocational training department (which eventually became the labor camps department). These two departments were the focus of Zionist activities, among them the Palestine Office and the youth movement administrations. Other departments in the center included those of finance, education and culture, social affairs, publications (with responsibility for publishing the bulletin *Vestnik*), statistics, general administration and archives, and converts to Christianity. A secretary-general was the chief administrator of this complex apparatus. The center maintained branches headed by *dovernici* (trustees) in various Jewish communities. The center's staff, who numbered several hundred, were not on a uniformly high level, some having been appointed to their posts only on the basis of their connections with center officials or the Slovak authorities. Some of these people gave the center a bad name. A large number of informants and collaborators were employed in the center.

The most prominent collaborator was Karel Hochberg, head of the department for special duties and, later, of the department of statistics. Statements about him are contradictory, but he had the reputation of being the confidant of Dieter WISLICENY, the SS adviser on Jewish affairs to the Slovak government. Hochberg was denounced in strong terms for his role in the 1942 deportations, when his department carried out the administrative aspects of the operation and thereby facilitated its implementation. The argument was that if the special-duties department had not cooperated, the deportations would have run into great difficulties. These administrative preparations, moreover, involved corrupt practices, fraud, and barter with human lives, and the department staff came to be hated by the Jews. In the fall of 1943, Hochberg was dismissed from his post on charges of corruption and was taken to the NOVÁKY camp, where he was beaten up. During the SLOVAK NATIONAL UPRISING, Hochberg was executed by Jewish partisans.

Some of those working in the center disagreed with the line taken by the *starosta*. Together with Jewish leaders who were not on the center's staff, they established their own circle, the PRACOVNÁ SKUPINA (Working Group), which led the struggle for the rescue of the surviving remnants of the community. Meetings of the Working Group were held in Gisi Fleischmann's office.

Sebestyen's servile and tractable character posed a danger to the Working Group and to the survival of the Jews who were left, and efforts were made to remove him from his post. These efforts succeeded in December 1943, when Neumann was appointed acting *starosta;* he stayed in the post until the fall of 1944, when the center was abolished by the German army. Under Neumann the center in effect operated on instructions from the Working Group. Some of the center officials joined the Jewish or general resistance movements.

The Jewish Center was different from the Judenräte (*see* JUDENRAT) that existed in the German-occupied areas, but it, too, faced the dilemma of collaboration. While the center made life easier for the Jews, without it the deportation and extermination operations of the Germans would have experienced great obstacles. Most of the blame lies with the department of special duties, but this, after all, was part of the center. Sebestyen's leadership lacked courage and vision, and he was not prepared to act in defiance of orders; the rest of the center followed his lead. When Neumann became acting *starosta* the situation changed, his appointment reflecting a new mood in Slovakia and radical political change.

BIBLIOGRAPHY

Dagan, A., et al., eds. *The Jews of Czechoslovakia.* Vol. 3. Philadelphia, 1984.

Grünhut, A. *Katastrophenzeit des slowakischen Judentums: Aufstieg und Niedergang der Juden von Pressburg.* Tel Aviv, 1972.

Neumann, J. O. *Im Schatten des Todes: Ein Tatsachenbericht vom Schicksalskampf des slovakischen Judentums.* Tel Aviv, 1956.

Rothkirchen, L. "The Dual Role of the 'Jewish Center' in Slovakia." In *Patterns of Jewish Leadership in Nazi Europe, 1933–1945.* Proceedings of the Third Yad Vashem International Historical Conference, edited by Y. Gutman and C. J. Haft, pp. 219–227. Jerusalem, 1979.

YESHAYAHU JELINEK

UZHGOROD (Hung., Ungvár; Slovak, Užhorod), city in the TRANSCARPATHIAN UKRAINE, in the southwest of the Ukrainian SSR. Jews began living in Uzhgorod at the end of the fifteenth century; it was a stronghold of Orthodox Jewry. At the end of World War I, the city became part of the Czechoslovak republic. By the terms of the first Vienna Award (November 2, 1938), it was annexed by HUNGARY on November 12, 1938; at the time, 9,576 Jews resided in Uzhgorod.

After the incorporation of Uzhgorod into Hungary, the Jews of the city suffered from Hungarian anti-Jewish legislation, which deprived many of them of their livelihood. With the outbreak of World War II, and especially after the start of deportations from neighboring SLOVAKIA in March 1942, refugees fled to the relative safety of Hungary. In Uzhgorod some eighty Jewish households harbored refugee Jews.

Three days after the Germans occupied Hungary (March 19, 1944), a half dozen trucks loaded with SS men entered Uzhgorod. Several days later they set up a Zsidó Tanács (Jewish Council), headed by Julius Laszlo, the Jewish community leader. The other members of the Zsidó Tanács were taken from the ranks of the community leadership. At the end of March, the Jewish community was ordered to hand over to the Germans 2 million pengö ($400,000 in 1941 values and $60,000 in 1945 values) within forty-eight hours. They managed to collect all but 60,000 pengö of the required sum. Over the next few days the authorities ordered the Jews to surrender their pianos, radios, and certain kinds of furniture. They also began to seize Jews at random for a day of forced labor. On March 31, an order was issued re-

quiring the Jews to wear a yellow badge (*see* BADGE, JEWISH) as of April 5. Around the same time, a curfew was imposed on the Jews.

Some eighteen thousand Jews from the surrounding area were taken to the Moskovits brickyard on Minai Street on April 14, the last day of Passover. Five days later, posters were put up in Uzhgorod warning the Jews of the city not to leave their homes. On the following day, April 20, gendarmes and local police entered Jewish homes and pillaged them of their valuables. Between April 21 and 23, the Jews of Uzhgorod were brought to the brick factory; when it could hold no more, they were concentrated in the Gluck lumberyard. The task of moving more than seven thousand Jews out of the city was carried out by the gendarmes, local police, members of the local administration, and two units of army trainees stationed in ORADEA, Transylvania, and Galanta, Slovakia. The Zsidó Tanács and its staff remained in the ghetto, now confined to about a dozen houses on one street.

The conditions in the brick factory and lumberyard were terrible; the Jewish internees suffered from overcrowding, lack of food, and poor sanitation, and most had no shelter whatsoever. They were guarded by gendarmes, local policemen, and Hungarian soldiers, the last armed with machine guns. The Zsidó Tanács and its staff did what they could to alleviate the plight of the Jews, chiefly by providing food. A very small number of Jews succeeded in escaping.

A letter from Rabbi Michael Dov WEISS-MANDEL of the Slovak underground rescue committee, the PRACOVNÁ SKUPINA (Working Group), was smuggled into Uzhgorod early in May to a Jew named Mendel Feldmann. The letter told of the extermination of the Jews and called on the Jews to resist ghettoization and deportation with all their might. Feldmann took the letter to the Zsidó Tanács, which tried unsuccessfully to prevent him from circulating it. Copies were smuggled into the two concentration points and to the towns of MUNKÁCS and Huszt. The response to this plea was negligible.

Uzhgorod was part of Zone No. 1 of the anti-Jewish operation (for the purpose of deportation, Hungary was divided into six zones). Beginning on May 14, 1944, the Jews of Uzhgorod and its vicinity were deported to AUSCHWITZ in seven transports. The first trainload reached the extermination camp on May 16, and the last left Uzhgorod on June 3. Some two thousand Jews from Uzhgorod survived the war; most subsequently immigrated to Israel.

BIBLIOGRAPHY

Braham, R. L. *The Politics of Genocide*. New York, 1981.

Dinur, D. *The Holocaust of Carpathorussian Jewry: Uzhgorod*. Jerusalem, n.d. (In Hebrew.)

ROBERT ROZETT

V

VA'ADAT HA-EZRA VE-HA-HATSALA BE-BUDAPEST. *See* Relief and Rescue Committee of Budapest.

VA'AD HA-HATSALA (Rescue Committee of United States Orthodox Rabbis), relief and rescue agency established in November 1939 by the Union of Orthodox Rabbis of the United States and Canada (the leading association of rabbis in the Orthodox community; otherwise known as the Agudat ha-Rabbanim). Its express purpose was to save the rabbis and yeshiva (rabbinical academy) students who had escaped from Poland to Lithuania following the outbreak of World War II.

During the initial two years of its existence, the Va'ad, led by its founder, Rabbi Eliezer Silver of Cincinnati, sent relief to the approximately 2,500 rabbis and yeshiva students who had fled to Lithuania, among them practically the entire faculty and student body of such well-known yeshivas as those of MIR, Kletsk, Radin, Kamenets, and BARANOVICHI. The Va'ad assisted in the emigration of about 650 of these rabbis and yeshiva students during the period from October 1940 to June 1941. Several of the scholars emigrated to the United States (among them rabbis Aron Kotler, Avraham Yaphin, Reuven Grazowsky, and Moshe Shatzkes) and to Palestine (among them rabbis Eliezer Yehuda Finkel and Eliezer Shach), but the majority, approx-imately 500, ended up in Shanghai, where almost all remained for the duration of the war. In the fall of 1941 the Va'ad obtained Canadian visas for 80 scholars, but only 29 succeeded in reaching Canada.

Several of the rabbis who arrived in the United States after the outbreak of the war, such as Abraham KALMANOWITZ and Aron Kotler, played an active role in the Va'ad's activities. After the Japanese attack on Pearl Harbor and the American entrance into the war on December 7, 1941, the Va'ad initially concentrated on assisting the refugee scholars in Shanghai, as well as several hundred rabbis and yeshiva students in Soviet Central Asia. The latter were among the thousands of Polish citizens, deported by the Soviets to Siberia prior to the Nazi invasion, who were released in the wake of the Polish-Soviet agreement (the so-called Sikorski-Stalin Pact) of August 1941. The Va'ad sent these groups funds as well as parcels of food and clothing, and thereby enabled the scholars to maintain their unique life-style and continue their Talmudic studies despite the difficult conditions in Shanghai and Central Asia.

Following the revelation throughout 1942 of the mass annihilation of European Jewry, the Va'ad engaged in political activity designed to rescue Jews under Nazi occupation. The highlights of these activities were a protest march of four hundred Orthodox rabbis to the White House on October 6, 1943, the only public demonstration by Jewish leaders in Washington during the war, and the efforts that contributed to establishing the WAR

REFUGEE BOARD. In early January 1944 the Va'ad officially decided that it would henceforth devote its efforts to rescuing all Jews, regardless of their religiosity or organizational affiliation, a decision that was prompted by the rabbis' realization of the scope of the disaster that had befallen European Jewry. During 1944 and 1945 the Va'ad, through its branches in Switzerland (the HIJEFS relief agency, headed by Recha and Isaac STERNBUCH), Sweden (Wilhelm Wolbe), Turkey (Yaakov Griffel), and Tangier (Renée Reichman), launched relief and rescue activities to assist the Jews under Nazi rule, and maintained contact with Orthodox leaders in Slovakia (Rabbi Michael Dov WEISSMANDEL) and Hungary. The culmination of these efforts was the rescue of 1,200 inmates of the THERESIENSTADT concentration camp, who were sent to Switzerland in February 1945 as a result of negotiations, initiated by the Va'ad, between Swiss politician Jean Marie Musy and SS chief Heinrich Himmler.

During the course of the war, the Va'ad's activities aroused considerable controversy within the American Jewish community and focused attention on several crucial issues related to rescue attempts. One of the most important was the priority the Va'ad accorded to rabbis and yeshiva students. The majority of the other American Jewish organizations preferred to allocate equal resources to all Jews in distress. Moreover, the aid that the Va'ad provided for the refugee scholars in Shanghai, and to a lesser extent in Central Asia, was in addition to the regular assistance received by the refugees and enabled the rabbis and yeshiva students to study on a full-time basis, while the other refugees had to work. Another issue that caused considerable controversy was that of rescue tactics. On various occasions the Va'ad used methods of transferring funds that violated the spirit, if not the letter, of American regulations, a policy adamantly opposed by other Jewish organizations, primarily the JOINT DISTRIBUTION COMMITTEE, which throughout the war maintained a policy of strict adherence to United States governmental directives. The Va'ad's willingness during the final stages of World War II to transfer funds into Nazi hands in return for the release of Jews also aroused controversy. The final issue of debate within the community concerned the Va'ad's fund-raising activities. Shortly before the Va'ad was established, fund raising in the American Jewish community for domestic and overseas needs had been unified under the United Jewish Appeal. The Va'ad's decision to launch a separate fund-raising effort broke community unity.

After World War II, the Va'ad played an active role in rehabilitating survivors, aiding Jewish children, and providing for religious needs. During the period from its establishment in late 1939 until the end of 1945, the Va'ad spent more than $3 million on relief and rescue work. It was involved in rescuing several thousand Jews during the war and in assisting thousands during the postwar period.

BIBLIOGRAPHY

Zuroff, E. "Rabbis' Relief and Rescue: A Case Study of the Activities of the Vaad ha-Hatzalah (Rescue Committee of the American Orthodox Rabbis), 1942–1943." *Simon Wiesenthal Center Annual* 3 (1987): 121–138.

Zuroff, E. "Rescue Priority and Fund Raising as Issues during the Holocaust: A Case Study of the Relations between the Vaad-Ha-Hatsala and the Joint, 1939–1941." *American Jewish History* 68/3 (1979): 305–326.

Zuroff, E. "Rescue via the Far East: The Attempt to Save Polish Rabbis and Yeshivah Students, 1939–1941." *Simon Wiesenthal Center Annual* 1 (1984): 153–184.

EFRAIM ZUROFF

VA'AD HA-HATSALA BE-KUSHTA. *See* Rescue Committee of the Jewish Agency in Turkey.

VAIVARA, concentration and transit camp in northeast ESTONIA. It was apparently established in 1943, close to the Vaivara railway station. Initially it served as a camp for Soviet prisoners of war. From August 1943 until

February 1944 it was the central camp of about twenty labor camps throughout Estonia. Through it passed some twenty thousand Jews brought from the ghettos of VILNA and KOVNO in Lithuania, and from Latvia. On arrival in Estonia the Jews were kept for some time in the Vaivara camp, which was consequently known also as a transit camp. In addition, Vaivara was a concentration camp, with an average of about thirteen hundred prisoners, the large majority of whom were Jewish (men, women, and children), with a minority of Russians, Dutch, and Estonians.

The camp commandant (*Lagerkommandant*) of the Vaivara camp, and thus of all the other camps for Jews in Estonia, was SS-Hauptsturmführer Hans Aumeier. The camp was directed by Hauptscharführer Max Dahlmann, Hauptscharführer Kurt Panike, and Helmut Schnabel, who held the rank of *Lagerführer;* the chief physician was Franz von Bothmann. The entire administrative staff was made up of SS TOTENKOPFVERBÄNDE (Death's-Head Units). The camp was guarded by an Estonian SS unit.

The prisoners worked from morning to night at different types of hard labor, such as constructing railways, digging antitank ditches, quarrying large stones and pounding them to gravel, and felling trees in forests and swamp areas where they stood up to their knees in half-frozen water. The daily food ration received by the prisoners consisted of seven ounces (200 g) of bread with margarine or ersatz jam, ersatz coffee, and vegetable soup.

After the labor and at night the prisoners huddled together in wooden huts with very thin walls. Each hut was divided into five sections, with 70 or 80 prisoners in each section, sleeping in triple-tier rows. Water was inadequate, and washing was allowed only infrequently. Consequently, lice and disease were rife in the camp. The sick and the weak among the Jewish prisoners, and all the old people and children who could not work, were killed after *Selektionen.* The first *Selektion* was held in the fall of 1943 on the parade ground of the camp: 150 Jewish men and women who had been found unfit for labor were transferred by truck to the nearby forest and shot. In the second *Selektion* about 300

Jews were taken out to their death, in particular those suffering from typhoid. In twenty other *Selektionen,* held approximately every two weeks, about 500 Jewish prisoners were killed. In one *Selektion,* the children, who until then had been kept together in a special hut, were killed. Many scores of other prisoners were killed and wounded by the blows and punishments of the SS. As the Red Army approached, several hundred of the remaining prisoners were taken from the Vaivara camp westward to Saki.

In 1968 Lagerführer Helmut Schnabel stood trial, and was sentenced to sixteen years' imprisonment; the following year his sentence was reduced to six years.

BIBLIOGRAPHY

Dworzecki, M. *Jewish Camps in Estonia, 1942–1944.* Jerusalem, 1970. (In Hebrew.)

DOV LEVIN

VALLAT, XAVIER (1891–1972), French coordinator of the Vichy government's anti-Jewish program in 1941 and 1942 (*see* FRANCE). Vallat's political career was shaped in the mold of Charles Maurras's movement, ACTION FRANÇAISE—militantly nationalist, Catholic, and authoritarian. A badly wounded war veteran in 1918, he was a right-wing parliamentarian before 1940.

In March 1941, Marshal Philippe Pétain appointed Vallat head of the COMMISSARIAT GÉNÉRAL AUX QUESTIONS JUIVES (Office for Jewish Affairs), which was charged with administering anti-Jewish policy and legislation. Committed to the elimination of Jews from French public life and to reducing their role in French society, Vallat stood for what he called *antisémitisme d'état.* This meant that French antisemitic policy was to serve the interests of the state, and not to follow the dictates of the Nazis. Vallat operated in a highly legalistic manner, although in rare instances he made exceptions, permitting distinguished French-born Jews to remain in French public life. Anti-German as well as anti-Jewish, he resisted following an antisemitic policy that would materially aid the

Reich. The Germans forced him out of office in May 1942, when their plans called for the deportation and killing of the Jews. Sentenced in 1947 to ten years in prison, Vallat was released two years later.

BIBLIOGRAPHY

Marrus, M. R., and R. O. Paxton. *Vichy France and the Jews.* New York, 1981.
Paxton, R. O. *Vichy France: Old Guard and New Order, 1940–1944.* New York, 1972.

MICHAEL R. MARRUS

VAN DER VOORT, HANNA, Dutch rescuer of Jewish children. Hanna van der Voort came from Tienray, in the Limburg province in the southern Netherlands. Together with Nico Dohmen, she helped find hiding places for 123 Jewish children in the southern Netherlands. Receiving these children through an extensive underground network with which they were affiliated, they sought out and arranged temporary and permanent places of refuge with private families, transferring children from place to place as circumstances warranted. The money for the upkeep by the host families originated with an underground organization. Dohmen, as a courier between the sheltering families and the underground, maintained close contact with the children and devoted much time and effort to counseling his wards and lifting up their spirits. They were given special courses on how to behave as Catholic children, but no one tried to convert them.

One account of the help received through Dohmen relates:

> Day and night he was at work to find placement with farmers who had many children of their own and who were willing to feed one more mouth. Nico usually had to speak to the local priest, who in turn convinced the farming family that it was a good deed to save a child. Nico was himself a Catholic and had an easy dialogue with the clergy. Nico played the role of "ersatz father" to dozens of children. In addition, he had to supply food coupons to the family for the child. These had to be stolen from the Germans by another division of the underground.

Hanna van der Voort was eventually arrested and tortured by the Germans, who failed to elicit information from her. Her sufferings in jail caused permanent damage to her health. Both Hanna van der Voort and Nico Dohmen were recognized by YAD VASHEM as "RIGHTEOUS AMONG THE NATIONS."

MORDECAI PALDIEL

VAPNIARKA, town in Vinnitsa Oblast (district), in the Soviet Ukraine; under the Romanian occupation (October 22, 1941, to March 1944) it was in TRANSNISTRIA. In October 1941 the Romanians established a detention camp in Vapniarka in the former barracks of a Soviet military school, at one end of the town. The seven hundred local Jewish inhabitants had fled or had been killed by the Germans and the Romanians. A first group of one thousand Jews was brought to the camp that month, mostly from ODESSA; it included Bessarabian Jews who had previously fled to Odessa. Some two hundred died in a typhus epidemic; the others were taken out of the camp in two batches, guarded by Romanian gendarmes, and shot to death in antitank ditches.

In 1942 another 150 Jews were brought to Vapniarka. They had been driven out of BUKOVINA and included Jews who had taken refuge there after fleeing from Poland in the fall of 1939. On September 16, a group of 1,046 Romanian Jews was brought to the camp. About half had been banished from their homes on suspicion of being Communists, but 554 of them had been included in the group on the demand of the authorities in the Romanian towns where they had lived, without any specific charges being raised against them. This was the last transport to arrive at the camp; thereafter its status was changed to that of a concentration camp for political prisoners, under the direct control of the Ministry of the Interior in Bucharest, rather than of the Transnistrian gendarmerie. In practice, Vapniarka was a concentration camp for Jewish prisoners only, since no other "politicals" were held there, the only other prisoners being Ukrainian criminal convicts. Of the 1,179 Jews in the camp, 107

were women, who were housed in two huts surrounded by a triple-apron barbed-wire fence.

Among the Jewish prisoners in the camp were 130 Communists, 200 Social Democrats, and also Trotskyists and Zionists. Most of the prisoners, however, did not belong to a political party or movement and had been arrested on purely arbitrary grounds. The prisoners established a camp committee whose main purpose was to help them survive despite the conditions prevailing in the camp —starvation, disease, hard labor, and physical and mental torture. Apart from the official committee the camp also had an underground leadership, and between the two they persuaded the prisoners to observe discipline voluntarily.

The camp commandant introduced severe restrictions on the supply of water and at times withheld it altogether. By keeping the camp meticulously clean, the prisoners were able to overcome the typhus epidemic, but they suffered from the poor quality of the food, which included a species of pea that was normally used to feed horses (*Latyrus sativus*), and barley bread that had a 20 percent straw content. Within a few weeks the

first symptoms of paraparesa spastica appeared, a disease that affects the bone marrow, causes paralysis of the muscles of the lower limbs, and then affects the functioning of the kidneys. By January 1943 hundreds of prisoners were suffering from the disease. The prisoners declared a hunger strike and demanded medical assistance. As a result, the authorities allowed the Jewish Aid Committee in Bucharest to supply them with medicine, and the prisoners' relatives in Romania were allowed to send parcels to the camp. It was only at the end of January that the prisoners were no longer being fed with the animal fodder that had caused the disease, but 117 Jews were paralyzed for life.

An investigation ordered by the authorities in March 1943 revealed that 427 Jews had been imprisoned for no reason whatsoever. These prisoners were moved to various ghettos in Transnistria, but only in December 1943 and January 1944 were they sent back to Romania and released. In October 1943, when the Soviet army was approaching, it was decided to liquidate the camp. The prisoners were divided into three groups. One group, consisting of 80 Jews, was among the 427 Jews who were sent to the ghettos in

Transnistria. A second group, made up of 54 Communists, was taken to a prison in Rabniţa, Transnistria; the prisoners stayed there for a while, only to be killed in their cells by SS men on March 19, 1944. The third group, which included most of the prisoners (565 persons), was moved to Romania in March 1944 and imprisoned in the Tîrgu-Jiu camp. These prisoners were held until August 24, when they were released after the fall of the Ion ANTONESCU government.

Many of the former prisoners in Vapniarka were appointed to senior posts in the new Romanian regime, among them Simion Bughici, who became foreign minister.

BIBLIOGRAPHY

Lavi, T., ed. *Rumania*, vol. 1. In *Pinkas Hakehillot; Encyclopaedia of Jewish Communities.* Jerusalem, 1969. (In Hebrew.)

JEAN ANCEL

VATICAN. *See* Christian Churches; Pius XII.

VEESENMAYER, EDMUND (b. 1904), German diplomatic envoy in the Balkans; collaborator with Adolf EICHMANN in the "FINAL SOLUTION." Born in Bad Kissingen, Veesenmayer studied economics and became a lecturer at the Munich Technical College and the Berlin School of Economy. He joined the Nazi party in 1925 and reached the rank of *Brigadeführer* in the SS in 1944. Veesenmayer entered the diplomatic service in 1932 and was active in the Balkans. His contacts as member of the board of the chemical firm Donauchemie AG in Vienna, of the Länderbank AG in Vienna, and of the Standard Elektrizitätsgesellschaft (Standard Electric Company) in Berlin stood him in good stead.

In the Balkans, where he was attached to the German legation at Zagreb beginning in 1941, Veesenmayer actively furthered the deportation of Serbian Jewry. This was his special area of responsibility, and he frequently complained to Joachim von RIBBENTROP of the failure of Hungary and Slovakia to pursue this policy consistently. In 1944 he was sent as Reich plenipotentiary to Hungary, where, between March and November, he de-

voted himself to the implementation of the "Final Solution" together with Eichmann, to whose activities he gave diplomatic cover. Although nominally responsible to Ribbentrop and the German Foreign Office, Veesenmayer reported directly to Ernst KALTENBRUNNER at the REICHSSICHERHEITSHAUPTAMT (Reich Security Main Office; RSHA) on his efforts to induce the Hungarian authorities to cooperate with the German police in liquidating Hungarian Jewry.

In April 1949 Veesenmayer was sentenced for war crimes to twenty years' imprisonment by the International Military Tribunal at Nuremberg (*see* NUREMBERG TRIAL), but in December 1951 the United States High Commissioner in Germany, John J. McCloy, procured his release through an act of clemency.

BIBLIOGRAPHY

Browning, C. *The Final Solution and the German Foreign Office: A Study of Referat D3 of Abteilung Deutschland, 1940–1943.* New York, 1978.

Karsai, E., ed. *Vadirat a nacizmus ellen: Dokumentumok a magyarorszagi zsidóuldoszes történetehez.* Vol. 3. Budapest, 1967.

Macartney, C. A. *October Fifteenth: A History of Modern Hungary.* Edinburgh, 1957.

LIONEL KOCHAN

VEIL, SIMONE (née Jacob; b. 1927), French Jewish political figure, born in Nice. On April 13, 1944, Simone Veil was deported from the DRANCY camp to AUSCHWITZ, where her parents and sister, who had been deported with her, perished. After the war Veil studied law and then worked for the Ministry of Justice. In 1974 she was appointed minister of health despite the fact that she had no political party affiliation. In 1979 she was elected president of the Council of Europe.

Simone Veil has participated in events held by Jewish organizations in support of Israel and of Soviet Jews' right to emigrate, and in protests against manifestations of antisemitism.

BIBLIOGRAPHY

Klarsfeld, S. *Mémorial de la déportation des Juifs de France.* Paris, 1978. (In French and English.)

LUCIEN LAZARE

VERNICHTUNGSLAGER. *See* Extermination Camps.

VERTUJENI, transit camp for Jews in BESSA-RABIA. Vertujeni was established in August 1941 in the village of that name—a predominantly Jewish place—on the Romanian bank of the Dniester, 6 miles (10 km) from Soroca, a district center (present-day Soroki, in the Moldavian Soviet Socialist Republic). Vertujeni was founded in 1838. In 1930 its Jewish population was 1,843, or 91 percent of the total; most of the Jews were farmers. When the Germans attacked the Soviet Union in June 1941, many Jews fled in horse-drawn carriages across the river to Soviet territory. Those Jews who remained disappeared without leaving any trace; most probably they were killed. Their houses were looted by their Romanian neighbors from the nearby villages.

In early August 1941, the military authorities decided on Vertujeni as the site of a transit camp, because of its location and because it was a Jewish village. The first Jews brought to the camp were those who had tried to escape from the German and Romanian armies and had been driven back from the Ukraine by German forces. Some thirteen thousand

Jews were packed into the camp on August 17, 1941. The following day another four thousand Jews were brought from Lipicani, and on August 21 several thousand more were imprisoned in the camp—survivors of the first wave of killings by the Romanian army in a number of small camps and villages in the Soroca district. The camp now had twenty-six thousand Jews.

Only a few housing structures were available in the camp, and the drinking water was not enough to serve the needs of the huge prisoner population. Conditions were so bad that even the camp commandant, Alexandru Constantinescu, was shocked. The average daily death toll was one hundred and seventy, the victims succumbing to hunger, thirst, disease, and exhaustion. Constantinescu would not accept the existing policy of deliberately causing the Jews to die (as he later put it, "I did not agree to what I was told to do"), and he resigned from his post. His successor, Col. Vasile Agapie; Agapie's deputy, Capt. Sever Buradescu; and Ioan Mihaiescu, an official of the National Bank of Romania who was posted to the camp to supervise the confiscation of valuables, had no such compunctions. They harassed and tortured the Jews, withheld water and food from them, personally killed individual Jews, raped women, seized Jewish property and valuables for their own benefit, and devised means of torture to force the Jews to surrender any remaining valuables still in their possession.

On September 10, 1941, an order was received by the camp administration to deport the Jews on foot to TRANSNISTRIA, at the rate of 1,600 per day. An additional, confidential, order, addressed to the camp commandant in person, ordered him to shoot the Jews while they were en route there. In accordance with these orders, two columns of Jews left Vertujeni every day for Rezina and Cosauti, each column numbering 800 persons. The last group left Vertujeni on October 6. The roads leading to the Dniester were filled with the corpses of Jews who had been shot; thousands of them were eventually buried in a common grave in the Cosauti Forest. The camp officials, Agapie, Buradescu, and Mihaiescu, were among the first Romanian war criminals to be put on trial, in early 1945. They were sentenced to life imprisonment.

VERTUJENI

Annexations from June to September 1940: (1) Bessarabia and (2) N. Bukovina to USSR; (3) N. Transylvania to Hungary; (4) S. Dobruja to Bulgaria.

BIBLIOGRAPHY

Ancel, J., ed. *Documents concerning the Fate of Romanian Jewry during the Holocaust.* Vols. 5, 6. Jerusalem, 1986.

JEAN ANCEL

VICHY. *See* France.

VICTIMS, NON-JEWISH. *See* Gypsies; Homosexuals in the Third Reich; Jehovah's Witnesses; Krimchaks; Prisoners of War, Soviet.

VIENNA. Until 1918, Vienna was the capital of the Habsburg Empire. A Jewish community was first established there in the twelfth century. In the nineteenth and twentieth centuries, Vienna was a center of Jewish learning and Hebrew literature. A variety of Jewish welfare institutions and sports organizations were founded there, and Jewish newspapers, including a daily, were published. Vienna was the center of the Zionist movement at its inception and the seat of the Zionist Executive. Jews and converts from Judaism played a highly significant role in local cultural life and, indeed, in world culture, as writers, composers, and scientists, including Arthur Schnitzler, Franz Werfel, Richard Beer-Hofmann, Stefan Zweig, Peter Altenberg, Gustav Mahler, Arnold Schönberg, Josef Popper-Lynkeus, and Sigmund Freud. Austrian Jews were leaders of the Social Democratic party. Among its main activists and theoreticians were Otto Bauer; Julius Tandler; Hugo Breitner; and Fredrick, Victor, and Max Adler. All except Bauer were atheists, and they made Vienna a citadel of socialism until their suppression in 1934.

In 1846 the Jewish population of Vienna was 3,740, but it increased rapidly as Jews from all over the Habsburg Empire poured into the capital. By 1923, Vienna's Jewish population numbered 201,513, the third largest in European cities; by 1936 it went down to 176,034, 9.4 percent of the population.

At the same time that Vienna became a great Jewish community and center of Jewish creativity, at the end of the nineteenth century, it also developed into a leading focus of modern antisemitism, which struck deep roots and engulfed large parts of the population. One of the city's best-known antisemites was Karl Lueger, who was elected mayor in 1896 as leader of the antisemitic Christian-Social party, and who served as a model for Hitler, using antisemitism as a means to achieve his political ends. AUSTRIA's annexation by Germany was enthusiastically welcomed by most of the Viennese, and the ensuing persecution of the Jews, in which a substantial part of the population participated, was even more brutal than in Germany.

Right after the German takeover, the ANSCHLUSS, in March 1938, the Jewish community and Zionist organization offices were closed and their board members were arrested and sent to the DACHAU concentration camp. Jewish public life, however, did not come to a complete standstill. The community secretary, Emil Engel, smuggled some 800,000 schillings belonging to the election fund out of the community building. In a café and on the Ha-Koah Sports Club premises, Engel, together with Rosa Rachel Schwarz, director of the youth social-welfare office, and Dr. H. Isider Körner, chairman of Ha-Koah, handed out financial assistance to the needy on the basis of a list that they improvised. The list of contributors, however, was found, and in retribution the Nazis imposed a fine of 500,000 reichsmarks on the Jewish community of Austria. This was the first such fine imposed on a Jewish community by the Nazis. With help from the American Jewish JOINT DISTRIBUTION COMMITTEE (the Joint), the number of meals provided daily by the soup kitchens rose from 800 to 8,000.

On May 2, 1938, the community offices were reopened, with emigration and social welfare now their major concern. The Joint in Paris and the COUNCIL FOR GERMAN JEWRY in London provided most of the foreign currency required for emigration operations, that is, the currency required by the Jewish emigrants for their travel expenses and for producing the required minimum amount on their arrival at their destination. Counterpart funds to the amount contributed by the Joint were then released by Adolf EICHMANN from the community's blocked account, mainly money collected through a special tax that Jewish emigrants were forced to pay in order to receive their passports. (Eichmann had been sent to Vienna to enforce the emigration of Austria's Jews by threats of arrest, through the ZENTRALSTELLE FÜR JÜDISCHE AUSWANDERUNG, the Central Office for Jewish Emigration. It was established on Jewish initiative in August 1938 but was converted by the Nazis into an instrument of their policies.) Another source for financing community operations was the amount that emigrants to Palestine were asked to pay for their "certificates" (visas), the well-to-do among them having to pay between two and five times the official value. This method for raising funds was introduced by the Jewish community's executive director, Dr. Josef LÖWENHERZ, to finance the increasing need for social care and emigration.

The number of soup kitchens in operation increased from sixteen in March 1939 to twenty-three in July of that year, dispensing free meals every day of the week; this was a result of the economic deterioration that followed in the wake of the November 1938 KRISTALLNACHT pogrom. One of the soup kitchens was kosher and also baked kosher bread. The number of persons who needed such assistance grew from 28,000 in March 1939 to 38,000 in March 1940. The soup kitchens were open from 8:00 a.m. to 6:00 p.m. in order to serve as a warm shelter for the poor and to provide them in the afternoon with another bowl of hot soup and a piece of bread. In March 1940, 43,000 persons (86 percent of the Jews of Vienna at that time) required assistance from the community, which did not receive any help from the city administration.

The Jewish community did not confine itself to assistance in material terms; in June 1938 it inaugurated vocational training and retraining courses to equip the Jews with a professional skill pending their emigration. In the course of a single year, 24,025 men and women attended 1,601 courses, which corresponds to the number of students enrolled in professional courses in all of Germany in the six years between the Nazi rise to power in

Memorial to the Jews who were forced to scrub the streets of Vienna after the Anschluss (March 13, 1938). It was dedicated in November 1988. [Geoffrey Wigoder]

The effects of the Vienna Jewish community offices are loaded on a truck under Gestapo supervision at the community's offices, 4 Seitenstettengasse, on March 18, 1938, when the Gestapo closed the Jewish offices and institutions and arrested their officers and leaders.

1933 and the outbreak of World War II in 1939. Löwenherz's circumspect handling of the courses enabled him to obtain the release of the artisans who had been arrested in the *Kristallnacht* pogrom, to save the tools and equipment used in the courses from being confiscated, and to circumvent the total ban, imposed in January 1939, on Jewish craftsmen working in their craft. The number of skilled craftsmen conducting the courses of instruction amounted to 3,054 in May 1939, representing 3.8 percent of the Jews with

professional qualifications. As late as May 1940, 1,151 courses were still in operation. They also played an important social role, by keeping occupied a large number of Jews—whose average age was becoming higher and higher—and by providing free repair and renewal of clothing, shoes, furniture, and even medical instruments. Some of the courses trained nurses and social workers. Until the suspension of the courses, on February 3, 1941, they were attended by 45,336 students. Language courses were kept up until July 1941.

The community also tried to keep the intelligentsia occupied. Following the closing of the Jewish newspapers and the dismissal of Jews from the Zionist and general press, a new periodical, the *Zionistische Rundschau* (edited by Dr. Emil Reich, who had been editor of the *Jüdische Rundschau*), was published, making its first appearance on May 20, 1938. A total of twenty-five issues were published, under Eichmann's strict supervision, until November 4 of that year. Following a failed attempt to revive the weekly after *Kristallnacht*, Viennese Jews had to make do with a supplement to the twice-weekly *Jüdisches Nachrichtenblatt*, published in Berlin, whose size gradually shrank until it was closed down in the middle of 1943. The paper reinforced the Jews' survival instinct and also provided valuable information on the welter of laws, bans, and demands imposed by the authorities upon the Jews, on the documents required for potential emigrants and the places to obtain them, and, most importantly, on emigration opportunities, the number of which declined from day to day.

Under pressure of international public opinion to find a solution to the refugee problem and to aid in the emigration of Jews from Germany and Austria, a conference on refugee problems was convened at Evian-les-Bains (*see* EVIAN CONFERENCE) on July 6, 1938, at which thirty-one nations were represented. The conference was attended by a delegation of Austrian Jewry, composed of Dr. Löwenherz; Professor Heinrich von Neumann, representative of Agudat Israel and a world-renowned doctor with international connections; and Berthold Storfer, a financial expert, who had been an Austrian adviser and representative at international gatherings and who in 1938 was the executive director of the overseas emigration bureau. These men had no illusions about the conference's potential contribution to alleviating the plight of the Jews in Germany and Austria, but they used the occasion for behind-the-scenes meetings. The aim of these was to secure aid from the Joint, the Council for German Jewry, the Central British Fund, the American Friends Service Committee (who gave help to Jews and Christians of Jewish descent), and HICEM—for identifying opportunities for emigration, and for assisting emigrants on the way to their destination. One important achievement was the merger of the German and Austrian immigration quotas to the United States into a single quota. Another was that the Nazis, through the YOUTH ALIYA office in Berlin (which distributed the seasonal allocation of immigration certificates to Palestine for Germany and Austria), agreed to make the entire allocation for the summer schedule of 1938 available to Austria.

In Vienna itself a sharp confrontation erupted between Willy Ritter, secretary of the He-Haluts Zionist pioneering movement, and Dr. Alois Rothenberg, head of the Palestine Office. Ritter demanded that all pioneers' certificates go to pioneers who had been on Zionist agricultural training farms and to organized professionals. Rothenberg, however, did not agree that young people should have preference over veteran Zionists, some of whom had been pioneers of Zionism since the turn of the century. This tragic conflict was caused by the pitifully small number of immigration certificates made available by the British; some of them, moreover, were earmarked for Jews who had been expelled from the Burgenland (one of the federal states of Austria on the Hungarian border).

The linkage between the pioneering movement and immigration certificates also worked to the disadvantage of members of the Zionist Revisionist movement, who in 1935 had seceded from the World Zionist Organization. They therefore resorted to "illegal" immigration projects (*see* ALIYA BET) and chose Vienna for their center because of its location. Beginning in the fall of 1937, Dr. Willy Perl, an attorney, and Moshe Krivoshein-Gallili, a journalist and adventurer, with the help of the Maccabi Zionist move-

ment in Paris sought ways of illegal emigration for young Jews from Austria, Poland, Latvia, Czechoslovakia, Yugoslavia, and Romania who were eager to go to Palestine. These young people were brought to Vienna, where they were organized and then sent to Palestine on small, antiquated Greek boats, some of which sank.

After the annexation of Austria, these groups grew larger and came to be known as the *Perl-Transporte* or Aliya Af-al-pi (the "despite" immigration). They were joined by the Maccabi ha-Tsa'ir movement, headed by Dr. Daniel Adolf ("Dolfi") Brunner. Agudat Israel representatives Julius Steinfeld and Moritz Pappenheim utilized these transports to secure the immigration of large groups of Burgenland expellees. When Greece gave in to British pressure and closed its doors to the "illegal" immigration, the refugee boats left from Yugoslav and Italian ports; and when these routes as well were closed to them, the boats went down the Danube, a free international waterway. They used for this purpose fictitious visas issued by consular representatives of Latin American countries to the organizers in return for a fee.

In view of the British policy against "illegal" immigration, every issue of the *Zionistische Rundschau* published a warning against using this route, which, the warning stated, was also being exploited by scoundrels. Behind the scenes, however, Löwenherz, with Eichmann's knowledge, cooperated with the organizers of these transports. The Mosad le-Aliya (the immigration branch of the Palestine Jewish community's underground organization, the Hagana) was also opposed to immigration by this method. It aimed at a well-planned and well-organized operation, and would not cooperate with Eichmann's tactics of forced emigration. Following *Kristallnacht*, however, the Mosad changed its approach, and its representative in Vienna, Moshe Averbuch-Agami, organized "illegal" immigration transports in cooperation with the Stern Bureau, headed by Berthold Storfer. (In 1939 Eichmann put Storfer in charge of a bureau that was located on Sterngasse [Stern Street] and that became known as the Stern Bureau. Storfer was responsible for overseas emigration from Germany, Austria, and the Protectorate of BOHEMIA AND

MORAVIA; when emigration ceased, Eichmann had Storfer deported to AUSCHWITZ.)

The Jews of Vienna used every means available to escape from the nonstop regime of terror that prevailed in their city. In the very first week of the Nazi takeover, Jewish men and women were forced to wash the sidewalks with water containing a strong solution of boric acid—a demeaning job, which was even more widely enforced in the week of the Passover holiday. At the end of May 1938, 2,000 Jews belonging to the intelligentsia were arrested, according to a readymade blacklist, and sent to the Dachau camp, in four transports. The dark streets of a blackout exercise in September 1938 were used for concerted attacks on Jews; so many were injured that the Jewish hospital courtyards could not hold them all.

It was in Vienna that the practice of attacking Jews on Jewish holidays was introduced. On October 4, 1938, the eve of the Day of Atonement, the Nazi party in Vienna decided to drive the Jews out of the city, with excited mobs demonstrating in the streets to express their support—a kind of grand rehearsal for the November 1938 pogrom. That evening, Nazi party members wearing plain clothes began taking Jews out of their apartments in well-to-do parts of the city, sealing the apartments, and leaving the Jews homeless, jesting to them that boats would take them to Palestine. On October 6 the operation was extended to include the outskirts of Vienna. It was brought to a halt on orders of the Gestapo and of Gauleiter Dr. Josef Bürckel, Reich commissioner for Austria's unification with Germany, who resented the party's action being taken behind his back.

The *Kristallnacht* events of November 1938 did not signify as dramatic a turn in Vienna as they did in Germany, but rather polarized the situation to the extreme. After mid-October 1938, not a single night passed without attacks on Jewish stores and schools and the desecration of synagogues. It became routine practice to close off streets in Jewish neighborhoods in the middle of the day and arrest the Jews. On *Kristallnacht*, forty-nine synagogues, as well as Hasidic prayerhouses and private prayer rooms, were destroyed in Vienna, and 3,600 Jews were deported to Dachau and BUCHENWALD, to be released only when their relatives were able to produce documentary proof that they were going to emigrate. The Nazi party membership in Vienna, led by Gauleiter Odilo GLOBOCNIK, played a significant part in the pogrom. In 1939 the expulsion of Jews from their apartments was accelerated, the Nazi policy being to concentrate the Jews in "Jewish" quarters. In the period from March to September 1939, 13,600 Jewish families were forced to vacate their apartments, and in the first half of that year, 9,500 formerly Jewish-owned apartments were turned over to "Aryan" owners.

After the occupation of Poland, the emphasis in the policy on Jews switched from emigration to deportation. Even young people with emigration papers in their possession were not released. In September 1939 the Jewish community was ordered to draw up an alphabetical list of all the Jews in the city. Early in October, 1,048 Polish and stateless Jews were deported to Buchenwald, including 122 residents of old-age homes, up to eighty-five years old. Under the Lublin Reservation resettlement project for the Jews of Germany, Austria, and the Protectorate, two transports with a total of 1,584 Jewish professionals left Vienna for Nisko, on the San River, on October 20 and 26, 1939 (*see* NISKO AND LUBLIN PLAN). Of them, no more than 198 persons were assigned to the job of setting up a barracks camp, while the rest were forced across the river into Soviet territory, with shots fired in the air. These activities suggest that Nazi anti-Jewish policy was in transition.

The deportation program was halted owing to the preparations being made for the offensive in western Europe. But it was reinstated in February 1941, and within three weeks more than five thousand Viennese Jews, in five transports, left for the KIELCE region of Poland. Once again the program came to a halt, this time because of the preparations for the invasion of the Soviet Union. Eichmann and his successor in Vienna, Rolf Günther, were prepared to allow emigration to continue and to exempt from deportation women, persons with special qualifications, and bearers of emigration papers, on condition that absolute obedience to orders was observed in preparing the candidates for deportation, in accordance with lists sent in by Gestapo headquarters in Berlin. In addition, Löwenherz had to provide substitutes for those who were exempted from deportation.

The interludes between pogroms and deportations and between one wave of deportations and the next were used by the Jews of Vienna to try and find a way of emigrating from the country and, as best they could, to bring some order into their lives. He-Haluts operations were at their height in July 1939, when 779 Zionist pioneers and teenagers were undergoing training in sixteen agricultural training camps and workshops and in three tree nurseries. At that point, 335 pioneers were on agricultural training in seven countries outside of Austria. Between November 1938 and June 1939, 2,500 youngsters were attending courses in agriculture and various trades (a total of sixty-five such courses) under Youth Aliya auspices. Of the 2,340 abandoned children left in Vienna in early 1940, only 338 were in the care of community institutions; 1,839 children, ranging in age from ten to eighteen, were attending the Youth Aliya school. Its moving spirit and organizer was Aron MENCZER, who had refused to join his parents and five brothers, all active Zionists, on their way to Palestine, choosing to stay behind and serve the children *in loco parentis* and as educator. In July 1940 the children held a handicrafts exhibition, and on September 1 they opened a Zionist exhibition, *Werk und Wege* (Work and Ways), for which they also prepared a catalog. On Jewish holidays Menczer arranged for youth services to be held, and on Passover he organized the children's own Seder service for them. In December of that year Menczer was invited to a Zionist youth convention in BĘDZIN to assist in organizing youth work in Upper Silesia.

Religious life, which had been conducted as usual—albeit on a more modest scale—up to the November 1938 pogrom, was subsequently continued clandestinely, with people gathering in quorums for services in private apartments. Requests by the community to permit services to be held in parts of the synagogues that had been left standing were turned down. In January 1939, spiritual ministration to Jewish prisoners was no longer permitted. Still, for the Jewish New Year of 5700 (1939/1940), a calendar was printed and distributed in 6,700 copies. The following year, 5701 (1940/41), booklets containing the Yizkor (memorial) service were also printed and made available. An attempt to bake matzoth (unleavened bread) for Passover failed. For the Festival of Tabernacles of 1940, the Joint office in Budapest provided Löwenherz with 150 *lulavim* (palm branches) and *etrogim* (citrons), two of the "four species" used in the festival, for distribution in Vienna and among Jewish communities and rabbis in Poland. Schlesinger's publishing house continued to supply religious books to foreign countries, from the Netherlands to Yugoslavia. In 1940 Löwenherz arranged for the Joint subsidies to Warsaw to be transmitted via Vienna, so as to benefit from the rate of exchange; a total of $1,700,000 was passed on in this manner, in seven installments. Löwenherz countered Eichmann's threats (of deportations and emigration stoppage) with a threat of his own, that such acts on Eichmann's part would mean an immediate end to the Joint's transfers of foreign currency.

On February 5, 1941, Alois BRUNNER, the successor to Eichmann and Günther, ordered the closing of He-Haluts. The two major agricultural training camps, Waidhofen and Doppl, were turned into labor camps, in which all the youth instructors were concentrated. The offices of Maccabi, the Mizraḥi religious Zionist movement, and the Zionist Organization were also closed down, following the termination of the Zionist Funds (the Jewish National Fund and the Palestine Foundation Fund) a few weeks earlier, in December 1940. On May 12, 1941, Brunner shut down the Youth Aliya offices and the Palestine Office and announced that young people interned in Dachau and Buchenwald would no longer be released for emigration.

On July 31, 1941, Vienna still had 43,811 Jews "by religion" living in the city, as well as 8,728 persons defined as Jews under the NUREMBERG LAWS (two-thirds of the latter figure were converts from Judaism). Further emigration of Jews between the ages of eighteen and forty-five was prohibited on August 5, 1941, and the final, systematic deportation of the Jews of Vienna was launched on October 15 of that year. By October 5, 1942, 5,000 Jews had been deported to ŁÓDŹ, 5,200 to RIGA, 6,000 to Izbica, and 10,476 to MINSK.

Most of them were shot to death or gassed; this was also the fate of the Jews who had been deported to Kielce in February 1941. The Jews selected for deportation were put into assembly camps, where they were held for weeks and months in subhuman conditions. Anton Brunner (no relation to Alois), a civilian official, was in charge of the deportations. He was unbelievably cruel and sadistic, separating family members from one another and deporting sick persons who had to be put on the train on stretchers. At first the deportations proceeded in accordance with Gestapo lists sent from Berlin; later, the Jews were deported by streets or by entire residential complexes. Couples in mixed marriages also had to display a Star of David sign on their entrance doors.

Worse even than the SS in their cruel behavior were the members of the Vienna JÜDISCHER ORDNUNGSDIENST, a kind of Jewish police that had its origin in the toughs employed by the Jewish community, beginning in 1938, to keep order in the long lines of people waiting to be admitted to the community offices. Three of these men were taken to Berlin to teach others how to round up people for deportation, and were so efficient in their jobs that even non-Jews were outraged at their behavior. The Jews were so afraid of the Jewish police that they spent the nights roaming the streets to escape being seized in their homes, only to be captured when they went to the soup kitchens for a meal. Jews whose hiding places had been destroyed by air attacks in 1942 and 1943, or whom hunger had forced out, waited helplessly in the street to be taken. Under the threat of deportation, Jewish community employees and Jews from the assembly camps were forced to take part in a Nazi antisemitic propaganda film (see FILMS, NAZI ANTISEMITIC) produced in 1942. In one scene a Jewish wedding was staged, complete with a wedding canopy, rabbi, and cantor, and in another, young women were filmed in the nude in the ritual bathhouse, sitting in the laps of old men (they had been taken out of the hospital) who were smoking thick cigars. Of all these "actors" only one woman survived.

In the period from June 20 to October 9, 1942, 13,776 Viennese Jews were deported to THERESIENSTADT. One of the transports, which left Vienna on September 23, was made up of "privileged" Jews, among them the last chairman of the Jewish community prior to the Anschluss, Dr. Desider Friedmann, and his deputy, the Zionist leader Robert Stricker. Both of these men had been arrested when the Jewish community offices were closed down, on March 18, 1938. They had been released from Dachau in the summer of 1939, on condition that they not leave Vienna and serve as hostages for the emigration of the Jews. (In October 1944, Friedmann and Stricker and their wives were deported to Auschwitz.) The transport of the "privileged" also contained the Zionist youth instructors, headed by Aron Menczer.

On November 1, 1942, the Jewish community organization was disbanded and changed to the Ältestenrat der Juden in Wien (Council of Elders of the Jews of Vienna). The remaining assets of the community, amounting to 6.5 million reichsmarks, were transferred to Prague, ostensibly to be used for the financing of the Theresienstadt ghetto. The Central Office for Jewish Emigration was closed down on March 31, 1943, and the responsibility for the deportations was transferred from one branch of the SS to another. For some time thereafter the Jewish community was still able to gain exemption from deportation for hospital patients, doctors, and senior officials, but it had to provide replacements. Usually these were younger employees of the community, with large families.

Much to the Nazis' disappointment, only 976 apartments were vacated in 1942, despite the large number of Jews who had been deported (32,721) or had been moved from their apartments to the "Jewish" quarters (a kind of open ghetto). The small number of apartments that became vacant indicates the cramped conditions in which the Jews were living—up to six families in a small three-room apartment—and how destitute they had become by that time.

In July 1944, approximately twenty-one thousand Jews from the Szeged and Debrecen areas of Hungary arrived at the Strasshof railway station, near Vienna. These were prospective candidates for exchange in an arrangement between Heinrich HIMMLER and the Western powers that Rezső KASZTNER had initiated. In Vienna, Hermann KRUMEY was in charge of this operation. Approximately half of these Jews were distributed among small labor camps that had been put up in school buildings and small stores, and the remainder in courtyards in towns and villages of Lower Austria. They were mostly women and minor children with their grandparents, suffering from malnutrition and disease. The Jewish community doctor, Dr. Emil Tuchmann, set up a clinic and maternity ward in the small Jewish hospital, and his assistants—ten physicians—walked for miles in order to visit each small group of Jews and supply the medicine they needed (the doctors were not allowed to use motorized transport). A Hungarian rabbi led a Passover Seder service at the hospital in 1945, and regular prayer services were held there.

Most of the Hungarian Jews who had been imprisoned in Vienna survived the war, whereas the greater part of those who had been distributed over the provincial towns were shot to death or perished during DEATH MARCHES. Some of them reached Theresienstadt and remained alive. A day before the liberation of Vienna by the Soviet army, on April 12, 1945, nine Jews who had been in hiding were shot to death by SS men about to make their escape from the city. As of December 31, 1944, 5,799 Austrian Jews still lived in Vienna. Of this number 3,388 were partners in so-called privileged mixed marriages (*privilegierte Mischlingen*), and 1,358, in regular mixed marriages. In Lower Austria there were 118 Jews. At the time of the liberation of Vienna, some 150 Jews remained in hiding, and a similar number survived who worked in the warehouses where confiscated Jewish possessions were stored, or as laborers in SS households. Also among the survivors were 35 Jewish community employees and 84 disabled war veterans, some of whom owed their lives to their Christian wives.

BIBLIOGRAPHY

Bauer, Y. *My Brother's Keeper: A History of the American Jewish Joint Distribution Committee, 1929–1939*. Philadelphia, 1974.

Botz, G. *Wohnungspolitik und Judendeportationen in Wien, 1938 bis 1945: Zur Funktion des Antisemitismus als Ersatz nationalsozialistischer Sozialpolitik*. Vienna, 1975.

Fraenkel, J., ed. *The Jews of Austria*. London, 1967.

Gedye, G. E. R. *Fallen Bastions: The Central European Tragedy*. London, 1942.

Rosenkranz, H. *Verfolgung und Selbstbehauptung: Die Juden in Österreich 1938–1945*. Vienna, 1978.

HERBERT ROSENKRANZ

VILNA (Lith., Vilnius; Pol., Wilno), capital of the Lithuanian SSR. From 1920 to 1939 Vilna was under Polish rule, and on the eve of World War II it had a population of about two hundred thousand.

Jews lived in Vilna from the first half of the sixteenth century. During the latter part of the eighteenth century, when the famous scholar Elijah ben Solomon Zalman (the "Gaon of Vilna") lived in the city, it became a center of Torah learning. In the nineteenth century Vilna was a hub of Jewish culture, with Jewish newspapers, publishing firms, and printing presses, and was known as "the Jerusalem of Lithuania." By the end of that century the city was also a focus of Jewish political life. In the interwar period, under Polish rule, the economic situation of the Jews there deteriorated and they also suffered from antisemitism. At the outbreak of World War II, Vilna's Jewish population was over fifty-five thousand.

On September 19, 1939, the Red Army entered Vilna, but a few weeks later the city was handed over to the Lithuanians. Vilna's Jews welcomed both the Soviet rule and the subsequent Lithuanian regime, since this meant the city would not come under German occupation. Some twelve thousand to fifteen thousand Jewish refugees from German-occupied Poland made their way there. In July 1940, Lithuania (and with it Vilna) was incorporated into the Soviet Union and became a Soviet republic. The Soviet regime outlawed the activities of Jewish organizations and political parties, and took over the Jewish schools and cultural institutions. Jewish studies—the Hebrew language as well as

Jewish religion and history—were prohibited. Nationalization measures by the Soviets were a severe blow to the livelihood of the Jews; the refugees, in particular, made efforts to emigrate to the West. In the period from September 1939 to the German invasion of the Soviet Union, sixty-five hundred Jewish refugees left Vilna for Palestine, the United States, China, Japan, and other places. Some of them were granted Soviet transit visas. On June 24, 1941, two days after invading the Soviet Union, the Germans occupied Vilna. Three thousand Jews were able to flee into the Soviet interior before the Germans took the city, at which time the Jewish population stood at fifty-seven thousand.

A few days later, the German military authorities and the Lithuanian administration that had been established issued a series of anti-Jewish decrees. Jews were ordered to wear the yellow badge (*see* BADGE, JEWISH); they were not allowed to use the sidewalks, and certain streets were put out of bounds; a night curfew was imposed; they could make their purchases only at certain times and in certain stores. On July 4 the Germans ordered the establishment of a JUDENRAT (Jewish Council), the composition of which was determined at a meeting held by a group of well-known Jewish figures. At first the Judenrat had ten members, with Shaul Trotzki as chairman and Anatol Fried as his deputy. Soon afterward, the military commander ordered that the membership be enlarged to twenty-four. In July, Einsatzkommando 9, assisted by *ypatingi buriai* ("the special ones"; Lithuanian volunteers who collaborated with the Germans), rounded up five thousand Jewish men from the streets and houses and took them to PONARY, 7.5 miles (12 km) from Vilna, to murder them there. The Jews in Vilna knew nothing of the fate of these men; there were only rumors that they were working somewhere in the east. Between the end of July and

The rich cultural life in the Vilna ghetto included theater performances. They were inaugurated at a gala opening on April 26, 1942, with a production of *Shlomo Molcho*, by David Pinski. Above is a scene from the production of Pinski's *The Eternal Jew* in June 1943.

early August, Lithuania was transferred from German military rule to German civil administration, as part of REICHSKOMMISSARIAT OSTLAND. Gebietskommissar (district commissioner) Hans Christian Hingst was appointed governor of Vilna. On August 6, as its first step, the new administration imposed a levy of 5 million rubles (500,000 reichsmarks) on the Jews.

In an *Aktion* carried out from August 31 to September 3, 1941, eight thousand more Jews were taken to Ponary and murdered, among them most of the members of the Judenrat. This *Aktion* became known among the Jews as "the great provocation," since it was preceded by the Germans' staging an attack on German soldiers, blaming it on the Jews, and presenting the *Aktion* that followed as a retaliatory move. In the following days, from September 3 to 5, the area from which the Jews had been evacuated for the *Aktion* was fenced in and two ghettos were set up there, Ghetto No. 1 and Ghetto No. 2, separated from each other by Deutsche (German) Street. On September 6 all the remaining Jews of Vilna were forced to move into the ghettos—some thirty thousand into Ghetto No. 1 and from nine thousand to eleven thousand into Ghetto No. 2. Another six thousand were taken to Ponary and murdered. On the following day the Germans established two Judenräte, one for each of the ghettos, with Anatol Fried appointed chairman in Ghetto No. 1 and Eisik Lejbowicz in Ghetto No. 2. The Judenräte had departments for food, health, lodging, education, and employment, and a general department for organizational and other affairs. A Jewish police force was also established, with Jacob GENS as its commander.

In the period from September 15 to October 21, families in which neither parent was employed in a place that issued *Scheine* (certificates—that is, work permits) were transferred into Ghetto No. 2. The other families—those in which at least one parent was in possession of a *Schein*—were put into Ghetto No. 1. It was during this period that the "Yom Kippur *Aktion*" (October 1, 1941) took place.

In three more *Aktionen*, on October 3–4, 15–16, and 21, Ghetto No. 2 was liquidated and its inhabitants taken to Ponary and murdered. The Germans distributed 3,000 "yellow *Scheine*" (so called by the Jews because of the color of the paper on which they were printed) among the Jews in Ghetto No. 1; distribution depended on the place where they worked and the priority each place had with the authorities. A "yellow *Schein*" enabled its bearer to register on it the other parent and no more than two children. The Germans planned to permit a maximum of 12,000 Jews to remain in the Vilna ghetto, out of the total of 27,000 to 28,000 surviving in Ghetto No. 1 at the time. On October 24 and November 3–5 the "yellow *Schein Aktionen*" took place, followed in December by further *Aktionen* on a smaller scale, the last on December 22. By the end of 1941, the Germans had killed 33,500 of the 57,000 Jews who had been in Vilna when the occupation began. A total of 12,000 "legal" Jews (those in possession of *Scheine*) were left in the ghetto, plus nearly 8,000 "illegals" who had gone into hiding. Another 3,500 had either fled to cities and towns in Belorussia, where the Jews were still living in relative safety, or had found a place to hide outside the ghetto.

For about a year, between the spring of 1942 and the spring of 1943, there were no mass *Aktionen*; the Jews referred to this as "the period of relative quiet." The ghetto, under Judenrat direction, became productive, with most of its inhabitants employed in jobs outside the ghetto or in workshops that had been established within it. The Judenrat's policy was based on the assumption that if the ghetto were productive and served German interests, it would be worthwhile, for economic reasons, for the Germans to keep it going. Toward the end of its existence, in the summer of 1943, the ghetto had fourteen thousand persons—over two-thirds of its population—employed in various jobs.

The dominant figure in the ghetto leadership was the Jewish police commander, Jacob Gens, who in July 1942 replaced Anatol Fried as Judenrat chairman. The ghetto had schools; a rich cultural life, including a theater; social-welfare institutions; soup kitchens; and a medical care system that sought to combat starvation and disease. Thanks to it the mortality rate was low, compared with that in other large ghettos. The police kept order, and there was a law court.

In the spring of 1943, the situation of the Jews in the Vilna area deteriorated. Four small ghettos—in Švenčionys, Mikališkes, Oshmiany, and Salos, with a total of five thousand Jews—were liquidated. Their inhabitants were told that they would be moved to the Vilna and Kovno ghettos, but only about a quarter reached Vilna; the rest were taken to Ponary and murdered. In June and July, labor camps in the Vilna area with Jews from the Vilna ghetto were liquidated. The liquidation of the small ghettos and the labor camps, and the murder of most of their inmates, caused great fear in the Vilna ghetto and undermined whatever faith the Jews there still had in the ghetto's future.

At the beginning of 1942, the underground FAREYNEGTE PARTIZANER ORGANIZATSYE (United Partisan Organization; FPO) had been established in the ghetto. During "the period of relative quiet" there was a more or less peaceful coexistence between the Judenrat and the underground, but this was broken in the spring of 1943, when the situation in the ghetto deteriorated amid increasing indications that the end was approaching. Gens's attitude toward the underground changed; in his eyes, smuggling weapons into the ghetto and maintaining contact with the partisans in the forests were a threat to the ghetto's continued existence. The first open clash occurred when Gens tried to remove the leaders of the underground—particularly Josef GLAZMAN, his former deputy and now vice-commander of the FPO—from the ghetto and send them to labor camps outside. Another serious confrontation took place in mid-July 1943, when Yitzhak WITTENBERG, the commander of the FPO, was freed by FPO members while under arrest. The Nazis demanded his return, threatening the ghetto population. After further threats by Gens, the FPO command agreed to surrender Wittenberg.

On June 21, 1943, Heinrich HIMMLER ordered the ghettos in the REICHSKOMMISSARIAT OSTLAND to be liquidated, those of their inmates who were fit for work to be sent to concentration camps, and the rest to be killed. In *Aktionen* on August 4 and 24 and September 1 and 4, over seven thousand men and women capable of working were rounded up and sent to concentration camps in Estonia.

During the September *Aktionen* the FPO called on the ghetto population to disregard the order to report for deportation and to rise up in rebellion. The inhabitants did not heed this call, believing that they were being sent to work camps in Estonia (which was, in fact, true) and not to Ponary to be murdered, as the FPO claimed. In the late afternoon of September 1, a clash broke out between the underground and the German forces that were combing the ghetto. In the ensuing exchange of fire, Yechiel Scheinbaum, the commander of "Yechiel's combat group," which had joined the FPO, was killed. In order to forestall more violence between the underground and the German forces, Gens, who believed that this would lead to the total liquidation of the ghetto, offered to provide the German authorities with the required quota for deportation to Estonia, on the condition that they pull their forces out of the ghetto. The Germans agreed, and as a result the clashes in the ghetto came to an end. Following the expulsions to Estonia, twelve thousand people were left. On September 14, Gens was summoned by the Gestapo and killed on the spot.

The final liquidation of the Vilna ghetto took place on September 23 and 24, 1943. Thirty-seven hundred men and women were sent to concentration camps in Estonia and Latvia; over four thousand children, women, and old men were sent to the SOBIBÓR extermination camp, where they were murdered. Several hundred old people and children were taken to Ponary to be killed. About twenty-five hundred Jews were left in Vilna, in the Kailis and Heeres Kraftfahrpark (Army Motor Vehicle Depot) labor camps and in two other, smaller, camps that provided labor for the German military. Over one thousand people had gone into hiding inside the ghetto, which was otherwise empty; in the ensuing months, most of them were caught. A few hundred members of the FPO succeeded in escaping from the ghetto during the September *Aktionen*, establishing themselves in two partisan groups in the Rudninkai and Naroch forests. Eighty Jewish prisoners were kept in Ponary to open up the mass graves and burn the bodies of the victims who had been buried there. On July 2 and 3, 1944, ten days before Vilna was liberated, the Jews in the local labor camps were taken to Ponary to be killed, though between one hundred fifty and two hundred were able to flee before the final liquidation and save themselves.

On July 13, 1944, Vilna was liberated; afterward, several hundred survivors gathered in the city. Of the fifty-seven thousand Jews who had been in Vilna when the Nazis occupied it, between two thousand and three thousand were left. About a third of them had taken refuge in the forests. The rest survived in concentration camps in Estonia and Germany, in hiding places, or by having had "Aryan" documents in their possession.

BIBLIOGRAPHY

Arad, Y. *Ghetto in Flames: The Struggle and Destruction of the Jews of Vilna in the Holocaust.* Jerusalem, 1980.

Dawidowicz, L. S. *From That Place and Time: A Memoir, 1938–1947.* New York, 1989.

Dworzecki, M. *Jerusalem of Lithuania in Revolt and Holocaust.* Tel Aviv, 1951. (In Hebrew.)

Korczak, R. *Flames in Ash.* Merhavia, Israel, 1946. (In Hebrew.)

YITZHAK ARAD

VILNIUS. *See* Vilna.

VINNITSA, regional center of Vinnitsa Oblast (district), Ukrainian SSR. Jews had been living in Vinnitsa since the sixteenth century; on the eve of World War II, the Jewish population was approximately 25,000, out of a total of 92,868. In the first few days after the German invasion of the Soviet Union, in June 1941, 17,500 of the city's Jews managed to flee to the east; when the German forces entered Vinnitsa, on July 19, they found 7,500 Jews there. A few days later hundreds of young Jews were apprehended, ostensibly in order to be sent to Palestine; in actuality, they were taken to the Jewish cemetery, where they were killed. The remaining Jews were put into a ghetto in the area of the military quarter (Voyenny Gorodok). At the end of September the skilled workers and professionals in the ghetto, together with their families—some five thousand people—were separated from the rest of

the Jews. The rest, consisting of two thousand old people, women, and children, were taken to the city outskirts and murdered.

At the beginning of 1942, Vinnitsa became the site of an advance field headquarters for Hitler, in his capacity as commander in chief. Tens of thousands of workers were brought in to set up the facility, and Vinnitsa Jews as well were put to work on the project. When it was completed a meeting was held, on July 14, at which an order was given that 20,000 of the Ukrainian workers were to be sent to work in the Reich and that the Jews were to be murdered. The meeting was attended by representatives of the SS, the German police (Ordnungspolizei), the SD (Sicherheitsdienst; Security Service), and the *Gebietskommissar* (district commissioner). The SD commander opposed killing the Jews, claiming that he needed them for maintaining the municipal services in Vinnitsa. He made a successful appeal to the *Höherer SS- and Polizeiführer* (Higher SS and Police Leader) of the Ukraine, Hans PRUTZMANN, to have the order rescinded. Nevertheless, in the following month some of the skilled workers, with their families, were killed. The remainder were transferred to a labor camp; of these, only a few survived. Vinnitsa was liberated on March 20, 1944.

BIBLIOGRAPHY

Gilbert, M. *The Holocaust.* New York, 1985.

SHMUEL SPECTOR

VISSER, LODEWIJK ERNST (1871–1942), Dutch jurist active in Jewish affairs. Visser held various posts in the Dutch legal system and in 1915 was appointed to the Dutch Supreme Court, becoming Chief Justice in 1939. He was active in the work of Jewish charitable organizations, especially those handling Jewish refugees. In 1933 he joined the Committee for Special Jewish Affairs (headed by Abraham ASSCHER), which had been founded in the wake of the Nazi rise to power in Germany. After the occupation of the Netherlands by the Germans in May 1940, Visser was suspended from his supreme court post (as were all Jews in government service), and

Lodewijk Ernst Visser.

the supreme court, by a vote of 12 to 5, decided not to oppose his suspension.

In December 1940 the major Jewish organizations in the Netherlands established the Joodse Coördinatiecommissie (Jewish Coordinating Committee) as the central organ for confronting the Germans' anti-Jewish policy. Visser became its chairman and in that capacity strongly criticized the action of Asscher and David COHEN in agreeing to set up the JOODSE RAAD (Jewish Council), as required by the Germans. Visser had profound differences of opinion with the leadership of the Joodse Raad over its policies; in October 1941, however, the Germans dissolved Visser's coordinating committee and made the Amsterdam Joodse Raad the sole representative body of Netherlands Jewry. Visser and Cohen had an animated and important exchange of letters, in which they aired their differing views on the policy to be pursued by Dutch Jewry. Cohen argued that the Jews had to cooperate with the Germans, since they ruled the country, while Visser stated his belief that the far-reaching concessions made by the Joodse Raad to the Germans were quite unjustified and only led to a deterioration in the situation.

Visser firmly believed that the Dutch administration should not be relieved of its constitutional obligation to protect the Jews, as Dutch citizens with equal rights. When he learned that, in retaliation for clashes between Jews and Dutch Nazis, Jewish youngsters had been deported to the MAUTHAUSEN camp, to perish there within a short while, Visser addressed passionate appeals to the secretaries-general of the Dutch government departments, calling on them to resist the German anti-Jewish measures. Later he protested against the evacuation of the Jews from various places. He was warned to desist from this campaign, at the risk of being put into a concentration camp. Three days after receiving a warning letter to this effect, Visser suffered a heart attack and died.

BIBLIOGRAPHY

De Jong, L. *Het Koninkrijk der Nederlanden in de Tweede Wereldoorlog.* Vols. 4, 5, 6. The Hague, 1969–1986.

Michman, J. "The Controversial Stand of the Joodse Raad in the Netherlands." *Yad Vashem Studies* 10 (1974): 9–68.

Michman, J. "The Controversy Surrounding the Jewish Council of Amsterdam." In *Patterns of Jewish Leadership in Nazi Europe, 1933–1945.* Proceedings of the Third Yad Vashem International Historical Conference, edited by Y. Gutman and C. J. Haft, pp. 235–258. Jerusalem, 1979.

Polak, J. A. *Leven en werken van Mr. L. E. Visser.* Amsterdam, 1974.

Presser, J. *The Destruction of the Dutch Jews.* New York, 1969.

JOZEPH MICHMAN

VITEBSK

VITEBSK, city in the northeastern region of the Belorussian SSR, known from the eleventh century. Jews lived in Vitebsk from the late sixteenth century, and the city was a center of Hasidism. Before World War II there were about fifty thousand Jews there.

On July 11, 1941, Vitebsk was occupied by the Germans and was partially destroyed and burned down in the battle. On July 24 many refugees, mostly Jews, were arrested and killed outside the city. Every day Jews were seized for forced labor; one day 300 young Jews among them were singled out, accused of arson, and put to death. Later, 27 Jews were caught, accused of not presenting themselves for work, and shot to death in the center of the city.

In the early days of the occupation a governing body was appointed in Vitebsk, and a JUDENRAT (Jewish Council) was charged with supplying Jews for forced labor. It had to organize the work gangs and equip them with work tools and food. The Judenrat was ordered to draw up a list of the Jewish population, including the offspring of mixed marriages. It was also responsible for concentrating the Jews in the ghetto, which was installed in the area of the railway station, a quarter where most of the houses had been destroyed and burned. The ghetto was surrounded by wire fences and about sixteen thousand people were crowded into it. The slaughter of Jews and of other groups continued.

Early in August 1941, 332 Jewish intellectuals were assembled and murdered. On September 4, 397 Jews imprisoned in the civilian prisoner camp were taken out, accused of organizing a revolt, and put to death. On October 1, 52 Jewish refugees from the town of Gorodok who were living in Vitebsk were killed. Jewish youngsters fled to the surrounding forests and joined units of the Soviet partisan movement. The liquidation of the Vitebsk ghetto began on October 8, on the pretext that it was a source of epidemics. The slaughter lasted three days. Jews were taken to the Vitba River and shot there. Their bodies were thrown into the river.

When Vitebsk was liberated by the Soviet army on June 26, 1944, there were no Jews in the city. About two years later, in 1946, some five hundred Jews were living there.

BIBLIOGRAPHY

Karuh, B., ed. *Vitebsk.* Tel Aviv, 1957. (In Hebrew.)

SHMUEL SPECTOR

VITTEL, detention camp near the town of Vittel in the Vosges Mountains, near Nancy, in northeastern FRANCE. The camp, established in 1940, was used to intern nationals of enemy and neutral countries whom the Germans wanted to exchange for their own nationals being held in countries at war with Germany. Unlike other Nazi camps, which consisted of wooden barracks, the Vittel camp consisted of luxurious hotels, located inside a park. The park was encircled by three rows of barbed-wire fence, with German patrols guarding the installation. The camp commandant was Hauptsturmführer Landhauser.

The internees were British subjects (numbering some two thousand at the end of January 1943), American citizens (of whom the first group arrived on January 25, 1943), and a third category that was entirely Jewish, whereas among the British and Americans the majority were not Jewish. In that third category, most were Polish by nationality and the rest were Belgian or Dutch Jews.

Some of these internees were in possession of Latin American passports; others had been promised visas, or had had other documents made out for them (free or against payment) by the consulates of Latin American countries in Bern, Switzerland, at the request of world Jewish organizations. The largest group had documents for Paraguay and Honduras: in mid-October 1943 three hundred adults and one hundred children fell into this group. One internee in the third category was the poet Itzhak KATZENELSON, who together with his son Zvi was in a group of sixty Jews from Warsaw brought to the camp; the Katzenelsons had Honduran papers in their possession. It was in Vittel that Katzenelson composed the famous "Lid fun Oysgehargetn Yidishn Folk" (Song of the Murdered Jewish People).

In January 1944, in response to a request made by Alois BRUNNER to Adolf EICHMANN, a special commission from Berlin was dispatched to examine the Latin American passports held by internees in the Vittel camp.

Jewish children at the Vittel detention camp in France. They were later transported to Auschwitz.

The commission declared the passports invalid. Since the Latin American countries involved also refused to acknowledge the validity of these passports, their Jewish holders were now in danger of losing their lives.

World Jewish organizations tried to help the Jews in Vittel and asked the American and British governments to put pressure on the Latin American countries concerned. Other organizations were also active, in various ways, in trying to save the Jews—the International RED CROSS, the American WAR REFUGEE BOARD, the London-based High Commission for Refugees, and also the Vatican, all the Latin American countries involved being Catholic. On March 19, 1944, the Vittel internees asked that they immediately be sent immigration visas ("certificates") to Palestine, this, in their opinion, being the only way their lives could be saved. Among the group of 282 Jews who disembarked in Haifa on July 19 of that year, with valid permits for entry into Palestine, 222 had come from BERGEN-BELSEN and 60 from Vittel. Efforts made by various governments and organizations were also successful, but they came too late for the other Jewish internees at Vittel. Recognition of the Latin American passports was renewed on March 31, 1944, but by then the tragedy of the Jews of Vittel had taken its course: 173 Vittel internees had been sent to the DRANCY camp on February 28 (among them Katzenelson and his son), and another 60 on May 16; from Drancy they were all deported to AUSCHWITZ-Birkenau. At the beginning of August the last 30 "Latin American nationals" among the Jews of Vittel were deported to their deaths.

The Vittel camp was liberated by the Allied forces on September 12, 1944. Shortly before, the camp commandant had received replies from several Latin American governments confirming the Latin American citizenship of some forty Vittel internees. The date of these communications from the Latin Americans, and the date on which the neutral countries involved in the negotiations—Switzerland, Spain, and Sweden—passed the renewed recognitions of the Vittel passports on to the German authorities, have not been accurately determined.

BIBLIOGRAPHY

Katzenelson, I. *Vittel Diary, May 22, 1943, to September 16, 1943*. Tel Aviv, 1964.
Wasserstein, B. *Britain and the Jews of Europe, 1939–1945*. Oxford, 1979. See pages 231–235.

ADAM RUTKOWSKI

VLASOV, ANDREI (1900–1946), Soviet army officer who collaborated with the Germans. Vlasov was born in a village in the Nizhni Novgorod district. In the Russian civil war he joined the ranks of the Red Army and eventually became a regular army man. He joined the Communist party in the early 1930s. In 1938 and 1939 he was in China, serving as military adviser to Chiang Kai-shek. In 1940 he commanded an elite division in the Kiev military district and rose to the rank of major general. When the Germans invaded the Soviet Union in June 1941, Vlasov was in command of the Thirty-Fourth Army, charged with the defense of Kiev, and he later commanded the Twentieth Army, which defended Moscow; he was promoted to lieutenant general and awarded the Order of Lenin and the Order of the Red Banner. In the spring of 1942 he was appointed commander of the Second ("Assault") Army on the Volkhov front; there he and his troops were encircled by the Germans. His attempts to break out of the trap failed, and on July 13 of that year he was taken prisoner.

Vlasov was interned in a prisoner-of-war camp for senior Soviet officers located near the advance headquarters of the German Army High Command. Following talks with senior German intelligence officers, Vlasov agreed to collaborate with the Germans against the Soviet regime. He was transferred to the propaganda branch of the Armed Forces High Command in Berlin. In September 1942 Vlasov issued three manifestos; in two of them he denounced Stalin, blaming him and his regime for the military defeats; attacked "Jewish capitalists," the "Jewish press," and the "Stalinist Bolshevik-Jewish dictatorship"; and called on Red Army soldiers to desert. In the other manifesto, Vlasov listed thirteen points on which to base a new regime that he would seek to establish in Russia. The plan was that this would be endorsed by the "Smolensk Committee" (a Russian public group that the headquarters of the German Central Army Group was in the process of organizing, to be headed by Vlasov). This plan was abandoned, however, on Hitler's orders, which also directed that Vlasov's activities be confined to propaganda.

In the period from November 1942 to the winter of 1944, Vlasov trained anti-Soviet propaganda agents at the Dabendorf camp, near Berlin, and drafted memorandums concerning his anti-Soviet movement. The agents were assigned to encourage Soviet prisoners of war to volunteer for the OSTBATAILLONE, and, at the front, to encourage Red Army personnel to desert. Several of the Ostbataillone were given badges to wear by the Wehrmacht, bearing the inscription ROA (the initials of RUSSKAYA OSVOBODITELNAYA ARMIYA, or Russian Liberation Army). The men serving in these units—and later on, also other categories of Soviet prisoners of war—were called "Vlasovtsy," but in fact no Vlasov army existed, since there was no unified command headed by Vlasov of the units made up of Soviet prisoners of war.

It was not until September 16, 1944, after a meeting with Heinrich HIMMLER, that Vlasov was permitted to set up the Komitet Osvobozhdeniya Narodov Rossii (Committee for the Liberation of the Peoples of Russia; KONR), to be recognized as an official representative body, and to form the "Russian Liberation Army," with Vlasov heading both the "army" and the "committee." Some of the minority groups in the Soviet Union, such as the Ukrainians, refused to join either Vlasov's army or his committee, and the Germans permitted them to establish similar organizations of their own. On November 14, 1944, Vlasov's KONR met in Prague and in an official ceremony issued the Prague Declaration, spelling out the political principles on which the Vlasov movement was based and the structure of the regime that it would set up—a combination of centralist socialism and capitalism.

On May 15, 1945, Vlasov and his staff were handed over to the Soviets. Radio Moscow announced on August 1, 1946, that he and his associates had been tried, sentenced to death, and executed by hanging.

BIBLIOGRAPHY

Andreyev, C. *Vlasov and the Russian Liberation Movement: Soviet Reality and Emigré Theories.* New York, 1988.
Dallin, A. *German Rule in Russia, 1941–1945.* London, 1981.
Fischer, G. *Soviet Opposition to Stalin: A Case Study in World War II.* Cambridge, Mass., 1952.
Strik-Strikfeldt, W. *Against Stalin and Hitler: Memoir of the Russian Liberation Movement, 1941–1945.* London, 1970.

SHMUEL SPECTOR

VLASOV ARMY. *See* Russkaya Osvoboditelnaya Armiya.

VOLDEMARAS, AUGUSTINAS (1883–1942), Lithuanian statesman. During World War I, Voldemaras was a professor of law at the University of Perm in Russia. In 1917 he was the Lithuanian representative at the Congress of Nations that took place in Kiev. He was influenced by the ideas of the Po'alei Zion leader, Ber Borochov, on the granting of "personal autonomy" to national minorities.

In 1918 Voldemaras became the first prime minister of independent Lithuania, serving also as foreign minister; he held these posts until 1922. He represented Lithuania at the Paris Peace Conference in 1919, and signed a declaration conferring far-reaching autonomy on the Jews of his country.

Following the 1926 military coup in Lithuania and the abolition of the democratic form of government, Voldemaras again became prime minister and foreign minister with the support of the National party, and in effect was a dictator. He founded and promoted the growth of Gelezinis Vilkas (Iron Wolf), a militant organization with a fascist and antisemitic ideology.

In September 1929 Voldemaras was ousted as a result of serious differences between him and the National party leadership, and Iron Wolf was outlawed. With Voldemaras's approval, his supporters assassinated several leading figures in the government and in 1934 staged an abortive coup. Voldemaras was exiled to a remote village and in 1938 was expelled from the country. His supporters went underground and, in the late 1930s, intensified their antigovernment operations and attacked Jews; the German Foreign Office provided them with regular financial support.

When the Soviet regime was established in Lithuania in June 1940, Voldemaras, to the general surprise, returned to the country, only to be arrested on the spot and exiled to Ordzhonikidze, in the Caucasus. At the time when the German army was advancing on this region, in November 1942, Voldemaras was put in prison, where, according to Russian sources, he died.

Voldemaras's supporters were among the leading collaborators with the Nazis, and took a very active part in killing Jews in Lithuania and elsewhere.

BIBLIOGRAPHY

Sabaliunas, L. *Lithuania in Crisis: Nationalism to Communism, 1939–1940.* Bloomington, 1972.

DOV LEVIN

VOLGOGRAD. *See* Stalingrad.

VOLKSDEUTSCHE, Nazi term for ethnic Germans living outside of Germany in countries of which they were nationals. They were not citizens of the Third Reich, that is, they did not hold German or Austrian citizenship as defined by the Nazi term *Reichsdeutsche* (Reich Germans).

Nazi Germany made every effort to win the support of the *Volksdeutsche*, who constituted German minorities in several countries. In 1931, prior to its rise to power, the Nazi party established the AUSLANDSORGANISATION DER NSDAP (Foreign Organization of the Nazi Party), whose task it was to disseminate Nazi propaganda among the German minorities living outside the borders of Germany. In 1936 the Volksdeutsche Mittelstelle (Ethnic Germans' Welfare Office), commonly known as VoMi, was set up under the jurisdiction of

the SS as the liaison bureau for the *Volksdeutsche*, headed by SS-Obergruppenführer Werner Lorenz. VoMi cooperated with Nazi-type organizations active in a number of places, such as the Deutsche Partei (German Party) in Slovakia, the Volksdeutsche Bewegung (Ethnic German Movement) in Luxembourg, and the Elsässischer Hilfsdienst (Alsace Auxiliary Service) in Alsace.

Nazi Germany endeavored to increase the number of *Volksdeutsche* in the conquered territories by a policy of Germanizing certain classes of the conquered people, mainly among the Czechs, Poles, and Slovenes. The Nazis encouraged the offspring of Germans, or persons who had family connections with Germans, to join the *Volksdeutsche*, on condition that they were not descended from Jews or GYPSIES. Those who joined enjoyed a privileged status and received special benefits.

In BOHEMIA AND MORAVIA, in addition to persons who had considered themselves as belonging to the German people during the period of the Czechoslovak republic, three other groups were recognized as *Volksdeutsche*: (1) *Deutschstämmige* (persons of German origin); (2) *Rückgedeutschte* (returning ethnic Germans); and (3) *Eingedeutschte* (persons affiliated with the German people).

In October 1939, after the occupation of Poland, the governor of the WARTHEGAU, Gauleiter Arthur GREISER, established a central bureau for the registration of *Volksdeutsche*. A new Nazi term was created to designate the register of those belonging to the *Volksdeutsche*—the *Deutsche Volksliste* (German Folk List), also known as the *Volksliste* or DVL.

At the beginning of 1940, distinctions were introduced to divide those registered in the *Volksliste* into four categories. The first group consisted of ethnic Germans active on behalf of the Third Reich; the second group, of other ethnic Germans; and the third and fourth groups, of Poles of German extraction (that is, who had Germans among their forebears) or who were related to Germans.

The German occupying authorities encouraged Poles to register with the *Volksliste*, and in many instances even forced them to do so, especially in the territories annexed to the Reich. Within these areas, a total of 959,000

The head of the Volksdeutsche Mittelstelle, SS-Obergruppenführer Werner Lorenz (left), at a meeting with Heinrich Himmler (seated, center) in the latter's office at the Gestapo headquarters in Berlin (1938). Also present were Reinhard Heydrich (second from left) and Karl Wolff (right). [Bildarchiv Preussischer Kulturbesitz]

persons in the first and second categories, who had considered themselves as belonging to the German minority living in independent Poland, were registered with the *Volksliste*. In the third and fourth categories, 1,861,000 Poles were recognized as having joined the ethnic Germans and were new *Volksdeutsche*. The number of *Volksdeutsche* living in the GENERALGOUVERNEMENT was estimated at 100,000. In addition, 350,000 ethnic Germans had settled in the western territories of occupied Poland between the beginning of the war and the spring of 1941; these *Volksdeutsche* had migrated from the Baltic countries and the Volhynia region, which had come under Russian rule.

The *Volksliste* was introduced into Yugoslavia following the Nazi occupation. In the Soviet territories, especially the Ukraine, conquered after the German invasion of Russia in the summer of 1941, the *Volksliste* was introduced in the same format as that instituted in Poland. In those countries decrees were issued granting the *Volksdeutsche* privileged status and material benefits.

Among its activities on behalf of the *Volksdeutsche*, VoMi organized large-scale looting of property, first that belonging to the Jews and Poles who in 1939 and 1940 had been deported from the Polish territory annexed to the Reich. The *Volksdeutsche* were given apartments, workshops, and farms that had belonged to Jews and Poles, with all their furniture and contents. They were also given hundreds of thousands of items of clothing taken from Jews who had been put to death in the extermination camps of CHEŁMNO, AUSCHWITZ, MAJDANEK, TREBLINKA, BEŁŻEC, and SOBIBÓR. In TRANSNISTRIA, the *Volksdeutsche* of Romania were given the apartments of Jews who had lived in the region, complete with all their furniture and contents.

Nazi Germany received far-reaching support from the *Volksdeutsche*. Hundreds of thousands of them joined the German forces. With the conquest of Poland in September

1939, armed self-defense units were organized from among the *Volksdeutsche* called Selbstschutz (Self-Defense); they cooperated with the EINSATZGRUPPEN in carrying out terrorist activities against Polish intellectuals and Jews. At the beginning of 1940, the Selbstschutz was disbanded and its members transferred to various units of the SS and German police. In Yugoslavia the "Prinz Eugen" Division of the Waffen-SS was formed from *Volksdeutsche* members, and was conspicuous in its operations against the partisans and in *Aktionen* among the population. About 300,000 *Volksdeutsche* from the conquered lands and the satellite countries volunteered for or were recruited to the Waffen-SS. From Hungary alone, some 100,000 ethnic Germans volunteered for service in the Waffen-SS and were released from military service in the Hungarian army. Among the populations in the Nazi-occupied lands, *Volksdeutsche* became a term of ignominy.

BIBLIOGRAPHY

Brown, M. "The Third Reich's Mobilization of the German Fifth Column in Eastern Europe." *Journal of Central European Affairs* 19/2 (July 1959): 128–148.

Lumans, V. "The Ethnic German Minority in Slovakia and the Third Reich, 1938–1945." *Central European History* 15/3 (September 1982): 266–298.

Lundins, C. L. "The Nazification of the Baltic German Minorities." *Journal of Central European Affairs* 7/1 (April 1974): 1–28.

McKale, D. M. *The Swastika outside Germany.* Kent, Ohio, 1977.

SHMUEL KRAKOWSKI

VOLKSDEUTSCHE MITTELSTELLE. *See* Volksdeutsche.

VOLOZHIN (Pol., Wołożyn), town in the Novogrudok district of the Belorussian SSR, which in the interwar period was part of Poland. In September 1939, when Volozhin was annexed to the Soviet Union, it had a Jewish population of thirty-five hundred. Volozhin was famous for its yeshiva (rabbinical academy), founded in 1803, which at its height had an enrollment of four hundred students.

The Germans entered Volozhin on June 25, 1941, and in August established a ghetto, consisting of fifty to sixty houses. The first *Aktion* took place on October 28, when 300 Jews were seized for "work" and killed. The Germans also extracted a payment from the Jews in the form of gold, coats, and furs. At the beginning of May 1942 the Germans demanded that the JUDENRAT (Jewish Council) chairman surrender 100 Jews to them, and when he refused he was shot dead in front of the Jews. On May 9 the Germans hitched the town rabbi, Hershel Rudensky, and several other Jews to a carriage loaded with policemen and forced them to pull it along and sing "Katiusha" (a Russian song) en route, with local residents looking on and mocking.

Another *Aktion* was launched on May 10, 1942, this one lasting for a whole week. With

VOLOZHIN

an SS-*Untersturmführer* by the name of Grabe in charge, the *Aktion* was carried out by Belorussian, Ukrainian, and Lithuanian policemen. When the Jews arrived at the assembly points, some of them wearing prayer shawls and phylacteries, groups of youngsters expressed scorn at the sight and ridiculed the Jews. One group of Jews, during a stop on the way, had filled their pockets with sand (at the suggestion of a Jew named Kushe), and when the Germans approached, the Jews threw sand in their eyes, making it possible for some to escape. About 1,700 Jews were assembled next to the bathhouse. They were all shot to death and their bodies cremated; babies were thrown alive into the flames. Another 800 Jews were assembled in the blacksmith's shop. Rabbi Reuben Hodosh of Olshan, who was among them, urged the Jews to dismantle the forges and attack the SS men with iron bars, bricks, and stones and try to make their escape. Rabbi Israel Lunin, a member of the Judenrat, objected on the ground that even a short span of life was worth living and must not be put at risk. When the Germans began shooting, the Jews tried to get away, and some managed to do so.

A third *Aktion* took place on August 29, in the course of which the last of the ghetto's Jews were murdered. About eighty Jews escaped; some of them later fought in the ranks of the Staritski partisan unit of the Tchkalov Brigade, and others joined the "Stalin," "BIELSKI," and other partisan units. One of the Volozhin Jews, Eliezer Rogovin, was in charge of the Staritski unit's demolition platoon.

Volozhin was liberated in mid-July 1944. Several dozen Jews returned to the town from the forests to which they had fled.

BIBLIOGRAPHY

Leoni, A., ed. *Wolozyn: The Story of a City and of "The Ets Hayyim" Yeshiva.* Tel Aviv, 1970. (In Hebrew.)

SHALOM CHOLAWSKI

VOMI. *See* Volksdeutsche.

VOORT, HANNA VAN DER. *See* Van der Voort, Hanna.

VRBA-WETZLER REPORT. *See* Auschwitz Protocols.

VUGHT, transit camp for Jews in the southern part of the NETHERLANDS, near 's Hertogenbosch. Established at the end of 1942, it was under the direct supervision of the WIRTSCHAFTS-VERWALTUNGSHAUPTAMT (Economic-Administrative Main Office; WVHA), which appointed the camp staff and named Karl Chmielewski as camp commandant. Chmielewski had previously served in the MAUTHAUSEN concentration camp, and when he was posted to Vught he brought along eighty Kapos from Mauthausen. At Vught, however, in contrast to Mauthausen, there were strict instructions to refrain from mistreating the prisoners.

The first Jewish prisoners came to Vught in January 1943, and by May their number had grown to 8,684; there were also non-Jewish prisoners, in a separate section. Conditions in the camp were very poor, and in response to complaints, the chairman of the country's JOODSE RAAD (Jewish Council), David COHEN, was given permission to visit Vught. On Cohen's recommendation, a Jewish professor of pediatrics from Amsterdam inspected the state of health of the children in the camp. Following his report, there was some improvement in the living conditions and sanitary arrangements.

Beginning in April 1943, male prisoners were sent to work outside the camp, where they were also used for the construction of fortifications. Most of the prisoners, however, were employed inside the camp, in the manufacture of clothing and furs. The most desirable places of work were the workshops of the Philips company, where 1,200 prisoners were employed. The company had insisted that its Jewish workers—including those who had not been on the payroll in peacetime—should enjoy decent conditions, have a hot meal every day, and not be subject to deportation. As of October 1943, the Jewish administration of the camp was headed by Dr.

One of the Philips workshops at the Vught transit camp.

Arthur Lehman, who did his best to care for the prisoners and was very popular with them. Lehman left behind a detailed report on the camp. For a time there were cultural and religious activities as well as a school in Vught, but this relatively positive situation underwent a change when SS-Sturmbann-führer Adam Grünewald was appointed camp commandant in October 1943. Grünewald was removed from his post in January 1944 because of the excessive punishments he meted out. His replacement, SS-Hauptsturm-führer Hans Hüttig, was a bureaucrat who made life miserable for the prisoners, owing to the harsh administrative measures he introduced.

From the very beginning of the camp's existence, prisoners from Vught were transferred to the WESTERBORK camp, but in the first few months, up to May 1943, this fate affected only about one thousand prisoners. From then on, the rate at which the transfers took place grew rapidly, as illustrated by figures showing the changes in the number of prisoners held in Vught:

May 7, 1943	8,684
May 15, 1943	7,874
June 11, 1943	4,158
June 14, 1943	7,088
June 25, 1943	4,276
July 9, 1943	2,778
September 10, 1943	2,707
September 17, 1943	1,724
October 15, 1943	1,770
November 12, 1943	2,492
November 19, 1943	776
March 24, 1944	387
June 2, 1944	496
June 3, 1944	The Jewish camp is liquidated.

Nearly all the prisoners transferred from Vught to Westerbork were deported to the AUSCHWITZ and SOBIBÓR extermination camps in the first available trains. The last group of deportees from Westerbork was made up of Philips employees from Vught, the company having failed to save them. But even in Auschwitz, these workers had a preferential status, being employed there by the German Telefunken firm under an agreement made between Telefunken and Philips. Nevertheless, most of the men among the workers perished. Of the 517 persons who made up the group of Philips employees and their families, 160 survived; of these, two-thirds were women and 9 were children.

BIBLIOGRAPHY

Koker, D. *Dagboek geschreven in Vught.* Amsterdam, 1977.

Prince Bernhard of the Netherlands, during his tour of the country's liberated areas, visits the transit camp at Vught. It was here that the Nazis built the "Black Hole," a cell measuring 8 feet by 12 feet, in which sixty-seven women were imprisoned for thirteen hours. Nineteen women died, three went mad, and thirty of the hysterical survivors were taken to a hospital. Prince Bernhard and members of his party look at the portable gibbet on the grounds of the camp on which, in a single day, twenty-two Dutch and Belgian partisans were hanged. [War Pool Photo]

Michman, J., H. Beem, and D. Michman. *The Netherlands*. In *Pinkas Hakehillot; Encyclopaedia of Jewish Communities*. Jerusalem, 1985. (In Hebrew.)

Presser, J. *The Destruction of the Dutch Jews*. New York, 1969.

JOZEPH MICHMAN

VYHNE, camp in SLOVAKIA, created early in 1940 near the town of Vyhne for 326 Jewish refugees from PRAGUE who had been interned in SOSNOWIEC, Poland. These Jews were brought to Slovakia through the efforts of Gisi FLEISCHMANN. By the start of the first wave of deportations from Slovakia, in March 1942, most of the inmates of Vyhne had been taken to safety in Palestine or other free countries.

After the NOVÁKY and SERED camps began to be used as Jewish work centers to safeguard Jews from deportation by proving their labor value to the Slovak government, Vyhne too was made into a Jewish labor camp. It was the smallest of the three such camps and suffered under a cruel Slovak administration. Still, living conditions were relatively good, and the camp proved its value to the Slovak government through the development of a textile industry. The inmates received sufficient rations, they could leave the camp occasionally, and the children studied in a government-approved school. There were no organized, coordinated preparations for armed resistance in Vyhne, although several resistance cells emerged. At the time of the SLOVAK NATIONAL UPRISING in August 1944, Vyhne, like the other labor camps, was liberated, and the inmates left. Many of the younger men joined the revolt, and most of the remaining Jews found refuge in the areas liberated by the rebels.

BIBLIOGRAPHY

Lipscher, L. "The Role of the Jews in the Antifascist Defensive War in Slovakia during World War Two." *Yalkut Moreshet* 14 (April 1972): 117–142. (In Hebrew.)

ROBERT ROZETT

W

WAGNER, HORST (1906–1977), Nazi official; head of the Inland II (Interior II) division of the German Foreign Office from April 1943 until the end of World War II. Born in Posen, Wagner joined the SS in 1936 and the Nazi party in 1937. He began working for Joachim von RIBBENTROP in 1936, with the particular task of escorting foreign visitors during the Olympics. Wagner was brought into the Foreign Office in 1938, working first in the protocol department and then on Ribbentrop's personal staff. When the Foreign Office was reorganized in April 1943, following the arrest of Under Secretary Martin LUTHER and the dissolution of Abteilung Deutschland (Division Germany), Wagner was appointed head of Inland II, the successor of Abteilung Deutschland. In that capacity he supervised Foreign Office matters related to the SS and police, Jews, and VOLKSDEUTSCHE (ethnic Germans). He escaped from an American internment camp in 1948 and lived in Italy, Argentina, and Spain before returning to Germany in 1956. Arrested in 1958, he managed, through an endless series of delaying tactics—sudden changes of lawyers and affidavits of medical unfitness—to avoid trial.

BIBLIOGRAPHY

Browning, C. R. *The Final Solution and the Foreign Office: A Study of Referat D3 of Abteilung Deutschland, 1940–1943.* New York, 1978.

CHRISTOPHER R. BROWNING

WALDHEIM, KURT (b. 1918), Austrian soldier and diplomat. Waldheim was born in a small village in AUSTRIA into a devout Catholic family. After finishing grammar school, he enlisted in a cavalry regiment. In 1937 he matriculated at the law faculty of the University of Vienna and at the Konsularakademie, where he was preparing for a diplomatic career. Following the ANSCHLUSS (the annexation of Austria to Nazi Germany), Waldheim joined the Nazi Students' Association and an SA (Sturmabteilung; Storm Troopers) cavalry unit. After being drafted into the WEHRMACHT, he took part in the invasion of the Sudetenland (October 1938), in the campaign in France, and, as a lieutenant, in the campaign against the Soviet Union. Wounded in Russia in December 1941, he returned for medical treatment to Austria. From 1942 to 1945 he served in the Balkans, first in Yugoslavia as an ordnance officer under the notorious Gen. Heinrich STAHL at the time of the Kozara offensive against the Yugoslav partisans and the accompanying massacre. He was then assigned to serve in Greece as an intelligence officer under Generaloberst Alexander Löhr, at the time of the deportation of Greek Jewry to the extermination camps.

In 1947 the Yugoslav government put Waldheim on the War Criminal List of the United Nations, but no further steps were taken against him. After his discharge from a prisoner-of-war camp he joined the diplomatic service of the new Austrian republic in 1945, and from 1968 to 1970 served as foreign minister. In 1971 he ran for the presidency of the Federal Republic of Austria but failed to be elected. However, that same year he was elected United Nations secretary-general,

Kurt Waldheim (second from left) in occupied Yugoslavia (May 22, 1943). [World Jewish Congress]

and five years later he was reelected for a second term. On August 6, 1986, he was elected president of Austria.

In April 1987 the United States Justice Department put Waldheim on the Watch List as a suspected war criminal. That July, at Waldheim's request, the Austrian government appointed an international commission of historians to establish the nature of his military service. The commission handed its unanimous report to the Austrian government on February 8, 1988. It concluded that Waldheim, although not personally responsible for or involved in murder or the issuing of orders for murder, knew of such unlawful activities. He was also close to persons who issued and carried out atrocities, but did nothing to try to disrupt them. Moreover, his passivity actually facilitated the carrying out of atrocities in several instances. In spite of the commission's findings, Waldheim refused to draw the proper conclusions and to resign.

BIBLIOGRAPHY

Herzstein, R. E. *Waldheim: The Missing Years.* New York, 1988.

JEHUDA L. WALLACH

WALLENBERG, RAOUL (1912–?), Swedish diplomat who saved the lives of tens of thousands of Jews in BUDAPEST. Wallenberg was born into a distinguished family of bankers, diplomats, and officers; his father, who died before he was born, was an officer in the Swedish navy. Wallenberg grew up in the house of his stepfather, Frederik von Dardell. He studied architecture in the United States, but then took up banking and international trade, which brought him to Haifa in 1936 for a six months' stay. On the recommendation of the Swedish branch of the WORLD JEWISH CONGRESS and with the support of the

American WAR REFUGEE BOARD, the Swedish Foreign Ministry, in July 1944, sent Wallenberg to Budapest, in order to help protect over 200,000 Jews who were left in the Hungarian capital after the deportation of 437,000 Hungarian Jews to AUSCHWITZ.

The Swedish legation in Budapest initiated its operation on behalf of the persecuted Jews a short while after the German occupation of Hungary, on March 19, 1944. At that time, Adolf EICHMANN and a special detachment under him, together with the Hungarian authorities, began organizing the deportation of the Jews to their death. The Swedish foreign minister, Ivar Danielsson, had proposed giving provisional Swedish passports to Hungarian Jews who had family ties or commercial connections with Swedish citizens. By the time Wallenberg arrived in Budapest, several hundred such "protective passports" had been issued. His arrival, on July 9, 1944, coincided with the stoppage of the deportations, a decision taken by the Hungarian government as a result of international pressure, including intervention by King Gustav V of Sweden.

The protective operation carried out by the Swedish legation, in conjunction with other diplomatic missions, was nevertheless maintained, and Wallenberg, the new legation attaché, was put in charge of a section created expressly for this purpose. Before taking up his post he had been given special authority, at his request, for certain arrangements to be left in his hands, such as the transmission of funds by means of the War Refugee Board (which in turn received the money from Jewish organizations in the United States).

The summer of 1944 was relatively quiet, but this quiet came to an end when the coup d'état of October 15 took place and the antisemitic fascist ARROW CROSS PARTY, headed by Ferenc SZÁLASI, seized power in the country. The Jews of Budapest now faced mortal danger, both from the Arrow Cross murder actions and from Eichmann's deportations. From that moment on, Wallenberg displayed his courage and heroism in the rescue actions he undertook. Over the course of three months he issued thousands of "protective passports." Most of the time, both the Hungarian authorities and the Germans honored the signature of the Swedish legation,

and the protective documents afforded protection for many Jews.

When Eichmann organized the DEATH MARCHES of thousands of Jews to the Austrian border, Wallenberg pursued the convoy in his car and managed to secure the release of hundreds of bearers of such passports and take them back to Budapest. His impressive and self-assured manner enabled him even to remove persons from the trains in which they were about to be sent to Auschwitz, or to release them from the MUNKASZOLGÁLAT (Labor Service System), into which they had been drafted.

The Jews were also in danger of being killed by Arrow Cross men, and to prevent this, Wallenberg set up special hostels accommodating fifteen thousand persons—an operation in which other diplomatic missions were also involved by issuing protective documents of their own. There were thirty-one protected houses, which together formed the "international ghetto," a separate entity,

Raoul Wallenberg.

Swedish Schutz-Pass. In order to protect Jews in Hungary from deportation, the Swedish legation issued protective passports. The Hungarian authorities promised that holders of these documents would not be deported and would be allowed to live in specially rented protected houses in the Pest district of Budapest. While serving as a diplomat in Hungary, Raoul Wallenberg issued such passes. He is credited with saving tens of thousands of Jewish lives in this way. [A Living Memorial to the Holocaust—Museum of Jewish Heritage, New York]

quite apart from Budapest's main ghetto. The management of these houses posed many complicated problems, since it involved the provision of food as well as sanitation and health services, all requiring much money; as many as six hundred Jewish employees were engaged in the administration and maintenance of the houses.

Both the "international ghetto" and the main ghetto were situated in Pest, which was the first part of Budapest to be occupied by the Soviets. Wallenberg made efforts to negotiate with the Soviets and to ensure proper care for the liberated Jews. The Soviets were highly suspicious of the Swedish mission and charged its staff with spying for the Germans. The large number of Swedish documents in circulation also raised doubt in their minds. When the Soviets requested him to report to their army headquarters in Debrecen, Wallenberg must have believed that he would be protected by his diplomatic immunity, especially since the Swedish legation had represented Soviet interests vis-à-vis the Germans, and he made his way to the Soviet headquarters. He returned to Budapest on January 17, 1945, escorted by two Soviet soldiers, and was overheard saying that he did not know whether he was a guest of the Soviets or their prisoner. Thereafter, all trace of him, and of his driver, Vilmos Langfelder, was lost. The other staff members of the Swedish legation were also held by the Soviets, but within a few months they all returned to Stockholm, via Bucharest and Moscow.

In the first few years following Wallenberg's disappearance, the Soviets claimed that they had no knowledge of a person named Wallenberg and were not aware that a person of that name was being held in any of their prisons. German prisoners of war, however, coming back from Soviet imprisonment, testified that they had met Wallenberg in prisons and camps in various parts of the Soviet Union. In the mid-1950s, on the basis of these accounts, Sweden submitted a strong demand to the Soviets for information on Wallenberg, to which the Soviets replied, in 1956, that they had discovered a report of Wallenberg's death in 1947 in a Soviet prison. Wallenberg's family, and especially his mother, did not accept this claim, which conflicted with testimonies from other sources.

As the years went by, public opinion, in Sweden and all over the world, became increasingly critical of the manner in which the

Swedish government had handled the issue. The subject of Wallenberg came up time and again, and with even greater force after the death of his mother in 1979. Books were published about Wallenberg and public committees were set up to deal with the case, especially in Britain, the United States, and Israel. The reports that were published revealed that in the final days preceding Budapest's liberation, Wallenberg, with the help of Hungarians and the Zsidó Tanács (Jewish Council), was able to foil a joint SS and Arrow Cross plan to blow up the ghettos before the city's impending liberation. Through this act—the only one of its kind in the Holocaust—some 100,000 Jews were saved in the two ghettos. In recognition of this rescue action on Wallenberg's part, the United States Congress awarded Wallenberg honorary American citizenship. Memorial institutions were created in his honor, streets were named after him, and films were produced about his work in Budapest. Wallenberg's name and reputation as a "RIGHTEOUS AMONG THE NATIONS" have become a legend.

BIBLIOGRAPHY

Anger, P. *With Raoul Wallenberg in Budapest: Memories of the War Years in Hungary.* New York, 1981.

Lindberg, H. *Svensk flyktingpolitik under internationelit tryck 1936–1941.* Stockholm, 1973.

Werbell, F. E., and T. Clarke. *Lost Hero: The Mystery of Raoul Wallenberg.* New York, 1982.

Yahil, L. "Raoul Wallenberg: His Mission and His Activities in Hungary." *Yad Vashem Studies* 15 (1983): 7–54.

LENI YAHIL

WANNSEE CONFERENCE, meeting held at a villa in Wannsee, Berlin, on January 20, 1942, to discuss and coordinate the implementation of the "FINAL SOLUTION." Heinrich HIMMLER's deputy and head of the REICHSSICHERHEITSHAUPTAMT (Reich Security Main Office; RSHA), Reinhard HEYDRICH, invited the state secretaries of the most important German government ministries to attend the meeting. While Heydrich, as well as his Jewish expert, Adolf EICHMANN, chaired consultations on Jewish policy both before and after the Wannsee Conference, this particular meeting was noteworthy for two reasons. First, it was the only one to involve the broad participation of such prominent members of the ministerial bureaucracy. Second, it was the point at which Adolf HITLER's decision to solve the so-called Jewish question through systematic mass murder was officially transmitted to this bureaucracy, whose participation was deemed necessary. It was not a meeting at which this decision was debated, but rather one at which the participants discussed the implementation of a decision already taken.

On July 31, 1941, Heydrich met with Hermann GÖRING, still the titular head for the coordination of Nazi Jewish policy. Heydrich brought for Göring's signature a document authorizing him to undertake preparations for a "total solution" to the Jewish question in Europe. Heydrich was to coordinate the activities of all the agencies of the German government whose jurisdiction was involved, and subsequently to submit the "overall plan" for the "final solution to the Jewish question."

At this time, Heydrich's EINSATZGRUPPEN were already engaged in the mass murder of Russian Jews by firing squads, but this method was clearly unsuitable for European Jewry outside the war zone. In the months following the July authorization, therefore, Heydrich's experts considered other options. Deportations of Jews from Germany began in mid-October 1941, and by November the construction of extermination camps with poison-gas facilities had begun at CHEŁMNO and BEŁŻEC. In late November Heydrich issued invitations to the state secretaries for a meeting on December 9, but it was subsequently postponed until January 20, 1942. The invitations included a copy of Heydrich's authorization from Göring. Since the meeting was scheduled for noon, refreshments were promised.

By the time of the meeting, most of the invitees were clearly aware that the Nazi regime was engaged in the mass murder of Jews. State Secretary Dr. Wilhelm STUCKART of the Interior Ministry had already discussed with his Jewish expert, Dr. Bernard LÖSENER, the massacre of German Jews deported to RIGA and had assured him that all this took place "on the highest orders." Dr. Josef Bühler, state secretary of the GENERAL-GOUVERNEMENT, had already traveled to Berlin for consultations in mid-December, after which his superior, Hans FRANK, had announced quite openly to his leading officials in Poland that they "must destroy the Jews." Under Secretary Martin LUTHER of the German Foreign Office had already sent his Jewish expert, Franz RADEMACHER, to SERBIA in October 1941 to facilitate a "local solution to the Jewish question" there through mass murder. He had also circulated copies of Heydrich's Einsatzgruppen reports on the mass murder of Russian Jewry to numerous Foreign Office officials. Gauleiter Alfred Meyer and Reichsamtsleiter Dr. Georg Leibbrandt were state secretary and chief of the political division, respectively, of the Reich Ministry for the Occupied Eastern Territories (Ostministerium). Leibbrandt had already been involved in correspondence concerning whether all Jews in the eastern territories were to be killed, regardless of sex, age, and economic considerations. The upshot of the correspondence was quite simply that economic interests were to be disregarded on principle in the solution to the "Jewish question." Representing the Justice Ministry was State Secretary Dr. Roland Freisler, the subsequent "hanging judge" of the notorious People's Court (*Volksgerichtshof*). Assistant Secretary Friedrich Wilhelm Kritzinger, reputedly one of the best-informed people in

Nazi Germany, represented the Reich Chancellery. Dr. Erich Neumann was present as state secretary of Göring's FOUR-YEAR PLAN office.

Various SS leaders were also in attendance: Heinrich MÜLLER of the Gestapo; Otto Hofmann of the SS RASSE- UND SIEDLUNGS-HAUPTAMT (SS Race and Resettlement Main Office; RuSHA); Dr. Karl Eberhard Schöngarth of the SS und Polizei (SS and Police) in Poland; Dr. Rudolf Lange of Einsatzgruppe A in the Baltic; SS-Oberführer Gerhard Klopfer, state secretary of Martin BORMANN's Party Chancellery; and of course Heydrich and his Jewish expert, Eichmann. No fewer than eight of the fifteen participants held Ph.D. degrees. Since most either had been involved in or had direct knowledge of the extensive massacres of Jews that had already taken place, Heydrich was not speaking to the uninitiated.

The January 20 meeting was held at the villa Am Grossen Wannsee 56–58, a former Interpol property that had been confiscated by the SS. Heydrich opened the conference with a long speech, based in large part on materials that Eichmann had compiled for him. In the first part of the speech, Heydrich reiterated his authority from Göring to coordinate—without regard to geographic boundaries—a "Final Solution" to the Jewish question and reviewed the policy of emigration that had led to the exit of 537,000 Jews from the German sphere until Himmler had forbidden further emigration in the fall of 1941.

Heydrich then made the transition to the second section of his speech. "In place of emigration, the evacuation of the Jews to the east has now emerged, after the appropriate prior approval of the Führer, as a further possible solution." A total of eleven million European Jews, including even those from Ireland and England, would be involved, according to Heydrich. The evacuations, however, were to be regarded "solely as temporary measures," for "practical experiences" were already being gathered that would be of great significance for the "imminent Final Solution of the Jewish question." Heydrich then went on to explain just what he meant by this. The Jews would be utilized for labor in the east. "Separated by sex, the Jews capable of work will be led into these areas in

The villa in Wannsee, Berlin, where the Wannsee Conference was held. [Geoffrey Wigoder]

large labor columns to build roads, whereby a large part will doubtless fall away through natural diminution. The remnant that finally survives all this, because here it is undoubtedly a question of the part with the greatest resistance, will have to be treated accordingly, because this remnant, representing a natural selection, can be regarded as the germ cell of a new Jewish reconstruction if released." Despite the euphemisms—separation of sexes, labor utilization leading to large-scale natural diminution, and, finally, appropriate treatment of the surviving remnant that could not be released to begin a renewal of the Jewish race—the genocidal implications were totally and unmistakably clear. If most of those attending the conference already knew that Jews were being killed in large numbers, they now had no further doubts about the intended scope of this murderous policy; it aimed at killing every last Jew in Europe, from Ireland to the Urals and from the Arctic to the Mediterranean.

Heydrich then moved into the third section of his speech, discussing some of the specific problems that would have to be dealt with. He proposed an old people's ghetto to ward off anticipated interventions over individual cases, and the sending of Jewish advisers to certain satellite countries to make preparations. But for Heydrich the most complex problem involved the fate of Jews in mixed marriages and their part-Jewish offspring. A major portion of the conference was spent exploring this problem, and it was only at this point that animated discussion began. Heydrich wanted to deport half Jews—that is, kill them—but to equate quarter Jews with Germans, provided neither their appearance nor their behavior was markedly Jewish. Jews in mixed marriages would either be deported to the east or sent to the old people's ghetto on a case-by-case basis, depending on the anticipated effect on the German relatives. Stuckart of the Interior Ministry pressed for compulsory sterilization of the half Jews rather than deportation, while Hofmann proposed giving the half Jews a choice between deportation and sterilization. To avoid endless administrative problems over mixed marriages, Stuckart also proposed compulsory divorce. These issues were not resolved, and were the subject of two further conferences in March and October 1942.

Thereafter, the discussion became quite freewheeling and unstructured. As Eichmann—who was sitting in the corner and supervising the stenotypists—related at his trial in Jerusalem, the conference had two parts, "the first part where everyone was quiet and listened to the various lectures, and then in the second part, everyone spoke out of turn and people would go around, butlers, adjutants, and would give out liquor. Well, I don't want to say that there was an atmosphere of drunkenness there. It was an official atmosphere, but nevertheless it was not one of those stiff, formal official affairs where everyone spoke in turn. But people just talked at cross vertices." Neumann asked that Jews important to the war economy not be deported until they could be replaced, and Heydrich concurred. Bühler, on the other hand, urged that the "Final Solution" begin in the Generalgouvernement, because there was no transportation problem there and most of the Jews there were already incapable of work. "He had only one request, that the Jewish question in this region be solved as quickly as possible."

At this point the protocol notes cryptically: "Finally there was a discussion of the various types of possible solutions." On Heydrich's instructions, Eichmann did not include the details of this portion of the meeting in the protocol, but in Jerusalem he testified as follows: "These gentlemen were standing together, or sitting together, and were discussing the subject quite bluntly, quite differently from the language that I had to use later in the record. During the conversation they minced no words about it at all . . . they spoke about methods of killing, about liquidation, about extermination."

At this time, of course, the Germans were still unsure about methods. The GAS VANS at Chełmno had only been in operation for six weeks. The camp at Bełżec, with gas chambers utilizing carbon monoxide from the exhaust gas of an engine, was still under construction. In the main camp at AUSCHWITZ, experiments with ZYKLON B pellets in Bunker 11 and in the crematorium had been undertaken in the fall of 1941. But the first farmhouse converted into a gas chamber at Birkenau was just being prepared for use.

Beyond the EUTHANASIA PROGRAM in Germany and the gas vans at Chełmno, therefore, the Nazis as yet had little experience in mass murder through gassing on the scale that would be required for the "Final Solution." The technological methods could not yet be taken for granted.

Heydrich closed the conference with a plea for the cooperation of all the participants. Eichmann later estimated that the whole meeting had taken between an hour and an hour and a half. Not everyone left immediately, however; some stood around in small groups "to discuss the ins and outs of the agenda and also of certain work to be undertaken afterward." In these more intimate circumstances, Heydrich "gave expression to his great satisfaction" and allowed himself a glass of cognac, though it was unusual for him to drink in front of others. He had cause for his satisfaction. As Eichmann recalled, Heydrich "more than anybody else [had] expected considerable stumbling blocks and difficulties." Instead he had found "an atmosphere not only of agreement on the part of the participants, but more than that, one could feel an agreement that had assumed a form which had not been expected." The state secretaries of the ministerial bureaucracy had not only not made difficulties, they were committed and enthusiastic about doing their part.

Following the conference, Eichmann prepared the protocol, which both Müller and Heydrich edited several times before approving it. Thirty copies were made, but only one, the sixteenth, was found after the war. It is presently kept in the archives of the German Foreign Office in Bonn.

BIBLIOGRAPHY

Arad, Y., Y. Gutman, and A. Margaliot, eds. *Documents on the Holocaust: Selected Sources on the Destruction of the Jews of Germany and Austria, Poland, and the Soviet Union.* Jerusalem, 1981. See pages 249–261.

CHRISTOPHER R. BROWNING

WARBURG, MAX (1867–1946), banker; a central figure in the leadership of German Jewry under the Third Reich. Warburg came from an old Jewish banking family, scions of eighteenth-century "court Jews" who had settled in Hamburg-Altona and branched off to Sweden, Britain, and the United States. His brother Felix was the first chairman of the administrative committee of the Jewish Agency, a founder and chairman of the JOINT DISTRIBUTION COMMITTEE, and active in international Jewish aid organizations. Under his brother's influence, Max Warburg too became interested in the Zionist effort, following a joint visit to Palestine in 1929.

Politically, Warburg was close to the conservative Right. In World War I he was a member of the Hamburg legislature and carried out assignments related to the organization of the German war economy. Together with the chief executive officer of the Hamburg-America Line, Albert Ballin, Warburg developed the merchant fleet. He was a member of the German delegation to the Paris Peace Conference, together with his banking partner, Karl Melchior.

Warburg was on the general board of the Reichsbank (the German state bank), and in March 1933 he and two other Jewish bankers affixed their signatures to the appointment of Hjalmar SCHACHT as governor of the bank, alongside the signatures of Adolf HITLER and Paul von HINDENBURG. Until his emigration to the United States in 1938, Warburg maintained close relations with Schacht. In his memoirs, *Aus meinen Aufzeichnungen* (From My Notes; 1952), Warburg relates that almost up to the time that he left Germany he was in favor of Jews' maintaining the economic position they held despite Nazi rule, since he believed there was hope for a better future. As time went on the Warburg bank had to reduce its scope and confine itself to Jewish clients and the transfer of their assets abroad, yet it was only in 1938 that Warburg reversed his earlier conviction. Acting on a hint from Schacht, he transferred his bank to non-Jewish hands, at a substantial loss to himself. His son Eric returned to Hamburg in the 1950s and joined the bank's management; since 1970 the bank has again been operating under the name of Warburg.

Max Warburg's activities in Jewish public affairs branched out into many fields. As a major philanthropist he belonged to Jewish charitable, cultural, and community institutions in Hamburg. In 1928 he became chairman of the HILFSVEREIN DER DEUTSCHEN JUDEN (Relief Organization of German Jews), and in 1933, together with Karl Melchior, he played a leading role in the establishment of the REICHSVERTRETUNG DER DEUTSCHEN JUDEN (Reich Representation of German Jews), becoming head of its ZENTRALAUSSCHUSS DER DEUTSCHEN JUDEN FÜR HILFE UND AUFBAU (Central Committee of German Jews for Relief and Reconstruction). Warburg's bank, together with the A. A. Wassermann Bank in Berlin, was the banking agent of Paltreu, the trust company that implemented the HAAVARA AGREEMENT, the transfer of Jewish assets from Germany to Palestine.

BIBLIOGRAPHY

Rosenbaum, E., and A. J. Sherman. *M. M. Warburg and Co., 1798–1938: Merchant Bankers of Hamburg.* London, 1979.

Sherman, A. "A Jewish Bank during the Schacht Era: M. M. Warburg and Co., 1933–1938." In *Die Juden in Nationalsozialistischen Deutschland 1933–1943,* edited by A. Pauker, pp. 167–172. Tübingen, 1986.

AVRAHAM BARKAI

WAR CRIMES. See Crimes against Humanity: Extradition of War Criminals; Genocide; Ludwigsburger Zentralstelle; Superior Orders; Trials of War Criminals; United Nations War Crimes Commission.

WAR CRIMES COMMISSION. See United Nations War Crimes Commission.

WAR CRIMES TRIALS. See Trials of War Criminals.

WAR CRIMINALS. See Extradition of War Criminals; Laws Punishing Nazis and Nazi Collaborators; Office of Special Investigations; Superior Orders; Trials of War Criminals.

WARHAFTIG, ZORAH (b. 1906), jurist and political figure. Warhaftig was born in Volkovysk, in western Belorussia, and studied law at the University of Warsaw. He was active in Jewish public life in Warsaw, especially in the religious Zionist Mizraḥi movement. Warhaftig was chairman of the head office of He-Haluts ha-Mizraḥi (Mizraḥi Pioneers) and vice-chairman of the Palestine Office. In the summer of 1939 he was a delegate to the Twenty-first Zionist Congress, which took place in Geneva, and returned to Warsaw a few days before World War II broke out.

Having served as vice-chairman of the Boycott of Nazi Germany Committee, Warhaftig had to flee and went to Lithuania. There he headed the Palestine Committee for Polish Refugees and devoted his time to the refugees' welfare and their settlement in Palestine. When Lithuania was occupied by the Soviets in 1941, Warhaftig made his way to JAPAN, where he kept up his work on behalf of the refugees, with special emphasis on the rescue of rabbinical students. In 1942 he went to the United States and was elected to the executive board of the WORLD JEWISH CONGRESS.

In 1947 Warhaftig settled in Palestine. He was put in charge of the Va'ad Le'ummi (National Council of the Jews in Palestine) legal department and in 1948 became a member of the Provisional State Council. From 1949 to 1981 he was a Knesset (parliament) member,

Zorah Warhaftig (right) and the "Righteous among the Nations" Sempo Sugihara.

representing Ha-Po'el ha-Mizraḥi (Mizraḥi Workers) and the National Religious party. He was deputy minister of religious affairs from 1952 to 1962, and minister of religious affairs from 1962 to 1974. Warhaftig was an expert on Jewish law and published important research papers on law and the administration of justice in the state of Israel.

Warhaftig published a memoir about his activities during the Holocaust, *Refugee and Survivor* (1988).

BIBLIOGRAPHY

Bauer, Y. "Rescue Operations through Vilna." *Yad Vashem Studies* 9 (1973): 215–223.

Gorka, J. *The Present in the Shadow of the Past.* Jerusalem, 1982. (In Hebrew.)

Zuroff, E. "Attempts to Obtain Shanghai Permits in 1941: A Case of Rescue Priority during the Holocaust." *Yad Vashem Studies* 13 (1979): 321–351.

Zuroff, E. "Rescue of Yeshiva Students in Poland through the Far East during the Holocaust." *Midor Lidor* 1 (1979): 49–76. (In Hebrew.)

JOSEPH WALK

WAR REFUGEE BOARD (WRB), United States government agency for rescuing and assisting World War II victims. In January 1944, Franklin D. ROOSEVELT issued an executive order establishing the War Refugee Board and charging it with carrying out the United States government's new policy of taking "all measures within its power to rescue the victims of enemy oppression who are in imminent danger of death." Roosevelt had waited to act fourteen months after the State Department (*see* UNITED STATES DEPARTMENT OF STATE) confirmed the news of the systematic extermination of the European Jews.

Beginning in November 1943, Congress debated the passage of a rescue resolution. Despite State Department attempts to prevent it, passage of such a resolution seemed likely in mid-January of 1944. If a rescue resolution were to be passed by Congress, its members would receive the credit, and not the Roosevelt administration. At the same time, the secretary of the treasury, Henry MORGENTHAU, Jr., was handed a report about State Department attempts to disrupt rescue. It was entitled "Report to the Secretary on the Acquiescence of This Government in the Murder of the Jews." Presented with an oral summary of the report, whose contents could result in a scandal for the government, and faced with the impending passage of a rescue resolution in Congress, Roosevelt quickly created the WRB.

On paper, the WRB had impressive powers. According to the executive order, all government agencies were to assist it, with special responsibility assigned to the State, Treasury, and War departments. In fact, only the Treasury Department, led by Morgenthau, fulfilled the mandate. The War Department was uncooperative, the State Department was frequently obstructive, and the other government agencies did almost nothing.

The WRB was also hurt by the president's lack of interest and support. Most important, the board was handicapped from the start by inadequate funding. Roosevelt allotted $1 million to be used for administering the WRB. For the actual rescue programs, which were far more expensive, the board had to turn to private Jewish organizations, especially the American Jewish JOINT DISTRIBUTION COMMITTEE. American Jews, through voluntary contributions to their organizations, provided close to $17 million for the government program. What was most needed—a major government commitment to rescue—was never realized. Instead, the board became a valuable, but limited, institution whose work was carried out in collaboration between the government and the private Jewish agencies, with the latter carrying most of the load.

Despite the difficulties they faced, the WRB's executive director, John Pehle, and his staff of thirty forged a wide-ranging rescue program. Its main contours included (1) evacuating Jews and other endangered people from Axis territory; (2) finding places to which they could be sent; (3) using psychological measures (especially threats of war crimes trials) to prevent deportations and atrocities; and (4) sending relief supplies into concentration camps. Much of this work was made possible by a handful of WRB representatives stationed overseas: Ira HIRSCHMANN in Turkey, Roswell McClelland in Switzerland, Iver Olsen in Sweden, and Leonard Ackermann in North Africa and Italy.

During much of 1944, the WRB was deeply

involved in efforts to save the Hungarian Jews. It played a crucial part in focusing international pressures on the Hungarian government and persuading it to stop the deportations before they encompassed the 230,000 Jews of BUDAPEST. Ultimately, somewhat more than half of these Jews survived the reign of terror inflicted by a later government under the fascist ARROW CROSS PARTY. The toll would have been much higher had it not been for the intrepid action of Raoul WALLENBERG in protecting the Budapest Jews. The young Swede had been sent to Budapest by the WRB, and his work there was funded by the board.

One of the most publicized WRB projects was the evacuation of 982 Jewish REFUGEES from Italy to a safe haven in an unused army camp at Oswego, New York (*see* FORT ONTARIO), in August 1944. The WRB had hoped to set up many such safe havens in the United States and to use these actions as a lever to pressure other countries to open

their doors as well. Roosevelt, however, agreed solely to the Oswego project. This tiny gesture only reinforced the adherence of other countries to their closed-door policies, and one of the WRB's main rescue strategies was thus crushed.

By the end of the war, the board had played a crucial role in saving approximately 200,000 Jews. About 15,000 were evacuated from Axis territory (as were more than 20,000 non-Jews). At least 10,000, and probably thousands more, were protected within Axis Europe by WRB-financed underground activities. The WRB's diplomatic pressures, backed by its program of psychological warfare, were instrumental in having the 48,000 Jews in TRANSNISTRIA moved to safe areas of Romania. Similar pressures helped end the Hungarian deportations; ultimately, 120,000 Jews survived in Budapest.

The results of other WRB programs, though they unquestionably contributed to the survival of thousands more, can never be quanti-

Photo taken in Secretary of State Cordell Hull's office on March 21, 1944, on the occasion of the third meeting of the War Refugee Board. Hull is at the left, Secretary of the Treasury Henry Morgenthau, Jr., is in the center, and Secretary of War Henry L. Stimson is at the right. [Franklin D. Roosevelt Library]

fied. These actions include the war crimes warnings and the shipment of thousands of food parcels into concentration camps during the last months of the war. On the other hand, numerous WRB plans that might have succeeded collapsed because the rest of the United States government would not cooperate.

BIBLIOGRAPHY

Feingold, H. L. *The Politics of Rescue: The Roosevelt Administration and the Holocaust, 1938–1945.* New Brunswick, N.J., 1970.
Wyman, D. S. *The Abandonment of the Jews: America and the Holocaust, 1941–1945.* New York, 1984.

DAVID S. WYMAN

WARSAW. [*The first article in this entry is an overview of the Nazi occupation of Warsaw. The second article,* Jews during the Holocaust, *deals with the fate of the Warsaw Jewish community.*]

General Survey

Warsaw is known from the thirteenth century; it became the capital of POLAND in 1596. It flanks both banks of the Vistula River, two-thirds of the city's area lying on the west bank and one-third on the east bank. In 1935 the city limits covered an area of 54 square miles (140 sq km), with a population of 1,300,000.

In early September 1939, a few days after the German attack on Poland and the outbreak of World War II, the Polish president, Ignacy Moscicki; the cabinet; and the chief of the General Staff, Marshal Edward Rydz-Smigly, all departed from Warsaw. The city's military defense was put in the hands of Gen. Walerian Czuma, who was succeeded by Gen. Juliusz Rommel. Civil defense was organized by the mayor, Stefan Starzyński. German forces reached the southern and western parts of Warsaw on September 8 and 9, and within a few days they had surrounded the city from all sides. Warsaw stood up to the German siege for three weeks. Air attacks and artillery shelling caused heavy damage to residential houses and ancient buildings and resulted in thousands of dead and wounded among the population.

On September 28 Warsaw surrendered, after it had despaired of receiving aid from the outside and in view of the existing living conditions and the rapid reduction of food supplies. For several weeks after the surrender the city was controlled by German army commanders. In late October, civil administration officials were also brought in, headed at first by a Reich commissar and later by a mayor. For short periods that post was held by Helmuth Otto and Oskar Dengel, successively, and from March 1940 to the end of the war Ludwig Leist was mayor. The city council, headed by the prewar deputy mayor, Julian Kulski, was subordinate to the mayor. The capital of the GENERALGOUVERNEMENT (the territory in the interior of occupied Poland), which was established on October 16, 1939, was KRAKÓW; Warsaw was only a district center, with Ludwig FISCHER serving as district governor.

The size of the city's German population, most of whom arrived after the war broke out, did not exceed thirty thousand. The number of military and police personnel varied from time to time, and generally was not more than twenty thousand. Warsaw was the seat of the Wehrmacht headquarters and an SS and police headquarters. The following served as *SS- und Polizeiführer* (SS and Police Leaders): SS-Gruppenführer Paul Moder, SS-Oberführer Arpad Wiegand, SS-Oberführer Ferdinand von Sammern-Frankenegg, SS-Brigadeführer Jürgen STROOP, SS-Brigadeführer Franz Kutschera, SS-Oberführer Herbert Böttcher, and SS-Brigadeführer Otto Geibel.

The German authorities terrorized the population in various ways—by arrests, murder in the streets, public and secret executions, deportations to concentration camps, and random seizures of persons for deportation to forced labor in the Reich. The headquarters of the terror operations was in the Sicherheitspolizei (Security Police) office, where persons were detained for questioning. The main terror center was the PAWIAK PRISON. There were several sites for public and secret executions in Warsaw and its environs, and they were put into use as early as the autumn of 1939. In the first stage the killings were carried out in areas near Warsaw, which were dubbed "Warsaw's circle of death"; one was the Palmiry Forest, where executions took place in the spring of 1940. They continued throughout the occupation of the city, reaching a climax in 1943. As of August 1, 1944, twenty-three thousand ethnic Poles had been deported to concentration camps and eighty-six thousand deported for forced labor in the Reich (*see* FORCED LABOR: FREMDAR-BEITER).

Apart from the direct terror operations, the Nazi authorities also imposed severe economic repression on the population. From August 1939 to 1944, the cost of living rose thirtyfold, whereas the official income rose only by 150 percent. Ration cards became compulsory and the rations supplied for them did not meet minimal needs. The inhabitants sought to combat hunger by taking on extra jobs, stealing from the German occupiers, engaging in black-market dealings, and, primarily, by smuggling in illegal food supplies, for which those caught were punished. A large part of the population was employed in armaments factories and other German-controlled enterprises.

Trading was one of the main preoccupations of Warsaw's economic life; people literally traded in everything, selling property extensively. On German orders, every person aged fourteen and over had to have an identity card in his possession and could be drafted for labor. Daily life in the city was severely handicapped by a curfew and by inadequate transportation facilities. All through the occupation, heating presented a serious problem; coal was hard to obtain, and people suffered from the cold. There was an acute shortage of housing, caused by the deliberate destruction of existing residential buildings. The Germans imposed strict limitations on cultural activities; the Polish press was liquidated, and in its place a Nazi propaganda daily, *Nowy Kurier Warszawski*, was published, as well as a few third-rate weeklies. The population was ordered to turn over their radios; from time to time, current news reports were broadcast by loudspeakers in the streets—"barkers," as people called them.

Concerts could be heard only in the coffeehouses. The films shown in the movie houses were nearly all German. Wide circles of the Polish population boycotted the official press, theater, and movies, but not all of the people joined in this campaign. Sports events too were prohibited. The educational system was restricted to elementary schools only, and even in them, history and geography lessons were excluded from the curriculum. Efforts by the Poles to establish comprehensive schools failed. The Germans permitted only vocational-training schools, to provide trained manpower for the Third Reich's economy. Technical colleges were also permitted to function, but the prewar universities were put out of action.

The reaction of the Poles to the restrictions on education and cultural activities was to organize clandestine classes and cultural events, in various forms. Secondary-school classes were conducted, in small groups, in private houses, with the participation of some twenty-five thousand students. College-level instruction was also provided, in similar form, with about ten thousand students attending.

Religious life was not officially restricted, but priests and religious orders were oppressed, like the rest of the population. The Warsaw inhabitants countered the German regime of terror with a broad resistance movement, consisting of a number of political and military organizations and a wide-ranging program of activities. Warsaw was the headquarters of the major Polish resistance organizations and an important scene for their undertakings.

The resistance movement was launched as early as September 1939. On September 26, the Służba Zwycięstwa Polski (Service for Polish Victory) was formed, which was later renamed the Związek Walki Zbrojnej (Union for Armed Struggle); in February 1942 it became the ARMIA KRAJOWA, the Polish Home Army.

Warsaw was also the center of the major political parties that supported the POLISH GOVERNMENT-IN-EXILE and formed the "London camp." These were the Stronnictwo Narodowe (National Front), the Stronnictwo Pracy (Labor Front), the Stronnictwo Ludowe (Popular Front), and the Polska Partia Socjalistyczna (Polish Socialist Party). Opposing these parties were fascist-type organizations, with antisemitic and anti-Soviet tendencies, which formed the NARODOWE SIŁY ZBROJNE (National Armed Forces). Among the leftist organizations the most active was the Polscy Socjalisci (Polish Socialists), which in 1943 became the Robotnicza Partia Polskich Socjalistów (Polish Socialist Workers' Party). Communist groups, which initially were small and not very active, increased their efforts when the Polska Partia Robotnicza (Polish Workers' Party; PPR) was founded, in January 1942. This was the beginning of the GWARDIA LUDOWA (People's Guard).

In the initial stage, the resistance movement found its expression in spreading propaganda, by means of some one thousand underground newspapers, and in storing up weapons, mainly for arms caches that had been created after the 1939 defeat, through purchases from German soldiers. Later, the resistance manufactured its own arms and ammunition, with emphasis on hand grenades. In a few instances, arms were parachuted by Allied aircraft and were stolen from Germans. For some time there was little armed action, what there was consisting mostly of liquidating spies and traitors. In 1943 relatively large-scale military actions were launched. Several particularly dangerous German officials were liquidated, among them the Higher SS and Police Leader Franz Kutschera. The Polish resistance movement also assisted in hiding Jews.

The resistance movement in Warsaw encompassed a broad section of the population, primarily among the intelligentsia and the working class, especially the young people. There were also separate YOUTH MOVEMENTS, of which the most active was that of the underground scouts, whose code name was "Gray Columns." Another movement for young people was the PPR-sponsored Związek Walki Młodych (Young People's Fighting Union); there were also Catholic, Socialist, and other youth movements. In 1943 and 1944 the number of sabotage acts and assassinations increased rapidly: a total of eight hundred military and sabotage actions of different kinds were carried out. Several dozen high-ranking occupation officials were liquidated in retaliation for the exceptional cruelty that they had practiced.

The resistance movement continued to ex-

pand, despite the resulting heavy loss of life and property owing to Nazi acts of reprisal, and it began preparations for a large-scale armed uprising. On August 1, 1944, the rebellion broke out on orders of the Armia Krajowa command, without coordination with the Armia Ludowa or the Soviet military command. When the WARSAW POLISH UPRISING erupted, Hitler wanted to bomb from the air the part of the city that was in the rebels' hands, but he gave up the idea. A few days later, after consultations with Heinrich HIMMLER, he ordered the total destruction of Warsaw, with a fortress to be constructed on the site.

Once the uprising was suppressed, the Germans ordered the civilian population to evacuate the city, sending them to the Pruszków, Ursus, and Piastów transit camps. Some 550,000 Warsaw inhabitants passed through these camps. More than 60,000 were sent on to concentration camps, and over 100,000 to labor camps in the Reich. Between October and December 1944 the Germans destroyed ancient shrines, many art collections, and other items of cultural importance, violating the promise they had given under the terms of the Polish surrender to respect these treasures in the city. Special squads of Germans blew up the buildings and systematically destroyed the abandoned city.

In January 1945, Soviet and Polish forces attacked the city from the south and north, crossing the Vistula and liberating Warsaw on January 17. The dimensions of the destruction and losses were unbelievably high. It is estimated that 80 percent of Warsaw's buildings were destroyed: 10 percent during the siege of the city in September 1939, 12 percent during the liquidation of the ghetto, 12 percent during the Polish uprising, and the rest in the deliberate destruction of the city after the collapse of the uprising.

Heavy losses were also inflicted on Polish cultural treasures. Approximately 90 percent of the churches were destroyed, 80 percent of the museums and theaters, 80 percent of the hospitals, and 70 percent of the schools. The losses in life included 20,000 in September 1939, and 32,000 by executions and other methods. The Jews murdered numbered 370,000, 166,000 persons were killed in the 1944 uprising, and 97,000 perished in the concentration and forced-labor camps. A total of 685,000 residents of Warsaw lost their lives during the Nazi occupation.

BIBLIOGRAPHY

Bartoszewski, W. *Warsaw Death Ring, 1939–1944.* Warsaw, 1968.

Cywilna obrona Warszawy we wrześniu 1939 r.: Dokumenty, materiały prasowe, wspomnienia i relacje. Warsaw, 1965.

Dunin-Wasowicz, K. *Warszawa w latach 1939–1945.* Warsaw, 1984.

Hanson, J. K. M. *The Civilian Population and the Warsaw Uprising of 1944.* Cambridge, 1982.

KRZYSZTOF DUNIN-WASOWICZ

Jews during the Holocaust

The earliest reports of the presence of Jews in Warsaw date from the fifteenth century. In the 1792 census, 6,750 Jews were found to be living there, about one-tenth of the city's total population. In the nineteenth century Warsaw's Jewish population grew rapidly; it became the largest Jewish community in Europe and, in the twentieth century, the second largest in the world, next only to New York. On the eve of World War I, the Jews in Warsaw numbered 337,000.

Just before World War II broke out, Warsaw's Jewish population was 375,000 (29.1 percent of the total). Jews were to be found in every part of the city, but its northern part contained a section that was predominantly Jewish, with many apartment houses and certain streets inhabited exclusively by Jews. According to 1931 data, 46.8 percent of the gainfully employed Jews worked in crafts and industry and 32.7 percent in commerce and finance; 8 percent of the total personnel in the liberal professions were Jewish. Apart from schoolteachers, hardly any Jews were employed by the national or city government offices; such posts in fact were generally barred to Jews. Government companies and private companies owned by Poles were reluctant to employ Jews, and this sometimes applied also to Jewish-owned enterprises (for a variety of reasons, such as the issue of working on the Sabbath). The antisemitic policy pursued by the Polish government, added to the generally poor state of the Polish economy, led to the pauperization of the Jewish population. On the eve of World War II, the situation of the Jews was marked by economic strangulation and a sense of being persecuted without having any place to which to emigrate, owing to the closed-door policy practiced by the target countries of emigration and the drastic limitations on immigration to Palestine, as of 1936.

Warsaw in those years was the capital of Polish Jewry and an important world Jewish center. The head offices of the political parties, of a great many welfare, educational, and religious institutions, and of the trade unions were located there. It was in Warsaw that most of the Jewish newspapers and periodicals were published in different languages, that the various educational trends received their central direction, and that sports organizations and youth movements had their headquarters. The cultural drive emanating from Warsaw, with its literary and artistic creativity, its publishing houses, theaters, and societies, was in stark contrast to the depressed status and abject poverty that constituted the lot of the masses of Warsaw's Jewish population. The growing political tension in the months preceding the outbreak of the war witnessed the beginnings of an understanding between Poles and Jews, who were both in a state of anxiety and insecurity. Although it had been expected, the war that broke out on September 1, 1939, found both Poles and Jews unprepared and helpless in the face of the Nazi war machine that was about to engulf them.

By the end of the first week of war, the German forces had managed to destroy Poland's military power, and the German army stood at the gates of Warsaw. At first the Polish high command resolved to make Warsaw an armed fighting fortress, but it later abandoned the plan. The civilian population, including many Jews, had been digging anti-tank ditches at the approaches to Warsaw in the early days of the war, and roadblocks had been put up inside the city. But at the same time that it was decided to defend the capital—a stand that Warsaw's mayor, Stefan Starzyński, proclaimed with great and compelling conviction—the spokesman of the commander in chief, Col. Roman Umiastowski, on the night of September 6–7 called on all men able to bear arms to leave the city. This call created a panic, with masses of people, mostly young and middle-aged men, crossing the Vistula bridges to the east bank. Adam CZERNIAKÓW, who was soon to become chairman of the Warsaw JUDENRAT (Jewish Council), made the following entry in his diary on September 7: "With a knapsack on their backs, all sorts of human beings left for the great unknown." The roads were jammed with people, presenting a convenient target for the low-flying aircraft that were strafing them with their automatic weapons.

The exodus from the city was joined by government cadres and top officials, as well as the leaders of the political and public organizations. Also swept along were Jewish public figures, leaders, and activists of the different political movements, among them Maurycy Mayzel, the appointed head of the Jewish Community Council. No meaningful preparations had been made for an evacuation, and no individuals or organizations were assigned to take the place of the persons who were abandoning the city in the emergency.

From the very first days of the war, Warsaw was subjected to air raids. By the end of the first week the antiaircraft defense had been put out of action, and the aircraft were able to drop bombs at will. Buildings collapsed on top of the people living inside; the cellars, which had been regarded as bombproof, became death traps. A growing number of refugees and travelers crowded the city—people who had fled or been driven out of the cities and towns of western Poland, as well as Warsaw residents whose homes had been destroyed and all their belongings lost. On September 24, Czerniaków confided in his diary: "All night long the guns keep on firing. There is no gas, no water, no electricity, and no bread; what a terrible day!" In the last week of September the city lay in ruins, a scene of chaos and death.

On September 28, Warsaw surrendered; the next day German forces made their entry into the city. There is no evidence that the Germans deliberately aimed their fire at the Jewish streets and the section that was densely populated with Jews. However, the Jews felt that they had been a special target. The hail of shells that landed on the High Holy Days (the New Year and the Day of Atonement) reinforced that impression. Chaim Aaron KAPLAN, a Jewish teacher in Warsaw who kept a detailed diary up to his last day in the ghetto, made the following entry on September 14: "Yesterday, between five and seven in the afternoon, as the Jewish New Year, 5700, was being ushered in, the northern section, populated mostly by Jews, suffered an air raid." Czerniaków, on September 22, stated: "Today is the Day of Atonement, truly the day of judgment. All night long the guns were shelling the city."

The written records and the memoirs reveal that the Jews had no idea of what the Nazis had in store for them. Many recalled the World War I German occupation, which was orderly and tolerant toward the Jews. From the very first days of this occupation, however, the Jews discovered that the German army that entered the city in 1939 was nothing like the troops that had been stationed there in World War I. The Jews were immediately subjected to attacks and discrimination. This started with Jews being driven away from food lines and seized for forced labor, with assaults on religious Jews who were wearing their traditional garb, and with the plunder of Jewish shops and of property that the Jews had hidden away in their homes. The indiscriminate seizure of Jews for forced labor, regardless of age or state of health, paralyzed Jewish life as Jews kept out of the streets. The main obstacle to the resumption of normal life was the "new order" that the occupier began to apply. Most of the business enterprises were not reopened, since the Jews were afraid to renew trade and display their wares in their shops. Teachers, craftsmen, professionals, journalists, and staff members of cultural and social-welfare institutions lost their positions, without receiving any compensation and without a prospect of finding a new place of work.

In November the first anti-Jewish decrees were issued, such as the introduction of a white armband with a blue Star of David (Magen David) on it to be worn by all Jews, the requirement of signs identifying Jewish shops and enterprises, the order to hand in radios, a ban on train travel, and so on. The hardest blows came with the decrees and regulations on economic affairs. On October

17 the district governor, Ludwig FISCHER, issued a decree prohibiting non-Jews from buying or leasing Jewish enterprises without obtaining a special permit for this purpose (a Jewish enterprise was defined as any enterprise in which Jews had a share of more than 25 percent). In November regulations were issued concerning the handling of money by Jews: Jews had to deposit all their money in a blocked bank account; the banks could release no more than 250 zlotys (the equivalent of about $2.50 during the war years) per week to the holder of the account. Kaplan recorded in his diary that no Jew was in a hurry to hand in his money, and he took pride in the fact that the Jews were not obeying the cruel and inhuman orders that were being issued by the occupying power. These orders, however, made it impossible for Jews to carry on economic activity in the open, and especially outside Jewish circles. Another decree, concerning the pensions of widows, the disabled, the elderly, and those retired from the various branches of government, excluded Jews from all welfare assistance. On February 4, 1940, Kaplan recorded: "The registration of Jewish assets (real estate, businesses, securities, offices, and private residences, exceeding 2,000 zlotys [about $20] in value), implemented in January, has now been followed by a new decree: every Jew who has a private residence containing clothing and household goods must hand in a detailed list of all the items he has in his home."

In addition to blocking Jewish accounts and putting a stop to economic activity by Jews, the Germans also embarked upon the confiscation of Jewish enterprises. An announcement published by Generalgouverneur Hans FRANK, the head of the GENERALGOUVERNEMENT (the territory in the interior of occupied Poland), laid down that any enterprise whose owner was absent or which was not being run in a proper manner could be seized by the authorities and have a custodian appointed to take care of it. This led to the confiscation of all Jewish enterprises, except for small stores in the Jewish area. In general, the custodians got rid of the Jewish owner and the Jewish employees, retaining the owner as an adviser only in special circumstances.

Even in the early stage of the occupation, the assets accumulated in the past served the Jews as their main source of subsistence. Jews with savings or goods that they had managed to conceal began trading them for food—a practice that was to continue throughout the war. As time went on the Jews' property and resources dwindled, and more and more Jews became penniless and faced a slow death, owing to the lack of food and other minimum requirements they needed merely to exist. It may be assumed that tens of thousands of Jews left Warsaw in the exodus that took place in the first few days of the war; on the other hand, an estimated ninety thousand Jews were added to the population, up until the establishment of the ghetto in November 1940—either as refugees or through being deported to Warsaw by the Germans. Many of these newcomers came from ŁÓDŹ, Włocławek, Kalisz, and other cities and towns in the western districts of Poland. They were housed in so-called *punkty* (shelter points), some of them very crowded, in buildings such as schools, public institutions, and even synagogues. The severe shortages, the overcrowded conditions and the despair that prevailed in the *punkty* caused their inhabitants to become the first victims of starvation and of the epidemics that were beginning to spread.

Judenrat Activities. The Jews were not permitted to reopen their schools, and for a while they were also barred from attending prayer services. The restoration of prewar institutions and organizations was strictly prohibited; even a small group of Jews was not allowed to meet without a permit. In place of the very many institutions of different kinds that had existed in the past, only two frameworks were allowed to function—the Judenrat and welfare institutions. The Judenrat was a new body set up by the Germans, in place of the traditional Jewish Community Council. On October 4, 1939, Czerniaków made the following entry in his diary: "I was taken to Szucha Street [Aleja Szucha, where the police, including the Gestapo, had its installations] and there I was told to appoint twenty-four persons to the Community Council and become its chairman." This was the first, and decisive, step toward the creation of the Judenrat, but at the time Warsaw's Jews

Before the establishment of the ghetto in November 1940, the Germans "resettled" about 90,000 Jews in Warsaw from other towns and cities in Poland. Housing had to be found for them in public buildings. This is a shelter in a synagogue at 27 Nowolipki Street for Jews who were expelled from Łódź and Alexandrów.

had no idea that they were witnessing an event that was to influence their lives for several years to come. Adam Czerniaków, although a member of the old Jewish Community Council, was not a well-known and established public figure among the Jews of Warsaw.

In September, when the fighting was at its height, the Polish mayor of Warsaw, Stefan Starzyński, had appointed Czerniaków to be the Jewish Community Council chairman, and Czerniaków's appointment to head the new body therefore seemed logical. In its original form the Judenrat was made up of persons who had held important posts in Jewish public life, as leaders of Jewish political parties and their representatives in the Polish Sejm (parliament). This meant that as initially formed the Judenrat carried more public weight than had the now defunct Jewish Community Council. Among its members were the Zionist leader Maximilian Hartglas, Moshe Kerner of the General Zionists, the ultra-Orthodox Agudat Israel leader Rabbi Isaac Meir Levin, and BUND leader Samuel

ZYGELBOJM. It was therefore quite natural for the Jewish population to regard the Judenrat at this stage as a continuation of the Community Council. Indeed, they referred to it as the Kehillah (community), all the more so since it had its offices on Grzybowska Street, in the same building where the former Kehillah had been housed.

Even when the prominent Judenrat members—including all the above except for Czerniaków—left Warsaw (they were among the last group to leave Poland legally in the first few months of 1940), the Kehillah-Judenrat still contained members who had enjoyed the respect and trust of the Jews in prewar Warsaw. Among these men were Abraham GEPNER, a merchant and industrialist who had headed the Jewish Merchants' Center and had been a member of the Warsaw City Council; Joseph Jaszunski, president of ORT (the Jewish organization for vocational education) in Poland and a member of the Yiddish cultural institution, YIVO; the engineer Stanisław Szereszewski, who had been chairman of Toporol, a society for the promotion of Jewish farming; Dr. Joseph Milijekowski, a leading physician and public figure; and Meshullam Kaminer, a prominent Agudat Israel activist. Later, when the ghetto came into being, the Judenrat would be burdened with increased responsibilities and its authority would be extended to all aspects of Jewish life. But even the first challenges that it had to face demonstrated its helplessness in face of the tragic dilemmas that confronted it, on issues such as forced labor, the collection of large "contributions," confiscations, and the indiscriminate arrests and executions of groups of Jews as retaliatory measures.

In the course of time it appeared that the random seizure of Jews for forced labor by the Germans would be replaced by an orderly procedure. The Judenrat proposed to the Germans that it would provide them with a fixed quota of men for work, in place of the haphazard kidnapings that had brought Jewish life to a total standstill. According to this arrangement, every Jew was assigned a fixed number of days per month for forced labor. As a result, the Judenrat, which did not have the financial resources to cover the wages of the forced laborers, was in financial straits at all times.

Mutual Aid. The other framework in which the Jews were allowed to remain active throughout the occupation and the existence of the ghetto was that of welfare and mutual help. As early as September 1939, during the fighting, a Polish emergency aid organization, the Stołeczny Komitet Samopomocy Społecznej (Municipal Committee for Social Welfare), had been formed; the Jews followed this example and set up a similar body of their own. The Poles had at their disposal funds for this purpose that the Polish government had left behind when it fled, and the Jews assumed that as Polish citizens and taxpayers they too were entitled to benefit from these financial resources. Before long, however, the Polish welfare agency informed the Jews that the Germans disapproved of Polish-Jewish cooperation, and the contacts between the two bodies were broken off. As a result, the Jews began to operate on their own.

The financial base for such operations consisted of funds that had been accumulated by the American Jewish JOINT DISTRIBUTION COMMITTEE (known as the Joint); these amounted to substantial sums and were available for welfare purposes under the new conditions. The Joint was registered as an American institution, and at this time the Germans still had to take that fact into consideration. The Joint took all the existing welfare institutions under its wing. Its representation in Poland, based in Warsaw, included a group of devoted and talented people who demonstrated their ability, courage, and dedication even during the war and the existence of the ghetto. Outstanding among them was Yitzhak GITTERMAN, a Lithuanian Jew who for years had been the moving spirit in the Joint's projects and activities. Others in this group were David Guzik, Leon Neustadt, Yitzhak Bornstein, and the historian Emanuel RINGELBLUM, who was to have a hand in many and varied activities during the war and in the underground. The Joint associated itself with welfare operations in a number of ways, including the care of refugees and the wounded during the fighting. Many unemployed members of the intelligentsia were employed by the welfare agencies that the Joint sponsored.

Before long it became evident that the number of needy cases was growing and that an organization had to be created, and properly equipped, that would be able to meet the requirements of the entire Jewish population. The Joint-sponsored Żydowskie Towarzystwo Opieki Społecznej (Jewish Mutual Aid Society; ŻTOS) lent assistance to 250,000 Jews during Passover of 1940. Its most important means of aiding masses of people were its soup kitchens, which doled out a bowl of soup and a piece of bread to all comers. When this operation was at its height, more than one hundred such soup kitchens were in existence in Jewish Warsaw. There were soup kitchens for certain trade unions, such as those for journalists and writers, and some kitchens were under the supervision of political parties and youth movements. In October 1939, 188,611 portions of soup were provided in Warsaw; the figure for March 1940 was 1,986,263. At the very beginning of the war, 15 percent of Warsaw's Jews needed the food ration that the soup kitchens handed out. In September 1940 the number of portions

CENTOS (Centrala Opieki nad Sierotami, or Organization for Care of Orphans). This is the CENTOS-run soup kitchen for children at 22 Nowolipki Street. [Foto Forbert]

given out by the kitchens dropped sharply, to 379,068, because the Joint's funds were running out.

During the course of 1940 the Joint spent approximately $1,500,000 for the Jews of Poland. In 1941 the amount spent was reduced by 20 percent, even though the economic situation of the Jews had become much worse. From 1942 the Joint faced enormous problems, since the United States had entered the war and it became increasingly difficult to ship food and transfer funds to an enemy state. Non-Jewish American organizations also extended relief, and even insisted that needy Jews should also benefit from their assistance. In an effort to maintain at least the most urgent, partial assistance, the Joint officials in Warsaw appealed to wealthy Jews who had managed to save some of their cash assets to lend money to the Joint, for which they would be reimbursed when the war was over.

Important instruments created by Jewish self-help, under the direction of Emanuel Ringelblum, were the Komitety Domowe, or House Committees. Such committees had been set up on an emergency basis during the September 1939 fighting, but Ringelblum and his associates felt that they could become a permanent feature for mutual help. The House Committees gained in importance when the early curfew hours were introduced, by which time all the tenants had to be in their homes; as a result, the ties among the tenants were strengthened. The committees were staffed by volunteer activists, who developed into an important local leadership group.

As the distress grew worse, the committees multiplied and gained in importance. At the end of April 1940 Warsaw had 778 such committees, in 878 apartment houses; by May 1940 the number had grown to 1,518, and by September some 2,000 House Committees were functioning. Ringelblum and his colleagues sought to make the House Committees into a network basing its work on social principles. The committees' first task was to take care of the penniless tenants in their buildings, but they also set up kindergartens and youth clubs and arranged cultural activities. The ŻTOS tried to extend the operations of the House Committees by requesting the better-off buildings to adopt shelter points or other buildings where the suffering was worse. When the situation did grow worse, however, and more and more people were in need, the activities of the House Committees went into a decline.

From its inception, the work of the ŻTOS was guided by social and political principles. It had a public council composed of representatives of the leaders of underground political bodies, and that council determined the aid policy and its goals. In this manner, the ŻTOS assumed a dual role: on the one hand it operated legally, with the knowledge and approval of the authorities, and on the other hand it maintained ties with the clandestine political organizations and lent its assistance to underground activities. Many people regarded the ŻTOS as an alternative to the Judenrat, an institution that represented the Jewish population vis-à-vis the official body controlled by the occupying power.

In the spring of 1940 the welfare section of the German administration headed by Generalgouverneur Hans Frank suggested the creation of a welfare institution for the entire population, including the Jews. This overall organization was indeed established, as the Naczelna Rada Opiekuńcza (Main Welfare Council). It included the Żydowska Samopomoc Społeczna (Jewish Self-Help Society), which developed into an autonomous Jewish agency; its head was Dr. Michael Weigert, who before the war had been active in the affairs of Jewish craftsmen and cultural institutions. Both the Main Welfare Council and the Jewish Self-Help Society had their head offices in Kraków.

The Jewish and Polish populations of Warsaw had hardly any contacts with each other on a public level. While not the capital of the Generalgouvernement, Warsaw was the capital of underground Poland. It was there that the underground military organizations were formed, that the political parties were clandestinely active, and that the DELEGATURA, representing the POLISH GOVERNMENT-IN-EXILE, had its main office. Warsaw Jews had ties with Poles on an individual basis and certain Jewish political groups were in contact with their Polish counterparts, but no links of any sort were created between the Polish underground forces, or the military and political branches of the Polish government-in-exile, and Jewish public bodies. No Jewish element became a recognized part of a Polish-sponsored underground framework, and no Jewish representative was ever invited to join a body established by official Polish underground organizations. At the beginning of the occupation, however, no serious anti-Jewish manifestations by Poles were recorded. The heads of the Main Welfare Council, the Polish welfare agency, took the situation of the Jews into account in their distribution of aid.

Ghetto Established. In January 1940 a wave of muggings and attacks on Jews was launched by Polish gangs, and individual Jews were robbed in the street without any interference by bystanders. These gangs were made up of hoodlums and underworld types who exploited the license they were given to rampage to their heart's content, with the Germans giving their tacit consent and encouragement, and perhaps even at their behest. During the Easter season these attacks turned into a real pogrom, which continued for eight days. The Jews did not dare defend themselves, fearing a possible German reaction. The Poles and the Polish underground did not come out with any vigorous denunciation, although individual Poles expressed their opposition and spoke out against the attackers. The rioting came to a sudden end, on German orders.

In mid-November 1940, the Jewish ghetto in Warsaw, surrounded by a high wall, was sealed off. It was situated in the heart of the Jewish quarter, in the northern section of the city, and encompassed the Jewish-inhabited streets. The first attempt to set up a ghetto had been made by the SS in November 1939, but at the time the military governor, Gen. Karl Ulrich von Neuman-Neurode, put a stop to the plan. In February 1940, however, Waldemar Schön, the official in charge of evacuation and relocation in the German district administration, was ordered to draw up plans for the establishment of a ghetto. Various possibilities were considered, one of them being the removal of the Jews from the city and their concentration in one of the suburbs. On October 12, 1940, the Day of Atonement, the Jews were informed of the decree establishing a ghetto. A few days later a map was published indicating the streets assigned to the ghetto area. Heavy pressure was brought to bear to cut down the size of

Żelazna Street; Jews are being moved into the ghetto (September–October 1940). The ghetto was sealed on November 15, 1940.

the projected ghetto, but some Poles called for Jewish-Polish cooperation to oppose this, in view of the situation that had been created, involving the evacuation of more than 100,000 Poles on the one hand, and of a corresponding number of Jews, on the other.

The construction of the wall surrounding the ghetto took many months, with the Judenrat obliged to defray the costs. Up to the very last day, the Jews did not know whether the ghetto would be open or sealed off from its surroundings. On November 16 the ghetto was in fact sealed off, and thousands of Jews who had left their remaining belongings on the other side of the wall no longer had access to them.

The Germans had planned for 113,000 Poles to be evacuated from their homes and resettled elsewhere, and for 138,000 Jews to take their place. As soon as the ghetto was set up, a flow of refugees converged upon it. Some 30 percent of the population of Warsaw was being packed into 2.4 percent of the city's area. According to German statistics, the density of population in the ghetto was six to seven people to a room. The apartment buildings in the ghetto area were in a poor state and lacked sanitary facilities, and there were no lawns or trees in sight. Of Warsaw's 1,800 streets, no more than 73 were assigned to the ghetto. The ghetto wall was 11.5 feet (3.5 m) high and topped by barbed wire. The 2,000 Warsaw Jews who had been converted to Christianity were also put into the ghetto and one church was left open, under a priest of Jewish parentage, who, with the rest of his flock, was regarded as Jewish under the racist laws. The Nazis did not use the term "ghetto," referring to it as the "Jewish quarter" (*Jüdische Wohnbezirk*). The ghetto cut the Jews off from the rest of the world and put an end to any remaining business ties with Poles.

The number of persons employed by the Judenrat increased rapidly and a 1,000-man Jewish police force (JÜDISCHER ORDNUNGS-

DIENST) was formed, which eventually was increased to 2,000. At its maximum size, the Judenrat staff consisted of 6,000 persons, compared to the 530 employed by the Jewish Community Council before the war. The daily food ration allocated to the Warsaw Jews consisted of 181 calories—about 25 percent of the Polish ration, and 8 percent of the nutritional value of the food that the Germans received for their official ration coupons. In November 1940, the month the ghetto was sealed off, there were 445 deaths in the ghetto. The number of deaths thereafter rose rapidly: in January 1941, to 898; in April, to 2,061; in June, to 4,290; and in August, to 5,560. The last number was the high-

est, the monthly figure thereafter fluctuating between 4,000 and 5,000 for as long as the ghetto existed. A substantial drop was registered in May 1942, at the time of the great deportation, when 3,636 deaths were recorded.

An economic structure was gradually created in the ghetto, sustaining a thin upper stratum made up of people who smuggled food into the ghetto and smuggled valuables out to the "Aryan" side, and of skilled craftsmen who made deals (legal or not legal) with German enterprises. However, the structure could not support the rest of the population, even those with full- or part-time employment. The pay received by the different cate-

Part of the ghetto wall, which was about 11 miles (18 km) long when the ghetto was sealed on November 15, 1940. The wall was 11.5 feet (3.5 m) high and 10.6 inches (27 cm) thick.

Jüdischer Ordnungsdienst (Jewish ghetto police).

gories of Jewish workers—who as time went on numbered tens of thousands—enabled not more than 10 percent of them to provide themselves and their families with the basic food requirements. Most of the population tried to subsist on their savings or on the proceeds of the sale of goods still in their possession. Having a job was important in itself, giving a sense of clinging to reality and helping to raise morale.

The pauperization proceeded at an ever-growing rate, with more and more people becoming completely penniless, even to the point of starving to death. One of the diarists, Stefan Ernst, made the following entry, at a time when the liquidation of the ghetto was drawing near: "The ghetto contains 20,000, maybe 30,000, persons who have enough to eat, and these are the social elite; at the other end of the ladder are about a quarter of a million people who are all beggars, completely bereft of everything, and who wage a daily struggle to postpone their death by starvation. In between these two extremes are about 200,000 people, the 'average,' who somehow manage, are still able to take care of themselves, look clean and dressed, and their bellies are not swollen from hunger." According to a calculation made by the ŻTOS, 65,000 persons in the ghetto had jobs, 55,000 of them drawing wages and the others self-employed. The same source put the number of people with no means of support of any kind at over 200,000.

The ghetto's ties with the outside world were handled by the Transferstelle (Transfer Office), a German authority that was in charge of the traffic of goods into and out of the ghetto. The first official to manage this office was Alexander Palfinger, a German

Woman selling armbands with the Star of David. This photograph was taken by Heinz Jöst, a soldier in the German army who was stationed at a camp near Warsaw. In September 1941 he wandered through the Warsaw ghetto taking photographs. Jews were required to wear these bands, and anyone caught without the band was severely punished. [Steidl Verlag]

who had previously served in the Łódź ghetto administration. He was succeeded by Max Fischer, a German economist who displayed great flexibility in carrying out his assignment.

In practice, only some goods—the food shipments into the ghetto and the products manufactured by the ghetto for clients on the outside—passed through the Transferstelle. The greater part of the economic activities in the ghetto were illegal, and the ghetto economy was essentially an illegal operation, made up of two basic elements: the smuggling of food into the ghetto and the illegal export of products fabricated inside it.

In June 1941, 333,000 zlotys' (about $3,330) worth of items manufactured in the ghetto passed through official channels. In the following months, the monthly average was 500,000 zlotys ($5,000), whereas the clandestine production, as calculated by an economist in the ghetto, amounted to approximately 10 million zlotys (about $100,000) in that same period. For two categories alone, carpentry work and brush manufacture,

goods in the amount of 7 million to 8 million zlotys ($70,000–$80,000) were manufactured illegally. The food smuggled into the ghetto, according to the quantity estimates made by Czerniaków, represented 80 percent of all the products brought in.

The German involvement in the ghetto took a number of forms. The German authorities' main interest was to plunder Jewish property and to make use of Jewish expertise in certain fields. From the earliest stage of the occupation, some Jews were employed in collecting scrap metal, feathers, and textiles. Later, growing numbers of Jews were dispatched to labor camps, where they were made to do backbreaking jobs and suffered from hunger, poor sanitary conditions, and wearisome and grueling discipline. In the summer of 1941, some 11,300 Jews were sent to camps in the Warsaw, Lublin, and Kraków districts, where the mortality rate and proportion of those who were disabled for life were all extremely high, as was the turnover. The 2,000 Jews with steady employment in German enterprises in Warsaw held service jobs in the military barracks, worked as porters in the railway station, and so on. They were able to smuggle some food, acquired at a low price, into the ghetto, for their families and for selling among their circle of friends. German entrepreneurs and factory owners soon became interested in the ghetto and the availability of cheap Jewish manpower, and they swooped down upon the ghetto in order to exploit it as a source of forced labor.

Jewish Labor, Legal and Illegal. German manufacturers appeared in the ghetto in the summer of 1941, having organized and obtained authorization to operate in the Warsaw area. First to appear on the scene was Bernard Hallmann, owner of a carpentry company, in July. In September, the Fritz Schulz Company, a Danzig-based fur establishment, became active in the ghetto. The most important among these operations, however, was conducted by a German named Walther Többens, a manufacturer of textile goods, who began his activities in the autumn. At first the German companies placed orders with existing Jewish workshops, but before long they put up their own workshops in the ghetto. In the early stage, relatively few Jews were prepared to work in the Ger-

Street scene in the ghetto.

man workshops; the pay received for a day's work was not enough to buy half a loaf of bread.

The Judenrat, seeking to play a role in these operations, encouraged the Jews to accept employment in the German manufacturing establishments, and formed a special department for this purpose. Its efforts were to no avail, however, and it was only the specter of possible deportations from the ghetto that eventually persuaded a growing number of Jews to accept such work. Various Polish trading companies, including some large enterprises, found themselves forced to establish clandestine connections with skilled craftsmen in the ghetto, in order to obtain supplies of haberdashery and other items they required. Even the Wehrmacht had such "secret" connections, to enable it to order beds, brushes, items of clothing, and so forth. The Jews proved themselves extremely skillful at inventing and improvising; they were able to make secondhand products look new and utilize all sorts of substitutes.

As a rule, the Jews preferred to work in places that manufactured goods for "illegal export," where they were treated better and where the pay was much higher than in the German-owned factories. Several methods were employed to carry out the smuggling operations, which never ceased as long as the ghetto remained in existence: through buildings that were connected with buildings on the "Aryan" side; across the wall, through camouflaged openings in the wall; and through subterranean canals. Smuggling on a large scale also went on through the ghetto gates, with the various policemen and guards —Germans, Poles, and Jews—involved in the conspiracy and receiving monetary bribes for letting the smuggled goods pass.

Smuggling on a small scale was also engaged in by children and women who, at the risk of their lives, crossed over to the Polish side in order to bring back some food for their families. The overall smuggling operation was a complex organization, maintaining ties with partners and accomplices on the Polish side. Each individual smuggling operation, involving dozens of packages, took no more than a few minutes, and every effort was made to leave no traces. However, hardly a day passed without people being caught and losing their lives. The casualties, however, did not deter the smuggling organization, and did not bring the smuggling to even a temporary halt. The organizers and the rank-and-file smugglers were not motivated by considerations of public interest or of defying the authorities. Their purpose was to stay alive and make a profit, although they also included many adventurous types.

The records and diaries kept in the ghetto all attest that the smugglers' operations played a vital role, thanks to which the ghetto was able to hold out and survive even in the face of the cruel steps taken by the Germans against the population. The children and women were a different type of smuggler; they operated on an individual basis, responding to the misery around them and seeking to save themselves and their relatives. Children aged seven or eight frequently gathered in the vicinity of the ghetto gates in order to look for a smuggling opportunity. Leon Berensohn, a prominent Jewish lawyer who belonged to the assimilationist circles and died in the ghetto, said that after the war the liberated survivors would have to put up a monument in memory of the Unknown Child—the smuggler in the Warsaw ghetto.

Attempts by the Germans to bring the smuggling to a complete stop met with the desperate resistance of human beings fighting for their lives. The Germans, who had no compunctions about the methods they were using, and for whom torture and murder were the accepted means of breaking resistance, could have stopped the smuggling by mass killings. Most likely, they resigned themselves to the continued smuggling, realizing that without it the ghetto population was doomed to death within a few weeks or months. The local administrative officials apparently decided that there was no point in trying to stamp out the smuggling entirely, and that sporadic raids, confiscations, and executions would keep it within acceptable bounds and under reasonable control.

Religion, Education, and Culture in the Ghetto. Among the prohibitions that the Germans did not enforce fully was the ban on gatherings, which applied even to the privacy of homes. For a while the ban also specifi-

Children in the Warsaw ghetto.

cally included public prayer services. This did not prevent Jews from holding daily services in private homes, with the prayer quorum of at least ten males, while on the Jewish festivals, thousands of persons attended prayer services. In the spring of 1941 the ban was abolished and the synagogues were permitted to reopen. The Great Synagogue on Tłomacki Street was reopened in June 1941, in a festive ceremony. Rabbi Kalonymos Kalmisch Shapira, the Hasidic rabbi of Piaseczno, maintained his flock of followers in the ghetto and preached to them on the Sabbath. His words not only expressed complete faith but also attempted to discover the meaning of the events that were taking place.

School instruction was prohibited in the ghetto. From time to time the Judenrat chairman, Czerniaków, asked the German authorities for permission to reopen the schools. In 1941 permission was granted to open the school year for several elementary-school classes. This "regular" school year, the only one that was observed in the ghetto, started in October 1941. When it was drawing to a close, sixty-seven hundred pupils were attending nineteen schools, belonging to the several educational systems that Warsaw Jewry had maintained before the war. The major educational effort, however, was an underground operation. Dozens, perhaps hundreds, of clandestine classes, on different levels, were held in private homes in the ghetto.

While regular schools were banned in the ghetto, the Judenrat was permitted to maintain the vocational training schools sponsored by the ORT organization. The first training courses were opened in 1940, but they reached their maximum development after the ghetto was established. In mid-1941, 2,454 students were attending such courses; under the cover of vocational training, courses were also given in the arts, architecture, and graphic art. One of the courses, conducted by former university professors, was in medicine.

Cultural life in the ghetto consisted of activities conducted by the underground organizations. The Idische Kultur Organizacje (Yiddish Culture Organization; IKOR), a clandestine organization for promoting Yiddish culture, in which Emanuel Ringelblum and Menahem Linder were active, sponsored literary evenings and special meetings to mark the anniversaries of noted Jewish writers. The members of Tekumah (Rebirth), also an underground organization, took an interest in the Hebrew language and Hebrew literature. The ghetto had clandestine libraries that circulated officially banned books. An eighty-member symphony orchestra had a repertoire that included the works of the great German composers; at one point it was warned to restrict itself to Jewish composers. Well-known writers and poets continued to create in the ghetto, including Itzhak KATZENELSON, Israel Sztern, Jehoszua Perle, Hillel ZEITLIN, Peretz Opoczynski, and Kalman Lis. Theatrical troupes gave performances, the actors including well-known personalities of the Polish stage (such as Michael Znicz) or the Yiddish stage (Zigmunt Turkow and Diana Blumenfeld). Only some

of these performances and programs drew upon serious dramas for their repertoire. The audiences consisted mostly of the ghetto's nouveaux riches, who wanted cheap entertainment that would help them forget the surrounding reality.

Underground Political Parties and Youth Movements. Underground activities by political circles and organizations had already begun around the time that the Germans entered Warsaw. Missing were the veteran and experienced Jewish leaders, who had left the city (and the country). Nevertheless, after Warsaw was occupied, members of youth movements and parties joined together and began to prepare plans of action. As time went on the underground embarked upon several courses of action, one of which was to provide assistance to persons who were in the most dire straits. At an early stage, the question arose as to whether political organizations could confine themselves to material aid and abandon political activity. Such activity, in its conventional meaning, was impossible, but at clandestine meetings in the soup kitchens, open discussions and debates were held and the different political positions were probed. The next step was to establish an underground press and to persist in efforts to communicate with political elements outside the country.

Jews serving various branches of the German administration as agents, individually or in organized groups, were supposed to submit up-to-date reports on what was happening in the ghetto. They did not, however, divulge to the Germans details on the underground and its activities and did not give away the names of underground members. This may have been because the Germans were primarily interested in information on property hidden in the ghetto and on illegal economic operations. But the failure to mention the underground operations in the reports prepared for the Germans—some of which are now available—was presumably also the result of the agents' determination to withhold information on the political underground activities from their German masters.

The Germans' lack of interest in the underground activities and the silence on the subject observed by their Jewish agents in the ghetto enabled the underground, prior to the

Children in the Warsaw ghetto.

spring of 1942, to engage in a broad range of activities without the Germans taking drastic steps to suppress them or to punish the participants. The underground press led to two results: It provided the news-hungry ghetto population with reliable information on international political developments and on the war fronts; and it raised political and ideological issues that encouraged polemics and discussions. All parties from the prewar Jewish political scene were also active in the ghetto underground. Especially prominent were the Bund and the Socialist Zionist Po'alei Zion Left. The members of each of these parties had maintained close relations among themselves, over and above their partisan political association, and these ties stood the two organizations in good stead and gave them more staying power, even in the underground.

In the ghetto, the Judenrat and the ŻTOS agreed to cooperate with the underground. Representatives of the Jewish political parties—Maurycy Ozech of the Bund, Shakhne ZAGAN of Po'alei Zion Left, Joseph Sak and Shalom Grajek of the Po'alei Zion Zionist Socialists, Menahem Kirschenbaum of the General Zionists, David WDOWINSKI of the Zionist

Revisionists, and Alexander Zishe Friedman of the religious Agudat Israel—cooperated with one another, constituting an advisory body to the ŻTOS and meeting at moments of crisis and change.

A unique and important enterprise created in the ghetto was the Ringelblum Archive, code-named ONEG SHABBAT by the underground. While it was not initiated directly by the political bodies, the archive depended in large measure on the support of the public leaders and the underground organizations. The extant material collected by the Ringelblum Archive consists of tens of thousands of pages—documents, notes, diaries, and a rich collection of underground newspapers—and is the most important source collection for research on the fate of the Jews under the Nazi occupation of Warsaw and of all of Poland.

The Jewish YOUTH MOVEMENTS and their leaders played an important role in the underground, especially in the later stages: following the great deportation, during the months of preparation for the uprising, and during the WARSAW GHETTO UPRISING itself. Among them the Zionist, and particularly the *haluts* (pioneering), movements constituted

Children in the Warsaw ghetto.

the driving force. During the war and in the ghetto the activities of the youth movements underwent a gradual change, as did their relative weight. They manifested a greater aptitude than did other movements for adapting to the changing circumstances and for taking dynamic action when necessary. The youth leaders assembled in Warsaw—among them Mordecai ANIELEWICZ, Yitzhak ZUCKERMAN, Zivia LUBETKIN, Josef KAPLAN, and Israel Geller—by virtue of their keen political instincts and leadership qualities were no longer mere leaders of youth groups, becoming instead the acknowledged leaders of the underground.

The youth movements did not confine their activities to the local scene. The leadership that had been formed in Warsaw extended its work to cover the undertakings of the different movements' branches and cells in all the ghettos and Jewish communities in occupied Poland. Many of their programs were attended not only by Warsaw residents but by members from ghettos in other parts of Poland. The maintenance of such a countrywide organization was made possible by a network of liaison officers—young men and women—using underground methods. These messengers, under false identities (especially the girls), provided the link to the isolated ghettos, cut off as they were from the rest of the world.

Prior to the stage in which the mass killings of Jews were launched, no basic differences existed among the political parties and the youth movements in the underground. The youth movements were more active and

more daring, and engaged in a wider variety of operations, but they did not offer themselves as an alternative to the underground's political leadership or even to the Judenrat. They accepted the authority of the political parties, acknowledging them as the senior element in the underground. There was a consensus which agreed that every effort had to be made to ensure physical survival, and although the youth movements occasionally voiced some objections, they were part of this consensus. In addition to the struggle for survival, however, the youth movements felt the need to stress ideological and spiritual factors, and they made the moral and spiritual condition of the ghetto youth their special concern.

A drastic change in the relationship between the component parts of the underground and the general power structure in the ghetto took place when the mass murders were launched and the first reports came in of the massacres at PONARY and elsewhere. At this point a new concept arose—that the Germans had embarked upon the total destruction of the Jews and that therefore the Jews had no choice other than to stand up and fight, even if this offered no prospect of survival.

In March 1942, at a meeting of the Warsaw Jewish leaders, Yitzhak Zuckerman, on behalf of the youth movements, sought to win agreement for the formation of an overall self-defense organization. His proposal was turned down. Some of those present refused to lend credence to the somber views expressed by the young people, while the Bund leaders refused to support a separate Jewish defense organization, favoring a struggle based on the Jewish and Polish working class. The failure of this meeting to arrive at an agreement led to the establishment of the Antifascist Bloc, sponsored by the Communists, and also including the Zionist Left. This organization, which was in existence during March and April 1942, had a military arm five hundred strong. Its plan of escaping to the forests was not put into operation and the arms that it had expected did not arrive; just before the target date, in May 1942, the whole structure collapsed. The Communist leaders of the bloc were imprisoned and the bloc went out of existence.

The Deportations. In the months preceding the mass deportation from the Warsaw ghetto, increasing nervousness was felt, under the impact of growing reports and rumors of deportations from other ghettos and places of Jewish habitation in occupied Poland. On the other hand, the economic situation improved, in relative terms, mainly because more employment became available. Coupled with encouraging news of German setbacks on the war fronts, this helped create a certain sense of stability, and even optimism on the chances of survival.

Unrest and panic were created and grave doubts were raised among the ghetto population by the night raids undertaken by the German police. These raids were carried out according to prepared lists; the persons on the list were seized in their homes, taken out, and shot at a nearby location. The first, and worst, such murderous raid took place on April 18, 1942, when fifty-two persons were killed that night, "the bloody night," as it came to be known in the ghetto. The names on the list were a mixed lot. They included underground leaders, such as Menahem Linder, Ringelblum's friend, who had been active in IKOR; persons engaged in legal economic activities, such as bakers; and even persons known to be German agents. Adam Czerniaków met with underground activists and tried to persuade them to stop publishing the underground newspapers, since the Germans had claimed that the existence of the underground press was the reason for the executions. The underground leaders, consulting on the subject, came to the conclusion that the Germans were lying, and decided that rather than stop publishing the underground press, they would intensify doing so. They pointed out that in other places, where no underground press and no widespread underground activities existed, the Germans had also made murder raids in advance of deportations. The first raid was followed by others, on a smaller scale; in the opinion of the underground activists, the purpose of these raids was to instill terror among the population and remove from the ghetto persons whom the Germans thought might take the lead in offering resistance.

Reports on the deportations are to be found in the underground press and in diaries.

Even in death there is no dignity. The ghetto hearse, carting emaciated bodies to the cemetery. [Steidl Verlag]

Czerniaków repeatedly recorded such rumors and fears in his diary. His entry of July 20, 1942, is of special significance. This date was two days before the deportation, when the German unit that was to carry it out was already present in Warsaw, ready for action. Czerniaków decided to turn to the Germans, with whom he had been in contact for nearly three years, and ask them what was really going on. He was sent from one official to the other, each claiming that they knew nothing and that there was no basis for the rumors.

Several days prior to the beginning of the planned *Aktion*, an SS officer, Hans Höfle, an aide of Odilo GLOBOCNIK and commander of the AKTION REINHARD unit, arrived in Warsaw. Together with the Gestapo section for Jewish affairs, Höfle drew up the plan for the deportation from the Warsaw ghetto. Several members of the Judenrat were arrested and held as hostages, and on the eve of the deportation, notices were posted listing the categories of Jews who were to be "evacuated." The Jews, full of fear and trepidation, interpreted the announcement to mean that 60,000 unemployed and starving Jews would be deported, while all those who were employed, including the sick among them, would not be affected. The *Aktion* began on July 22, 1942, and continued until September 12. On July 23, Adam Czerniaków committed suicide. He had been ordered to provide a daily quota of 7,000 Jews for deportation, and to include children in this number. Czerniaków was not prepared to have anything to do with turning over Jews, and preferred to put an end to his life. He was replaced by the deputy chairman, the engineer Marek Lichtenbaum.

Czerniaków's death, which cast a pall over the ghetto, led to a decline in the Judenrat's standing and its ability to function. The Germans used the Jüdischer Ordnungsdienst to help them in the deportation. The commander of the Jewish police, Joseph Szerynski (a convert from Judaism), was in jail at the time, facing charges of illegally trading in furs that he had been ordered to confiscate. The acting commander, a lawyer named Jacob Lejkin, undertook the assignment, and with the help of two thousand to twenty-five hundred policemen carried it out with precision and determination. Lejkin's excuse was that it was better for the operation to be in the hands of Jews, because if it were handled by the Germans and their Ukrainian and Latvian helpers, far more brutal methods would be applied and no distinction would be made between those earmarked for deportation and those exempt.

In the first few days of the deportation, the ghetto inhabitants streamed into the German factories (which were called "shops") or into workshops that were under German protection; there, they thought, they would be safe from deportation. The Jews used whatever savings they had left to buy their way into employment in a "shop"; one popular method was to be in possession of work tools, especially a sewing machine. In the first few days the permits exempting Jews from deportation were honored, and the Germans indiscriminately stamped the large number of work permits that were submitted to them. On the second day, 7,300 Jews were seized; on the third day, 7,400; and on the fourth, 7,350. The columns of Jews were taken on foot to the UMSCHLAGPLATZ (transfer point) at the northern end of the ghetto, on the corner of Zamenhof and Niska streets. Once there, the deportees were packed into freight trains,

100 Jews per car; the next day the train was back, empty, and ready to take on another "transport." The *Umschlagplatz*, or *Umschlag*, as it was generally referred to, was from the start of the deportations the scene of the worst crises and the greatest fear in the tragic history of the Warsaw Jewish community.

In the first ten days, sixty-five thousand Jews were taken from the ghetto. This meant that the Germans had filled the quota they had announced. Even in this first phase, which lasted to the end of July, there were several instances, when the daily quota had not been met, of the SS, the German police, and their Ukrainian and Latvian helpers' breaking into the ghetto alleys, rounding up people at random in the streets, and dragging them out of their homes, without paying any heed to the paper in their possession or to the exempt status they had by virtue of the permits they held.

In the second phase, from July 31 to August 14, the German forces and their helpers took direct charge of the *Aktion* and the roundups, with the Jewish police in a secondary role. The German police and the auxiliary police, made up of Ukrainians, Latvians, and Lithuanians—a force of some two hundred armed men—saw the *Aktion* through, day after day. On Saturday, August 1, Abraham Lewin wrote in his diary: " 'Outside, the sword deals death, and inside, terror' (Lamentations 1:20). This is the eleventh day of the *Aktion*, which becomes more terrible and more cruel from one day to the next. The Germans are clearing whole buildings and entire sections of streets of their inhabitants . . . today's sufferings are worse than any that preceded them."

Rumors, of unknown origin, were rife in the ghetto that the *Aktion* would be over in a day or two, but they were false. An announcement was made that people who reported voluntarily on August 2, 3, or 4 would be issued 6.6 pounds (3 kg) of bread and 2.2 pounds (1 kg) of jam, and that their families would be kept together. In the first week of August, 200 children were taken out of Janusz KORCZAK's orphanage. Dr. Korczak and his team of assistants went to the railway cars together with the children, the elderly educator refusing offers to help him save himself. Ringelblum recorded in his diary: "Korczak set the tone: everybody [all the instructors at the orphanage] was to go to the *Umschlag* together. Some of the boarding-school principals knew what was in store for them there, but they felt that they could not abandon the children in this dark hour and had to accompany them to their death."

The third phase of the deportation began on August 15 and ended on September 6. At this point the deportation took on the character of a total evacuation. The Germans and their helpers conducted a manhunt, combing the streets and the apartment houses, seizing every person they found at home, looking into every corner, and hardly taking note of the papers and exemptions produced by the Jews. Jews who were employed in the "shops" sought refuge there with their families, but the Germans showed no mercy for any of them. First to be deported were the unskilled workers, and then it was the turn of the skilled workers, entire "shops" being emptied of their work force. It became increasingly difficult to round up people, and the Germans compelled every Jewish policeman to bring in a daily quota of five Jews per day; a policeman who failed to fill the quota had his mother, wife, and children taken away. A growing number of policemen deserted the force, and some went into hiding. From mid-August, individuals who had managed to escape from the TREBLINKA extermination camp (in the freight cars carrying out the victims' clothing collected in the camp) succeeded in infiltrating back into the ghetto, and reported on the fate in store for the deportees when they reached their destination.

The final phase began on September 6. The "shops" and the Judenrat were allotted a number of permits; 35,000 such permits were issued, meaning that the Germans intended to leave in the ghetto 10 percent of its pre-deportation population. The bearers of the permits were assembled in a street bottleneck in the David Quarter, where they had to pass through a final inspection and selection. Their bundles too were inspected. In their memoirs, some of the victims recorded that from time to time, when the guards stuck their bayonets into bundles carried on the back of some of the people in the line, the sound of a baby's cry would ring out from the bundle.

In addition to the 35,000 who had permits, another 25,000—and perhaps more—managed to remain in the ghetto. This was a new ghetto, consisting of three separate parts. The central area contained several "shops"; the Judenrat, whose authority was curtailed or completely abolished; several installations belonging to the Judenrat; and Jews who were in the employ of Germans outside the ghetto. The second, smaller part was named the "shops area" and contained two large factories, those of Többens and Schultz. The third part was a small enclave that also contained one of the "shops." During working hours Jews were not allowed in the street. The three parts were not connected with one another and the residents of one could not cross over to another, even after working hours. In effect, this was no longer a ghetto but a labor camp.

The Jews who were left, mostly women and young men, the last remnants of their families, went through a great psychological change. As long as the deportations were going on, the Jews had been in a constant state of tension, concentrating all their strength on one goal: to survive where they were, and not be put into the deportees' column and taken to the *Umschlag*. When the deportations came to a halt, they had time to take stock of their situation. It was clear to all that their lives were as much in danger as before, and that all they had was a short period of grace before another deportation would take place—the final one. They were lonely and deeply troubled by a sense of guilt, at having forsaken their dear ones and failed to protect them. They were ashamed of not having offered any resistance, of not having used force to defend themselves, and of not having even raised a hand against the hated Jewish policemen. More and more of them said that they would not surrender to the Germans without a fight.

The Underground and the Ghetto. On July 23, the day after the deportation was launched, a meeting was called of underground leaders and public figures who were close to the underground. The representatives of the youth movements and of some of the political factions, including the Bund, favored forming a defense organization that would resist the deportation by force. The leading public figures participating were reluctant to take such a step or opposed it outright. The historian Ignacy (Yitzhak) SCHIPER argued that armed resistance would put the whole ghetto in jeopardy; this was not the first time in history that the Jewish people had to sacrifice some of its sons in order to assure its continued existence as a people, and such a sacrifice had also to be made this time. Alexander Zishe Friedman, the popular Agudat Israel representative, put his faith in God, who would not forsake His people; resistance offered no hope. On the seventh day of the deportation, July 28, representatives of Ha-Shomer ha-Tsa'ir, Dror, and Akiva held a meeting at which they decided to form the ŻYDOWSKA ORGANIZACJA BOJOWA (Jewish Fighting Organization; ŻOB). Included in the group of founders were Yitzhak Zuckerman, Josef Kaplan, Samuel Breslaw, Zivia Lubetkin, Mordechai TENENBAUM-Tamaroff, and Israel Kanal. A headquarters was set up and it was decided to send a delegation, headed by Arie WILNER, to the "Aryan" side. Mordecai Anielewicz, who was to be the ŻOB commander in its formative stage and the leader of the revolt, was absent from the meeting, having left Warsaw on a mission to Zagłębie.

Although the organization was founded, it had no means at its disposal and had as yet to adopt a clear policy on the way it would conduct the struggle. One of the ŻOB's first steps was to publish and distribute leaflets informing the public of the fate of the deportees and what Treblinka stood for. The ghetto population does not seem to have taken kindly to the publication of these leaflets, regarding them as a provocative act that would give the Germans a pretext for the total liquidation of the ghetto.

When the deportation was in full swing, the Bund sent one of its men, Zalman Friedrich, on a mission to ascertain the destination of the deportation trains and gather information on that destination. Friedrich managed to get close to Treblinka, collect information on what was happening there, and return safely to the ghetto. On the basis of his report, the Bund put out a special issue of its underground paper, giving precise details of the fate that lay in store for the deportees.

The first steps taken were to try to acquire weapons and to draw up a plan of action. An attempt to establish ties with the ARMIA KRAJOWA (Home Army), the Polish military underground organization, did not succeed, since the man through whom Arie Wilner had hoped to set up such ties broke off all contacts. The Communists were more willing to help, and it was with their assistance that the ŻOB obtained its first arms shipment—five pistols and eight hand grenades.

The ŻOB passed a death sentence on Szerynski, the Jewish police commander, who had been released from jail in order to help the Germans in the deportation. The attempt made on Szerynski's life, in which he was wounded, had a tremendous impact on the ghetto, but only the underground members and those close to the organization knew who was responsible for the attempt. On September 3, 1942, the ŻOB faced its first crisis. In a surprise raid by the Gestapo on a "shop" where the ŻOB had its principal base, Josef Kaplan, one of the organization's leaders, was arrested. Another prominent member, Samuel Breslaw, who tried to set Kaplan free, was shot in the street. In another incident, a young woman member of the ŻOB, who was transferring the organization's weapons from Mila Street to another location, was caught by the Germans with the entire store of the ŻOB's arms on her person. A deep sense of frustration set in among the ŻOB members, and youngsters among them demanded that they all take to the streets, seize anything they could use as a weapon, and put an end to the ghetto's placid acceptance of the situation. This was opposed by several of the ŻOB leaders, who persuaded the youngsters to drop the idea and utilize the expected lull for thorough preparations for the final struggle.

When the wave of deportations came to an end, the ŻOB began operating under different conditions. Mordecai Anielewicz returned to the ghetto and assumed a leading role in the organization's activities. Arie Wilner established contacts with the Armia Krajowa, which led to its recognition of the ŻOB as a fraternal organization in league with it, and to its supplying a modest quantity of pistols to the Jewish fighters. Most of the ŻOB's arms, however, were acquired by purchasing them from middlemen, who had bought or stolen them from Germans or their helpers. A profound change in public opinion had taken place in the ghetto, and as a result, underground groups of different political orientations were now willing to join the Jewish Fighting Organization. By October the ŻOB had been consolidated and enlarged, with the addition of youth movements and splinter groups of underground political parties of all persuasions, from Zionists to Communists. A ŻOB command was formed, made up of representatives of the founding organizations and the fighting groups.

In addition to the ŻOB, the Żydowski Komitet Narodowy (Jewish National Committee) was formed, composed of prominent public figures, which gave the ŻOB its support. The Bund was not prepared to join a public body together with Zionists, but it agreed to establish a joint Coordinating Committee with the national committee. It was this Coordinating Committee that was the ghetto underground's overall representative body vis-à-vis the Poles and that also sought support and resources on behalf of the ŻOB from among the ghetto population. One of its important achievements was to raise funds for the purchase of arms. Many of the contributors gave money of their own free will, others only after pressure and threats. The fund-raising, in its different forms, was in the hands of the Jewish National Committee and the Coordinating Committee.

In that period another organization came to be formed in the ghetto, under Revisionist (Zionist) auspices. The Zionist Betar movement and the Revisionist underground did not integrate into the ŻOB or the national committee, for various reasons, and their members set up their own fighting organization, the ŻYDOWSKI ZWIĄZEK WOJSKOWY (Jewish Military Union), headed by Pawel Frankel. The union also established ties with one of the groups in the Polish underground, and used methods similar to those employed by the ŻOB to raise money and acquire arms. For some time there was serious tension between the two bodies, but shortly before the revolt they began to coordinate their activities, with the Jewish Military Union accepting the ŻOB's authority. The ŻOB operated primarily in Warsaw, but it also established branches in other large ghettos and helped to transform the Jewish youth organization into fighting formations.

Deportation and Resistance in January 1943. The second wave of deportations was launched on January 18, 1943. This time, however, the Jews who were ordered to assemble in the courtyards of their apartment houses to have their papers examined refused to comply and went into hiding. The first column that the Germans managed to round up, in the first few hours, consisting of some one thousand persons, offered a different kind of resistance. A group of fighters led by Mordecai Anielewicz and armed with pistols deliberately infiltrated the column that was on its way to the Umschlag, and when the agreed-upon signal was given, the fighters stepped out of the column and engaged the German escorts in hand-to-hand fighting. The column dispersed, and news of the fight, which had taken place in the street of the central ghetto, soon became common knowledge.

That first day the Germans also met with armed resistance on Zamenhof Street, from an apartment in which a group of Dror members, including Yitzhak Zuckerman, had taken up positions. The resistance, especially the fight that had taken place in the street, left its imprint on the January deportations. These continued until January 22, by which time the Germans had rounded up five thousand to six thousand Jews from all parts of the ghetto; after the events of the first day, hardly any Jews responded to the German order to report.

The fact that the *Aktion* was halted after only a few days, and that the Germans had managed to seize no more than 10 percent of the ghetto population, was regarded, by Jews and Poles alike, as a German defeat. The Warsaw Jews who had lived through the first great wave of deportations had believed that the next deportation would be the last, and that the ghetto would be liquidated. The actual outcome was regarded as a German retreat, caused by the resistance they encountered from the fighters and from the general population of the ghetto. It is now known that the Germans had not intended to liquidate the entire ghetto by means of the January deportations. In fact, they were carrying out an order given by Heinrich HIMMLER, after a visit he made to Warsaw on January 9, to remove 8,000 Jews from the ghetto and reduce its population to the level the Germans had decided on after the great deportation in the summer and fall of 1942.

The deportations and other events that took place in January were to have a decisive influence on the last months of the ghetto's existence, up to April and May of 1943. The Judenrat and the Jewish police lost whatever control they still had over the ghetto. In the central part of the ghetto it was the fighting organizations that were obeyed by the population. Globocnik appointed one of the German "shop" owners, Többens, as ghetto commissar. His assignment was to transfer the machinery and workers of the major "shops" in the Warsaw ghetto to labor camps in the Lublin area. Többens, however, ran into opposition from the workers, who were taking their instructions from the ŻOB.

The Jewish resistance also impressed the Poles, and they now provided more aid to the Jewish fighters than in the past. The fighting organizations used the few months they had left before the final liquidation to consolidate, equip themselves, and prepare a plan for the defense of the ghetto. The ŻOB now had twenty-two fighting squads, of fifteen fighters each; the Military Union had about half the number of fighters, but it operated in a similar manner.

The ghetto as a whole was engaged in feverish preparations for the expected deportation, which all believed would be the last and the final one. The general population concentrated on preparing bunkers. Groups of Jews, made up mostly of tenants of the same building, went to work on the construction of subterranean bunkers; such shelters, on a subterranean level or in the cellars, had proved very useful during the January deportation. However, there was more than that to the preparation of bunkers in the period from January to April 1943. The January experience gave new hope to the ghetto population, who felt that the Germans might perhaps want to hold back and avoid a military clash with the Jews of the ghetto in a large city that was the capital of Poland and contained the hard core of the Polish resistance movement. Many Jews were now ready to entertain the hope that the combination of resistance and hiding out might provide the route to rescue. The fighters and the general population now had a common interest, with each having its allotted task. The ŻOB was to be the armed force that would battle in the open, and the masses of the people were to hide out in the bunkers, in what would be another form of joint resistance.

The fighters and their commanders were under no illusion and did not believe that their fighting would lead to rescue. They were preparing for a revolt that would be a final act of protest, a last sign of life that they would send to the Jews and all of humanity in the free world. For this reason they made no attempt to prepare retreat or escape routes that would be available when the fighting was over, their decision being that the only choice open to them was the readiness to fight until the last breath in their bodies.

The network of bunkers in the ghetto was being expanded, and a substantial part of the ghetto population was kept busy at night digging the hideouts and communication trenches under the ground. Much thought and sophistication went into the planning of the entries and exits of the subterranean hiding places. Bunkers and wooden bunks were installed in them, and air circulation was provided for, as well as electricity and water supplies, food, and medicines to last for months. The preparation of bunkers became a mass movement in the central ghetto area, and as the final deportation drew near, every inhabitant of the ghetto had two addresses—one on the ghetto surface and a subterranean one in a bunker.

Final Liquidation and Revolt. The final liquidation of the ghetto began on Monday, April 19, 1943, the eve of Passover. This time the deportation did not come as a surprise. The Jews had been warned of what lay ahead and they were ready. The Germans had a substantial military force on the alert for the deportation, but they do not seem to have expected the direct confrontation of street battles. The German authorities did not rely on SS-Oberführer Ferdinand von Sammern-Frankenegg, the *SS- und Polizeiführer* (Higher SS and Police Leader) of the Warsaw district. They called in SS and Police General Jürgen STROOP, who had had experience in fighting the partisans, to supervise the deportation and liquidation of the ghetto. Stroop's daily reports on the battle against the ghetto and his final summing-up when the revolt had

WARSAW GHETTO UPRISING, APRIL 19, 1943

© Martin Gilbert 1982

come to an end constitute the basic historical documentation of the resistance offered by the Jews and the methods used by the Nazis to overcome it.

According to Stroop, the *Grossaktion* (major *Aktion*) began on April 19, when a strong police force surrounded the ghetto at 3:00 a.m. The German armed force that had been readied for the operation consisted of 850 men and 18 officers, under the command of Sammern-Frankenegg. It entered the ghetto in two sections, met with armed resistance, and was forced to retreat.

On the first day, and even more effectively in the days that followed, the Germans became aware of the kind of uprising they were facing. The central ghetto, which had a population of more than thirty thousand, was completely empty—not a soul was to be seen in the streets or in the buildings, except for a Jewish police unit and a handful of Judenrat members. No Jews could be rounded up for deportation, and the freight cars that had been brought in and were waiting for the Jews in the *Umschlagplatz* had to remain empty. The magnitude of the hiding operation took the Germans as much by surprise as the dimensions of the armed resistance.

In the first three days, street battles were fought in the ghetto. The systematic burning of the ghetto, building by building, did, however, force the fighters to abandon their positions, to take refuge in the bunkers, and to go over to a different method of fighting the Germans, by making sorties in small groups of fighters and taking the Germans by surprise. In the first two nights no German soldier was to be seen in the ghetto.

The ghetto was now one great burning torch. It was enveloped in dense smoke and permeated by stifling odors, its very air seeming to burn. The bunkers became infernos. Situated underground, with buildings or ruins of buildings on top, the bunkers and the air in them reached the boiling point; the food was spoiled by the devastating heat, the water was warm, and it stank. The Jews inside had taken off their clothes, could hardly breathe or talk, and were on the verge of going mad. Even so, they would not surrender to the Germans. Under cover of darkness they tried to move from the living hell their bunkers had become to other bunkers where conditions were slightly better—although these too were bound to suffer the same fate and become uninhabitable within a few days.

In the second week of the uprising, the bunkers were the main arena of resistance. In this fight, the Germans had to struggle for each bunker, one by one. By throwing hand grenades into the bunker, or by forcing in tear gas or poison gas, in the end they compelled the Jews to emerge. In many instances the Jews kept on fighting when they came out; barely conscious from the poisoned and scorching darkness, they fired their pistols at the first German they saw.

On May 16, Stroop announced that the *Grossaktion* had been completed. To celebrate the victory, he ordered Warsaw's Great Synagogue, which was situated outside the ghetto, to be burned down and destroyed. In his daily dispatch Stroop made it a point to brag: "The Jewish quarter of Warsaw no longer exists" ("Das ehemalige jüdische Wohnviertel Warschau besteht nicht mehr").

The fact is that even after May 16, Jews were still hiding out in bunkers and continued to live there. There were also reports of armed clashes taking place amid the ruins of what had once been the ghetto. As much as a year later, during the WARSAW POLISH UPRISING that was launched in August 1944, individual Jews were still found in the labyrinth of the ghetto's bunkers.

In his final report on the military campaign that he led against the ghetto revolt, Stroop provided the following data: "Of the total of 56,065 Jews who were seized, 7,000 were destroyed during the course of the *Grossaktion* inside the former Jewish quarter; in the deportation to T2 [the Treblinka extermination camp] 6,929 were exterminated, which adds up to 13,929 Jews destroyed. In addition to the 56,065, another 5,000 to 6,000 lost their lives in explosions and fires." Stroop's figures are exaggerated. His report also mentions that the German losses were sixteen killed and eighty-five wounded; these figures do not tally with the daily casualty reports that Stroop submitted during the fighting. Some sources believe that the German losses were much higher.

In the last few months of its existence, some twenty thousand Jews left the ghetto to seek refuge on the Polish side. A special organization, ZEGOTA, was created by the underground Polish political parties, within the Polish underground movement, to extend aid to Jews. It did this with great devotion, and approximately four thousand Jews benefited from Zegota's assistance at various times. In Poland it was more difficult to help Jews than in other occupied countries; offering shelter to a Jew was punishable by death. The main reason why only a small number of Jews were able to hide out was the proliferation of extortionists, Poles who out of greed or for other reasons made it their business to turn Jews over to the Germans. In addition to the "RIGHTEOUS AMONG THE NATIONS" who helped Jews out of humanitarian motives, quite a few Poles sheltered Jews for money. No data are available on the number of Jews who were saved by hiding or by posing as Poles. Many of these Jews fell in battle or were killed during the Warsaw Polish uprising, in which Jews also took an active part.

The revolt in the ghetto had tremendous reverberations among the remaining Jews of Poland, among the non-Jews in the country, and in all of Europe. Even while the war was still in progress, the story of the Warsaw ghetto uprising became a legend that was passed on, with awe and emotion, as an event of rare historical significance.

Warsaw Jews who were forced out of the bunkers or otherwise fell into German hands during the uprising were not all murdered on the spot, nor were all the people transported from the *Umschlagplatz* in April and May 1943 taken straight to their death. Transports made up of Jews from the "shops area," where resistance had not been so fierce, were sent to PONIATOWA and TRAWNIKI. From the central ghetto, many transports had MAJ-DANEK and BUDZYŃ as their destination. Most of these Jews were killed in early November 1943, in the "ERNTEFEST" murder operation. Several thousand Jews who were taken to the Majdanek concentration camp were deported, after a short stay there, to AUSCHWITZ and to labor camps in the western parts of occupied Poland. When all the *Selektionen*, transfers, and evacuations were over, no more than one thousand to two thousand of these Jews had survived.

When the war ended the surviving Jews made their way back to the cities where they had lived before the war. Some two thousand survivors gathered in Warsaw within a few months, and were given first aid by the Jewish Committee that began functioning in the city. Warsaw did not attract a large concentration of Jews, Lublin being preferred, as the place where the Polish administration and a new life were gaining hold. It was only when the reconstruction of Warsaw had progressed and the Polish institutions were reestablished there that the central Jewish organizations followed suit and moved to Warsaw.

The ŻYDOWSKI INSTYTUT HISTORYCZNY (Jewish Historical Institute), which was set up in a wing of the building housing the Institute of Jewish Studies, embarked upon what became a highly important effort of collecting documents and mementos of the Jews of Poland and the Holocaust period. Warsaw became the seat of the Central Committee of the Jews of Poland, followed, in 1950, by the Cultural and Social Union of the Jews of Poland. Eventually, twenty thousand to thirty thousand Jews settled in Warsaw, most of whom had not lived there before the war. The great majority of these Jews left in the waves of Jewish emigration from Poland in the postwar period.

Only a few sites of Jewish Warsaw have remained, the most important being the Jewish cemetery on Okopowa Street and the Nozik synagogue on Twarda Street. Much work has been invested in rehabilitating and maintaining the cemetery, and some of the street names, such as Anielewicz Street, serve as reminders of the past and of the last days of Jewish life in the city. The site of the bunker where the ŻOB had its headquarters, on Mila Street, is marked by a memorial tablet. On the fifth anniversary of the ghetto revolt, in 1948, a monument by the sculptor Nathan Rapaport was dedicated on Ghetto Heroes' Square, a site that had once been in the heart of the Jewish quarter. Later a memorial boulevard was established, to mark the path of suffering taken by the Jews who were making their way from their ancient quarter to the *Umschlagplatz,* now also marked by a memorial.

BIBLIOGRAPHY

Gutman, Y. *The Jews of Warsaw, 1939–1943: Ghetto, Underground, Revolt.* Bloomington, 1982.

Hersey, J. *The Wall.* New York, 1967.

Hilberg, R., et al. *The Warsaw Diary of Adam Czerniakow: Prelude to Doom.* New York, 1979.

Kaplan, C. A. *Scroll of Agony: The Warsaw Diary of Chaim A. Kaplan.* London, 1966.

Mark, B. *The Uprising of the Warsaw Ghetto.* New York, 1975.

Ringelblum, E. *Notes from the Warsaw Ghetto: The Journal of Emanuel Ringelblum.* New York, 1958.

ISRAEL GUTMAN

WARSAW GHETTO UPRISING, the first urban uprising in German-occupied Europe, and, among the Jewish uprisings, the one that lasted the longest, from April 19 to May 16, 1943. In the spring of 1942 some members of the Jewish underground of the Warsaw ghetto, especially those in the Zionist pioneering movements, under the impact of the reports of a mass murder campaign in the east had come to the conclusion that a defense force had to be formed that would go into action if an attempt were made to deport the Jews from the ghetto. Efforts to organize such a force met with resistance from various groups in the underground, and by the time the mass deportations from the Warsaw ghetto were launched on July 22, 1942, no unified Jewish resistance force had come into being. A resistance organization called the Antifascist Bloc had been formed in April 1942 and operated for a while, but it included only some of the underground elements, and failed to attain the goals it had set for itself.

When the deportations began, renewed efforts were made to establish a fighting organization, consisting of the various underground factions operating in the ghetto; but this attempt too was quashed by some of the ghetto leaders, who believed that armed resistance posed an intolerable threat and could lead to the end of the entire Jewish ghetto population, including those who might otherwise be saved. Nevertheless, the ŻYDOWSKA ORGANIZACJA BOJOWA (Jewish Fighting Organization; ŻOB) was founded on July 28, on a more modest scale, consisting only of the three Zionist pioneering movements, Ha-Shomer ha-Tsa'ir, Dror, and Akiva. The operational plans of the new organization in the summer of 1942 had little effect, and initial attempts to establish contact with the Polish military underground ARMIA KRAJOWA (Home Army) were also unsuccessful. Indeed, in that early period of its existence the ŻOB suffered serious debacles, and lost many of its fighters and leaders in the deportations. The deportations came to a halt in mid-September, by which time about 300,000 Jews had been removed from the ghetto, 265,000 of them deported to the TREBLINKA extermination camp. This left a Jewish population of 55,000 to 60,000 in the ghetto.

These survivors felt isolated and bitter. Most of them were young people who now blamed themselves for not having offered armed resistance against the deportation of their families. They were also well aware that having survived that first wave of deportations, they had not yet been saved, and that they were experiencing merely a temporary lull between one wave of deportations and the next.

This mood was shared by the factions in the ghetto underground. In October more of them joined the ŻOB, which now represented all the active forces in the underground, with the exception of Betar and the Revisionists, who set up a fighting organization of their own, the ŻYDOWSKI ZWIĄZEK WOJSKOWY (Jewish Military Union; ŻZW). At that point the ŻOB emissaries finally succeeded in establishing contact with the Armia Krajowa, the major element in the Polish military underground, gaining its recognition and obtaining from it a very small quantity of arms—ten pistols and some explosive charges. This was a far cry from what the ŻOB needed to equip its members, but it was an important boost to morale. A headquarters was established for the ŻOB, under the command of Mordecai ANIELEWICZ; it embarked upon the training of the fighters and laid plans for resistance.

On Monday, January 18, 1943, before the ŻOB had completed its preparations, the Germans launched the second wave of deportations, the "January *Aktion*." It was this second *Aktion* in the ghetto by the German police and SS that became the ŻOB's first military test. Judging by what it had experienced in the first wave of deportations, which had taken 83 percent of the Jews in the ghetto, the surviving Jewish population assumed that the second *Aktion* was to be the final deportation of Warsaw's Jews. German documents that have since come to light reveal that this was not so, and that the second *Aktion* was planned to remove from the ghetto no more than 8,000 Jews. The *Aktion* came as a surprise, and the ŻOB leadership was unable to meet and decide on a coordinated reaction. Even so, the *Aktion* did not proceed as the Germans had planned and expected. The two companies that were equipped with arms—Ha-Shomer ha-Tsa'ir and Dror—went into action. The main operation, commanded by Mordecai Anielewicz, took place in the street. A group of Ha-Shomer ha-Tsa'ir men, armed with pistols, deliberately broke into a column of Jews that were being marched to the UMSCHLAGPLATZ (assembly point), and when the agreed sign was given they confronted the German escorts in a face-to-face battle. That fight was the first in which Germans were attacked in the ghetto. Most of the Jewish fighters fell in the battle, although Anielewicz was able to overcome the German soldier with whom he was struggling and was saved. The long column of Jews scattered in all directions. News of the battle soon reached the rest of the beleaguered Jews; in one place, a building on Zamenhof Street, a squad of Dror men, commanded by Yitzhak ZUCKERMAN, lay in waiting, and when the Germans appeared on the scene they were met by a hail of fire.

That day, January 18, 1943, was not only the ŻOB's baptism of fire. In the course of the *Aktion* that the Germans launched that day and which lasted for four days, there was a decisive change in the ghetto population's pattern of behavior. When the first column had dispersed, the Germans were no longer able to set up another one, since the Jews refused to respond to the shouts ordering them to get out of their houses and report to the assembly points. The majority of the ghetto Jews were concealed in improvised hiding places. The Germans also acted in a different manner, desisting from their usual ear-splitting cries, moving quietly, and keeping away from places where Jews might be hiding. When the *Aktion* ended, on the fourth day, five thousand to six thousand Jews had been caught. The Jews interpreted the early discontinuation of the *Aktion* by the Germans as a sign of weakness and a retreat before the force that had confronted them; the Polish underground also assumed that the Jewish resistance had compelled the Germans to interrupt the *Aktion*.

These events in January had a decisive impact on the preparations that were being made for the next uprising; the three months from January to April were utilized for feverish activities to put the ŻOB in a state of readiness for the forthcoming test on the field of battle. One of the lessons that the ŻOB had learned from the January events was that the ghetto might once again be taken by surprise with an *Aktion* and that therefore the ŻOB

Facing page: In the four weeks between April 19 and May 16, 1943, a group of young Jewish men and women armed with little more than pistols faced a heavily armed German force three times larger. Gen. Jürgen Stroop (fourth from the right, second photo on left) was the "leader of the grand operation." Unable to capture the Jewish fighters, the Germans burned the ghetto down building by building, forcing the Jews hiding in bunkers inside to come out (second and third photos on right). Hans Frank, the governor-general of Poland, visited the ghetto during the uprising (front center, smiling, bottom photo on left). "The Jewish Quarter of Warsaw Is No More!" was the text on the title page of *The Stroop Report*, a commemorative album bound in leather. It was in three parts: a descriptive introduction; daily communiqués on the progress of the "operation"; and a series of fifty-four photographs. Three sets were prepared. One was presented to Himmler, one to Gen. Friedrich Wilhelm Krüger, *Höherer SS- und Polizeiführer Ost*, and one to Stroop. The bottom photo on right shows the ghetto in flames as seen from the Polish side. [*The Stroop Report*]

and all its fighters had to be on a permanent alert. A total of twenty-two fighting units were formed in that period, based on the movements to which their members belonged. They were each assigned to apartments controlled by the ŻOB, located in the immediate vicinity of the positions that the ŻOB planned to occupy when the time came. Another "January lesson" was that the enemy had to be taken unaware by the attacks and that these had to be launched from well-prepared positions in the maze of the ghetto buildings and roof attics. Accordingly, the ghetto, or parts thereof, was divided into fighting sectors with designated positions, with a fighting unit attached to each. Anielewicz was in overall command of the ŻOB and the ghetto; Israel Kanal commanded the central area, Yitzhak Zuckerman (followed by Eliezer Geller) the factory units (the "shops"), and Marek EDELMAN the units in the area of the brushmakers' stores. A ŻZW force, commanded by Pawel Frenkiel, entrenched itself in the Muranowski Square area.

The weapons in the hands of the fighting organizations were mostly pistols—the personal weapon of the individual fighter; some of them had been obtained from Polish organizations, but for the most part they had had to be purchased. The ŻOB also had automatic weapons and rifles that its men had seized from the Germans, and the ŻZW had obtained weapons from Polish sources. In addition, hand grenades were manufactured in the ghetto, and these were to play an important role in the fighting during the uprising. In this waiting period between January and April, the ŻOB could have recruited many new members to its ranks, but a real expansion of the force was precluded by the lack of arms. Shortly before the uprising was launched, the ŻOB's armed and organized force consisted of twenty-two fighting platoons, with a total of 500 fighters. The ŻZW had 200 to 250 fighters, and the total Jewish fighting forces in the ghetto numbered 700 to 750.

The civilian population of the ghetto also underwent a transformation that was to have a decisive impact on the course of events during the uprising. The Jews in the ghetto believed that what had happened in January was proof that by offering resistance it was possible to force the Germans to desist from their plans. Many thought that the Germans would persist in unrestrained mass deportations only so long as the Jews were passive, but that in the face of resistance and armed confrontation they would think twice before embarking upon yet another *Aktion*. The Germans would also have to take into account the possibility that the outbreak of fighting in the ghetto might lead to the rebellion spreading to the Polish population and might create a state of insecurity in all of occupied Poland. These considerations led the civilian population of the ghetto, in the final phase of its existence, to approve of resistance and give its support to the preparations for the uprising. The population also used the interval to prepare and equip a network of subterranean refuges and hiding places, where they could hold out for an extended period even if they were cut off from one another. In the end, every Jew in the ghetto had his own spot in one of the shelters set up in the central part of the ghetto. Many of these civilian shelters also had a cache of defensive weapons. The civilian population and the fighters now shared a common interest based on the hope that, under the existing circumstances, fighting the Germans might be a way to rescue.

The ŻOB command did not share the optimistic appraisal that armed resistance might deter the Germans from carrying out their plans, but it encouraged the digging of bunkers and their being equipped for a long stay. The ways in which preparations proceeded for the forthcoming crucial test—the military measures undertaken by the fighting organizations, the attitude of the general population, and the network of bunkers that it prepared—turned the uprising on April 19, coinciding with the last *Aktion*, which was launched on that day, into a widespread popular revolt, with far-reaching consequences.

The three months between January and April were used for intensively training the fighting forces, acquiring weapons, and drawing up a strategic plan for the defense of the ghetto. The last *Aktion* and the resistance campaign that came to be known as the Warsaw ghetto uprising began on April 19, 1943, which was the eve of Passover. The ghetto fighters had been warned and had advance knowledge of the timing of what was to be the final deportation. There is no doubt that the chief of the SS and police in the Warsaw district, Obergruppenführer Ferdinand von Sammern-Frankenegg, was aware of the existence of a Jewish defense formation, but he apparently did not dare admit to his superiors in Kraków that a significant Jewish fighting force had been established in the ghetto. Heinrich HIMMLER did not rely on Sammern-Frankenegg, and on the eve of the final deportation he replaced him with a man who had had experience in fighting partisans, SS- und Polizeiführer (SS and Police Leader) Jürgen STROOP, whose task it became to suppress the uprising and bring the ghetto to its knees.

In the twenty-seven days that the uprising lasted, the Nazis deployed a considerable military force, including tanks, that in the first days of the fighting consisted, on the average, of 2,054 soldiers and policemen and 36 officers. Facing them were 700 to 750 young Jewish fighters who had had no military training or battle experience and who for all practical purposes were armed with no more than pistols.

On the morning of April 19, when the German forces entered the ghetto they did not find a living soul in the central part, except for a group of policemen. The entire Jewish population had taken to the hiding places and bunkers, and by refusing to comply with the Germans' orders they became part of the uprising. That day, following the first clash, the Germans were forced to withdraw from the ghetto. They lost a tank and an armored vehicle that had been hit by Molotov cocktails, and they were unable to capture the ŻOB and ŻZW position on Muranowska Square, where two flags were raised on top of a building—the flag of Poland and a blue-and-white Jewish national flag. In the first of his daily reports on the fighting in the ghetto, Stroop stated: "As soon as the units were deployed they were attacked by coordinated fire from the Jewish bandits; the tank that had been sent into battle and the two armored vehicles had Molotov cocktails thrown at them. The tank caught fire twice. This enemy assault at first compelled our forces to withdraw. Our losses in this first operation were twelve (six SS men and six TRAWNIKI men)."

The face-to-face fighting lasted for several days. The Germans were not able to capture or hit the Jewish fighters, who after every clash managed to get away and retreat by way of the roofs; nor could the Germans lay hands on the Jews hiding in the bunkers. The Germans therefore decided to burn the ghetto systematically, building by building; this forced the fighters to take to the bunkers themselves and to resort to partisan tactics by staging sporadic raids. The flames and the heat turned life in the bunkers into hell; the very air was afire, the food that had been stored up spoiled, and the water was no longer fit to drink. Despite everything, the bunker dwellers refused to leave their hideouts.

Stroop's report for April 22 contains the following passage:

> The fire set during the night forced the Jews who, despite all the search operations, were still hiding—under the roofs, in cellars, and other secret places—to appear in front of the housing blocks in an attempt to find some way of escaping the flames; large numbers of Jews, entire families at a time, their clothes afire, jumped from the windows or tried to climb down on bed sheets that they had tied together, or in some other fashion. We made sure that these Jews, like all the others, were liquidated on the spot.

The bunker war—the burning of the bunkers—turned out to be the Germans' most difficult and troublesome task. Time and again Stroop claimed in his daily reports that he had overcome resistance and that the uprising was dying out, only to report the next day that there was no end to the attacks and the losses suffered by his troops.

Gradually, however, the Jews' power of resistance declined. On April 23 Mordecai Anielewicz wrote to Yitzhak Zuckerman, the member of the ŻOB command who was on the "Aryan" side:

> I cannot describe to you the conditions in which the Jews are living. Only the chosen few will hold out; all the others will perish, sooner or later. The die is cast. In the bunkers where our comrades are hiding out no candle can be lit at night because of the lack of air. . . . From all the companies in the ghetto, only one person was killed, Yehiel; that, too, is a victory of sorts. . . . Peace be with you, my dear friend; perhaps we shall still meet again. The main

thing is that my life's dream has been realized: I have lived to see Jewish defense in the ghetto in all its greatness and glory.

One of the fighters' most vulnerable points was their lack of arms, both qualitatively and quantitively. The small-caliber pistols in their possession were not suitable for street fighting, and, in spite of the fighters' stubborn persistence and daring, the losses they inflicted on the Germans were quite small. The people in the bunkers put up a desperate fight, but their cause was hopeless from the outset when the entire ghetto was in flames and all inside were trapped. The Poles reported that units of the Polish military underground undertook to rally to the help of the Jews; some of these fighters fell in the attempt, but not a single group was able to penetrate the wall and get into the ghetto.

On May 8 the headquarters bunker of the ŻOB at 18 Mila Street fell, and with it also Mordecai Anielewicz and a large group of fighters and commanders. The ŻOB fighters had not made any plans for a retreat from the ghetto, their assumption being that the battle would go on inside the ghetto until the last fighter had fallen. Thanks to a rescue mission arranged by the ŻOB men on the Polish side that made its way through the sewers of the city, several dozen fighters were saved.

The fighting in the ghetto lasted nearly a month. The Jews in the bunkers who were not discovered by the Germans' dogs or by means of special search instruments the Germans used kept up their resistance as long as they were alive. The Nazis also threw gas grenades into the bunkers, when the Jews inside refused to leave even after they had been forced open.

On May 16 Stroop announced that the fighting was over and that "we succeeded in capturing altogether 56,065 Jews, that is, definitely destroying them." He stated that he was going to blow up the Great Synogogue on Tłomacka Street (which was outside the ghetto and the scene of the fighting) as a

Survivors of the Warsaw ghetto uprising are arrested by German soldiers (September–October 1944). [National Archives]

The Ghetto Uprising monument in Warsaw by the Israeli sculptor Nathan Rapaport, unveiled in 1948. The other side of the monument is called "The Last March" and depicts the deportation of the Jews from Warsaw. A replica of this monument was created by Rapaport for Yad Vashem in Jerusalem. It is located at the edge of a large plaza where official remembrance ceremonies are held. [Geoffrey Wigoder]

symbol of victory and of the fact that "the Jewish quarter of Warsaw no longer exists."

Even after May 16 there were still hundreds of Jews in the subterranean bunkers of the ghetto, which was now a heap of ruins. They sneaked out of the bunkers during the night in search of food and water and kept in touch with one another. The last survivors among these fighters succeeded in establishing contact with the Poles and escaping to the "Aryan" side. Only a handful held out in the bunkers until the WARSAW POLISH UPRISING in August 1944.

The Warsaw ghetto uprising was the first instance in occupied Europe of an uprising by an urban population. Its unique feature was the fact that it was a general rebellion, in which armed fighters took part together with masses of Jews hiding out in bunkers and refuges. The common fate that the fighters and "civilians" knew they shared and their utter determination made the Warsaw ghetto, starved and humiliated though it was, a bastion of resistance and fighting that battled the forces of Nazi Germany and stood up against them for a longer period than some independent countries in Europe had held out.

[*See also* Ghetto; Resistance, Jewish.]

BIBLIOGRAPHY

Friedman, P. *Martyrs and Fighters.* New York, 1954.

Gutman, Y. *The Jews of Warsaw, 1939–1943: Ghetto, Underground, Revolt.* Bloomington, 1982.

Hersey, J. *The Wall.* New York, 1967.

Lubetkin, Z. *In the Days of Destruction and Revolt.* Tel Aviv, 1981. (In Hebrew.)

Lubetkin, Z. "The Last Days of the Warsaw Ghetto." In *The Fighting Ghettos*, edited by M. Barkai, pp. 64–87. Philadelphia, 1962.

Mark, B. *The Uprising of the Warsaw Ghetto.* New York, 1975.

Milton, S., and A. Worth, eds. *The Stroop Report: The Jewish Quarter of Warsaw Is No More.* New York, 1979.

Sakowska, R., et al. *The Warsaw Ghetto: The Forty-fifth Anniversary of the Uprising.* Warsaw, 1988.

ISRAEL GUTMAN

WARSAW POLISH UPRISING, the Polish uprising against the Germans in the summer of 1944. It broke out on August 1, on the instigation of the ARMIA KRAJOWA, the largest Polish resistance organization, which took orders from the POLISH GOVERNMENT-IN-EXILE in London. The aim of the uprising was to seize control of Warsaw before the Red Army entered the city, a development that was expected to take place shortly. The rebel forces amounted to some twenty-three thousand ill-equipped troops. They were facing tens of thousands of German troops and police, who were plentifully supplied with arms and equipment.

The uprising did not come as a surprise to the Germans. In the first few days it extended over large parts of central Warsaw, as well as the more distant quarters of several suburbs and a number of points on the right bank of the Vistula River. Not a single bridge or enemy stronghold was captured by the attacking Polish force.

Four days later the Germans launched a counterattack, with the help of reinforcements. The attack, under the command of Erich von dem BACH-ZELEWSKI, was accompanied by mass terror and inhuman methods of fighting. The aid that came to the Poles from the western Allies did not amount to more than a few arms drops. In the early stages of the revolt, the Soviets hindered the Allied aid. Only in the later stages, in mid-September, did the Soviets themselves drop some supplies.

Most of the Polish fighters were young people. Several smaller leftist resistance organizations led by the Armia Ludowa (*see* GWARDIA LUDOWA) joined the uprising. The Armia Ludowa also included a group of Jews, mem-

Dr. Władysław Bartoszewski and Countess Tarnowska, both of the Polish Red Cross, acting as Gen. Tadeusz Bor-Komorowski's delegates. They are seeking a truce with the Germans after sixty-three days of resistance.

bers of the ŻYDOWSKA ORGANIZACJA BOJOWA (Jewish Fighting Organization; ŻOB), who had succeeded in leaving the ghetto after the Jewish revolt there had been quashed the previous year (*see* WARSAW GHETTO UPRISING). Other Jews as well took part in the uprising.

On August 4 the rebels liberated several hundred Jewish prisoners (from Greece and Hungary) from the concentration camp on Gesia Street, and the latter joined in the fighting. The civilian population of the city gave strong support to the uprising, by publishing newspapers, providing first aid, organizing supplies and postal services, and so on. On September 14, Polish army units that had previously been parachuted into Warsaw seized control of the right bank of the Vistula and managed to transfer several battalions to the left bank, suffering heavy losses in the process. They could not, however, bring relief to the insurgents. The besieged city center fell on October 2, and this marked the end of the uprising.

Polish losses came to between 16,000 and 20,000 fighters killed and missing, 7,000 wounded, and 150,000 civilians killed. The last figure included several thousand Jews who had been in hiding with the Polish population after the liquidation of the ghetto. German losses were 16,000 dead and missing, and 9,000 wounded.

The Germans expelled most of the surviving civilians to nearby camps, and 65,000 of them were subsequently transferred to concentration camps. About 100,000 were conscripted for forced labor in the Reich and the rest were dispersed over the GENERALGOUVERNEMENT. Following the insurgents' surrender, the Germans burned and razed those parts of the city that were still intact. The uprising and the total destruction of Warsaw also caused great losses to Poland's cultural and spiritual treasures.

BIBLIOGRAPHY

Grunspan, R. *The Uprising of the Death Box of Warsaw*. New York, 1978.

Hanson, J. K. M. *The Civilian Population and the Warsaw Uprising of 1944*. Cambridge, 1982.

Korbonski, S. *The Polish Underground State: A Guide to the Underground, 1939–1945*. New York, 1969.

Zawodny, J. K. *Nothing but Honor: The Story of the Warsaw Uprising, 1944*. Stanford, 1978.

KRZYSZTOF DUNIN-WASOWICZ

WARTHEGAU (Wartheland), territorial administrative unit established by the German occupiers in October 1939 in the Polish territories annexed to the Reich; it existed until Poland and the adjoining territories were liberated in January 1945. The term "Warthegau" originated from the name of the river Warthe (Pol., Warta). At first the region was called Reichsgau Posen (Reich District Posen), which on January 9, 1940, was changed to Reichsgau Wartheland.

The area of the Warthegau was 16,966 square miles (43,942 sq km) and included the prewar Posen region (now the Poznań province) and parts of the districts of Bydgoszcz, ŁÓDŹ, Pomerania (Pol., Pomorze), and WARSAW. The region was divided into three districts: Posen, Hohensalza (Pol., Inowrocław), and Kalisz (as of April 1940, Łódź), and into thirty-eight rural and six urban subdistricts. The Warthegau was the largest administrative district in the Reich.

During the first weeks of World War II, 4,922,000 persons were living in the area, of whom 385,000 were Jews and 325,000 Germans. The administrative head throughout the occupation was Arthur GREISER, the president of the DANZIG senate. From September 14 to October 25, 1939, Greiser was the head of the civil administration attached to the military commander of Posen (Zivilverwaltung beim Militärbefehlshaber Posen), and later was the local Reich commissioner (*Reichsstatthalter*). Hitler also appointed Greiser regional Nazi party leader (*Gauleiter*) of the Warthegau. Under Greiser's management the Warthegau was planned as an example of the development of National Socialist relations for the entire Reich. For this reason Greiser declared the region to be an area of experimentation in National Socialism (*Exerzierplatz des Nationalsozialismus*), the purpose of which was to try out methods of dealing with the local population. He divided up the population according to race into "superior persons" (*Übermenschen*) and "inferior persons" (*Untermenschen*), assigning the Ger-

WARTHEGAU

mans to the first group and Poles, Jews, and GYPSIES to the second. Within a few weeks, the *Übermenschen* had taken over all the managerial positions at all levels of political, business, and economic administration. In their everyday life, the *Übermenschen* enjoyed a variety of economic, political, and cultural privileges. A comprehensive network of primary and secondary schools (and, as of 1941, universities as well) was established exclusively for them. During the first months of the German occupation and the setting up of the Warthegau administration, hundreds of cinemas and scores of theaters and museums were made available to the *Übermenschen*; concerts and other cultural events were organized for *Übermenschen* only.

In most of the restaurants and coffee-houses, special sections were set apart "for Germans only" (*nur für Deutsche*). Only they were allowed to enter hotels, first- and second-class railway carriages, and the better streetcars, and only they were allowed to fre-

quent public baths, the seashore, and public parks.

The attitude of the German authorities toward the Poles was that they were to be persecuted and some even killed. During the occupation more than seventy thousand Poles were killed, and others were sent to CONCENTRATION CAMPS. Other means of persecution included curtailing the Polish birthrate by breaking up families through sending one of the spouses to forced labor in the Reich; preventing couples from marrying; expulsion; maximum exploitation of ability to work; starvation wages; meager rations of food and clothing; arduous living conditions; and deficient welfare and health services.

The German authorities in the Warthegau discriminated against the Poles in the economic area as well. They expropriated 95.5 percent of all Polish property; closed down the education network, the publishing houses, and all Polish organizations; prohibited Poles from going to libraries, public reading rooms, theaters, concerts, and other cultural events; and prevented them from visiting public swimming pools, certain seashores, and parks. Children were forbidden to use playgrounds; the use of the Polish language was restricted in public affairs; serious limitations were imposed on holding religious ceremonies; and in 1941 religious life was divided up according to nationality. The Germans demanded that Poles were not to be addressed by the term *Pan* (Mr.); Poles were not allowed to have contacts with Germans other than official ones, and Germans were not permitted to greet Poles with handshakes. Other actions against the Poles included the imposition of curfews, and bans on travel, on changing one's address without permission of the authorities, on the use of public telephones, on possession of radios, and on the mailing of parcels without prior police inspection. In some places the local Nazi authorities demanded that Poles make way for Germans on the pavements and at times not even greet them. Owing to all these harsh measures, the Germans called the region the "Warthegau punishment camp" (*Straflager Warthegau*), a definition also used at times by the SD (Sicherheitsdienst; Security Service) in official documents.

One of the most tragic chapters in the German policy toward the inhabitants was the annihilation of the Jews in the region. The fate of the Jews can be divided into four periods: (1) up to the end of 1939; (2) from the beginning of 1940 to the middle of December 1941; (3) from the end of 1941 to August 1944; and (4) from September 1944 to the end of the occupation.

Even in the first four months of the war, the German authorities were discriminating against the Jews and had begun a process that was to culminate in annihilation. During the first weeks of the occupation, decisions were taken to designate the Jews by making them wear a Jewish BADGE (the Star of David), to expel them, to expropriate their property, to send them to forced-labor camps, to forbid them to change their domicile without permission, and to restrict or ban their use of public transport and communications. Jews were to immediately cease their involvement in political, cultural, and educational activities, and a ban was placed on their religious ceremonies. During these four months, the occupation authorities in some places did not confine their activities to routine discriminatory practices, but initiated acts of murder against the defenseless Jewish inhabitants. Only a few hours into the occupation, Jews were shot by Wehrmacht soldiers out of racial hatred. At first the Germans dealt with the Jews living in small towns: some were shot or bayoneted to death and the rest were herded into the synagogues, which were then burned down or destroyed by hand grenades being tossed into them.

During the second phase, the Germans concentrated the Jews in 173 forced-labor camps or ghettos. Many died of starvation, torture, atrocious hygienic conditions, enforced hard labor, lack of medical attention, and so forth. In 1940 several thousand Jews were brutally murdered.

In the third phase, after the construction of the extermination camp at CHEŁMNO, the majority of the Warthegau's Jewish population was annihilated. In Chełmno approximately 310,000 Jews from the region were put to death, including several tens of thousands who had been transported from Germany,

Austria, and Czechoslovakia to the Łódź ghetto. Some 70,000 Jews were sent from the Warthegau to AUSCHWITZ, and the great majority perished there. During the final period of the occupation, the rate of extermination of the Jews remaining in the Warthegau was reduced, because the Germans had decided to exploit their professional expertise for the benefit of the German economy.

A total of 380,000 Jews in the region were put to death. Only 5,000 Jews remained alive, constituting 1.3 percent of the prewar Jewish population. As part of the annihilation of the "alien racial element," several hundred Gypsies living in the Warthegau were murdered, as were a further 5,000 Gypsies who had been transported from other areas to Chełmno.

Throughout the entire period of the occupation, 450,000 persons were killed and another 20,000 died as a result of military operations. The German authorities expelled more than 630,000 persons from the region, and 450,000 were relocated to hard-labor camps in the Reich. Twenty-five thousand fell ill with chronic diseases and 15,000 were physically disabled, mainly as a result of spending extended periods in concentration camps and prisons. The value of the damage to property in the Warthegau totaled several billion zlotys (according to prewar values, one dollar was equivalent to 5 zlotys).

BIBLIOGRAPHY

Dobroszycki, L., ed. *The Chronicle of the Lodz Ghetto, 1941–1944.* New Haven, Conn., 1984.

Luczak, C. *Przyczynki do gospodarki niemieckiej w latach 1939–1945.* Poznań, 1949.

Nawrocki, S. *Policja hitlerowska w Kraju Warty w latach 1939–1945.* Poznań, 1970.

Pospieszalski, K. M., ed. *Hitlerowskie prawo okupacyjne w Polsce.* Vol. 1. Poznań, 1952.

CZESŁAW LUCZAK

WDOWINSKI, DAVID (1895–1970), one of the founders and leaders of the ŻYDOWSKI ZWIĄZEK WOJSKOWY (Jewish Military Union; ŻZW) in the WARSAW ghetto. Wdowinski was born in Będzin, and at the end of World War I was active in a Jewish self-defense organization in Lvov. He studied at the universities of Vienna, Brno, and Warsaw, and became a psychiatrist. At the request of Vladimir JABOTINSKY, the leader of the Zionist Revisionist movement, Wdowinski gave up his professional practice and devoted all his time to working in the leadership of the Revisionist movement in Poland.

Wdowinski was an active member of the Warsaw ghetto underground and represented his movement in the advisory body of the Żydowskie Towarzystwo Opieki Społecznej (Jewish Mutual Aid Society). In the summer of 1942 he helped found the ŻZW, which was headed by members of Betar (the youth wing of the Revisionist movement), and he was apparently responsible for formulating the ŻZW's policy lines. Following the WARSAW GHETTO UPRISING, Wdowinski was imprisoned in concentration camps. After the war he emigrated to the United States. He published a book of memoirs, *And We Are Not Saved* (1963), which recounted his activities and those of the Betar movement in the Warsaw ghetto. Wdowinski was a witness at the EICHMANN TRIAL in Jerusalem in 1961. He died of a heart attack during a memorial meeting for the Warsaw ghetto uprising, in Tel Aviv in 1970.

BIBLIOGRAPHY

"Warsaw Ghetto Recollections." In *Anthology on Armed Resistance, 1939–1945.* edited by I. Kowalski, pp. 127–138. New York, 1984.

ISRAEL GUTMAN

WEHRMACHT, the armed forces of GERMANY in the period from 1935 to 1945. The name was adopted when the military draft was introduced on March 16, 1935 (in violation of the Treaty of Versailles), replacing the name Reichswehr, which had been its designation under the Weimar Republic. In April 1938 the Wehrmacht's land forces consisted of twenty-eight divisions. By the beginning of World War II this number had grown to seventy-five, consisting of 24,000 officers and 2.7 million men of other ranks on active service, as compared with the 100,000 military personnel, including 4,000 officers, that had been the official total of the Reichswehr.

In 1938 Hitler established the OKW (Oberkommando der Wehrmacht, or Armed Forces High Command) under Wilhelm KEITEL, as a consulting organization. It was to coordinate the activities of the OKH (Oberkommando des Heeres; Army High Command), the OKL (Oberkommando der Luftwaffe; Air Force High Command), and the OKM (Oberkommando der Kriegsmarine; Navy High Command). When the war broke out, most of the actual fighting was in the hands of the OKH because the war was largely land-based. As the war progressed, Hitler transferred divisions from the OKH to the OKW, turning the latter into a combat high command. By the end of 1941 all the theaters of the land war were under the jurisdiction of the OKW except for the eastern front, which remained under the OKH. In 1943, when the Wehrmacht was past its prime, especially with regard to equipment, it still had 13,555,000 personnel under its command (*see* Table 1).

Nazi indoctrination of the Wehrmacht gathered momentum in 1938 at the latest, after Hitler's spectacular successes in annexing territories without resorting to war (AUSTRIA; the Sudetenland, followed by BOHEMIA AND MORAVIA; and MEMEL) and the drafting of Nazi-trained age groups from the HITLERJUGEND and the Reich labor services. Any disapproval of Nazi atrocities committed in the wake of the September 1939 campaign in Poland was for the most part silenced after the spectacular victory over France in May and June of 1940. Hardly any opposition was voiced to the criminal orders issued by Hitler in connection with the "ideological war" against the Soviet Union that he launched in June 1941. It was only in the fall of 1941 that objections were raised in the Wehrmacht to Hitler's policy, when it became apparent that the original timetable of "Barbarossa" (the code name for the invasion of the Soviet Union in 1941) could not be kept and that, at best, a drawn-out war was a likelihood.

Only a very small number of Wehrmacht officers opposed Hitler's destructive policy at its inception. Part of this group was immobilized at an early stage, while the rest made prolonged but futile efforts to create a broad-based military opposition to him and to win support abroad for a coup d'état. On the

TABLE 1. *Wehrmacht (1943)*

COMBAT TROOPS	
Feldheer (Land Forces)	4,647,000
Luftwaffe (Air Force)	990,000
Kriegsmarine (Navy)	170,000
Heere in der Heimat und Ostgebieten (Forces in the Reich and in the East)	526,000
Luftwaffensoldaten in der Heimat und Ostgebieten (Air Force in the Reich and the East)	393,000
Ersatzheer (Army Reserves)	1,767,000
Luftwaffe Ersatz und Ausbildungseinheiten (Air Force Reserves and Training Units)	363,000
Kriegsmarine Ersatz und Ausbildungseinheiten (Naval Reserves and Training Units)	617,000
Waffen-SS	280,000
Ersatz Waffen-SS (Reserve Waffen-SS)	70,000
Total Combat Troops	9,823,000
OTHER PERSONNEL	
SS und Polizei (SS and Police Forces)	600,000
Ostruppen, Hilfswillige, Legionen, und Italienische Neuaufstellungen (Ostbattalione, Volunteer Auxiliaries, Legions, and "New Italian Drafts")	939,000
Wehrmachtsgefolge (Wehrmacht "Retinue")[1]	967,000
Kriegsgefangene und Internierte (Prisoners of War and Internees)	1,226,000
Total Other Personnel	3,732,000
Grand Total	13,555,000

[1]"Retinue" personnel included the Reich labor service, Organisation Todt, German Red Cross, and Reich railway, postal, and customs services.

other hand, the Wehrmacht was witness to the mass-murder actions committed by the Einsatzgruppen, and Wehrmacht units were employed in support of these actions. Some of the senior Wehrmacht commanders, such as Walter von REICHENAU, justified the murder campaign against the Jews in their orders to the troops. Again and again, and even in 1943 and 1944, efforts to organize an action by the German officers' corps against Hitler came to naught because of a vain hope for victory, quarrels among the field marshals and among the various branches of the service, and the fear that such an action would lead once again to the creation of a DOLCHSTOSSLEGENDE ("stab-in-the-back" myth). The renowned homogeneity of a "conservative" officers' corps no longer existed, not even in the army, where it was reputed to have been particularly strong. Any remaining doubt was removed when, in the wake of the abortive July 20, 1944, attempt on Hitler's life, the senior generals set up a court of honor and promptly dismissed those colleagues suspected of having had even the faintest connection with the attempt, handing them over to the Gestapo and to the People's Court (*Volksgerichtshof*).

The claim made after the war that the Wehrmacht was unaware of the "Final Solution" and the other Nazi atrocities is easily refutable, at least as far as the OKW and the OKH are concerned.

[See also Abwehr.]

BIBLIOGRAPHY

Barnett, C. *Hitler's Generals*. London, 1986.
Goerlitz, W. B. *History of the German General Staff, 1657–1945*. New York, 1953.

Wehrmacht Day, Nuremberg (1935). Left to right: Adolf Hitler; Generaloberst Hermann Göring, commander in chief of the Luftwaffe; Generalfeldmarschall Werner von Blomberg, commander in chief of the Wehrmacht; Generaloberst Werner von Fritsch, commander in chief of the army; Generaladmiral Erich Raeder, commander in chief of the navy; (?); Generalmajor Wilhelm Ritter von Leeb.

Messerschmidt, M. *Die Wehrmacht im NS-Staat: Zeit der Indoktrination.* Hamburg, 1969.

Schramm, P. E., ed. *Kriegstagebuch des Oberkommandos der Wehrmacht: Wehrmachtsführungsstab 1940–1945.* 8 vols. Munich, 1982.

Taylor, T. *Sword and Swastika: Generals and Nazis in the Third Reich.* New York, 1952.

Wheeler-Bennet, J. W. *The Nemesis of Power: The German Army in Politics, 1918–1945.* London, 1953.

HANS-HEINRICH WILHELM

WEHRMACHT INTELLIGENCE SERVICE.
See Abwehr.

WEILL, JOSEPH (1902–1988), French activist in the underground and in welfare organizations. Born in Bouxwiller, Alsace, Weill was the son of Rabbi Ernest Weill, a leading French scholar. Weill was a physician, and before the war he directed a private hospital in Strasbourg. At the outbreak of World War II he was recruited into the army and was responsible for health services for the inhabitants of the French region bordering on Germany, who had been dispersed throughout central France. The temporary resettlement had been carried out by the French authorities in order to protect these civilians.

When France fell, in June 1940, Weill was the medical adviser of the Jewish organization OEUVRE DE SECOURS AUX ENFANTS (Children's Aid Society; OSE). Thanks to his extensive connections in government circles, he was allowed access to the detention camps in the south of France, where the Vichy government had assembled tens of thousands of Jews with their families in degrading conditions of distress and malnutrition. The detailed and exact reports that Weill circulated on the condition of these detainees alerted Swiss and American humanitarian organizations to the need for assistance. As a direct consequence, the French authorities released from the camps hundreds of old people and thousands of children, a process involving many months of negotiations and not completed until the spring of 1941. Most of those released were taken into OSE institutions.

When deportations from France to eastern Europe began, Weill and his helpers rescued hundreds of Jewish children from the hands of the police. Weill showed his aides how to prepare forged identity cards for these children in order to hide their Jewish identity. He created an underground organization, the Réseau Garel (Garel Network), which placed the children with Christian and nonreligious families and institutions involved in saving Jews.

Activists in the Réseau Garel kept in constant touch with each child and paid his or her monthly maintenance. They worked to bolster the children's spirits and helped them to maintain their attachment to Judaism. In all, the Réseau Garel cared for four thousand children, and smuggled over one thousand of them into Switzerland. Not one of the children entrusted to this organization was lost.

In May 1943, with the Gestapo on his trail, Weill was compelled to flee to Switzerland. There, he dealt with the absorption of the Jewish children smuggled out of France and, with the aid of the smuggling network, was responsible for transferring JOINT DISTRIBUTION COMMITTEE funds to Jewish underground workers in France. On Weill's initiative, extension courses in local medical schools were authorized in the first half of 1944 for about two hundred Jewish doctors interned in refugee camps in Switzerland. Weill also brought about sixty young people from these camps into an abridged social-work course taught by Dr. Paul Baerwald, in an effort to prepare a professional labor force to care for survivors of the Nazi camps.

After the war, Weill served as president of the Consistoire Israélite, the umbrella organization of the Jewish communities of Alsace.

His autobiography, titled *Déjà . . . Essai autobiographique*, was published in 1983.

BIBLIOGRAPHY

Keren-Patkin, N. "Jewish Children: Salvation Projects in France." *Yalkut Moreshet* 36 (1983): 101–150. (In Hebrew.)

Kieval, H. J. "Legality and Resistance in Vichy France: The Rescue of Jewish Children." *Proceedings of the American Philosophical Society* 124 (1980): 339–366.

Lazare, L. *La résistance juive en France.* Paris, 1987.

Weill, J. *Contribution à l'histoire des camps d'internement dans l'anti-France.* Paris, 1946.

LUCIEN LAZARE

WEIMAR REPUBLIC. *See* Germany.

WEISSMANDEL, MICHAEL DOV (1903–1956), rabbi; one of the leaders of the PRACOVNÁ SKUPINA (Working Group), a Jewish underground organization in SLOVAKIA. Born in Debrecen, Hungary, Weissmandel attended rabbinical academies in Trnava and Nitra in Slovakia. In 1935 he accompanied his teacher Rabbi Samuel David Ungar (who was also his father-in-law) on a trip to Palestine, together with an ultra-orthodox Agudat Israel delegation headed by Unger.

In October 1940 a JUDENRAT, the ÚSTREDŇA ŽIDOV (Jewish Center), was established in Slovakia. Between March and October 1942, 40,000 of Slovakia's 90,000 Jews were deported to the Lublin reservation in Poland, and 18,000 to the AUSCHWITZ extermination camp. The Pracovná Skupina was set up at the height of the deportations, and it became the central agency for rescuing Jews, aiding deportees in Polish camps, gathering and disseminating information on the extermination of Jews in Poland, and establishing links to Jewish and non-Jewish organizations abroad.

Together with Gisi FLEISCHMANN, the head of the Pracovná Skupina, Weissmandel tirelessly sought ways of rescuing Jews, and he pleaded for help from every possible source, in Slovakia and abroad. In his letters to Jewish organizations and individuals, written in rabbinic Hebrew, he voiced harsh criticism of

Michael Dov Weissmandel.

their failure to respond without delay to his demands.

In the summer of 1942, Weissmandel favored the proposal of some activists within the Ústredňa Židov to pay a ransom to Dieter WISLICENY, Adolf EICHMANN's deputy in Slovakia, in exchange for the cessation of deportations from Slovakia to extermination camps; a sum between $40,000 and $50,000 was in fact paid, in two installments. Weissmandel and the other members of the Pracovná Skupina believed that it was these payments that stopped the deportations from Slovakia. After the Holocaust, others claimed that the cause of the stoppage was opposition from Slovak cabinet ministers and influential persons, together with pressure brought to bear by the Catholic church and public opinion.

Basing themselves on their experience with Wisliceny, the members of the Pracovná Skupina believed that negotiations for the rescue of Jews from all parts of occupied Europe in exchange for money stood a chance of succeeding. This program came to be known as the EUROPA PLAN. When the group failed in its efforts to come up with a down payment of $200,000 toward the total sum of $2 million to $3 million, as demanded by Wisliceny, Weissmandel sought to gain time by deception. Using official stationery that he had obtained from Switzerland, he produced fictitious letters containing positive replies to his requests for money, signing them "Ferdinand Roth," supposedly a "representative of world Jewry."

On March 19, 1944, Weissmandel wrote to friends in Budapest to inform them of his contacts with Wisliceny, who had been posted there following the Nazi seizure of HUNGARY. But by the time the deportations of Hungary's Jews were launched, in May of that year, Weissmandel had changed his mind regarding contacts with the Nazis, and he advised these same friends to "beware of deceit and trickery"—to try to escape and offer resistance, but under no circumstances to enter the ghettos.

On April 7, 1944, two Jews from Slovakia, Walter Rosenberg (Rudolf Vrba) and Alfred Wetzler, managed to escape from Auschwitz. They reported to the Pracovná Skupina on the death factory in operation there, and also produced a precise sketch of the camp layout (see AUSCHWITZ PROTOCOLS). A few weeks later, on May 27, two more Jews, Czesław Mordowicz and Arnost Rosin, escaped from Auschwitz, confirmed the evidence given by Rosenberg and Wetzler, and reported on the destruction of Hungarian Jewry. This information was passed on to Jewish organizations abroad, as well as to the government of Slovakia and to the Catholic church in that country. Gisi Fleischmann and Weissmandel took the lead in organizing this information campaign. Weissmandel repeatedly demanded that the Allies bomb Auschwitz—the camp, the railway lines leading to it, and the bridges and tunnels en route. These efforts were in vain (see AUSCHWITZ, BOMBING OF).

The deportations from Slovakia were resumed in the fall of 1944, following the suppression of the SLOVAK NATIONAL UPRISING and the occupation of the country by the Germans. Weissmandel and his family were put on a train to Auschwitz. He managed to jump off during the journey, went into hiding in the Bratislava area, and eventually left Slovakia in a train, organized by Rezsö (Rudolf) KASZTNER, that took him and other Jews to Switzerland. From there he left for the United States.

In Mount Kisco, New York, Weissmandel reestablished the Nitra *yeshiva*, and it was from there that he issued a manifesto in which he virulently denounced Zionism and the premature establishment of a Jewish state, "before the Almighty willed it and sent the Messiah." His book *Min ha-Metzar* (*From the Depths*), containing his memoirs and views, was published posthumously in 1960.

BIBLIOGRAPHY

Forst, S. "Biographical Fragments and Aspects of the Life of Michael B. Weissmandel." *The Jewish Observer* 2 (June 1965): 9–13.

Fuchs, A. *The Unheeded Cry.* New York, 1984.

Neumann, O. J. *In the Shadow of Death: The Campaign for the Rescue of the Jews of Slovakia.* Tel Aviv, 1958. (In Hebrew.)

SHLOMO KLESS

WEIZMANN, CHAIM (1874–1952), statesman and scientist; first president of the state of Israel. Born in Motol, in the Pale of Settlement in Russia, Weizmann moved at the age of eleven to nearby Pinsk. In 1892 he went to Germany, and for two years, in 1892 and 1893, studied at the Darmstadt Polytechnic. He then (until 1897) studied dye chemistry at the Charlottenburg Polytechnic in Berlin. In 1897 Weizmann entered Fribourg University in Switzerland, from which he received his Ph.D. in chemistry in 1899. He settled in Manchester, England, in 1904, and by 1913 had risen at the University of Manchester to the rank of reader in biochemistry; he had also assumed key roles within the World Zionist Organization and the English Zionist Federation.

Following the entry of Turkey into World War I, Weizmann decided that the cause of Zionism had to be tied to Great Britain. He made an outstanding and unique contribution to the British war effort with his fermentation process yielding acetone, a solvent necessary in arms production. Weizmann was the key Zionist negotiator in the attainment, on No-

vember 2, 1917, of the Balfour Declaration, which offered British support for the creation of a Jewish national home in Palestine. In 1920 he was elected president of the World Zionist Organization, and he initiated the establishment of an enlarged Jewish Agency in 1929.

In August 1933, the Zionist Congress nominated Weizmann, then out of office, to head the Jewish Agency's Department for the Settlement of German Refugees. Weizmann's first action was to try to coordinate all Jewish relief activities and to streamline the strategies of the Jewish organizations involved in such work. His efforts met with little success, since the differences in the philosophies and orientations of the various Jewish groups were too deep to be bridged within a brief period. Weizmann opposed mere philanthropy; he always wished to bring about an organized, carefully controlled immigration of German Jews and other refugees to Palestine, to the extent that the country could absorb them. Nevertheless, in light of the increased persecution of German Jews, he did not adopt a rigid policy. On the contrary, he hoped that a large influx of immigrants would greatly enhance the Zionist enterprise in Palestine. He felt that the young Jews, who had no future in Germany, should be given preference and that as much of their property as was possible to save ought to be transferred to Palestine. Although he was not personally involved in the details of the HAAVARA AGREEMENT, he supported it. Weizmann also expended much effort in trying to persuade outstanding scientists to emigrate to Palestine; besides wishing to save their lives, he wanted to establish Palestine as an international center of scientific research.

Returning to office as president of the World Zionist Organization in 1935, Weizmann used his diplomatic connections to try to blunt the racial persecution of Jews in Germany and elsewhere. Shortly after Hitler assumed the chancellorship in 1933, Weizmann had met with Ramsay MacDonald, the prime minister of Great Britain, and other British ministers. He also turned repeatedly for help to Benito MUSSOLINI, with whom he met, to Jan Christian Smuts, the prime minister of South Africa, and to French diplomats. To all of them, as well as in various international

Chaim Weizmann (standing) at a meeting of Jewish Agency leaders in Jerusalem (1945). [Central Zionist Archives, Jerusalem; Beth Hatefutsoth]

forums, he protested against the racial, civil, and economic discrimination against Jews.

On the eve of World War II, Weizmann pledged full Jewish cooperation against Hitler to the British prime minister, Neville Chamberlain, and he proposed the establishment of a Jewish fighting division under its own flag within the British military forces. As the Nazi destruction of European Jewry proceeded, Weizmann was involved in trying to organize desperate rescue efforts, all declined by Great Britain. An example was his plea, in September 1939, for the suspension of the WHITE PAPER regulations severely limiting Jewish immigration to Palestine during this period of emergency, so that European Jews might find refuge there. In February 1943 Great Britain also rejected a proposal, probably emanating from the Romanian government, asking for $3.5 million—$50 per person—as "security" in exchange for transferring 70,000 Jews to a place of refuge, preferably Palestine.

In May 1944, Joel BRAND, a Zionist official in Budapest, brought a report to Palestine that the Germans were prepared to halt the wholesale murder of European Jewry and to evacuate one million Jews in return for 10,000 trucks and quantities of tea, coffee, cocoa, and soap. The British detained Brand on a trumped-up charge of being a Nazi agent. In July of that year, Weizmann met with British foreign secretary Anthony Eden and pleaded for a positive response to the Brand mission, if only to gain time. His plea did not result in any action being taken. He also requested the bombing of the EXTERMINATION CAMPS. The British replied that technical difficulties made this unfeasible.

After the war, Weizmann, ill and half-blind, was shunted to the periphery of the Zionist movement by David BEN-GURION and Abba Hillel SILVER. In December of 1946 he was removed from the presidency of the World Zionist Organization. Nevertheless, he continued to perform indispensable services for the movement, and when the state of Israel was established he was appointed its first president. In 1949 he published his autobiography, *Trial and Error.*

BIBLIOGRAPHY

Gorni, Y., and G. Yogev, eds. *A Statesman in Times of Crisis: Chaim Weizmann and the Zionist Movement, 1900–1948.* Tel Aviv, 1977. (In Hebrew.)

Halpern, B. *A Clash of Heroes: Brandeis, Weizmann, and American Zionism.* New York, 1987.

The Letters and Papers of Chaim Weizmann. 25 vols. New Brunswick, N.J., 1968–1984.

Reinharz, J. *Chaim Weizmann: The Making of a Zionist Leader.* New York, 1985.

Rose, N. *Chaim Weizmann: A Biography.* New York, 1986.

JEHUDA REINHARZ

WEIZSÄCKER, ERNST VON (1882–1951), German Foreign Office official. The son of a Württemberg government official, Weizsäcker was a naval officer in World War I and joined the Foreign Office in 1920. His political views throughout his career manifested numerous inconsistencies. Critical of the Kaiser's prewar diplomacy, the Pan-Germans, annexationism, and unrestricted submarine warfare, he nonetheless did not believe that Germany bore the major blame for the outbreak of war. Though he never lent credence to the DOLCHSTOSSLEGENDE ("stab-in-the-back" myth), he wanted a quick end to reparations payments, occupation of the Rhineland, and German disarmament. He criticized Foreign Minister Gustav Stresemann for not achieving these objectives more quickly, yet he supported Stresemann's Deutsche Volkspartei (German People's Party).

While he abhorred Nazi demagogy and extremism, fearing that the Nazis would lead Germany to war and defeat, Weizsäcker nevertheless became state secretary of the Foreign Office under Joachim von RIBBENTROP in 1938, the year in which the Foreign Office began expelling Jews of Polish citizenship from Germany. In 1938 and 1939 he wanted concessions from the Allies, but also wanted them to be firm enough to induce Germany to behave reasonably. Although opposed to the German attack on Poland, the occupation of Norway, the western offensive, and the invasion of the Soviet Union, he never found any occasion to cease serving the regime with whose policies he disagreed so strongly. Wishing for the removal of Adolf Hitler, he still wanted to avoid the German defeat necessary for that end, and sought to keep many of the dictator's ill-gotten gains.

Ernst von Weizsäcker, German diplomat, testifying at his trial by the Nuremberg Military Tribunals (The Ministries Case, November 15, 1947, to April 14, 1949).

Weizsäcker's involvement in Nazi Jewish policy was scarcely less ambivalent. He opposed the arrest of Jews of North and South American citizenship because of potential reprisals against German citizens abroad, but he did not oppose the arrest of European Jews in German-occupied territories, since Germany did not fear retaliation in these cases. On one occasion he stated that in principle the Foreign Office always favored "the more lenient" alternative in Jewish policy. When asked by the SS whether the Foreign Office had any objections to deporting Jews from France to AUSCHWITZ, Weizsäcker amended the reply to the effect that the Foreign Office "did not raise" rather than "did not have" any objections. When the prime minister of Slovakia, Vojtech TUKA, requested more German pressure to help him continue the deportation of Slovak Jews in June 1942, Weizsäcker altered the Foreign Office's answer to read that a halt in deportations would "cause surprise" rather than "leave a bad impression" in Germany. In such equivocal ways Weizsäcker tried to serve country and conscience simultaneously.

In the aftermath of a 1943 reorganization of the Foreign Office, Weizsäcker was appointed ambassador to the Vatican. When the deportation of eight thousand Jews from ROME was ordered in October of that year, Weizsäcker is believed to have passed on warnings that reached the Jewish community. He also warned Berlin that the arrests "on the Pope's doorstep" might turn the Pope against Germany and would certainly be exploited by Allied propaganda. But at the same time, to forestall any papal pronouncement detrimental to the German cause, he warned the Vatican that protest would only worsen the situation.

After the war, Weizsäcker was convicted by the Nuremberg Military Tribunals (Trial 11, The Ministry Case) on counts of crimes against both peace and humanity (*see* SUBSEQUENT NUREMBERG PROCEEDINGS). The latter charge was based on the replies he had signed stating that the Foreign Office did not raise any objection to Jewish deportations. Conviction on the first count was overturned on appeal, but Weizsäcker was sentenced to seven years for the second count. In 1950, after eighteen months in jail, he was released. He published his apologetic memoirs, *Erinnerungen* (Recollections), that year. Weizsäcker's son, Richard von Weizsäcker, became president of the Federal Republic of Germany in 1984.

BIBLIOGRAPHY

Browning, C. R. *The Final Solution and the German Foreign Office: A Study of Referat D3 of Abteilung Deutschland, 1940–1943.* New York, 1978.
Hill, L. E. "The Vatican Embassy of Ernst von Weizsäcker." *Journal of Modern History* 39/2 (1967): 138–159.

CHRISTOPHER R. BROWNING

WELTSCH, ROBERT (1891–1982), Zionist writer, editor, and journalist. Born in Prague, Weltsch in his youth joined the Zionist student society Bar Kochba. After serving in World War I in the Austro-Hungarian army, he became a member of the Zionist Executive, representing the Ha-Po'el ha-Tsa'ir labor party. From 1920 to 1938, Weltsch edited the journal of the Zionist Organization of Germany, the *Jüdische Rundschau*. His article "Wear the Yellow Badge with Pride," published on April 4, 1933, had a deep impact on German Jewry, raising its morale and helping it to cope with the Nazi persecution.

Following his arrival in Palestine in 1938, Weltsch edited the *Mitteilungsblatt*, the weekly of the German-speaking immigrants' organization, and also wrote for the Hebrew daily *Haarets*. During the NUREMBERG TRIAL he served as the *Haarets* correspondent in Germany, and later wrote for it from London. He was one of the founders of the LEO BAECK INSTITUTE and was chairman of its London branch. From 1956 to 1980 he edited twenty-five volumes of the institute's *Year Book*, summarizing the content of each in his introduction.

Weltsch was a close follower of Chaim WEIZMANN, whose Zionist policies he supported as a journalist. Regarding the Arab question, however, he backed the line of the Berit Shalom circle, advocating the idea of a binational Arab-Jewish state in Palestine. He opposed David BEN-GURION's policies as formulated in the BILTMORE RESOLUTION of 1942, which demanded the formation of a Jewish state, and after the establishment of the state of Israel in 1948 he wrote critically of its domestic and foreign policy.

In the festschrift dedicated to Weltsch on his seventieth birthday, the educator Ernst A. Simon wrote, concerning the article "Wear the Yellow Badge with Pride": "It had to be him who in this black hour gathered the strength to find the unique word of courage, of resistance, and of solace. Rightly, this slogan will always be connected with his name."

BIBLIOGRAPHY

Poppel, S. M. *Zionism in Germany, 1897–1933: The Shaping of a Jewish Identity.* Philadelphia, 1976.

DAVID BANKIER

WERWOLF (Werewolf), code name of a Nazi organization for sabotage operations behind the Red Army lines. The decision to establish the group was taken by the Nazis in September 1944, after their defeats at the hands of the Soviets and in the face of the Red Army advance to the German border. Obergruppenführer Hans-Adolf PRÜTZMANN was put in command, and three thousand to four thousand men were recruited, mostly from the SS and the HITLERJUGEND (Hitler Youth). Werwolf teams began operating in January 1945, but scored little success; before long most of the men were caught and liquidated. A few small teams tried to operate after the war was over, mainly against the Polish authorities in Silesia. The last of these groups was eliminated by the Polish security services in 1947.

BIBLIOGRAPHY

Reitlinger, G. *The SS: Alibi of a Nation.* Englewood Cliffs, N.J., 1981.

SHMUEL KRAKOWSKI

WESTERBORK, camp situated in the northeastern NETHERLANDS, near the town of that name in the province of Drenthe. From 1942 to 1944 Westerbork served as a transit camp for Jews who were being deported from the Netherlands to eastern Europe. The camp had been established in October 1939 by the Dutch government to house Jewish refugees who had entered the country illegally, and a Dutch official from the Ministry of Justice was put in charge of it. The costs of putting up the camp and maintaining it, totaling 1.25 million gulden, were charged to the Jewish Refugee Committee in the Netherlands (established in 1933), which paid them off in yearly installments of 200,000 gulden. When the Germans invaded the Netherlands on May 10, 1940, there were 750 refugees in the Westerbork camp; they were moved to Leeuwarden, only to be taken back to the camp following the Dutch surrender. Subsequently, refugees from other camps were moved to Westerbork, and in 1941 it had a population of 1,100, accommodated in two hundred small wooden houses.

At the end of 1941 the German administration decided to use Westerbork as a transit camp for Jews who were being deported to the east. A barbed-wire fence was put up around the camp and twenty-four large wooden barracks were constructed, the costs of the new construction and the camp's maintenance now financed by the proceeds from confiscated Jewish property; in 1942 and 1943 these costs amounted to over 10 million gulden. In the first six months of 1942, some four hundred German Jews were transferred to Westerbork from cities in the Netherlands from which Jewish residents of Dutch nationality had been moved to Amsterdam.

On July 1, 1942, the German Sicherheitspolizei (Security Police) took over control of the Westerbork camp, and an SS company was sent in to reinforce the Dutch military police guarding the camp. Erich Deppner, an official in the German administration of the Netherlands, was appointed camp commandant. It was he who handled the first transport from Westerbork to AUSCHWITZ and caused a riot when, in order to fill the required quota of 1,000 deportees, he included in the transport children without their parents and women who happened to be standing in line for admittance into the camp (their husbands had already been registered for the camp, and were not included in the transport).

On September 1, 1942, Deppner was replaced by an SS officer, Josef Hugo Dischner; but the latter too failed in his task when he showed himself unable to deal with the sudden influx of 13,000 Jews who had been seized in a raid. On October 12, Dischner was succeeded by SS-Obersturmführer Albert Konrad Gemmeker. Gemmeker generally managed to run the camp without having to resort to drastic measures, while still fully complying with the orders he received from German headquarters in The Hague. He left the day-to-day operation of the camp in the hands of the German Jews—who had been in charge of it from the beginning—and this did not change even when the majority of the camp inmates were Jews of Dutch nationality, since the German Jews retained all the responsible posts.

The systematic transfer to Westerbork of

TABLE 1. *Destinations of Jews Deported from Westerbork*

DESTINATION	NUMBER OF TRAINS	NUMBER OF JEWS
Auschwitz	68	54,930
Sobibór	19	34,313
Theresienstadt	7	4,771
Bergen-Belsen	9	3,762
Total	103	97,776

Jews from all other parts of the Netherlands was launched on July 14, 1942, and on the following day their deportation to Auschwitz was set in motion. A total of almost 100,000 Jews were deported from Westerbork, as indicated in Table 1.

The timetable for the trains, the size of the transport, and its destination were determined by Adolf EICHMANN's office; Gemmeker left in the hands of the Jewish camp leadership the responsibility of compiling the lists of those to be deported. The leadership, however, was not allowed to include in the lists camp residents who were under a *Sperre* (a "ban"; that is, they were exempted from being moved). These included Jews of foreign nationality and, in particular, the veteran inmates, numbering 2,000, who had been given special status about two weeks before the de-

portations were launched. As of February 2, 1943, the deportation trains left Westerbork every Tuesday, turning the preceding night in the camp into a time of horror and panic.

Thus the Westerbork camp led a double life. There was the "permanent" population, who remained in place for a considerable length of time, ran their own affairs, and, in a peculiar way, led a near-normal life, especially in months when no deportations took place; and there were the masses who were brought into the camp from time to time, stayed there for a week or two, and were then dispatched to the east.

The camp administration consisted of ten subdivisions. Outstanding among the subdivision heads was Kurt Schlesinger, a businessman in his earlier life, who became Gemmeker's right-hand man. On August 12, 1943,

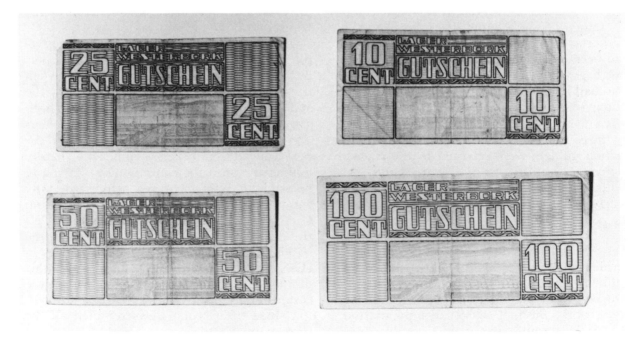

Scrip from the Westerbork transit camp. [A Living Memorial to the Holocaust—Museum of Jewish Heritage, New York]

Lighting the candles at the Hanukkah festival (during the month of December) in the Westerbork transit camp.

Schlesinger was appointed head of the principal subdivision, which was also in charge of the main card index—the key instrument for the compilation of the lists of persons to be deported. Another subdivision was the Jewish police (JÜDISCHER ORDNUNGSDIENST); at its full strength, it consisted of 200 young men, divided evenly between Dutch Jews and Jews from Germany. It was employed in arranging the transports, in addition to its duty of maintaining order inside the camp. The camp inmates were supposed to work for the war effort, but the will to work was very low. In 1943, when the permanent population was at its peak, the people employed in the camp, both Jews and non-Jews, worked at the following occupations:

OCCUPATION	NUMBER EMPLOYED
Metalworking	1,196
Health services	1,128
Outside employment	921
Workshops	716
Women's service	578
Inside jobs	352
Technical department	286
Education and welfare	284
Ordnungsdienst (police)	129
Central kitchen	382
Camp headquarters	63
Total	6,035

As seen from these figures, the number of persons employed in health services was exceptionally large. Westerbork had a hospital with 1,800 beds; 120 doctors and another 1,000 employees; laboratories, drug dispensaries, and so on. Heading the hospital was Dr. F. M. Spanier, who had much influence over Gemmeker, both hailing from Düsseldorf. The camp commandant also encouraged entertainment activities—concerts, operas, and cabaret performances—in which outstanding artists among the camp population took part. There were no shortages in the camp, since the Dutch administration provided it with a regular supply of commodities. The camp commandant also had at his disposal a fund for additional purchases, which had its source in the Jewish property that had been confiscated.

On April 12, 1945, when Allied forces were approaching Westerbork, Gemmeker officially handed the camp over to Kurt Schlesinger. On that day the camp had 876 inmates, of whom 569 were Dutch nationals; the rest belonged to various other nationalities or were stateless. After the war, a Dutch court sentenced Gemmeker to ten years in prison.

A memorial and a permanent exhibition were set up on the site of the Westerbork camp.

BIBLIOGRAPHY

Boas, J. H. *Boulevard des Misères: The Story of Transit Camp Westerbork.* Hamden, Conn., 1985.

De Jong, L. *Het Koninkrijk der Nederlanden tijdens de Tweede Wereldoorlog.* Vol. 8. The Hague, 1978. See pages 725–767.

Hillesum, E. *Etty: A Diary, 1941–1943.* London, 1983.

Hillesum, E. *Letters from Westerbork.* New York, 1986.

Machanicus, P. *Waiting for Death: A Diary.* London, 1968.

Paape, A. H. *Commemoration Centre Camp Westerbork.* Amsterdam, 1984.

Presser, J. *The Destruction of the Dutch Jews.* New York, 1969. See pages 406–464.

JOZEPH MICHMAN

WESTERWEEL, JOOP (1899–1944), Dutch Christian rescuer of Jews. Westerweel took part in Christian Socialist movements as a young man and engaged in the antifascist struggle. He taught in a modernist school in Bilthoven that absorbed many German refugee children in the 1930s.

In the early stages of the deportations of Dutch Jews to Poland, Westerweel became acquainted with Joachim ("Schuschu") Simon (1919–1943), one of the counselors of a group of *halutsim* (Zionist pioneers) living on a farm near his school. Together they created an underground movement for concealing the *halutsim* from the two principal farms in the Netherlands, Loosdrecht and Gouda. From August 10 to 16, 1942, hiding places were found for sixty pioneers, forty-eight of them from the Loosdrecht training farm. Subsequently, Westerweel and "Schuschu" began to organize an escape route for the *halutsim* over the border and into neutral Switzerland and Spain.

In October and November 1942, "Schu-schu" traveled to France to establish contacts with the Jewish underground there, and between December 1942 and January 1943 the first *halutsim* were smuggled into France through Belgium, prior to transferral to Spain. After taking three pioneers to Switzerland, "Schuschu" returned to organize further escapes. Several young pioneers were introduced as workers in the ORGANISATION TODT, which built fortifications in western France. In May 1943 the first "workers" arrived in France, maintaining contact with the heads of the group. On one of his many journeys into France to organize escapes into Spain and Switzerland, "Schuschu" was arrested in the south of the Netherlands (January 24, 1943) while in possession of material that might jeopardize his colleagues. After succeeding in informing them of his arrest, "Schuschu" committed suicide in prison. His work was carried on by his comrades, and the Westerweel group expanded to twenty members. In a memorable farewell speech delivered to a group of *halutsim* in the Pyrenees in February 1944, Westerweel urged

Joop Westerweel.

that on their arrival in Palestine they remember their comrades who had fallen on the way.

On March 11, Westerweel and a friend were captured by the Germans while attempting to transfer two young girls to the Belgian border crossing. Westerweel was taken to the VUGHT camp where, despite severe torture, he refused to betray his group. He was executed on August 11, 1944. His group continued its activities, smuggling a total of 150 to 200 Jews into France, including about 70 *halutsim*. A Westerweel Forest was planted in Israel in 1954.

BIBLIOGRAPHY

Avni, H. "The Zionist Underground in Holland and France and the Escape to Spain." In *Rescue Attempts during the Holocaust*. Proceedings of the Second Yad Vashem International Historical Conference. Jerusalem, 1977. See pages 555–590.
Cochavi, A., ed. *Underground of the Zionist Youth in Holland*. Tel Aviv, 1969. (In Hebrew.)
Habas, B., ed. *His Inner Light: The Life and Death of Joop Westerweel*. Haifa, 1964. (In Hebrew.)
Regenhardt, J. W., and C. Groot. *Om nooit te vergeten*. N.p., 1984.

JOZEPH MICHMAN

WHITE PAPER OF 1939 (also known as the MacDonald White Paper, after the British colonial secretary, Malcolm MacDonald), British statement of Palestine policy issued on May 17, 1939. As the persecution of German Jewry reached a crescendo, the YISHUV (the organized Jewish community in Palestine) was thrown into turmoil. In April 1936 Palestine's Arab community, goaded by Italian and German propaganda, declared a general strike to protest the increase in Jewish immigration after the Nazi rise to power in 1933. The strike soon turned into an all-out revolt against the British Mandate and the Jewish community. Over the next three years dozens of Jewish settlements were attacked by roving Arab bands, and the defensive resources of the Yishuv were stretched to their limits.

The British adopted a dual policy of using troops to quell the violence, even to the extent of cooperating with the Hagana (the underground Jewish army), and engaging in diplomatic endeavors designed to find a peaceful settlement of the endemic hostility between Arab and Jew. These peace feelers included overtures to the governments of Egypt and Iraq, but they were almost complete failures. As a last-ditch effort, the British Mandatory authorities called a London conference (the St. James Conference, February–March 1939) to try and hammer out a mutually acceptable agreement between the two claimants to Palestine. Arab refusal to even sit in the same room with the Jewish representatives, however, doomed the conference to complete failure.

At this point British policy changed radically. Although committed to the creation of a Jewish national home through the Balfour Declaration (November 2, 1917) and the League of Nations Mandate (April 25, 1920), with war looming in Europe the British concluded that the development of the Yishuv no longer coincided with imperial interests. The British cabinet concluded that Arab support, or at least neutrality, was vital in the upcoming anti-Nazi struggle; Jewish support, given Hitler's antisemitic policy, was taken for granted. As a result a new White Paper was published that, in effect, repudiated all previous British commitments to Zionism. First, Jewish immigration was to be limited to 15,000 per annum for five years; thereafter, any new immigration was contingent on Arab approval. Second, Jewish land acquisition was severely restricted in over 90 percent of the mandated territory. Finally, the British declared their intention (in the so-called constitutional clause) to establish an Arab-Palestinian state in 1949.

The Jewish protests fell on deaf ears. The British government in London had established its Middle Eastern policy and stubbornly refused to modify its approach, even when the situation showed how morally bankrupt appeasement of the Arabs actually was. The Hagana and Irgun Tseva'i Le'ummi underground movements planned to actively resist the White Paper, but these plans were abandoned when World War II broke out on September 1, 1939. Nevertheless, the entire Yishuv saw the White Paper as a direct threat to Jewish rights and, with regard to

Jewish refugees fleeing Nazi-occupied Europe, to Jewish survival. As such, it provided the impetus for the adoption of an independent policy, as represented by ALIYA BET ("illegal" immigration) and the BILTMORE RESOLUTION of May 11, 1942. The latter declared the goal of Zionism to be the establishment of a Jewish commonwealth in Palestine.

BIBLIOGRAPHY

Bauer, Y. *From Diplomacy to Resistance.* New York, 1970.

Wasserstein, B. *Britain and the Jews of Europe, 1939–1945.* Oxford, 1979.

ABRAHAM J. EDELHEIT

WHITE RUSSIA. *See* Belorussia.

WIENER LIBRARY. *See* Documentation Centers: Wiener Library.

WIESEL, ELIE (Eliezer; b. 1928), writer; 1986 Nobel Peace Prize laureate. Raised in a religious home in SIGHET MARMAŢIEI, Transylvania, Wiesel tenuously held on to his faith in God after being deported to AUSCHWITZ with his family in 1944. Liberated from BUCHENWALD, he later took up studies at the Sorbonne in Paris, and became a foreign correspondent for the Israeli daily newspaper *Yediot Aharonot.* In his memoir *Un di Velt Hot Geshvigen* (1956), written in Yiddish and adapted and translated into eighteen languages (Fr., *La Nuit;* Eng., *Night*), Wiesel epitomizes the experience of a concentration camp inmate in a unique style and syntactic structure that have provided a verbal resource for discourse about the Holocaust. He has written twenty-five novels whose underlying artistic *modus operandi* is to bring to life pictures drawn from the Jewish annals, transforming them into vibrant human experiences.

While his novels and discursive prose deal with the fragility of the human condition, the anguished memories of his ordeals, woven into the text of the story, express the collective loss of a seared generation. Always mindful of the suffering of the other victims, Wiesel has nevertheless continuously pointed out the uniqueness of the Jewish experience, stated in a memorable formulation: "While not all victims were Jews, all Jews were victims."

On accepting the Congressional Medal from President Ronald Reagan in 1985, Wiesel appealed to the president not to visit the cemetery in Bitburg, Germany, in which forty-seven SS men are buried. "Your place, Mr. President, is with the victims," he declared. This impulse to boldly jolt the conscience of society earned Wiesel the Nobel Peace Prize. In his presentation address, Egil Aarvik, the chairman of the Norwegian Nobel Committee, summed up Wiesel's message to humanity: "Do not forget, do not sink into a new blind indifference, but involve yourselves in truth and justice, in human dignity, freedom, and atonement."

In his tenure as chairman of the U.S. HOLOCAUST MEMORIAL COUNCIL between 1980 and 1986, Wiesel instituted national Days of Remembrance in the United States, and his leadership inspired the introduction of Holocaust curricula in numerous states, cities, and counties. In his words and deeds, Wiesel has helped to bring the Holocaust to the frontiers of American consciousness. He is a professor in the humanities at Boston University.

BIBLIOGRAPHY

Abrahmson, I., ed. *Against Silence: The Voice and Vision of Elie Wiesel.* 3 vols. New York, 1985.

Fine, E. S. *Legacy of Night: The Literary Universe of Elie Wiesel.* Albany, N.Y., 1982.

Rosenfeld, A. H., and I. Greenberg, eds. *Confronting the Holocaust: The Impact of Elie Wiesel.* Bloomington, 1978.

ELI PFEFFERKORN

WIESENTHAL, SIMON (b. 1908), investigator of Nazi war criminals. Born in Buchach (Pol., Buczacz), Galicia, Wiesenthal studied architecture at the Prague Technical University and was living in Lvov, Poland, when World War II began. He was arrested by Ukrainian police and spent most of the war

Simon Wiesenthal.

in concentration and forced-labor camps, among them JANÓWSKA (Lvov), PŁASZÓW, GROSS-ROSEN, and BUCHENWALD. He was liberated in MAUTHAUSEN on May 5, 1945, by the United States Army.

After the war Wiesenthal devoted himself to the investigation of Nazi war criminals. He worked initially for the War Crimes section of the United States Army in Austria, and in 1947 established the Jewish Historical Documentation Center in Linz. Public interest in Nazi war criminals waned, and Wiesenthal therefore closed his Linz center in 1954. He resumed his work in Vienna in 1961 in the wake of the EICHMANN TRIAL, which generated renewed interest in the prosecution of Nazi war criminals.

Among the most prominent Nazis whom Wiesenthal helped discover and/or bring to justice were Franz STANGL, commandant of the TREBLINKA and SOBIBÓR extermination camps; Gustav Wagner, deputy commandant of Sobibór; Franz Mürer, commandant of the VILNA ghetto; and Karl Silberbauer, the policeman who arrested Anne FRANK. In 1977 the SIMON WIESENTHAL CENTER for Holocaust Studies was established at the Yeshiva University of Los Angeles in honor of Wiesenthal's life's work. Besides his efforts to prosecute Nazi war criminals, Wiesenthal has played an important role in commemorating the victims of the Holocaust. His works on the Holocaust include *The Murderers among Us; Sunflower; Max and Helen;* and *Every Day Remembrance Day: A Chronicle of Jewish Martyrdom.*

[*See also* Extradition of War Criminals.]

BIBLIOGRAPHY

Cooper, A. "Simon Wiesenthal: The Man, the Mission, His Message." In *Genocide: Critical Issues of the Holocaust,* edited by A. Grobman and D. Landes, pp. 384–388. Los Angeles, 1983.

EFRAIM ZUROFF

WILNER, ARIE (1917–1943), one of the founders of the ŻYDOWSKA ORGANIZACJA BOJOWA (Jewish Fighting Organization; ŻOB) in his native WARSAW, and the ŻOB's liaison officer with the Poles. When World War II broke out, Wilner was a member of the Zionist youth movement Ha-Shomer ha-Tsa'ir in Warsaw, and his plan to emigrate to Palestine was postponed because of the training assignments he was given. In September 1939 he was among those who escaped from Warsaw and made their way to Vilna, which had been occupied by the Soviet Union and became part of Lithuania. Wilner was active in Vilna until its conquest by the Germans in June 1941. He returned to Warsaw and was one of the first to warn of the significance of the massacres that were being carried out in the east.

Wilner became involved in underground activities, and his Polish appearance enabled him to travel and make frequent visits to the ghettos in occupied Poland. In June 1942 he was among the founders of the ŻOB and became its representative on the "Aryan" side of the city. He established contact with the main Polish underground organization, the ARMIA KRAJOWA (Home Army), and obtained from it recognition of the ŻOB. A close relationship developed between Wilner and Henryk WOLINSKI, who was in charge of the Jewish section in the Armia Krajowa; but Wilner

Arie Wilner.

and sent him to a nearby concentration camp, from which he was rescued in a daring operation led by Henryk Grabowski, a member of the Polish Catholic Scout movement. When the WARSAW GHETTO UPRISING broke out, Wilner was suffering from a wounded leg, but he later took an active part in the fighting. Wilner was in the ŻOB command bunker when it was discovered; according to eyewitnesses, he called on the fighters to commit suicide, and he himself was among those who perished in the bunker. His parents and sisters were hidden with Poles in Warsaw and were saved.

BIBLIOGRAPHY

Gutman, Y. *Revolt of the Besieged: Mordechai Anilevitch and the Uprising of the Warsaw Ghetto.* Merhavia, Israel, 1963. (In Hebrew.)
"Portrait of a Combatant (Aryeh Wilner)." *Yalkut Moreshet* 8 (March 1968): 104–117. (In Hebrew.)

ISRAEL GUTMAN

WILNO. *See* Vilna.

also kept in touch with the Communist underground, the Armia Ludowa (*see* GWARDIA LUDOWA), and used every means available to acquire arms and bring them into the ghetto. Although the center of Wilner's activities lay outside the ghetto, he participated in the major decision making of its underground and in resistance operations. After the crisis experienced by the ŻOB in September 1942, Wilner contributed to its reconsolidation, and in January 1943 he took part in an armed uprising.

On March 6, 1943, Wilner was arrested by the Germans during a search of his apartment on the "Aryan" side, in which he was found to be in possession of arms. The Germans thought he was a member of the Polish underground; they interrogated and tortured him, but he gave no one away. His arrest, however, led to tension between the Armia Krajowa and the ŻOB, and contact between the two was broken off for a short time. The Germans discovered that Wilner was a Jew,

WIRTH, CHRISTIAN (1885–1944), SS major and head of the concentration camp organization in Poland. Wirth was born in Württemberg and trained as a carpenter, later serving in World War I and receiving high decorations. He entered the police force after the war and became notorious for his methods of interrogation. A member of the Nazi party from 1931, by 1939 he was a *Kriminalkommissar* in the Stuttgart criminal police, a department of the Gestapo.

At the end of 1939, Wirth began to specialize in the "treatment" of the insane by means of euthanasia (*see* EUTHANASIA PROGRAM), and at this time performed the first known gassing experiments on Germans certified as incurably insane. In 1940 he became an inspector of euthanasia establishments in Greater Germany, and in 1941 this led to Wirth's assignment to Lublin, where he set up a new euthanasia center, the first outside the Reich. He followed this with the establishment of five extermination camps in Poland, of which the first to become operational was at CHEŁMNO.

During the next year and a half, Wirth was made responsible for supervising the killing of more than 1.5 million Jews in the camps of BEŁŻEC, SOBIBÓR, and TREBLINKA, in cooperation with Odilo GLOBOCNIK and the SS police headquarters in Lublin. This assignment involved the introduction of new gassing techniques. When the camp at Bełżec was closed in the fall of 1943, Wirth was promoted to SS-Sturmbannführer and sent to Trieste, where his task was to expedite the deportation of the Jews. He was killed by partisans while on a journey to Fiume.

BIBLIOGRAPHY

Klee, E. *"Euthanasie" im NS-Staat: Die Vernichtung lebensunwerten Lebens.* Frankfurt, 1983.

LIONEL KOCHAN

WIRTSCHAFTS-VERWALTUNGSHAUPT-AMT

WIRTSCHAFTS-VERWALTUNGSHAUPT-AMT (Economic-Administrative Main Office; WVHA), the central administration for SS economic activities, based in Berlin. The WVHA was formed on February 1, 1942, replacing the Verwaltung und Wirtschaft and Haushalt und Bauten (Budget and Construction) main offices, which had been in charge of budgets, building projects, and the SS economic enterprises. The Haushalt und Bauten main office had administered the official Reich budget allocations to the SS, which covered most of the financial requirements of the Verfügungstruppen (militarized SS formations; later renamed the Waffen-SS, or Armed SS) and the TOTENKOPFVERBÄNDE (Death's-Head Units), employed as concentration camp guards. The Verwaltung und Wirtschaft main office handled the funds that the SS received from the Nazi party, as one of its subdivisions. Owing to the proliferation of economic activities conducted by the SS and the growth of the Waffen-SS, the existing setup became complicated, and for this reason the two offices were merged and reorganized. As part of the reorganization, the inspectorate of concentration camps, which until then had come under the SS-Hauptamt (SS Main Office), was moved to the WVHA, becoming Amtsgruppe (Branch) D of the new organization.

SS-Obergruppenführer Oswald POHL, who had held the top post in both Verwaltung und Wirtschaft and Haushalt und Bauten, was appointed head of the WVHA, and SS-Brigadeführer Richard GLÜCKS, who had been the *Inspekteur der Konzentrationslager* (Inspector of CONCENTRATION CAMPS), became the officer in charge of WVHA Branch D, keeping its offices in Oranienburg, outside Berlin.

A similar administrative structure existed for the concentration camps. The *Arbeitseinsatzführer* (supervisor of labor in the camp), although subject to the authority of the camp commandant, also received technical instructions from Branch II D, and a similar relationship existed between the camp doctor and Branch III D. It was only the political section in the concentration camps that received its technical orders from the REICHS-SICHERHEITSHAUPTAMT (Reich Security Main Office; RSHA), the competent authority for the imprisonment of persons in concentration camps (and, when the situation arose, for their release). The political section was especially dreaded by the prisoners, because it was responsible for their interrogation and frequent mistreatment.

The incorporation of the concentration camps in the WVHA resulted from the expanded role that concentration camp prisoners were expected to play, as of 1942, in the manufacture of armaments. Their successful performance of technically complicated manufacturing processes requiring precision led to a revised evaluation of their work capacity. This, in turn, required that the system under which the prisoners were deployed be reorganized and that economic considerations be allotted greater weight. Until the formation of the WVHA, the use of prisoners for production had been in the hands of Haushalt und Bauten, the relevant section being headed by SS-Hauptsturmführer Wilhelm Burböck; it now became Section II in WVHA Branch D, headed by SS-Standartenführer Gerhard Maurer. It was this office, II D, that negotiated WVHA contracts with industrial firms for the use of concentration camp prisoners—the number of prisoners to be employed by them, the kind of work they would perform, the food and accommodation they would receive, and the financial compensation that the firms would make per prisoner per day. (The latter depended on the

A group of defendants in Trial 4, The Pohl Case, heard before the Nuremberg Military Tribunals at the Subsequent Nuremberg Proceedings. All are former members of the SS Wirtschafts-Verwaltungshauptamt (Economic-Administrative Main Office; WVHA). Oswald Pohl, former chief of the WVHA, is in the front row at the left.

job requirements and ranged from two to six reichsmarks.)

The efforts made by the WVHA to increase the SS contribution to war production by using concentration camp prisoners at first had the effect of improving living conditions for the majority of the prisoners. This improvement, however, did not last long. On the one hand, the WVHA management was constantly seeking to raise the volume of war-production work done by prisoners; on the other hand, it did not make corresponding efforts to provide for their accommodation and nourishment and for the proper training of SS personnel and job supervisors in charge of the prisoners. The net result was that the WVHA came to resort to brute force and draconian punishments in order to raise the prisoners' output, in the process causing their total exhaustion. Replacements for the prisoners were readily available, since the RSHA kept on supplying the concentration camps with an unending stream of contingents from the occupied territories. The prisoners were overexploited to an unbelievable

degree, primarily those who were put on earth-moving and construction projects. Prisoners employed in the manufacture of valuable technical products were less affected.

Pohl himself, on September 15, 1942, made an agreement with Reichsminister Albert SPEER, providing—as a first step—for the supply of "fifty thousand able-bodied Jews" in the AUSCHWITZ extermination camp, who were to be "siphoned off from the migration in the east," that is, to be temporarily saved from murder. Pohl played a decisive role in expanding Auschwitz into a huge industrial and extermination complex. As far as the WVHA was concerned, the exploitation of prisoners as forced labor and their extermination were equal elements of Nazi rule; the "subhumans" were only there to serve the Nazis' own ideological and economic purposes.

In the summer of 1944, the WVHA faced immense difficulties in supplying the concentration camp commandants with even the barest minimum of food and clothing for the prisoners. At the same time, the WVHA arranged for even more work projects. Speer made efforts to check the growing influence that the WVHA was gaining in the armaments industry by its control of the allocation of manpower at a time of severe shortage. In October 1944, he ordered that any further use of prisoners must have his personal approval; but this did not prevent him from approving the transfer of industrial armaments plants into bombproof mines, an operation that the WVHA promoted and carried out at an enormous cost of life to the prisoners used in the project. The SS officer in charge of this operation was Obergruppenführer Hans Kammler, the chief of SS construction, which included the industrial plants, the concentration camp installations, and the prisoners' barracks.

BIBLIOGRAPHY

Billig, J. *Les camps de concentration dans l'économie du Reich hitlérien.* Paris, 1973.

Georg, E. *Die wirtschaftlichen Unternehmungen der SS.* Stuttgart, 1963.

Speer, A. *Infiltration.* New York, 1981.

FALK PINGEL

WISE, STEPHEN SAMUEL (1874–1949), American Jewish leader. Wise left his mark as a religious leader, a founder of and activist in the Zionist movement in the United States, and a spokesman for the cause of civic betterment. Much of the criticism of the role of the American Jewish community during the Holocaust focuses on his leadership.

After serving as a Reform rabbi in Portland, Oregon, Wise came to the east and in 1907 founded the Free Synagogue in New York, remaining its spiritual leader until his death. In 1922 he established the Jewish Institute of Religion (JIR), an academy for training Reform rabbis, and was its president until its merger with the Hebrew Union College of Cincinnati in 1948. Wise was a crusader for social causes. His sermons and speeches focused on every civic cause of the 1920s and 1930s, including municipal corruption and labor's right to organize. It was his campaign to compel the corrupt James Walker, mayor of New York, to resign that brought him into

conflict with Franklin D. ROOSEVELT, who was governor of New York from 1928 to 1932. This rupture lasted until the presidential election of 1936, when Wise became a staunch supporter of the administration.

Wise played a key role in establishing the American Zionist movement. In 1897 he helped found the New York Federation of Zionists, which became the Federation of American Zionists a year later. Together with Louis D. Brandeis, he helped convince President Woodrow Wilson to support the Balfour Declaration. He was a spokesman for the Zionist cause at the Paris Peace Conference of 1919–1920 and assumed the presidency of the Zionist Organization of America that same year, heading it from 1918 to 1920 and again from 1936 to 1938. Wise was among the organizers of the American Jewish Congress, founded in 1920, and in 1936 he established the WORLD JEWISH CONGRESS, of which he was president until his death. The leadership role that Wise sought to fill proved increasingly difficult after 1933, when the Nazis came to power in Germany. American Jewry was weak and divided. In 1933, Wise enlisted the support of the American Jewish Congress for the movement to boycott German products (*see* BOYCOTTS, ANTI-NAZI), seeing this as the morally correct thing to do. At the same time, he

Stephen S. Wise. [American Jewish Archives, Hebrew Union College]

wavered in his support for the HAAVARA AGREEMENT that existed between Germany and the YISHUV, the organized Jewish community in Palestine.

Abba Hillel SILVER, a fellow Reform rabbi and Zionist but a Republican supporter, had been radicalized by the events in Europe. He had made an agreement with the more moderate Wise (who was under Roosevelt's influence) to avoid confronting the administration publicly. In 1943 Silver broke the agreement by arousing American public opinion on behalf of Zionism. The aging Wise was at the same time confronted by the Revisionist Zionists, whose cause (aiding the Irgun Tseva'i Le'ummi) had been considerably strengthened by a group of Palestinian Jews headed by Peter Bergson (alias of Hillel Kook). Wise came into open conflict with the Revisionist BERGSON GROUP, which, he was convinced, was intending to take over the American Zionist movement. At the same time, he faced opposition from the newly organized anti-Zionist constituency within the Jewish community. Clearly, the American Jewish community had, in the crucial year of 1943, become more fragmented than ever. Wise's attempt to play the role of conciliator came to naught. The divisions within the community were too great, as was the gap between what the Jewish rescue advocates sought and what the Roosevelt administration was willing to give during wartime. Because of his leadership position, Wise was ultimately compelled to bear much of the onus for that failure.

By 1943, some felt Wise's leadership to be inconsistent and weak. He found it difficult to plead the special case for the rescue of European Jewry before the Roosevelt administration at a time when the nation faced such awesome dangers. He agreed that Under Secretary of State Sumner Welles should corroborate the news of the "FINAL SOLUTION" contained in the RIEGNER CABLE before making it public, lest Jews be accused of atrocity-mongering. By 1944, Wise had become deeply disillusioned. The establishment of the Jewish state a year before his death gave him considerable gratification, but as the radical losses suffered by European Jewry became known, his despair intensified. His autobiography, *The Challenging Years: The Autobiography of Stephen Wise*, was published in 1949.

BIBLIOGRAPHY

Ganin, Z. "Activism versus Moderation: The Conflict between Abba Hillel Silver and Stephen S. Wise during the 1940s." *Studies in Zionism* 5/1 (Spring 1984): 71–96.

Urofsky, M. I. *A Voice That Spoke for Justice: The Life and Times of Stephen Wise.* Albany, N.Y., 1982.

Voss, C. H., ed. *Stephen S. Wise: Servant of the People.* Philadelphia, 1969.

HENRY L. FEINGOLD

WISLICENY, DIETER (1911–1948), SS *Hauptsturmführer*; Adolf EICHMANN's deputy in the Jewish Section (Section IV B 4) of the REICHSSICHERHEITSHAUPTAMT (Reich Security Main Office; RSHA) in SLOVAKIA, GREECE, and HUNGARY and organizer of the mass deportation of Jews from these countries between 1942 and 1944. Wisliceny joined the SS in 1934 and entered the SD (Sicherheitsdienst; Security Service) the same year. Beginning in September 1940 he acted as "adviser on Jewish affairs" to the Slovak government and soon became known for his intelligence and opportunism.

During the deportations from Slovakia in the summer of 1942, Wisliceny was bribed by the Bratislava-based underground PRACOVNÁ SKUPINA (Working Group) to delay the deportation of Slovak Jews. He entered into negotiations on the so-called EUROPA PLAN, initiated by Rabbi Michael Dov WEISSMANDEL, to save the remaining Jews in Europe in return for a ransom of $2 million to $3 million, to be made available by Jewish organizations abroad. Wisliceny accepted a sum between $40,000 and $50,000 (the exact amount is not known) as a first installment and transmitted it to higher SS authorities.

In 1943 and 1944, Wisliceny headed the Sonderkommando für Judenangelegenheiten (Special Commando for Jewish Affairs) in SALONIKA and was instrumental in the liquidation of Greek Jewry. In March 1944 he joined Eichmann's Sonderkommando in BUDAPEST to organize the deportations of Hungarian Jews and became involved as liaison in the "Blood for Goods" negotiations with the RELIEF AND RESCUE COMMITTEE OF BUDAPEST.

After the war, Wisliceny served as a witness

for the prosecution at the NUREMBERG TRIAL and was extradited to Czechoslovakia. While awaiting his trial in the Bratislava prison, he wrote several important affidavits on the "FINAL SOLUTION"; on Eichmann's role; on the mufti of Jerusalem, Hajj Amin al-HUSSEINI; and on the negotiations over the Europa Plan and the "Blood for Goods" proposal. Wisliceny's testimony was used by the prosecution at the EICHMANN TRIAL in Jerusalem in 1961. Condemned to death, he was hanged in Bratislava in February 1948.

BIBLIOGRAPHY

Bauer, Y. *American Jewry and the Holocaust: The American Jewish Joint Distribution Committee, 1939–1945.* Detroit, 1981.
Fuchs, A. *The Unheeded Cry.* New York, 1984.
Molho, M., and J. Nehama. *The Destruction of Greek Jewry, 1941–1944.* Jerusalem, 1965. (In Hebrew.)

LIVIA ROTHKIRCHEN

WITTENBERG, YITZHAK (Leo Itzig; 1907–1943), the first commander of the FAREYNEGTE PARTIZANER ORGANIZATSYE (United Partisan Organization; FPO) in VILNA. Born into a working family, Wittenberg was a tailor and, from an early age, a member of the Communist party. During the short-lived Soviet regime in Lithuania (June 1940 to June 1941), he made a name for himself as a Communist activist. Under the German occupation and in the Vilna ghetto, Wittenberg became a leader of the Communist underground. He was one of the sponsors of the FPO, and his willingness to join with Zionists in a united organization—which included the anti-Communist Zionist Revisionists—is an indication of his personality and his strong ties with the Jewish population. In January 1942, when the FPO came into being, Wittenberg was elected its commander, on the basis of his personal qualities, his experience in underground operations, and his ties with Communist circles outside the ghetto. He soon won the respect of all the elements of the organization.

One of the Vilna Communists, who lived outside the ghetto, gave Wittenberg away when he himself was imprisoned by the Ger-

Yitzhak Wittenberg.

mans, although the latter were apparently unaware of the existence of the FPO and Wittenberg's role in it. The JUDENRAT (Jewish Council) was asked to surrender Wittenberg, and its chairman, Jacob GENS, had a sharp confrontation on the issue with the FPO. Wittenberg was arrested by the Lithuanian police, only to be set free by armed FPO members, and he went into hiding in the ghetto. The incident threatened to develop into an open struggle for power. Gens appealed to the ghetto population, claiming that the FPO's attitude was jeopardizing all the Jews, and as a result many Jews turned against the FPO and its commanders. This exposure to mass pressure, and the recognition that the time was not ripe for a general uprising, persuaded the FPO command to decide on the difficult step of surrendering Wittenberg to the Judenrat.

Wittenberg accepted the decision when he learned that it had the support of the underground Communist party leadership in the ghetto. "Wittenberg Day" in the Vilna ghetto—July 16, 1943, a day that had a far-reaching impact on the FPO—ended with Wittenberg surrendering to the Jewish police. He apparently committed suicide in prison, by taking poison.

BIBLIOGRAPHY

Arad, Y. *Ghetto in Flames: The Struggle and Destruction of the Jews in Vilna in the Holocaust.* Jerusalem, 1980.

ISRAEL GUTMAN

WOLFF, KARL (1900–1984), senior SS and police officer. Wolff was born in Darmstadt, where his father was a district court judge. In World War I Wolff served as a lieutenant and earned an Iron Cross, First Class. After the war he fought in the ranks of the Freikorps in the state of Hesse. From 1920 to 1933 he held various business posts and then set up his own public relations firm in Munich.

In 1931 Wolff joined the Nazi party and the SS, and in July 1933 he was appointed Heinrich HIMMLER's adjutant. In 1936 he was elected to the Reichstag as a member from Hesse.

Wolff advanced rapidly up the SS ladder, being appointed *Standartenführer* in January 1934, *Gruppenführer* in the Waffen-SS in May 1940, and SS-*Obergruppenführer* and *General-oberst* (senior general) in 1942. He was awarded the Nazi party's gold medal on January 30, 1939.

It was Wolff who, with Himmler's help, obtained the necessary deportation trains from the German RAILWAYS administration for transporting innumerable thousands of Jews to the TREBLINKA extermination camp. In September 1943, Wolff became military governor of northern Italy and plenipotentiary of the Reich to Benito MUSSOLINI's Fascist government. In February 1945 Wolff contacted United States intelligence agent Allen Dulles in Zurich and arranged for the surrender of the German forces in northern Italy.

After the war Wolff appeared as a witness for the prosecution in trials of Nazi criminals. He was tried by a German court and sentenced to four years' imprisonment with hard labor in 1946, but was released a week later. Wolff then became a highly successful public relations agent. In 1961, at the time of the EICHMANN TRIAL, he drew attention to

SS-Standartenführer Karl Wolff (right foreground, facing the camera), adjutant to Heinrich Himmler (left, with binoculars), at an SS cavalry display in June 1934. [Bildarchiv Preussicher Kulturbesitz]

himself with an interview that he gave to a German magazine in May of that year.

Wolff was put under arrest in January 1962. He was charged with the murder of Jews, and with direct responsibility for the deportation of 300,000 Jews to Treblinka. On September 30, 1964, he was sentenced to fifteen years in prison and ten years' loss of civil rights; in 1971, however, he was released for good behavior.

BIBLIOGRAPHY

Reitlinger, G. *The SS: Alibi of a Nation.* Englewood Cliffs, N.J., 1981.

SHMUEL SPECTOR

WOLINSKI, HENRYK (1901–1986), Polish jurist. Prior to World War II, Wolinski was employed in central government institutions in Warsaw. In February 1942 he became a member of the ARMIA KRAJOWA (Home Army; AK), under the code names Wacław and Zakrzewski, heading the section for Jewish affairs in the operational command of the AK's Information and Propaganda Office. Wolinski prepared reports on German policy for the extermination of the Jews. These reports were intended for the AK command and for the POLISH GOVERNMENT-IN-EXILE in London. In the fall of 1942 the Jewish Fighting Organization (ŻYDOWSKA ORGANIZACJA BOJOWA; ŻOB) contacted Wolinski, subsequently maintaining this contact for the AK command through Arie (Jurek) WILNER and Yitzhak (Antek) ZUCKERMAN. Wolinski fervently pleaded the Jewish cause before the AK commanders and participated in the Rada Pomocy Żydom (Council for Aid to Jews), known as ZEGOTA, subsequently creating a council cell in the AK operational command that aided many Jews in hiding. After the war Wolinski was a legal adviser and attorney in Katowice.

In 1974 he was accorded the title "RIGHTEOUS AMONG THE NATIONS" by YAD VASHEM.

BIBLIOGRAPHY

Bartoszewski, W., and Z. Lewin, eds. *Righteous among Nations: How Poles Helped the Jews, 1939–1945.* London, 1969.

Henryk Wolinski.

Blumenthal, N., and J. Kermish. *Resistance and Revolt in the Warsaw Ghetto: A Documentary History.* Jerusalem, 1965. (In Hebrew.)

TERESA PREKEROWA

WOŁOŻYN. *See* Volozhin.

WOMEN. *See* Concentration Camps; Ravensbrück.

WORKING GROUP. *See* Pracovná Skupina.

WORLD JEWISH CONGRESS (WJC), international Jewish body founded in 1932 but in existence only from 1936. The WJC was a successor organization to the Comité des Délégations Juives (Committee of Jewish Delegations), which had been established to put forward Jewish claims at the Paris Peace Conference after World War I.

Among the WJC's affiliates was the American Jewish Congress (AJC), which had been formed on a temporary basis during World War I, and reorganized on a permanent basis in 1922. The AJC opposed what it saw as a plutocratic, assimilatory German Jewish leadership in the United States, and attempted to replace it with a mass following of American Jewry organized on a democratic basis.

Premised upon the concept of the Jews as a nation, the WJC was organized as an attempt to create a worldwide defense of Jewry against Nazism and antisemitism. The AJC and the WJC, under the leadership of the American rabbi Stephen S. WISE, were among the first and most active groups to fight Nazism. As early as March 1933 the AJC organized a mass rally in Madison Square Garden in New York against Nazi terrorization of Jews, and in May of that year it sponsored a parade protesting the burning of books in Germany. The AJC joined the boycott of German goods (see BOYCOTTS, ANTI-NAZI) and became the mainstay of the boycott movement. It attempted to influence the government administration to relax immigration restrictions in order to allow a greater influx of Jewish refugees. Along with other Jewish organizations, however, it hesitated to press for legislation that would permit larger quotas, for fear that such an act would lead only to further restrictions.

After the outbreak of World War II in Europe, the executive of the WJC was relocated from Europe to the United States. It carried on its work from there, using the officers of the AJC as its conduit to gain access to government officials. Nahum GOLDMANN headed the WJC's administrative committee; Leon Kubowitzki (later, Aryeh Kubovy) was in charge of rescue attempts; Arieh Tartakower ran its relief department; and Maurice Perlzweig was in charge of its political department. Relief efforts of the WJC were hampered not only by the United States government's refusal to allow food to be sent through the blockade of Europe and to permit money to be transferred to occupied countries, but also by the limited funds available to the WJC. Nonetheless, both the WJC and the AJC maintained constant pressure on the United States government and the embassies of the Allies, through lobbying efforts and mass demonstrations, for action that would alleviate the plight of European Jewry. The AJC organized mass rallies in Madison Square Garden in New York and in other cities around the United States in July 1942 and again in March 1943 to publicize the plight of European Jews and to call for action by the United States and Allied governments to save the remnants of Jewry. A cable sent in August 1942 by the WJC representative in Geneva, Dr. Gerhart Riegner, outlining the German plans for the "FINAL SOLUTION," was the main factor in creating an awareness in America of what had befallen the Jews of Europe (see RIEGNER CABLE). Throughout the war, the respresentatives of the WJC in Europe were the main source of information regarding the fate of European Jewry.

Rabbi Wise, who was president of both organizations, was the leading Jewish activist with connections in government circles, though his access to and influence upon President Franklin D. ROOSEVELT were very limited. He and Dr. Goldmann did succeed, however, in obtaining Roosevelt's consent, in July 1943, to send funds to ROMANIA for the relief and rescue of Jews. Wise was also largely responsible for informing Secretary of the Treasury Henry MORGENTHAU, Jr., of the tragedy overwhelming European Jewry and for gaining his sympathy for rescue attempts. These two factors were probably the most crucial ones leading to the creation of the WAR REFUGEE BOARD in 1944. It was the procrastination of the State Department over the transfer of funds, and later the Treasury Department's report to the president, that led to the establishment of the board.

BIBLIOGRAPHY

Eppler, E. "The Rescue Work of the World Jewish Congress during the Nazi Period." In *Rescue Attempts during the Holocaust*. Proceedings of the Second Yad Vashem International Historical Conference, edited by Y. Gutman and E. Zuroff, pp. 47–70. Jerusalem, 1972.

Kubowitzki, L. *Unity in Dispersion: A History of the W.J.C.* New York, 1948.

ARIEL HURWITZ

WORLD WAR II. The war that engulfed a large part of the earth between 1939 and 1945 involved most of the world's nations. It began with the German invasion of Poland on September 1, 1939, and ended in Europe with the German surrender on May 7, 1945, and in the Pacific theater with the Japanese surrender on September 2, 1945. There are no generally accepted casualty figures. The estimates for Europe run between 30 million and 35 million dead, and perhaps up to 55 million the world over, soldiers and civilians, among whom between 5 and 6 million were Jews who died in the Holocaust.

Background. The economic crisis that began in 1929 and continued in different forms until the outbreak of war critically sharpened the economic and political conflicts in the world. Germany, devastated by the aftereffects of World War I, suffered especially, and this was the main element in the background to the rise of the National Socialist movement there. The aftereffects included the disintegration of the prewar German social structure, the weakness of the liberal and centrist forces that supported a democratic society, and the discomfiture caused by the defeat of 1918, which brought with it the rise of a strident nationalistic response. National Socialism offered a dictatorship—a new style of government with the abolition of parliamentary squabbling—national pride, the struggle for a predominant position in Europe, and, mainly, the pulling together of all levels of society in order to emerge from the economic crisis that in 1932 caused the unemployment of seven million Germans. The assumption of power by the Nazis at the end of January 1933 was viewed with sympathy by the British government, which was worried about the security of its empire in the face of the spread of communism. The Nazis too defined communism as a primary enemy. The French government, while apprehensive about German revanchism, reflected the mood of its population when it assumed a mainly passive stand vis-à-vis the German threat.

In the decade prior to 1939, the Soviet Union, busy with its internal upheavals, at first neglected the Nazi threat altogether and continued its attack on social democracy as well as on the capitalist West. But it changed its policy in 1935 to advocate the establishment of "popular fronts," uniting antifascist groups, mainly of the Left, while maintaining Communist predominance in them.

In the end, however, it was the desire of the Nazi leadership for a war that proved to be the cause of its outbreak. The Nazi aim was to establish the predominance of the Germanic-Nordic peoples of the "Aryan" race in Europe, and thereby to control, in effect, the world. For that purpose LEBENSRAUM ("living space") was aspired to in eastern Europe, in line with Nazi ideology as formulated by Adolf HITLER and others. To achieve it, the perceived enemies of Germany—Bolshevik Russia, liberal France, plutocratic America—all of whom were controlled by "international Jewry," in Nazi eyes, ultimately had to be defeated in a war. War was a desideratum of Nazi ideology both as a means and an end, in the spirit of Social Darwinism: only war would show who was strong and who therefore had the right to rule. In the end, it was not economic, military, or political reasons that instigated the most terrible of wars to date. Economically, by 1938 or 1939, Germany had largely recovered; militarily, it threatened others but was under no danger of attack; and politically, it was already the predominant power in Europe. Nazi Germany wanted a war for ideological reasons. In a memorandum to Hermann GÖRING, instructing him to prepare Germany for war within four years, Hitler wrote in the summer of 1936:

> Since the beginning of the French Revolution the world has been drifting with increasing speed toward a new conflict, whose most extreme solution is bolshevism, but whose content and aim is only the removal of those strata of society that gave the leadership to humanity up to the present, and their replacement by international Jewry. . . . Germany has a duty to make its own existence secure by all possible means in the face of this catastrophe and to protect itself against it . . . a victory of bolshevism over Germany would not lead to a Versailles Treaty, but to the final destruction, even the extermination, of the German people.

The ideals of *Lebensraum* and antisemitism were closely linked, and while no operative plans for a total annihilation of the Jewish people existed before 1941, the germ of

Delegation of Japanese officers visiting the Sachsenhausen concentration camp (c. 1936). [Bildarchiv Preussischer Kulturbesitz]

the Holocaust was contained in Nazi ideology, which was the motivating force leading to war.

Antecedents. The German army, which even prior to 1933 had circumvented, mainly with Soviet help, the provisions of the Versailles Treaty limiting its size and equipment, began rearming in 1934. In 1935 the industrial Saar area, which had been under French supervision, was regained by Germany through a plebiscite, and in the same year a naval agreement was signed with Britain that enabled Germany to increase its navy. German diplomacy established the Rome-Berlin Axis with Italy in 1936 and 1937 and engineered the Anti-Comintern Pact between Germany, Japan, and Italy, directed against the Soviet Union. Germany's anti-Communist image weakened Western opposition to Nazi expansionism, although Germany, despite its rearmament efforts, was not ready for war before the summer of 1939.

In 1936, the German army entered the demilitarized Rhineland area, which had been under effective French influence, but the French did not react. Austria was annexed, in March 1938 because Italy no longer objected to that step (*see* ANSCHLUSS), amid acclamation by most Austrians. The annexation of the Sudeten area of Czechoslovakia in the wake of the MUNICH CONFERENCE of September 1938 effectively emasculated the power of the Czech army, which had its fortifications there. In March 1939, Czechoslovakia was finally destroyed: Bohemia and Moravia became a German protectorate, Slovakia became an independent state under German tutelage, the Transcarpathian Ukraine was annexed by Hungary, and Memel was annexed from helpless Lithuania. The following month, the Italians occupied hitherto independent Albania.

During the 1930s, the British government tried to deflect German expansionism toward the east. In 1937, when Neville Chamberlain became prime minister, he introduced the policy of appeasement vis-à-vis Germany (*see* GREAT BRITAIN: APPEASEMENT OF NAZI GERMANY). Until 1938, the Franco-Soviet and Franco-Czechoslovak military pacts were still valid, and they provided for a military balance against the rising German might. The Munich agreement destroyed this balance, and the British policy of directing Germany

EUROPE — 1937

© Martin Gilbert 1982

toward the east was a central factor in this development. After Munich, war became at least very probable.

The entry of German troops into Prague on March 15, 1939, convinced Chamberlain that his trust in Hitler had been misplaced. Serious preparations for war had been started by Secretary of State for War Leslie Hore-Belisha earlier, and in March 1939 Britain,

and a rather reluctant France, issued guarantees of Western support to all the states between Germany and the Soviet Union. British forces, however, were very weak; only 2 or 3 divisions were stationed in the British Isles, and the plan was to increase these to 19 divisions (some 300,000 men). France, on the other hand, relied on the Maginot Line fortifications on its border with Germany, and was making some rather tentative attempts to extend the fortifications along its border with Belgium. It had, on paper, 110 divisions, of which 85 (some 5 million men) could actually be mobilized within a short time. This force included 5 cavalry and 2 mechanized divisions, and one armored division. There were no strategic plans for offensive operations at all.

Overall Nazi strategy was revealed to the top German leadership on November 5, 1937, when Hitler addressed a meeting of political and military leaders. It was there that the future annexations of Austria and Czechoslovakia were announced and the eastern direction of expansion outlined. In the spring of 1939, pressure was directed against Poland, after some hesitations. The Free City of DAN-ZIG (Gdańsk) was demanded by Germany, as well as freedom of movement through the Polish Corridor, which separated the bulk of German territory from East Prussia. Poland, faced by this threat, signed a military pact with France in May. Military and political negotiations among Britain, France, and the Soviet Union (April to August 1939) broke down because of Western unwillingness (and inability) to promise the Soviets real support, and because of the Polish refusal to permit Soviet troops to enter Polish territory to fight against the Germans. Mutual suspicions between the West and the Soviet Union caused Joseph STALIN to turn to the Nazis. Hitler was interested in a rapprochement in order to guarantee the isolation of Poland and to obtain a free hand in the West. In addition, an agreement with the Soviet Union would assure a supply of raw materials essential for the pursuit of war. A neutrality pact, known as the NAZI-SOVIET PACT, was signed on August 23, 1939. It provided for the effective partition of Poland, and the inclusion of Lithuania, at a later stage, in the German sphere of influence.

Poland relied on its military strength—thirty first-line divisions and ten reserve divisions, as well as twelve cavalry divisions, for a total of 2.5 million men. However, this force was on paper, for it lacked mobility and armor. On the other side, on paper, stood ninety-eight German divisions, of which fifty-two consisted of first-line troops. Of these, six were armored, four motorized, and another four mechanized divisions. These fourteen divisions made all the difference, and to this was added the control of the skies by the German air force.

Polish Campaign and "Phony War." The Polish army was destroyed within a few days, despite great bravery on the part of many Polish units, and mopping-up operations ended with the surrender of Warsaw on September 28, 1939, after an epic defense. Soviet troops had entered Poland on September 17, and annexed the eastern parts of the country. By an addendum to the neutrality pact (September 28), Nazi Germany and the Soviet Union agreed to include Lithuania in the Soviet sphere of influence together with Latvia and Estonia, and some corrections of the demarcation line in Poland were made in German favor. Vilna was "ceded" by the Soviets to Lithuania in October.

Western promises of help to Poland were broken, and the large French army scarcely moved during the Polish campaign. A static warfare with little action on the western front lasted until May 1940, giving Germany the time needed to turn its army into an extremely strong force. By the spring of 1940, 133 Allied divisions—103 French, 9 British, and miscellaneous Belgian, Dutch, and Polish (in exile)—were facing 136 German divisions. The Germans had 10 armored and 7 motorized infantry divisions, as against 6 and 8 Allied divisions, respectively, and 2,700 tanks as against 3,000 Allied ones. The Luftwaffe (the German air force) had a total of 1,050 fighters, 280 dive-bombers, and 1,100 medium bombers, as against 735 Allied fighters, 49 dive-bombers, and 414 medium bombers. In actual fact the Allies had large numbers of additional planes, but for various reasons these remained unused. Qualitatively, German machinery was superior, but the edge was not very large. However, the new military tactics of massed armor accompanied by air superiority, although tested and demonstrated in Poland, were not understood by Western military leaders.

The Communist and fascist elements in the West, each for their own reasons, sabotaged the willingness to fight. This also became clear during the Russo-Finnish War, which

Count Galeazzo Ciano, foreign minister of Italy (left, smiling and shaking hands with Gen. Wilhelm Keitel), arrives in Berlin after the collapse of Poland.

lasted from November 30, 1939, to March 13, 1940. The Soviets aimed at a widening of the security belt north of Leningrad, the annexation of some strategically important islands in the Gulf of Finland, and access to the northern port of Petsamo. Some 330,000 Finns succeeded in holding out against a force of 450,000 Soviet soldiers for three months, inflicting heavy defeats on the Soviets. A reorganization in the Soviet command, combined with massive Soviet reinforcements, broke the resistance of the Finns. Finland, however, remained an independent state.

The Western powers viewed the Soviet Union as an ally of Germany and tried to help the Finns, but failed. In December 1939, the Soviet Union was excluded from the League of Nations. Germany made peace overtures to the West at the time, and the prospect of a Western crusade against the Soviet Union appeared a possibility.

Invasion of Denmark and Norway. Western warfare against Germany was mainly economic. The British fleet (under Winston CHURCHILL, First Lord of the Admiralty from September 1939 until May 1940) tried to blockade Germany and decided to prevent the shipment of Swedish iron ores to Germany via the Norwegian port of Narvik under the protection of Norwegian neutrality. On April 7, 1940, the British announced that they would mine Norwegian waters, and a British invasion of Norway seemed possible. The Germans were preparing an invasion of their own, and they invaded Denmark and Norway on April 9. Despite heavy Norwegian resistance (the Danes had no real army), which cost the Germans three heavy cruisers and other losses, Norway was conquered in a few weeks, although Narvik continued to be held by the Allies until June 10.

Campaign in the West. While the Scandinavian operation was still proceeding, the Germans attacked in the west (May 10), with an improved version of the Schlieffen Plan of 1914. They approached France with a wide sweep through the Netherlands and Belgium, ignoring these countries' neutrality. Using a new tactic, the *Blitzkrieg* (lightning war), in which armored divisions moved into enemy territory quickly and powerfully, they conquered the Netherlands in five days, after devastating bombing attacks and the surprise capture of the sluices, some with the help of Dutch collaborators. Western strategists decided to have their armies meet the Germans in Belgium. The Allied forces were outflanked by a surprise move through the Ardennes that brought the Germans behind the Allied armies. The Germans reached the Channel coast, and the surrounded Allied forces fought a losing battle against overwhelming odds. Belgium capitulated on May 28. Under the protection of the Royal Air Force (RAF), the British troops, with some French and Belgians (a total of some 350,000), managed to escape from Dunkerque in about ten days (May 26 to June 4) with the help of British civilian craft, leaving their equipment behind. The decision of Hitler not to use all available forces to destroy and capture the British force, and his subsequent decision not to invade Britain immediately, saved the British from total defeat. Meanwhile, Chamberlain had resigned on May 10, and Churchill became prime minister.

Faced with the loss of a large army, with German air superiority, and with a concentration of highly mobile German armor and artillery units, the French retreated. Paris fell on June 14, and a new government under the aged Marshal Philippe PÉTAIN was set up to negotiate a French surrender. Italy had joined the war on June 10, and though its troops made no headway on the border with France, it became a co-victor with Germany. On June 22, 1940, an armistice was signed with Germany, and on June 24 with Italy. Most of the French military equipment was handed over to the Germans, and most of the French navy was locked up at Toulon; France was divided into a northern zone occupied by the Germans, and a smaller southern zone under French administration. The new capital was Vichy. French colonies were ordered to desist from cooperating with the British. British attempts to convince the French generals to continue the struggle proved futile, except in the case of Charles de GAULLE, who established the Free French forces from London. French naval forces at Oran, Algeria, were attacked by the British to prevent their falling into German hands; other French naval forces outside of Europe were put under British control.

Battle of Britain. In July and August 1940, Britain was practically defenseless: it had eight partly equipped divisions and another fifteen that were just beginning to train. No armor was available. Originally, the Germans planned to invade Britain on September 15, but the date was postponed again and again because of mounting difficulties. Ships bringing food to Britain were attacked, but enough food got through. The Luftwaffe was sent to soften up Britain for the invasion. The RAF had 2,913 aircraft; the Germans, 4,549. In practice, between 550 and 650 British Hurricanes and Spitfires, equipped with an increasingly efficient radar system, had to deal with some 1,700 German aircraft, of which 864 were bombers. The German ME 109 fighters, matching the Spitfires, had a limited range that just barely included London. As the Luftwaffe encountered more difficulties, Hitler postponed the invasion date. In the end, it could not overcome the RAF, and without that no invasion was possible. Between July and the end of October, the Germans lost 1,722 planes as against 915 British fighters lost.

The Baltic States and the Balkans. On June 15, 1940, Soviet troops entered Lithuania, Latvia, and Estonia, and over the course of the following two months put an end to these countries' independence. On June 28, the Soviets occupied Bessarabia and northern Bukovina after giving an ultimatum to Romania, with the Germans passive in both cases. The Soviet Union believed that it was now in a much better position vis-à-vis Germany than previously.

In the meantime, Germany continued to penetrate the Balkans. Germany's arbitration between Hungary and Romania in August 1940 awarded northern Transylvania to Hungary. It also resulted in the demise of the royal Romanian government of Carol II and the emergence of the authoritarian government of Ion ANTONESCU, who ruled in a coalition with the fascist IRON GUARD until January 1941, when he rid himself of them. Both Romania and Hungary were now firmly under German influence. Italy, not to be outdone, plunged into an adventure in October when it attacked Greece from Albania, but it could make no headway; the small Greek army even penetrated into Albania early in 1941.

In November 1940, Germany tried to reach an arrangement with the Soviets. The Russian foreign minister, Viacheslav MOLOTOV, on a visit to Berlin, agreed in principle to a pact between Germany, Japan, Italy, and the Soviet Union. But faced with Hitler's suggestion to turn toward India, he demanded German agreement to a declaration of Finland, Bulgaria, Iran, and the Dardanelles as Soviet spheres of influence. This finally turned Hitler against the Soviets. He had been planning an attack on the Soviet Union since September, and this meant that the Balkan flank had to be secured first, and his Italian allies bailed out of Greece. Romania and Bulgaria joined the Axis early in 1941, but in Yugoslavia, which had signed a similar agreement, the government was toppled by an anti-German military group under Gen. Dušan Simović. As a result, German plans were changed, and on April 6 they invaded Yugoslavia and Greece, where a British force landed to help the Greek army. In a lightning advance, Yugoslavia was defeated and Greece conquered. Out of the 60,000-strong British army, 45,000 were evacuated to Crete (by May 1), but on May 20, 15,000 German paratroopers descended on the island and conquered it, suffering heavy losses in the process. Some 16,000 British troops managed to escape to Egypt.

The Middle East and Africa. The Italians, who controlled Libya, Eritrea, and Ethiopia, hoped to conquer Egypt and the Suez Canal, but in a lightning campaign that started on December 9, 1940, mobile British troops under Gen. Archibald Wavell defeated a much larger Italian force in the Western Desert and occupied Cyrenaica. In early 1941 a British force advanced from southern Sudan into Eritrea and, after conquering the Italian key position at Cheren, occupied Ethiopia by the end of May. It then reinstated Emperor Haile Selassie, who had fled after the Italian conquest of his country in 1935 and 1936. The Italian army surrendered.

In February 1941, Gen. Erwin Rommel arrived in Libya with 35,000 German troops, and in a sudden attack in March defeated the British, whose army had been depleted by a force sent to Greece. German armaments were far superior to those of the British, whom the Germans pushed back to the Egyptian border, leaving only an enclave of British troops in the port of Tobruk, which the Germans were unable to occupy. In November, after Wavell had been relieved by Gen. Claude Auchinleck, a numerically superior British force (85,000 British troops, compared to 55,000 Germans) drove the Germans out of Cyrenaica again, relieving Tobruk.

Meanwhile, in the Middle East, most of the independent and semi-independent states showed marked sympathy for the Axis powers. In Iraq a government under the pro-German Rashid Ali al-Gaylani was in power from March 1940. He was forced by the British to resign in January 1941, but returned to power in a putsch on April 2. The British landed troops at Basra, in accordance with the British-Iraqi treaty, and the Iraqi forces surrounded the British air base at Habbaniya. Small British forces routed the numerically superior Iraqis and occupied Baghdad on May 30, putting a stop to a major anti-Jewish pogrom that had been in progress there. The leader of the Palestinian Arabs, the mufti of Jerusalem, Hajj Amin al-HUSSEINI, who supported Rashid Ali, fled to Berlin with him.

The French protectorates of Syria and Lebanon were under Vichy control, and Syrian airfields were put at the disposal of German aircraft. Despite a much stronger French force there, the British, aided by a Free French force (and guided by some Palestinian Jewish underground volunteers), invaded Syria on June 8, 1941, and brought about the surrender of the Vichy forces on July 10.

Invasion of the Soviet Union. Unable to defeat Britain, wary of a possible attack by the Soviet army (the only major land force still left in Europe), and disturbed by Soviet demands in the Balkans, Hitler decided to invade the Soviet Union and on December 18, 1940, gave orders to prepare Operation "Barbarossa." The preparations included a series of commands given in March 1941, one of which was the basis for the so-called KOMMISSARBEFEHL, which provided for the murder of all political commissars who were officers of the Soviet army and then, by extension, of all Soviet officials viewed as bearers of the Communist ideology. Soviet areas were to be economically exploited and despoiled, and the fact that mass death through starvation would result from this policy was taken into account. Hitler had originally intended to deal with Britain first, but now that he planned to attack the Soviet Union he saw the struggle as a war of ideologies (*Weltanschauungskrieg*), which would be conducted by the Germans not as an ordinary military struggle but as a war of extermination. He saw Bolshevism as a Jewish ideology and the Soviet Union as controlled by Jews; hence the elimination of the Soviet Union became wedded to the annihilation of the Jews.

The date of the attack had to be postponed from mid-May to June 22, 1941, because of the German attack in the Balkans. Some historians have advanced the thesis that this delay saved the Soviet Union from defeat because it did not give the German forces enough time to defeat the Soviets before the winter set in.

The German forces numbered some three million men and included Finnish, Romanian, and Hungarian units, since these countries joined in the attack—Finland and Romania to regain territories lost in 1940, and Hungary to maintain its territorial gains. The Germans had 102 infantry divisions, 14 motorized, one cavalry, and 19 armored divisions with 3,550 tanks. They were initially opposed by two million Soviet soldiers in 88 infantry, 7 cavalry, and 54 tank and armored divisions. German equipment was generally far superior. The Luftwaffe gained air superiority by destroying Soviet airfields early in the fighting. Three main armies, those of Wilhelm von Leeb in the north, Fedor von Bock in the center, and Gerd von Rundstedt in the south, attacked in the directions of Leningrad in the north; Minsk-Smolensk-Moscow in the center, which received predominance in German planning; and Kiev in the south. Although they offered determined resistance in many places, the Soviet troops, unprepared by their political leadership for the battle, were outgunned, outmaneuvered, encircled, and wiped out in their millions, although more millions were being mobilized in the rear and thrown into the fray. In July the Baltic states were overrun, with local populations actively aiding the Germans, but the latter were stopped by the Soviet army before Leningrad. In the south, the Germans conquered Kiev in September. Odessa fell on October 16, and Kharkov on October 24. In November the Crimea was invaded and conquered, and on November 15 the Germans laid siege to Sevastopol, which held out until July 2, 1942.

The main thrust in the center brought the Germans in July 1941 to Minsk, followed by Smolensk. Then, despite stiff Soviet resistance, they conquered Viazma and Briansk in October. Both in the Ukraine and in the Briansk-Viazma region, huge Soviet armies numbering many hundreds of thousands were defeated and most of the soldiers taken prisoner. In November the advance on Moscow continued, but it was stopped at Mozhaisk, some 37 miles (60 km) from Moscow. Advance units actually came within sight of the city. A Soviet counteroffensive started on December 6 with fresh reserve troops and pushed the Germans back, liberating Kalinin on December 16. The Soviet advance caused very large German casualties and confounded all the plans carefully laid in the previous spring. German confidence was shaken.

The Soviet government, although it had been explicitly warned of the forthcoming German attack and its date, had not prepared its forces to meet it. Despite the mutual mistrust between the Soviet Union and the West, Churchill declared his readiness to aid the Soviets. Western policies concerning Nazi Germany were formulated in the Atlantic Charter, conceived and signed by Franklin D. ROOSEVELT and Churchill on August 14, 1941, and the Soviet Union then cosigned the declaration. An Anglo-Soviet treaty was signed on July 13, and talks led to the establishment of the United Nations with the United States, after the Japanese attack on Pearl Harbor of December 7, 1941.

In March 1941, the United States Congress had approved the Lend-Lease Act, empowering the president to provide goods and services to nations whose defense was deemed vital to the interests of the United States. The Soviet Union now became the recipient of

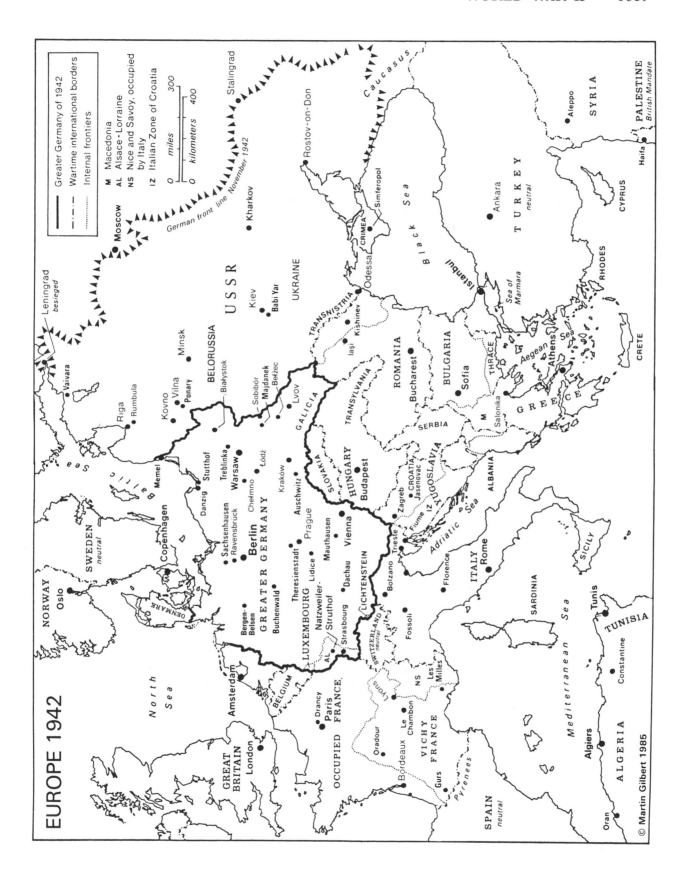

EUROPE 1942

Greater Germany of 1942
Wartime international borders
Internal frontiers

M   Macedonia
AL Alsace-Lorraine
NS Nice and Savoy, occupied by Italy
IZ Italian Zone of Croatia

0   300   miles
0   400   kilometers

German front line November 1942

© Martin Gilbert 1985

massive American Lend-Lease assistance ($1 billion in 1941 and 1942). Aid arrived through the north in naval convoys, and through Iran, which had been occupied in August by a combined Soviet-British invasion.

In late 1941 the Soviet command, which had been hard hit by the Stalinist purges of 1937 and 1938, was revamped. Semyon Timoshenko, commander of the western (central) front, relieved Semyon Budenny in the south. Georgi Zhukov, who had defended Leningrad, moved to the western front and organized the great Soviet counteroffensive in December 1941. This counteroffensive was possible because the Soviets had become convinced that Japan would maintain its neutrality and that it would therefore be safe to remove troops from East Asia.

In the spring of 1942, the Germans began their offensive, which was designed to deal a decisive blow to the Soviet army. Conquering the Don basin, they took Voronezh on July 7 and Rostov on July 24, and reached the outskirts of the crucially important city of Stalingrad, on the Volga River, on August 20. In September they broke out of the Crimean peninsula, took Novorossisk on September 6, and occupied the Caucasian oil fields in October. By mid-September they had penetrated into Stalingrad itself, but the Soviet troops there hung on desperately. However, on November 19, 800,000 Soviet troops with 900 tanks began a pincer attack that closed, on November 23, on twenty-two German divisions with some 300,000 men. In November they attacked at Rzhev in the central sector, and in December near Kharkov. In January 1943, another Soviet offensive relieved the seventeen-month siege of Leningrad. On February 2, the German Sixth Army of Field Marshal Friedrich von Paulus at Stalingrad capitulated, with 91,000 survivors. Soviet T-34 tanks, as well as large amounts of Western armaments (3,276 tanks, 2,665 aircraft, and 70,000 tons of fuel), had been the material underpinning of the Soviet successes.

German Rule in Occupied Europe. Nazi ideologists and politicians devised the concept of the "New Order" in Europe under Nazi domination. Ethnic groups defined by Nazi ideology as "subhuman" or "racially worthless," especially the Poles and most other Slavs (with the exception of Slovaks, Croats, and Bulgarians), were treated with great brutality. From late 1941, intellectuals associated with the SS began developing an overall German genocidal plan for the restructuring of eastern Europe called GENERALPLAN OST. Its different versions provided for the selective mass murder of millions, mainly the intellectual elites of the Slavic nations; the resettlement of others; the "Germanization" of many; and the enslavement of the rest. The plans included massive resettlement of Germans as the controlling minority in eastern Europe.

German policy in Poland was radically genocidal, aiming at the elimination of the Polish nation as such; the disappearance of its educational, religious, and economic base; mass expulsion from strategic areas; and massive enslavement. As a result, it is estimated that more than three million ethnic Poles died during the war. Similar policies were pursued in the Ukraine, in Belorussia, and on Russian ethnic territory, as well as in Serbia. In some of these areas, especially the Ukraine and the Baltic republics, large segments of the population at first welcomed the Germans as liberators from Soviet rule, and supported the annihilation policy followed against the Jews. However, German brutality slowly brought about a change in attitude. Some of Germany's allies, especially the Croat fascist USTAŠA regime under Ante PAVELIĆ, engaged in parallel policies; in Croatia, some 800,000 Serbs and 90,000 GYPSIES, in addition to the Jews, were murdered by the fascist militia.

The German armed forces did not follow the prewar conventions, such as the Geneva Convention, in their treatment of Soviet PRISONERS OF WAR (POWs). The formal claim was that the Soviet Union had never signed these conventions. In fact, a decision was taken by the Nazi ideologists to use the Soviet POWs as slaves and to kill most of them by starvation, overwork, or both. According to accepted figures, about 3.3 million Soviet POWs perished in this way during the war.

In the West, far milder policies were followed. French, Belgian, and Dutch POWs were at first used, in accordance with international law, as working forces. Later, local labor forces were recruited, either in agreement with local collaborators (as in France, in February 1943) or by force, to work in German industries and in agriculture. "Germanic" countries (the Netherlands and Switzerland) were ultimately slated to become parts of Germany, as were Bohemia and Moravia. Other areas, especially France, were to be kept as satellite countries with a measure of internal autonomy.

Apart from the Jews, it is probable that the Nazis intended to annihilate totally the Gypsy (Romany) population of Europe, although the evidence is still unclear. Several thousand Gypsies were gassed, together with Jews, at CHEŁMNO and AUSCHWITZ; others were murdered, especially in Poland and Croatia. Estimates place the number of Gypsies killed at between 250,000 and 400,000, out of a total of 3 million to 5 million European Gypsies. The Gypsies were seen as a "mixed" group of nomads of partially Aryan origin. German scientists argued in favor of annihilating the Gypsy "mixed bloods," and keeping alive the "racially pure" Gypsies, but this policy was not followed everywhere.

The Holocaust should be seen in this context, although with regard to the Jews, the policy was not of selective murder and enslavement but of total physical annihilation of every person with more than two Jewish grandparents. Mass murder began with the special mobile killing units of the REICHS-SICHERHEITSHAUPTAMT (Reich Security Main Office; RSHA)—the four EINSATZGRUPPEN in the Soviet Union—starting in early July 1941. They were joined by police battalions of the ORDNUNGSPOLIZEI and three special SS brigades of the Kommandostab Reichsführer-SS (Command Staff of the Reich Leader of the SS), as well as by some WEHRMACHT (army) units. Together, these forces murdered at least 1.5 million and perhaps up to 2 million Jews by the end of 1942. In the conquered Soviet areas, killings were carried out largely by machine-gunning, except near Minsk, where a gassing installation was set up at MALY TROSTINETS. The Jews from the other parts of Europe were killed largely in the gassing installations of Chełmno, BEŁŻEC, Auschwitz, SOBIBÓR, and TREBLINKA. Hundreds of thousands of others died in the CONCENTRATION CAMPS, among them the camp at MAUTHAUSEN, where people

were killed by forced labor. Others died as a result of starvation, disease, and on-the-spot executions (especially the very young, the old, and the sick), or after discovery in hiding places, in all the occupied countries.

While the decision to kill the Soviet Jews must have been taken before the invasion of the Soviet Union, its extension to the rest of Europe is documented in an authorization from Göring to Reinhard HEYDRICH of July 31, 1941. The administrative and technical measures necessary for implementing the entire program previewed in that document were agreed upon at a meeting of top bureaucrats from the different ministries that took place on January 20, 1942, in the Berlin suburb of Wannsee (*see* WANNSEE CONFERENCE).

As a result of the German wartime policies, resistance movements sprang up throughout Europe. In Poland the main group, the ARMIA KRAJOWA (Home Army), was directed by the London-based POLISH GOVERNMENT-IN-EXILE. A smaller, Communist-led armed underground, the GWARDIA LUDOWA, was directed from Moscow. The Armia Krajowa refused to engage in open combat against the Germans until the latter were weakened, and it attempted to fight both against Germany and against a Communist takeover. A Soviet-oriented underground sprang up behind German lines in the occupied Soviet territories. Armed groups fighting against Soviets, and, in some measure, against Germans as well, arose in the Ukraine (the Bandera bands). In Yugoslavia, the Communist-led partisans became a real force engaging large German forces, while a royalist armed force, the CHETNIKS, collaborated to some extent with the Germans and Italians. Politically diverse French underground forces were united in 1943 under de Gaulle, and they prepared to participate actively in the liberation of France. Armed urban guerrillas and partisan movements existed in Greece (on a very large scale), in Italy after the entry of German forces into the country in September 1943, in Scandinavian countries, in Austria, in the Protectorate of BOHEMIA AND MORAVIA and Slovakia, and in the Benelux countries. The first major revolt in a city was the WARSAW GHETTO UPRISING, which broke out on April 19, 1943. In addition there were a number of other armed actions in the ghettos of CZĘ-

STOCHOWA, BIAŁYSTOK, VILNA, KRAKÓW, MIR, LACHVA, TUCHIN, and many other places, and in the Sobibór, Treblinka, and Auschwitz-Birkenau camps.

Entry of the United States into the War. Japanese designs to become the predominant power in East Asia were first manifested in 1931 with the invasion of China, which by 1941 had led to the occupation of China's main cities and most of its industrial and agricultural centers. However, the Chinese Nationalist (Kuomintang) government under Chiang Kai-Shek, as well as its Communist adversary under Mao Tse-tung, were offering determined resistance to the Japanese invaders. Britain and France tried to compromise, out of weakness. Japan concluded a neutrality pact with the Soviet Union on April 13, 1941, to free its flank and concentrate on eliminating Western influence in Asia. A carefully prepared surprise attack on the United States naval fleet at Pearl Harbor in Hawaii on December 7, 1941, initiated hostilities. The United States declared war on Japan the following day, and on December 11, Germany and Italy declared war on the United States. The weakened American fleet was unable to defend Guam and Wake islands, which fell on December 13 and 20, respectively. The Philippines were invaded in late December and fell in January, the United States forces holding out on the Bataan peninsula and Corregidor until May.

In January, too, the Japanese invaded and conquered the Netherlands East Indies (present-day Indonesia), sinking most of the Allied navy in the Battle of the Java Sea (February 27 to March 1). On December 25 the British in Hong Kong surrendered. The British defeat in Malaya was precipitated by the sinking of the two British battleships, *Repulse* and *The Prince of Wales*. Malaya was then overrun, and Singapore fell on February 15. Thailand joined Japan as an ally. However, the Allies, mainly Australians and New Zealanders, checked the Japanese advance in New Guinea; in the indecisive Battle of the Coral Sea (May 7, 1942), some 100,000 tons of Japanese shipping were sunk.

In March 1942, the Japanese conquered Burma and threatened India. However, the British forces managed to halt the Japanese advance. The turning point in the Pacific came with the American naval victory in the Battle of Midway (June 4 to 7), which put an end to Japanese dreams of defeating the United States. The tide began to turn against the Japanese, and American troops landed on the Solomon Islands in August. In November, a Japanese fleet was defeated there, while the Battle of Guadalcanal took the lives of large numbers of Americans and Japanese. In 1943, American and British Commonwealth troops began the slow reconquest of the Pacific islands and invaded Burma, where British general Charles Orde Wingate's commando troops harried the Japanese. Allied soldiers taken as POWs, as well as interned Allied civilians, were treated with extreme brutality by the Japanese, who also carried out medical experiments on Chinese prisoners in Manchuria. In Malaya and elsewhere, thousands of internees and prisoners died of starvation and maltreatment. There, too, the treatment was based on racism, in this case an anti-Western and anti-Chinese ideology.

El Alamein and North Africa. In Cyrenaica, inferior armor caused General Auchinleck's forces to yield ground to a new German offensive that started in January 1942. In June, Tobruk, with a garrison of 30,000, fell to Rommel's army. Only in July were the German tanks stopped, at El Alamein, about 60 miles (96 km) from Alexandria. With greater reserves in troops, armor, and fuel, Rommel would probably have taken Egypt, the Suez Canal, and Palestine. However, the Mediterranean was a secondary theater of war for the Germans. Under the overall command of Sir Harold Alexander, the Eighth Army under Gen. Bernard Montgomery, with greatly improved tanks and more guns, began its major attack on October 23, 1942. By November 4, Rommel's army was in full retreat, which continued until it reached the Tunisian border in late January 1943. Between January 17 and 27, Roosevelt and Churchill met at Casablanca and took the decision not to end the war without unconditional German surrender.

On November 8, 1942, Anglo-American troops invaded North Africa, held by pro-Vichy French forces; 850 ships under Gen. Dwight D. EISENHOWER brought units that took over Algeria and Morocco, in some places against stiff French resistance. Algiers was occupied by a local anti-Nazi detachment largely composed of and commanded by local Jews. Adm. François DARLAN, a French pro-Nazi collaborator, who happened to be in Algiers, arranged for a French surrender. He was assassinated on December 24, and a compromise French administration, which kept the anti-Jewish Vichy laws intact for some months, was set up by Gen. Henri Giraud. In stages, control was taken over by de Gaulle's supporters.

The Anglo-American forces advanced on Tunis, where the Germans and Italians managed to organize defensive positions. After bitter fighting, the Axis forces surrendered on May 12, 1943. An estimated 950,000 Axis troops were killed or captured, and 8,000 planes and 2.4 million tons of shipping were lost.

That July, the Anglo-Americans under Eisenhower invaded Sicily, leading on July 25 to the resignation of Benito MUSSOLINI and the establishment in Italy of the military government of Marshal Pietro BADOGLIO. Badoglio sued for an armistice, the Allies invaded Italy on September 2, and Italy surrendered on September 8. However, in a daring coup, a German commando freed Mussolini from detention, and a Fascist government was set up in northern Italy that claimed to be carrying on the war at the side of Germany. Since this government had no power, German troops invaded Italy and raced southward to face the Allies. Stubborn German resistance, especially at Monte Cassino, was overcome only in 1944. Rome fell on June 4 and Florence was liberated on August 12, but German troops held northern Italy until May 1945.

The Battle of the Atlantic. In 1939, the merchant shipping of the countries that were to fight Nazi Germany amounted to about 43 million tons, as against 13 million tons owned by Germany, Italy, and Japan. Between 35 million and 40 million tons of shipping were sunk in World War II.

At the outbreak of the war, Germany had fifty-six submarines, one fewer than the British. While the German surface navy never managed to become a deadly threat (although it attracted much of Britain's naval efforts), the submarine threat to Britain's supplies from the Western Hemisphere was

real enough. By the end of 1939, 114 ships —more than 420,000 tons—had been sunk by German U-boats. In early 1940 British destroyers seemed capable of containing the German threat, but with the fall of France and with air bases in southern Norway available to the Germans, their long-range bombers (the Focke-Wulf 200) could sink ships approaching Ireland and Scotland. The U-boat menace increased again, and in October 1940, 63 ships (350,000 tons) were sunk. In September the United States had agreed to hand over 50 American destroyers to the British, in exchange for the lease of British bases on the American side of the Atlantic. By February 1941, there were only twenty-one German U-boats left, out of fifty-six in the previous summer, but German building programs were speeded up. In the following month, surface attacks, air strikes, and the U-boats accounted for the destruction of 139 Allied ships, with over half a million tons. The rates of sinking continued to be very high, but with the approval of the Lend-Lease Act in March, American warships now patrolled part of the sea route to Britain, thus relieving the hard-pressed Royal Navy. Canadian warships also helped a great deal. However, as new U-boats appeared faster than the rate of sinking, the threat to Britain's lifeline increased. In 1942, 7,790,000 tons of Allied shipping were lost, most of it to U-boats, and only seven million tons' worth of new ships came into service. At this rate, Britain might well have been defeated. The peak of the German successes came in March 1943, but by May, German losses had reached about one-third of the U-boat strength, as a result of improved Allied naval tactics and better equipment. The Germans withdrew the U-boats from the Atlantic. In the summer of 1943, the bulk of the German U-boats were sunk by Allied forces. After that, while the threat remained, it was contained.

Soviet Victory. While continuing to press the western Allies for an invasion of the European continent in order to create a second front, the Soviets carried on their advance in early 1943, driving the Germans out of the Caucasus and liberating most of the Ukraine. This took place despite a German counteroffensive in March leading to the reoccupation

Anthony Eden, British foreign secretary (right), with Viacheslav Molotov, People's Commissar for Foreign Affairs (left), reviews a guard of honor at the Moscow airport. Eden had come to attend the Moscow Conference of Foreign Ministers in October 1943.

of Kharkov, which had been taken by the Soviets in February. On July 5, the German armies opened up a massive tank attack in the Kursk area, but they were contained and then defeated in a tremendous Soviet push westward. The Kursk tank battle was the last German attempt to take the offensive on the eastern front. Advancing steadily against stubborn German resistance, the Soviets reached the prewar Polish border in February 1944. In their spring offensive they liberated Poland as far as the Vistula River, and in their advance southward they caused the Romanian king to stage a palace revolution; depose the pro-Nazi dictator, Ion Antonescu; surrender to the Allies; and join the fight against Germany, on August 23. On September 5 the Soviet Union declared war on Bulgaria; Bulgaria surrendered, and Sofia was occupied on September 16.

The Soviet forces were aided by the development of partisan units behind the German front, mainly on occupied Soviet territory, and to a lesser degree in Poland and Slovakia. Originally, scattered groups of Soviet soldiers behind German lines had attempted to maintain themselves, but they were mostly wiped out by German troops and local pro-German inhabitants. However, Communist cadres, as well as Soviet POWs fleeing from German camps and Jews escaping from ghettos, formed the foundations of permanent partisan units. There was little direction from the unoccupied parts of the Soviet Union at first, but it was reorganized in May 1942, mainly for the forested region of Belorussia, under Panteleimon Ponomarenko. Trained Soviet troops were parachuted or infiltrated, most of them through the swamps of the so-called Briansk gap. Gradually, local inhabitants joined them, having experienced German brutality. By the spring of 1944, according to official estimates, some 400,000 pro-Soviet PARTISANS were operating behind German lines. While the measure of actual damage to the German war effort is disputed, substantial German forces were required to fight the partisans, and the insecurity behind the lines was a morale factor of significance. Railway and telephone lines were destroyed, and the local population was won over to the Soviet side. Jews, who had been one of the main recruiting sources at first, despite prevalent antisemitism among the partisans

Maj. Gen. Ivan Susloparov presenting Soviet awards to British Royal Air Force men. The latter were parachuted into Yugoslavia as part of a British mission establishing contact with the partisans and later linking up with the Soviets.

themselves, largely fell victim to the German antipartisan offensives in 1942 and 1943. Out of as many as forty thousand Jews in the forests, only a fraction survived.

Jews were also members of partisan units in Poland, although almost solely in the pro-Communist underground; the mainstream Armia Krajowa refused to accept Jews, and the right-wing underground, which joined the Armia Krajowa in 1943, killed any Jews it found. In Slovakia, a national uprising (*see* SLOVAK NATIONAL UPRISING) took place in late August 1944, led by a coalition of pro-Western and Communist forces. Probably some two thousand Jews took part in this uprising, which was defeated by German forces in October.

In Yugoslavia, the Communist partisans under TITO had liberated most of the country (nearly five thousand Jews were members of these forces), aided mainly by the British. Together with the Soviets, they liberated Belgrade and the rest of the country in October. German forces managed an orderly retreat from Greece and Yugoslavia.

Relations between the Soviet Union and the Polish government-in-exile in London, under Premier Władysław SIKORSKI, had been established in August 1941. A Polish army under Gen. Władysław Anders had been set up, composed of Polish nationals in the Soviet Union, including a large number of Jews. The relationship was uneasy, however, and the Anders army was allowed to leave the Soviet Union in 1942 in order to fight in Italy. Despite rampant antisemitism in the Anders forces, several thousand Jewish soldiers, as well as some of their relatives, managed to leave the Soviet Union at that time.

In 1943, the Germans uncovered mass graves of between eight thousand and ten thousand Polish officers who had been shot in 1940 at KATYN, in the western part of the Soviet Union. The Soviets were accused—rightly, as it turned out—of responsibility for this murder. They denied it at the time, and Polish-Soviet relations were severed. A pro-Communist Polish committee was established in the Soviet Union that later developed into a Polish provisional government with its center in Lublin (July 1944), under President Bolesław Bierut. In 1943 a Polish army under Soviet command was set up under Gen. Zygmunt Berling, and it participated in the liberation of Poland.

Faced with the attempts of the Hungarian government under Miklós KÁLLAY to arrange for a separate peace with the Allies, German forces invaded Hungary in March 1944 and forced the regent, Miklós HORTHY, to appoint a pro-German government under Döme SZTÓJAY. Sztójay was removed in August, and Horthy tried to arrange for a surrender of Hungary to the Soviets (October 1944). The Germans arrested him and established a fascist government under Ferenc SZÁLASI, which collaborated with them until the German collapse early in 1945. This was the framework for the destruction of most of Hungarian Jewry.

Bombardment of Germany and Invasion of France. Before the war, British air strategy had propounded the theory that the war could be decisively influenced by strategic bombing. However, while the number of bombers produced in Britain was double that of fighters, the Germans had many more bombers than the British in 1940. A change in British military thinking in the late 1930s had led to a larger fighter force, which saved Britain in 1940. British bombing raids on Germany took place at night because of the efficient daytime German air defense and despite the inaccuracy of nighttime bombing. In 1942, while indiscriminate carpet bombing of German cities undoubtedly affected German morale, the British losses were high (up to 5 percent of the participating aircraft), and the three 1,000-bomber raids against Cologne, Essen, and Bremen in May and June did not damage German industry in any significant way. German armaments production increased by 50 percent in 1942. Britain lost 1,014 bombers in that year.

The American air force, technically better equipped, concentrated on daytime bombing of military and industrial targets, while the British continued to devastate German cities. The Ruhr cities were attacked between March and July 1943, and the Hamburg area between July and November, the latter involving 17,000 bomber sorties. On August 17, the rocket experimental station at Peenemünde was raided. Between November 1943 and March 1944 Berlin was the main target.

However, this did not defeat Germany. Allied losses were very high (over 5 percent each raid), and German military production kept rising. On February 25, 1944, the Schweinfurt ball-bearing plant was attacked, causing real damage to the German war effort.

The crucial element in permitting the Allies to continue bombing was the development of the long-range (1,500 miles) Mustang fighter, superior to anything the Germans had at the time. The Mustangs became operational in December 1943, and by the end of the war, 14,000 had been produced. In 1943, 200,000 tons of bombs were dropped on Germany, nearly five times as much as in 1942. Yet German armaments production rose by another 50 percent. In 1944 the Allied air forces, now operating from Italy (and later also from France), achieved complete supremacy in the air. Oil refineries were the main American targets, while the British concentrated largely on the German transportation system in France and elsewhere. In late 1944 and early 1945, German production began to flag; parallel to this, blanket attacks against civilian centers were resumed, leading to the mid-February 1945 attack on Dresden, in which close to 100,000 civilians died.

German production had kept growing until late 1944, partly through the dispersal of the armaments industry (such as the attempt to build an oil refinery at Monowitz, part of the Auschwitz camp) and partly by the building of underground factories (such as those at DORA-MITTELBAU). All this was done with the help of slave laborers supplied by the SS, among them many Jews. German rockets (the V1 and V2) were directed at Britain, but they did not achieve any reversal of the situation. Albert SPEER was the engineer of German resilience in the production of arms.

After long preparations, and in the face of considerable technical and logistic difficulties, about 250,000 Allied soldiers went ashore in Normandy on June 6, 1944 (D-Day)—a force that was to grow to 2.2 million men, with 450,000 vehicles and 4 million tons of supplies landed from artificial harbors by late June. Victory was assured by the superiority of the Allied air forces, with some ten thousand planes. They were opposed by fifty-eight German divisions, including ten armored ones. On July 31, American forces

First Cairo Conference, November 22 to 26, 1943. Winston Churchill and Franklin D. Roosevelt discussed the Normandy invasion, and with Chiang Kai-shek they issued a declaration on the status of territories conquered by Japan. Seated, in front: Chiang Kai-shek, Roosevelt, and Churchill.

broke through the German defense lines, and the whole of France was liberated by the end of August. However, the Allies were checked in the southern part of the Netherlands, after an unsuccessful paratroop attack at Arnhem on the Rhine in September.

While preparing for a final attack on Germany, the western Allies under Eisenhower were taken by surprise in December 1944 when German forces under von Rundstedt attempted to break through American defense lines in Belgium and repeat their feat of 1940. Again, their armored equipment proved superior to that of the Allies, but with the clearing of the skies, the Allied air force, coupled with the spirited defense put up by the Americans, stopped and then reversed the German advance (the Battle of the Bulge).

The Battle for Germany. German resistance continued until the total Allied victory. There was widespread identification in Germany with the Nazi dictatorship: because of the fear of Soviet revenge for what the Germans had done in the Soviet Union; because of identification with the Nazi ideology; because of the Nazi terror machine; because of the lack of a viable political or military alternative; and because the Allied policy of unconditional surrender appeared to leave no other option. A group of rightist officers, supported by a coalition of largely conservative politicians, plotted to assassinate Hitler and establish a military government that would negotiate with the western Allies. However, the attempt on Hitler's life by Count Claus von Stauffenberg (July 20, 1944) failed, and the conspirators were caught and executed.

Final victory was assured not only by the overwhelming power of the Allied land forces, but by their control of the skies, despite the development of superior German jet planes (the ME 262). Had the war lasted longer, the Allied air superiority would have been seriously challenged. As it was, more than one thousand German planes were destroyed in January and February 1945, out of a total of fifty thousand German planes lost throughout the war.

Pvt. First Class Andrew E. Dubill, 141st Infantry Regiment, speaks with two Jewish girls who had been held prisoner by the Germans. In the railway cars in the background are bodies of prisoners slaughtered by SS troops at Seeshaupt, Germany. [United States Army]

A rebellion led by the Polish underground broke out in WARSAW on August 1, 1944, while the Soviet army was camped on the other side of the Vistula River. The Poles hoped to stake a claim for their postwar independence, but the Soviets refused to help them. Western efforts to supply arms to the rebels were futile, and they had to surrender on October 2, having sustained heavy losses and with Warsaw in ruins.

On January 12, 1945, the Soviets began a powerful offensive, taking Warsaw five days later. It brought them onto German territory by March. Budapest was liberated in January and February, and Vienna was taken in early April. The stubborn German defense of lost positions on Hitler's orders meant that their losses were multiplied against all military logic. On March 7 the Americans finally crossed the Rhine, and in April the Allies, from west and east, made their way through Germany. In the process, they discovered and liberated the concentration camps, beginning with Auschwitz in January (by the Soviets), and then BERGEN-BELSEN (April 14, by the British), BUCHENWALD (April 11, by the Americans), and others. Hundreds of thousands of concentration camp inmates who had been

marched through Germany at the last moment, with awesome loss of life (at least 250,000 Jews, if not more, died in this way), were liberated during these last days of the Reich. Adolf Hitler, in his fortified bunker in Berlin, committed suicide on April 30; his testament centered on his antisemitic phobia, and he demanded of the Germans that they fight "international Jewry" in the future. Mussolini was shot by Italian anti-Fascist partisans on April 28. Soviet forces conquered Berlin in early May, and the Germans surrendered on May 7. May 8 was proclaimed as the day of victory (VE-Day).

End of the War in the Pacific. Allied forces under Gen. Douglas MacArthur, advancing from one chain of Pacific islands to another, slowly gained naval and air supremacy. In October 1944 American forces began the liberation of the Philippines, and in a naval battle taking place from October 23 to 26, they sank a large part of the Japanese fleet. Air raids on the Japanese islands started in November, while British forces began the reconquest of Burma. In February and March 1945, the Americans suffered many casualties during the conquest of the island of Iwo Jima, 750 miles (1,207 km) from Yokohama. On April 1, Okinawa was invaded, and another Japanese fleet was destroyed, despite a new tactic of suicidal Japanese air raids by kamikaze pilots. The struggle for Okinawa lasted until June, again with large American casualties.

On August 6, the first atomic bomb was dropped, on Hiroshima. More than eighty thousand people were killed immediately, and many more died later of the aftereffects of radiation. Three days later, another bomb was dropped, on Nagasaki. On August 8, the Soviet Union joined the war against Japan in order to gain some disputed territories. Faced with the prospect of the mass destruction of the Japanese people, Emperor Hirohito intervened and ordered his generals to surrender. The surrender terms were accepted on August 14, and on August 26, American occupation forces under MacArthur landed in Japan. The formal surrender to the United States, Great Britain, and the Soviet Union was signed on September 2, and the surrender to the Chinese, on September 9.

BIBLIOGRAPHY

Churchill, W. S. *The Second World War.* 6 vols. London, 1948–1953.

Dallin, A. *German Rule in Russia, 1941–1945: A Study of Occupation Policies.* London, 1957.

Erdmann, K. *Die Zeit der Weltkriege.* Stuttgart, 1960.

Fuller, J. F. C. *The Second World War, 1939–1945: A Strategical and Tactical History.* New York, 1949.

Langer, W. L., and S. E. Gleason. *The Undeclared War.* New York, 1952.

Liddell-Hart, B. H. *History of the Second World War.* London, 1970.

Snyder, L. L. *The War: A Concise History, 1939–1945.* New York, 1961.

Werth, A. *Russia at War, 1941–1945.* London, 1964.

YEHUDA BAUER

WRB. *See* War Refugee Board.

WROCŁAW. *See* Breslau.

WURM, THEOPHIL (1868–1953), Evangelical theologian who was appointed bishop of Württemberg in 1933. At the time of the Nazi rise to power, Wurm supported the German Christians (Deutsche Christen), a faction that supported the Nazis. Late in 1933, however, when the Nazis wanted to enforce the *Gleichschaltung* (coordination under Nazism) law—that is, to subject the church institutions to Nazi ideology and organization—Wurm went into the opposition. He joined the Confessing Church (Bekennende Kirche) and violently opposed the appointment of Ludwig Müller as Reich bishop of the Evangelical Church (Evangelische Kirche), an appointment made to ensure support of the Nazis by the Protestant church and opposition to the Confessing Church. Because of his position, Wurm was placed under house arrest in 1934. Following a public protest, Wurm, like Bernhard LICHTENBERG and Clemens August Graf von GALEN, violently attacked the EUTHANASIA PROGRAM and the persecution of the Jews.

After the war, in 1945, Wurm was chairman of the Evangelical Church Council in Germany and one of the authors of the "Stuttgart Confession," which acknowledged that church clergy had not done enough in the struggle against the Nazis.

BIBLIOGRAPHY

Littell, F. H., and H. G. Locke, eds. *The German Church Struggle and the Holocaust.* Detroit, 1974.

ZVI BACHRACH

WVHA. *See* Wirtschafts-Verwaltungshauptamt.

Y

YAD VASHEM (English name, The Holocaust Martyrs' and Heroes' Remembrance Authority), Israeli national institution of Holocaust commemoration. The idea of establishing a memorial in Palestine for the Jews who fell victim to the Holocaust was conceived during World War II, when reports were received of the mass murder of Jews in the German-occupied countries. It was first proposed in September 1942, at a board meeting of the Jewish National Fund, by Mordecai Shenhavi, a member of Kibbutz Mishmar ha-Emek. Shenhavi proposed "the commemoration of the Holocaust in the Diaspora, and of the participation of the Jewish people in the Allied armies." He also proposed the name "Yad Vashem" (lit., "a monument and a name"), from Isaiah 56:5: "I will give them, in my house and in my walls, a monument and a name, better than sons and daughters; I will give them an everlasting name that shall never be effaced."

When the war came to an end and the full extent of the catastrophe was revealed, Shenhavi's proposal gained momentum. On May 2, 1945, he submitted it to the Jewish National Institutions in Jerusalem, under the title "Yad Vashem Foundation in Memory of the Lost Jewries in Europe—Outline of a Plan for the Commemoration of the Diaspora." The proposal was made public on May 25. This led to a joint meeting of the Jewish National Council (Va'ad Le'ummi) and the National Institutions on June 4, at which Shenhavi's and other proposals were discussed. The meeting recommended the adoption of Shenhavi's proposal, including the es-

tablishment of a center in Jerusalem to consist of an eternal light for the victims; a registry of their names; a memorial for the destroyed Jewish communities; a monument for the fighters of the ghettos; a memorial tower in honor of all the Jewish fighters against the Nazis; a permanent exhibit on the concentration and extermination camps; and a tribute to the "RIGHTEOUS AMONG THE NATIONS." The proposal also recommended the planting of memorial forests and the building of educational institutions for the children of the survivors.

The plan was discussed at a Zionist meeting in London on August 15, 1945, and it was decided to set up a provisional board, made up of the Zionist leaders David Remez (as chairman), Shlomo Zalman Shragai, and Baruch Zuckerman, in addition to Shenhavi. For about a year negotiations continued between the National Institutions, the Hebrew University, and the Chief Rabbinate of Palestine, centering mostly on the plan's financial and operational aspects. In February 1946 Yad Vashem opened an office in Jerusalem and a branch office in Tel Aviv. On June 1, 1947, it convened its first plenary session, and the following day the plan of "Yad Vashem for the Diaspora" was put on public exhibition. On July 13 and 14, 1947, the First Conference on Holocaust Research was held at the Hebrew University in Jerusalem. At the conference it was decided that the Holocaust documentation center would be located in Jerusalem, and that a thirty-one-member council and a scholarly committee would be set up. The outbreak of the Israeli War of

Aerial view of the Yad Vashem Holocaust Martyrs' and Heroes' Remembrance Authority, located on the Mount of Remembrance (Har ha-Zikaron) in Jerusalem: (1) main entrance; (2) cafeteria; (3) administration building, archives, and library; (4) World Center for Teaching the Holocaust; (5) Children's Memorial; (6) Historical Museum; (7) Hall of Names; (8) synagogue; (9) Art Museum; (10) auditorium; (11) Hall of Remembrance; (12) Wall of Remembrance, Ghetto Uprising monument, and "The Last March," by Nathan Rapoport; (13) Soldiers', Partisans', and Ghetto Fighters' monument, by Bernie Fink; (14) Avenue of the Righteous; (15) Garden of the Righteous; (16) Valley of the Destroyed Communities (under construction). [Pantomap, Jerusalem]

Independence in May 1948, however, brought Yad Vashem operations to an almost complete standstill.

In 1950, when the fighting had come to an end and armistice agreements had been signed, Shenhavi resumed his activities in behalf of the establishment of Yad Vashem, now addressing himself to the institutions of the state of Israel. He asked that priority be given to resuming the registration of Holocaust victims, on which a start had been made earlier, and that a law be enacted granting commemorative citizenship to the victims. The Israeli government appointed a special committee for this and the subject also came up for discussion at the Twenty-third Zionist Congress, which met in Jerusalem in the summer of 1951. The jurists who had been asked to deal with the legal aspects of the citizenship proposal had not arrived at a clear-cut decision, and the government therefore decided to continue preparations for the establishment of a Martyrs' and Heroes' Remembrance Authority that would also put the citizenship issue on the agenda. In 1952 the minister of education, Professor

Ben-Zion Dinur, presented to the Knesset (the Israeli parliament) a bill for the establishment of the authority, and on May 18, 1953, the Knesset unanimously passed the Yad Vashem Law, establishing the Martyrs' and Heroes' Remembrance Authority, with all the members rising and observing a minute of silence in memory of the Holocaust victims. The law passed its final reading on August 19, and was published on August 28, 1953.

The Yad Vashem Law states that the authority is established to commemorate the six million Jews murdered by the Nazis and their helpers; the Jewish communities and their institutions that had been liquidated and destroyed; the valor and heroism of the soldiers, the fighters of the underground, and the prisoners in the ghettos; the sons and daughters of the Jewish people who had struggled for their human dignity; and the "Righteous among the Nations" who had risked their lives in order to save Jews. Among the tasks that the law assigns to Yad Vashem are to establish memorial projects; to gather, research, and publish testimony of the Holocaust and its heroism and to impart its lessons; to grant commemorative citizenship to the victims; and to represent Israel on international projects aiming at perpetuating the memory of the victims of the Holocaust and of World War II.

The authority was set up as a corporate institution, administered by a council and a directorate. Under the law, the government undertook to participate in the costs of its construction and maintenance, but the authority was also permitted to accept allocations, income, and contributions from other sources. The law also provided that the minister of education issue regulations for the authority's method of operation. Ben-Zion Dinur, one of the outstanding Jewish historians of his generation, was appointed Yad Vashem's first chairman, serving in that post from 1953 to 1959. He was succeeded by Dr. Aryeh Kubovy, who held the post until his death in 1966. From that time, the posts of chairman of the council and of the directorate were separated; Gideon HAUSNER was chairman of the council from 1968 to 1988 and was succeeded by Dr. Joseph Burg; Katriel Katz served as chairman of the directorate from 1968 to 1972 and was succeeded by Dr. Yitzhak Arad.

A hill in west Jerusalem—part of the Mount Herzl complex—was chosen as the site of Yad Vashem. Architect Aryeh Elhanani designed the memorial buildings, and architects Benjamin Idelson and Aryeh Sharon the administration building. The building housing the archives, the library, and the administrative offices was completed in 1957, and Yad Vashem moved in that same year. On April 13, 1961, the Hall of Remembrance was dedicated, symbolizing the six million. Its walls are made of huge basalt slabs and it has a tent-shaped roof (hence its Hebrew name, Ohel Yizkor, or Tent of Remembrance); its two gates were sculpted by Israeli artists David Palombo and Bezalel Schatz, respectively. Alongside the Ohel Yizkor is the Historical Museum, which contains a permanent exhibition of authentic photographs, artifacts, and documents relating to the Holocaust and heroism.

On May 1, 1962, the first trees were planted on the Avenue of the Righteous among the Nations, and a public committee was appointed by Yad Vashem to determine who was entitled to the Righteous among the Nations medal. The award is given to those non-Jews who, at the risk of their own lives and for humanitarian reasons, saved the lives of Jews. Most of the trees on the avenue have been planted by the rescuers themselves, visiting Israel as guests of the Holocaust survivors whose lives they had saved, or on their own. By now the avenue encompasses Memorial Hill from all sides.

The Hall of Names was dedicated on April 7, 1968, to serve as the depository of the pages of testimony in which the names of the Holocaust victims are registered by surviving relatives and friends.

In April 1982 the building with the art museum and the auditorium commemorating the Jews who fell in the French Résistance was opened to the public, and on May 8, 1985, the Soldiers', Partisans', and Ghetto Fighters' monument, by Bernie Fink, was dedicated. Nandor Glid created a monument to the millions of Jews who perished in the extermination camps. It is situated on the northwestern edge of the large plaza between the museum and the Hall of Remembrance.

On June 28, 1987, the Children's Memorial, designed by architect Moshe Safdie, was dedicated, commemorating the one and a half million Jewish children who perished in the Holocaust.

The western end of Memorial Hill is the Valley of the Destroyed Communities, its walls, designed by architects Lipa Yahalom and Dan Zemach, consisting of large stones on which are engraved the names of the destroyed Jewish communities. The southern section of Memorial Hill contains Warsaw Ghetto Square and the Ghetto Uprising monument by Nathan Rapaport. It is on this site that the official opening assembly of Martyrs' and Heroes' Remembrance Day (on the Hebrew date, 27 Nisan) is held every year, attended by the president of Israel.

The Yad Vashem Archive contains millions of pages of documents, testimonies, and memoirs in many languages and is one of the largest and most important collections relating to the Holocaust period. The library has 80,000 volumes, mainly dealing with the Holocaust period but also including works on the growth of modern antisemitism, fascism, and Nazism, on the background of World War II, and on the fate of the Holocaust survivors. In 1973 Yad Vashem inaugurated a Holocaust Teaching Department, which has developed into a teaching center for Holocaust studies with two branches, in Jerusalem and at Volhynia House in Givatayim. It holds seminars for teachers from Israel and abroad, as well as study days for high school students, soldiers, and others, reaching tens of thousands each year.

From the outset Yad Vashem has engaged in historical research, conducted by the Research Department under the guidance of a

The Garden of the Righteous at Yad Vashem in Jerusalem, lined with carob trees planted by gentiles who risked their lives to save Jews during the Holocaust. [Zvi Reiter]

The interior of the Hall of Remembrance at Yad Vashem. The hall, designed by the Israeli architect Aryeh Elhanani, is a rectangular building with walls of basalt boulders and a concrete marquee ceiling. A gray mosaic floor is inscribed with the names of the twenty-two largest Nazi concentration and extermination camps. The central focus of the hall is the Eternal Light, designed by Kosso Eloul, which is shaped like a broken bronze cup. In front of the Light is a vault holding ashes of the martyrs, gathered from most of the extermination camps and brought to Israel. Commemorative and solemn state ceremonies are held in this hall.

scholarly advisory board made up of representatives of Holocaust research institutes in Israel's universities. One of the Yad Vashem Research Department's first undertakings was the Bibliographical Series on the Holocaust, numerous volumes of which have been published in cooperation with the Yivo Institute for Jewish Research in New York.

Since 1957 *Yad Vashem Studies,* an annual in Hebrew and English, has been published, with leading research scholars in Israel and abroad among its contributors. The publications division issues collections of documents and articles, memoirs, research studies, and the Dr. Janusz Korczak Book Series for youth. Yad Vashem is engaged in two major multivolume projects: *Pinkas Hakehillot* (Record Books of Jewish Communities), an encyclopedia of Jewish communities from their earliest beginnings to the time of their destruction; and a *Comprehensive History of the Holocaust,* each volume of which will deal with a particular country or subject. Yad Vashem has also participated in the preparation of the *Encyclopedia of the Holocaust.*

From April 7 to 11, 1968, Yad Vashem held its first scholarly congress, on "Jewish Resistance in the Holocaust," and since then has hosted congresses every few years, each dealing with a central subject of Holocaust research.

Yad Vashem has become a major national shrine, and more than a million people, from Israel and abroad, visit it every year. A visit to Yad Vashem is part of the program for official guests on state visits to Israel.

[*See also* Documentation Centers; Museums and Memorial Institutes.]

BIBLIOGRAPHY

Dinur, B. "Problems Confronting Yad Vashem in Its Work of Research." *Yad Vashem Studies* 1 (1957): 7–30.

Leshinsky, Y. "Yad Vashem as Art." *Ariel* 55 (1983): 7–25.

Zuroff, E. "Yad Vashem: More than a Memorial, More than a Name." *Shoah* 1/3 (Winter 1979): 4–9.

SHMUEL SPECTOR

YELIN, HAIM (1913–1944), writer and anti-Nazi fighter. Yelin was born in the town of Vilkija, Lithuania. At the end of World War I, his family settled in KOVNO and earned its livelihood by importing Yiddish books and managing the Libhober fun Vissen (Pursuers of Wisdom) library. In 1932, Yelin graduated from the Hebrew *Realgymnasium* in Kovno. He was found physically unfit for military service. For a short while he was active in No'ar Tsiyyoni Halutsi (Zionist Pioneering Youth; NETSAH), but left it when he became attracted to the Communist party (which was illegal), during his studies in the faculty of economics at Kovno University (1934–1938). He was a regular contributor to the Communist daily *Folksblat* and the monthly *Shtrala*.

After the incorporation of Lithuania into the Soviet Union in July 1940, Yelin was appointed to a senior post in the government printing office. During the first few days of the German invasion, in June of 1941, he and his family tried to escape into the Soviet interior, but they failed and on their return were put into the Kovno ghetto. For a time Yelin lived under an assumed name in the ghetto, and he also changed his appearance, out of fear that if recognized he would be charged with the Communist activities he had engaged in under the Soviet regime.

At the end of 1941, together with some of his friends who were also veteran Communist sympathizers, Yelin established a group that called itself the Antifascist Struggle Organization; he was elected its commander. His duties included managing the group's internal affairs, and liaison with elements outside the ghetto. Disguised as a peasant or a railway worker, he would leave the ghetto, seeking to establish contact with remnants of the Communist party, as well as with the Soviet PARTISANS who were becoming active in the area.

It was not until the summer of 1943 that Yelin succeeded in establishing permanent contact with the partisans. He became a member of the Communist party and was permitted to enter the partisans' base in the Rudninkai Forest, 90 miles (145 km) east of Kovno. As a result of his efforts a united front was formed of all the underground groups in the ghetto, including the Zionists, with the aim of enabling Jewish youths to join the partisan units in the forests. Yelin himself accompanied the first few groups who left the ghetto for this purpose. The operation, which enabled 350 young Jews to join the partisans, made Yelin a leading figure in the Kovno underground. On April 6, 1944, while on a mission outside the ghetto, he was ambushed by Gestapo agents, and later executed.

BIBLIOGRAPHY

Olieski, Y., et al., eds. *Haim Yelin: Ghetto Fighter and Writer*. Tel Aviv, 1980. (In Hebrew.)

DOV LEVIN

YELLOW BADGE. *See* Badge, Jewish.

YIDDISH LITERATURE IN THE HOLOCAUST. *See* Literature on the Holocaust: Yiddish Literature.

YIDISHER ARBETER-BUND. *See* Bund.

YISHUV, the Jewish community in Palestine. On the eve of World War II, the Yishuv was beset by a deep political crisis caused by a combination of two factors: (1) the deterioration of the legal status and economic condition of the Jews of central and eastern Europe; and (2) the strained relations with the British Mandatory power, which reached their nadir with the publication of the 1939 WHITE PAPER. The latter restricted Jewish immigration into Palestine to a total of 75,000 for the following five years, thus imposing further limitations on the capacity of the community of 470,000 to provide a haven for at least a part of European Jewry. As a result, ALIYA BET ("illegal" immigration) became one of the principal means that the Yishuv used in its struggle with the British, with the latter attacking the boats with "illegal" immigrants on board and interning the immigrants in camps. When the war broke out, the British intensified their drive against "illegal" immigration, claiming that this form of immigration could be serving the Axis powers by smuggling into Palestine spies posing as Jewish refugees. Disasters such as the sinking of the *Patria* and the STRUMA became the landmarks of that struggle.

Despite the conflict with the British over immigration, the Jews of Palestine regarded themselves as a natural ally of the countries that were fighting Hitler, and as soon as the war broke out, the Yishuv's institutions declared that they were rallying to the Allies' side. Some thirty thousand Jewish Palestinians, men and women, volunteered for service in the British army, even though the British systematically sought to put a brake on such enlistment and to keep the Jewish volunteers from getting proper military training and battle experience. Only in September 1944 was approval given for the formation of the JEWISH BRIGADE GROUP, which was eventually to see action in Italy under its own flag.

This conflict between the British attitude toward the Zionist enterprise and the "illegal" immigrants, on the one hand, and, on the other hand, the fact that the Yishuv had no choice but to stand at the Allies' side in the war became the principal issues at stake in the relations between the organized Jewish community of Palestine and the British, as well as between the Yishuv institutions

A Jewish Brigade soldier teaches Hebrew to Jewish refugee children at the Rishonim training farm in Bari (in southeastern Italy, on the Adriatic Sea). This was the first training farm established by Palestinian Jewish soldiers (1944). [Beth Hatefutsoth]

and the dissident underground movements, the Irgun Tseva'i Le'ummi and the Stern group, LOHAMEI HERUT ISRAEL.

Another cardinal problem was to understand the real truth behind the reports coming in from Europe concerning the situation of the Jews. In the first few months of the war a great many reports reached the Yishuv about developments in Europe, conveyed by the media, Jewish organizations, and the thousands of refugees who still managed to reach Palestine. At that stage, the fate of the Jews of Europe was interpreted as a side effect of the war: in every war the civil population had suffered, especially the Jewish population. Lower-rank Germans, it was thought, were giving vent to their instincts, especially in countries with a tradition of antisemitism where the local population was collaborating with the Germans. In the second half of 1940 and in 1941, the prevailing view in Palestine was that the situation of the Jews in the occupied areas was very serious but that it had stabilized, and that most of the Jews, including those in the ghettos in Poland, would survive, albeit at the price of terrible suffering, loss of life, and loss of property. No one foresaw that what was taking place would develop into all-out systematic mass murder. It appears, moreover, that it was only in the spring of 1941, on the eve of the invasion of Soviet Russia, that the Nazi leadership itself decided on the physical destruction of all the Jews of Europe. In the Yishuv institutions, decreasing attention was paid to the reports arriving from occupied Europe, and instead they concentrated mostly on the problem of the millions of Jews who, it was assumed, would be penniless and destitute when the war was over, a problem for which Zionism would have to come up with a quick solution. The leadership of the Yishuv was of the opinion that for the time being, until the end of the war, aid to the Jews of Europe should be provided by the great Jewish world organizations with financial means and political contacts, such as the American Jewish JOINT DISTRIBUTION COMMITTEE, the AMERICAN JEWISH COMMITTEE, the American Jewish Congress, the WORLD JEWISH CONGRESS, and Western Jewry in general. Up until that time, the Yishuv itself had depended on help and support from Jews elsewhere, and was not re-garded as capable of aiding millions of Jews in Europe.

Following the invasion by Germany of the Soviet Union in June 1941, the systematic mass murder of Jews was launched in the newly occupied territories. The Yishuv had by then established channels for communications from Europe; nevertheless, it had no clear picture of what was transpiring, and its assumption was that the fate of Soviet Jews would be similar to that of the Jews of Poland. It was only at the beginning of 1942 that factual reports began coming in to the Yishuv—and, for that matter, to the entire free world. The sources were official quarters, such as the Soviet foreign minister and the POLISH GOVERNMENT-IN-EXILE in London. In the summer of 1942, the RIEGNER CABLE was received from Switzerland, where Jewish representatives had a reliable German source, stating that all indications pointed to the systematic and total extermination of the Jews by scientific methods.

At this very time the German forces in North Africa, under the command of Gen. Erwin Rommel, were advancing on Alexandria, and came within 62 miles (100 km) of the Egyptian port. The British made it clear that if Alexandria fell, they would abandon Palestine and withdraw all the way to Iraq. To the Yishuv leaders it was clear that the British withdrawal, followed by a German conquest of Palestine, would mean the end of the Yishuv, with the Arabs assisting the Germans in destroying the Zionist enterprise and the Jewish population. Both the leadership and the general public were resolved that the Jews would not evacuate Palestine, not children and women, nor any of the public figures, and that they would make a stand on Mount Carmel, with its natural features and its proximity to the Haifa port, and hold out there up to the end.

It was at this critical point that shocking reports about the fate of European Jewry reached the Yishuv. Faced with the imminent threat of a German invasion, the Yishuv, unable to relate to European Jewish reality in terms of rescue, could only empathize in a fraternity of fate. It was only when Rommel retreated and the Western Desert front gradually receded that the Yishuv was able to breathe. In the fall of 1942 a group of Palestinian Jews arrived in the country, repatriated in an exchange of Jews and Germans. Their reports shocked the Yishuv, confirming the information previously received and complementing it with a clearer, and terrifying, picture. The Jewish Agency Executive published an official communiqué describing the situation of the Jews in Europe, but in hindsight, one can see that even then, despite the shock and the change that had taken place in the Yishuv's awareness, there was still no full realization of the true situation. This was due to the difficulty in grasping the events of the Holocaust both in their human and moral implications and in their implications for the future of the Jewish people.

Reaction and Internal Organization. With the realization of the seriousness of the situation in Europe, the Yishuv went into mourning and held demonstrations, expressing both deep despair and self-blame. This was coupled with a sharp internal debate on the nature of its relations with Jews in the diaspora and the relations between Zionism and the Jewish heritage. Secular Socialist Zionists questioned whether fasting and prayers were the appropriate expression for the deep anger and pain that the Yishuv was experiencing.

There was also a debate as to whether days of mourning, demonstrations, and protest strikes in the British military installations were contributing to the concrete goal, the rescue of the Jews of Europe. The political leadership of the Yishuv was concerned that demonstrations in cities with a mixed Arab-Jewish population might lead to a renewal of the Arab attacks on the Yishuv that had taken place from 1936 to 1939, and that the British might exploit the demonstrations and strikes as a pretext for harassing the Yishuv, whose assistance and army volunteers it no longer needed, after Rommel's retreat and the general improvement in the Allies' military situation in the Middle East.

Following three days of mourning, the Yishuv leadership considered plans for the internal organization of rescue efforts. In January 1943 the JOINT RESCUE COMMITTEE of the Jewish Agency (Va'ad ha-Hatsala ha-Meuhad she-le-yad ha-Sokhnut ha-Yehudit) was set up. The establishment of this committee seemingly indicated the Yishuv's desire to overcome partisan differences, and the Jewish Agency's determination to establish a separate body for rescue efforts. In practice, the committee had neither the authority nor

Moshe Shertok (Sharett), head of the Jewish Agency's Political Department, visits the soldiers of the Jewish Brigade in Italy (March 1945). [Beth Hatefutsoth]

the means that it required. The committee, and especially its chairman, Itzhak GRUENBAUM, came in for heavy criticism. Gruenbaum carried out his assignment with many hesitations and public debates, which did not reflect his deep distress and his many exertions on behalf of the rescue of the Jews.

Political contacts linked with rescue efforts and the immigration of refugees were maintained by the Jewish Agency's Political Department, headed by Moshe Shertok (Sharett), and by its Immigration Department, headed by Eliyahu Dobkin. At the end of 1942 an operational center was established in Istanbul, staffed by about a dozen representatives of the Yishuv institutions and political parties. This was in addition to the existing office in Geneva, which from the beginning of the war had included representatives of the Yishuv and of Jewish organizations such as the World Jewish Congress, the He-Haluts Center, and the Immigration Department. In both these centers the representatives, together with the operatives of the Mosad le-Aliya Bet (organization for "illegal" immigration), were in close communication with Palestine, and especially with the Histadrut (the General Federation of Labor), where most contacts with the youth movements and parties were concentrated. The Histadrut was also the headquarters for the leaders in charge of the Yishuv's security and its confidential contacts with the diaspora: Eliyahu Golomb, Shaul Meirov, Zvi Yehieli (Schechter), and, in an advisory capacity, Berl Katznelson and Yitzhak Tabenkin.

There was an unending internal wrangle over the finances to be allocated for the rescue operation. Many members of the leadership—in the Va'ad Le'ummi (National Council), in the top trade union echelon, in Mapai (the Labor party), and in other political parties—were of the opinion that substantial funds had to be allocated at once, even for rescue projects that might appear farfetched and with little prospect of success. Among the advocates of this approach were David Remez, then the Histadrut secretary-general, Golda Meyerson (Meir), and Yaakov Hazan, the Ha-Shomer ha-Tsa'ir leader. But the Jewish Agency Executive, and especially its chairman, David BEN-GURION, Shertok, and the treasurer, Eliezer Kaplan, held that

the Yishuv's meager resources had to be handled carefully and with restraint, especially after the early years of the war, which in economic terms had been very difficult for the Yishuv. These leaders were of the opinion that the dimensions of the Holocaust and the fact that it was taking place far away from Palestine made doubtful the chances of successful rescue efforts. They felt that finances should be made available only for concrete projects with clear prospects of succeeding.

In mid-1943, when it became clear that rescue at that stage meant providing the means simply to keep Jews alive in the occupied territories, the Jewish Agency Executive was persuaded to allocate more funds. The Yishuv's economic situation was improving, and it was ready to contribute to the rescue efforts; individuals, agricultural settlements, and institutions were offering contributions even before being asked to do so by the Yishuv leadership. Most of the Jewish population was made up of persons who had come from Europe, especially eastern, southeastern, and central Europe, in the six years preceding the war, and it was their relatives, personal and political friends, and the communities in which they had grown up that were to be rescued.

Large sums were allocated outside the budget of the Jewish Agency Executive. They were collected from private individuals; from the well-to-do by special drives, regular deductions from salaries, and taxation (by agreement) of existing assets. The Histadrut stood at the helm of the fund-raising campaigns and also made substantial contributions from its own resources.

From February 1, 1943, to the end of the war, the sum of 1,325,000 Palestinian pounds (equivalent to $32 million in the late 1980s) was expended on rescue efforts. Two-thirds of this sum was expended inside occupied Europe and one-third on bringing Jews to Palestine; the latter began to a serious extent in March 1944, when emigration via Romania became possible. This sum constituted 34 percent of the Joint Mobilization and Rescue Campaign (the official fund established by the national institutions to cope with wartime emergencies), and was equivalent to 26 percent of the total expenditures made by the Jewish Agency.

The Yishuv leadership felt that the financial burden of the help and rescue efforts should be borne mainly by the Jewish communities in the free world. At the end of 1942, Ben-Gurion and Zalman Rubashov (Shazar) proposed that the Joint Distribution Committee should provide the finances and the Yishuv should provide the volunteers required for the various operations. For most of the war years the Joint's board of directors rejected this idea, but its representatives in Europe found it easier to reach an understanding with the Yishuv's representatives than did the executive boards of the two bodies. The Joint provided half a million Palestinian pounds ($12 million) in various ways, representing some 39 percent of the total expenditures made by the Yishuv on rescue efforts.

The response of the Jewish communities in the free world—in Britain, South Africa, and elsewhere—did not match that of the Joint; their total contribution amounted to 170,000 Palestinian pounds ($4,080,000), no more than 13 percent of the total. There were several reasons for this modest result: concern that such contributions might be regarded as violating Allied regulations forbidding the transfer of funds and materials to enemy territory; fear of antisemitic reactions; divisiveness and quarrels; the absence of one central address for the disunited Jewish people and the refusal to accept the Yishuv and the Zionist movement as such an address; and a lack of understanding of the situation of the Jews of Europe and the extreme urgency of the rescue efforts. However, Jews in Switzerland and Turkey did lend the Yishuv representatives sizable sums for rescue efforts, on the mere assurance that these sums would be paid back at some future date.

When the Yishuv had organized for the rescue effort, at the beginning of 1943, rescue programs began to emerge both in Palestine and in the Jewish communities of the occupied countries. The Yishuv institutions, mainly the Jewish Agency Executive and the Histadrut Executive Council, handled a number of these programs at the same time.

1. At the end of 1942 a proposal was received from Romania according to which the seventy thousand surviving Romanian Jews, who had been expelled to TRANSNISTRIA, would be permitted to emigrate in return for several tens of millions of dollars. The Jewish Agency Executive maintained contacts with Romanian representatives, despite its doubt that Romania, a German ally, would be permitted to operate on its own, in a manner that contradicted the "FINAL SOLUTION." It is now known that the Romanians informed the Germans of the proposal before establishing contact with Jewish organizations in Romania and Palestine, and that the Germans foiled it. All that Romanian Jewry (which had been actively engaged in rendering aid to the expellees) and the Jewish Agency were able to accomplish was to facilitate the transfer of material help to Transnistria. In addition, in 1944, they managed to have the survivors (including thousands of orphans) brought back to Romania. Later, some were taken to Palestine.

2. In the fall of 1942, members of the Slovak Jewish Rescue Committee, the PRACOVNÁ SKUPINA (Working Group), proposed to Dieter WISLICENY, a German representative in Bratislava, the EUROPA PLAN—the payment of a substantial sum in return for the Germans' halting the deportations of Jews, from all over Europe, to extermination camps. Wisliceny, one of Adolf EICHMANN's close aides, informed the authors of the plan that his chief, Heinrich HIMMLER, was prepared in principle to negotiate such an arrangement for two million to three million dollars, provided a payment on account were first made. For a time the Jewish Agency, which had received the call for money to be transferred for this purpose, was unable to decide whether this was a serious proposal and not just a fraud, because the sum in question was so much less than what the Romanians had asked for. In May 1943 Wisliceny reconfirmed Himmler's consent, and in June the Jewish Agency Executive decided to pay $200,000 as an advance sum. In August its emissary in Istanbul, Teddy Kollek, on instructions from Shertok, delivered a large part of this sum to a courier who was leaving for Bratislava. At that point, however, the Germans informed their Jewish contacts that the proposal was no longer being considered.

3. At the end of 1942 the British government agreed to a request made by the Jewish Agency to make available a total of 29,000 immigration certificates to Palestine for Jewish children in the occupied countries of Europe; this was the number of certificates still remaining from the 75,000 that had been allocated on the eve of the war. Reports from Europe stated that children were the first among the Nazis' victims. This British agreement, however, was a sham; in the course of 1943 it turned out that not only did the Germans have no intention of letting the children go, but the British were doing their best to torpedo the efforts of the Agency, Histadrut, and Yishuv emissaries to rescue the children, because of their concern that when the quota was exhausted they would face a sharp confrontation with the Yishuv over a new quota of immigration visas. This chapter revealed British policy in all its callousness, causing bitter disappointment and a profound feeling of helplessness in the Yishuv.

4. Further proposals were raised by the Jewish Agency Executive and other Jewish bodies in the free world, such as the idea of distributing hundreds of thousands of "protective passports," under the imprimatur of the Allied powers, among the Jews in the occupied countries; giving them the status of prisoners of war; exchanging them for Germans living in the Allied countries (*see* EXCHANGE: JEWS AND GERMANS); transferring them from Europe to transit camps in North Africa; or keeping them in transit camps in their countries of origin, under the protection of the International RED CROSS, with the financing to be provided by the Jewish people. Most important of all was the proposal that the Allied powers demand of the Germans, by way of neutral countries such as Switzerland and Sweden, that they put an immediate end to the annihilation of the Jews, coupled with an unequivocal warning of the consequences to Germany if it failed to heed this call. The Allied powers, for reasons of their own, did not assiduously pursue these proposals, claiming that only the end of the war would bring an end to the Jewish plight and that nothing should be done to divert the Allies from the measures they were taking to achieve that purpose as quickly as possible.

5. In the second half of 1943, in the wake of the BERMUDA CONFERENCE, the Yishuv institutions came to the bitter conclusion that chances of the rescue of Jews on a large scale were very poor, if not close to nil. The German extermination machine was operating relentlessly and speedily; the rescue of Jews was a low priority in the eyes of the Allied powers; and the Jewish world remained disunited and helpless. The Yishuv therefore concluded that the main effort would have to be directed toward the "small rescue," as it was called in the Rescue Committee, which had been continuing all the time alongside the grand schemes. This meant sending food parcels, medicines, money, and various documents to the occupied countries; helping to smuggle individuals across borders, especially from the occupied countries into neutral or satellite states; arranging for the exchange of small groups of Jews for Germans; and maintaining contact by mail and printed materials, as a means of encouragement and hope.

These efforts were for the most part directed by the Yishuv emissaries in Istanbul and Geneva, who had succeeded in setting up a manifold program of activities—an impressive achievement, in relation to their small number, which did not exceed more than twenty or thirty individuals. They succeeded, even though personal or political relations among them often left much to be desired, because they were young, dedicated, and resourceful, and, above all, because they were deeply affected by the suffering of the Jews of Europe.

The "illegal" immigration organization operated out of Istanbul. Between February 1942, when the *Struma* sank in the Bosphorus, and the spring of 1944, the organization had not been able to get hold of a single boat, but by the end of that year it had transported 3,500 to 5,000 persons into Palestine by sea, and another 1,500 had come in by the overland route, mostly on their own.

6. In the spring of 1944, when the deportation of Hungarian Jews to AUSCHWITZ was launched, an SS proposal was submitted to the Yishuv leadership for the release of a million Jews, by way of Spain and Portugal, in exchange for ten thousand trucks and dozens of tons of other essential goods. This offer came to be known by the name that Eichmann gave it, "Blood for Goods." After the war this proposal became part of the bitter dispute involving the activities of Dr. Rezső

KASZTNER, who had led the negotiations with SS representatives in Hungary. The Jewish Agency's assessment was that the Germans were more interested in making a separate peace with the West, before they were defeated in the war and before the Soviets conquered a substantial part of Germany, than they were in stopping the newly inaugurated murder of the Jews of Hungary.

Basing itself on its experience with similar plans that had been brought up in the past, the Jewish Agency leadership was convinced that the Allied powers would not agree to the shipment of material aid to Germany. Nevertheless, the Jewish leaders assumed that negotiations, even as a pretense, might put a stop to the deportations. This consideration led Dr. Chaim WEIZMANN and Shertok to make repeated appeals to the Allied powers, which, however, were of no avail. The United States, which at first had taken a positive attitude on opening negotiations, relented in the face of adamant Soviet opposition to the idea. Britain, which believed that the German proposal was an attempt at blackmail and psychological warfare, on several occasions deliberately misled the Jewish leaders and their representatives in order to prevent any contact between them and the Germans from taking place. Negotiations on the issue never reached the concrete state that would have made it possible to determine whether or not the Nazis were indeed prepared to release Jews in exchange for goods.

7. In the summer of 1944 the Jewish Agency Executive made repeated appeals to the Allies to bomb the extermination installation of Auschwitz and the railway lines leading to the camp. These appeals were rejected, one after the other, on technical and other grounds, despite the very strong feelings on the issue in public opinion, Jewish and non-Jewish. Today it is clear that it would have been possible to launch air attacks on the installations and destroy them by precision bombing (see AUSCHWITZ, BOMBING OF).

8. At the end of 1942, the Jewish Agency submitted various proposals of a military nature to the British, at the core of which was the idea of parachuting into the occupied countries hundreds of young people—who had come to Palestine from these countries and were familiar with their languages, local customs, and geography—the purpose being to raise the morale of the Jews there and persuade them to rise up against their persecutors. There was no lack of volunteers for this kind of mission, but the British did not want the Yishuv's military capability to grow by providing such training to its best-qualified young people. The British therefore used delaying tactics, and in the end only thirty-five men and two women parachuted or were infiltrated into Europe (see PARACHUTISTS, JEWISH). Most of them left on their mission in the spring of 1944 or thereafter, but because of their small and late appearance on the scene, close to the end of the war, the significance of their deed was mainly symbolic. However, in the last few months of the war and the immediate postwar period, they succeeded in rescuing and encouraging Jewish survivors and in laying the groundwork for their immigration to Palestine. The contact with and aid to the Jews was seen by the parachutists as their main task, and their allegiance to their British uniforms and the furthering of the overall war aims, as a secondary objective. Their appearance in Europe and their generally high moral and human qualities made them a legend, and names such as Hannah SZENES and Enzo SERENI became part of the Jewish national mythology.

The Yishuv leadership and the members of the Jewish Agency Executive were in a trap during the Holocaust period. The Germans' implacable determination to carry out the "Final Solution"; the terrible indifference shown by the Allied powers and the absence of any alternative source of political support; the difficulties caused by the wartime conditions; the divisions and quarrels among the Jewish people, of whom the Zionists were only a small part; and, above all, the Yishuv's lack of any military, financial, and political means of its own for independent action—all of these combined to make it impossible to save millions. And so the Yishuv concentrated on the saving of thousands. The "small rescue" was conducted alongside the principal efforts of the Yishuv: settling on the land, maintaining security, and seeking to assure the political future. In those years, the leadership concentrated on strengthening the Yishuv, so that when the war ended it would be capable of taking in the surviving remnants and maintaining the struggle for its political goals.

[See also Beriḥa; Rescue Committee of the Jewish Agency in Turkey.]

BIBLIOGRAPHY

Bauer, Y. From Diplomacy to Resistance: A History of Jewish Palestine, 1939–1945. New York, 1973.

Eliash, S. "The Rescue Policy of the Chief Rabbinate of Palestine before and during World War II." Modern Judaism 3/3 (October 1983): 291–308.

Gelber, Y. "Zionist Policy and the Fate of European Jewry, 1943–1944." Studies in Zionism 7 (Spring 1983): 133–167.

Gelber, Y. "Zionist Policy and the Fate of European Jewry (1939–1942)." Yad Vashem Studies 13 (1979): 169–210.

Porat, D. An Entangled Leadership: The Yishuv and the Holocaust, 1942–1945. Tel Aviv, 1986. (In Hebrew.)

Slutzky, Y. "The Palestine Jewish Community and Its Assistance to European Jewry in the Holocaust Years." In Jewish Resistance during the Holocaust. Proceedings of the Conference on Manifestations of Jewish Resistance, pp. 414–426. Jerusalem, 1971.

Vago, B. "Some Aspects of the Yishuv Leadership's Activities during the Holocaust." In Jewish Leadership during the Nazi Era: Patterns of Behavior in the Free World, edited by R. L. Braham, pp. 45–65. New York, 1985.

DINA PORAT

YITZHAK KATZENELSON GHETTO FIGHTERS' HOUSE COMMEMORATING THE HOLOCAUST AND THE REVOLT.
See Museums and Memorial Institutes: Bet Loḥamei ha-Getta'ot.

YIZKOR BOOK, a book commemorating a Jewish community destroyed in the Holocaust; about nine hundred such books have been written. The books are dedicated to the larger communities, but often contain chapters on neighboring small communities. Thousands of people, from all walks of life, have participated in the commemoration project—ranging from political and intellectual leaders to any person possessing information about the community in which he or she had lived.

The authors of the Yizkor books have recorded primarily the period of the Holocaust, as well as the preceding decades, approximately from the beginning of the twentieth century—a period during which the Jewish communities that were later annihilated reached unprecedented heights in every sphere of life, including the economy, politics, culture, education, science, and the arts. There was a danger that important information on these manifold activities and achievements would be lost forever, because most of the archives, the collections of books, and the artworks had disappeared during the Holocaust. To save this knowledge, more than ten thousand authors and over one thousand editors and publishers participated in the enterprise, with the number of publishing and fund-raising committees involved also reaching the thousands.

In most cases the editing was entrusted to men of letters who came from the community to which the specific Yizkor book was dedicated. In some instances the editing was done by historians, writers, and professionals, who produced outstanding historical monographs; they included Philip Friedman, Nathan Michael Gelber, Joseph Schatzky, Raphael Mahler, Isaiah Trunk, and Nachman Blumental. A number of outstanding historians, such as Ben-Zion Dinur, Joseph Kermish, Chone Schmeruk, Shmuel Ettinger, and Yehoshua Goldberg, published many scholarly contributions. Yizkor books also reprinted rare works by leading Jewish historians of the period preceding the Holocaust—Meir Balaban, Ignacy SCHIPER, Simon DUBNOW, and Emanuel RINGELBLUM—thereby making these studies available to a large reading public. Many articles on rabbis and Hasidic "rebbes," and on Hasidism, liturgical music, and the religious life of the communities were written by Meir Shimeon Geshuri. David Davidowitz contributed much to historical research on the synagogues in the communities of Poland.

Most of the books are dedicated to the Jewish communities of eastern Europe: POLAND (in its pre–World War II borders), the SOVIET UNION, ROMANIA, LITHUANIA, LATVIA, Czechoslovakia (see SLOVAKIA and BOHEMIA AND MORAVIA, PROTECTORATE OF), and HUNGARY. Jews of western European origin, mainly from Germany, followed in the footsteps of their original communities' historiographical tradition, publishing some one hundred memorial volumes, mainly in the form of monographs or anthologies, written for the most part in German, by a single author.

A memorial volume published in New York in 1937, dedicated to the martyrs of the community of Felsztyn, who were slaughtered in 1919—*Felshtin Sammelbuch zum Andenk fun di Felshtiner Kedoishim* (Felsztyn Anthology; Memorial to the Felsztyn Martyrs)—may be regarded as the archetype of the Yizkor book. The prototype Yizkor book was published in New York in 1943, when the Holocaust was still raging; this was the *Lodzer Yizkor Buch*, published by the Fareynikter Rettungskomitet (United Rescue Committee). An unusual Yizkor book is the one dedicated to the Sierpc community in Poland, published in a DISPLACED PERSONS' camp in Munich in 1947. It was written in Yiddish, but for lack of Hebrew print, Latin characters were used for the Yiddish text. Generally, the Yizkor books are written in Hebrew or Yiddish, or both; sometimes they also contain a synopsis in English, or, in a few cases, in another European language.

The Yizkor books include articles on the history of the community concerned, from its beginning until its destruction, but the more significant subjects are those dealing with the Holocaust and the following years: the life of the community up to the time that ghettos were established; life in the ghettos; the liquidation of the communities and the annihilation of their members; the uprisings and resistance; concentration camps, labor camps, and extermination camps; the attitude of the local population toward the Jews; collaborators with the Nazis and the "Righteous among the Nations"; the fate and fortunes of Jewish refugees and the displaced persons; the She'erit ha-Peletah ("surviving remnant"); "illegal" immigration into Palestine; the postwar history of the community; and information on members of the community living in Israel or those who had made their home in other countries. Articles dealing with community life up to 1939 include descriptions of the way of life, local color, cultural and religious life, demographics, economics, politics, and social institutions.

Of special importance are the documents published in the Yizkor books—diaries, letters, poems, and literary items dating from the Holocaust period. No less valuable are testimonies and memoirs put on paper by Holocaust victims or by survivors, during the occupation or shortly thereafter. The illustrations found in the books are also, for the most part, important and rare items, providing further documentation of the Holocaust and the years that preceded it.

As is to be expected in a project of such vast dimensions, the Yizkor books contain methodological and factual errors, some of quite a serious nature, especially in the books edited and supervised by laymen. Some stories and notes in the books tend to be banal or apologetic. Occasionally the editors have tampered with documents, either to absolve Holocaust victims of real or imagined guilt, or to protect the reputation of survivors. Descriptions of life in the Jewish communities prior to the Holocaust are often full of nostalgia and deal only with the positive aspects of their life, to the total exclusion of the seamy side. Some of the books are careless with dates and data.

Such deficiencies, however, do not detract from the inestimable importance of the immense Yizkor book project. The effort continues to this day, but now on a more modest scale than previously. The Yizkor books are especially precious to the survivors from the various communities, to their families, and to their children and grandchildren who wish to learn more about their own roots. Future historians, writers, scholars, ethnographers, and folklorists will find in them an inexhaustible resource.

BIBLIOGRAPHY

Edelheit, A. J., and H. Edelheit. *Bibliography on Holocaust Literature.* Boulder, 1986.

Piekarz, M. *The Holocaust and Its Aftermath: Hebrew Books Published in the Years 1933–1972.* Vol. 2. Jerusalem, 1974. (In Hebrew.)

ABRAHAM WEIN

YOUTH ALIYA (Youth Immigration), movement for the transfer of children and young people, initially from Germany and subsequently from other countries, to Palestine (Israel). The idea of Youth Aliya was originally propounded by Recha Freier, to deal with distressed Jewish youth in Germany who had been dismissed from employment. Her intention was to bring these young people to Palestine and to provide them with education and agricultural vocational training in rural settlements, principally in the kibbutzim.

At first, Youth Aliya was operated through the Jüdische Jugendhilfe (Jewish Youth Help) organization and the Committee for Cooperation with Children and Youth Aliya. After the Nazi rise to power in Germany in 1933, the Youth Aliya Office was created under the auspices of the Jewish Agency in Jerusalem. The office was headed by Henrietta Szold, founder of the Hadassah Women's Zionist Organization in the United States. This organization bore most of the financial burden of the Youth Aliya undertaking. The first group of youth immigrated to Palestine from Germany in February 1934, with immigration permits obtained for this purpose from the British Mandatory government.

From 1933 until the final absorption of survivors after World War II, 30,353 children and young people immigrated to Palestine and were brought up with the help of Youth Aliya. Out of this number 5,012 had immigrated by the outbreak of the war (1934–1939), 9,342 during the war (1939–1945), and 15,999 after the war (1945–1948). These figures place Youth Aliya at the head of the projects to rescue children and youth in the Holocaust period.

Youth activities, incorporating study with work, were created in the kibbutz movements. Youth counselors were trained for care of the young people, who came from different countries, knew no Hebrew, and arrived without families. Youth Aliya expanded into an institution and helped to supervise and aid the newcomers in kibbutzim and many other places. Some of the youth were sent to *moshavim* (cooperative settlements), where they were taken in by adoptive families. The percentage of those remaining in the *moshavim* upon reaching adulthood was very high.

As the situation of German Jewry deteriorated, the number of Youth Aliya candidates increased, particularly after the KRISTALLNACHT pogrom took place in November 1938. In Germany, a number of educational organizations were created for the young people, in addition to the already existing He-Haluts and Berit Halutsim Datiyyim agriculture training centers and the "intermediate training" centers for youths aged fourteen and fifteen from the pioneer youth movements. Some young people from these centers and organizations, including the training kibbutzim, were evacuated to transit points in neighboring countries—in Great Britain, the Netherlands, and Sweden.

After the outbreak of the war, Youth Aliya exploited every opportunity to bring to Palestine the youth for whom immigration permits had been obtained and who had been prevented from immigrating by the prevailing situation. Efforts were also made to obtain immigration permits that had been frozen in British consulates in the Greater German Reich (Germany, Austria, and Czechoslovakia). During the war years, Youth Aliya constantly pressed the Mandatory government to accept increased quotas of immigration permits. The permits received were sent, through the central office in Geneva or the Palestine Office of the Jewish Agency, to countries from which it was still possible to bring groups of youth. In this way, youth were brought from Romania, Italy, Sweden, Denmark, Yugoslavia, Bulgaria, Hungary, Turkey, and Cyprus. The best-known immigration episodes are those of the "TEHRAN CHILDREN" and the "Transnistrian children."

After the war Youth Aliya counselors were sent to Europe, where they helped organize homes for children and young people in the DISPLACED PERSONS' camps in Europe and assisted in educational administration of those institutions. A special extension was active in the CYPRUS DETENTION CAMPS.

BIBLIOGRAPHY

Adiel, S. *Literature about Youth Aliyah: A Selected, Sorted, and Edited Bibliography (1934–1984).* Jerusalem, 1984. (In Hebrew.)

Dash, J. *Summoned to Jerusalem: The Life of Henrietta Szold.* New York, 1979.

Freier, R. *Let the Children Come: The Early History of Youth Aliyah.* London, 1961.

Gelber, Y. "The Origins of Youth Aliyah." *Studies in Zionism* 9/2 (Autumn 1988): 147–171.

Haestrup, J. *Passage to Palestine: Young Jews in Denmark, 1932–1945.* Odense, 1983.

Leshem, P. *Strasse zur Rettung, 1933–1939: Aus Deutschland vertrieben bereitet sich jüdische Jugend auf Palästina vor.* Tel Aviv, 1973.

CHAIM SCHATZKER

YOUTH MOVEMENTS. [*The seven articles in this entry review the history of Jewish youth movements before and during the Holocaust:*

General Survey
Bohemia and Moravia
France
Germany and Austria
Hungary
Romania
Slovakia

See also the entries on specific youth organizations and youth leaders mentioned herein.]

General Survey

The independent organizing of youth, by youth, in European countries had its start in the early years of the twentieth century. Sociopolitical developments in central and western Europe provided the background for the rise of youth movements. Established traditional society was promoting conservatism and continuity, and regarded youth as a preparatory stage for the obligations and tasks of adulthood. In the course of the nineteenth century, however, the authority of conservative society and the traditional family had been undermined, and it was this process of erosion that made it possible for young people to organize on their own. Their desire for independent organization was motivated by their discontent with the existing state of affairs and their rejection of bourgeois values and the bourgeois way of life, which, in the eyes of the youth, was wholly dedicated to the achievement of material gains, its manners and mores often consisting of falsehood and pretense. The emerging youth movements sought to introduce simplicity and sincerity into their new framework, and, above all, to tear down the walls of alienation separating human beings from one another. Aspiring to freshness and purity, the young people were attracted to the outdoors, away from the cities, to roam the countryside and draw close to nature. In their search for roots they were fascinated by folklore, popular poetry and music, and romantic literature.

The first youth organizations that came into being, and that formed a kind of prototype for youth movements in general, were the *Wandervögel* ("birds of passage") groups and later the *Bünde* (leagues), founded in Germany at the turn of the century. It was in these organizations that the life-style of youth movements, with their distinct pattern of education and of relationships with the opposite sex, first took shape. Among German youth, only a relatively small group, numbering no more than sixty thousand and mostly from bourgeois families, belonged to youth movements. Their protests and their yearning for new challenges did not develop into a call for social change. They expressed much longing for the liberation of the individual from the conventional fetters of society, much admiration for *völkisch* literature, and, as a result of the penchant for the past and for romantic literature, a strong attraction to nationalism. These movements did not, however, greatly affect social development in Germany, and their impact was limited, for the most part, to the revival of folklore motifs in music, poetry, and the arts. In general, the graduates of the youth movements regarded their former membership in them as a pleasant adventure of their youth; when it came to an end they adjusted to German society as it was and found their place in it. It was only a fraction of them who, on their return from the battlefields of World War I, could find no peace and veered toward extreme political movements, either the radical Left or the nationalist Right, the latter in the form of Nazism.

It was in Germany (and also in Poland; see below) that the first Jewish youth movements came into being. The initial cause for their emergence in Germany was that Jewish boys and girls were not welcome in the German movements. Later, the Jewish youth movements, under the impact of political developments, fostered their own cultural and ideological patterns of activities, based on Jewish motifs and tradition and also expressing their specific distress as Jews. The first Jewish youth movements to be formed in Germany after World War I were Blau-Weiss

Jewish youth studying Hebrew at the Palestine Office of the Zionist Organization in Berlin (1935). [Central Zionist Archives, Jerusalem]

(Blue-White), Ha-Bonim (The Builders; a movement attracted to the idea of Zionist pioneering), and the Kameraden (Comrades) movement, which was assimilationist until one of the factions deriving from it, the Werkleute (Working People), became Zionist, adopted a radical pioneering ideology, and founded Kibbutz Ha-Zore'a in Palestine. In 1931 and 1932 the Ha-Shomer ha-Tsa'ir and Betar Zionist movements were established in Germany, their members, for the most part, coming from Jewish families of eastern European origin who were then living in Germany (the so-called *Ostjuden*).

Jewish Youth Movements in Eastern Europe. In eastern Europe, Jewish youth movements played a particularly important role, both in the influence they exercised on the conduct of their own members and their organizations, and in their impact on the general Jewish public, as an independent and active factor seeking to cope with the challenges and trials of those days. The youth movements that came into existence in Poland after the end of World War I learned many lessons from the experience of the youth movements in Germany and Austria and were influenced by them. But

it was from eastern European Jewry that they drew their strength and inspiration and became consolidated as effective organizations against the background of the dynamic changes those Jewish communities were experiencing in the interwar period. The outstanding characteristic of the Zionist youth movements in Poland was their rejection of the existing state of affairs and their refusal to adapt themselves to the way of life and the passivity of the adult Jewish society. Under the guidance of young instructors, these movements broke out of the narrow, closed circle of Jewish life and developed their own life-style, with the emphasis on youth, the outdoors, sports, and song, and on direct (albeit self-restrained) contact with the opposite sex. It was not, however, the changes in the behavior of the individual that determined the significance of these movements; rather, it was their search for Jewish and human content that would provide the answer to their longing for change, and their resolve to apply their findings in practice. Generally speaking, the youth movements did not follow an established political program and are not to be seen as political bodies. Their ideology derived from different sources, from which they absorbed all sorts of ideas—some of them contradictory in nature—that they fused into a single whole, in an original, if not always organic, manner.

The first Jewish youth movement in eastern Europe arose in Galicia. This was Ha-Shomer ha-Tsa'ir, a Zionist movement that eventually arrived at an ideology combining maximalist Zionism and leftist social radicalism. Most of its members came from a petit bourgeois background and were students. Dror, a movement whose outlook in certain respects was close to that of the Ha-Shomer ha-Tsa'ir, recruited its members mostly from among the poorer strata of Jewish society. Gordonia adopted a moderate Zionist Socialist program, whereas the Ha-No'ar ha-Tsiyyoni and Akiva movements focused on Zionism and Hebrew culture. Betar, which became a mass youth movement, identified with and was loyal to a political movement, Zionist Revisionism, and thus had a clearly defined political character.

As time went on, the pioneering youth movements laid down a program of education and of gradual progress varying from one age group to the next. The graduates of these movements joined agricultural training projects, in which they passed through a stage that was to be followed by their immigration to Palestine. The Zionist youth movements, with the exception of Betar, were linked to kibbutz movements in Palestine, and on arriving there most of their former members joined a kibbutz belonging to the movement with which they had been associated. This system was applied by the youth movements in Poland and in most of the eastern European countries, imparting a character quite different from that of the youth movements in western Europe. The internal cohesion achieved by the eastern European youth movements, their range of activities, and the values to which they adhered accounted for the appeal these movements had for their members, which lasted into adult-

Members of a Jewish youth movement in Będzin, Poland (March 1, 1940).

hood and contained the basic elements of a lifelong identification with the particular movement's content and goals.

According to this concept, real life was to begin only when the youth movement members had immigrated to Palestine, and, for many, only when they had jointed a kibbutz. Their training and preparations in the diaspora were only a preliminary phase, and during this phase the movements generally kept aloof from political life. In the period between the two world wars a very large number of young people were organized in the Jewish youth movements in Poland, and while they never included the majority of Jewish youth there, they numbered about 60,000, which constituted most of the organized youth; the rest were affiliated with the youth sections of Jewish political parties, Zionist and non-Zionist. Among the non-Zionist parties, it was the BUND that had the largest youth section. On the eve of World War II, when the youth movements were at their numerical height, they are estimated to have had a membership of 100,000.

The Holocaust in Eastern Europe. Under the Nazi occupation regime, the Jewish youth movements played a significant role in Jewish community life, and over the course of time they became a major factor in the Jewish resistance movement. When the war broke out and the German occupation regime was installed, a new chapter began in the story of the Jewish youth movements in Poland. In the first few months the youth movements, like most other organizations and institutions, were in disarray; the existing frameworks were breaking up and the emissaries from Palestine, who had served as instructors in the movements and dealt with immigration, all returned to Palestine. Like the heads of the central Jewish political parties and institutions, the leaders of the youth movements left Warsaw and other large cities in central and western Poland and made their way to the eastern provinces, which the Soviet Union had seized. Unlike the political parties, however, the youth movement leadership decided to send some of their senior members back to the German-occupied areas, to revive the movements there and reorganize them for an under-

ground existence. Among those who went back in early 1940 were Mordecai ANIELEWICZ and Yitzhak ZUCKERMAN, who became the leaders of the movements in the underground and in time also the leaders of the ŻYDOWSKA ORGANIZACJA BOJOWA (Jewish Fighting Organization; ŻOB) and of the WARSAW GHETTO UPRISING.

Like other organizations that went underground, the youth movements made changes in their aims and methods. Unlike the large political bodies, however, the youth movements, because they were based on small and intimate cells, were able to preserve their distinctive character and, in the prevailing atmosphere of helplessness and disintegration, insist on retaining their traditional principles and moral strength. After their reorganization, and now operating clandestinely, they embarked on a remarkably intensive range of activities. They were responsible for most of the underground press published in Warsaw, both before and after the ghetto was set up, they conducted courses of study as a substitute for the regular schools, and they organized seminars, ideological symposiums, and other activities. The youth movements operated a network of couriers, most of them girls, who made illegal trips to the closed-off and isolated ghettos and thereby gave their branches, spread all over the occupied country, the sense that they were part of a centralized movement, directed from its headquarters in Warsaw.

In the underground the youth movements no longer adhered to their former position of abstaining from public community activities but participated in the life of the ghetto underground. This does not mean, however, that their leaders aspired to leadership of the community. Like the other underground political organizations, the youth movements had no intention of taking the place of the Judenräte (Jewish councils; see JUDENRAT), but they were opposed to the methods of the Judenräte, which tended to victimize the poorest sectors of the population and submit blindly to the Germans. Apart from the general goal of survival, the youth movements set themselves the objective of trying to prepare the youth for the challenges in store for them once the war, the humiliation, and the persecution came to an end. Up to the time that the "FINAL SOLUTION" was launched by the Nazis, the youth movements had no intention of trying to take the place of the existing organizational pattern in the ghettos, overt or covert, and were only one component in the array of organizations working together in the struggle for survival.

The turning point in the underground youth movements' policies of action coincided with the overall change in the situation of the Jews under the German occupation. When the Germans invaded the Soviet Union on June 22, 1941, they also embarked upon a mass murder drive, and in early 1942 the murder drive spread to the Polish areas that had been incorporated into the Reich and to the GENERALGOUVERNEMENT. These fateful developments caused a sharp and bitter debate in the ghettos, where opinions differed concerning their implications, the conclusions to be drawn from them, and the ways in which the ghettos should meet the new situation confronting them.

The Jews of VILNA suffered heavy blows at the very beginning of the murder campaign. It was in that city that the youth movement leaders first expressed an appraisal of the new situation—in surprisingly precise terms—and that the first Jewish fighting organization, made up of the youth movements, came into being. At a meeting of Zionist pioneering youth movements held on the night of December 31, 1941–January 1, 1942, Abba KOVNER's proclamation was presented. It stated: "All those who have been removed from the ghetto were taken to their death. . . . Hitler plans to annihilate all the Jews of Europe. . . . The Jews of Vilna have been selected to be the first in line. . . . The only way to respond to the enemy is to resist . . . we must resist up to our dying breath." The bold and far-reaching assertions made in the manifesto were not based on proven information but on intuition and a penetrating insight into the course of events. The call for armed resistance was not presented as a means of deterring the Nazis or of possible rescue, but as an action that had to be taken. It was clear that there was no chance of survival and that resistance, by a national Jew-

ish fighting unit that had faith in freedom and in the future of the Jewish people, was the only plausible response for organized Jews who were part of the anti-Nazi alliance.

In the large ghettos, the Judenräte and their close associates, as well as most of the members of the underground political parties, believed that the mass murders in the east were the result of an eruption of wild hatred on the battlefront, or of local initiative; they rejected the claim that the murders were the beginning of a drive that had as its aim the physical destruction of all Jews. The veteran Jewish leaders also feared that the youth movements' bold ideas and their transformation into a fighting force might bring disaster to the great majority, who would be the victims of the Nazi practice of retaliation by means of collective punishment. Some of the Judenrat chairmen, who were used to taking the lead and were confident of their own ability to cope with the situation, came up with the concept that rather than risking human lives and the murder of masses, the Jews should work harder and prove their efficiency. The Germans would then realize that the Jewish workers were making an invaluable contribution to their needs, and would put an end to the cruel oppression and murder. This concept, to which Judenrat chairmen such as Jacob GENS (Vilna), Efraim BARASZ (Białystok), and Mordechai RUMKOWSKI (Łódź) subscribed, obviously did not take into account the apparently remote possibility that an overall decision had been taken for the murder of the Jews, a decision that was motivated by racist ideology; they felt that what was happening was the work of individual irresponsible Nazis and was based on pragmatic and morally unrestrained considerations. This was in sharp contrast to the position taken by most youth movement leaders, who were convinced that the murder drive was ideologically motivated and based on a clear-cut, central, and high-level decision; hence the youth movements' resolve to prepare for resistance to the deportations, which they believed were bound to affect every ghetto.

These two opposing views, of the Judenräte on the one hand and the youth movements on the other, inevitably led to confrontations and sharp disputes, which in some ghettos assumed the form of violent clashes. In most instances, the leadership of the underground political parties, at least in the early phases of the implementation of the "Final Solution," opposed the youth movements' positions; this forced the movements' leaders to operate on their own in order to gain support for their course of action. In the final phase this turned the youth movements into a kind of alternative ghetto leadership and, in the Warsaw ghetto, into the replacement of the existing one, guiding and directing the course of activities in the ghetto's last days. The youth movements spread the idea of resistance to the different ghettos, sending emissaries from Warsaw to BIAŁYSTOK, KRAKÓW, CZĘSTOCHOWA, and Zagłębie to help organize resistance and take part in the struggle. Youth movement leaders also established contact with Polish and Lithuanian underground fighting organizations and tried to obtain help from them, in the form of arms, supplies, training, and communciation with the free world.

The "pioneering" Zionist youth movements Ha-Shomer ha-Tsa'ir, Dror, and Akiva were very active in the fighting organizations. They helped to initiate and plan resistance and the struggle that was waged in all the ghettos that had a fighting body, and members of these movements headed the fighting organizations in the main ghettos. Betar participated in the FAREYNEGTE PARTIZANER OR-GANIZATSYE (United Partisan Organization) in Vilna, a group of its members took part in the resistance in Białystok, and in Warsaw, Betar had its own fighting body. Akiva joined the ŻOB in Warsaw, and was the major element of HE-HALUTS HA-LOHEM in Kraków. Ha-Noar ha-Tsiyyoni and Gordonia also took part in the fighting organizations in most of the ghettos, the former making a particularly strong impact in the towns of the Zagłębie area. The Bund and the Communist youth were active in the fighting bodies in most of the ghettos. In the Warsaw and Vilna ghettos, two fighting organizations were established, reflecting (at least in Warsaw) the differing political outlooks of the constituent movements. Thus it happened that even in the last phase the movements were sometimes inca-

pable of overcoming all their political differences. It is equally true, however, that at no point, and in no other framework, did the various political movements and bodies attain the kind of far-reaching cooperation achieved in the fighting organizations. About two thousand members of the youth movements were active in the fighting organizations of the main ghettos in occupied Poland.

The goal of the fighting organizations founded by the youth movements was to offer armed resistance or to rise in revolt in the ghettos, in face of the impending final deportation of the Jews to the EXTERMINATION CAMPS, even while being fully aware that all their fighters were fated to fall in battle. Armed resistance and uprising were both fully put into effect in the Warsaw ghetto uprising of April 1943; in other ghettos, among them those of Vilna and Białystok, the concept applied was that when the ghetto was confronted with the final deportation an armed struggle would be launched, but some of the fighters would try to make their way to the forests to join the partisans with the object of continuing the struggle even after the fighting in the ghetto was over. In Kraków the fighting organization waged its armed struggle outside the ghetto, so as to avoid endangering the lives of the Jews inside, and its revenge operations were carried out in the part of the city that lay outside the ghetto. In the towns of the Zagłębie area the fighting organizations (except for occasional attempts at armed resistance) put their emphasis on rescue operations, either by fleeing across the nearby border to Slovakia, or by using foreign passports to go abroad.

In areas outside Poland, as in KOVNO, Lithuania, the youth movements prepared for escaping into the forests and joining the partisan movement, and did not have a consistent policy of staging a revolt in the ghetto. In MINSK, Belorussia, where none of the Jewish youth movements existed and the initiative for action was in the hands of the Communists, a resistance organization was formed that maintained close ties with the partisans in the forests and succeeded in getting thousands of Jews out to join the latter or to take refuge in the FAMILY CAMPS IN THE FORESTS. Youth movement members and former members played a significant role among the activists behind the spontaneous uprisings in and escapes from the small towns of Belorussia and the Ukraine. Members of youth movements in Slovakia took a very active part in daring rescue operations, were organized within the labor camps, and joined the SLOVAK NATIONAL UPRISING of 1944 in separate Jewish units. They distinguished themselves as fighters during the uprising and, after its suppression, as partisans.

Retrospectively, it is evident that neither the Judenräte nor the youth fighting organizations were able to save masses of Jews. This, it appears, would have been possible only if elements beyond the inner Jewish circle had extended help. The eastern European youth movements had no pretensions of paving the way for mass rescue, and they regarded their struggle as one last act, deriving its inspiration from human and national considerations, by a community that was condemned to total extermination. The writings and manifestos of youth movement members published in the last phase of the Holocaust show that at a time when all existing social and communal frameworks were disintegrating, and every person was on his own facing a bitter fate, it was the youth movements that held on to an organized solid and disciplined structure, and whose thoughts and actions were guided by criteria based on social and national Jewish considerations.

BIBLIOGRAPHY

Gutman, I. *Fighters among the Ruins.* Washington, D.C., 1988. See chapter 2.

Gutman, Y. *The Jews of Warsaw, 1939–1943.* Bloomington, 1980.

Gutman, Y. *Struggle in Darkness: Studies in Holocaust and Resistance.* Tel Aviv, 1985. (In Hebrew.)

Hechalutz Halochem, Organ of the Chalutz Underground Movement in Occupied Cracow: August–October, 1943. Naharia, Israel, 1984. (In Hebrew.)

Kermish, J., ed. *The Jewish Underground Press in Warsaw.* 3 vols. Jerusalem, 1979, 1984. (In Hebrew.)

Perlis, R. *The Hehalutz Youth Movements in Occupied Poland.* Naharia, Israel, 1987. (In Hebrew.)

ISRAEL GUTMAN

Bohemia and Moravia

The German occupation of truncated Czechoslovakia and its partition into the Protectorate of BOHEMIA AND MORAVIA and the independent Slovak state caused a radical change among the Jews of the Protectorate. The relatively rapid separation of the Jews (and of persons classified as Jews by the Nazi racist legislation) from their sources of livelihood and their traditional social frameworks had a unifying effect on them, with the Jewish community assuming a growing number of welfare functions that under normal circumstances would have been the responsibility of the state. The German occupation authorities, for their own reasons, encouraged this process and urged it also on other Jewish organizations. As a result, the Zionist movement became an emigration agency and the central factor in the reorganization of Protectorate Jewry.

The youth movements, which showed greater enterprise than others in coping with the pressing problems facing the Jews, played an active and leading role in this process, which was not confined to the youth and came to affect the entire Jewish population.

The He-Haluts Center engaged in training dozens of *hakhshara* (pioneering) groups, mainly in agriculture; in vocational training and retraining; in coordinating operations among the different movements; and in organizing immigration to Palestine. The Youth Aliya (Immigration of Children and Youth into Palestine), in addition to organizing the emigration of young people and children, also took part in education and vocational training, at the MI-HA agricultural training school, the Youth Aliya school in Prague, and an agricultural training school in Denmark.

The youth movements that were active in Bohemia and Moravia varied in character and in the pattern of their programs. Some followed the example of youth movements in central Europe, while others drew their inspiration primarily from the Polish and Lithuanian models. Tehelet Lavan (Blue-White), the oldest youth movement in Czechoslovakia, had most of its strength in the western part of the country. It followed the pattern of scoutlike activities on the German model, and its ties in Palestine were with No'ar Tsiyyoni Halutsi (NETSAH) and the socialist kibbutz movement Ha-Kibbuts ha-Me'uhad. He-Haluts ha-Tsa'ir (The Young Pioneer) had most of its members in pioneering training, many of whom were from the TRANSCAR-PATHIAN UKRAINE, and its ties in Palestine were also with NETSAH and ha-Kibbuts ha-Me'uhad. El-Al (Upward) drew most of its membership from the Czech-speaking intelligentsia, and in ideology was close to Tehelet Lavan. Ha-Shomer ha-Tsa'ir, which had established itself relatively late in the western part of Czechoslovakia, placed the emphasis in its educational program on class warfare and revolution, and on settlement in Palestine in the framework of the Marxist settlement movement Ha-Kibbuts ha-Artsi. Maccabi ha-Tsa'ir (Young Maccabi), whose major development followed its unification with the Gordonia Zionist youth movement, eventually grew into the largest pioneering and educational scout movement in Bohemia and Moravia. It called for settlement in Palestine within the socialist Hever ha-Kevutsot kibbutz movement.

Notwithstanding the heated ideological debates they conducted with one another, to a great extent all the youth movements cooperated, including the religious Bnei Akiva group, which was affiliated with the He-Haluts Mizrachi religious pioneering movement. Their ways parted only shortly before the first groups were about to be taken to THERESIENSTADT, when the Ha-Shomer ha-Tsa'ir council advised its members to go underground or escape to Slovakia or Hungary. The other movements decided not to abandon their junior members, their families, and the community as a whole, and many of them felt that Ha-Shomer ha-Tsa'ir's decision was selfish or even amounted to a betrayal. Both camps based their positions on value judgments. Retrospectively, it would appear that the activist line adopted by Ha-Shomer ha-Tsa'ir, despite the painful separation that it involved, was based on a more realistic analysis of what the future held in store.

In the early stage of their occupation, the Germans regarded emigration as a good way of ridding the Protectorate of Jews. The youth movements were able to operate without interference and without taking safety precautions. In July 1940, however, the movements and all the other Zionist organizations were outlawed, and Jewish children were also barred from the schools. Education now went underground, with the professional educators and youth movement instructors enlisted for this assignment. This became a countrywide operation, organized by the Prague Jewish community, which from August 1940 was the only institution authorized to deal with the affairs of the Jews in Bohemia and Moravia. Its deputy director was Jacob EDELSTEIN, a He-Haluts member and the outstanding personality among the community leaders.

In the fall of 1941 the Germans decided to concentrate the Protectorate's Jews in Theresienstadt, and Edelstein undertook to head the project of transferring them there. Even earlier, the Prague Jewish community had prepared a project for moving the Jews to several towns in Bohemia and Moravia, on the assumption that by working for the Germans they would be saved from destruction. A special department was set up to work out detailed plans for transferring the Jews to nearby locations where they would work in factories. The team chosen by Edelstein for his project was made up mostly of fellow He-Haluts members.

In an attempt to change what was a deportation to a ghetto into a preparatory stage for emigration to Palestine, Edelstein appointed He-Haluts members to take charge of the children and the youth, and to organize the labor force of the ghetto. Erich Österreicher, a Tehelet Lavan member, was appointed head of the labor service, and he chose He-Haluts members for his staff of assistants. Österreicher and his staff sought to assign jobs that would be useful for a future life in Palestine. The same principle guided the team in charge of the children and youngsters. The youth department was headed by Egon Redlich, a Maccabi ha-Tsa'ir member, and, in the initial stage, also by his fellow Maccabi ha-Tsa'ir member, Fredy Hirsch. Together with a staff of youth movement instructors, they dealt with all the children and youths aged four to seventeen.

A gathering of a He-Haluts group in the town of Dvale, 10 miles (16 km) south of Prague, in 1940.

The group is singing "Am Yisrael Ḥai" (The People of Israel Live!).

Three kindergartens were established, one Hebrew-speaking. The over-seventeen age group lived together in "junior homes." Specialized institutions, such as a home for retarded children and a children's convalescent home, were also set up. The most intensive educational effort was made in the "children's homes," dormitories in which children lived with their teachers and where all facilities were provided, from medical care to clothing repairs. A normal school curriculum was followed, under the guise of activities that had not been outlawed by the Germans, such as drawing, singing, and gymnastics. About four hundred pupils were accommodated in each of the three large children's homes. The basic educational unit was the *Heim* (home), each holding twenty to thirty children. Some of these *Heime* had teachers who were not Zionists; the Communists, for example, provided first-rate educators.

The frequent transports that left Theresienstadt for camps in the east and the dread of being included in one of them, as well as the distressing living conditions, made it extremely difficult to engage in educational work. The youth movements nevertheless did all they could to counter the prevailing conditions of fear and suffering. The adult pioneers also took up cultural activities, and Hebrew lessons were obligatory, but the main concern was mutual help, such as distributing food to those in need.

On November 10, 1942, a He-Haluts conference was held in Theresienstadt. At the end of three days of discussions it was decided to merge the different movements into one, to be known as He-Haluts he-Ahid (Unified He-Haluts). This was done largely at the initiative of Jenda Kaufmann. A fourteen-member board was elected, made up of representatives of Bnei Akiva, Ha-Shomer ha-Tsa'ir, and the other youth movements; a four-member executive board was also elected.

In February 1943 the new unified movement held a "census day," and 40 grams of sugar were collected as a membership fee from each person wanting to be counted as a member of the movement. On Lag Ba-Omer 1943, to celebrate the opening of a sports field on the walls of the Theresienstadt fortress, a Scouts' Day was observed. A rally was held to mark the birthday of the founder of modern Zionism, Theodor Herzl (May 2), and the international workers' day, May 1. Speeches were made in Czech and Hebrew, and six thousand members took part in the event.

With Jacob Edelstein's knowledge, the chairman of the executive, Gert Körbel, was charged with setting up an underground defense organization, aided by a member who had been an officer in the Czechoslovak reserves. Reluctance to cooperate with the Communist underground, the fear of collective punishment, and the inclusion of key people in the major deportations of the fall of 1943 soon put an end to this project.

In August 1943 a group of 1,200 children from the BIAŁYSTOK ghetto was brought to Theresienstadt, apparently in preparation for an exchange arrangement. The emaciated, lice-infested children were not permitted to meet with the ghetto inhabitants. On German orders, teachers were assigned to the children (one was Aron MENCZER), and they lived with them in complete isolation from the rest of the ghetto. Fredy Hirsch was arrested by the Germans when he tried to establish contact with the children, and in September 1943 he was deported to AUSCHWITZ-Birkenau with a transport of 5,000 Jews, consisting mostly of former residents of the Protectorate and including a large number of pioneers. On arrival in the concentration camp, contrary to the usual practice, no *Selektion* was made, and all the men, women, and children in the transport were put together into the "family camp."

The "children's block" in the Birkenau family camp, in which 600 children lived together with their teacher-counselors, was the final and perhaps the most touching chapter in the story of the Czechoslovak pioneering youth movement. Hirsch received permission to gather all the children over eight in one block, Block 31; later, the adjacent block also became available for children, those over

five. In this terrible setting, within sight of the smoking chimneys of the crematoria, the teachers, nearly all of whom were members of the youth movements, managed to create the atmosphere of a bearable life, with the children studying, playing, helping one another, and willingly keeping order—an atmosphere that to some degree enabled them to forget their hunger and disregard the reality of the camp. Six months to the day after their arrival, thirty-eight hundred survivors of that transport from Theresienstadt, children and teachers alike, were sent to the gas chambers. Fredy Hirsch, who was to have led an uprising organized by the underground, committed suicide.

Following Hirsch's death, Seppl Lichtenstein (one of the leaders of the Prague branch of Tehelet Lavan), together with teachers from a December 1943 transport, now took charge of the block. These children, together with the survivors of the December 1943 and May 1944 transports, shared the fate of their predecessors in July 1944, except that on this occasion those fit for work, including the instructors, were sent to labor camps in Germany.

The visit of the International RED CROSS to Theresienstadt on June 22, 1944, had no effect on the ghetto, and life went on as before. In August a second He-Haluts conference was held in Theresienstadt and a new executive was elected, consisting of twenty-eight members. The conference confirmed the Zionist pioneering movement's aims in the ghetto: to train the children and young people for cooperative living, universal and national Jewish values, and socialist Zionism. The practical issue was whether to permit members of the movement to volunteer for the transports in order to join their parents on their way to Auschwitz, or to insist that they stay in the ghetto to continue their work for the common good.

The realities of life did not leave much room for airing such questions. In September the Germans launched the evacuation of the Theresienstadt ghetto. Left there were old people of sixty-five and over, and a handful of young people to take care of them and perform essential jobs for the Germans. Hardly any of the pioneers remained.

BIBLIOGRAPHY

Bondy, R. *"Elder of the Jews": Jakob Edelstein of Theresienstadt.* New York, 1989.

Bondy, R., ed. *Life as If: The Diaries of Egon Redlich from the Theresienstadt Ghetto (1942–1944).* Naharia, Israel, 1983. (In Hebrew.)

Goshen, S. "Zionist Students' Organizations." In vol. 2 of *The Jews of Czechoslovakia*, pp. 173–184. New York, 1971.

Schmiedt, S. "Hehalutz in Theresienstadt: Its Influence and Educational Activities." *Yad Vashem Studies* 7 (1968): 107–126.

WILLY GROAG

France

On the eve of World War II the Haluts (Pioneer) Youth movements and the Federation of Religious Youth had small branches active in FRANCE. They suffered from a lack of instructors, and most of their members came from immigrant and refugee families; only a few were native-born Frenchmen. The oldest Jewish youth movement was the ECLAIREURS ISRAÉLITES DE FRANCE (French Jewish Scouts), founded in 1923 by the seventeen-year-old Robert GAMZON. At first, the movement was joined by the children of native-born French Jews, but Gamzon introduced a pluralistic admissions policy and accepted both religious and secular youth, Zionists and anti-Zionists. As a result, within a few years the scout movement was the only framework that encompassed Jewish youth from all sectors of the Jewish population, including the children of immigrant and refugee families. Activities on behalf of the Jewish National Fund and the singing of songs of the Jews of Palestine became parts of the movement's program. The Orthodox Jewish community had a small youth organization of its own, named Yeshurun.

After the fall of France in June 1940, all youth movements in the German-occupied northern part of the country were abolished by German decree. The scouts and the Zionist movement Ha-Shomer ha-Tsa'ir, however, resumed their activities under the guise of community clubs. In the Vichy-controlled south, the youth movements continued to operate openly for another two years. During the summer of 1942, with the mass arrests and deportations of the Jews of France, the Jewish youth movements went underground.

At a meeting held in Montpellier in May 1942, the leaders of the various Zionist youth movements agreed to give up their separate political identities. This made it possible for a Zionist youth movement to be set up on a unified rather than a federative basis, and for a leadership to be elected that was not based on a party key. The Montpellier meeting had been convoked on the initiative of Simon LÉVITTE, the secretary-general of the scout movement and a member of its board, and Lévitte—himself not identified with any particular Zionist party—was elected secretary-general of the new Zionist youth movement. A year later, two senior members of the scout movement, Gamzon and Chimon Frederic Hammel, joined the board of the new movement.

The Zionist youth movement established an underground organization, under the code name "Physical Training" (Education Physique). The scout movement also set up its own underground, code-named "Sixth" (La Sixième), the two undergrounds fully cooperating with each other. Once the new Zionist youth movement had come into being, Zionist youth became an active element in the community and made a great contribution to its organization and success. (Immediately after the war, however, the unified movement disbanded and each of its component parts reverted to its original identity.)

Organized Jewish youth in France recorded significant achievements in three spheres—education, rescue, and guerrilla warfare. In addition to the educational activities that were usual for youth movements, the Jewish youth movement in occupied France organized study groups in which some adults took part and which also served as training seminars for instructors. The scout movement conducted special seminars for new instructors, whom it selected from among the teachers dismissed from their posts under the decrees issued by the French government in Vichy. These were people who had hitherto regarded Judaism as belonging to their forefathers—a culture, they believed, of the past. Youngsters who were unable to attend the courses because of the distance they would have had to travel received the contents in correspondence courses.

The rescue efforts made by the youth movements concentrated on the forging of documents and their distribution; surveys, carried out under difficult conditions, in areas remote from urban concentrations, for the purpose of identifying non-Jewish families and institutions that would take in Jewish families or individual Jewish children; the care of children; and the readying of groups of children for travel to and passage across the Swiss or Spanish border. Three out of four Jews who were in France in the summer of 1940 were saved, tens of thousands of them rescued partly owing to the Jewish youth movements. The outstanding achievement of the youth movements' underground activity was the care taken of over 7,000 children whose parents had been deported; some 1,500 of these children were smuggled into Switzerland and 88 into Spain, while the others were placed with non-Jewish families and institutions that took care of them (for payment). Every such child had an underground member assigned to him or her, and this person made regular visits (once a month), was responsible for the child's physical and moral welfare, and made sure that the child remained aware of his or her Jewish heritage. Dozens of the young men and women who made up the Jewish underground teams were caught and murdered, but not a single child for whom they were responsible came to harm. After the liberation, children whose parents had perished during the war were placed in the care of the organized Jewish community.

The events of September 1943 in Nice were a severe test for the Jewish youth movements. As long as the Italians were in occupation of the zone, they protected the Jews from the French officials, withstood pressure from the Germans, and gave refuge to the thirty thousand Jews who fled there from other parts of France. When, however, the Italians signed a cease-fire agreement with the Allied forces (September 8, 1943), they abandoned the military positions they had held in France, and these were taken over by German military forces and police. The Jews in Nice and its environs were caught in a trap; moreover, the leaders and officials of the local Jewish organizations (which until then had operated in the open) vanished from the scene overnight, and the only ones left to look after the Jews and find safe havens for them were the underground activists of the youth movements. They suffered heavy losses, but within a relatively short period the youth movements' representatives equipped many of the Jews with forged documents and provided them with new places of refuge.

The ARMÉE JUIVE (the Jewish resistance movement), which Zionist activists had organized in Toulouse, recruited fighters among the members of the youth movements and trained them in the use of arms and in guerrilla warfare. In April 1944, a partisan unit in Nice liquidated a gang of informers and Gestapo collaborators. Partisan units were also active in Lyons, Toulouse, and PARIS. The underground set up an intricate network to smuggle fighters to Palestine, by way of Spain, and three hundred youngsters reached Palestine in this fashion in 1944. They included several dozen members each from the Zionist movement's agricultural training farms, the scout movement, and the Dutch He-Haluts youth movement (the latter having first managed to cross into France). Operations of this nature took a heavy toll.

The organization of partisan units sponsored by the Armée Juive and the scout movement began in the winter of 1943–1944. The most significant battle in which Jewish units participated was an ambush on an armored train, in the vicinity of Castres, in southern France; after a night of heavy fighting, on August 19–20, 1944, the train was captured, and, as a consequence, 3,500 German officers and men surrendered to the Résistance units. Armée Juive units also took part in the liberation of Paris and other major French cities.

BIBLIOGRAPHY

Hammel, F. C. *Souviens-toi d'Amalek: Témoignage sur la lutte des Juifs en France (1938–1944)*. Paris, 1982.

Latour, A. *Jewish Resistance in France (1940–1944)*. New York, 1981.

Lazare, L. *La résistance juive en France*. Paris, 1987.

LUCIEN LAZARE

Germany and Austria

By the time the Nazis came to power, at the end of January 1933, the Jewish youth movements in GERMANY had crystallized their respective ideologies and organizational patterns and institutions. Ideologically, the Jewish youth movements consisted of two branches: the Zionist pioneering movements and the non-Zionist movements. The Zionist movements were Ha-Bonim, founded in 1933 by the merger of the Jung-Jüdischer Wanderbund (Young Jewish Hiking Society) and Kadimah; Werkleute (Toilers), an offspring of the Kreis (Circle), which in turn was a group in the Kameraden (Comrades), a non-Zionist movement that had broken up in 1932; and Ha-Shomer ha-Tsa'ir. In 1934 another Zionist youth movement was formed, the Jewish Scouts–Maccabi ha-Tsa'ir, based on the amalgamation of the two organizations contained in its name.

The non-Zionist Jewish youth movements were the Bund Deutsch-Jüdischer Jugend (German Jewish Youth Society), the assimilationist element in the Kameraden movement; and DEUTSCHER VORTRUPP, GEFOLGSCHAFT DEUTSCHER JUDEN (German Vanguard, German Jewish Adherents), an anti-Zionist and assimilationist movement founded by Hans Joachim Schoeps. Jewish sports clubs included the Zionist-oriented Bar Kochba, which was affiliated with the international Jewish sports organization, Maccabi; and the non-Zionist sports club of the REICHSBUND JÜDISCHER FRONTSOLDATEN (Reich Union of Jewish Frontline Soldiers). Other youth organizations were not really youth movements but the youth sections of political parties, such as the religious Zionist Young Mizrachi Youth Society; the ultra-Orthodox non-Zionist Agudat Israel Youth Groups; Betar-Jüdisch-Nationale Jugend Herzlia (Jewish National Youth, Herzlia); He-Haluts, a general organization for all Zionist pioneering movements that had the task of providing agricultural training facilities and vocational training, and of organizing emigration to Palestine (also for pioneers who were not members of any of these youth movements); and Berit Halutsim Datiyyim (Bahad), the religious pioneering organization.

All the Jewish youth movements were com-

Members of the Baḥad youth movement in Germany studying the Talmud. [Abraham Pisarek Archive, Berlin]

pelled by the authorities to belong to the Reichsausschuss der Jüdischen Jugendverbände (Reich Committee of Jewish Youth Organizations). The committee had been in existence since 1924, but it was no more than a loose and voluntary umbrella organization of Jewish youth movements and youth organizations in Germany. It became powerful and important only when the Nazi authorities and the Reichsjugendführung (Reich Youth Leadership) made it the sole representative of all Jewish youth organizations, the channel of communication for all orders, and the body responsible for the implementation of such orders, designed to carry out Nazi policy on Jewish youth affairs.

Nazi policy on Jewish youth organizations and youth movements was not consistent. Various prohibitions were issued, repealed, and reissued, and the regulations applied in different parts of the country were not uniform. Some general policy aims did prevail, including the concentration of all Jewish youth organizations and youth movements in a single association; the isolation of the Jewish youth from German youth and the general population; strict control of Jewish youth movements and all their activities; an attempt to discourage the efforts of those Jewish bodies and movements that called on the Jews to stay put in Germany; encouragement of the work of organizations providing vocational retraining for purposes of emigration; and the refusal to grant any special consideration to Jewish youth outside the overall Nazi policy on the Jews of Germany and their ultimate fate.

The development of Jewish youth movements in Germany and their activities in the Nazi period stemmed from their ideological attitude toward the traumatic change that had taken place in the situation of German Jewry. The non-Zionist movements, whose members continued to regard themselves as Germans and planned to stay in the country (or, possibly, to emigrate to any country that would admit them), broke up or were disbanded by the authorities, whose sole interest was in organizations that exclusively promoted Jewish emigration.

The Zionist youth movements, on the other hand, experienced a tremendous growth in their membership after 1933. These movements, which in the 1920s had been only marginal phenomena on the Jewish scene in Germany, now became its main core. They showed the Jews a way out of their predicament—not by headlong flight, as humble refugees from one exile to another, but through a solution based on national pride: emigration to the Jewish homeland.

The Zionist pioneering youth movements maintained their own way of life and their social, ideological, and cultural activities as best they could, despite deteriorating conditions and the restrictions imposed on the Jews. They went on hikes; engaged in ideological discussions, sports, and the study of Hebrew and Jewish history; and published their own newspapers. Their main emphasis, however, was to attract as many youth groups as possible to their ideal of preparing for physical work in Palestine. As Nazi pressure on the Jews grew and the plight of German Jewry worsened, the Zionist youth movements sought to organize their immigration to Palestine in whatever form presented itself: YOUTH ALIYA, ALIYA BET ("illegal" immigration), sending their members to training farms in other countries, illegal border crossings, and so on. Although many of the young people were drafted into forced-labor battalions, they managed to maintain contact with their movements and even to hold clandestine assemblies. Several of the youth movements' leaders were murdered by the Nazis even before the members remaining in Germany were deported to the extermination camps.

The Jewish youth movements in AUSTRIA went through a social, ideological, and educational development which was very similar to that of their German counterparts. A significant difference, however, was the impact of the influx of eastern European Jewish immigrants on the Austrian Jewish youth after World War I. Following the ANSCHLUSS in 1938, only the Zionist He-Haluts youth movements continued to exist in Vienna, fulfilling the same role as their German counterparts. They organized and prepared Jewish youth in the framework of He-Haluts for immigration to Palestine by all means possible, including illegal ones. Until the outbreak of World War II, they were supported clandestinely by the German Jewish youth movements, which already had experience with semi-legal activity under Nazi rule.

Bnei Akiva youth movement troop in a youth camp established by UNRRA in Germany (August, 1946). [Leibowitz family; Beth Hatefutsoth]

BIBLIOGRAPHY

Maoz, E. "The Werkleute." *Leo Baeck Institute Year Book* 4 (1959): 165–182.

Schatzker, C. "The Jewish Youth Movement in Germany in the Holocaust Period." *Leo Baeck Institute Year Book* 32 (1987): 157–182; 33 (1988): 301–325.

Schwarzner, Y. *The Halutz Underground in Nazi Germany.* Tel Aviv, 1969.

Strauss, H. "The Jugendverband: A Social and Intellectual History." *Leo Baeck Institute Year Book* 6 (1961): 206–235.

CHAIM SCHATZKER

Hungary

In the 1930s there were several small Zionist youth movements in HUNGARY, with a total of between fifteen hundred and two thousand members: Ha-Shomer ha-Tsa'ir, Dror-Habonim, Maccabi ha-Tsa'ir, Ha-No'ar ha-Tsiyyoni, and the religious Bnei Akiva —all united together in the He-Haluts federation—and a small Betar group. None of them significantly influenced either the Jewish community in Hungary or the Zionist movement. The incorporation into Hungary of southern Slovakia, the Transcarpathian Ukraine (Carpatho-Ruthenia), and northern Transylvania, between 1938 and 1941, created a further source of membership. An important change in the character of these movements was caused by the considerable number of refugees from neighboring Slovakia who came to Hungary after March 1942, fleeing the deportations from Slovakia to the Nazi camps in Poland. Those who had been members of Zionist youth movements in their own country were absorbed by the local Hungarian counterparts.

To aid their comrades who had escaped deportation, the members of the Hungarian Zionist youth movements had to use illegal underground methods, such as forging false identity papers, previously inconceivable for local Jews considering themselves good Hungarian patriots. These were the first steps toward what later became the Haluts resistance. By the end of 1942, BUDAPEST had become an important center for rescue operations and for conveying information from Nazi-occupied Europe.

Before March 1944, Hungarian Jewry lived in relative tranquillity in spite of the country's three consecutive anti-Jewish laws, and the youth movements grew in strength even though they were declared illegal shortly after Hungary joined World War II. In December 1943, the government allowed the Zionist youth movements to return to legal activity. Just prior to this change in the government's position, a wave of refugees, mainly from Poland, reached Hungary. They had left the ghettos at the peak of the extermination and had witnessed the Warsaw ghetto uprising, and they transmitted information to their Hungarian comrades about the destiny of the Polish Jews.

After the German invasion of Hungary on March 19, 1944, the Zionist youth movements were the main (or only) segment of Hungarian Jews with a fairly clear understanding of what to expect from Nazi rule. They tried various means of saving lives until Hungary was liberated by the Soviet army. During April and May 1944, while most of Hungarian Jewry was being herded into ghettos, the young people tried, with the help of false "Aryan" identity papers of their own creation, to contact friends in the provinces and help them escape the ghettos. They also tried to warn the Jews of the dangers of deportation to Auschwitz. Although they did save hundreds of lives, their attempt to warn the masses of Jews was a total failure, since they were met with mistrust in most of the provincial communities.

A much wider and more successful phase of their activity was that of the Tiyyul (the Hebrew word means "excursion") organization, which smuggled refugees across the border, primarily to Romania, between May and August 1944. Tiyyul was comprised of several groups in Budapest that prepared the candidates for crossing the border and provided them with false papers for traveling. Near the Transylvanian border, activists of the Haluts resistance awaited them and made contact with the smugglers. The Haluts resisters were not the only ones to organize escape routes to Romania; numerous Transylvanian Jews escaped on their own initiative. Although many Jews were arrested before or just after a border crossing, some seven thousand men and women were saved in this way, and between two thousand and three thousand of them were brought over directly by the Haluts resistance organization.

On July 7, 1944, the Hungarian regent,

Adm. Miklós HORTHY, ordered the cessation of the deportations and offered to allow several thousand Jews to emigrate from Hungary (*see* HORTHY OFFER). The emigration plan itself was unsuccessful, but it enabled some neutral powers to issue a document called a "protective pass" (*Schutzpass*), which essentially placed its bearers under the protective custody of the nation that had issued it. This protection was based on the idea that those holding the passes were potential immigrants.

On October 15, after the ill-fated Hungarian attempt at a reversal in policy and the establishment of the purely fascist regime, deportations were resumed, taking the form of DEATH MARCHES. The Zionist youth resistance and some devoted neutral diplomats succeeded in saving several thousand Jews, thanks to genuine or false protective passes.

Owing to these deportations, thousands of children of all ages were left behind with no one to care for them. The Haluts resistance met this challenge and took charge of the children under the official cover of Section A (headed by Ottó KOMOLY) of the International RED CROSS. From October 1944 until the liberation in January 1945, nearly forty children's homes were set up, protecting five thousand to six thousand children and approximately two thousand adults. At the same time, the Swiss consulate's office for Jewish emigration (known as the "Glass House") became a document distribution center, one of the Haluts headquarters, and a hiding place for some three thousand Jews. A complex organization was set up to feed the inhabitants of this center, the children's homes, and the Budapest ghetto after its establishment in November 1944.

The resistance acted in an equally clear and efficient manner with regard to the printing and distribution of protective passes. Approximately 100,000 false passes were circulated, undoubtedly saving many lives. The Haluts resistance during the last months of the war also became one of the main sources of documents and food for the Hungarian resistance movement. During the fascist reign, young Haluts resisters, disguised as ARROW CROSS PARTY men, succeeded by cunning or by force in saving some of the Jews attacked by the fascist militia.

BIBLIOGRAPHY

Cohen, A. *The Halutz Resistance in Hungary, 1942–1944.* New York, 1986.
Rozett, R. "Child Rescue in Budapest, 1944–1945." *Holocaust and Genocide Studies* 2/1 (1987): 49–59.

ASHER COHEN

Romania

Zionist youth movements played an important role in Zionist affairs in ROMANIA, not because of their size but because of their organizational strength, their ideology, the values they represented, and the significant proportion of their members who settled in Palestine.

In Romania between the two world wars, nearly all the major Zionist youth movements had a foothold: Bnei Akiva, Gordonia, Dror-Habonim, Ha-No'ar ha-Tsiyyoni, Ha-Shomer ha-Tsa'ir, Berit ha-Kannaim, and Betar. In the period when King Carol II ruled as dictator, from 1938 to 1940, He-Haluts was not permitted by the authorities to function, and as a result the youth movements no longer had a legal basis for their existence. They therefore resolved to operate in a semi-clandestine manner, under the cover of "training of prospective immigrants," an activity that dovetailed with the Romanian regime's policy of encouraging emigration, whether to Palestine or to other places. Following the occupation of Poland in September 1939, Jews from Poland took refuge in Romania, and the Zionist youth movements, expecting a similar fate to overtake Romania in whole or in part, accelerated their clandestine activities and preparations for immigration to Palestine.

In June 1940 the Soviet Union occupied northern BUKOVINA and BESSARABIA, which meant that a large number of former Zionist youth movement members were now under Soviet rule. Some of the Youth movements, particularly Ha-No'ar ha-Tsiyyoni and Ha-Shomer ha-Tsa'ir, remained active clandestinely, but before long the Soviet authorities arrested the Ha-Shomer ha-Tsa'ir leaders and exiled them to Siberia. This effectively put an end to the remaining activities of the youth movements. When the fascist regime

Members of a Zionist youth movement in Vatra Dornei, a city in southern Bukovina (Romania).

under Ion ANTONESCU came to power in Romania in September 1940, the Zionist youth movements were subjected to persecution and violent acts of terror. The *hakhsharot* (agricultural-training schools) were dissolved, causing hundreds of Zionist youth to concentrate in Bucharest.

The persecution of the Zionist youth movements came to a peak during the IRON GUARD rebellion and its suppression. Dozens of the movements' members were imprisoned and tortured; Moshe Orechowski, executive director of the Palestine Office in Bucharest, was murdered. The persecution of the movements and the imprisonment of their members were accompanied by grotesque charges against them. In 1941 the last emissaries from Palestine, as well as the last immigrants, left Romania for Palestine, a development that led to the emergence of youth leaders, both among the Zionist youth movements and in the Romanian Zionist organization. Under the impact of these events, a coordinating body, the Berit ha-No'ar (Youth Union), was formed, to coordinate all operations relating to immigration to Palestine, mutual aid, and the gathering and dissemination of informa-

tion. The Berit ha-No'ar also tried to establish contact with youth movement members in German- and Soviet-occupied Poland, but with little success.

Romania's participation in the German invasion of the Soviet Union in June 1941 had immediate effects on the situation of the Jews. It led to the tightening of anti-Jewish laws, the IAŞI pogrom of July 29 of that year, and the deportation of the Jews of Bessarabia and Bukovina to TRANSNISTRIA, where most of them perished. Under these circumstances, the youth movements were forced to go underground and to restrict their operations to some of the cities: Bucharest, Iaşi, Timişoara, the CHERNOVTSY ghetto, and a few other places. Since there was no possibility of leaving for Palestine and since Zionist activities were risky, the former members of the youth movements, more than any other group, conducted Zionist activities as an underground operation.

These activities, such as the training of new members, were severely limited in scope, because of the persecution to which the Jews were subjected, the anti-Jewish laws, and the forced-labor draft. The activists were therefore compelled to use forged documents; only a few of the leaders were granted exemption from forced labor in 1942 and 1943, through an arrangement with the CENTRALA EVREILOR (Jewish Center).

The infiltration of Communist elements into its ranks was a permanent risk faced by the Zionist underground. The Communists' aim was to drag the youth movements into spectacular antifascist actions, a risk that they had no good reason to take upon themselves. In March 1943 three Communist youths were arrested in Bucharest, and they implicated sixteen Ha-Shomer ha-Tsa'ir members, aged ten to twenty, who had taken part in writing antifascist slogans on Romanian paper money. Some of them were sentenced to death, and the majority were given prison terms of ten to twenty-five years.

Beginning in 1942, the Zionist youth movements' work concentrated on the following operations:

1. They maintained regular contact with the RESCUE COMMITTEE OF THE JEWISH AGENCY IN TURKEY in Istanbul, and with the Jewish Agency office in Geneva. These contacts were of vital importance for the movements, both as a means of keeping up morale by being informed on developments in Palestine, and for practical purposes, which took the form of money transfers. The Rescue Committee gave the underground youth movements guidance on various issues, such as emigration to Palestine and rescue efforts; the youth movements, in turn, passed on information to the Rescue Committee on the extermination of Jews in Poland.

2. They maintained contact between the headquarters of the movements and their dispersed members, so as to sustain morale and lend assistance to those members who needed it. Of great importance was the contact with the Chernovtsy ghetto and the deportees in Transnistria. The contact with Chernovtsy was kept up by Zionist youth who traveled back and forth from Bucharest with forged identification papers, taking money to the ghetto and helping refugees to make their way to Bucharest. Not much could be done with regard to Transnistria, because of the immense suffering being experienced by the Jews there. Activities there were restricted to personal contacts (as was the case with Ha-No'ar ha-Tsiyyoni). Most of the contacts with Transnistria were effected through non-Jews, who at best took money and small quantities of medicine and food from Bucharest to the deportees. Ha-No'ar ha-Tsiyyoni was represented on the delegation that went to Transnistria in 1943 to arrange for the repatriation of orphans.

3. In Chernovtsy, the Zionist youth movement underground provided aid and shelter for refugees from Poland who had managed to arrive there, by way of Sniatyn. When the Soviet army was drawing near, in 1943, the refugees were no longer safe in Chernovtsy—and the movements tried to transfer them to Bucharest. There was a mishap in the operation, however, as a result of which some of the youth movement leaders and some veteran Zionist leaders were arrested. At the beginning of 1944 a dangerous situation was created, which was compounded by information about the Zionist movement that fell into Nazi hands with the help of a Swiss journalist, Hans Welti. Welti had acted as a courier between the Jewish and Zionist organizations in Bucharest and Geneva, and had been seized by the Germans. They set him free only after he let them photocopy letters from Bucharest addressed to the Jewish Agency in Geneva.

Gustav RICHTER, the attaché on Jewish affairs at the German legation in Bucharest, planned to stage an anti-Zionist show trial and thereby liquidate the Zionist underground in Romania. However, before a trial could be staged, the impact of the events on the war front brought a change in Romania's pro-German orientation, and the Romanian authorities were not prepared to cooperate with the Germans on this affair. With the help of strong pressure from Jewish leaders and international organizations, most of the prisoners were released.

4. In March 1944, when Hungary was occupied by the Germans and a campaign was launched for the extermination of Hungary's Jews, the Zionist youth movement members, with the help of the Romanian Jewish communities and the Zionist organization, arranged a rescue effort to save Hungarian Jews. At Turda, Arad, and other points along the border with Hungary, rescue teams were put in place to help smuggle refugees and Zionist youth from Hungary into Romania. Thousands of Jews were saved in the two-month operation.

5. When the Soviet army was advancing on Romania, the Zionist youth movements took measures designed to prevent the Germans from avenging themselves on the Jews before German forces withdrew from the country. It was the parachutists (*see* PARACHUTISTS, JEWISH) from Palestine dropped in Romania between October 1943 and the summer of 1944, and especially Itzhak Ben-Efraim (Menu), in charge of self-defense, who helped persuade the Zionist youth to organize to defend the Jewish population of Romania. During the uprising against Antonescu in August 1944, several companies of Zionist youth, numbering two hundred to three hundred, stood ready to defend the Jewish quarter in Bucharest. They were commanded by Ben-Ephraim and Berl Schieber, a member of Ha-No'ar ha-Tsiyyoni. Such a defense, fortunately for the Jews, never had to be undertaken.

BIBLIOGRAPHY

Avrahami, A. *The "Noar Hatzioni" in Romania.* Tel Aviv, 1984. (In Hebrew.)

Goren, D. *Twice on the Accused Bench—The Hashomer Hatzair Movement in Rumania: Chapters of Life and Struggle.* Tel Aviv, 1980. (In Hebrew.)

Levnon, Y. *Grace Found in the Desert: Chapters in the History of Religious Zionism in Romania.* Haifa, 1962. (In Hebrew.)

Zeit, M. *Stories from the Gordonia–Maccabi Hatzair Movement in Romania.* Hulda, Israel, 1978. (In Hebrew.)

EFRAIM OFIR

Slovakia

After World War I, Jews from Poland who were passing through SLOVAKIA on their way to Palestine established a scout movement in Bratislava that they named Ha-Shomer (The Watchman). This movement was active in western Slovakia, where assimilation was rife among the Jews and German cultural influence was strong. In the TRANSCARPATHIAN UKRAINE and eastern Slovakia, where the Jews were steeped in Jewish tradition (and under Hungarian cultural influence), the Kadimah (Forward) organization was formed, modeled on a Jewish scout movement of the same name that had existed in prewar Hungary. The two movements merged, forming Ha-Shomer–Kadimah, a religious scouting organization. In 1927 the movement split over the issue of the obligation to settle in Palestine, on which some of the members insisted. These members went on to form a branch of Ha-Shomer ha-Tsa'ir, and the rest became the nucleus of other Zionist youth movements: Betar, Bnei Akiva, and Maccabi ha-Tsa'ir.

During the early 1930s the existing agricultural-training camp facilities were expanded and became especially attractive (as did the Communist party) in view of the economic depression. In March 1939, following the creation of independent Slovakia, with its fascist clerical antisemitic regime, the Jews were expelled from the secondary schools and the universities. Thousands of Jewish youngsters now sought an escape from antisemitic hostility in a social framework that offered a possible solution and engaged in meaningful social and cultural activities. They found what they were looking for in the Zionist youth movements. The great influx of new members compelled the movements to assume completely new tasks: to provide Jewish youth with educational opportunities in place of the schools from which they had been expelled, to help families cope with the economic problems confronting them, and to seek opportunities for "illegal" immigration to Palestine. The Zionist youth movements flourished in this period (1939–1942), establishing branches and cells, running summer and winter camps for teenagers and younger children, and training cadres of youth leaders and instructors. Additional training-camp facilities were set up for agricultural and other forms of training, and vocational courses were held, financed by the American Jewish JOINT DISTRIBUTION COMMITTEE and with the assistance of the ÚSTREDŇA ŽIDOV (Jewish Center).

The last effort to organize "illegal" immigration to Palestine was made in April 1940, when two ships with 736 passengers aboard

(103 belonging to pioneering Zionist youth movements) waited for transit visas that would enable them to proceed to the Black Sea. The effort failed; the visas did not arrive, and the passengers disembarked on Slovak soil, penniless and in desperate straits. The borders of Slovakia were now closed.

In late March 1942 the deportation of Slovakia's Jews to the extermination camps in Poland was launched. The deportees included a large number of Zionist youth movement members, pioneers who had been in agricultural training, and younger children belonging to the movements, with their families. The movements organized escape routes to Hungary; hundreds of their members made their way to Budapest, where they were made welcome by members of fraternal movements in the Hungarian capital.

When the deportations came to a stop in the fall of 1942, the Zionist youth movements went underground. Their members were drafted into labor camps, served in the SIXTH SLOVAK BRIGADE, or lived in the cities with forged "Aryan" papers. On December 31, 1943, and January 1, 1944, the Ha-Shomer ha-Tsa'ir council met in the home of Rabbi Abba (Armin) Frieder, spiritual leader of the Jewish community of Nové Mesto nad Váhom. Frieder was in touch with the Slovak minister of the interior, and received information from him on the Slovak cabinet's deliberation concerning Jewish affairs. The council decided to take part in the Slovak underground's armed struggle. It also gave its approval for several of its members to cross over into Hungary. The latter eventually joined the He-Haluts underground in Budapest, and played a prominent role in its activities.

The SLOVAK NATIONAL UPRISING broke out on August 29, 1944. Members of the underground Zionist youth movements in the labor camps and in the cities joined the fighting units on all fronts. Parachutists from Palestine (see PARACHUTISTS, JEWISH) were dropped over the liberated area and took up aid and rescue operations, under the direction of the movements' headquarters. The Germans brought large forces in to suppress the uprising. Banská Bystrica, the center of the rebellion, fell on October 27. The parachutists and the movements' headquarters withdrew in-

to the forests and took up positions at the foot of Mount Prasiva. The Germans attacked their camp; among those who fell in the fighting was Egon Roth, a Ha-Shomer ha-Tsa'ir leader. The three parachutists, Haviva REIK, Rafael Reiss, and Zvi Ben-Yaakov, were caught and executed.

The Germans seized control of all of Slovakia and deported the remnants of the Jewish population to the extermination camps. An underground remained active in the capital, BRATISLAVA, headed by members of Maccabi ha-Tsa'ir, which supplied funds and forged documents to the Jews who were in hiding.

Slovakia was liberated in April 1945. The Zionist youth movements were revived and functioned until 1949, when most of the surviving Jews of Slovakia left for Israel to settle there.

BIBLIOGRAPHY

Kornniansku, J. *On the Pioneers' Mission.* Naharia, Israel, 1979. (In Hebrew.)

Nir, A. *Paths in a Ring of Fire.* Merhavia, Israel, 1967. (In Hebrew.)

AKIVA NIR

YUGOSLAVIA. As a nation, Yugoslavia was established in 1918, after World War I. Its core was SERBIA (which had already been independent), joined by Montenegro (another independent country) and former Austro-Hungarian areas inhabited by southern Slavic peoples. On the eve of World War II, Yugoslavia had a population of 15,500,000, 43 percent of whom were Serbs, 34 percent Croats, 7 percent Slovenes, and 7 percent Macedonians; the rest were Germans, Hungarians, Albanians, Jews, and Gypsies. By religion, 49 percent belonged to the Orthodox church, 37 percent were Catholics, 11 percent Moslems, 2 percent Protestants, and 0.5 percent Jews.

According to the 1922 constitution, Yugoslavia was to be a unified state, headed by the Serbian royal house of Karageorgević; in practice, the largest single ethnic group, the Serbs, ruled the other peoples, creating a situation that became a source of constant tension. The major opposition to the Serbs came from the Croats, the second largest group in

YUGOSLAVIA, 1941 to 1945

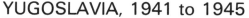

the country. The ethnic differences were exacerbated by the economic gaps between the north of the country—CROATIA and Slovenia, a relatively developed area—and the backward south; by the different religions, Orthodox versus Catholic, and by the conflicting national aspirations of the Serbs, on the one hand, and the Croatians and Macedonians, on the other. To these internal pressures were added pressures from beyond the country's borders: in the early years, from Italy and Hungary, which had irredentist claims on Yugoslav territory; and later, from Nazi Germany, as it developed its drive for the conquest of Europe. At the beginning of 1929, after the assassination of the Croatian leader Stjepan Radić, King Alexander seized power and created an authoritarian regime. In

October 1934 Alexander was assassinated in Marseilles, while on an official visit to France, by Macedonian and Croatian nationalists. Prince Pavel, who became regent for Crown Prince Peter (still a minor), took over, and ruled the country with the support of the army commanders and Serbian politicians.

Before Hitler's rise to power, Yugoslavia was a member of the Little Entente, a French-oriented league of three states, the other two being Romania and Czechoslovakia. Later in the 1930s, when Germany became a powerful country and took over Austria and Czechoslovakia, Yugoslavia began looking for new political patrons. Until early 1941, it managed by political maneuvering to avoid joining the AXIS powers, but on March 25 of that year, it was forced to do so. Two days later a pro-Western military coup took place in Belgrade; Prince Pavel was ousted, Crown Prince Peter was declared king, and the agreement on Yugoslavia joining the Axis was not implemented. Within a few days, on April 6, Germany and its allies—Italy, Hungary, and Bulgaria—invaded Yugoslavia, and on April 18 resistance by the Yugoslav army came to an end.

At this point Hitler decided to destroy Yugoslavia as a political entity and divide it among the states that had taken part in the invasion. Germany annexed northeastern Slovenia and set up a military administration in Serbia. Bulgaria annexed MACEDONIA, and Hungary the BAČKA region. Montenegro and most of the Adriatic coast were handed over to Italy, while Croatia, Bosnia, and Herzegovina together were formed into a puppet state, the Independent State of Croatia, in which the USTAŠA movement was put in power.

The Jews of Yugoslavia. In the 1931 census, the last to be taken before the occupation, the Jewish population numbered 73,000. By 1941 the number had risen to 80,000, and included 4,000 refugees from Germany, Austria, and other countries, baptized Jews, and Jews who had not been willing to declare themselves as Jewish but were counted as such under the anti-Jewish legislation then in force. The distribution of the Jewish population, by area of occupation, is shown in Table 1.

The main centers of Jewish population were BELGRADE (11,000), Zagreb (11,000), SARAJEVO (10,000), and Osijek, Bjelovar, Skopje, and Bitola (Monastir). Among Yugoslav Jewry, 58.8 percent were employed in commerce, finance, and transportation (compared to 4 percent of the general population); 12.7 percent in industry and crafts (10.7 percent); 11.6 percent in office work and the professions (4.6 percent); only 0.6 percent in agriculture, forestry, and fishing (76.3 percent); and 16.3 percent in other occupations. Most of the Jews belonged to the middle class; their economic situation was good, but very few of them were rich. In some places, mainly in Macedonia, the Jewish communities were poor.

By community origin, 60 percent of Yugoslavia's Jews were Ashkenazic and 40 percent Sephardic, but despite the differences in origin, mentality, education, tradition, and so on, it had taken Yugoslav Jewry only a short time to merge into a unified community after the Yugoslav state came into being. A young leadership group emerged in the 1920s and took over the community institutions. They were motivated by Zionist ideology rather than community origin, and their integration was well demonstrated by the considerable number of Ashkenazic-Sephardic intermarriages.

Yugoslav Jewry was headed by the Union of Communities, an umbrella organization comprising all the local communities, which represented the Jews before the authorities and dealt with all national Jewish affairs. The Chief Rabbi of Yugoslavia, Dr. Isaac Alcalay, was appointed to the senate. The attitude of the Yugoslav regime toward the Jewish population was benevolent, and the Jews felt secure and protected. There was an extensive network of Jewish institutions of welfare, education, culture, sports, and youth. Zionist activities were at the center of Jewish life.

Before Hitler came to power, antisemitism was a marginal phenomenon in Yugoslavia, existing mainly in nationalist Catholic clerical circles (in Croatia) and among profascist populist groups, such as the Zbor party in Serbia. As the persecution of Jews grew in

TABLE 1. *Distribution of Jewish Population in Yugoslavia*

		PERISHED IN HOLOCAUST	
AREA	NUMBER OF JEWS IN 1941	NUMBER	PERCENTAGE
Croatia	40,000	30,000	75
Serbia (including Banat)	16,000	15,000	94
Bačka	16,000	14,000	88
Macedonia	8,000	7,000	88
Total	80,000	66,000	83

Germany, Yugoslav antisemitism also intensified in various manifestations. German-financed hate publications along the lines of *Der* STÜRMER were distributed, and antisemitic propaganda newspapers founded. None of these efforts, however, made much of an impact on the public. Antisemitism reached a new height after the war broke out in September 1939, as a result of the growing German pressure on Yugoslavia. The Yugoslav government, in the belief that anti-Jewish legislation would appease the Germans, in October 1940 enacted two anti-Jewish laws, one establishing a *numerus clausus* (quota) for Jews in secondary schools and universities, and the other excluding Jews from trading in certain food items. These laws were severely criticized by intellectuals and by the Serbian public. The Union of Communities launched a public drive against the anti-Jewish legislation, spearheaded by the Jewish weekly journal, *Židov*.

In the period from 1933 to 1941, some fifty thousand Jews fleeing from the Nazis on their way to seek refuge in other countries passed through Yugoslavia. Yugoslav Jewry made great financial and organizational efforts to help the refugees, contributing $750,000 (in 1941 value) to their maintenance. Yugoslav Jewry also assisted in the Haapala ("illegal" immigration into Palestine) that was being conducted in that period in the lower Danube basin.

Destruction of Yugoslav Jewry. It was the division of the country into separate areas that determined the pace at which the extermination of Yugoslav Jewry was to proceed: its timing, the methods employed, and the reactions. In each area the process was different.

Serbia. The German military administration in Serbia, a regime of unmitigated terror, implemented the extermination of the Jews in its area with dispatch and thoroughness. In the very first days of the occupation the Jews were ordered to register, and anti-Jewish regulations were issued, including restrictions on freedom of movement, economic measures, and the introduction of identifying insignia. For several months afterward, most of the male Jews were put on forced labor. After the outbreak of the revolt in Serbia in July 1941, all the male Jews were put in con-

centration camps, most of them (including the Jewish men from the Banat) in Topovske Šupe, in the Belgrade suburbs, and others in the Šabac camp and in Niš. In August the murder of the Jewish men was launched, as part of the retaliation measures for the attacks by the resistance on Germans, and by November of that year most of the men had been killed by German military units. The turn of the women and children came at the beginning of December 1941, when they were imprisoned in the SAJMIŠTE concentration camp, on the outskirts of Belgrade. In March 1942 a gas van was brought in, and eight thousand women and children from the Sajmište camp were murdered between March and May. This in effect marked the end of Serbian Jewry. Responsible for these deeds were the leading officials of the German administration of Serbia, Harold Turner, Wilhelm Fuchs, Emanuel Schäfer, and August Meissner; the army commanders in the Balkans, Generals Wilhelm List and Walter Kuntze; and the commander of the army in Serbia, Gen. Franz Böhme.

Croatia. (including Bosnia and Herzegovina). Croatia was a puppet state, in which Jews were persecuted as soon as it came into being. The persecution was part of the genocide of what were designated in Croatia as "foreign elements": the Serbs (over a million), Jews, and GYPSIES. The Jews suffered more than the other categories. Croatia adopted the NUREMBERG LAWS, which left the Jews with no legal escape, such as conversion. In the first few months of the Croatian state's existence, many anti-Jewish measures were enacted that isolated the Jews economically and socially and forced them to wear identifying badges. Large-scale arrests were begun in June 1941, and by the end of the year about two-thirds of the Jews of Croatia were imprisoned. Most of them were killed by the Ustaša in the large JASENOVAC concentration camp. In August 1942, five thousand Jews from Croatia were deported to AUSCHWITZ, in accordance with a Croatian-German agreement, and in May 1943 another two thousand Jews were deported to the east. Most Croatian Jews who survived had managed to escape into the Italian zone of occupation.

Macedonia. Macedonia was under Bulgar-

Viktor Meshulam, a Jewish commander of a partisan group in Yugoslavia. [Beth Hatefutsoth]

ian rule, and the persecution of its Jews began in the fall of 1942, with the enactment of a series of anti-Jewish measures. In February 1943 the German and Bulgarian governments negotiated an agreement providing for the deportation of the Jews of Macedonia (and other areas) to extermination camps. On March 11 of that year, all the Jews of Macedonia were arrested by Bulgarian police and imprisoned in a transit camp in Skopje. Most of them were deported to the TREBLINKA extermination camp between March 22 and 29 and killed in the gas chambers there. A total of 7,144 Macedonian Jews were killed, and fewer than 1,000 survived.

Bačka. This area was annexed by Hungary and its Jews came under Hungarian laws, including the anti-Jewish legislation that had been introduced before the Germans occupied that country. The first heavy blow fell in the course of a killing operation known as the "great raid," which took place from January 21 through 23, 1942. The military command-

ers and administrative officials on the scene had asked the authorities in Budapest for permission to "purge" the area of "unreliable foreign elements." This meant, above all, the Jews, and, to a lesser degree, the Serbian inhabitants. The "purge" was staged in the tense atmosphere resulting from the Serbian uprising against the Germans and the ensuing punitive measures. When permission was received from the top echelon, units of the army, the gendarmerie, and the police went on a rampage of pillage and murder, which culminated in the mass slaughter of the Jews of Novi Sad, the district capital. About thirteen hundred persons were murdered in the raid, of whom nine hundred were Jews. The onslaught was halted by the intervention of Hungarian politicians. The men responsible for this operation were put on trial, but escaped to Germany before sentence was passed.

Many of the young Jews of Bačka were drafted into the labor service battalions (*see* MUNKASZOLGÁLAT) operated by the Hungarian army and had to carry out hard tasks, under difficult and degrading conditions, on the eastern front. The extermination of the Jews of Bačka took place as part of the general policy against Hungarian Jewry after the Germans occupied the country in March 1944. The Bačka Jews were first concentrated in three camps: Bacska-Topolya, Baja, and Bácsalmás (in Hungary). Deportations to the east began in early May of that year and came to an end a month later, by which time more than ten thousand persons had been deported to Auschwitz and killed there.

Rescue Efforts. Most of the Yugoslav Jews who survived the war did so by escaping to the Italian zone of occupation on the Adriatic coast. The Italian government, the Italian military commanders in Yugoslavia, and the Italian foreign ministry officials together worked out a policy to protect the Jews from the Germans. There were several reasons for this stand: opposition, in principle, to the murder of the Jews; the desire to safeguard Italian prestige and standing in occupied Yugoslavia; and the growing realization that the war was turning in favor of the Allies. The Germans and their Croatian allies sought to pressure the Italians to hand over the Jews, but could not move them; up to the

Jewish soldiers from Palestine meet with Jewish refugees in Yugoslavia (May 1945). [Beth Hatefutsoth]

Italian surrender in September 1943, the Jews in the Italian zone continued to enjoy Italian protection. In the summer of that year, all four thousand of the Jews in the coastal zone were concentrated in the RAB camp, which saved their lives when the Italians surrendered and the island fell into the hands of the PARTISANS. Some five thousand Jews were saved by the Italians. Other Jews survived by fleeing to Hungary, hiding in Yugoslavia, or joining the partisans. Several hundred Jews who were married to non-Jews or were persons of mixed blood according to the Nazi criteria were left unharmed.

Jews in the Struggle against the Germans and Collaborators. The struggle against the German invaders began in July 1941 with the Serbian uprising. Soon, the Communists took over the leadership of the struggle, and in the ensuing four years the leftist (partisan) move-ment increased in strength. By the middle of 1943 the movement had over 200,000 fighters in its ranks. At the height of the struggle, no fewer than twenty German divisions were fighting the partisans, with assistance from collaborators of various nationalities, including the SS Handzar division, which had been recruited among the Muslim minority in Croatia. Along with the struggle against the Germans and the other occupiers, Yugoslavia was also the scene of a civil war between various forces, foremost among them the Communist-oriented partisans. The latter, while not letting up in their fighting against the Germans, fought the CHETNIKS, Serbian groups supporting the monarchy whose fight against the partisans led them to collaborate with the Italians and Germans. Other collaborators included gangs of armed robbers and highway bandits, the Ustaša, and the Serbian quisling, Gen. Milan Nedić, with his associate Dimitrije Ljotić and their men, who fought with the Germans against the partisans. The fight against the Germans and in the civil war was exceedingly cruel, with tremendous loss of life; some 1,500,000 Yugoslavs were killed in the war.

Jewish participation in the resistance movement led by TITO was very large, in relative terms, despite the tremendous difficulties the Jews encountered in reaching the remote areas in which the fighting took place, and despite the fact that when the struggle began in the fall of 1941, and especially by the time the partisans had gained in strength (the second half of 1942), most of Yugoslavia's Jews had already been liquidated. The list of Jews who fought in the resistance movement contains 4,572 names. Three thousand Jews served in combat units and the others in auxiliary units; 1,318 Jews fell in battle; 150 were given the Partizanska Spomenica 1941 medal, awarded to the original group of fighters, and 10 received the highest Yugoslav distinction, that of Narodni Heroj Jugoslavije (National Hero of Yugoslavia). A considerable number of Jews held high ranks of command; one was Gen. Voja Todorović, who commanded the land forces in the post-war period, and another, Dr. Roza Papo, was the first woman to be given the rank of general. Jews played a major role in establishing the partisans' medical corps, which was headed by Dr. Herbert Kraus, and in creating the logistic infrastructure for the various branches of the partisan army. The partisan leadership manifested friendship toward the Jews and gave them support; specific orders were issued to extend them special aid and try to rescue them. Expressions of antisemitism were severely curbed.

When the war was over, many of the fifteen thousand Yugoslav Jewish survivors returned to the country, but within a few years, when the state of Israel was established, most of them left to make their home in the Jewish state. At present about five thousand Jews live in Yugoslavia, mostly in Belgrade, Zagreb, and Sarajevo.

BIBLIOGRAPHY

Freidenreich, H. P. *The Jews of Yugoslavia: A Quest for Community.* Philadelphia, 1979.

Romano, J. *The Jews of Yugoslavia, 1941–1945: Victims of Genocide and Freedom Fighters.* Belgrade, 1982.

MENACHEM SHELAH

Z

ZABINSKI, JAN (b. 1897), Polish agricultural engineer and zoologist who saved many Jews in WARSAW. On the eve of the German occupation, Dr. Zabinski was director of the Warsaw zoo. The Germans appointed him superintendent of the city's public parks as well. Availing himself of the opportunity to visit the Warsaw ghetto, ostensibly to inspect the state of the flora within the ghetto walls, Zabinski maintained contact with prewar Jewish colleagues and friends and helped them escape and find shelter on the "Aryan" side of the city.

Many cages in the zoo had been emptied of animals during the September 1939 air assault on Warsaw, and Zabinski decided to utilize them as hiding places for fleeing Jews. Over the course of three years, hundreds of Jews found temporary shelter in these abandoned animal cells, located on the western

Jan Zabinski (fourth from right), together with some of the people he saved, at a tree-planting ceremony at Yad Vashem in Jerusalem (October 30, 1968).

bank of the Vistula River, until they were able to relocate to permanent places of refuge elsewhere. In addition, close to a dozen Jews were sheltered in Zabinski's two-story private home on the zoo's grounds. In this dangerous undertaking he was helped by his wife, Antonina, a recognized author, and their young son, Ryszard, who nourished and looked after the needs of the many distraught Jews in their care. At first, Zabinski paid from his own funds to subsidize the maintenance costs; then money was received through the Jewish Committee, headed by Dr. Adolf Berman, Jerzy Zemian, and Rachel Auerbach.

An active member of the Polish underground ARMIA KRAJOWA (Home Army), Zabinski participated in the WARSAW POLISH UPRISING of August and September 1944. Upon its suppression, he was taken as a prisoner to Germany. His wife continued his work, looking after the needs of some of the Jews left behind in the ruins of the city.

In 1965, Jan and Antonina Zabinski were recognized by YAD VASHEM as "RIGHTEOUS AMONG THE NATIONS."

BIBLIOGRAPHY

Bartoszewski, W., and Z. Lewin, eds. *Righteous among Nations: How Poles Helped the Jews, 1939–1945*. London, 1969.

Berman, A.-A. *The Jewish Resistance*. Tel Aviv, 1971. (In Hebrew.)

MORDECAI PALDIEL

ZAGAN, SHAKHNE (1892–1942), Zionist leader and one of the prime movers in the creation of the WARSAW ghetto underground. Born in Kraków, Zagan in his youth was active in the Zionist Socialist movement and in 1920 became a leader of the radical wing in the Po'alei Zion party headquarters in Warsaw. He involved himself in editing periodicals and in party organization and propaganda. Zagan was one of the few party leaders who did not join the mass exodus from Warsaw in September 1939, and was among those who took the lead in organizing welfare and mutual aid activities for refugees and establishing soup kitchens for the needy. He was a member of the Żydowskie To-warzystwo Opieki Społecznej (Jewish Mutual Aid Society), a political advisory council.

In the ghetto underground, Zagan devoted himself to educational affairs and to the publication of underground newspapers. Po'alei Zion Left distinguished itself with multifaceted activities in the underground, and Zagan led his comrades in most of the initiatives and operations they launched. He was one of the founders and leaders of the Antifascist Bloc, the first armed organization set up in Warsaw. In the summer of 1942, when the mass deportation of Jews from Warsaw was launched, Zagan was inclined to support organized resistance, but he did not take a resolute and consistent stand. In early August of that year, when the deportation was in full swing, Zagan and his family were seized and taken to the TREBLINKA extermination camp.

BIBLIOGRAPHY

Ringelblum, E. *Writings from the Warsaw Ghetto, 1942–1943*. Vol. 2. Tel Aviv, 1985. See pages 103–122. (In Yiddish.)

ISRAEL GUTMAN

ZAGŁĘBIE. *See* Silesia, Eastern Upper.

ZAMOŚĆ (Russ., Zamoste), province in eastern POLAND. Prior to World War II, Zamość formed the southern part of the Lublin district, situated between the Bug and Vistula rivers. Its major city, Zamość, was founded at the end of the sixteenth century. The area covers some 2,317 square miles (6,000 sq km) and before World War II was divided among four districts—Zamość, Tomaszów Lubelski, Hrubieszów, and Biłgoraj—with more than 1,660 population centers and about 510,000 inhabitants—340,000 Poles, 110,000 Ukrainians, and 60,000 Jews. The Ukrainians, for the most part, lived in the rural areas of Tomaszów Lubelski and Hrubieszów, whereas the Jews were concentrated in the towns, forming 51 percent of the urban population; in some towns they accounted for over two-thirds of the population. Jews constituted the majority in a number of the cities, including Zamość, Tomaszów Lubelski, Tarnogród, Tyszowce, Krasnobród,

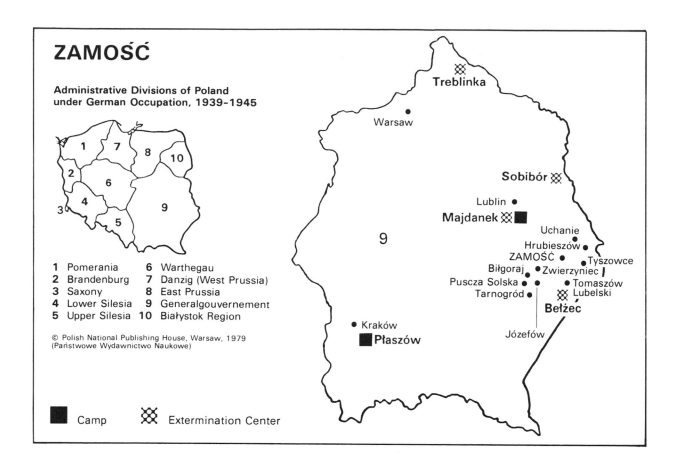

ZAMOŚĆ

Administrative Divisions of Poland
under German Occupation, 1939-1945

1 Pomerania   6 Warthegau
2 Brandenburg   7 Danzig (West Prussia)
3 Saxony   8 East Prussia
4 Lower Silesia   9 Generalgouvernement
5 Upper Silesia   10 Białystok Region

© Polish National Publishing House, Warsaw, 1979
(Państwowe Wydawnictwo Naukowe)

■ Camp   ⊠ Extermination Center

Józefów, and Uchanie. The area was predominantly agricultural, a large part of the land belonging to feudal landlords; a considerable area was forest land (such as Puscza Solska and Lasy Roztecza).

Under the German occupation the Zamość population underwent exceptionally harsh treatment: the AB-AKTION; the murder of Jews in the ghettos; massacres; and deportations to the BEŁŻEC extermination camp (the last on the initiative of Odilo GLOBOCNIK). Following these events, on November 12, 1942, the Zamość area was declared the GENERALGOUVERNEMENT's "First Resettlement Area" (Erster Siedlungsbereich), and in the wake of that decision some three hundred villages were evacuated of their Polish population of 110,000, consisting of peasant families. Ten thousand people perished in the course of the evacuation. The survivors were taken to transit camps in Zamość and Zwierzyniec, to the AUSCHWITZ and MAJDANEK extermination camps, to the Reich for forced labor, or to villages in the Lublin and Warsaw districts. More than 30,000 children were

taken away from their Polish parents and handed over to strangers. Some of them died in Auschwitz or in the course of the deportation, and some were designated for "Germanization" in the Reich.

These genocidal operations led to the strengthening of the resistance and partisan movement in the Zamość area, with numerous partisan units engaging the Germans in clashes and battles, for example in Wojda, Zaboreczno, and Osuchy. In order to suppress resistance and continue the expulsion of the Polish population and its replacement by German settlers, the Nazis resorted to collective punishment. They made an example of selected areas, in which numerous villages were completely wiped out, including Sochy, Szarajowka, and Kitow. Large police and military forces took part in these operations, code-named Aktion Werwolf and Aktion Sturmwind; in Sturmwind alone, three divisions were deployed. While these operations were under way, the Nazis also hunted down people who had gone into hiding in the forests, some of whom were Jews.

In the spring of 1944, the southeastern part of the Zamość area was the scene of heavy fighting between the UKRAINSKA POVSTANSKA ARMYIA (Ukrainian Insurgent Army) and units of the Polish resistance. Both sides incurred heavy losses in the fighting, and the districts of Hrubieszów and Tomaszów Lubelski were emptied of their inhabitants.

The Zamość area was liberated by the Red Army in July 1944.

BIBLIOGRAPHY

Bernstein, M. *Zamosc Record in Memoriam.* Buenos Aires, 1957. (In Yiddish.)

Madajczyk, C., ed. *Zamojszczyzna—Sonderlaboratorium SS: Zbiór dokumentów polskich i niemieckich z okresu okupacji hitlerowskiej.* 2 vols. Warsaw, 1977.

Mankowski, Z. *Między Wisła a Bugiem, 1939–1944.* Lublin, 1978.

Myslinski, K., ed. *Zamość i Zamojszczyzna w dziejach i kulturze polskiej.* Zamość, 1969.

Tamar, M., ed. *Zamosc in Its Glory and Destruction.* Tel Aviv, 1953. (In Hebrew.)

ZYGMUNT MANKOWSKI

ZBĄSZYŃ, Polish town that before World War II was in the Poznań province, on the border with Germany. Between November 1938 and August 1939 Zbąszyń was the site of a camp for Jews who had been expelled from Germany.

The town's population in 1938 was 5,400, including 360 Germans and 52 Jews. On October 27, 1938, the Germans began arresting Jews of Polish nationality in Germany, in order to expel them to Poland. The immediate cause for this decision by Germany was a decree that the Polish Ministry of the Interior had issued on October 6, 1938, according to which the passports of Polish citizens residing abroad would have to be checked and revalidated; passports not revalidated by October 29, 1938, would no longer entitle their bearers to return to Poland.

According to a report submitted by the Polish consulate in Oppeln (now Opole), the German police came to the homes of the Jews at night to present them with the expulsion orders, forcing the Jews to get dressed on the spot and taking them to the Polish border,

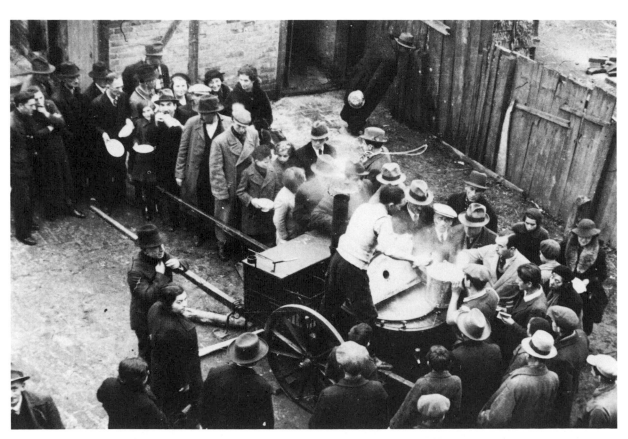

Jewish deportees in Zbąszyń lining up for soup at a mobile cooking facility (November 1938).

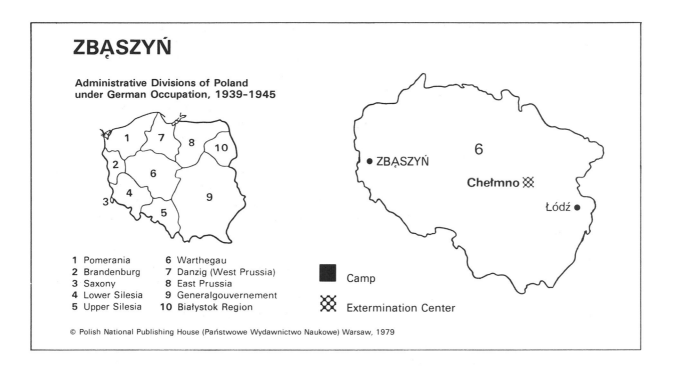

ZBĄSZYŃ

Administrative Divisions of Poland
under German Occupation, 1939–1945

1 Pomerania
2 Brandenburg
3 Saxony
4 Lower Silesia
5 Upper Silesia
6 Warthegau
7 Danzig (West Prussia)
8 East Prussia
9 Generalgouvernement
10 Białystok Region

■ Camp

✕✕ Extermination Center

© Polish National Publishing House (Państwowe Wydawnictwo Naukowe) Warsaw, 1979

which the Jews had to cross illegally. The expellees were given no time to arrange their affairs or hand over their businesses. When they reached the border the German escorts sometimes fired into the air, frightening the Jews even more and causing them to drop their belongings and sustain injuries in a headlong flight.

Such expulsions took place all over Germany, but the actions taken by the police differed from one place to another. Most often only the head of the family was expelled, but sometimes wives and children were also included. The deportees were taken by train to the Polish border, usually in the vicinity of Zbąszyń and Beuthen. The Germans estimated that some seventeen thousand persons had been deported, but precise figures were not available. The German action took the Polish authorities by surprise. Some Polish consulates (such as the one in Frankfurt am Main) advised the Jews to comply with the German orders, while others tried to help in various ways. The Polish consul in Lipsk, Feliks Chiczewski, permitted the candidates for expulsion to take refuge in the building and garden of his office. In this way the expulsion of about half the Polish Jews in the city was foiled, according to German police estimates.

Local Polish authorities estimated the number of Jews expelled to the Zbąszyń district on October 28 and 29, 1938, at sixty-one hundred; data obtained from other sources indicate that the number of expellees who passed through Zbąszyń was ten thousand. Most came by train, but large groups also arrived on foot and were beaten up by the Germans to force them to cross the border into Poland. Among the deportees were elderly people, some of whom died en route; there were also cases of suicide. Many of the arrivals had to be hospitalized.

The deportees included the Grynszpan family from Hannover; in revenge, their son, Herschel GRYNSZPAN, shot a German diplomat in Paris, an act that the Nazis used as a pretext to launch the KRISTALLNACHT pogrom. The deportees were allowed to take along only ten reichsmarks per person, and no valuables or securities; for lack of funds they were unable to proceed to places in the Polish interior.

In the first days of the expulsion the Polish police stopped groups of Jews who had illegally crossed the border and sometimes forced them back into Germany, especially those among the expellees who were really German nationals. At first, most of the deportees coming over the border near Zbąszyń were kept close to the point where they had crossed into Poland, but later on they were taken to Zbąszyń. Some of the people made their way into the Polish interior, but many who had no place to go remained in the railway station, on a nearby lot, or in the streets. From the beginning, the local authorities put abandoned barracks (former stables) at the disposal of the deportees.

By October 31, 1938, the police had listed 5,799 expellees arriving in Zbąszyń. On that day the central Polish authorities issued an order forbidding Jews to leave the town. They hoped that the concentration of large numbers of Jews expelled from Germany near the border would put pressure on the Germans and induce them to begin negotiations to hasten the return of the Jews to the homes from which they had been driven.

In the initial stage, the local inhabitants of Zbąszyń responded to the authorities' appeal and provided the refugees with warm water and some food. On the afternoon of October 30, help arrived from Warsaw, supplied by Emanuel RINGELBLUM and Yitzhak GITTERMAN of the JOINT DISTRIBUTION COMMITTEE, who were to form the General (Jewish) Aid Committee for Jewish Refugees from Germany in Poland, established several days later (November 4, 1938). A committee to help the refugees was also set up in Zbąszyń, headed by a Jewish flour-mill owner named Grzybowski. The refugees were housed in army barracks and in buildings forming part of a flour mill, and fifteen hundred of them were accommodated in private dwellings. Expenses were covered by the aid committee.

The restriction on the movement of the refugees, confining them to Zbąszyń, was a violation of their civil rights and led to protests. Some were able to get away, in spite of the precautions taken by the police, at times with the help of local inhabitants. The Polish authorities did not consider the ban on some refugees' leaving Zbąszyń as anything other than a temporary measure, and when negotiations with the Germans dragged on, the refugees were issued permits to leave the town. At the end of November 1938 the authorities decided to close down the camp in stages. At this time there were about four thousand refugees in Zbąszyń. The refugees sought out relatives and friends in Poland, and many Jewish communities rallied to their aid. Some of the refugees obtained emigration visas and left the country; a number of the young people joined the agricultural training camps of the He-Haluts Zionist movement.

The expenses of maintaining the camp were borne by a national committee, supported by local committees (2.8 million zlotys), and by the Joint Distribution Committee (700,000 zlotys). A variety of institutions were formed in the camp to serve the refugees, by a delegation from the national committee and the Joint working in cooperation and headed by Emanuel Ringelblum. They provided the refugees' needs and gave support to the local offices, which could not have handled all the many requirements on their own. The camp was run by a main office, with sub-offices for supplies, housing, legal affairs, information, registration, emigration, mail, and employment; departments for children, cultural activities, *Landsmannschaften* (immigrant benevolent organizations), welfare, health, supervision, and control; and a court of honor. A fifty-bed hospital was set up, as were a dental clinic and a first-aid station, workshops, vocational and language courses, classes for children, and even sports clubs, which played local Zbąszyń teams.

Ringelblum, in a letter written on December 6, 1939, described the period he spent in Zbąszyń working with the refugees:

I have neither the strength nor the patience to describe for you everything that has happened in Zbąszyń. Anyway, I think there has never been so ferocious, so pitiless a deportation. . . . In five weeks we (in the first few days Yitzhak Gitterman, Ginsberg, and myself, but then Gitterman left) put up a whole town, with a supply department, hospital, workshops for carpenters, tailors, shoemakers and barbers, a legal section, an emigration office, our own post office (with fifty-three clerks), a welfare department, a court of arbitration, a committee for law and order, a control service (both overt and covert), a sanitary commission, a network of health services, etc. In addition to ten to fifteen persons who have come here from other parts of Poland, nearly five hundred refugees are employed on the various tasks I have listed. The important thing is that there is no line here dividing donors from beneficiaries; the refugees see in us brothers coming to their aid at a time of trouble and distress. Most of the responsible jobs are held by refugees, and we have the most cordial relationship with them. . . . A far-flung network of cultural activities has been created here; the first thing we did was to introduce the use of Yiddish, and this has really become the fashion in the camp. We are running courses in Polish, which are attended by nearly two hundred students. Other courses are also being held. We have several reading rooms, a library, and the religious refugees have organized a Talmud Torah [religious school]. Concerts are being held and a choir has been founded.

(Arad et al., pp. 123–124)

Negotiations between the Poles and the Germans came to an end by January 24, 1939, when an agreement was signed under which the deportees were permitted to go back to Germany, in groups not exceeding one hundred at a time, for a limited stay to settle their affairs and liquidate their businesses. The proceeds of such liquidation would have to be deposited in blocked accounts in Germany (from which, practically speaking, no withdrawals could be made). The Polish government, for its part, enabled the families of the deportees to join them in Poland. These arrangements took until the summer of 1939, and, most probably, a small number of refugees were still on their temporary stay in Germany when war broke out on September 1, 1939.

BIBLIOGRAPHY

Arad, Y., et al. *Documents on the Holocaust.* Jerusalem, 1981.

Gelbard, D. "From Zbonshin to Palestine." *Yalkut Moreshet* 2 (April 1964): 35–45. (In Hebrew.)

Mahler, R. "The Ringelblum Letters." *Yalkut Moreshet* 2 (April 1964): 17–31. (In Hebrew.)

JERZY TOMASZEWSKI

ZDZIĘCIÓŁ. *See* Diatlovo.

ZEGOTA, code name of Rada Pomocy Żydom (Council for Aid to Jews), an underground organization in occupied POLAND. Zegota was in operation from December 1942 until the liberation of Poland in January 1945. It was preceded by the Tymczasowy Komitet Pomocy Żydom (Provisional Committee for Aid to Jews), founded on September 27, 1942, on the initiative of Zofia KOSSAK-SZCZUCKA, who

also became its chairperson. Made up of democratic Catholic activists, the Provisional Committee had 180 persons under its care. On December 4, 1942, it became a permanent council, known as Zegota.

Zegota had on its board representatives of five Polish and two Jewish political movements. Julian GROBELNY represented the right-wing Socialist movement (Polska Partia Socjalistyczna–Wolność, Równość, Niepodległość); Piotr Grajewski, the left-wing Socialist movement; Tadeusz Rek, the Stronnictwo Ludowe (Popular Party); Ferdynand Arczyński, the Stronnictwo Demokratyczne

A "Righteous among the Nations" certificate issued by Yad Vashem to the Zegota organization. The text reads: "Today, the 10th of Heshvan 5723 (October 28, 1963), at our invitation a tree was planted on the Avenue of the Righteous at the Memorial Mount in Jerusalem by Maria Kann and Władysław Bartoszewski of the Zegota executive, whose members risked their lives to save Jews during the period of Nazi persecution. Israel will never forget their nobility and courage."

(Democratic Party); and Władysław Barto-szewski, the Front Odrodzenia Polski (Front for Poland's Renewal). The two participating Jewish organizations were the Żydowski Komitet Narodowy (Jewish National Committee) and the BUND, represented by Adolf Abraham BERMAN and Leon FEINER, respectively. Grobelny was elected chairman of the council, and when he was arrested in May 1944 he was replaced by Roman Jablonowski; in late 1944 Leon Feiner became president. Feiner and Rek were deputy chairmen; Adolf Berman, secretary; and Arczyński, treasurer of the council. Zegota established a children's section, a medical section, and a regional section. Witold Bienkowski, director of the Jewish section of the DELEGATURA (the representation of the POLISH GOVERNMENT-IN-EXILE in Poland), was the Delegatura's representative with Zegota, although from time to time this function was taken over by Bartoszewski. Zegota had branches in Kraków and Lvov, headed by Stanisław Dobrowolski and Władysława Chomsowa, respectively.

Zegota did not establish a regional network of its own, utilizing instead the existing clandestine organizations of its member movements, or of other groups that were in contact with it, such as the Związek Syndikalistów Polskich (League of Polish Syndicalists) and the headquarters group of the ARMIA KRAJOWA (the Polish Home Army).

The Delegatura made allocations to Zegota that in 1943 ranged from 150,000 to 750,000 zlotys ($4,000 to $8,000, in 1939 values) per month, and in 1944 from 1 million to 2 million zlotys ($7,000 to $8,000) per month, totaling 28.75 million zlotys ($215,000) for the whole period. Between July 1943 and June 1944 Zegota also received subsidies from the Bund and the Jewish National Committee, totaling 3.2 million zlotys ($26,000), but it repaid these allocations late in 1944, adding a contribution of its own. In the fall of 1943 Zegota repaid a sum of $23,000 to the International Organization of Polish Jews.

In January 1943 Zegota provided financial assistance to three hundred persons, and by the end of the year to two thousand; that figure was doubled to four thousand by the summer of 1944. A chronic shortage of funds precluded a further rise in the number of aid recipients. The monthly allocation per person ranged from 400 to 700 zlotys ($15, according to the black-market rate of exchange), which was barely enough for subsistence. Similar monthly payments, however, were made by the Armia Krajowa to the families of its members who had fallen in battle. In cases of special danger or exposure to blackmail, the council made an effort to provide additional aid.

The major contribution made by Zegota was to provide, free of charge, "Aryan" documents for the Jews under its care, and frequently also for Bund and National Jewish Committee personnel. At first, Zegota used the facilities of the Armia Krajowa and other political organizations for this purpose, but it later accomplished the forging on its own, producing false baptismal, marriage, and death certificates, identity cards, and employment cards. Tens of thousands of forged documents of the highest quality were provided by Zegota to the Jews it was looking after (each person required several such documents).

Concealing Jews was punishable in Poland by death for all the persons living in the house where they were discovered, including their children. The most difficult aspect was therefore to find hiding places for persons who looked Jewish. Zegota was on a constant lookout for suitable accommodations, utilizing for this purpose its members' ties with other organizations. It also helped in the construction of shelters inside or outside apartments, to be used by Jews either on a permanent basis or in critical moments. No estimate can be given of the magnitude of this form of aid by Zegota, but it appears to have been on a large scale.

Children were put in the care of foster families, or, where Zegota had the necessary connections, into public orphanages or similar institutions maintained by convents. The foster families were told that the children were relatives, distant or close, and they were paid by Zegota for the children's maintenance. In Warsaw, Zegota had twenty-five hundred children registered whom it looked after in this way.

Medical attention for the Jews in hiding was made available thanks to Zegota's connections with the clandestine Komitet Lekarzy Demokratów i Socjalistów (Democratic and Socialist Doctors' Committee). This committee maintained an efficient network that made it possible for Jewish patients to be seen by specialists at short notice.

Zegota had ties with the PIOTRKÓW TRYBUNALSKI, Radom, Pionki, and SKARZYSKO-KAMIENNA camps, and Zegota's representatives in Warsaw helped transmit money and letters to these camps on behalf of the Bund and the Jewish National Committee. In Kraków, Zegota had similar ties with the PŁASZÓW camp and with Lvov.

Zegota also made numerous efforts to induce the Polish government-in-exile and the Delegatura to appeal to the Polish population to help the persecuted Jews, and to impose sanctions on Polish informers who were turning over Jews to the Germans for money. The council published three leaflets dealing with this issue, as well as press releases on the struggle of the Jews and the fate they were facing, and it lodged protests against the antisemitic acts of some factions in the Polish underground.

Among the few organizations in occupied Europe that were active in giving aid to Jews, Zegota was the only one that was run jointly by Jews and non-Jews from a wide range of political movements, and the only one that, despite the arrests of some of its members, was able to operate for a considerable length of time and to extend help to Jews in so many different ways.

BIBLIOGRAPHY

Bartoszewski, W., and S. Lewin, eds. *Righteous among Nations*: *How the Poles Helped the Jews, 1939–1945*. London, 1969.

Gutman, Y., and S. Krakowski. *Unequal Victims*: *Poles and Jews during World War Two*. New York, 1987.

Prekerowa, T. *Konspiracyjna Rada Pomocy Żydom w Warszawie 1942–1945*. Warsaw, 1982.

TERESA PREKEROWA

ZEITLIN, HILLEL (1871–1942), religious thinker, journalist, scholar, and writer. Born in Korma, in the Mogilev district of Belorus-

sia, Zeitlin moved in 1907 to Warsaw, where he was among the founders of the two major Yiddish dailies, *Haynt* and *Der Moment*, and a contributor to both. A student of kabbala and Hasidism, Zeitlin sought to attract his contemporaries to the sources of Judaism and Jewish thought, and wrote (in both Hebrew and Yiddish) about problems of religious belief; in his own attitude he passed from fervent and ecstatic faith to heresy and back again to religious faith. He was the outstanding figure among a group of pre–World War II writers—including Uri Zvi Greenberg, H. Leivick, Itzhak KATZENELSON, and his own son, Aaron Zeitlin—who foretold the approaching end of European Jewry.

For Zeitlin, the anticipation of the Holocaust emerged from his religiosity. He criticized modern attempts to interpret life and based his view of the world on traditional Jewish sources, expressing in his works a sense of guilt and a clear feeling of an impending catastrophe. After 1917 he wrote descriptions of his dreams and visions, interpreting them as forewarnings of coming events. A dream of his own death and another of a sinking ship, with the Jews aboard dying as martyrs, were described in his writings and also in a lecture he gave in 1931 ("Why Is the Ship of Salvation Unable to Reach the Shore?"). Yet another dream he described involved a deportation train with Jews aboard. In July 1939, a few weeks before the war broke out, Zeitlin gave a detailed account of a vision of total destruction that he had experienced—of the Nazi enemy going from city to city, from town to town, from one Jewish community to the other, destroying the Jews of Poland, brutally attacking the old and the young, and leaving no remnant. He related this vision to a group of friends and disciples, and the account was then published in *Der Nayer Ruf*, a periodical dedicated to religious revival and national unity.

The little that is known about Zeitlin's life and work in the Holocaust years is culled from diaries and memoirs written by others. Up until the mass deportation from Warsaw at the end of July 1942, he lived in his apartment in the "small ghetto" there, writing voluminously and translating the Book of

Psalms into Yiddish, but he took no part in public life and did not publish his writings. The latter were all lost when he was forced to leave his house without prior notice. For a while he stayed in the Jewish hospital, until the Jewish New Year (September 12 in 1942), when that institution was liquidated. Zeitlin is said to have been shot to death on the UMSCHLAGPLATZ.

BIBLIOGRAPHY

Frimer, N. "A Vignette of Rabbi Hillel Zeitlin and the Holocaust." *Tradition* 15/1–2 (Spring–Summer 1975): 80–88.

Holtz, A. "Hillel Zeitlin: Publicist and Martyr." *Jewish Book Annual* 28 (1970): 141–146.

Lensky, M. *The Life of the Jews in the Warsaw Ghetto: Memories of a Physician.* Jerusalem, 1983. See pages 205–215. (In Hebrew.)

Malachi, E. R. "A Bibliography of the Works of Hillel Zeitlin." *Hatekufah* 32–33 (1948): 848–875. (In Hebrew.)

Urbach, S. B. *The Story of One Soul.* Jerusalem, 1953. (In Hebrew.)

YECHIEL SZEINTUCH

ZEMUN. *See* Sajmište.

ZENTRALAUSSCHUSS DER DEUTSCHEN JUDEN FÜR HILFE UND AUFBAU (Central Committee of German Jews for Relief and Reconstruction),

center for economic and social rehabilitation among German Jewry that was active from 1933 to 1938. The committee was founded in April 1933, to fill the urgent social needs that arose following Hitler's rise to power. It was created by the political, communal, and social organizations and the central welfare institutions of German Jewry. A factor in its establishment was the demand of Jewish welfare institutions outside Germany, especially in Great Britain, for a coordinating center to deal with all the aid funds being provided both outside and within Germany. The committee was headed by Rabbi Leo BAECK. The director-general until his death in November 1933 was Ludwig Tietz, one of the prominent young leaders of the CENTRALVEREIN DEUTSCHER STAATSBÜRGER JÜDISCHEN GLAUBENS (Central Union of German Citizens of Jewish Faith). A group of young people, Zionists, and Centralverein members were the committee activists. They were experienced in social rehabilitation work, including work in the institutions for productive rehabilitation that had been created for the absorption of the waves of immigrants from eastern Europe. The group included, in addition to Tietz, Friedrich Brodnitz, Friedrich Borchardt, Werner Senator, Cora Berliner, Max Kreuzberger, Salomon Adler-Rudel, and Paul EPPSTEIN.

The first and most urgent task of the committee was the economic rehabilitation of Jews who had been deprived of their livelihood by discriminatory laws. In this activity stress was placed on vocational training, since the committee's objective was not yet solely to prepare for emigration. From its creation it worked in close collaboration with the REICHSVERTRETUNG DER DEUTSCHEN JUDEN (Reich Representation of German Jews), and on April 1, 1934, it was incorporated into that body, together with several other organizations. Its work became more efficient and the Reichsvertretung was strengthened, with its powers expanded and its capacity of action increased. Upon its incorporation into the Reichsvertretung, the committee assumed the administration of the latter's financial affairs, including centralization of the assistance money given by Jewish bodies abroad, principally by the JOINT DISTRIBUTION COMMITTEE and the Central British Fund. The committee also continued to collect money from German Jews, and was one of the important instruments for aid and mutual security. Its detailed annual reports for the years 1933 to 1939 appeared from 1935 in the name of the Reichsvertretung.

[*See also* Appendix, Volume 4.]

BIBLIOGRAPHY

Adler-Rudel, S. *Jüdische Selbsthilfe unter dem Naziregime 1933–1939, im Spiegel der Berichte der Reichsvertretung der Juden in Deutschland.* Tübingen, 1974.

Birnbaum, M. *Staat und Synagoge, 1918–1938: Eine Geschichte des Preussischen Landesverbandes Jüdischer Gemeinden.* Tübingen, 1981.

YEHOYAKIM COCHAVI

ZENTRALE STELLE DER LANDESJUSTIZ-VERWALTUNGEN ZUR AUFKLÄRUNG VON NS-VERBRECHEN LUDWIGSBURG.

See Ludwigsburger Zentralstelle.

ZENTRALSTELLE FÜR JÜDISCHE AUS-WANDERUNG (Central Office for Jewish Emigration),

staff established by the Sicherheitspolizei (Security Police) and SD (Sicherheitsdienst; Security Service) that dealt with the emigration and expulsion of the Jews of AUSTRIA and, later, also of the Jews of the Protectorate of BOHEMIA AND MORAVIA.

The Vienna office of the Zentralstelle was established on August 26, 1938, by the Reich commissioner for Austria, Josef Bürckel, and was headed by Adolf EICHMANN, who was posted to VIENNA for this assignment from the Jewish Section of the SD. It was Eichmann who introduced into the Zentralstelle the methods that were later to be applied to the expulsion of Europe's Jews. Eichmann concentrated all the Jews of Austria in Vienna, fixed quotas and put the onus of filling them on the Jewish community organization, removed bureaucratic obstacles, and forced the wealthier Jews to finance the costs of expelling Jews who had no means of their own.

Following a recommendation made by Reinhard HEYDRICH on November 12, 1938, which was sanctioned by Hitler and became a *Führerbefehl* (Führer's order), Hermann GÖRING ordered a similar establishment to be set up in Germany (on January 24, 1939), to be headed by Heydrich. On January 30, Heydrich advised all those concerned that the new office, to be named the Reichszentrale für Jüdische Auswanderung (Reich Central Office for Jewish Emigration), would be headed by Heinrich MÜLLER, chief of Section II of the GESTAPO. Heydrich planned to establish branch offices of the Zentralstelle in Berlin, Hamburg, Frankfurt, and Breslau, but this was not carried out.

After the Nazi occupation of Bohemia and Moravia, a Zentralstelle on the model of the one in Vienna was set up in PRAGUE, on July 26, 1939. The new office was run by Hans Günther, who had been Eichmann's deputy in Vienna, but Eichmann was in charge of both the Vienna and the Prague offices. The new office followed the pattern worked out in Vienna, adapted to local conditions, and eventually handled the expulsion of the Protectorate Jews to THERESIENSTADT.

When Poland was occupied by the Nazis, Heydrich charged Eichmann with the task of expelling the population of those parts of western Poland that were being annexed to Germany. On December 21, 1939, Heydrich appointed Eichmann "officer in charge of all Security Police affairs relating to the clearance of the eastern areas." Eichmann was transferred to Berlin, where he was also put in charge of the Reichszentrale für Jüdische Auswanderung; the offices in Vienna and Prague were put under the central office in Berlin. The staff that Eichmann had recruited to implement Heydrich's orders was incorporated into the Reichszentrale and became a regular section of the REICHSSICHER-HEITSHAUPTAMT (Reich Security Main Office; RSHA). Its designation at first was Section IV D 4, later changed to IV B 4; this was the section that was to trap Europe's Jews and deport them to extermination camps.

BIBLIOGRAPHY

Adler, H. G. *Der verwaltete Mensch: Studien zur Deportation der Juden aus Deutschland.* Tübingen, 1974.

Kulka, A. D. "Toward a Clarification of the SD Jewish Policy in the First Conquered Countries." *Yalkut Moreshet* 18 (November 1974): 163–184. (In Hebrew.)

Rosenkranz, H. "Austrian Jewry: Between Forced Emigration and Deportation." In *Patterns of Jewish Leadership in Nazi Europe, 1933–1945.* Proceedings of the Third Yad Vashem International Historical Conference, edited by Y. Gutman and C. Y. Haft, pp. 65–74. Jerusalem, 1979.

YEHOYAKIM COCHAVI

ZHETL. *See* Diatlovo.

ZHITOMIR, regional center of Zhitomir Oblast (district), Ukrainian SSR; one of the oldest Russian cities. In the nineteenth century, Zhitomir had a government-sponsored rabbinical seminary and a well-known Hebrew printing press. On the eve of World War II over thirty thousand Jews lived there, out of

a total population of ninety-five thousand. Most of the Jews fled the city before its conquest by the Germans, and when the Nazis entered it, on July 9, 1941, they found some ten thousand Jews remaining.

In July and August of that year five thousand of Zhitomir's Jews were murdered in groups on various pretexts. The remaining five thousand were put into a ghetto located near the city marketplace. At a meeting held on September 18, attended by representatives of Einsatzkommando 4a (of Einsatzgruppe C), the military administration, and the municipality, it was decided that "the Jews of Zhitomir must be liquidated, radically and finally." The next day at dawn, the ghetto was cordoned off by German and Ukrainian police, and the Jews were taken ten kilometers outside of the city on the Novograd-Volynski highway to pits prepared in advance, where they were all killed and buried, in six mass graves.

Zhitomir was liberated on December 31, 1943. A local war crimes investigation committee had the graves opened and found that they contained the bodies of 9,263 victims.

SHMUEL SPECTOR

ZIMAN, HENRIK (Genrikas Zimanas, known as "Hanak"; 1910–1987), Lithuanian Jewish scientist, journalist, Communist leader, and partisan commander. Ziman came from a family of Jewish landowners in southern LITHUANIA. He taught Lithuanian at Jewish secondary schools in Ukmergė and at the same time majored in biology at the University of Kovno. A Communist activist from 1932, in 1934 he was put in charge of the party's clandestine publications, in several languages. Following the annexation of Lithuania by the Soviet Union in the summer of 1940, Ziman directed the Sovietization of the country's culture and played an important role in the liquidation of the existing Zionist and Hebrew-language institutions.

When the Nazis invaded Lithuania in June 1941, Ziman fled to the Soviet interior. In Moscow he conducted anti-Nazi propaganda on behalf of the Soviet Lithuanian government, and in November 1942 he was appointed deputy chief of staff of the Lithuanian partisan movement. Six months later—by which time he had been given the nom de guerre "Jurgis"—he was parachuted into an area of Belorussia, close to the Lithuanian border, that was controlled by the partisans. In October 1943, Ziman arrived at the Rudninkai Forest in southern Lithuania (*see* PARTISANS), where he assumed command of a partisan brigade that also included units made up of fighters from the VILNA and KOVNO ghettos. Ziman did not as a rule favor the existence of separate Jewish partisan units, in line with the policy of the Soviet partisan movement.

After the war, Ziman resumed his activities in the Communist party and in the government institutions of Soviet Lithuania. He held a number of senior posts in the Central Committee of the Lithuanian Communist party and Supreme Soviet. From 1945 to 1970 he was editor in chief of *Tiesa*, a daily newspaper published by the party; later he also edited *Komunistas*, the party's ideological organ. Ziman published hundreds of articles on cultural and political subjects, in some of which he harshly criticized the Zionist movement and its policy during and after the Holocaust period.

BIBLIOGRAPHY

Levin, D. "Ziman (Zimanas): The Life of a Jewish Communist Leader in Lithuania." *Shvut* 1 (1973): 95–100. (In Hebrew.)

DOV LEVIN

ZIMETBAUM, MALA (1922–1944), escapee from AUSCHWITZ. Zimetbaum was born in Poland and as a child moved with her family to Belgium. In September 1942 she arrived in Auschwitz with a transport of Belgian Jews and, following a *Selektion*, was put into a women's camp in Birkenau. Because of her fluency in several languages she became an interpreter in the camp, gaining the confidence of the SS women in charge. Despite the advantages and the status that went with the position she held, Zimetbaum went to great lengths to help rank-and-file prisoners and was one of the few prisoners holding official appointments to gain general sympathy among the inmates.

In the camp Zimetbaum met Adek Galinski, a young Polish prisoner who had come to Auschwitz with the first transport. Galinski was in contact with the underground and was preparing his escape from the camp. In June 1944 Zimetbaum and Galinski escaped from Auschwitz; she was the first woman to do so. Because of the position she had held, her escape had a great impact on the prisoners. The two escapees reached the Slovak border, but were apprehended there and within a few weeks were sent back to the camp. Both were sentenced to be hanged —Zimetbaum in the women's camp and Galinski in the men's camp—but both committed suicide while being taken to the gallows. Mala Zimetbaum had a concealed razor blade, and she cut an artery on one of her wrists. When the SS man holding her tried to wrest the blade away she slapped his face with her bleeding hand.

BIBLIOGRAPHY

Kagan, Raya. *Hell's Office Women: Oswiecim Chronicle.* Merhavia, Israel, 1947. (In Hebrew.)
Sobański, Tomasz. *Ucieczki Oświęcimskie.* Warsaw, 1966.

ISRAEL GUTMAN

Mala Zimetbaum.

ZIONISM. *See* Aliya Bet; Beriḥa; Biltmore Resolution; Gruenbaum, Itzhak; Jabotinsky, Vladimir; Silver, Abba Hillel; Weizmann, Chaim; White Paper of 1939; Wise, Stephen Samuel; Yishuv; Zionist Movement in Germany, 1933–1939.

ZIONIST MOVEMENT IN GERMANY, 1933–1939. Never a mass movement in a largely assimilated Jewish community, Zionism became a major force among Jews in GERMANY after 1933.

The Zionistische Vereinigung für Deutschland (German Zionist Federation; ZVfD) was founded in October 1897, shortly after the first Zionist Congress in Basel, as an umbrella organization for existing Zionist groups in Germany. It embraced all Zionist parties until the secession in 1931 of the small Revisionist organization headed by Richard Lichtheim, which then reconstituted itself in 1934, with Georg Kareski as leader. Under Felix Rosenblüth (Pinhas Rosen, who settled in Palestine in 1931), Alfred Klee, Alfred Landsberg, and Kurt Blumenfeld (who immigrated to Palestine in 1933), the ZVfD attracted more adherents during the Weimar Republic, particularly among the youth, as a result of the establishment of the Jewish national home in Palestine and the growing virulence and public tolerance of antisemitism in German society. Prior to the rise of the National Socialist movement and the spectacular gains of the Nazi party, the ZVfD enjoyed respectable growth and good relations with the governments of the Weimar Republic, and it intensified the Zionist impact on the Jewish community.

After 1933, Nazi determination to remove the Jewish community in Germany, coupled with the traditional Zionist rejection of emancipation as the solution to the Jewish question and Zionist promotion of Jewish immigration to Palestine, created a role for the ZVfD in Nazi Jewish policy. The nature of that role was exploitative rather than collaborative; the regime considered the Zionists "useful Jews," not allies. It encouraged the ZVfD to promote Zionism in the Jewish community and to organize Jewish emigration, albeit within the context of overall policies that isolated and pauperized the Jewish community as a whole. In reaction to the Nazi seizure of power, the Jewish public turned to Zionism as one of the possible avenues of escape. The official paper of the ZVfD, *Die*

The Palästina-Amt (Palestine Office) in Berlin, registering applicants for emigration (1935).

Jüdische Rundschau, greatly increased its circulation, and its chief editor, Robert WELTSCH, became a major Jewish spokesman whose articles encouraged the persecuted and humiliated Jews. In 1933, hundreds of Jews crowded the Palästina-Amt (Palestine Office) of the ZVfD seeking immigration certificates to Palestine. Unfortunately, the office did not have a sufficient number of certificates for those people without capital who wished to enter Palestine.

The HAAVARA AGREEMENT, however, concluded in August 1933 between the German government, representatives of the ZVfD, and the Anglo-Palestine Bank, enabled Jews planning to immigrate to Palestine to take a certain portion of their assets in the form of German exports. The Nazis endorsed the Transfer Agreement to promote Jewish emigration and German exports, and to neutralize the international anti-Nazi boycott movement (*see* BOYCOTTS, ANTI-NAZI).

The authorities tolerated separate Jewish social, educational, and cultural institutions because Jews had been legislated out of every facet of the larger German society. Zionist institutions and activities were especially encouraged because the Nazis had prohibited organizations promoting the German national identity of Jews and their continued presence in Germany. German Zionists were permitted to send representatives to the Zionist Congresses in 1933 (Prague), 1935 (Lucerne), and 1937 (Zurich). At least until the end of 1935, German authorities facilitated the entry into Germany of Zionist officials from abroad to assist in preparing Jews for immigration to Palestine. Most of these emissaries were sent by the Jewish labor movement in Palestine and came from the kibbutzim. They became active in the youth organizations, whose members prepared themselves for immigration to Palestine, where most of them intended to join the kibbutz movement.

Under Nazi rule the Zionist youth movements of Germany played a significant role, and their influence on the Jewish youth far exceeded their numerical strength. They became the driving force in the organization of YOUTH ALIYA and in the pioneer organization He-Haluts, which established the *hakhsharot* (training farms) where the young people pre-

An agricultural training program sponsored by the Jewish community of Frankfurt. The farm was located near the Jewish cemetery (1937).

pared themselves vocationally and socially for their future life in the kibbutzim. Many who had no previous affiliation joined He-Haluts, hoping to immigrate to Palestine. In addition, the Zionist movement fostered the wide network of general vocational training and retraining that was established by the Reichsvereinigung der Juden in Deutschland (Reich Association of Jews in Germany; *see* REICHSVERTRETUNG DER DEUTSCHEN JUDEN). The Nazis encouraged these Zionist endeavors, and from 1938 to 1941 the SS even supported the organization of the so-called illegal immigration of Jews from the Reich to Palestine.

From 1933 to 1937, during the tenure of Siegfried Moses as president of the ZVfD, the organization was forced to continue its work under the most unfavorable conditions. German Zionists were coerced into denying to the outside world that Jews were being mistreated. With difficulty, they persuaded most Zionists outside of Germany to reject the international anti-German boycott, and to embrace the Haavara agreement as the best way to save German Jews and Jewish assets. The Zionist premise was that there was no future for Jews in Germany and no alternative but to cooperate with the Nazis in order to obtain the best conditions for safe Jewish emigration. Most difficult was the task of effectively preparing Jews for emigration to Palestine in an environment of intimidation, fear, coercion, and growing economic deprivation.

The ZVfD sought to persuade the Nazis that Zionist efforts to promote Jewish national consciousness and emigration to Palestine were in Germany's national interest, and that these efforts required the protection of the civil rights and economic livelihood of the Jewish community during the process. For the most part, the Nazis incorporated the Zionist goal, but not the desired means, into their policies. The ZVfD worked closely with non-Zionists in the Reichsvertretung, which they jointly formed in the fall of 1933 to care for the collective interests of all the Jewish organizations in Germany. The ZVfD also played an important role in cultural institutions and in the growing educational network that was established by the Reichsvertretung as a remedy for the expulsion of Jews from German public schools. The introduction of modern Hebrew in the school curriculum was one of the ZVfD's achievements.

In 1938, Hitler's preparations for war, together with the new forced emigration procedures initiated by the SS in Austria and eventually throughout the Reich, and the KRISTALLNACHT pogrom in November, resulted in the dissolution of the remaining Jewish organizations, including the ZVfD. The Palästina-Amt continued to function through 1941, until the beginning of the deportations to the east.

BIBLIOGRAPHY

Eloni, Y. "German Zionism and the Rise to Power of National Socialism." *Studies in Zionism* 6/2 (1985): 247–262.

Feilchenfeld, W., et al. *Haavara Transfer nach Palästina und Einwanderung deutscher Juden 1933–1939.* Tübingen, 1972.

Nicosia, F. R. "Revisionist Zionism in Germany (II): Georg Kareski and the Staatszionistische Organisation, 1933–1938." *Leo Baeck Institute Year Book* 32 (1987): 231–269.

Nicosia, F. R. *The Third Reich and the Palestine Question.* London, 1985.

Reinharz, J. "Hashomer Hazair in Germany (II): Under the Shadow of the Swastika, 1933–1938." *Leo Baeck Institute Year Book* 32 (1987): 183–231.

Reinharz, J. "The Zionist Response to Antisemitism in Germany." *Leo Baeck Institute Year Book* 30 (1986): 105–140.

Schatzker, C. "The Jewish Youth Movement in Germany in the Holocaust Period." *Leo Baeck Institute Year Book* 32 (1987): 157–181; 33 (1988): 301–325.

FRANCIS R. NICOSIA

ZIONIST ORGANIZATION OF AMERICA. *See* American Zionist Emergency Council.

ZIONIST ORGANIZATIONS. *See* American Zionist Emergency Council; Bergson Group; Front of the Wilderness Generation; Irgun Berit Zion; Loḥamei Ḥerut Israel; Youth Aliya.

ZŁOCZÓW. *See* Zolochev.

ŻOB. *See* Żydowska Organizacja Bojowa.

ZOLOCHEV (Pol., Złoczów), town in Lvov Oblast (district), Ukrainian SSR; between the two world wars it was part of Poland. On the eve of World War II the town had a Jewish population of over seven thousand. In September 1939 it was annexed to the Soviet Union, and many hundreds of Jews took refuge there, especially from the parts of Poland occupied by the Germans. In June 1940, some of the refugees were expelled from Zolochev to the Soviet interior. Only a few Jews, however, managed to escape from Zolochev to the east after the German invasion of the Soviet Union on June 22, 1941. The Germans occupied the town on July 2, and two days later the Ukrainians went on an anti-Jewish rampage. The pogrom lasted for three days and three thousand Jews were murdered. In August of that year the Jews of Zolochev were ordered to pay a ransom of four million rubles. The JUDENRAT (Jewish Council), which had been set up in July and was headed by Zigmunt Mayblum (a leader of the community and former deputy mayor), had to implement a variety of decrees, such as supplying manpower for forced labor; collecting valuables, furniture, and other household equipment and handing them over to the Germans; and ensuring observance of the curfew and regulations on the movement of Jews in and outside the town. From time to time members of the Judenrat were taken hostage as a guarantee that German orders would be carried out.

In the fall of 1941 the Germans began to seize Jews at random and send them to work camps that had been established in the vicinity. In November, two hundred Jews were abducted and taken to the camp in Lackie Wielkie, and in the following weeks many others were apprehended and taken to various camps—in Kozaki, Korowice, Yaktorov, Pluhow, and Sasow. The Judenrat and the families of the men in the camps tried to help, mainly by sending them food and clothes, but as time went on they lost touch. Most of the camp inmates were killed or died

from mistreatment, hunger, or epidemics.

In the spring of 1942 the Judenrat made efforts to find employment for the Jews in projects of importance to the German economy, in the town or nearby, in the hope that this would put a stop to the random seizure and removal of Jews to forced labor in the work camps. In mid-August of that year the Judenrat was ordered to draw up a list of three thousand Jews for deportation from the town. Most of the members of the Judenrat refused to comply and even warned the Jewish population of the impending *Aktion*. On August 28 the Germans launched the *Aktion*, which lasted for two days. Close to twenty-seven hundred Jews were deported to the BEŁ-ŻEC extermination camp on August 30.

Another *Aktion* took place on November 2–3, and when it was over another twenty-five hundred Jews were loaded on a freight train and also taken to the extermination camp at Bełżec; this number included Jews from the vicinity of Zolochev who had been brought to the town just before or during the course of the *Aktion*. A ghetto was set up on December 1, 1942, and into the small area allotted to it were crowded the surviving

Jews of Zolochev, as well as the remnants of nearby Jewish communities, including those of Olesko, Sasow, and Biały Kamien. Many died from starvation and contagious diseases. Groups of youngsters in the ghetto made attempts to organize an escape to the forest to join the partisans; most of these efforts failed because of the hostile attitude of the local Ukrainian population.

On April 2, 1943, the ghetto was liquidated. The Germans and their Ukrainian helpers rounded up the Jews in the market square. There were some instances of resistance; the Judenrat chairman, Mayblum, was asked to sign a document stating that the ghetto was being liquidated because of a typhoid epidemic; he refused to sign and was killed on the spot. From the market square the last of the town's Jews were taken to Jelechowice, a village 2.5 miles (4 km) from Zolochev, to pits that had been dug in advance, and there they were killed.

BIBLIOGRAPHY

Lask, I. M., "The City of Zloczow." English section of *Sefer Kehilat Zloczow*, edited by B. Kora', pp. 11–208. Tel Aviv, 1967.

Mayer, S. *Der Untergang fun Zloczow*. Munich, 1947. (In Yiddish, in Latin characters.)

AHARON WEISS

ZORIN, SHALOM (1902–1974), Jewish partisan commander. Born in MINSK, Zorin was a carpenter by trade. Between 1917 and 1920 he fought in the Civil War as a Communist partisan. After Minsk was occupied by the Germans in late June of 1941, Zorin lived in the Minsk ghetto and worked in the local prisoner-of-war camp, where he made the acquaintance of a captured Soviet officer, Semyon Ganzenko. In late 1941 they both escaped to the forests in the Staroe Selo area, about 19 miles (30 km) southwest of Minsk. With others they formed a legion of partisans called Parkhomenko, with 150 members, many of whom were Jews.

As the number of Jews in the unit increased, antisemitism intensified and there were many clashes between Jews and non-Jews. Zorin defended the Jews, and conse-

Shalom Zorin.

quently Ganzenko, who was the commander of the brigade, charged him with forming a Jewish partisan unit, "Unit 106" (subsequently called the "Zorin Unit"), to absorb Jews who escaped from the ghettos. Unit 106 began with sixty men and fifteen guns. With the passage of time the unit grew to eight hundred men. After successive attacks by the Belorussian police units and the Germans in the Staroe Selo region, the Zorin Unit transferred its base to the Naliboki Forest, close to the bases of many partisan units. Zorin's chief of staff was Anatoly Wertheim; his commissar was Chaim Fogelman; and the head of the special department charged with internal security was a partisan named Melzer. The contact with the Minsk ghetto was maintained through eleven- to fifteen-year-old boys, who also brought to the forest large groups of Jews who had escaped from the ghetto.

The Zorin Unit had a Jewish civilian camp, with artisans who established workshops in the forest and served the partisan units throughout the area. They provided a sewing workshop, a shoemaker's workshop, a bakery, a sausage factory, a workshop for repair of arms and bomb production, a flour mill, and a large hospital with doctors from Minsk. Soviet and Jewish holidays (including Passover and Hanukkah) were celebrated in the camp, and a school was created, with seventy pupils of different ages. There were about one hundred men in the combat unit. Zorin was outstanding in his fatherly concern for all the members in his unit, and he believed the saving of Jewish lives to be his principal task.

In a battle fought in July 1944 with a retreating German unit, seven of Zorin's men were killed and Zorin received a leg wound. He immigrated to Israel in 1971.

BIBLIOGRAPHY

Even-Shoshan, S., ed. *Minsk, Jewish Mother-City: A Memorial Anthology.* Vol. 2. Jerusalem, 1985. (In Hebrew.)

Greenstein, Y. *A Remnant from Jubilee Square: A Chronicle of a Partisan from the Minsk Ghetto.* Tel Aviv, 1968. (In Hebrew.)

The Jewish Partisans. Merhavia, Israel, 1958. (In Hebrew.)

Kohanovich, M. *The Fighting of the Jewish Partisans in Eastern Europe.* Tel Aviv, 1954. (In Hebrew.)

SHALOM CHOLAWSKI

ZUCKERMAN, YITZHAK (Antek; 1915–1981), one of the founders and leaders of the ŻYDOWSKA ORGANIZACJA BOJOWA (Jewish Fighting Organization; ŻOB) in WARSAW. Zuckerman was born in Vilna, the son of an observant family. On graduating from the Hebrew high school in Vilna, he joined the Zionist YOUTH MOVEMENTS He-Haluts and He-Haluts ha-Tsa'ir. In 1936 he was invited to join the He-Haluts head office in Warsaw, and in 1938, when the united youth movement Dror–He-Haluts was formed, Zuckerman became one of its two secretaries-general. He took an interest in Yiddish and Hebrew literature, and in education in the spirit of pioneering Zionism and socialism. Zuckerman toured Jewish communities in towns and cities, especially in eastern Poland, organizing branches of the movement and youth groups, and offering them guidance for their activities.

When World War II broke out in September 1939, Zuckerman, together with his comrades—activists in He-Haluts and in the youth movements—left Warsaw for the east, the parts of Poland that had been occupied by the Soviet Union. There he engaged in organizing underground branches of the movement. In April 1940 he crossed back into the German-occupied territory, on instructions from his movement, in order to promote underground activities there. He became one of the outstanding underground leaders in Warsaw and indeed in all of Poland; he helped to found and edit the underground press, organized clandestine seminars and conferences, and set up the Dror high school. Zuckerman also established the pattern of his movement's activities in underground conditions, making secret visits to ghettos in German-occupied territory. He took part in organizing and guiding the

branches and cells of the movement in the provincial towns, and in setting up surreptitious *hakhsharot* (agricultural training farms). He helped create frameworks for coordinating activities with other youth movements operating illegally, especially the Zionist-Marxist Ha-Shomer ha-Tsa'ir. It was in this period that Zuckerman became close to Zivia LUBETKIN; the two underground leaders eventually married and became partners in various undertakings and in the great struggle.

In his memoirs, *Chapters from the Legacy*, Zuckerman records that when the reports reached Warsaw in the fall of 1941 concerning the mass murders being carried out by the EINSATZGRUPPEN in the areas that the Germans had taken from the Soviets, underground educational activities no longer seemed to be worthwhile or important. "There was no point to them . . . unless such activities went hand in hand with an armed Jewish resistance force." He was among

Yitzhak Zuckerman (center, tallest) and members of the Warsaw "Kibbutz I" at a memorial for their comrades (1945). The sign in Polish reads: "Honor to the Fallen Heroes."

those who initiated contacts with the various Jewish underground factions in Warsaw, in early 1942, for the creation of a unified military resistance movement. These efforts, however, failed at this time. Zuckerman joined the Antifascist Bloc, established in the spring of 1942, and was one of its activists. The organization did not last long, however, and had no achievements to record.

When the mass deportation of Jews from Warsaw was launched, on July 22, 1942, a group of public figures in the ghetto held an emergency meeting. Zuckerman demanded on behalf of He-Haluts that the seizure of the Jews be resisted by force. His proposal was turned down, and no agreement was reached on any other issue. On July 28 Zuckerman took part in a meeting attended only by the leaders of the three pioneering movements, Ha-Shomer ha-Tsa'ir, Dror, and Akiva. It was at this meeting that the decision was taken to set up the ŻOB, and Zuckerman became a member of its staff headquarters. The new organization was not able to carry out large-scale resistance operations in the ghetto while the deportations were taking place, but it kept together a nucleus of determined activists and spread the ideas of armed resistance and appropriate preparation to other ghettos besides Warsaw. In December 1942 the ŻOB sent Zuckerman on a mission to KRAKÓW, to discuss with the resistance movement there possible avenues for its operations. On the night of December 22, following a military action by the Kraków organization, Zuckerman was wounded in the leg, and managed only with great difficulty to make his way back to Warsaw.

On January 18, 1943, when the second phase of deportations from the ghetto was launched, a group of fighters, with Zuckerman at their head, barricaded themselves in a building in the ghetto and opened fire on the Germans. As a member of the enlarged ŻOB staff Zuckerman participated in the intensive preparations for a revolt that continued from the end of January to April 1943, and was appointed commanding officer of one of the three main fighting sectors into which the ghetto was divided. As the time for the revolt drew close, Zuckerman was ordered to cross over to the Polish side of Warsaw, as the authorized representative of the ŻOB and as its liaison officer with the fighting organizations belonging to the Polish underground. At the time when the WARSAW GHETTO UPRISING was in full swing, Zuckerman made efforts to supply arms to the fighters, and in the final days of the revolt he and other members of the organization formed a rescue team that made its way through the sewers into the ghetto, which was now going up in flames.

After the revolt, Zuckerman, together with some other survivors, was active in the Żydowski Komitet Narodowy (Jewish National Committee), which gave aid to Jews in hiding and maintained contact with Jews in some of the forced-labor camps and Jewish partisan units based in the forests in central Poland. In March 1944 Zuckerman drew up a summary report on the establishment of the ŻOB and its record; that May, the report was transmitted to London, through the channels of the Polish underground. Zuckerman and other Jewish leaders who were in hiding with the Poles were the signatories of appeals for help and of situation reports concerning the remnants of Polish Jewry. In the last two years of the war these were forwarded to London and to authoritative Jewish organizations, by way of the Polish underground. During the WARSAW POLISH UPRISING of August 1944, Zuckerman was in command of a group of Jewish fighters, remnants of the underground and the ŻOB.

In January 1945, Zuckerman and his wife, Zivia, were liberated by the Soviet forces, and he at once applied himself to relief work among the surviving remnants of Polish Jewry. He took part in the restoration of the He-Haluts movement and the mass exodus of Jews from Poland in 1946 and 1947, known as the BERIḤA.

Zuckerman left for Palestine in early 1947. He was one of the founders of Kibbutz Lohamei ha-Getta'ot (the Ghetto Fighters' Kibbutz) in western Galilee and one of the sponsors of BET LOHAMEI HA-GETTA'OT (the Ghetto Fighters' Museum), established to perpetuate the memory of the fighters and the study of the Holocaust. For the rest of his life he kept a loving eye on the development of the latter project. Appearing as a witness in the EICHMANN TRIAL in 1961, Zuckerman read to the court the last letter he had received from

Mordecai ANIELEWICZ, the commander of the Warsaw ghetto revolt, on April 23, 1943, when the fighting was at its height.

BIBLIOGRAPHY

Lubetkin, Z. *In the Days of Destruction and Revolt.* Tel Aviv, 1981.

Yitzhak Zuckerman: A Year after His Death. Naharia, Israel, 1983. (In Hebrew.)

Zuckerman, I. "The Jewish Fighting Organization, ZOB: Its Establishment and Activities." In *The Catastrophe of European Jewry,* edited by Y. Gutman and L. Rothkirchen, pp. 518–548. Jerusalem, 1976.

Zuckerman, Y. *Chapters from the Legacy.* Naharia, Israel, 1982. (In Hebrew and Yiddish.)

Zuckerman, Y. "From the Warsaw Ghetto." *Commentary* (December 1975): 62–69.

ISRAEL GUTMAN

ŻYDOWSKA ORGANIZACJA BOJOWA (Jewish Fighting Organization; ŻOB [Yi., Yidishe Kamf Organizatsye]), Jewish armed group established in WARSAW on July 28, 1942, when mass deportations from the ghetto were in full swing, to enable the Jews to defend themselves and offer armed resistance to the Nazi enemy. First to join the ŻOB were the pioneering YOUTH MOVEMENTS—Ha-Shomer ha-Tsa'ir, Dror, and Akiva. The first command of the ŻOB consisted of Yitzhak ZUCKERMAN, Josef KAPLAN, Zivia LUBETKIN, Shmuel Braslav, and Mordechai TENENBAUM (Tamaroff). Arie WILNER was deputized to be the organization's representative with the Polish underground, his task being to establish contacts with the latter's fighting organizations and obtain assistance from them.

The establishment of the ŻOB was preceded by negotiations and discussions among political groups in the Warsaw ghetto concerning the formation of a military defense organization. These talks had been going on since March 1942, in reaction to various reports received in the ghetto concerning the massacres that the EINSATZGRUPPEN were perpetrating in Soviet territories occupied by the Germans in the second half of 1941; the reports on the emergence of the FAREYNEGTE PARTIZANER ORGANIZATSYE (United Partisan Organization) in Vilna; and the eyewitness accounts of the mass murders taking place in the CHEŁMNO camp, which reached Warsaw at the beginning of 1942. In the discussions, the political factions and their leaders were unable to reach agreement. Some of the leaders and prominent public figures taking part rejected the proposal because they believed that Warsaw Jews were not in danger of being deported, and even if that danger did materialize, the greater part of the ghetto population who were engaged in productive work or were fit for such work, might escape, whereas military organization and resistance in the ghetto might lead to its immediate and total liquidation. Until the deportations, the BUND representatives opposed any separate Jewish organization, believing that the Jews should join the general Polish underground. For a long time the Bund members also opposed forming part of a general Jewish organization together with Zionist and bourgeois groups, their political antagonists. These considerations—to which must be added the refusal of Polish underground elements to recruit Jews to their ranks and establish their own branches in the ghetto—precluded the creation of a broadly based fighting organization prior to the deportations.

The first such fighting organization to be set up in the Warsaw ghetto was the Antifascist Bloc. Formed at the end of March and in early April 1942, on the initiative of the Communists, it also attracted factions from the Zionist left. The Zionist partners in the bloc assumed that the Communists enjoyed the support of the Soviet Union and had at their disposal military power and equipment that would be available for arming and strengthening the defense organization in the ghetto. It turned out, however, that the Communists in the GENERALGOUVERNEMENT territory had no direct link with the Soviet Union, that they possessed few resources of their own, and that their standing among the Polish population was negligible. The Communists wanted to use the ghetto as a manpower reserve for partisan operations, and did not support resistance in the ghetto itself—a position contrary to that of the Zionists, and especially the Zionist youth movements, for whom the struggle in the ghetto was the main purpose of any defense organization. Before long it also turned out that the Communists' promises to transfer groups of fighters from the ghetto to partisan units in the forests were groundless, because at that time the Communist organization had no footholds there; all attempts under Communist direction to transfer people to the forests ended in disaster. On May 30, 1942, several Communist activists in the ghetto were arrested, one of them Andrej Schmidt (his real name was Pinkus Kartin), a parachutist who had come from the Soviet Union and taken charge of the military arm of the Antifascist Bloc in the ghetto. The arrests of Schmidt and his associates were the result of their political activities as Communists and had nothing to do with the bloc, but they caused shock and fear among the movements that had joined the bloc, and led to its dissolution.

The great wave of deportations from the Warsaw ghetto took place from July 22 to September 12, 1942, and saw close to 300,000 Jews uprooted from the ghetto and 265,000 of them taken to the TREBLINKA extermination camp. During this period the ŻOB called on the Jews in the ghetto to stand up for themselves and resist deportation; but the call was not heeded by the fear-ridden population, whose mind was on survival. Because of the lack of weapons and the atmosphere of terror in which the deportations took place, the ŻOB was unable to carry out any large-scale attacks and revenge actions. On August 20 Israel Kanal, a member of ŻOB, shot and severely wounded Joseph Szerynski, the commandant of the Jewish ghetto police, which had taken an active part in the deportations. ŻOB members set fire to several warehouses belonging to German factories in the ghetto, and in various places interfered with the hunt for the Jews. On September 3 the ŻOB was dealt a heavy blow when two of its leaders, Josef Kaplan and Shmuel Braslav, were captured and killed; on the same day, the ŻOB's pitiful collection of arms—five pistols and eight hand grenades—fell into German hands. In the eyes of the ŻOB members this setback was a decisive blow, and many of them demanded that instead of wasting more time they should fight with their bare hands, since there was no chance of a real battle being waged. It was only the influence of the senior members, Yitzhak Zuckerman and Arie Wilner, that held the others back and prevented them from giving vent to their disappointment and despair. The two leaders argued that after the mass deportation there would be a lull, which could be used for obtaining arms and planning a revolt.

When the wave of deportations came to an end, the ŻOB's methods and its standing among the remaining population underwent a change. Some fifty-five thousand Jews were now left in the ghetto, thirty-five thousand of whom were recognized as workers in factories that belonged to the Germans and were under German supervision; the other twenty thousand had succeeded in eluding deportation and going into hiding. The tension of the preceding months was gone and was replaced by a sense of anticlimax. The vacuum created by the disappearance of family and friends, the reports that were finally understood about what was happening in Treblinka, and the news from places that had gone through one or more deportations and were experiencing it once again—all of this proved to the survivors that they were living on borrowed time and their end, too, was near. Many now said out loud that they regretted not having offered resistance to the deportations, and insisted that they would fight if an *Aktion* were again launched.

This situation enabled the ŻOB to enter a new stage of growth and entrenchment. In October 1942 negotiations with the underground political groups were concluded, and from these a broader ŻOB emerged, now based also on Po'alei Zion Zionist Socialists, Po'alei Zion Left, the Bund, Gordonia, Ha-No'ar ha-Tsiyyoni (The Zionist Youth), and Communists, in addition to the founding pioneering Zionist youth movements. For a while, Betar and the Revisionist Zionists also belonged to the ŻOB, but disagreement over the allocation of posts and the structure of the organization led to the Revisionist camp's secession and the establishment of their own military formation, the ŻYDOWSKI ZWIĄZEK WOJSKOWY (Jewish Military Union; ŻZW). Individuals from other political groups also joined the ŻZW, as did some who had previously not belonged to any underground organization. In this period of intensive operations there was great tension and frequent confrontation between the ŻOB and the ŻZW, and they were on the verge of armed clashes. In the end, however, representatives of the two bodies held talks and reached an agreement in which the ŻZW undertook to coordinate any action they were planning with the ŻOB.

A strategic plan was also agreed upon regarding armaments, arms procurement, and the division of sectors and positions in the ghetto between the two organizations, in preparation for the struggle that would be waged when, as expected, the Germans renewed the *Aktion*. Mordecai ANIELEWICZ (of Ha-Shomer ha-Tsa'ir) was appointed the commander of ŻOB; the other members of the command were Yitzhak Zuckerman (Dror), Berk Schajndemil (Bund; later replaced by Marek EDELMAN), Yohanan Morgenstern (Po'alei Zion Zionist Socialists), Hersh Berlinski (Po'alei Zion Left), and Michael Rosenfeld (Communists). The Zionist factions that had joined and supported ŻOB decided to set up a civilian body as well, made up of well-known personalities. This was duly established, as the Żydowski Komitet Narodowy (Jewish National Committee). It played an important role in legitimizing the ŻOB in the final stages of the ghetto's existence, collected funds for the procurement of arms, and gave ŻOB the authority of a general Jewish organization representing the Jews before the Polish underground leaders. The Bund, which had hesitated to join the ŻOB and did so only after overcoming internal differences, refused to take part in the National Committee, but its leaders agreed to the formation of a Coordinating Committee (Komitet Koordynacyjny), in which the Zionist factions and the Bund took part. Abrasha Blum was the leading Bund personality pressing, under the new circumstances, for amalgamation and coordination. The veteran Zionist leaders who played an active role in the National Committee included Menahem Kirschenbaum, of the General Zionists. ONEG SHABBAT, the underground archive established by Emanuel RINGELBLUM, became affiliated with the National Committee.

The ŻOB was created in Warsaw, which was the center of its operations. From the very beginning, however, the ŻOB made efforts to spread the concept of resistance and preparation for a revolt to the provinces, especially to cities with a strong underground core. In pursuit of this objective, Mordechai Tenenbaum was dispatched to BIAŁYSTOK, where he brought about the unification of the Jewish forces and led the uprising there. Zvi Brandes and Frumka PLOTNICKA were sent to Zagłębie (Będzin), and Avraham Leibovich ("Laban") to KRAKÓW.

The ŻOB's principal emissary on the "Aryan" side of Warsaw was Arie Wilner, who was assisted by two representatives of the Coordinating Committee—Adolf Abraham BERMAN of Po'alei Zion Left and Leon FEINER of the Bund. Wilner was able to establish ties with both the ARMIA KRAJOWA (Home Army; AK), the military arm in Poland of the POLISH GOVERNMENT-IN-EXILE in London, and the Armia Ludowa (People's Army), the Communists' fighting force among the Poles. The AK recognized ŻOB officially, but the arms it provided to the forces in the ghetto were negligible; it also trained ŻOB members to make their own hand grenades out of explosives. Helping the Jewish fighters was Henryk WOLINSKI, head of the AK's Jewish section, on whom Wilner made a deep impression. In his official report Wolinski stated that the ŻOB addressed "dogged and unflagging appeals to the army, which, however, treated these appeals with distrust and the utmost reserve."

One of the first operations undertaken by the ŻOB, even before its base was broadened, was to purge the ghetto of elements that had assisted the Germans in the *Aktion*: the Jewish ghetto police commanders (*see* JÜDISCHER ORDNUNGSDIENST) and the agents who reported to the Germans on developments in the ghetto. Before the first uprising, which took place in January 1943, the acting chief of the Jewish police at the time of the deportations, Jacob Lejkin, was executed; later, in the wake of the uprising, such activity was extended. It reached, among others, Dr. Alfred NOSSIG, a man of great talent and a noteworthy past as an active Zionist and a Territorialist, who in his last days in the Warsaw ghetto had become a Nazi informer. The ŻOB's original aim had been simply to take revenge, but in the event their punitive actions also struck fear into the hearts of the collaborators and neutralized them. In the last weeks of the ghetto's existence, Marek Lichtenbaum, Adam CZERNIAKÓW's successor as chairman of the JUDENRAT (Jewish Council), was asked why he did not impose law and order. His answer was that he was no longer in control and that the real ruler was now the ŻOB.

[*See also* Resistance, Jewish.]

BIBLIOGRAPHY

Blumenthal, N., and J. Kermisz. *Resistance and Revolt in the Warsaw Ghetto*. Jerusalem, 1965. (In Hebrew.)

Gutman, Y. *The Jews of Warsaw, 1939–1943*. Bloomington, 1980.

Zuckerman, I. "The Jewish Fighting Organization, ZOB: Its Establishment and Activities." In *The Catastrophe of European Jewry*, edited by Y. Gutman and L. Rothkirchen, pp. 518–548. Jerusalem, 1976.

ISRAEL GUTMAN

ŻYDOWSKI INSTYTUT HISTORYCZNY. *See* Documentation Centers: Żydowski Instytut Historyczny.

ŻYDOWSKI ZWIĄZEK WOJSKOWY (Jewish Military Union; ŻZW), a military organization created, like the ŻYDOWSKA ORGANIZACJA BOJOWA (Jewish Fighting Organization; ŻOB), in the WARSAW ghetto. The ŻZW was organized by members of the Betar Zionist youth movement and of the Revisionist Zionist movement, which took part in the WARSAW GHETTO UPRISING of April 1943. The exact date of the ŻZW's creation and the motives inspiring it are not clear. Unlike the ŻOB, whose founding, organizational stages, and operations are documented, there is no original documentation for the ŻZW that permits a continuous and reliable reconstruction of its history.

During the major deportation of Warsaw's Jews, from July to September 1942, the main Warsaw Betar leaders were absent from the ghetto, living in fairly tolerable conditions as a work group on a farm near the town of Hrubieszów. In September, following the *Aktion* in Hrubieszów and its vicinity, in which local Jews were deported to the extermination camps, the Betar members who had managed to evade the *Aktion* returned to Warsaw, where they created the founding cell of the ŻZW.

The Betar nucleus never fully unified with the ŻOB, which already existed in the fall of 1942 and which was at that time expanding and consolidating. It would seem, from testimonies of people connected with the ŻZW, that the ŻOB command refused to integrate them in its structure as an organized group, unlike the other political organizations of which it was composed, and permitted them to join the general organization only as individual members. On the other hand, survivors from the ŻOB command maintain that the Betar members, who included persons with prior military training, wanted to take over the command. This pretension was rejected, leading to a split of the fighting force in the ghetto into two separate groups.

The ŻZW was apparently created in September and October 1942. It was backed by a public committee that included prominent members of the Revisionist movement in Poland—Dr. David WDOWINSKI, Dr. Michael Strykowski, and the journalist Leon (Arie) Rodal. The military command was headed by Pawel Frenkiel, who had a Betar background. There is some doubt regarding the membership of the command, since various publications give different names. In addition to the Betar members who formed its core, individuals without political affiliations were absorbed, as were groups with other political attachments, including Communist sympathizers. The size of the organization's membership is also unclear, although it is thought to have totaled about two hundred and fifty.

The ŻZW maintained contacts with Polish groups and individuals affiliated with networks of the Polish underground organization, the ARMIA KRAJOWA (AK). It received arms through the assistance of Henryk Iwanski, known as Bystry ("quick"), a Polish officer serving in the Korpus Bezpieczeństwa (Security Unit), an AK unit charged with defense tasks. Iwanski, for personal reasons, maintained contact and helped the ŻZW to obtain arms. Another officer of the Polish military underground, Cezary Ketling, also supplied arms to the ŻZW, apparently for financial gain. Unlike the ŻOB, whose contacts with the Polish underground and the AK were of an official nature and were approved by the latter's supreme command, the ŻZW's ties were based mainly on personal contacts, were not debated in the AK institutions, and were not authorized by the AK leadership.

According to existing sources, the ŻZW assembled a sizable quantity of arms and had far more automatic weapons than the ŻOB, although members of both organizations were equipped primarily with pistols. The ŻZW had its command in one of the buildings on Muranowska Square, bordering on the area outside the ghetto. It was linked to the "Aryan" side by a tunnel, through which its arms were brought into the ghetto. The ŻZW, like the ŻOB, imposed levies on the wealthier Jews of the ghetto and also carried out forced expropriations. This duplication of levies, and the conflicts over arms acquisitions, led to tension between the two organizations that bordered on confrontation. Negotiations were conducted to resolve methods of arms allocation and division of combat sectors for the anticipated battle; the ŻZW was integrated into the strategic plan developed by the ŻOB, and it worked in coordination with the latter and accepted its authority.

The ŻZW did not take part in the ghetto insurrection of January 1943. In the Warsaw ghetto uprising that April, its forces fought one of the major battles in the vicinity of Muranowska Square, and its fighters distinguished themselves by their courage and firepower. A blue-and-white flag and the Polish national flag were raised from the roof of the building constituting the central position of the ŻZW. A force of the ŻZW also operated during the April uprising, in the "Brushmakers'" area and the area of the large stores.

According to reliable sources, the ŻZW combat force, with its command, fled through the tunnel to the "Aryan" side after the major combat in Muranowska Square. The anticipated aid was not forthcoming, and the union, which had no foothold on the "Aryan" side, lost its active members in a clash with the German forces while in hiding. [*See also* Resistance, Jewish.]

BIBLIOGRAPHY

Halperin, A. *Betar's Role in the Warsaw Ghetto Uprising.* Jerusalem, 1976.
Litani, C. L. *Muranowska 7: The Warsaw Ghetto Rising.* Tel Aviv, 1966.
Mark, B. *Uprising in the Warsaw Ghetto.* New York, 1975.

ISRAEL GUTMAN

ZYGELBOJM, SAMUEL ARTUR (1895–1943), a leader of the Polish BUND. Zygelbojm was born in Borowice, a village in the Lublin district, into a family of ten children; his father was a teacher and his mother a seamstress. At the age of eleven Zygelbojm had to give up school in order to help provide for the family. After World War I and the establishment of independent POLAND, Zygelbojm moved to Warsaw, where he became the Bund-appointed secretary of the Union of Metal Workers. From 1924 he was a member of the Bund central committee and secretary of the Central Council of Jewish Trade Unions. As of 1930 he also edited *Arbeter Fragen* (Workers' Issues), the trade unions' journal. In 1936 he was transferred to Łódź to run the Bund branch there, and in 1938 he was elected to the Łódź city council.

When World War II broke out, Zygelbojm returned to Warsaw. He was one of the two Jews among the twelve hostages that the Germans took in Warsaw at the beginning of the occupation (the other was Abraham GEPNER). After his release he was among the group of Bund members who organized an underground center of the party, and he was delegated by the Bund to represent it in the first JUDENRAT (Jewish Council) set up in Warsaw. At the end of December 1939, when he was in danger of being arrested, Zygelbojm left the country in a semilegal way and went to Belgium. There he gave a report to a Socialist International meeting on the persecution of the Jews in the early stage of the Nazi occupation of Poland. When Belgium fell into German hands, Zygelbojm fled to France, and in September 1940 he left France for New York. In March 1942 he was sent to London as a member of the National Council of the POLISH GOVERNMENT-IN-EXILE, which now became the central arena of his activities.

Zygelbojm adhered to the hard line of his party, and his uncompromising anti-Zionist position did not make it easier for the other Jewish member of the council, the Zionist Ignacy Isaac SCHWARZBART, to cooperate with Zygelbojm. In the meetings of the National Council, Zygelbojm stressed his belief in a free Poland in which an egalitarian and just society would rid itself of the evil of antisemitism. When, however, more and more reports came in of the murder campaign that was being conducted in Poland, Zygelbojm, with tremendous zeal and devotion, took up the task of letting the world know what was happening. He mobilized aid for the perse-

Samuel Artur Zygelbojm.

cuted Jews and, with the help of the Polish government-in-exile, appealed to public opinion in the free countries, and especially to the organized Socialist movement, to provide aid and effective means of rescue. Zygelbojm maintained close ties with Socialists in the government-in-exile and its institutions, and as a result he sometimes received information that had been withheld from Schwarzbart.

In May 1942 a report reached Zygelbojm from the Bund in Warsaw on the mass murder of Jews in Poland. This report, which had been passed on to London by the Polish underground, was one of the first sources of information concerning the mass slaughter and its dimensions. It contained a list of the places in which *Aktionen* had been carried out, identified the sites of the extermination camps, and gave an estimate of the number of Jews who had by then been killed—seven hundred thousand. In public appearances Zygelbojm made constant efforts to draw attention to what was taking place in Poland and to appeal to the conscience of the world. In an address broadcast by the BBC, on June 2, 1942, Zygelbojm spoke of "the Jews in the ghettos who day by day see their relatives being dragged away en masse to their death, knowing only too well that their own turn will come." "It will be a disgrace to go on living," Zygelbojm said in that speech, "to belong to the human race, unless immediate steps are taken to put a stop to this crime, the greatest that history has known." In another speech, in September 1942, Zygelbojm disclosed that reports were reaching the Polish government in London of seven thousand Jews being deported daily from Warsaw.

In October 1942 Zygelbojm met with Jan KARSKI, the liaison officer between the Polish underground and the government-in-exile. Karski had just come from Poland, and before leaving had seen one of the camps and visited the Warsaw ghetto. (He believed that he had seen the Bełżec camp, but many years after the war it became clear that he had been to some other camp in the Lublin area.) Karski was the bearer of a message from two Jewish representatives with the underground on the Polish side of Warsaw, one of them Leon FEINER, a member of the Bund, and the other, apparently, Arie WILNER. Feiner, so Karski said, had asked him to report:

> We are full of hate for all those who saved themselves and are now there, because they are not helping us . . . are not doing enough. We know that over there, in the free world, they cannot believe what is going on here; so something must be done to force the world to believe. . . . We here are all dying, so let them die there too; let them besiege the Churchill government and the other governments, declare a hunger strike and die on the doorstep of these governments, and refuse to move from there until the governments believe what is going on here and take steps to save the remnants that are still alive.

As Karski reported it, Zygelbojm's reaction was: "But that's impossible! If I do that, they'll send two policemen to arrest me for breaking the peace; I am sure they would take me to some institution for a psychiatric examination. That's just impossible."

Zygelbojm, at an increasing rate and with an ever-growing sense of urgency, kept on making appeals. The statements he made at the time were each an SOS. He felt that he was racing against time, and became increasingly aware of his helplessness and his failure to communicate to his interlocutors the tempest raging in his own soul. He appealed to Churchill and Roosevelt and made sharp accusations in meetings of the Polish National Council. In a speech on the BBC in December 1942, Zygelbojm declared: "If Polish Jewry's call for help goes unheeded, Hitler will have achieved one of his war aims—to destroy the Jews of Europe irrespective of the final military outcome of the war."

Zygelbojm's last letters, to the Polish Bund's office in the United States and to his brother in Australia, speak with despair of the futility of his rescue efforts; he states in them that he "belongs to those who are over there." On May 12, 1943, when word came of the liquidation of the last Jews of Warsaw—among them his wife, Manya, and his sixteen-year-old son, Tuvia—Zygelbojm put an end to his life. In farewell letters addressed to the president of the Polish republic, Władysław Raczkiewicz, and to the prime minister of the Polish government-in-exile, Władysław SIKORSKI, Zygelbojm wrote:

> Responsibility for the murder of the entire Jewish population of Poland lies primarily with the murderers themselves, but indirectly humanity as a whole is responsible, all the Allied nations and their governments who to date have done nothing to stop the crime from going on. . . . The Polish government did much to rouse world opinion, but it was not convincing enough. . . . I cannot keep quiet, I cannot live, while the remnants of the Jewish people in Poland, who sent me here, are being destroyed. My comrades in the Warsaw ghetto have died a hero's death in the final battle, with a weapon in their hands. I did not have the honor to fall like them. But I belong to them and to their grave—their mass grave. May my death be a resounding cry of protest, against the indifference with which the world looks at the destruction of the Jewish world, looks on and does nothing to stop it. I know that a human life is of little value nowadays, but since I did not succeed in accomplishing anything while I was alive, I hope that my death will shock those who have been indifferent, shock them into action in this very moment, which may be the last moment for the remnants of Polish Jewry.

BIBLIOGRAPHY

Johnpoll, B. K. *The Politics of Futility: The General Jewish Workers' Bund of Poland, 1917–1943.* Ithaca, N.Y., 1967.

Ravel, A. *Faithful unto Death: The Story of Arthur Zygielbaum.* Montreal, 1980.

Stein, A. S. *Comrade Arthur: Personalities and Chapters from the Life of the Bund.* Tel Aviv, 1953. (In Hebrew.)

ISRAEL GUTMAN

ZYKLON B, commercial name of hydrogen cyanide (HCN), a highly poisonous cyanic gas that was used in the EUTHANASIA PROGRAM and subsequently in the Nazi EXTERMINATION CAMPS, especially AUSCHWITZ. The gas was delivered to the camps in crystalline (pellet) form, hermetically sealed in tin canisters. As soon as the crystals were exposed to air they turned into lethal gas, and any person breathing it was asphyxiated within minutes. An SS man wearing a gas mask emptied the crystals through a small opening (provided with a cover) into the hermetically sealed gas chamber in which the victims had been packed (*see* GAS CHAMBERS).

Ordinarily, Zyklon B was used as an insecticide. Rudolf HÖSS, the Auschwitz camp commandant, in the report that he wrote in prison after the war, relates how in the summer of 1941 he was ordered to prepare for the mass killing of Jews in the camp in the framework of the "FINAL SOLUTION," and how he and Adolf EICHMANN looked for a lethal gas that would be suitable for this purpose. They were aware that the method of GAS VANS (gassing with carbon monoxide fumes introduced by way of an exhaust pipe into a hermetically sealed trailer truck), used in the CHEŁMNO camp and the three camps serving AKTION REINHARD (BEŁŻEC, SOBIBÓR, and TREBLINKA), was not suitable for killing on the scale that was planned for Auschwitz. On September 3, 1941, an experiment was carried out at the Birkenau site in Auschwitz on a group of Russian prisoners of war to determine whether Zyklon B, which the camp storehouses carried for purposes of fumigation, was an effective means of mass killing. The experiment proved this to be so, and from then on Zyklon B was used in Birkenau for the gassing of the Jews who were brought there by masses from all over occupied Europe.

The manufacture of Zyklon B and its supply to the camps were handled by DEGESCH (Deutsche Gesellschaft für Schädlingsbekämpfung mbH, or German Vermin-combating Corporation) in Frankfurt, a firm controlled by I.G. FARBEN, and by the Tesch and Stabenow Company in Hamburg. Because of the greater demand for Zyklon B, I.G. Farben's dividends on the DEGESCH investment for the years from 1942 to 1944 were double those of 1940 and 1941. The management of DEGESCH could not have been unaware of the use to which their Zyklon B was being

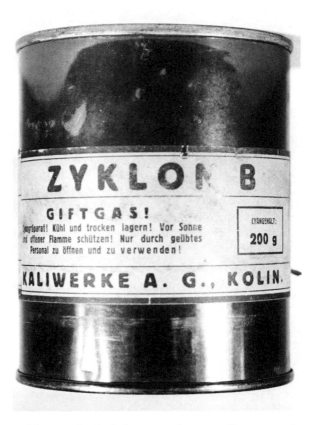

Zyklon B, the lethal gas used especially at Auschwitz and made without the "indicator," a warning odor.

put. The SS ordered that the special odor, required by German law as a warning, be removed. This odor was intended to alert humans to the lethal presence of the gas. Ordering its removal was a clear indication of the purpose it was to serve.

[*See also* Trials of War Criminals: Zyklon B Trial.]

ISRAEL GUTMAN

Glossary

*Abwehr The intelligence service of the German armed forces' high command.

Agudat Israel (Union of Israel) Orthodox worldwide Jewish movement and political party founded in 1912 in Katowice, Upper Silesia.

Aktion (pl., *Aktionen*) Raid against Jews, often in a ghetto, primarily to gather victims for extermination.

Aliya Jewish immigration to Palestine and, later, to the state of Israel.

*Aliya Bet Organized "illegal" immigration to Palestine.

Ältestenrat (Council of Elders) Another name for **Judenrat**. The Ältestenräte existed primarily in Theresienstadt, in Kovno, and in the territories incorporated into the Reich.

Altreich (Old Reich) Nazi term for Germany before 1938.

Angriff, Der (The Attack) Nazi newspaper published and edited by Joseph Goebbels in Berlin from 1927 to 1945.

*Anschluss The annexation of Austria by Germany on March 13, 1938.

Anti-Comintern Pact Agreement signed in Berlin on November 25, 1936, by Germany and Japan. They were joined in 1937 by Italy, and later by Bulgaria, Hungary, Romania, Spain, and other states. The signatories agreed to fight the Communist International (Comintern), that is, the Soviet Union.

"Arbeit macht frei" ("Work liberates") Slogan above the entrance gate to **Auschwitz I** and other concentration camps.

*Armée Juive (Jewish Army) The French Zionist resistance movement.

*Arrow Cross Party A Hungarian fascist party.

Aryan The name, used by the Nazis and others, of the "race" of people speaking languages thought to be derived from Sanskrit. Aryans were viewed by the Nazis as a superior race.

Aryanization The expropriation of Jewish businesses by the German authorities.

Ashkenazim Yiddish-speaking Jews from northern France and western Germany who migrated to eastern Europe in the fifteenth and sixteenth centuries.

Auschwitz I The main Auschwitz camp.

Auschwitz II Birkenau, the extermination center at Auschwitz.

Auschwitz III Buna-Monowitz, a slave labor camp at Auschwitz, and also the numerous Auschwitz subcamps.

Aussenpolitisches Amt (Foreign Policy Office) Branch of the Nazi party.

*Axis Germany, Italy, and Japan, powers that signed a pact in Berlin on September 27, 1940, to divide the world into their spheres of respective political interest. They were later joined by Bulgaria, Croatia, Hungary, Romania, and Slovakia.

*badge, Jewish Badge worn by Jews in the occupied countries, on Nazi orders, in order the distinguish them from the rest of

---

*Names preceded by an asterisk are entry titles.

the population. Most commonly, it was a yellow Star of David with or without the word "Jew" in the local language. It was usually worn both on the chest and on the back.

"Barbarossa" Code name for the German attack against the Soviet Union, which began on June 22, 1941.

Beer-Hall Putsch (also called the Hitler Putsch or the Munich Putsch) A failed attempt by Hitler and the Nazis to take over the Bavarian government on November 9, 1923.

Befehlshaber der Ordnungspolizei (BdO) Commander of the Ordnungspolizei, or German regular police; also, the commander's office.

Befehlshaber der Sicherheitspolizei (BdS) Commander of the **Sicherheitspolizei,** or Security Police; also, the office of the commander.

*Beriḥa (Heb.; "flight") "Illegal" emigration movement (1944–1948) from eastern Europe into central and southern Europe, with the ultimate aim of immigration into Palestine.

blood libel The accusation that Jews kill gentiles to obtain their blood for Jewish rituals.

*Bund Jewish socialist, non-Zionist organization founded in Vilna in 1897 and active mainly in Poland between the two world wars.

Bund Deutscher Mädel (German Girls' League; BDM) The Nazi organization for girls, parallel to the **Hitlerjugend.**

CENTOS (Centralne Towarzystwo Opieki nad Sierotami, or Central Agency for Care of Orphans) Jewish welfare agency in Poland.

Central Museum of the Extinguished Jewish Race Projected Nazi museum in Czechoslovakia.

collaboration Cooperation between citizens of a country and its occupiers.

D-Day Code name of the Allied invasion of France on June 6, 1944.

*death marches Forced marches of concentration camp inmates (usually Jews) during the German retreat near the end of World War II.

DEGESCH (Deutsche Gesellschaft für Schädlingsbekämpfung mbH, or German Vermin-combating Corporation) German firm that oversaw the distribution of **Zyklon B** gas.

Delasem (Delegazione Assistenza Emigranti Ebrei) Italian organization aiding Jewish refugees in the occupied areas of Italy.

*Deutsche Ausrüstungswerke (German Armaments Industry) **SS** branch that exploited forced labor from concentration camps.

*displaced persons (DPs) Persons driven out of their countries of origin during World War II.

Drang nach Osten (drive to the east) Expression of German foreign policy and actions with regard to eastern Europe and the Soviet Union. The term originated in the first half of the nineteenth century.

Drobitski Yar (Drobitski Ravine) Site, near Kharkov, of massacres of Jews.

Durchgangslager (Dulag) Transit camp.

*Einsatzgruppen ("action squads") Mobile units of the SS and **SD**. The Einsatzgruppen accompanied the advancing German army into Poland in September 1939 and into the Soviet Union from June 22, 1941. Their official tasks were to wipe out political opponents and seize state documents. In the Soviet Union in particular, they carried out mass murders, primarily of Jews.

Einsatzkommando Sub-unit of an Einsatzgruppe.

*"Final Solution" (in full, *Endlösung der Judenfrage in Europa*, or final solution of the Jewish problem in Europe) Nazi code name for the physical extermination of European Jewry.

free professions Professions requiring university-level training, such as medicine, the law, engineering, and university teaching.

Freikorps Volunteer armies organized beginning in 1918 by former army officers in Germany after its defeat in World War I. Their goals were to protect Germany's eastern borders and crush revolutions at home. The Freikorps dissolved in 1921.

Freiwillige (volunteers) Non-German collaborators who joined the Waffen-SS.

Führer (Leader) Adolf Hitler's title in Nazi Germany.

Galicia   Region in southeastern Poland and the northwestern Ukraine; former Austrian crown land. Now divided between Poland and the Ukrainian SSR.

Gau (district)   Main territorial unit in the Reich during the Nazi period.

Gauleiter   Nazi party head of a *Gau*.

Gebietskommissar   German head of a *Gebiet* (territory).

Gebietskommissariat (District Commissariat)   Lowest level of the German civil administration in the occupied territories of the Soviet Union.

Gendarmerie   Regional or rural police.

Generalbezirk (also Generalkommissariat, or General Commissariat)   Intermediate level of the German civil administration in the occupied territories of the Soviet Union.

*****Generalgouvernement**   The Germans' name for the administrative unit comprising those parts of occupied Poland that were not incorporated into the Reich. It included five districts: Galicia, Kraków, Lublin, Radom, and Warsaw.

*****Gestapo** (Geheime Staatspolizei, or Secret State Police)   Together with the **Kriminalpolizei**, the Gestapo constituted the Sicherheitspolizei.

Gleichschaltung   Coordination; that is, elimination of opposition and the Nazifying of the German state.

*****Haavara**   Trade company established in Germany for the transfer of Jewish capital to Palestine in the form of goods.

Hagana   The underground military organization, founded in 1920, of the Yishuv, the Jewish community in Palestine.

hakhshara (pl., *hakhsharot*)   The organized agricultural training of young people prior to immigration to Palestine.

haluts (pl., *halutsim*)   A pioneer in Palestine.

Heeres Kraftfahrpark (Army Motor Vehicle Depot)   The German maintenance services for military vehicles.

Herrenvolk (master race)   The Nazis' racial definition of the German people.

*****Hilfswillige**   Soviet prisoners of war and civilians in Nazi-occupied territories who volunteered for or were drafted into the German army.

*****Hitlerjugend** (Hitler Youth)   The Nazi youth organization for boys, founded in 1922.

*****Hlinka Guard**   SS-influenced armed militia of the Slovak People's Party, named after Andrej Hlinka, Slovak nationalist leader.

Höherer SS- und Polizeiführer (Higher SS and Police Leader)   Senior commander of SS and police in an occupied area; Heinrich Himmler's personal representative.

*****Horst Wessel Song**   Nazi party anthem written in 1929 by Horst Wessel, an **SA** member who was killed (in a private quarrel) by a Communist. The Nazis elevated him to the status of a hero.

*****Iron Guard**   The Romanian fascist movement.

judenfrei ("free of Jews")   Nazi term for the absence of Jews in a given area as a result of deportation and extermination operations.

*****Judenrat** (Jewish Council)   Council of Jewish leaders established on Nazi orders in an occupied place.

judenrein ("cleansed of Jews")   *See* **judenfrei**.

*****Jüdischer Ordnungsdienst**   Jewish ghetto police.

Julag (from *Judenlager*, Jewish camp)   Nazi camp for Jews.

*****Kapo** (probably from Ital. *capo*, "chief")   Supervisor of inmate laborers in a concentration camp.

*****Kriminalpolizei** (Criminal Police; Kripo)   German criminal police. Together with the Gestapo, they formed the Sicherheitspolizei.

*****Kristallnacht** ("Night of the Broken Glass")   Organized pogrom against Jews in Germany and Austria on November 9–10, 1938.

Land (pl., *Länder*)   The former sovereign states of Germany under the **Weimar Republic**.

Lebensborn (Fountain of Life)   SS association established in 1936. Its main tasks were to facilitate the adoption of "racially appropriate" children by childless SS couples and to encourage the birth of "racially sound" children.

Lebensraum (living space)   Principle of Nazi

ideology and foreign policy, expressed in the drive for the conquest of territories, mainly in the east.

Lend-Lease American program for the supplying of military goods to the Allies during World War II.

Luftwaffe The German air force.

*__Madagascar Plan__ Nazi plan, formulated in the spring of 1940, for the expulsion of the European Jews to the island of Madagascar, off the southeastern coast of Africa. The plan was abandoned that autumn.

*__Mein Kampf__ (My Struggle) Adolf Hitler's book expounding his ideology, published in two volumes (July 1925 and December 1926).

*__Mischlinge__ Nazi term for persons having one or two Jewish grandparents.

Mit brennender Sorge (With Burning Concern) Encyclical issued by Pope Pius XI on March 14, 1937, assailing racism and the cult of the state.

Mosad le-Aliya Bet (Organization for "Illegal" Immigration) The immigration branch of the Yishuv's underground organization, the **Hagana**.

Munich Putsch *See* **Beer-Hall Putsch**.

*__Muselmann__ Concentration camp term for an inmate on the verge of death from starvation and exhaustion.

*__Nacht und Nebel__ (Night and Fog) Code name for the rounding up of suspected members of the anti-Nazi resistance in occupied western Europe.

Naczelna Rada Opiekuńcza (Main Welfare Council) Organization in the **Generalgouvernement** that coordinated Polish, Jewish, and Ukrainian welfare activities under the auspices of the Nazi authorities.

National Legionary Government Government established in Romania in 1940 by Ion Antonescu and Horia Sima (chief of the Iron Guard) with the goal of drawing close to Germany and Italy.

*__Nazi-Soviet Pact__ Two agreements signed by Germany and the Soviet Union on August 19 and 23, 1939, dealing with economic and political issues. A secret protocol divided Nazi and Soviet spheres of interest in the Baltic states and Poland.

Neolog One of the three trends of Judaism in Hungary, akin to Reform Judaism.

"Night of the Long Knives" (*Nacht der langen Messer*) Nazi purge of the SA on June 30–July 1, 1934.

numerus clausus The quota of Jews permitted, as in a university.

*__Nuremberg Laws__ Two laws issued in 1935 to further the legal exclusion of Jews from German life. The first removed the Jews' citizenship; the second defined the Jews racially and prohibited them from engaging in marital and other relations with Germans. The laws were proclaimed at the annual Nazi party rally in Nuremberg on September 15, 1935.

*__Nuremberg Trial__ Trial of twenty-two major Nazi figures in Nuremberg in 1945 and 1946. They were tried by the International Military Tribunal.

Oberkommando der Wehrmacht (OKW) Armed Forces High Command; eventually, the high command of all the German armed forces.

Oberkommando des Heeres (OKH) Army High Command.

Oblast (district) Administrative unit in the Soviet Union.

Odessa (Organisation der SS-Angehörige, or Organization of SS Members) One of the groups that helped engineer the escape of Nazis from Germany after World War II.

Old Kingdom (also called Old Romania or the Regat) Romania in its pre-1918 borders.

Ordnungsdienst. *See* **Jüdischer Ordnungsdienst.**

*__Organisation Todt.__ Semi-militarized agency that made use of forced labor. It was headed by Dr. Fritz Todt beginning in 1933 and was named after him upon his death in 1942.

ORT International organization, founded in Russia in 1880, for developing skilled trades and agriculture among Jews through vocational training.

Ostarbeiter (eastern worker) Slave laborer from the eastern occupied territories.

*__Ostbataillone__ (Ostlegionen, Osttruppen) German army units made up of Soviet collaborators (prisoners of war and Soviet citizens). They numbered about a million men.

Ostjuden Jews from eastern Europe who had settled in Germany.

Ostland The eastern European territories occupied by the Nazis, consisting of the Baltic states (Estonia, Latvia, and Lithuania) and the western half of Belorussia.

Palästina-Amt (Palestine Office) Office of the Jewish Agency that dealt with immigration to Palestine.

Pale of Settlement Area in the western part of the Russian empire in which Russian Jews were confined from 1835 to 1917.

Palmaḥ The assault forces of the Hagana.

Paltreu Trust company implementing the **Haavara** transfer of goods to Palestine.

*partisans Guerrilla fighters.

Potsdam Conference Meeting held by Winston Churchill, Joseph Stalin, and Harry S. Truman from July 17 to August 2, 1945, in Potsdam, Germany. Its purpose was to discuss the political and economic problems arising after Germany's surrender.

Protektorat Böhmen und Mähren (Protectorate of Bohemia and Moravia) Nazi designation for the parts of Czechoslovakia occupied in 1939.

quisling A traitor; a term taken from the name of Vidkun Quisling, the pro-Nazi Norwegian leader. It usually refers to the leader of an enemy-sponsored regime.

rampa A Polish word; the railway platform for arriving trains at a concentration or extermination camp.

Rassenschande (racial defilement) Nazi term for sexual contact between an Aryan and a Jew.

*Rasse- und Siedlungshauptamt (Race and Resettlement Main Office) Nazi office that supervised the racial purity of SS members, as well as the colonization of SS settlers in the eastern occupied territories.

Razzia (pl., *Razzien*) A roundup of Jews.

Red Army (full name, Rabochya Krestyanskaya Krasnaya Armiya, or Workers' and Peasants' Red Army) Official name of the Soviet army until June 1945, when it was changed to Soviet Army.

Regat *See* **Old Kingdom**.

Reichsbahn The German state railways.

Reichsfluchtsteuer An emigration tax that Jews had to pay before leaving Germany.

Reichsführer-SS (Reich Leader of the SS) Heinrich Himmler's main title.

Reichskommissariat (Reich Commissariat) Major territorial division of the German civil administration in the occupied areas of the Soviet Union.

*Reichskommissariat für die Festigung des Deutschen Volkstums (Reich Commissariat for the Strengthening of German Nationhood) SS agency concerned with ethnic Germans.

*Reichskommissariat Ostland The German civil administration of the **Ostland**.

*Reichssicherheitshauptamt (Reich Security Main Office; RSHA) Nazi administrative office formed on September 22, 1939, from the union of the SD and the Sicherheitspolizei (the latter included the Gestapo and the Kriminalpolizei).

Reichssippenamt The Reich Genealogical Office.

Reichstag The German parliament.

Reichswehr Name of the German army from 1919 until 1935, when it became the Wehrmacht.

Reichszentrale für Jüdische Auswanderung (Reich Central Office for Jewish Emigration) The Nazis' central agency for matters relating to Jewish emigration. Its original functions ceased in October 1941, when further emigration of Jews was prohibited.

Réseau Garel (Garel Network) Underground organization in France that placed Jewish children with Christian families and with institutions involved in saving Jews.

Restgetto The residual ghetto after an *Aktion*.

Revisionists Members of the New Zionist Organization, founded by Vladimir Jabotinsky in 1925.

*"Righteous among the Nations" Title given by **Yad Vashem** to non-Jews who risked their lives to save Jews in Nazi-occupied Europe.

*Rote Kapelle (Red Orchestra) Soviet spy

ring that operated in Germany, Belgium, and France during World War II.

*Russkaya Osvoboditelnaya Armiya German-sponsored military units of Russian collaborators.

*SA (Sturmabteilung; Storm Troopers) Shock units founded by the Nazi party in 1921; also called Brownshirts.

Schwarze Korps, Das The official SS newspaper.

*SD (Sicherheitsdienst; Security Service) The SS security and intelligence service, established in 1932 under Reinhard Heydrich and incorporated in 1939 into the Reichssicherheitshauptamt.

Selektion (pl., Selektionen) The process of selecting, from among Jewish deportees arriving at a Nazi camp, those who were to be used for forced labor and those who were to be killed immediately. The term also refers to the selecting, in ghettos, of Jews to be deported.

Sephardim Jews expelled from Spain and Portugal in 1492; they and their descendants migrated to North Africa, Italy, western Europe, the Balkans, the Near East, and the Americas.

She'erit ha-Peletah The "surviving remnant" of Europe's Jews after the Holocaust.

sho'ah The Hebrew term for "holocaust"; the mass destruction of Jews by the Nazis.

Sicherheitspolizei (Security Police; Sipo) Nazi security police, composed of the Gestapo and the Kriminalpolizei.

Sonderbehandlung ("special treatment") Euphemism for the killing of detainees.

*Sonderkommando ("special squad") SS or Einsatzgruppe detachment; also refers to the Jewish units in extermination camps who removed the bodies of those gassed for cremation or burial.

"The Soviet Paradise" Anti-Soviet exhibition held in Berlin in 1942.

*SS (Schutzstaffel, or Protection Squad) Originally, guard detachments formed in 1925 as Hitler's personal guard. In 1929, under Himmler, the SS developed into the elite units of the Nazi party.

SS- und Polizeiführer SS and Police Leader; one rank below the Höherer SS- und Polizeiführer.

Stahlhelm (Steel Helmet) Nationalist organization of former German soldiers, founded in 1918.

Stalag (from Stammlager, or base camp) Prisoner-of-war camp.

Status Quo Ante Jewish communities in Hungary that followed neither the Neolog nor the Orthodox trend.

*Stürmer, Der (The Attacker) Antisemitic weekly newspaper edited by Julius Streicher.

*Subsequent Nuremberg Proceedings Twelve trials, held in Nuremberg from 1946 to 1949, of Nazi criminals. They were tried by the Nuremberg Military Tribunals, composed of American judges.

swastika Ancient symbol originating in South Asia; appropriated by the Nazis as their emblem.

Székely Land Former autonomous district in northern Transylvania.

Tarbut (Heb.; "culture") Zionist-oriented secular school movement in eastern Europe, especially influential in Poland.

*Third Reich The official name of the united German state was the Reich. The first Reich was the Holy Roman Empire, and the second Reich was created by Otto von Bismarck, first chancellor (1871–1890) of the German Empire. The Third Reich was proclaimed by Adolf Hitler and lasted twelve years.

Tiyyul (Heb.; "excursion") The loosely organized escape of Jews, during World War II, from Slovakia to Hungary, and from Hungary to Romania, Slovakia, and Yugoslavia.

Transferstelle Nazi office in Warsaw that implemented the exchange of goods between the ghetto and the "Aryan" side of the city.

*Transnistria Province in the southern part of the Ukraine that was occupied and governed by Romania from 1941 to 1944.

Trianon Hungary Hungary according to the 1920 Treaty of Trianon, which deprived Hungary of more than two-thirds of its territory and about 60 percent of its population after World War I.

*Umschlagplatz Place in Warsaw where freight trains were loaded and unloaded.

During the deportations from the Warsaw ghetto, it was used as an assembly point where Jews were loaded onto cattle cars to be taken to Treblinka.

*United Nations Relief and Rehabilitation Administration (UNRRA) An organization established on November 9, 1943, by forty-four member nations of the United Nations. After World War II it aided millions of **displaced persons.**

*Ustaša Croatian nationalist terrorist organization that came to power in April 1941, with the establishment of the Croatian state. It was responsible for the mass murder of Serbs, Jews, and Gypsies.

Vernichtung durch Arbeit (extermination through work) Deliberate policy of gradually killing prisoners in some Nazi camps through starvation and overwork.

Vichy Spa town in central France; the capital of unoccupied France and the headquarters of the regime headed by Marshal Philippe Pétain. The Germans occupied Vichy France in November 1942.

Völkischer Beobachter (People's Observer) Main newspaper of the Nazi party.

*Volksdeutsche (ethnic Germans) Germans living outside Germany.

Volksdeutsche Mittelstelle (VoMi) SS welfare and repatriation office for ethnic Germans.

Volksgemeinschaft "Folk community" of Germans.

Waffen-SS Militarized units of the SS.

*Wannsee Conference Meeting called by Reinhard Heydrich and held at Wannsee, a suburb of Berlin, on January 20, 1942, to coordinate the "Final Solution."

*War Refugee Board United States agency established in January 1944 by order of President Franklin D. Roosevelt, to rescue people from Nazi-occupied territories.

*Warthegau (Wartheland) Western Polish district annexed to the Reich after September 1939.

*Wehrmacht The combined German armed forces.

Weimar Republic The German republic (1919–1933) established after the end of World War I, with its capital in the city of Weimar.

Wissenschaft des Judentums Judaic studies.

*Yad Vashem Holocaust memorial in Jerusalem.

Yalta Conference Conference held in Yalta, in the Crimea, from February 4 to 11, 1945. Attended by Churchill, Roosevelt, and Stalin, its purpose was to discuss the last stage of the war against Germany.

Zentrum The Catholic Center party in Germany.

*Zyklon B (hydrogen cyanide) Pesticide used in the Euthanasia Program and later, especially in the gas chambers of Auschwitz-Birkenau.

Chronology

February 24, 1920	The Nazi party platform is written.
November 9, 1923	In Munich the Nazis, headed by Adolf Hitler, unsuccessfully try to take over the Bavarian government, in what becomes known as the Beer-Hall Putsch.
September 14, 1930	The Nazis receive over 18 percent of the vote in a Reichstag election.
July 31, 1932	The Nazis receive over 37 percent of the vote in a Reichstag election.

1933

January 30	Hitler becomes chancellor of Germany after a Reichstag election in which the Nazis receive approximately 33 percent of the vote.
February 27	The German Reichstag building is set on fire; the next day, a national emergency is declared.
March 20	A concentration camp is established at Dachau, and the first prisoners arrive the next day.
March 24	The Enabling Law (*Ermächtigungsgesetz*) is passed by the Reichstag and is used by Hitler to help establish his dictatorship.
April 1	A one-day nationwide boycott of Jewish businesses is carried out in Germany.
April 7	Quotas are applied in Germany to the number of Jewish students allowed in institutions of higher education, and laws prohibiting Jews from working in government offices are promulgated.
April 21	Ritual slaughter is outlawed in Germany.
May 10	Books are publicly burned throughout Germany.
May 17	The Bernheim petition, against Nazi anti-Jewish legislation in German Upper Silesia, is presented to the League of Nations in Geneva. On June 1, 1933, the petition is granted.
August 25	The Haavara (transfer) agreement is signed between Jewish leaders from Palestine and the Nazi authorities.
September 22	In Germany, Jews are removed from the fields of literature, music, art, broadcasting, theater, and the press.

1934

January 26	Germany and Poland sign a ten-year nonaggression pact.
June 30	Hitler orders the SS, under Heinrich Himmler, to purge the SA leadership. Many are murdered, including Ernst Röhm, in what becomes known as the "Night of the Long Knives."
July 25	Chancellor Engelbert Dollfuss is killed when the Nazis unsuccessfully try to seize power in Austria.
August 2	The German president, Paul von Hindenburg, dies, leaving the way open for Hitler to establish a dictatorship.

1935

January 13	The Saarland is retaken by Germany.
March 16	In violation of the Versailles Treaty, conscription is resumed in Germany.
September 15	The Nuremberg Laws are decreed at a Nazi party rally, defining who may be a citizen of Germany and banning marriage and other forms of contact between Jews and Germans.
October 3	Italy attacks Ethiopia.
December 31	Jews are dismissed from the civil service in Germany.

1936

March 7	German forces enter the Rhineland.
May 5	Ethiopia surrenders to Italy.
October 25	The Rome-Berlin Axis agreement is signed.

1937

March 21	Pope Pius XI issues the encyclical *Mit brennender Sorge,* a statement against racism and nationalism.
July 16	A concentration camp is established at Buchenwald.
November 25	Germany and Japan sign a military and political pact.

1938

March 13	German forces occupy Austria in what becomes known as the Anschluss.
March 23	The Jewish community organizations in Germany lose their official status and are no longer recognized by the government.
April 24	A decree calling for the registration of all Jewish property is promulgated in Germany.
April 26	Directives for the expropriation of Jewish property are issued in Austria.
May 16	In Austria, the first group of inmates begins work in the Mauthausen quarries.
May 29	The First Anti-Jewish Law is promulgated in Hungary, restricting the Jewish role in the economy to 20 percent.
June 15	Fifteen hundred German Jews are put into concentration camps.
June 25	German Jewish physicians are permitted to treat only Jewish patients.

1938

July 6–15	A conference is held at Evian-les-Bains during which representatives from thirty-two nations discuss the refugee problem but take little action toward solving it.
July 8	On Nazi orders, the Great Synagogue in Munich is torn down.
August 17	All Jewish men in Germany are required to add "Israel" to their name, and all Jewish women, "Sarah."
August 26	In Vienna, the Central Office for Jewish Emigration (Zentralstelle für Jüdische Auswanderung) is set up under Adolf Eichmann.
September 27	Jews are barred from practicing law in Germany.
September 29	The Munich agreement is signed.
October 5	The passports of German Jews are marked with the letter *J*, for *Jude*.
October 6	As a result of the Munich agreement, the Sudetenland is annexed by Germany and the Czechoslovak Republic is established, with autonomy for Slovakia.
October 8	The Hlinka Guard is established in Slovakia.
October 28	Between 15,000 and 17,000 stateless Jews are expelled from Germany to Poland; most are interned in Zbąszyń.
November 2	Under the provisions of the first Vienna Award, parts of Slovakia and the Transcarpathian Ukraine are annexed by Hungary.
November 9–10	Following the assassination of Ernst vom Rath, a secretary at the German legation in Paris, by a Jewish youth, Herschel Grynszpan, the *Kristallnacht* pogrom takes place in Germany and Austria; some 30,000 Jews are interned in concentration camps.
November 12	In the wake of the *Kristallnacht* pogrom, a fine of 1 billion reichsmarks is levied on the Jews of Germany.

1939

January 1	The Measure for the Elimination of Jews from the German Economy is invoked, banning Jews from working with Germans.
March 2	Eugenio Pacelli becomes Pope Pius XII.
March 11	A law permitting the establishment of the Hungarian Labor Service System (Munkaszolgálat) is enacted.
March 14	Slovakia is declared independent.
March 15	German forces enter Prague; Aktion Gitter (Operation Bars) is launched in the Protectorate of Bohemia and Moravia, and Jews, German emigrés, and Czech intellectuals are arrested.
March 22	Germany annexes Klaipėda (Memel), Lithuania.
April 7	Italy invades Albania.
May 5	The Second Anti-Jewish Law is promulgated in Hungary, defining who is a Jew and restricting Jewish participation in the economy to 6 percent.
May 15	The Ravensbrück concentration camp for women is established in Germany.

1939

May 17	The MacDonald White Paper, severely restricting Jewish immigration to Palestine, is issued by the British government.
July 4	The Reichsvereinigung der Juden in Deutschland (Reich Association of Jews in Germany) replaces the Reichsvertretung der Juden in Deutschland (Reich Representation of Jews in Germany).
August 23	The Nazi-Soviet Pact is signed.
September 1	A curfew is imposed on Jews throughout Germany, forbidding them to be out of doors after 8:00 p.m.
	German forces invade Poland.
September 2	In Poland, Stutthof is established as a camp for "civilian prisoners of war."
September 3	France and Great Britain declare war on Germany.
September 6	Kraków is occupied by the Germans.
September 8	German forces occupy Łódź, Radom, and Tarnów.
September 14	German forces occupy Przemyśl.
September 17	Parts of eastern Poland are annexed by the USSR.
September 18	Economic sanctions are promulgated against the Jews in Łódź.
September 21	Reinhard Heydrich meets with Einsatzgruppen commanders and Adolf Eichmann. He orders the establishment of Judenräte (Jewish councils) in Poland, the concentration of Polish Jews and a census of them, and a survey of the Jewish work force and Jewish property throughout Poland.
September 27	The Reichssicherheitshauptamt (Reich Security Main Office; RSHA) is established.
September 28	Poland is partitioned by Germany and the USSR; German forces occupy Warsaw.
October 1	The Polish government-in-exile is formed in France (it later moves to London).
October 8	The first ghetto established by the Nazis is set up, in Piotrków Trybunalski (Poland).
October 16	Kraków is designated the capital of the Generalgouvernement.
October 18–27	Fourteen hundred Jews from Mährisch Ostrau, 1,875 from Katowice, and 1,584 from Vienna are deported to the Lublin area.
November 9	Łódź is annexed to the German Reich.
November 12	The deportation of Jews from Łódź to other parts of Poland begins.
November 15–17	All the synagogues of Łódź are destroyed by the German authorities.
November 23	Hans Frank, the governor-general of the Generalgouvernement, orders that all Jews in the Generalgouvernement must wear the yellow badge by December 1, 1939.
November 28	A regulation establishing Judenräte in the Generalgouvernement is promulgated.

1939

November 30– March 13, 1940	Invasion of Finland by the USSR, followed by the Winter War.
December 5–6	Jewish property in Poland is seized by the German authorities.

1940

February 8	The establishment of a ghetto in Łódź is ordered.
April 9	German forces invade Denmark and Norway.
April 12	Hans Frank declares that Kraków must be *judenfrei* ("free of Jews") by November. By March 1941, 40,000 out of 60,000 Jews have been deported from Kraków.
April 27	Himmler orders the establishment of a concentration camp at Auschwitz. Early in June the first prisoners, mostly Poles, are brought there.
April 30	The Łódź ghetto is sealed.
May 10	The German offensive in Belgium, Luxembourg, and the Netherlands begins.
	Neville Chamberlain resigns as British prime minister and Winston Churchill assumes the post.
May 12	German forces cross the French border.
May 14	The Luftwaffe bombs Rotterdam heavily; the Dutch surrender to the Germans.
May 16	In France, German forces break through the French lines at Sedan.
	Hans Frank orders the launching of the AB-Aktion, in which thousands of Polish intellectuals and leaders are killed.
May 17	German forces occupy Brussels.
May 25	Himmler sends a memorandum to Hitler suggesting that the Jews in the eastern occupied areas be sent to Africa.
May 26–June 4	British forces retreat across the English Channel to Great Britain.
May 28	Belgium surrenders to Germany.
June 10	Italy enters the war on Germany's side, declaring war on Great Britain and France, and invading France.
June 14	German forces occupy Paris.
June 15	The USSR occupies the Baltic states.
June 22	Germany and France sign an armistice.
June 24	Italy and France sign an armistice.
June 27	Romania cedes Bessarabia and Bukovina to the USSR.
June 30	Two hundred Jews in Dorohoi are killed by a Romanian infantry battalion.
July 9	The German blitz (bombing) of London begins.
July 16	The expulsion of Jews from Alsace and Lorraine to southern France is initiated.

1940

July 19	Telephones are confiscated from Jews in Germany.
August 2	A civilian administration under Gauleiter Gustav Simon is installed in Luxembourg.
August 3	Northern Transylvania is annexed by Hungary.
September 6	King Carol II flees Romania, his son Michael I becomes king, and a National Legionary Government is set up under Ion Antonescu.
September 7	Romania cedes southern Dobruja to Bulgaria.
September 20	The first prisoners arrive at the Breendonck camp in Belgium.
September 26	The Ústredňa Židov (Jewish Center) is established in Bratislava.
September 27	Germany, Italy, and Japan sign the ten-year Tripartite Pact, also known as the Pact of Berlin.
October 3	The first *Statut des Juifs* is promulgated in Vichy France.
October 5	Legislation for the confiscation of Jewish property is passed by the Romanian government.
October 7	The Law for the Protection of Nations is issued in Bulgaria, curbing the rights of Jews.
October 22	Jewish businesses are registered throughout the Netherlands.
October 22–25	The Jews of Baden, the Palatinate, and Württemberg are sent to the Gurs camp in France during Aktion Burckel.
October 28	Italy invades Greece.
November 4	Jewish civil servants are dismissed throughout the Netherlands.
November 15	The Warsaw ghetto is sealed.
November 20–25	Hungary, Romania, and Slovakia become members of the Tripartite Pact.
December 19	In North Africa, British forces begin a battle that will end in their capture of Cyrenaica.

1941

January 10	All the Jews of the Netherlands are registered.
January 21–23	The Iron Guard unsuccessfully attempts a coup in Romania, accompanied by riots against the Jews.
February 5	The Law for the Protection of the State is passed in Romania, making Romanian Jews subject to double the punishment meted out to other Romanians for crimes committed.
February 13	The Joodse Raad (Jewish Council) meets for the first time in Amsterdam.
February 17	Ion Antonescu abolishes the National Legionary Government in Romania.
February 22	A total of 389 Jewish males from the Jewish quarter of Amsterdam are sent to Buchenwald.
February 25	A general anti-Nazi strike is held in Amsterdam.

1941

March 1	Bulgaria joins the Tripartite Pact.
	Himmler orders the construction of a camp at Birkenau (Auschwitz II). Construction begins in October 1941 and continues until March 1942.
March 3–20	A ghetto in Kraków is decreed, established, and sealed.
March 11	The United States government approves the Lend-Lease Act.
March 25	Yugoslavia joins the Axis.
March 27	A pro-Allied coup is carried out in Yugoslavia.
April 1	A pro-Nazi government is established in Iraq by Rashid Ali al-Gaylani.
April 6	German forces invade Greece and Yugloslavia.
April 7	The 30,000 Jews of Radom are placed in two ghettos.
April 9	German forces occupy Salonika.
April 10	Riots break out in Antwerp against Jews.
	The Croatian state is set up by the Germans and Italians.
April 13	The governments of Japan and the USSR sign a neutrality pact.
	German forces occupy Belgrade.
April 14	More anti-Jewish riots break out in Antwerp.
April 18	Yugoslavia capitulates to the Germans.
April 24	The Lublin ghetto is sealed.
May 11	Rudolf Hess, Hitler's deputy, lands in Glasgow on what he terms "a private peace mission."
May 15	A law is passed in Romania permitting Jews to be drafted for forced labor.
May 19	A pogrom against the Jews of Baghdad takes place.
May 30	Baghdad is taken by the British.
June 1	British forces withdraw from Crete.
June 2	The second *Statut des Juifs* is promulgated in Vichy France.
June 6	The *Kommissarbefehl* (Commissar Order) is issued in preparation for the invasion of the USSR. It states that political officers in the Soviet army must be singled out and killed.
June 8	British forces invade Vichy-controlled Syria.
June 18	Turkey and Germany sign a friendship treaty.
June 21	In Romania, Jews are expelled from the towns and villages of southern Bukovina.
June 22	The Germans launch Operation "Barbarossa," invading the USSR. They take Kishinev and Kovno, among other places.
	Zagreb Jews are arrested and sent to the Pag and Jadovno concentration camps.

1941

June 23	The Einsatzgruppen begin their killings in the USSR, and submit reports of their activities almost daily.
June 24	German forces occupy Vilna.
June 25	About 15,000 Jews are killed in Iaşi in a pogrom.
June 26	German forces occupy Dvinsk (Daugavpils).
June 27	Hungary enters the war on the side of the Axis powers.
	The Germans occupy Białystok and kill 2,000 Jews.
June 28	German forces occupy Minsk and Rovno and reoccupy Przemyśl.
June 29	Several thousand Jews are shot in the courtyard of the Iaşi police headquarters. This day becomes known as "Black Sunday."
June 29–July 2	All Jewish males from sixteen to sixty years old are arrested in Dvinsk.
June 30	Germans forces occupy Lvov.
July 1	German forces occupy Riga.
July 1–August 31	Einsatzgruppe D, Wehrmacht forces, and Escalon Special, a Romanian unit, kill between 150,000 and 160,000 Jews in Bessarabia.
July 2	German forces occupy Ternopol; in Lvov, local Ukrainians commit atrocities against Jews.
July 3	German forces occupy Novogrudok.
July 4	German forces occupy Pinsk.
	Latvians serving in German units set fire to the central synagogue in Riga.
	A Judenrat is established in Vilna. About 5,000 Vilna Jews are killed during the month of July by Einsatzkommando 9 and local collaborators.
July 4–11	Five thousand Ternopol Jews are killed in a pogrom.
July 9	German forces occupy Zhitomir.
July 10	Vichy French forces surrender to the British in Syria.
	Latvia is cleared of Soviet troops.
July 13–August 9	A total of 9,012 Jews from Dvinsk are killed.
July 16	Up to this date, 2,700 Jews have been shot outside Riga.
July 16–29	The Germans and Soviets fight at Smolensk, with the Germans eventually victorious.
July 20	A ghetto is established in Minsk.
July 21	Hermann Göring signs an order giving Heydrich the authority to prepare a "total solution" to the "Jewish question" in Europe.
	Romanian forces occupy Bessarabia.
July 24	A ghetto is established in Kishinev; some 10,000 Kishinev Jews have already been killed.

1941

July 25–27	Local Ukrainians rampage against the Jews in Lvov in a pogrom that becomes known as the Petliura Days.
July 26	After twenty-five days of fighting, Mogilev, in Belorussia, falls to German forces.
August 1	The Białystok ghetto is established.
August 4–5	A Jewish Council is established in Kovno under Elchanan Elkes and told by the German authorities that it is responsible for the transfer of the Jews to the ghetto.
August 5	Eight thousand Jewish men from Pinsk are killed.
August 7	Between 2,500 and 3,000 Pinsk Jews are murdered.
August 14	Roosevelt and Churchill sign the Atlantic Charter, an eight-point declaration of peace aims and terms.
	Smolensk is occupied by German forces.
August 17	Thirteen thousand Jews are interned in the Vertujeni camp.
August 19	Einsatzkommando 8 and local collaborators in Mogilev kill 3,726 Jews.
August 21	Four thousand more Jews are interned in the Vertujeni camp.
August 21– August 17, 1944	Seventy thousand Jews pass through the Drancy transit camp.
August 25	Soviet and British forces enter Iran.
August 27–28	At Kamenets-Podolski, 23,600 Jews are massacred by German forces under Friedrich Jeckeln; at least 14,000 of them had recently been deported from Hungary.
August 31–September 3	Eight thousand Vilna Jews are killed in Ponary.
September 1	The Euthanasia Program is officially ended; between 70,000 and 93,000 people have been killed in the German Reich during the course of the program.
September 3	The first experimental gassing at Auschwitz is carried out on Soviet prisoners of war.
September 3–6	Two ghettos are established in Vilna.
September 4	Fifteen hundred young Jews from Berdichev are shot just outside of town.
September 9	The *Židovsky Kodex* (Jewish Code) is invoked in Slovakia, defining who is a Jew.
September 10	The Vertujeni camp inmates are deported on foot to Transnistria.
September 15	In the Netherlands, laws are invoked banning Jews from many public places.
	Approximately 18,600 Jews are killed outside Berdichev.
September 15– October 13, 1942	At least 150,000 Jews from Bessarabia and Bukovina are deported to Transnistria, and some 90,000 die there.

1941

September 19	The Jews in the Reich are required to wear the yellow badge in public.
	Kiev is captured by Germans; 10,000 Jews have been killed in Zhitomir.
September 27	Heydrich arrives in Prague as *Reichsprotektor*.
September 29–30	At Babi Yar, 33,771 Kiev Jews are killed by Einsatzkommando 4a.
October 1–December 22	In *Aktionen* in Vilna, 33,500 Jews are killed.
October 6–March 16, 1945	A total of 46,067 Prague Jews are deported to the "east" and to Theresienstadt.
October 8	The Vitebsk ghetto is liquidated and more than 16,000 Jews are killed.
October 11	A ghetto is established in Chernovtsy.
October 12	German forces reach the outskirts of Moscow, and the city is partly evacuated.
	Obersturmbannführer Martin Sandberger of Sonderkommando 1a reports that Jewish men over the age of sixteen are being killed by his Sonderkommando in Estonia; by the beginning of 1942, 936 Jews have been killed.
	Three thousand Jews are killed at Sheparovtse, near Kolomyia.
October 13	Twenty thousand Jews in Dnepropetrovsk are killed.
October 15	Jews are deported from Austria and Germany to Kovno, Łódź, Minsk, and Riga.
October 16	German forces occupy Odessa.
October 19	Jews are murdered in Belgrade.
October 19–September 28, 1943	Luxembourg Jews are deported to Łódź in eight transports.
October 23	Further Jewish emigration from Germany is prohibited.
	Nineteen thousand Jews are killed in Odessa.
October 24	German forces occupy Kharkov.
October 28	Nine thousand Jews are killed in an *Aktion* outside Kovno at the Ninth Fort; 17,412 Jews remain in the Kovno ghetto.
October 30	Four thousand of the 4,500 Jews of Nesvizh are killed, and the remaining Jews are put into a ghetto.
November 1	In Poland, the construction of an extermination center at Bełżec begins.
November 7	Twelve thousand Jews of Minsk are killed at Tuchinka.
November 7–8	Twenty-one thousand Jews are killed in the Sosenki pine grove outside Rovno.
November 7–9	More than three thousand Jews are killed in Pogulanka, outside Dvinsk.

1941

November 8	The establishment of a ghetto in Lvov is ordered.
November 10	The Nazis finalize their plans for Theresienstadt.
November 15– July 2, 1942	After a battle lasting seven months, Sevastopol falls to the Germans.
November 20	Twenty thousand Minsk Jews are killed at Tuchinka.
November 20– December 7	Thirty thousand Jews are killed in the Rumbula Forest outside Riga, during the so-called Jeckeln Aktion.
November 24– April 20, 1945	A total of 140,937 Jews of Bohemia and Moravia are deported to Theresienstadt; 33,539 die and 88,196 are deported farther.
November 25	The Association des Juifs en Belgique (Association of Jews in Belgium) is established.
	The deportation of Polish Jews from Breslau begins, continuing intermittently until April 1944.
November 29	The Union Générale des Israélites de France (Union of French Jews), the organization of French Jewry, is formed.
December 6	Great Britain declares war on Romania.
	A Soviet counteroffensive begins outside Moscow.
December 7	Hitler issues the *Nacht-und-Nebel-Erlass* (Night and Fog Decree) for the suppression of anti-Nazi resistance in occupied western Europe.
	Japanese forces attack the American naval base at Pearl Harbor.
December 8	Malaya and Thailand are invaded by the Japanese.
	The first transport of Jews arrives at the Chełmno extermination camp, and transports continue to arrive until March 1943. The camp reopened for operation in April 1944. About 320,000 Jews were killed at Chełmno.
	Four thousand Jews of Novogrudok are killed.
December 10	Germany and Italy declare war on the United States, and the United States declares war on them.
December 13	Bulgaria and Hungary declare war on the United States.
December 21–31	Fifty-four thousand Jews are killed in the Bogdanovka camp, and 200 are left alive.
December 22	The Japanese invade the Philippines.
	Churchill arrives in Washington for a conference with Roosevelt.
December 23	In Kolomyia 1,200 Jews, holders of foreign passports, are arrested and subsequently killed at Sheparovtse.
December 25	Hong Kong capitulates to the Japanese.

1942

January 10–11	The Japanese invade the Netherlands East Indies.
January 14	The concentration of the Dutch Jews in Amsterdam begins. First to arrive are the Jews of Zaandam.

1942

January 16	Deportations from Łódź to Chełmno begin, and continue until September 1942.
January 20	In the Berlin suburb of Wannsee a conference, presided over by Heydrich and attended by top Nazi officials, is held to coordinate the "Final Solution" (the extermination of the Jews).
January 21	The Germans begin a counteroffensive in North Africa.
	The Fareynegte Partizaner Organizatsye (United Partisan Organization) is created by Jews in Vilna.
January 24	Four hundred Jewish intellectuals are arrested and subsequently killed in Kolomyia.
February 1	The SS Wirtschafts-Verwaltungshauptamt (Economic-Administrative Main Office; WVHA) is established, under Oswald Pohl.
	A nationalist government is formed in Norway under Vidkun Quisling.
February 8	The first transport of Jews from Salonika is sent to Auschwitz.
February 15	The British surrender Singapore to the Japanese.
February 23	The *Struma*, a ship loaded with Jewish refugees refused entry to Palestine, sinks off the coast of Turkey; 768 passengers drown and 1 survives.
March 1	In Poland, construction of the Sobibór extermination camp begins. Jews are first killed there early in May 1942.
March 2	Five thousand Jews from Minsk are killed.
March 3	Jews in Belgium are drafted for forced labor.
March 7	The British evacuate Rangoon.
March 12–April 20	Thirty thousand Jews are deported from Lublin to Bełżec.
March 17	Killings begin at the Bełżec extermination camp, the first of the Aktion Reinhard camps to be put into operation.
March 19	The Intelligenz Aktion is carried out in Kraków; fifty Jewish intellectuals are killed.
March 19–end of March	Fifteen thousand Jews are deported from Lvov to Bełżec.
March 25	A ghetto is established in Kolomyia, containing about 18,000 Jews.
March 26	The first transport of Jews sent by Adolf Eichmann's office goes to Auschwitz.
March 26–October 20	More than 57,000 Slovak Jews are deported.
March 28	The first transport of French Jews is sent to Auschwitz.
April 3	A total of 383 Jews from Munich are deported to Piaski, near Lublin.
April 3–4	Five thousand Jews from Kolomyia are deported to Bełżec, and 250 are killed in the Kolomyia ghetto itself.
April 6	More than 600 Jews attempt to flee from Diatlovo (Zhetl) to the forest during the final *Aktion*.

1942

April 9	American forces surrender to the Japanese at Bataan.
April 18	In Warsaw, fifty-two Jews are murdered in what becomes known as the "Bloody Night."
April 27–28	Seventy Jewish men are shot in Radom and 100 are deported to Auschwitz.
April 29	The Jews of the Netherlands are ordered to wear the yellow badge.
April 30	The Jews of Pinsk are ordered to establish a ghetto within one day. About 20,000 Jews move into it.
	Twelve hundred Jews are killed in Diatlovo during an *Aktion*. The Jews offer armed resistance but to no avail.
May 1	The Dvinsk ghetto is virtually liquidated, with only 450 Jews remaining. They are transferred to Kaiserwald late in October 1943.
May 7	In the Battle of the Coral Sea, the Allies sink over 100,000 tons of Japanese shipping.
May 10	Fifteen hundred Jews are deported from Sosnowiec to Auschwitz.
May 27	In Belgium, the wearing of the yellow badge is decreed. The decree goes into effect on June 3.
	Heydrich is severely wounded in Prague by the "Anthropoid" team. He dies of his wounds on June 4.
May 28–June 8	Six thousand Kraków Jews are deported to Bełżec and 300 are killed in the city itself.
June 4	The United States declares war on Romania.
June 4–7	United States forces defeat the Japanese at Midway, in the Pacific.
June 7	The Jews in occupied France are required to wear the yellow badge.
June 10	In reprisal for the assassination of Heydrich, the village of Lidice, in Czechoslovakia, is razed. All 192 of the men from the village are killed, as are 71 women; the rest of the women are sent to Ravensbrück.
June 11	Eichmann's office orders that the deportation of Jews from the Netherlands, Belgium, and France begin in a few weeks.
	Thirty-five hundred Jews are deported from Tarnów to Bełżec.
June 15–18	Ten thousand more Tarnów Jews are deported to Bełżec, and many Jews are murdered in the vicinity of Tarnów.
June 18	One thousand Jewish men are deported from Przemyśl to the Janówska camp in Lvov.
June 20–October 9	From Vienna, 13,776 Jews are deported to Theresienstadt.
June 21	German forces take Tobruk from the British.
June 22	The first transport from the Drancy camp in France leaves for Auschwitz.
June 25	Churchill and Roosevelt confer in Washington.

1942

June 26	A transport from Brussels is sent to the Organisation Todt labor camps in northern France.
	In the Netherlands, an active schedule of deportations to Westerbork begins, and from Westerbork to Auschwitz.
July 1	The Sicherheitspolizei takes over the Westerbork internment camp.
July 8	Seven thousand Lvov Jews are interned in the Janówska camp.
July 11	Nine thousand Jewish males from Salonika between the ages of eighteen and forty-five are drafted into the Organisation Todt labor battalions in Greece.
July 13–14	Jews are deported from Antwerp to northern France for forced labor.
July 14	The systematic transfer of Dutch Jewry to the Westerbork camp begins.
	A closed ghetto is set up in Przemyśl.
July 15	The first transport leaves Westerbork for Auschwitz.
July 16–17	A total of 12,887 Jews of Paris are rounded up and sent to Drancy; in all, about 42,500 Jews are sent to Drancy from all over France during this *Aktion*.
July 19	Himmler orders that the extermination of the Jews of the Generalgouvernment be completed by the end of the year.
July 20	An armed Jewish uprising takes place in Nesvizh.
July 22	The Treblinka extermination center is completed; by August 1943 some 870,000 Jews have been killed there.
July 22–September 12	During the mass deportation from Warsaw, some 300,000 Jews are deported, 265,000 of them to Treblinka. About 60,000 Jews remain in the Warsaw ghetto.
July 23	Adam Czerniaków, the head of the Warsaw Judenrat, commits suicide rather than assist the Nazis in deporting the Warsaw Jews.
July 24	In Derechin an *Aktion* against the Jews takes place.
July 27, 31; August 3	On three separate days, more than 10,500 Przemyśl Jews are deported to Bełżec. The first day of the *Aktion*, Wehrmacht lieutenant Dr. Alfred Battel rescues Jews in the employ of the Wehrmacht.
July 28	The Żydowska Organizacja Bojowa (Jewish Fighting Organization; ŻOB) is formed in Warsaw.
July 28–31	Thirty thousand German Jews who had been sent to Minsk are murdered at Maly Trostinets.
August 5	The smaller ghetto in Radom is liquidated and 6,000 Jews are sent to Treblinka. Two thousand more are sent from the larger ghetto.
August 6– December 29, 1943	Jewish inmates from the Gurs camp in France are deported to Auschwitz and Sobibór by way of Drancy.
August 8	In Geneva, Gerhart Riegner cables Rabbi Stephen S. Wise in New York and Sidney Silverman in London about Nazi plans for the

1942

extermination of European Jewry. The United States Department of State holds up delivery of the message to Wise, who finally receives it from Silverman on August 28.

Twenty-five hundred Jews of Novogrudok are killed.

August 9	During the liquidation of the Mir ghetto, Jews offer armed resistance. Over the next three days, some 10,000 Jews from Będzin, Sosnowiec, and Dąbrowa are selected and deported.
August 10	The Yeheskel Atlas Jewish partisan brigade attacks a German garrison in Derechin.
August 10–23	Fifty thousand Jews are deported from Lvov to Bełżec.
August 11	Two thousand Jews are killed in Rostov-on-Don.
August 12	Churchill, Stalin, and Averell Harriman meet in Moscow and affirm their goal of destroying Nazism.
August 12–18	Five thousand Jews from Będzin and 8,000 from Sosnowiec are deported to Auschwitz.
August 13–14	Jews lacking Belgian nationality are seized in Antwerp and sent to the Malines camp.
August 13–20	The majority of Croatian Jews are deported to Auschwitz.
August 15	Jews from Antwerp are deported to northern France for forced labor.
August 16–18	The large Radom ghetto is liquidated. Eighteen thousand Jews are deported to Treblinka and 1,500 who resist deportations are shot on the spot. Four thousand Jews are put into a special labor ghetto in Radom.
August 20–24	Eighteen thousand of the 20,000 Jews of Kielce are deported to Treblinka.
August 27–30	Three thousand Jews are sent from Ternopol to Bełżec.
September 2	The Lachva ghetto is surrounded by German forces and an uprising breaks out. Six thousand Jews flee, but most are caught and quickly killed.
September 3–4	The last transports of Belgian nationals are sent from Antwerp to the Malines camp.
September 4	The Jews of Macedonia are required to wear the yellow badge.
September 7	Seven thousand Jews from Kolomyia are deported to Bełżec and 1,000 are killed in the Kolomyia ghetto itself.
September 8	Eight thousand Jews are deported from Tarnów to Bełżec; about six weeks later another 2,500 are sent there.
September 9	Two thousand Lublin Jews are deported to Majdanek.
September 10–12	Jews not of Belgian nationality are seized in Antwerp. They are sent to the Malines camp and to perform forced labor in northern France.

1942

September 12	The German Sixth Army and Fourth Panzer Army reach the suburbs of Stalingrad; the Battle of Stalingrad begins.
September 24–26	An uprising breaks out in Tuchin when the Germans move to liquidate the ghetto. Most of the Jews escape, but they are subsequently found and killed.
September 30	The Ternopol Judenrat is ordered to hand over 1,000 Jews to the Nazis, and refuses. The Nazis and their helpers arrest Jews and deport 800 of them to Bełżec.
October 2	The deportation of Dutch Jewry is intensified.
October 9	The Italian racial laws are enforced in Libya.
October 13–21	Twenty thousand Jews from Piotrków Trybunalski are deported to Treblinka and 500 escape to the forest. In July 1944 the ghetto is liquidated, and the Jews are sent to labor camps or to Auschwitz.
October 16	Over 1,000 Jews are arrested by the Nazis in Rome and deported to Auschwitz.
October 24	A total of 252 friends and relatives of persons from Lidice are murdered in Mauthausen in reprisal for the assassination of Heydrich.
October 25	Eighteen hundred Lublin Jews are deported to Majdanek.
October 27–28	Seven thousand Kraków Jews are deported to Bełżec, and 600 are shot in Kraków.
October 29–November 1	Almost all the Jews of Pinsk are murdered.
November 1	The deportation of Jews from the Białystok district to Treblinka begins.
November 2	British forces take El Alamein from the Germans.
November 8	American and British forces invade North Africa; Operation "Torch" is under way.
November 9	German and Italian forces occupy Tunisia.
November 11	Southern France is occupied by the Germans and Italians.
	Four thousand Jews are deported from Kolomyia to Bełżec.
November 18	The Germans order 8,000 Przemyśl Jews to gather for deportation, but only 3,500 do so; 500 more are found hiding. All told, 4,000 Jews are deported to Bełżec.
November 18– January 12, 1943	Some 15,000 Jews are killed in the Lvov ghetto, which becomes a Julag (*Judenlager*, or camp for Jews) in January 1943.
November 19	Soviet forces begin a counterattack near Stalingrad.
November 20	Nine hundred and eighty Jews from Munich are deported to Riga.
November 24	Rabbi Stephen S. Wise releases to the press the news contained in the Riegner cable.
December 4	Zegota (the Council for Aid to Jews) is established in Poland.

1942

December 6	The German authorities order the Jewish leadership of Tunisia to recruit 2,000 Jews for forced labor. Eventually, 5,000 are placed in labor camps.
December 10	The Polish government-in-exile asks the Allies to retaliate for the Nazi killing of civilians, especially Jews.
December 16	A ghetto is established in Kharkov. Three weeks later approximately 15,000 Jews are killed in the Drobitski Ravine.
December 17	An Allied declaration is made condemning the Nazis' "bestial policy of cold-blooded extermination."
December 23	The last Jews in Pinsk are killed.

1943

January 1	Dutch Jews are no longer permitted to have private bank accounts, and all Jewish money is put into a central account.
January 13	Fifteen hundred Jews are deported from Radom to Treblinka.
January 14–24	Roosevelt and Churchill meet at Casablanca and declare the unconditional surrender of Germany to be a central war aim.
January 18–22	More than 5,000 Jews are deported from Warsaw and are killed. The first Warsaw ghetto uprising breaks out.
January 23	In Libya, British forces liberate Tripoli.
February 2	Ninety-one thousand German soldiers under Field Marshal Friedrich von Paulus surrender to the Soviet army at Stalingrad.
February 5–12	In Białystok, 2,000 Jews are killed and 10,000 deported to Treblinka; Jews offer armed resistance.
February 13	In Tunisia, the Jews of Djerba are forced to pay 10 million francs to the German authorities.
February 24	A ghetto is established in Salonika.
February 26	The first transport of Gypsies reaches Auschwitz. They are placed in a special section of the camp called the Gypsy Camp.
February 29	The Kolomyia ghetto is liquidated and 2,000 Jews are killed.
March 4–9	Nearly all the 4,000 Jews of Bulgarian Thrace are arrested and sent to Treblinka.
March 11	A total of 7,341 Macedonian Jews are concentrated in Skopje. Most are subsequently deported to Treblinka.
March 13	Ostindustrie GmbH is founded by the SS to exploit Jewish labor in the Generalgouvernement.
	Two thousand Jews are deported from Kraków to Płaszów.
March 14	Twenty-three hundred Kraków Jews are deported to Auschwitz and 700 are shot in Kraków.
March 17	Fifteen hundred Lvov Jews are killed and 800 are deported to Auschwitz.
March 20–August 18	Transports from Salonika arrive at Auschwitz.

1943

April 8–9	One thousand Jews are murdered near Ternopol.
April 13	Mass graves are discovered at Katyn, Poland, the site of a massacre of Polish officers by the Soviets.
April 19–30	British and American representatives confer in Bermuda about rescue options and fail to come up with significant rescue proposals.
April 19–May 16	The Warsaw ghetto uprising takes place and the Warsaw ghetto is destroyed.
May 5–10	The last two transports of Jews are sent from Croatia to Auschwitz.
May 7	An *Aktion* takes place in Novogrudok, after which only 233 Jews of the original 7,000 remain alive. Three weeks later, 100 of the remaining Jews successfully escape and join partisan units.
May 8	Mordecai Anielewicz and other leaders of the Warsaw ghetto uprising are killed in a bunker at 18 Mila Street during the fighting.
May 11–27	Churchill and Roosevelt confer in Washington.
May 12	Samuel Zygelbojm, a Jewish representative of the Polish government-in-exile in London, commits suicide as an expression of solidarity with the Jewish fighters in Warsaw, and in protest against the world's silence regarding the fate of the Jews in Nazi-occupied Europe.
May 13	Tunisia is liberated by the Allies.
June 1	The final liquidation of the Lvov ghetto begins. When the Jews resist, 3,000 are killed. Seven thousand are sent to Janówska.
June 20	Except for a handful of workers, the Ternopol ghetto is liquidated and Jews are killed in and around the city.
June 25	Jews in Częstochowa resist the Germans with arms.
July 5	Himmler orders that Sobibór, an extermination camp, be made a concentration camp.
July 9–10	Allied forces invade Sicily.
July 20	Seventeen hundred Jews are transported from Rhodes to Athens.
July 21	Himmler orders the liquidation of the Reichskommissariat Ostland ghettos by sending the Jewish workers to labor camps and killing the rest of the Jews.
July 22–early August	The remaining Jewish workers from Ternopol are killed.
July 25	Mussolini falls from power and Pietro Badoglio forms a new government in Italy.
August 1	The final liquidation of the Będzin and Sosnowiec ghettos is begun and most of the Jews are deported to Auschwitz; Jews offer armed resistance.
August 2	The uprising at Treblinka takes place.
August 4–September 4	Seven thousand Jews are deported from Vilna to Estonia for forced labor.

1943

August 15–20	Nazi forces under Odilo Globocnik surround the Białystok ghetto, and its 30,000 remaining Jews are ordered to appear for evacuation. A Jewish uprising breaks out in the ghetto.
August 17	By way of Athens, 120 Jews of Rhodes arrive in Auschwitz.
August 18–21	The final deportation of Białystok Jewry takes place.
September 1	An uprising is attempted in the Vilna ghetto but is aborted. During the rest of September the fighters escape to the partisans.
September 2–3	Thirty-five hundred Jews are deported from Przemyśl to Auschwitz.
September 2	The final liquidation of the Tarnów ghetto is launched. Seven thousand Jews are deported to Auschwitz and 3,000 to Płaszów. The 300 workers who remain are deported to Płaszów at the end of the year. The Jews offer armed resistance.
September 3–4	The last Jews of Belgium are deported as part of Operation "Iltis."
September 3	The Allies invade southern Italy.
September 8	German forces occupy Athens; Italian forces capitulate to the Germans in Rhodes.
	The Badoglio government in Italy signs an armistice with the Allies.
September 11	One thousand Jews discovered hiding in Przemyśl are murdered.
September 11–14	The Minsk ghetto is liquidated and almost all of its Jews are killed.
September 20	A Judenrat is set up in Athens under Moses Sciaki.
September 23–24	The Vilna ghetto is liquidated. Thirty-seven hundred Jews are sent to labor camps in Estonia and 4,000 are deported to Sobibór.
September 28	The Jews of Rome deliver a levy of 50 kilograms of gold to the Gestapo.
September 29	The last 2,000 Amsterdam Jews are sent to Westerbork.
October 1–2	In Denmark, German police begin rounding up Jews for deportation. The Danish population begins the rescue of 7,200 Danish Jews.
October 2–3	Throughout the Netherlands the families of Jewish men drafted for forced labor are sent to Westerbork.
October 13	Italy declares war on Germany.
October 14	The Sobibór uprising takes place.
October 16	Mass arrests of Jews begin in Rome.
October 18	In Rome, 1,035 Jews are deported to Auschwitz.
October 21	During the final *Aktion* in Minsk, 2,000 Jews are killed at Maly Trostinets.
October 25	Dnepropetrovsk is liberated.
October 26	Twenty-eight hundred Kovno Jews are sent to German labor camps.
November 3	Jews are arrested in Genoa, Italy.
	Aktion "Erntefest" (Operation "Harvest Festival") is launched, liq-

1943

uidating the Poniatowa and Trawniki camps and the remaining Jews in the Majdanek camp. Other Jews brought to Majdanek from the Lublin area are killed as well. In all, between 42,000 and 43,000 Jews are killed during the operation.

November 6–9	Jews are arrested in Florence, Milan, and Venice.
November 9	The United Nations Relief and Rehabilitation Agency (UNRRA) is founded.
November 14	Jews are arrested in Ferrara, Italy.
November 19	The Sonderkommando 1005 prisoners in the Janówska camp revolt. Several dozen escape and the rest are killed.
November 28– December 1	Churchill, Roosevelt, and Stalin confer in Tehran.
November 30	The authorities order the concentration of all Italian Jews in camps.

1944

January 15	Berdichev is liberated by Soviet forces.
January 25	The Allies carry out a successful air attack on the Schweinfurt ball-bearing factory, causing great damage to the German war effort.
March 15	Soviet forces begin the liberation of Transnistria, crossing the Bug River and reaching the Dniester on March 20.
March 17	A group of 99 prisoners breaks out of the Koldichevo camp. Twenty-four are recaptured and 75 reach partisan units, primarily the Bielski unit.
March 19	German forces occupy Hungary after an Hungarian attempt to pull forces back from the eastern front.
March 27	Eighteen hundred Kovno Jews, mostly elderly people and children, are killed.
April 5	Jews in Hungary begin wearing the yellow badge.
April 7	Alfred Wetzler and Rudolf Vrba escape from Auschwitz and reach Slovakia, bearing detailed information about the killing of Jews in Auschwitz. Their report, which reaches the free world in June, becomes known as the Auschwitz Protocols.
April 15	During an escape attempt from Ponary, where they had been employed burning corpses, fifteen prisoners succeed in escaping and sixty-five others are killed.
April 16	In Hungary, the concentration of the Jews of the Transcarpathian Ukraine begins.
May 2	The first transport of Jews from Hungary arrives at Auschwitz.
May 2–9	Two ghettos are established in Oradea.
May 9	Twenty-five hundred men in Oradea are assembled for forced labor.
May 15	Between May 15 and July 9, 437,000 Hungarian Jews are deported, primarily to Auschwitz. Most of those sent to Auschwitz are gassed soon after their arrival.

1944

May 23	An Allied offensive begins at Anzio, in Italy.
May 24–June 3	The Jews of Oradea are deported, mainly to Auschwitz.
June 4	Rome is captured by the American Fifth Army.
June 6	D-Day. Allied forces land in Normandy with the largest seaborne force in history.
	Eighteen hundred Jews from Corfu are arrested and sent to Auschwitz.
June 17–24	The Jews of Budapest are confined to specially marked "Jewish buildings."
June 23–July 14	Transports from Łódź reach Chełmno.
July 8	The Kovno ghetto is liquidated. Two thousand Jews are killed and 4,000 are marched to Germany.
July 9	The Hungarian regent, Miklós Horthy, orders an end to the deportations from Hungary. Two days later they cease.
July 10	From Bergen-Belsen, 222 Jews with immigration certificates reach Haifa.
July 13	Vilna is liberated by Soviet forces.
July 20	An unsuccessful attempt is made to kill Hitler.
	Two thousand Jews from Rhodes are sent to Auschwitz.
July 21–25	Children's homes in France operated by the Union Générale des Israélites de France are raided. Three hundred Jewish children, in addition to adult staff, are sent to Drancy and from there to Auschwitz.
July 23	A delegation of the International Red Cross visits Theresienstadt.
July 25	Lublin is liberated by the Soviet army.
July 26	The remaining Jews of Radom are sent to Auschwitz.
July 27	Dvinsk is liberated by Soviet forces. Twenty Jews remain in the city.
July 28	The first major death march begins, with the evacuation of the Gesia Street camp in Warsaw. Thirty-six hundred prisoners set out on foot for Kutno; 1,000 are killed on the journey of 81 miles (130 km).
July 31	American forces break through German lines in France. By the end of August, France is liberated.
August 1	The Polish rebellion begins in Warsaw.
	Kovno is liberated by the Soviet army.
August 7–30	Deportations from Łódź to Auschwitz take place.
August 11	American forces take Guam from the Japanese.
August 12	Allied forces occupy Florence.
August 23	Paris is liberated.

1944

August 23	The regime of Ion Antonescu is overthrown and Romania joins the Allies.
August 28–29 to October 27	The Slovak national uprising takes place and is suppressed by the SS.
September 3	The last transport of Jews leaves Westerbork.
September 4	Antwerp is liberated.
September 5	The USSR declares war on Bulgaria.
September 9	Churchill and Roosevelt confer in Quebec.
September 12	Soviet forces begin their attack on Budapest.
September 16	Bulgaria surrenders to the USSR.
September 18–19	Twenty-nine hundred Jewish inmates and 100 Soviet prisoners of war from the Klooga camp are shot at Lagedi.
September 28	The Klooga camp is liberated by Soviet forces. Eighty-five prisoners are found alive, having survived in hiding.
October 2	The Warsaw Polish uprising is quashed.
October 6–7	In the Sonderkommando uprising at Auschwitz, one of the gas chambers is destroyed before the uprising is quelled.
October 13	Soviet forces liberate Riga.
October 15	Ferenc Szálasi and his Arrow Cross Party come to power in Hungary.
October 17	Soviet forces liberate Oradea.
November 8	Deportations from Budapest are resumed.
November 13	A ghetto is established in Budapest for Jews without international protection.
December 16	German forces launch an offensive, the Battle of the Bulge, in the Ardennes forest.
December 26	The Soviet encirclement of Budapest that began on September 12, 1944, is complete.

1945

January 9	American forces land in Luzon.
January 16	Soviet forces liberate Kielce; twenty-five Jews are in the city at the time.
January 17	The SS is ordered to evacuate Auschwitz, and on the following day begin leaving. Sixty-six thousand prisoners are marched on foot toward Wodzisław, to be sent from there to other camps, and 15,000 die on the way. Forty-eight thousand men and 18,000 women prisoners are still in Auschwitz and its satellite camps at this time.
	Soviet forces liberate Warsaw.
	Raoul Wallenberg is arrested by the Soviets.
January 18	The Soviets take Pest.

1945

January 19	Łódź is liberated by the Soviet army.
January 25	Four thousand Jews are evacuated by foot from the Blechhammer camp toward the Gross-Rosen camp; 1,000 die on the way.
	From Bergen-Belsen, 136 Jews with South American passports reach Switzerland.
January 25–April 25	Fifty thousand Jews are evacuated by foot from the Stutthof camp and its satellites; 26,000 of them perish.
January 27	Soviet forces enter Auschwitz and find 7,650 prisoners there.
February 3	American forces invade Manila.
February 4–12	Churchill, Roosevelt, and Stalin meet at Yalta.
February 5	Twelve hundred Jews from the Protectorate of Bohemia and Moravia are transferred to Switzerland with the help of the International Red Cross.
February 13	Buda is taken by the Soviets.
February 19	Iwo Jima is invaded by American marines.
March 7	American forces cross the Rhine.
April 1	American forces invade Okinawa.
April 4	All German forces are expelled from Hungary.
April 5–6	More than 28,250 inmates are evacuated from Buchenwald, and from 7,000 to 8,000 others are killed.
April 9	The evacuation of Mauthausen begins.
April 11	The Buchenwald concentration camp is liberated by American forces.
April 12	Roosevelt dies and Harry S. Truman succeeds him as president.
April 15	With the help of the International Red Cross, 413 Danish Jews in the Protectorate are transferred to Sweden.
	Bergen-Belsen is liberated by British forces, who find the inmates in the midst of a typhus epidemic.
April 21	Except for the sick and their caretakers, all the inmates of the Ravensbrück camp have been evacuated.
April 25	The United Nations meets in San Francisco.
April 28	Mussolini is shot by Italian partisans while trying to escape to Switzerland.
April 29	Dachau is liberated by the American Seventh Army.
	Slovakia is occupied by the USSR.
April 29–30	Ravensbrück is liberated. In the camp are 3,500 sick women.
April 30	Hitler and Eva Braun commit suicide in Hitler's bunker in Berlin.
May 2	Soviet forces take Berlin.
	German forces in Italy surrender to the Allies.

1945

May 3	The Nazis hand over Theresienstadt, with 17,247 Jewish inmates, to the International Red Cross.
May 4	The SS leave Mauthausen.
May 7	The Germans surrender to the Allies.
May 8	VE-Day. The war in Europe is officially over.
June 26	The United Nations charter is signed in San Francisco; it goes into effect on October 24, 1945.
August 6	The United States drops the first nuclear bomb, on Hiroshima.
August 8	The USSR declares war on Japan.
August 9	The second nuclear bomb is dropped by the United States, on Nagasaki.
August 14	Japan accepts the Allied surrender terms. World War II is over.
September 2	The Japanese sign the American and British surrender terms in the Tokyo harbor, aboard the USS *Missouri*.
September 9	Japan signs the Chinese surrender terms.

1948

May 14	The new state of Israel, the Jewish national homeland, is established.

Compiled by ROBERT ROZETT
June 14, 1989

Appendix

1. Major Jewish Organizations in Germany, 1893–1943
2. Structure of the Einsatzgruppen from June 22, 1941
3. Nuremberg Trial
4. Subsequent Nuremberg Proceedings
5. Subsequent British Trials
6. Estimated Jewish Losses in the Holocaust

1. Major Jewish Organizations in Germany, 1893–1943

ESTABLISHED		ESTABLISHED		ESTABLISHED	
1893	Centralverein Deutscher Staatsbürger Jüdischen Glaubens (Central Union of German Citizens of Jewish Faith)				
				1933	Zentralausschuss der Deutschen Juden für Hilfe und Aufbau (Central Committee of German Jews for Relief and Reconstruction)
		September 1933	Reichsvertretung der Deutschen Juden (Reich Representation of German Jews)		
1935	Centralverein der Juden in Deutschland (Central Union of Jews in Germany)	1935	Reichsvertretung der Juden in Deutschland (Reich Representation of Jews in Germany)		
1936	Jüdischer Centralverein (Jewish Central Union)	July 4, 1939	Reichsvereinigung der Juden in Deutschland (Reich Association of Jews in Germany)		
November 1938	Jüdischer Centralverein ceases to function and amalgamates with	June 10, 1943			

2. Structure of the Einsatzgruppen from June 22, 1941

Einsatzgruppen and Their Operational Areas	Commanders	Einsatzkommandos/ Sonderkommandos	Commanders
Einsatzgruppe A: The Baltic states (Estonia, Latvia, Lithuania) and the territory between their eastern borders and the Leningrad district. Einsatzgruppe A was attached to Army Group North.	Dr. Franz Walter Stahlecker (until his death on March 23, 1942) Heinz Jost (March 24 to September 9, 1942) Dr. Humbert Achamer-Pifrader (September 10, 1942, to September 4, 1943) Friedrich Panzinger (September 4, 1943, to May 1944)	Sonderkommando 1a (on December 3, 1941, its name was changed to Kommandantur der Sicherheitspolizei und des Sicherheitsdienstes Estland, or Office of the Commander of the Security Police and Security Service in Estonia)	Dr. Martin Sandberger (until autumn 1943) Bernhard Baatz (October 31, 1943, to October 15, 1944)
		Sonderkommando 1b (on December 3, 1941, its name was changed to Kommandantur der Sicherheitspolizei und des Sicherheitsdienstes Weiss-Ruthenien, or Office of the Commander of the Security Police and Security Service in Belorussia)	Dr. Erich Ehrlinger (until December 3, 1941) Dr. Eduard Strauch (December 3, 1941, to June 2, 1943) Dr. Erich Isselhorst (June 3 to October 1943)
		Einsatzkommando 2 (on December 3, 1941, its name was changed to Kommandantur der Sicherheitspolizei und des Sicherheitsdienstes Lettland, or Office of the Commander of the Security Police and Security Service in Latvia)	Rudolf Batz (until early November 1941) Dr. Eduard Strauch (November 4 to December 3, 1941) Dr. Rudolf Lange (from December 3, 1941)
		Einsatzkommando 3 (on December 3, 1941, its name was changed to Kommandantur der Sicherheitspolizei und des Sicherheitsdienstes Litauen, or Office of the Commander of the Security Police and Security Service in Lithuania)	Karl Jäger (until autumn 1943) Dr. Wilhelm Fuchs (September 15, 1943, to May 6, 1944) Hans Joachim Böhme (May 11, 1944, to January 1, 1945)

Einsatzgruppe B: Belorussia and the Smolensk district up to the outskirts of Moscow. Einsatzgruppe B was attached to Army Group Center.		
Arthur Nebe (until November 1941) Erich Naumann (from November 1941 to March 20, 1943) Horst Böhme (March 12 to August 28, 1943) Dr. Erich Ehrlinger (August 28, 1943, to April 1944) Heinz Seetzen (April 28 to August 1944) Horst Böhme (from August 12, 1944)	Sonderkommando 7a	Dr. Walter Blume (until September 1941) Eugen Steimle (September to December 1941) Karl Matschke (as Steimle's representative from December 1941 to February 1942) Albert Rapp (February 1942 to January 28, 1943) Helmut Looss (June 1943 to June 1944) Dr. Gerhard Bast (June to October or November 1944)
	Sonderkommando 7b	Gunther Rausch (until February 10, 1942) Adolf Ott (mid-February 1942 to January 1943) Karl Rabe (January or February 1943 to October 1944)
	Sonderkommando 7c (also known as Vorkommando Moskau, or Forward Commando Moscow). Sonderkommando 7c was joined to Sonderkommando 7a in December 1943.	Dr. Franz Six (until August 20, 1941) Waldemar Klingelhöfer (as Six's representative from August 21 to October 1941) Dr. Erich Körting (October to December 1941) Wilhelm Bock (December 1941 to June 1942) Rudolf Schmücker (as Bock's representative from June to late autumn 1942) Dr. Walter Blume (late autumn 1942 to July 1943) Wilhelm Eckardt (July to December 1943)

(cont.)

2. *Structure of the Einsatzgruppen from June 22, 1941 (cont.)*

Einsatzgruppen and Their Operational Areas	Commanders	Einsatzkommandos/ Sonderkommandos	Commanders
		Einsatzkommando 8	Otto Bradfisch (until April 1, 1942) Heinz Richter (April 1 to September 1942) Dr. Erich Isselhorst (September to November 1942) Hans Schindhelm (November 13, 1942, to October 1943)
		Einsatzkommando 9	Dr. Alfred Filbert (until October 20, 1941) Oswald Schäfer (October 20, 1941, to February 1942) Wilhelm Wiebens (February 1942 to January 1943) Dr. Friedrich Buchardt (January to March 1943)
Einsatzgruppe C: Southern and Central Ukraine. Einsatzgruppe C was attached to Army Group South.	Dr. Emil Otto Rasch (until October 1941) Dr. Max Thomas (October 1941 to August 28, 1943) Horst Böhme (September 6, 1943, to the end of March 1944)	Sonderkommando 4a	Paul Blobel (until January 13, 1942) Dr. Erwin Weinmann (January 13 to July 1942) Eugen Steimle (August 1942 to January 15, 1943) Theodor Christensen (January to December 1943)
		Sonderkommando 4b	Günther Herrmann (until September 1941) Fritz Braune (October 1, 1941, to March 21, 1942) Dr. Walter Haensch (March 21 to July 1942) August Meier (July to November 1942) Friedrich Suhr (November 1942 to August 1943) Waldemar Krause (August 1943 to January 1944)

Group	Unit	Commander(s)
	Einsatzkommando 5 (disbanded in January 1942)	Erwin Schulz (until September 1941) August Meier (September 1941 to January 1942)
	Einsatzkommando 6	Dr. Erhard Kröger (until November 1941) Robert Mohr (November 1941 to mid-September 1942) Ernst Biberstein (mid-September to May 1942) Friedrich Suhr (August to November 1943)
Einsatzgruppe D: Southern Ukraine, Crimea, and Ciscaucasia (Krasnodar and Staun districts). Einsatzgruppe D was attached to the Eleventh Army. At the end of March 1943 it became known as Kampfgruppe Bierkamp (Fighting Group Bierkamp). As of May 1943, only Sonderkommando 10a and Einsatzkommandos 11b and 12 continued to function. Professor Otto Ohlendorf (until June 1942) Walter Bierkamp (July 1942 to July 1943)	Sonderkommando 10a	Heinz Seetzen (until July 1942) Dr. Kurt Christmann (August 1, 1942, to July 1943)
	Sonderkommando 10b	Alois Persterer (until February 1943) Edward Jedamzik (February to May 1943)
	Einsatzkommando 11a (in July 1942 it was disbanded and part of it was attached to Sonderkommando 11b, now called Sonderkommando 11)	Paul Zapp (until July 1942)
	Einsatzkommando 11b	Unknown (until July 1941) Bruno Müller (July to October 1941) Dr. Werner Braune (October 1941 to September 1942) Paul Schulz (September 1942 to February 1943)
	Einsatzkommando 12	Gustav Nosske (until February 1942) Dr. Erich Müller (February to October 1942) Günther Herrmann (October 1942 to March 1943)

3. Nuremberg Trial (*International Military Tribunal*)

The Indictment

The United States of America, The French Republic, The United Kingdom of Great Britain and Northern Ireland and The Union of Soviet Socialist Republics *against* Hermann Wilhelm Göring, Rudolf Hess, Joachim von Ribbentrop, Robert Ley, Wilhelm Keitel, Ernst Kaltenbrunner, Alfred Rosenberg, Hans Frank, Wilhelm Frick, Julius Streicher, Walter Funk, Hjalmar Schacht, Gustav Krupp von Bohlen und Halbach, Karl Dönitz, Erich Raeder, Baldur von Schirach, Fritz Sauckel, Alfred Jodl, Martin Bormann, Franz von Papen, Arthur Seyss-Inquart, Albert Speer, Konstantin von Neurath, and Hans Fritzsche, individually and as members of any of the following groups or organizations to which they respectively belonged, namely: Die Reichsregierung (Reich Cabinet); Das Korps der Politischen Leiter der Nationalsozialistischen Deutschen Arbeiterpartei (Leadership Corps of the Nazi Party); Die Schutzstaffeln der Nationalsozialistischen Deutschen Arbeiterpartei (commonly known as the "SS") and including Der Sicherheitsdienst (commonly known as the "SD"); Die Geheime Staatspolizei (Secret State Police, commonly known as the "Gestapo"); Die Sturmabteilungen der NSDAP (commonly known as the "SA"); and the General Staff and High Command of the German armed forces, all as defined in Appendix B of the Indictment.

DEFENDANTS

The Accused

Name	Position	Sentence
1. Martin Bormann	Deputy Führer, Head of the Chancellery	Death
2. Karl Dönitz	Supreme Commander of the Navy (1943), Chancellor (1945)	Ten years
3. Hans Frank	Governor-General of the Generalgouvernement	Death
4. Wilhelm Frick	Minister of the Interior	Death
5. Hans Fritzsche	Head of the Radio Division, Propaganda Ministry	Acquitted
6. Walther Funk	President of the Reichsbank (1939)	Life imprisonment
7. Hermann Göring	Reich Marshal and Commander in Chief of the Luftwaffe	Death
8. Rudolf Hess	Deputy Führer (1939)	Life imprisonment
9. Ernst Kaltenbrunner	Chief of the Sicherheitspolizei and SD; Head of the RSHA	Death
10. Wilhelm Keitel	Chief of the OKW (Armed Forces High Command)	Death
11. Alfred Jodl	Chief of the OKW Operations Staff	Death
12. Konstantin von Neurath	Minister of Foreign Affairs (1932–1938); Reich Protector of Bohemia-Moravia (1939–1943)	Fifteen years
13. Franz von Papen	Chancellor (1932); Ambassador to Vienna (1934–1938), Ambassador to Turkey (1939–1944)	Acquitted
14. Erich Raeder	Supreme Commander of the Navy (1928–1943)	Life imprisonment
15. Joachim von Ribbentrop	Reich Foreign Minister	Death
16. Alfred Rosenberg	Reich Minister for the Eastern Occupied Areas	Death
17. Fritz Sauckel	Plenipotentiary General for Manpower	Death
18. Hjalmar Schacht	Minister of Economics (1933–1936); President of the Reichsbank (until 1939)	Acquitted
19. Baldur von Schirach	Leader of the Hitler Youth; Gauleiter of Vienna	Twenty years
20. Arthur Seyss-Inquart	Reich Commissioner for the Occupied Netherlands	Death
21. Albert Speer	Minister of Armaments and War Production	Twenty years
22. Julius Streicher	Founder of *Der Stürmer*; Gauleiter of Franconia	Death

4. Subsequent Nuremberg Proceedings

Trial 1, The Medical Case
October 25, 1946–August 20, 1947

Defendant	Verdict or Sentence	Outcome
Karl Brandt	Death by hanging	Executed 1948
Siegfried Handloser	Life imprisonment	Sentence reduced by Clemency Board to twenty years
Paul Rostock	Not guilty	Acquitted
Oskar Schröder	Life imprisonment	Sentence reduced to fifteen years
Karl Genzken	Life imprisonment	Sentence reduced by Clemency Board to twenty years. Fined by denazification court, 1955.
Karl Gebhardt	Death by hanging	Executed 1948
Kurt Blome	Not guilty	Acquitted
Rudolf Brandt	Death by hanging	Executed 1948
Joachim Mrugowsky	Death by hanging	Executed 1948
Helmut Poppendick	Ten years' imprisonment	Released January 31, 1951
Wolfram Sievers	Death by hanging	Executed 1948
Gerhard Rose	Life imprisonment	Sentence reduced by Clemency Board to fifteen years
Siegfried Ruff	Not guilty	Since 1952 head of the Institute for Aeronautical Medicine of the German Air Navigational Experiment Center. Since 1954 professor at University of Bonn.
Hans Wolfgang Romberg	Not guilty	Acquitted
Georg August Weltz	Not guilty	Since 1952 professor at University of Munich
Konrad Schäfer	Not guilty	Acquitted
Waldemar Hoven	Death by hanging	Executed 1948
Wilhelm Beiglböck	Fifteen years' imprisonment	Sentence reduced to ten years
Adolf Pokorny	Not guilty	Acquitted
Herta Oberheuser	Twenty years' imprisonment	Released April 1952
Fritz Ernst Fischer	Life imprisonment	Sentence reduced to fifteen years
Viktor (Victor) Brack	Death by hanging	Executed 1948
Hermann Becker-Freyseng	Twenty years' imprisonment	Sentence reduced to ten years

Trial 2, The Milch Case
November 13, 1946–April 17, 1947

Defendant	Verdict or Sentence	Outcome
Erhard Milch	Life imprisonment	Sentence reduced by Clemency Board to fifteen years; released 1954

Trial 3, The Justice Case
January 4, 1947–December 4, 1947

Defendant	Verdict or Sentence	Outcome
Josef Altstötter	Five years' imprisonment	
Wilhelm von Ammon	Ten years' imprisonment	Sentence reduced to time served as of January 31, 1951
Paul Barnickel	Acquitted	
Hermann Cuhorst	Acquitted	
Karl Engert	Not tried owing to ill health	
Günther Joel	Ten years' imprisonment	
Herbert Klemm	Life imprisonment	Sentence reduced by Clemency Board to twenty years
Ernst Lautz	Ten years' imprisonment	Sentence reduced to time served as of January 31, 1951
Wolfgang Mettgenberg	Ten years' imprisonment	
Günther Nebelung	Acquitted	
Rudolf Oeschey	Life imprisonment	Sentence reduced to twenty years

(cont.)

Trial 1 (*cont.*)

Hans Petersen	Acquitted	
Oswald Rothaug	Life imprisonment	Sentence reduced by Clemency Board to twenty years; pensioned.
Kurt Rothenberger	Seven years' imprisonment	Released August 1950; pensioned
Franz Schlegelberger	Life imprisonment	Released on medical probation after recommendation of Clemency Board, 1951
Carl Westphal	Not tried	Committed suicide before arraignment

Trial 4, The Pohl Case
January 13, 1947 — November 3, 1947

DEFENDANT	VERDICT OR SENTENCE	OUTCOME
Oswald Pohl	Death by hanging	Executed 1951
August Frank	Life imprisonment	Sentence reduced by Clemency Board to fifteen years
Georg Lörner	Death by hanging	Sentence commuted by tribunal to life; reduced by Clemency Board to fifteen years. Upon release, acquitted by Bavarian Denazification Court, 1954.
Heinz Karl Fanslau	Twenty-five years' imprisonment	Sentence reduced by tribunal to twenty years; further reduced by Clemency Board to fifteen years
Hans Lörner	Ten years' imprisonment	Sentence reduced by Clemency Board to time served as of 1951
Josef Vogt	Acquitted	
Erwin Tschentscher	Ten years' imprisonment	Sentence reduced by Clemency Board to time served as of 1951
Rudolf Scheide	Acquitted	
Max Kiefer	Life imprisonment	Sentence reduced by tribunal to twenty years; further reduced by Clemency Board to time served as of 1951
Franz Eirenschmalz	Death by hanging	Sentence commuted by Clemency Board to nine years
Karl Sommer	Death by hanging	Sentence commuted by military governor to life; further reduced by Clemency Board to twenty years
Hermann Pook	Ten years' imprisonment	Sentence reduced by Clemency Board to time served as of 1951
Hans Heinrich Baier	Ten years' imprisonment	Released January 31, 1951
Hans Karl Hohberg	Ten years' imprisonment	Sentence reduced by Clemency Board to time served as of 1951
Leo Volk	Ten years' imprisonment	Sentence reduced by Clemency Board to eight years
Karl Mummenthey	Life imprisonment	Sentence reduced by Clemency Board to twenty years
Hans Bobernin	Twenty years' imprisonment	Sentence reduced by tribunal to fifteen years; freed by Clemency Board, 1951
Horst Klein	Acquitted	

Trial 5, The Flick Case
February 8, 1947 – December 22, 1947

DEFENDANT	VERDICT OR SENTENCE	OUTCOME
Friedrich Flick	Seven years' imprisonment	Released August 24, 1950
Otto Steinbrinck	Five years' imprisonment	
Odilo Burkart	Acquitted	
Konrad Kaletsch	Acquitted	
Hermann Terberger	Acquitted	
Bernhard Weiss	Two and one-half years' imprisonment	Vice president, Bundesverband Deutschen Industrie, Cologne

Trial 6, The I.G. Farben Case
May 8, 1947–July 30, 1948

DEFENDANT	VERDICT OR SENTENCE	OUTCOME
Carl Krauch	Six years' imprisonment	
Hermann Schmitz	Four years' imprisonment	Chairman, Rheinische Stahlwerke, 1955
Georg von Schnitzler	Five years' imprisonment	
Fritz Gajewski	Acquitted	
Heinrich Hörlein	Acquitted	
August von Knieriem	Acquitted	
Fritz ter Meer	Seven years' imprisonment	Released 1950. Deputy chairman, T.G. Goldschmidt A.G., Essen; Board of directors, Bankverein Westdeutschland A.G., Düsseldorf; Board of directors, Düsseldorfer Waggonfabrik, 1955.
Christian Schneider	Acquitted	
Otto Ambros	Eight years' imprisonment	Board of directors, Bergwerkgesellschaft Hibernia; Board of directors, Süddeutsche Kalkstickstoffwerke; Board of directors, Grünzweig und Hartmann, 1955
Max Brüggemann	Not tried owing to ill health	
Ernst Bürgin	Two years' imprisonment	
Heinrich Bütefisch	Six years' imprisonment	Board of directors, Deutsche Gasolin A.G., Berlin; Board of directors, Feldmühle, Papier und Zellstoffwerke, Düsseldorf; Director, Technical Committee of Experts, International Convention of Nitrogen Industry, 1955
Paul Häfliger	Two years' imprisonment	
Max Ilgner	Three years' imprisonment	Chairman, Board of directors, Freundeskreis der Internationalen Gesellschaft für Christlichen Aufbau, 1955
Friedrich Jähne	One and one-half years' imprisonment	Decorated with the Distinguished Service Cross with Star of the Order of Merit by West German government
Hans Kühne	Acquitted	
Carl Lautenschläger	Acquitted	
Wilhelm Mann	Acquitted	
Heinrich Oster	Two years' imprisonment	
Karl Wurster	Acquitted	
Walter Dürrfeld	Eight years' imprisonment	Board of directors, Scholven-Chemie A.G. Gelsenkirchen, 1955
Heinrich Gattineau	Acquitted	
Erich von der Heyde	Acquitted	
Hans Kugler	One and one-half years' imprisonment	Member of Central Committee of the Chemical Industry

Trial 7, The Hostage Case
May 10, 1947–February 19, 1948

DEFENDANT	VERDICT OR SENTENCE	OUTCOME
Wilhelm List	Life imprisonment	Released on medical parole, 1951
Maximilian von Weichs		Indicted; too ill to be tried
Lothar Rendulic	Twenty years' imprisonment	Sentence reduced by Clemency Board to ten years; released 1952
Walter Kuntze	Life imprisonment	Medical parole; released February 10, 1953
Hermann Förtsch	Acquitted	
Franz Böhme		Committed suicide after indictment and prior to arraignment

(cont.)

Trial 7 (*cont.*)

Helmuth Felmy	Fifteen years' imprisonment	Sentence reduced by Clemency Board to ten years; released 1952
Hubert Lanz	Twelve years' imprisonment	Sentence reduced by Clemency Board to time served as of 1951
Ernst Dehner	Seven years' imprisonment	Released January 31, 1951
Ernst von Leyser	Ten years' imprisonment	Released January 31, 1951
Wilhelm Speidel	Twenty years' imprisonment	Sentence reduced by Clemency Board to time served as of 1951
Kurt von Geitner	Acquitted	

Trial 8, The RuSHA Case
July 1, 1947–March 10, 1948

DEFENDANT	VERDICT OR SENTENCE	OUTCOME
Ulrich Greifelt	Life imprisonment	Died 1949
Rudolf Creutz	Fifteen years' imprisonment	Sentence reduced to ten years
Konrad Meyer-Hetling	Given credit for time served from May 27, 1945, until sentencing, March 10, 1948	
Otto Schwarzenberger	Given credit for time served from May 2, 1945 until sentencing, March 10, 1948	
Herbert Hübner	Fifteen years' imprisonment	Released January 31, 1951
Werner Lorenz	Twenty years' imprisonment	Sentence reduced by Clemency Board to fifteen years
Heinz Brükner	Fifteen years' imprisonment	Released January 31, 1951
Otto Hofmann	Twenty-five years' imprisonment	Sentence reduced by Clemency Board to fifteen years
Richard Hildebrandt	Twenty-five years' imprisonment	Reportedly free, 1955
Fritz Schwalm	Ten years' imprisonment	Released January 31, 1951
Max Sollmann	Given credit for time served from July 6, 1945, until sentencing, March 10, 1948	
Gregor Ebner	Given credit for time served from July 5, 1945, until sentencing, March 10, 1948	
Günther Tesch	Given credit for time served from May 13, 1945, until sentencing, March 10, 1948	
Inge Viermetz	Acquitted	

Trial 9, The Einsatzgruppen Case
July 3, 1947–April 10, 1948

DEFENDANT	VERDICT OR SENTENCE	OUTCOME
Ernst Biberstein	Death by hanging	Sentence commuted by Clemency Board to life
Paul Blobel	Death by hanging	Executed 1951
Walter Blume	Death by hanging	Sentence commuted by Clemency Board to life
Werner Braune	Death by hanging	Executed 1951
Lothar Fendler	Ten years' imprisonment	Sentence reduced by Clemency Board to eight years
Matthias Graf	Time already served	Released
Walter Hänsch	Death by hanging	Sentence commuted by Clemency Board to fifteen years

Trial 9 (*cont.*)

Emil Haussman	Not tried	Committed suicide July 31, 1947
Heinz Jost	Life imprisonment	Sentence commuted by Clemency Board to ten years
Waldemar Klingelhöffer	Death by hanging	Sentence commuted by Clemency Board to life
Erich Naumann	Death by hanging	Executed 1951
Gustav Nosske	Life imprisonment	Sentence reduced by Clemency Board to ten years
Otto Ohlendorf	Death by hanging	Executed 1951
Adolf Ott	Death by hanging	Sentence commuted by Clemency Board to life
Waldemar von Radetzky	Twenty years' imprisonment	Sentence reduced by Clemency Board to time served as of 1951
Otto Rasch	Not sentenced	Died November 1, 1948
Felix Rühl	Ten years' imprisonment	Sentence reduced by Clemency Board to time served
Martin Sandberger	Death by hanging	Sentence commuted by Clemency Board to life
Heinz Schubert	Death by hanging	Sentence commuted by Clemency Board to ten years
Erwin Schulz	Twenty years' imprisonment	Sentence commuted by Clemency Board to fifteen years
Willy Seibert	Death by hanging	Sentence commuted by Clemency Board to fifteen years
Franz Six	Twenty years' imprisonment	Sentence commuted by Clemency Board to ten years
Eugen Steimle	Death by hanging	Sentence commuted by Clemency Board to twenty years
Eduard Strauch	Death by hanging	Execution stayed because of defendant's insanity

Trial 10, The Krupp Case
August 16, 1947–July 31, 1948

DEFENDANT	VERDICT OR SENTENCE	OUTCOME
Alfried Felix Alwyn Krupp von Bohlen und Halbach	Twelve years' imprisonment; forfeiture of all property, both real and personal	Sentence reduced by Clemency to time served and restoration of assets
Ewald Oskar Ludwig Löser	Seven years' imprisonment	Sentence reduced by Clemency Board to time served as of 1951
Eduard Houdremont	Ten years' imprisonment	Sentence reduced by Clemency Board to time served as of 1951
Erich Müller	Twelve years' imprisonment	Sentence reduced by Clemency Board to time served as of 1951
Friedrich Wilhelm Janssen	Ten years' imprisonment	Sentence reduced to time served as of 1951
Karl Heinrich Pfirsch	Acquitted	
Max Otto Ihn	Nine years' imprisonment	Sentence reduced by Clemency Board to time served as of January 1951
Karl Adolf Ferdinand Eberhardt	Nine years' imprisonment	Sentence reduced to time served as of January 31, 1951
Heinrich Leo Korschan	Six years' imprisonmnt	Sentence reduced by Clemency Board to time served as of 1951
Friedrich von Bülow	Twelve years' imprisonment	Sentence reduced to time served as of January 31, 1951
Werner Wilhelm Henrich Lehmann	Six years' imprisonment	Released August 24, 1950
Hans Albert Gustav Kupke	Two years' imprisonment	

Trial 11, The Ministries Case
November 4, 1947–April 13, 1949

DEFENDANT	VERDICT OR SENTENCE	OUTCOME
Ernst von Weizsäcker	Seven years' imprisonment	Sentence reduced by tribunal to five years; released 1950. Died 1951.
Gustav Adolf Steengracht von Moyland	Seven years' imprisonment	
Wilhelm Keppler	Ten years' imprisonment	Sentence reduced by Clemency Board to time served as of 1951.
Ernst Wilhelm Bohle	Five years' imprisonment	
Ernst Wörmann	Seven years' imprisonment	Sentence reduced by tribunal to five years
Karl Ritter	Four years' imprisonment	
Otto von Erdmannsdorff	Acquitted	
Edmund Veesenmayer	Twenty years' imprisonment	Sentence reduced by Clemency Board to ten years
Hans Heinrich Lammers	Twenty years' imprisonment	Sentence reduced by Clemency Board to ten years
Wilhelm Stuckart	Three years, ten months, and twenty days, or time served (owing to ill health)	Fined 500 marks by denazification court. Killed in automobile accident, 1953.
Richard Walther Darré	Seven years' imprisonment	Released August 24, 1950
Otto Meissner	Acquitted	
Otto Dietrich	Seven years' imprisonment	Released August 24, 1950
Gottlob Berger	Twenty-five years' imprisonment	Sentence reduced by Clemency Board to ten years
Walter Schellenberg	Six years' imprisonment	Released before serving sentence. Died in Italy, 1952.
Lutz Schwerin von Krosigk	Ten years' imprisonment	Sentence reduced by Clemency Board to time served.
Emil Johann Puhl	Five years' imprisonment	
Karl Rasche	Seven years' imprisonment	Released 1950
Paul Körner	Fifteen years' imprisonment	Sentence reduced by Clemency Board to time served as of 1951; pensioned
Paul Pleiger	Fifteen years' imprisonment	Sentence reduced by Clemency Board to nine years
Hans Kehrl	Fifteen years' imprisonment	Sentence reduced to time served as of 1951

Trial 12, The High Command Case
November 28, 1947–October 28, 1948

DEFENDANT	VERDICT OR SENTENCE	OUTCOME
Wilhelm von Leeb	Three years' imprisonment	
Hugo Sperrle	Acquitted	
Georg Karl Friedrich Wilhelm von Küchler	Twenty years' imprisonment	Sentence reduced by Clemency Board to twelve years
Johannes Blaskowitz		Committed suicide in prison, February 5, 1948
Hermann Hoth	Fifteen years' imprisonment	Released on medical parole, April 8, 1954
Hans Reinhardt	Fifteen years' imprisonment	Released July 27, 1952
Hans von Salmuth	Twenty years' imprisonment	Sentence reduced by Clemency Board to twelve years
Karl Hollidt	Five years' imprisonment	
Otto Schniewind	Acquitted	
Karl von Roques	Twenty years' imprisonment	Died 1949
Hermann Reinecke	Life imprisonment	Released October 1954
Walter Warlimont	Life imprisonment	Sentence reduced by Clemency Board to eighteen years
Otto Wöhler	Eight years' imprisonment	Released January 31, 1951
Rudolf Lehmann	Seven years' imprisonment	Released August 24, 1950

5. Subsequent British Trials

The Belsen Trial
September 17, 1945 – November 17, 1945

DEFENDANT	VERDICT OR SENTENCE	OUTCOME
Josef Kramer	Death by hanging	Executed December 13, 1945
Dr. Fritz Klein	Death by hanging	Executed December 13, 1945
Peter Weingartner	Death by hanging	Executed December 13, 1945
George Kraft	Not guilty	
Franz Hössler	Death by hanging	Executed December 13, 1945
Juana Bormann	Death by hanging	Executed December 13, 1945
Elisabeth Volkenrath	Death by hanging	Executed by December 13, 1945
Herta Ehlert	Fifteen years' imprisonment	Reduced to twelve years; released May 7, 1953
Irma Grese	Death by hanging	Executed December 13, 1945
Ilse (Else) Lothe	Not guilty	
Hilde Lohbauer (Lobauer)	Ten years' imprisonment	Reduced to seven years; released July 15, 1950
Josef Klippel	Not guilty	
Nikolas Jenner (Jonner)	Unable to stand trial owing to sickness	
Oscar Shmedidzt (Schmitz)	Not guilty	
Karl Flrazich (Francioh) (Franzisch)	Death by hanging	Executed December 13, 1945
Paul Steinmetz	Unable to stand trial owing to sickness	
Ladislaw Gura	Took ill during proceedings and was withdrawn	
Fritz Mathes	Not guilty	
Otto Calesson (Kulessa)	Fifteen years' imprisonment	Sentence suspended; released September 10, 1954
Medislaw Burgraf	Five years' imprisonment	Released August 11, 1949
Karl Egersdorf	Not guilty	
Anchor Pinchen (Ansgar Pichen)	Death by hanging	Executed December 13, 1945
Walter Otto	Not guilty	
Walter Melcher	Unable to stand trial owing to sickness	
Franz Stofel	Death by hanging	Executed December 13, 1945
Heinrich Schreirer	Fifteen years' imprisonment	Sentence suspended September 10, 1950
Wilhem Dor (Dorr)	Death by hanging	Executed December 13, 1945
Eric Barsch (Basch)	Not guilty	
Erich Zoddel	Life imprisonment	Sentenced to death by a military government court and executed for an offense commited after the liberation of Belsen
Ignatz Schlomoivicz	Not guilty	
Ilse Forster	Ten years' imprisonment	Released December 21, 1951
Ida Forster	Not guilty	
Vladislav Ostrowoski (Ostrowski)	Fifteen years' imprisonment	Sentenced suspended September 10, 1954
Antoni Aurdzieg	Ten years' imprisonment	Released March 20, 1952
Klara Opitz	Not guilty	
Charlotte Klein	Not guilty	
Herta Bothe	Ten years' imprisonment	Released December 21, 1951
Frieda Walter	Three years' imprisonment	Served; released November 16, 1948

(cont.)

The Belsen Trial (*cont.*)

Irene Haschke	Ten years' imprisonment	Released December 21, 1951
Gertrud Fiest	Five years' imprisonment	Released August 11, 1949
Gertrud Sauer	Ten years imprisonment	Released December 21, 1951
Hilde Lisiewitz	One year imprisonment	Served; released November 16, 1946
Johanne Roth	Ten years' imprisonment	Released July 15, 1950
Anna Hempel	Ten years' imprisonment	Released December 21, 1951
Hildegarde Hahnel	Not guilty	
Helene Kopper	Fifteen years' imprisonment	Released February 25, 1952
Anton Polanski	Not guilty	
Stanislawa Staroska (Starostka)	Ten years' imprisonment	Suicide on May 10, 1946, or reduced to five years (Foreign Office files offer conflicting evidence, but the latter is probably correct)

The Natzweiler Trial
May 29, 1946–June 1, 1946

DEFENDANT	VERDICT OR SENTENCE	OUTCOME
Wolfgang Zeuss	Not guilty	
Magnus Wochner	Ten years' imprisonment	Released May 10, 1953
Emil Meier	Not guilty	
Peter Straub	Thirteen years' imprisonment	Tried on other charges by another British court; sentenced to death; executed October 11, 1946
Fritz Hartjenstein	Life imprisonment	Reduced to twenty-one years. Tried on other charges by another British court; sentenced to death by shooting; commuted to life; reduced to ten years. Extradited to France; tried and sentenced to death; commuted to life. Tried on other charges by the French; sentenced to death; died of illness October 20, 1954.
Franz Berg	Five years' imprisonment	Tried on other charges by another British court; sentenced to death; executed October 11, 1946
Werner Rohde	Death by hanging	Executed October 11, 1946
Emil Bruttel	Four years' imprisonment	Extradited to France; returned to British zone and released March 4, 1950
Kurt aus dem Bruch	Not guilty	
Walter Herberg (Harberg)	Not guilty	

The von Falkenhorst Trial
July 29, 1946–August 2, 1946

DEFENDANT	VERDICT OR SENTENCE	OUTCOME
Nikolaus von Falkenhorst	Death by shooting	Commuted to twenty years. Sentence suspended; released July 13, 1953.

The Velpke Trial
March 20, 1946–April 3, 1946

DEFENDANT	VERDICT OR SENTENCE	OUTCOME
Heinrich Gerike	Death by hanging	Executed October 8, 1946
Georg Hessling	Death by hanging	Executed October 8, 1946
Werner Noth	Not guilty	
Hermann Müller	Not guilty	
Gustav Claus	Not guilty	
Richard Demmerich	Ten years' imprisonment	Reduced to seven years; released December 2, 1950
Fritz Flint	No finding, since accused died.	
Valentina Bilien	Fifteen years' imprisonment	Sentence suspended; released January 23, 1954

6. Estimated Jewish Losses in the Holocaust

Introduction. The statistics presented here are an attempt to provide a well-founded and comprehensive picture of the losses incurred by the Jews of Europe as a direct result of Nazi persecution. This is not the first attempt at a full summation of Jewish losses during the Holocaust. Since the end of World War II, statistical data for individual countries, as well as a total figure, have appeared several times. Best known are the tables published by Jacob Lestchinsky, Raul Hilberg, Jacob Robinson, and Martin Gilbert. These researchers compiled statistics for the Jewish population in each European country before the war and for the number of survivors in those countries after the war. Yet they arrived at very different conclusions.

The Jewish sociologist Lestchinsky, basing his figures on Jewish populations in Europe as of 1939, arrived at a total figure of 5,957,000 Jewish victims, whereas Raul Hilberg, in the revised edition of his book *The Destruction of the European Jews* (New York, 1985), determined that 5,100,000 Jews perished in the Holocaust, basing himself on Jewish populations as of 1937. Hilberg also gave figures for the mortality in the camps, ghettos, and killing sites that led him to the same total. He noted in his explanation that the figures for the ghettos of eastern Europe, for shooting in open areas, and for Auschwitz had been rounded to the nearest thousand; figures for other types of killing had been rounded to the nearest 50,000.

In his article for the *Encyclopaedia Judaica* (Jerusalem, 1972), Jacob Robinson wrote that the simplest method of arriving at a total for Jewish losses during the Holocaust (including persons killed directly or indirectly and those who committed suicide) is to add up the figures in wartime statistical reports on ghettos, labor camps, extermination camps, and specific *Aktionen* perpetrated by the Nazis and their collaborators. Robinson calculated that 5,820,960 Jews were killed in the Holocaust. He stated that very reliable numbers are available for the deportations to extermination camps from Germany, France, Belgium, the Netherlands, and Theresienstadt. Robinson added, however, that figures are not available for all the different *Aktionen*, and that the statistics for other countries are less exact, as are those in the Einsatzgruppen reports and for the extermination camps. It is probable that these statistics were in Adolf Eichmann's office but were destroyed or disappeared; as is well known, Eichmann gave a total figure of 6,000,000 Jewish victims. Reasonably reliable figures are also available for Austria, Czechoslovakia (the Protectorate of Bohemia and Moravia, and Slovakia), Hungary, Luxembourg, Italy, Norway, Romania, Yugoslavia, and Greece. Significant difficulties arise regarding Poland and the Soviet Union, especially since the latter controlled the Baltic countries, part of Poland, and part of Romania during the war, which was not the case prior to 1939.

Since Robinson's research was published, many scholars in different lands, particularly in Israel, have devoted much time and energy to determining figures for those countries for which the data are less exact, especially Poland and the Soviet Union. For Poland, the estimated population of the Jews at the outbreak of the war has been studied, taking into account many diverse factors. The flight of the Jews in the wake of the Nazi advance was considered, and the figure arrived at includes the number of Jews who escaped to the south (Hungary and Romania), as well as the handful that reached the free world and the thousands who fled with troops and with non-Jewish Poles to Soviet territory. There are also dependable figures for the number of Polish Jews who survived the Nazi camps and for those who remained alive in Poland itself, either with the help of the local population or by passing themselves off as Christians, in civilian areas or in partisan units.

The number of Jews who returned to Poland from the Soviet Union during the wave of repatriation has also been taken into account in studies on Polish Jewish losses. In these calculations an error of several thousand may have been made, especially since the Jewish origin of children who survived in Polish religious institutions or among religious Poles was not always divulged after the war. On the other hand, people whom the Nazis considered to be Jews and who consequently perished, but who in actuality were Christians, are not included in statistics for the Jewish population in 1939. This too is a source of statistical inaccuracies. Moreover, mistakes were undoubtedly made during the registration carried out by the Jewish communities in Poland after the war; many survivors who traveled in search of surviving relatives were included in numerous community registers. It is also plausible that a certain number of Polish Jewish refugees who married and began families while living in the Soviet Union gave up their right to be repatriated to Poland and remained where they were. As a further complication, among the Jews repatriated to Poland there were spouses of Soviet origin, as well as Jews from the Baltic states who simply declared that they were Polish. Even if all these factors may appear to balance themselves out, it seems that the figures given for the number of survivors in Poland may be too large.

Conscientious research has also been devoted to calculating Jewish losses in the Soviet Union. These efforts have been based on the statistics for the number of Jews in the cities and towns of the areas forming part of the Soviet Union in 1939, in which the number of Jewish refugees was quite small. The number of Jews killed by the Einsatzgruppen has also been calculated, as has the estimated number of Jews believed by the Soviet authorities or by numerous witnesses to have escaped.

An attempt has been made in the statistics to clarify a number of issues and problems. Important subjects needing clarification included the changes in borders and the population exchanges in central Europe (Bohemia and Moravia, Slovakia, Hungary, and Romania) during the 1930s and 1940s. A thorough investigation was also made of the statistics on Germany, for which several versions exist. These versions reveal significant differences in the number of Jews who emigrated, as well as in the number who lived in Germany from 1939 through October 1941, when further emigration from Germany was forbidden. Not all the statistics here include figures for Jews who were considered such by racial definition and who were killed as Jews. The birthrate of Jews during the war years was generally not taken into account, nor was the potential birthrate, which was reduced because of the Nazi oppression. Because all scholars do not agree on the figures, those presented here sometimes differ slightly from figures found elsewhere in the encyclopedia.

The statistics here are of special importance because they are not the work of a single researcher trying to encompass all of Europe; rather, they are the work of a number of scholars, each working in his own area of expertise. This method is of substantial advantage, since it permits a much deeper and more detailed analysis for each country and eliminates many distortions caused by overlapping data.

Obviously, the data in Table 1, despite the substantial time and effort that went into compiling them as exactly as possible, are only estimates. But it may be said that they are closer to the true picture than previously published statistics, and that the error factor is no more than a few percent.

TABLE 1. *Estimated Jewish Losses in the Holocaust*

COUNTRY	INITIAL JEWISH POPULATION	MINIMUM LOSS	MAXIMUM LOSS
Austria	185,000	50,000	50,000
Belgium	65,700	28,900	28,900
Bohemia and Moravia	118,310	78,150	78,150
Bulgaria	50,000	0	0
Denmark	7,800	60	60
Estonia	4,500	1,500	2,000
Finland	2,000	7	7
France	350,000	77,320	77,320
Germany	566,000	134,500	141,500
Greece	77,380	60,000	67,000
Hungary	825,000	550,000	569,000
Italy	44,500	7,680	7,680
Latvia	91,500	70,000	71,500
Lithuania	168,000	140,000	143,000
Luxembourg	3,500	1,950	1,950
Netherlands	140,000	100,000	100,000
Norway	1,700	762	762
Poland	3,300,000	2,900,000	3,000,000
Romania	609,000	271,000	287,000
Slovakia	88,950	68,000	71,000
Soviet Union	3,020,000	1,000,000	1,100,000
Yugoslavia	78,000	56,200	63,300
Total	9,796,840	5,596,029	5,860,129
Rounded	9,797,000	5,596,000	5,860,000

Losses by Country

Austria. Jewish population in 1938: 185,000; losses, 50,000. Fifty thousand Jews were deported from Austria or died there; another 15,000 were deported from other European countries to which they had fled, and are included in their statistics. Most of the remaining Jews managed to leave Austria after the Anschluss for a safe haven as long as emigration was possible.

Belgium. Jewish population prior to the start of deportations: 65,700; losses, 28,900. Of the Jews living in Belgium on the eve of the war, fewer than 10 percent were Belgian Jews of long standing, the rest being classified as recent immigrants or refugees. A total of 34,800 Jews were imprisoned in Belgium or deported, and of them 28,900 died. Although the figures for Belgium are quite reliable, there may be a small overlap between the Belgian statistics and those for some of the countries from which Jewish refugees emigrated to Belgium. German, Austrian, and Czech refugees to Belgium are included here, and not in the statistics of their countries of origin.

Bohemia and Moravia, Protectorate of. Jewish population in 1939: 118,310; losses, 78,150. About 26,000 Jews escaped from the area before the start of the deportations, leaving 92,200, and 78,150 perished during the Holocaust.

Bulgaria. Jewish population at the start of the war: 50,000; no losses from deportations, but an undetermined number died because of Nazi persecution. The Jews of Bulgaria proper, some 50,000, were generally spared the fate of most of the Jewish communities in the occupied countries or in countries aligned with the Nazis. Virtually all of the more than 11,000 Jews in the areas of Macedonia (annexed from Yugoslavia) and Thrace (annexed from Greece) were deported to their death by the Bulgarian regime. They are not included in the figures for Bulgaria but in those of their countries of origin.

Denmark. Jewish population in 1940: 7,800; losses, 60. According to a definition of who was considered a Jew by race, about 7,800 Jews were living in Denmark on the eve of the deportations. Sixty-three hundred were Danish Jews, and 1,500 were refugees. A total of 7,220 Jews were rescued and found refuge in Sweden; 475 were deported to Theresienstadt, most of whom returned. At least 50 Jews hid successfully in Denmark. Fifty Danish Jews died in Nazi camps, and perhaps 10 more died in Denmark itself owing to Nazi persecution.

Estonia. Jewish population in 1941: 4,500; losses, 1,500 to 2,000. About 500 Jews were deported to Siberia by the Soviet authorities before the Nazis entered Estonia, and between 2,000 and 2,500 Jews fled in the wake of the Nazi advance. The figure for Estonia does not include Polish refugees in Estonia, who are included in the statistics for Poland.

Finland. Jewish population in 1939: 2,000; losses, 7. About 2,000 Jews lived in Finland before the outbreak of the war, including about 200 refugees from Germany. Twenty-three Jewish soldiers lost their lives fighting in the Finnish armed forces. In November 1942, 28 Finns, among them 8 Jews, were handed over to the Gestapo. Only one of the Jews survived. The statistics on refugees from Germany in Finland are included here and not in the German figures.

France. Jewish population before the start of deportations: 350,000 (including refugees from Belgium and central Europe); losses, 77,320. The figures for the losses suffered by French Jewry are well documented. More than 77,000 Jews were either deported to their death from France or died on French soil as a result of Nazi-fostered persecution. About one-third of them were French citizens of long standing, and the rest were Jews who had immigrated into France from eastern Europe after World War I, or Jews who had fled to France in the wake of Hitler's rise to power.

Germany. Jewish population in 1933 following a definition of who was a Jew by race: 566,000; losses (including German Jews who were deported from other countries), 193,500 to 200,000. The figure for German Jewish losses given in Table 1 (between 134,500 and 141,500) does not include those German Jews who before the advent of the "Final Solution" emigrated or were expelled to countries from which they were later deported. Of the 137,500 deported from Germany directly to the ghettos of eastern Europe (such as those of Łódź, Riga, and Minsk) and to various camps, at least 128,500 perished. Another 6,000 Jews were killed in concentration camps in Germany and in the Euthanasia Program or committed suicide (chiefly to avoid being deported). At least 65,000 of the 98,000 German Jews who were in other countries (from which they were later deported) perished during the Holocaust; they are included in the statistics for those countries in Table 1.

Greece. Pre-Holocaust Jewish population: 77,380; losses, 60,000 to 67,000. In 1940 the Jewish population of Greece was 77,380 (including Thrace, which was under Bulgarian rule during the war and had over 2,600 Jews). Of this total, over 62,000 Jews were deported. In 1947, 10,230 Jews were living in Greece, among them some 2,000 who had returned from the deportations. This means that perhaps 60,000 deportees were killed, leaving about 7,000 Greek Jews for whom there is no accounting. It is plausible that some perished as forced laborers in Greece and others in partisan units or during the deportation drives. Still others may have died of natural causes during the war years. Some of the 7,000 may have survived the war, but they had left Greece or had not returned there by the time the statistics were compiled.

Hungary. Jewish population in 1941, including annexed territories: 825,000; losses, 550,000 to 569,000. A total of 725,000 Jews, by traditional definition, lived in Hungary in 1941, according to the census of that year. The figure of 100,000 more usually offered for persons who were considered Jews by racial standards is only a rough estimate. The main issue regarding the statistics for Jewish losses from Hungary during the war is that of the territorial changes that involved Hungary and its neighbors Romania, Czechoslovakia (including the Transcarpathian Ukraine, now in the Soviet Union), and Yugoslavia. In the table, the Jews of northern Transylvania have been included in the figures for Hungary (not Romania), the Jews of the Banat region in Hungary (not Yugoslavia), and the Jews of the Transcarpathian Ukraine in Hungary (not Czechoslovakia or the Soviet Union), according to the available statistics, although it might seem more logical to have included them in the countries where they lived prior to the outbreak of World War II. Some figures, like the number of forced laborers killed or imprisoned in the Soviet Union, or the number of Jews who escaped from Hungary in 1944, are available for Hungary only after 1941, and therefore those given for Hungary reflect its borders after the wartime annexations. Between 255,000 and 265,000 Jewish survivors were in Hungary and its former territories shortly after the war. These figures do not include the thousands of Hungarian Jewish laborers trapped in the Soviet Union until early 1947 and the Jews who had survived but did not return to Hungary or to former Hungarian territory (such as some of the 8,000 to 10,000 who fled to Romania). In the areas under Hungarian authority from 1941 to 1945, between 550,000 and 569,000 were killed, most during and after the deportations of 1944.

Italy. Pre-Holocaust Jewish population: 44,500; losses, 7,680. These figures include Rhodes, which was an Italian possession until after the war.

Latvia. Jewish population in 1941: 91,500; losses, 70,000 to 71,500. The figure for Latvia's Jewish population at the time when the Germans invaded includes 90,000 native Jews and another 1,500 refugees from Germany, Austria, and Bohemia and Moravia. Jewish refugees from Poland, however, are not included among the refugees in Latvia but in the statistics for Poland. On the eve of the German occupation, the Soviet authorities deported about 5,000 Jews to Siberia. Between 14,000 and 15,000 Jews fled as the Germans advanced, and about 70,000 native Jews, together with the above-mentioned 1,500 refugees, were actually trapped in Latvia. Some 68,500 to 69,000 native Latvian Jews were killed, as were nearly all the refugees.

Lithuania. Jewish population in 1941: 168,000; losses, between 140,000 and 143,000. On the eve of the German occupation, the Soviet authorities deported about 7,000 Jews to Siberia. Some 14,000 to 15,000 Jews fled from Lithuania during the German advance. When the occupation began about 145,000 Lithuanian Jews and some 3,000 German, Czech, and Austrian Jewish refugees were in Lithuania. The statistics for Lithuania do not include the Vilna area, which is included in the figures for Poland, nor do they include the Polish refugees who were in Lithuania. If these figures are added, the pre-Holocaust population of Lithuania amounts to about 265,000, with losses proportionate to this increase.

Luxembourg. Jewish population in 1940: 3,500; losses, 1,950. The figures for Luxembourg are well documented, although there is an overlap of several hundred, representing Jews who fled Luxembourg and were deported from other countries.

Netherlands. Jewish population in 1940: 140,000; losses, 100,000. The figures for the Netherlands are reliable, but as with other countries that Jewish refugees entered, the problem of overlapping statistics remains. Some 15,000 Jewish refugees were in the Netherlands at the time of the German invasion, and the largest group, German Jews, is included in the statistics for the Netherlands, not for Germany. Two thousand Dutch Jews who had fled to France and Belgium were also killed during the Holocaust, and are included in the figures for those countries.

Norway. Pre-Holocaust Jewish population: 1,700; losses, 762. Since the Jewish community was quite small (the figure of 1,700 includes 200 refugees), the statistics for Jewish losses in Norway are precise: 762 Jews perished.

Poland. Jewish population in 1939: 3,300,000; losses, 2,900,000 to 3,000,000. This population figure applies to Poland according to its boundaries before September 1, 1939, and includes the areas that later became part of the Soviet Union. Polish refugees who perished in the areas of the Soviet Union that came under Nazi control are included in the figures for Poland.

Romania. Jewish population in 1941: 609,000, not including northern Transylvania; losses, 271,000 to 287,000. The changes in the boundaries of Romania make statistics here problematic. Of the 609,000 Jews living in Romania after northern Transylvania was ceded to Hungary in 1940, about 20,000 successfully escaped from Bessarabia and Bukovina during the German advance. Some 150,000 to 160,000 Jews were killed on the spot in Bessarabia and Bukovina, between 105,000 and 110,000 were killed during the deportations to Transnistria and in Transnistria itself, about 12,000 were killed during the Iaşi pogrom, and between 4,000 and 5,000 were killed in other parts of Romania owing to Nazi-inspired persecution.

Slovakia. Jewish population at the start of 1942: 88,950; losses, 68,000 to 71,000. The parts of Slovakia ceded to Hungary are included in the Hungarian (not the Slovak) figures. It is impossible to determine an exact number for the losses of Slovak Jewry: many Jews from other countries who were en route to Palestine under Aliya Bet auspices passed through Slovakia before the deportations, and some were trapped there; hundreds of Polish Jewish refugees were in Slovakia at the time of the deportations and after the war as displaced persons; hundreds of German Jewish refugees were trapped in Slovakia during the war; and many Slovak Jews left Slovak territory before and during the deportations and immediately after liberation.

Soviet Union. Jewish population within the borders of the Soviet Union as of 1939: 3,020,000; losses, 1,000,000 to 1,100,000. Not including Polish refugees, about 2,100,000 Jews were in the areas of the Soviet Union destined to be taken over by the Germans. More than 1.5 million were in the western Ukraine, nearly 400,000 in Belorussia, and 200,000 in other parts of the Soviet Union occupied by the Germans. About 1,000,000 fled in the wake of the Nazi offensive or were mobilized into the Soviet army; virtually all the rest were killed. As with Poland, because of the large size of the Jewish population, it is impossible to determine exact numbers. The figures in the table include Jewish soldiers in the Soviet army who were taken prisoner by the Germans and singled out for death, but they do not include Jewish soldiers who died in battle. Polish refugees who died in the Soviet Union are not included in these statistics.

Yugoslavia. Pre-Holocaust Jewish population: 78,000; losses, 56,200 to 63,300. Macedonia is included in the figures for Yugoslavia, but statistics for the Banat region are reflected in the Hungarian figures. Including the Jews of the Banat, up to 67,000 Jews were killed within the borders of what is now Yugoslavia.

Compiled by YEHUDA BAUER
and ROBERT ROZETT

Index

Numbers in **boldface** refer to the main entry on the subject.

A

Aarvik, Egil, 1650
Abadie, Moussa, 1082
AB-Aktion, **1**
Abandonment of the Jews, The (Wyman), 671
Abegg, Elisabeth, **1–2**, 1282
Abetz, Otto, **2–3**
Ables, Ernst, 1183
A Boym in Polyn (Segalowicz), 892
Abrahám, Samu (Shimon), 1466, 1467
Abrahamson, Arye, 1024
Abromeit, Franz, 327
Abs, Hermann, 1258
Abschiebung (term), 1399
Abstammungsbescheid (certificate of Aryan descent), 49
Abugov, Aleksandr, **3**, 1119
Abwanderung (term), 1399
Abwehr, **3–5**, 409, 1246, 1337
  and Arab leadership, 704
  Lithuanian nationalists' cooperation, 876
  Soviet intelligence infiltration, 1234
  Soviet Jewish prisoner-of-war policies, 1191
Accounting for Genocide (Fein), 670
Account Settled (Schacht), 1330
ACCR. *See* American Committee for Christian German Refugees
Ackermann, Leonard, 1596
Action Française, **5–6**, 1213, 1411, 1559
Adamowicz, Irena, **6**, 783, 826, 1282
Adams, Henry, 57
Adan Ben-Kelev (Kaniuk), 882
Adas Israel (Berlin), 197, 200
Adenauer, Konrad, 589, 1256–1258, 1275, 1498
Adler, Cyrus, 35
Adler, Fredrick, 1564
Adler, Jacob (Yankel), 900
Adler, Karl, 844, 984
Adler, Max, 1564

Adler, Stanisław, 373
Adler, Victor, 1564
Adler-Rudel, Salomon, 1255, 1438, 1732
Ad Lo Or, Mi-Kol ha-Ahavot (Kovner), 824
ADL. *See* Anti-Defamation League (U.S.)
Adnei ha-Nahar (Appelfeld), 882
Adorno, Theodor, 880, 1024
Adrianovitsch, Georg, 1361
A. E. G. (Allgemeine Elektrizität Gesellschaft), 777
Af der Vakh (Kharik), 893
Af Gekirtste Vegn (Zabare), 894
Africa, North. *See* Algeria; Libya; Morocco; North Africa; Tunisia
AFSC. *See* American Friends Service Committee
After Auschwitz (Rubenstein), 750
Agami, Moshe, 1261
Agapie, Vasile, 1563
Agencja Narodowa (publication), 1032
Aglona (Euthanasia Program), 453
Agrarian Party (Romania). *See* Partidul Agarar (Romania)
Agrarian Party (Slovakia), 1370, 1371
Agudat ha-Rabbanim. *See* Union of Orthodox Rabbis of the United States and Canada
Agudat Israel, 40–41, 383, 1260, 1710
Aharonovits, Aharon, 1117
Ahlen (war crimes trial), 1497, 1505
Ahnenerbe, **6–9**, 1402
Aḥoti ha-Ketanna (Kovner), 824, 883
Aid Committee for Jewish War Victims (Belgium), 80, 252
Aide aux Israélites Victimes de la Guerre (Belgium), *See* Aid Committee for Jewish War Victims (Belgium)
Aid to Jews
  by American nonsectarian organizations, 1065–1066

  by Belgians, 44, 164–165, 251–252, 1059–1060
  by Britons, 607–610
  by Bulgarians, 266, 268–272
  by Christian organizations, 1108
  by consular offices, 1264–1265, 1272, 1280
  by Czechoslovak government-in-exile, 333
  by Danes, 209, 270, 363–365, 369
  by the Dutch, 225–226, 401–402, 641, 1048, 1052–1053, 1055, 1077, 1100, 1307, 1560, 1648–1649
  by the French, 24, 355–356, 512, 586, 650, 859–860, 1324
  by German diplomacy in Denmark, 409
  by German occupation, 1131–1132, 1202, 1333
  by Germans, 1–2, 201, 231, 573, 599–600, 654, 1202, 1331–1332
  by Greeks, 105, 319, **454**, 613, 614, 615–616
  by Hungarians, 1090, 1138–1139, 1449–1450
  by Italians, 155–156, 328, 612, 614, 615, 724, 725, 729–730, 1138, 1709
  by Latvians, 876–877
  by Lithuanians, 151–152, 217, 232–233, 846, 1358
  by neutral nations, 258–259
  by Poles, 3, **9–10**, 151, 289–290, 299, 481, 578–579, 618–619, 789, 821, 828–829, 886, 1167, 1172, 1339–1340, 1624, 1629, 1659, 1723–1724
  by Polish government-in-exile, 1177–1178
  by Protestant churches, 294–295
  by Roman Catholic Church, 183, 293–294, 299, 578–579, 821, 1322–1323, 1362–1363
  by Romanians, 305

Central Consistory of French Jews. *See* Consistoire Central des Israélites de France

Central Defense Committee against Jewish Atrocity and Boycott Propaganda. *See* Zentralkomitee zur Abwehr der Jüdischen Greuel- und Boykotthetze

Central Historical Commission. *See* Tsentraler Historisher Komisiye

Central Jewish Committee for the Reconstruction of Religious Life in Belgium. *See* Comité Central Israélite pour la Reconstruction de la Vie Religieuse en Belgique

Central Jewish Council (Budapest), 533

Central Jewish Historical Commission, 396

Central Jewish Office for Slovakia. *See* Židovska Ústredňa Uradovna pre Slovensko

Central Jewish Relief Society (Belgium). *See* Oeuvre Centrale Israélite de Secours

Centralne Towarzystwo Opieki nad Sierotami (Poland). *See* CENTOS

Central Office for Jewish Emigration. *See* Zentralstelle für Jüdische Auswanderung

Central Office for the Solution of the Jewish Question in Bohemia and Moravia. *See* Zentralamt für die Regelung der Judenfrage in Böhmen and Mähren

Central Resettlement Office. *See* Umwandererzentralstelle

Central Union of German Citizens of Jewish Faith. *See* Centralverein Deutscher Staatsbürger Jüdischen Glaubens

Centralverein der Juden in Deutschland. *See* Centralverein Deutscher Staatsbürger Jüdischen Glaubens

Centralverein Deutscher Staatsbürger Jüdischen Glaubens, 196, **281–282,** 559, 560, 566, 643
  leadership, 663
  Wiener Library, 395

Central Welfare Council (Warsaw). *See* Rada Głowna Opiekuńcza

Central Welfare Organization of German Jews. *See* Zentralwohlfahrtstelle der Deutschen Juden

Central Yiddish Schools Organization. *See* CYShO

Centre de Documentation Juive Contemporaine (France), **392**

Centro di Documentazione Ebraica Contemporanea (Italy), **393**

Cernăuţi. *See* Chernovtsy

Certificates of nationality. *See* Protective documents

Ceuta, 993

CFGJ. *See* Council for German Jewry

CGD. *See* Comité Général de Défense

CGQJ. *See* Commissariat Général aux Questions Juives

Chagall, Marc, 96, 99, 886

Chalcis, 614, 615

Chamberlain, Houston Stewart, 62, 69, **282–283,** 1210–1211, 1305

Chamberlain, Joseph P., 1187

Chamberlain, Neville, 300, 600–601, 603–605, 1642, 1663, 1666
  Munich conference, **1001–1006**

Chambers, gas. *See* Gas chambers

Chambéry, 1082

Chambon-sur-Lignon. *See* Le Chambon-sur-Lignon

Chapayev partisan battalion, 1116

Chapuisat, Edouard, 1232

Charcot, Jean-Martin, 1211–1212

Charleroi, 160

Charlotte (film), 488

Charnel House (Picasso), 93, 95, 96 *ill.*

Checiny, Judenrat, 769 *ill.*

Chełm, Palestinian Jewish prisoner-of-war camp, 1191

Chełmno, 11, 159, 220, 234, **283–286,** 461–463, 493, 618, 1150, 1284
  Austrian Jews in, 131
  confiscation of prisoners' property, 214–215
  Czech Jews in, 230
  establishment of, 310, 1652
  gassings, 539, 542, 544, 1130, 1168, 1591, 1593, 1672, 1750
  Grojanowski report, 621
  Gypsies in, 636, 1672
  Łódź deportations to, 904–905, 908, 1313
  memorials and monuments, 1014
  Oneg Shabbat report on, 285, 1086
  Sonderkommando, 1378
  songs from, 892
  war crimes trials, 1506, 1515
  Warthegau Jews in, 1635

Chepilovo, massacre, 1363

Cherche, 1287

Cherkessk, gas vans, 543–544

Chernaia kniga. See Black Book of Soviet Jewry, The

Chernigov, 1118, 1244

Chernovtsy, 262, **287–288**
  deportations, 942, 1474–1475
  ghetto, 1274, 1714
  Jewish partisan survivors, 192–193

Chernyshev, Vasily Yehimovich. *See* Platon, General

Cherven, 173, 974

Chetniks, **288–289,** 1673, 1721

Chiang Kai-shek, 1673

Chiczewski, Feliks, 1727

Chief Rabbi's Fund (France), 318

Chief Rabbi's Religious Emergency Council (Great Britain), 608, 609, 1334

Child of Our Time, A (oratorio), 1024

Children
  in Auschwitz-Birkenau, 171, 1707
  Austrian refugees, 129–130
  Belgian rescue efforts, 44, 79, 103, 167, 251–252, 1059–1060
  British asylum for Jewish refugees, 607, 608–610, 1334
  British proposal for Palestinian immigration, 1692
  in Buchenwald, 255, 256
  in Cyprus detention camps, 330, 331–332
  deportation from Lidice to Chełmno, 286
  deportations of French, 150, 1537
  deportations of Serbian, 740
  diaries, 373, 884, 886, 888, 1166
  Dutch hiding and rescue of, 401–402, 1055, 1056, 1077, 1560
  Euthanasia Program for, 1128
  French Jewish aid for, 479–480, 538–539
  French rescue efforts, 32, 293, 304, 356, 414, 741, 1107, 1335, 1637–1638, 1709
  French survivors, aid for, 518, 920
  gas vans, 544
  "Germanization" designation for selected Polish, 1224
  Hitlerjugend organization, **677–679**
  Holocaust memorial for, 1684
  of Holocaust survivors, 99, **1432–1435**
  Hungarian Jewish emigration plan, 690
  Hungarian rescue efforts, 259, 924, 1253, 1449–1450, 1712
  international protection in Hungary, 815
  Italian rescue efforts, 155–156
  Jewish international welfare organization, 1081
  Kielce massacre, 802, 803
  Korczak's work with, 817–818
  Latvian massacre, 410
  Lidice and Lezaky massacres, 430, 872
  Lithuanian shelters, 151–152
  Marseilles deportations, 1538
  Polish rescue efforts, 290, 299, 578–579, 1340, 1730
  Quaker relief aid, 34
  Roman Catholic aid for, 293, 299
  sterilization experiments, 965
  survivors, recovery of Jewish orphans, 30, 1412
  Tehran children (Polish), **1454–1455**
  in Theresienstadt, 971

Children (*cont.*)
U.S. aid and rescue efforts, 1065–1066, 1262–1263
Warsaw ghetto, 1612 *ill.*, 1613 *ill.*, 1615 *ill.*, 1618
Youth Aliya, **1695–1696**
see also Youth movements
Children of Holocaust Survivors, First Conference on (1979), 1434
Children's Aid Society. *See* Oeuvre de Secours aux Enfants
Children's Inter-Aid Committee (Great Britain), 608, 609
Chile
Jewish refugees, 83
war criminal asylum, 1225
China
UN War Crimes Commission, 1541
World War II, 1673
Chişinău. *See* Kishinev
Chkalov partisan brigade, 1115
Chmielewski, Karl, 632, 1584
Chodel, deportations to Opole Lubelskie, 1088
Chodorov, 1287
Cholawski, Shalom, 1013, 1044, 1110 *ill.*
Choms, Władysława, **289–290**
Chomsky, Marvin, 488
Chomsowa, Władysława, 1730
Chorazycki, Julian, 1487
Chor Synagogue (Riga), 1277
Chortkov, **290–291**, 1119
Chorzów, 648–649
Chounio, Edgar, 1326
Christian churches, **291–299**
aid to French Jewish children, 1082
aid to Jews in Denmark, 364
aid to Jews in Hungary, 258, 1449–1450
aid to Jews in Netherlands, 1052–1053, 1100
aid to Jews in Norway, 1068
aid to Jews in Romania, 1322–1323
and Aryanism, 283, 1211
blood libel accusations, 63, 265, 563, 1156, 1248
British aid to Jews, 1108
Chernovtsy Jewish conversions, 288
clergymen interned at Dachau, 339
converts, Jewish badge regulations for, 140, 142–143
crucified Jesus as Holocaust symbol, 96
German, anti-Nazi, 4, 150, 231, 294, 296, 375–376, 568, 575, 576, 1061, 1674
German, Jewish conversions, 560
German, reaction to anti-Jewish policies, 572–573
and German refugees from Nazism, 32–33, 34

historiography of aid to Jews, 670–671
in Poland, 1149, 1347–1348
post-Holocaust attitude toward Jews, **295–299**
reaction to Euthanasia Program, 452–454
"Stuttgart Confession of Guilt" (1945), 296, 1061, 1679
theological opposition to antisemitism, 231, 1060–1061, 1108
theological support for Judaism, 150–151
theology as source of antisemitism, 55–56, 60, 63, 291–292
U.S. efforts for European Jews, 191, 1060–1061, 1065–1066
see also Protestantism; Roman Catholic church; Vatican; specific denominations
Christian Friendship (France). *See* Amitié Chrétienne (France)
Christian National Defense League (Romania). *See* Iron Guard
Christian National Party (Romania). *See* Partidul National Crestin
Christian Reformed Church (Netherlands), 297
Christians Concerned for Israel (U.S.), 298
Christianstadt, 625
Christian Study Group on Israel and the Jewish People (U.S.), 298
Christian X, King (Denmark), 142, 364
Christmann, Kurt, 1489
Christophersen, Thies, 682
Chronicles of the Łódź ghetto, **909–910**
Chrzanów, 972, 1352, 1354
Chuikov, Vasily, 1407
Chumak, Paul, 358
Chuprynka, General. *See* Shukhevych, Roman
Church aid. *See* Christian churches; Protestantism; Roman Catholic church; specific denominations and religious orders
Church Dogmatics (Barth), 150
Churchill, Winston, **299–301**, 359, 417, 545 *ill.*, 601, 602, 605, 745, 747, 787, 944, 1304 *ill.*, 1392
Auschwitz bombing proposal, 119
and Polish government-in-exile, 1153
on war crimes trials, 1495, 1496
World War II, 1665, 1666, 1670, 1674
Church World Service, 33
Chvalkovsky, František, 490
Chwojnik, Abraham, 274
Ciano, Galeazzo, 695, 936, 1002 *ill.*, 1667 *ill.*

Cicognani, Amleto, 1138
Ciechanów, 114, 336, 648–649
Cieszyn, 648–649
CIMADE (France), 295
Cinema. *See* Films
Ciolkosz, Adam, 1178
Ciscaucasia, Einsatzgruppe D, 436, 437, 543–544
Citizens' Committee on Displaced Persons (U.S.), 387
City of the Immaculata (Poland), 811
Ciudei, 418
Civic Self-Defense Organization (Poland). *See* Społeczna Organizacja Samoobrony
Civil Service, Law for the Restoration of the Professional (Germany). *See* Law for the Restoration of the Professional Civil Service
Civil Struggle Directorate (Poland), 357
Civitella del Tronto, 866
Claims Conference (1951–1952), 595, 755, 1257–1258
Class, Heinrich von, 65
Clauberg, Carl, 111, **301–302**, 650, 965–966, 966, 1131, 1132, 1227, 1326
Clauss, Ludwig Ferdinand, 1214
Clay, Lucius D., 809, 1544
Cleansing of the Ground (Romania). *See* Curatirea Terenului
Clemency, for war criminals, **1497–1499**, 1504, 1505
Netherlands, 1057, 1512
Romania, 1512
Clermont-Tonnerre, Stanislas de, 57
Clerq, Staf de, 164
Cleveland, Ohio, 357, 358
Cluj, **303–304**, 719, 787, 788, 790, 1476, 1477
Co czytałem umarlym (Szlengel), 1449
Codreanu, Corneliu, 74, 329, 477, 719, 720, 1215, 1289
Cohen, Alfred, 223
Cohen, Arthur A., 750–751
Cohen, Aryeh, 718
Cohen, Benjamin V., 991
Cohen, David, 100, **303**, 757, 758, 759 *ill.*, 760, 770, 1047–1048, 1051, 1052, 1053, 1056, 1512, 1576, 1584
Cohen, Haim Efraim, 454
Cohen, Herman, 559
Cohen, Jacob, 900
Cohen, Richard, 670
Cohen, Sam, 639
Cohen, Sir Samuel, 123
Cohen, Yohanan, 193
Cohn, Marianne, **304**
Collaborators
historiography on, 670

Jewish Center for Adult Education (Germany). *See* Mittelstelle für Jüdische Erwachsenenbildung

Jewish Center (Romania). *See* Centrala Evreilor

Jewish Center (Slovakia). *See* Ústredňa Židov

Jewish Central Information Office (Amsterdam), 395

Jewish Chaplaincy (France). *See* Aumônerie Générale Israélite

Jewish Colonization Association, 1237

Jewish Committee (Hanover), 382 *ill.*

Jewish Committee for Social Action and Reconstruction (France). *See* Comité Juif d'Action Social et de Reconstruction

Jewish Community Council (Lublin), 915, 916, *see also* Judenrat (Lublin)

Jewish Community Council (Warsaw), 1606

Jewish Community Cultural Society (Lublin), 919

Jewish Community Office (Austria), 128

Jewish Community Organization (Munich), 1000

Jewish Conquest of the World, The (Bey), 63

Jewish Consistory (Sofia), 266, 267 *ill.*, 269

Jewish Coordinating Committee (Netherlands). *See* Joodse Coördinatiecommissie (Hague)

Jewish Council. *See* Judenrat

Jewish Council of Hungary. *See* Zsidó Tanács

Jewish Council in the Netherlands. *See* Joodse Raad

Jewish Council in Romania. *See* Consiliul Evreesc

Jewish Council of the World, The, 737

Jewish Cultural Association. *See* Kulturbund Deutscher Juden

Jewish Cultural Society (Poland), 1234

Jewish Defense Committee (Belgium). *See* Comité de Défense des Juifs

Jewish Defense Committee (France). *See* Comité Général de Défense

Jewish Democratic Committee (Romania). *See* Comitetul Democrat Evereesc

Jewish Fighting Organization (France). *See* Organisation Juive de Combat

Jewish Fighting Organization (Poland). *See* Żydowska Organizacja Bojowa

Jewish-German exchanges. *See* Exchange, Jews and Germans

Jewish Ghetto Police. *See* Jüdischer Ordnungsdienst

Jewish Historical Institute (Poland). *See* Żydowski Instytut Historyczny

Jewish history. *See* Documentation centers; Historiography; specific country names

Jewish homeland. *See* Homeland, Jewish; Israel, state of; Palestine; Zionist movement

Jewish Labor Committee (U.S.), 36, 37, 43, **748** anti-Nazi boycott, 237, 752

Jewish Law (France). *See* Statut des Juifs

Jewish Material Claims Conference, 714

Jewish Military Union (Poland). *See* Żydowski Związek Wojskowy

Jewish Museum of Prague, 230, 1187

Jewish Mutual Aid Society (Poland). *See* Żydowskie Towarzystwo Opieki Społecznej

Jewish National Committee (Poland). *See* Żydowski Komitet Narodowy

Jewish National Fund, 206

Jewish Newspaper. See Yiddishe Zeitung (publication)

Jewish parachutists. *See* Parachutists, Jewish

Jewish People's Fraternal Order, 748

Jewish People's Party (Germany). *See* Jüdische Volkspartei

Jewish police. *See* Jüdischer Ordnungsdienst

Jewish prisoners of war. *See* Prisoners of war, Jewish

Jewish Refugees Committee (Great Britain), 608

Jewish Religious Congregation (Prague), 229 *see also* Ältestenrat der Juden in Prag

Jewish Representation Council (Great Britain), 237

Jewish Rescue Committee. *See* Pracovná Skupina

Jewish responses to the Holocaust, **748–751**

Jewish Scouts, French. *See* Eclaireurs Israélites de France

Jewish Self-Help Society (Poland). *See* Żydowska Samopomoc Społeczna

Jewish Settlement Association, 1069

Jewish Socialist Party. *See* Bund

Jewish Social Self-Help Society. *See* Jüdische Soziale Selbsthilfe (Kraków)

Jewish Telegraph Agency, 204

Jewish Theological Seminary (Germany), 243

Jewish Trade Union Federation, 26

Jewish War Veterans (U.S.), anti-Nazi boycott, 237, 752

Jewish Welfare Bureau. *See* Jüdische Unterstützungsstelle

Jewish Winter Relief (Breslau). *See* Jüdische Winterhilfe

Jewish Youth Front. *See* Front of the Wilderness Generation

Jewish Youth Movements. *See* Youth Movements

Jewish Youth Organizations, Reich Committee of. *See* Reichsausschuss der Jüdischen Jugendverbände

Jews. *See* "Final Solution"; Judaism (for religious aspect); specific countries and aspects of Holocaust

Jews: Kings of the Period, The (Toussenel), 59

Jews of Warsaw, The (Gutman), 670

Jews Were Expendable, The (Penkower), 671

JFO. *See* General Jewish Fighting Organization (Kovno)

Jihlava, 227

JLC. *See* Jewish Labor Committee

Joachim of Fiore, 1464

Job paradigm (Old Testament), 749–750

Jodenvereeniging van Belgie. *See* Association des Juifs en Belgique

Jodl, Alfred, **751–752**, 1490–1491

John Paul II, Pope, 299, 683, 1139

John XXIII, Pope, 297, 666

Joint, The. *See* Joint Distribution Committee, American Jewish

Joint Boycott Council (U.S.), 237, **752**

Joint Distribution Committee, American Jewish, 426, 483, 495, 616, 664, **752–755**, 788, 802, 935, 955, 1237, 1254, 1283, 1540, 1558 administration, 752–754, 1335–1336, 1594 apolitical relief work, 34, 39, 43, 156–157 Austrian Jewish aid, 129, 913, 914 Belgian Jewish aid, 250 *beriha* aid, 193 and Bermuda Conference, 204 and British Council for German Jewry, 319 and Cyprus detention camps, 331–332, 755 and displaced persons, 379 and forced Jewish emigration, 426 French Jewish aid, 479, 512, 514, 515, 1639 and French resistance, 88 in Generalgouvernement, 1165 German Jewish relief aid, 1732

Memorials and monuments (*cont.*)
Yizkor books, 895, 1694–1695
see also Museums and memorial
institutes
Memorial for the Unknown Jewish
Martyr (France), 392
Menczer, Aron, **971**, 1569, 1707
Mendel, Max, 645
Mendelsohn, Sh!omo, 273
Mendelssohn, Moses, 196
Mengele, Josef, 111, 391, 464, 650,
964, **971–972**, 1018, 1131
U.S. investigation of, 1083
Mennecke, Friedrich, 1128
Mentally ill. *See* Euthanasia Plan
Menten, Pieter, 1512
Merchants' Association (Bulgaria),
266
Merder fun Felker (Ehrenburg), 218,
425
Merin, Chaim, 973
Merin, Moshe, 767, **972–974**, 1160,
1352–1353, 1354–1355, 1378–
1379
Merkaz la-Gola. *See* Diaspora Center
(Italy)
Merlin, Samuel, 190
Mersik, Zvi, 212, 1456
Merton, Maximilian, 613, 1326
Merzdorf, 624
Meserlitz-Oberwald, Euthanasia
Program, 453
Meshulam, Viktor, 1719 *ill.*
Messerschmitt Aircraft Company,
1038
Mestrović, Ivan, 96
Metaxas, Ioannis, 610, 1325
Meyer, Alfred, 1592
Meyer, Eduard, 1054
Meyer-Hetling, Konrad, 550, 551, 552
Meyerhof, Otto, 862
Meyerhoff, Harvey M., 1551
Meyerson, Golda. *See* Meir, Golda
(Meyerson)
Meytes, Eliyahu, 893
Michael I, King (Romania), 74, 75,
1290, 1293
Michalcze, 599
Michalovce, 1366
Michels, Robert, 475, 476
Middle East. *See* Arab-Israeli conflict;
Palestine; specific country names
Midway, Battle of (1942), 1673
Miechowice. *See* Miechowitz
Miechowitz, forced labor, 1094
Mihaiescu, Ioan, 1563
Mihăileni, 400, 401
Mihajlović, Draža, 288 – 289
Mikališkes, 1574
Mikashevichi, 847
Mikhoels, Shlomo, 743, 744, 745,
1388–1389
Mikołajczyk, Stanisław, **974**, 1153,
1154, 1177

Mikula Konishchuk partisan group,
1119
Milaković, Branko, 1327
Milan
deportations of Jews, 727
documentation center, **393**
Milbertshausen, 1001
Milch, Erhard, 8, 1503
Mildenstein, Leopold von, 1338
Milijekowski, Joseph, 1606
Military. *See* Army; Partisans;
Resistance; World War II
Military Works (Tito), 1469
Milkhome (Markish), 893
Milkhome Tsayt (Gordon), 894
Miller, Arthur, 888, 889
Milorg (Norwegian underground
army), 1067
Milos (ship), 29, 943
Milosz, Czesław, 884
Miloszyce, 624, 1094
Mi-Ma'amakim (publication), 799,
800, 1349
Mineralnye Vody, gas vans, 543–544
Minkowski, Eugène, 1081, 1426
Minsk, **974–978**
deportations from, 1123, 1377,
1378
deportations to, 131, 201, 230, 529,
572, 645, 1186, 1569
Einsatzgruppe B in, 438
Euthanasia Program, 453
family camps in forests, **467–469**
gas vans, 543
German occupation, 1669, 1670
ghetto, 579, 581, 582, 1244
ghetto resistance, 767, 1267
Jewish leadership, 1021–1022
Jewish population, 172–173, 174
Judenrat, 767
massacre of Jews, 173, 940
Nazi administration, 843
partisans, 1113, 1115, 1270, 1703,
1740
Reichskommissariat Ostland,
1243–1245
underground, 975, 976–977
Mińsk Mazowiecki, 619, **978–979**,
1271
Mintz, Binyamin, 756
Mintz, Lipek, 973
Mir, **979–980**
ghetto uprising, 1270, 1673
Jewish refugees in Shanghai, 1346
partisans, 1115
rabbinic scholars' escape via East
Asia, 1263–1265, 1557
underground, 1311
Mira, Gola, 832
Miranda de Ebro camp, 1391, 1392
Miravek, Augustin, 1368
Mirbeth, Josef, 32
Mire, Gola, 652
Miriam, Rivka, 883

Mir Lebn (Rabin), 894
Mirovshchina, 783
Mir Yeshiva, 779, 1557
Mischlinge, 48–49, 51, 53, 69, 428,
574, 912, 913, 965, **981–983**,
1216, 1501, 1503
Gypsies, 635, 636, 638
Heydrich's plan for, 1593
Netherlands, 1047
Miskolc, **983–984**
Mit brennender Sorge (papal
encyclical), 292, 1136
Mitn Punim tsu der Zun (Spiegel),
1397
Mitrani, Michel, 487
Mitteilungen an den Adel (Plessen),
881
Mitteilungsblatt (journal), 1644
Mittelbau. *See* Dora-Mittelbau
Mittelsteine, 625
Mittelstelle für Jüdische
Erwachsenenbildung, 563, **984**,
1247
Mittelwerk, 1096
Mittleman, Yaakov, 1090
Mixed Board for War Criminals,
1498–1499
Mixed marriages. *See* Intermarriage
Mizoch, massacre, 1528 *ill.*
Mizrachi (religious Zionist
movement), 43, 196
Mizrahi, Moshe, 487
Mizraḥi. *See* American Zionist
Emergency Council
MJS. *See* Mouvement de la Jeunesse
Sioniste (France)
Mlotek, Chana Gorden, 893
Mobile killing units. *See*
Einsatzgruppen
Moczarski, Kazimierz, 1417
Model Childhood, A (Wolf), 880
Modrzejów, 1355
Moeller van den Bruck, Arthur,
1464
Moeser, Hans Karl, 400
Mogilev, 172, 174, **985**
Einsatzgruppe B in, 438
Euthanasia Program, 453
massacre of Jews, 173
partisans, 1113, 1115
transit camp, 173–174
Mogilev-Podolski, **985–987**
Mohammed al-Mounsaf, Bey Sidi,
1521
Moja walka o życie (Nowakowska),
885
Molczadski, Chaim, 158, 973
Moldavia
deportations to Transnistria, 1474–
1475
Romanian pogroms, 1295
see also Bessarabia
Möllhausen, Eitel Friedrich, 1301
Molodowsky, Kadia, 893

ORT (Organization for Rehabilitation through Training), 105, 203, 379, 383, 1105, 1614
Orthodox churches, aid to Jews, 105, 271, 454, 614, 616
Orthodox Jews. *See* Judaism; specific organizations
Orthodox Nepasztal (Hungary), 806
Orthodox Rabbis, Rescue Committee of United States. *See* Va'ad ha-Hatsala
Ortiz, Roberto M., 81
Osenbashli, Ahmed, 706
OSE. *See* Oeuvre de Secours aux Enfants (France)
Osherowitz, Hirsh, 893
Oshmiany, 556, 1574
Oshry, Efraim, 799, 800
OSI. *See* Office of Special Investigations (U.S.)
Osijek, 323, 327, 328
Osijek Bjelovar, Jewish population, 1718
Oslo, 1068
Osmancea, 305
Osobka-Morawski, Edward, 1153
OSS. *See* Office of Strategic Services (U.S.)
Ostara (publication), 1214
Ostashkov, 790
Ostbahn. *See* Railways
Ostbataillone, 660, 706, **1098–1099**
Ostdeutsch Landbewirtschaftungs, 649
Oster, Hans, 4, 5, 278, 1043
Österreicher, Erich, 1706
Osti. *See* Ostindustrie GmbH
Ostindustrie GmbH, **1099**, 1403, 1480, 1502
Ostland. *See* Reichskommissariat Ostland
Ostlegionen. *See* Ostbataillone
Ostrava, 228
Ostrog, 1529
Ostrowiec-Świętokrzyski, escapes, 1271, 1516
Ostrowski, Bernard, 909
Oswald, Josef. *See* Rufajzen, Oswald
Oswego, N.Y. *See* Fort Ontario
Oświęcim (town), 1352, 1353
    Jewish leadership, 972
    see also Auschwitz
Oszmiana. *See* Oshmiany
Other Victims: Non-Jews Persecuted and Murdered by the Nazis (conference; 1987), 1551
Otter, Baron Göran von, 575
Otto, Helmuth, 1598
Otwinowski, Stefan, 884
OUN. *See* Orhanizatsyia Ukrainskykh Natsionalistiv
OUN "B," 1097
OUN "M," 1097
OUN-Melnyk, 969

OUN-R. *See* Revolutionary OUN (Ukraine)
Our Partisan Course (Kovpak), 828
Our Struggle (Slovakia). *See* Nas Boj
Ovadia, Estreja, 933 *ill.*
Overduijn, Leendert, **1100**
Oyg af Oyg (Vergelis), 893
OZE. *See* Oeuvre de Secours aux Enfants
Ozech, Maurycy, 1615
Oziewicz, Ignacy, 1031, 1032

P

Pa'amonium ve-Rakavot (Amichai), 882
Paape, Harry, 394
Pacelli, Eugene. *See* Pius XII
Pachtmann, Eduard, 128–129
Pacific (ship), 29, 943
PAC. *See* President's Advisory Committee on Political Refugees (U.S.)
Padenie Parizha (Ehrenburg), 425
Paderewski, Ignacy, 1177
Pag, 325, 326
Paget, Reginald Thomas, 941
Pagis, Dan, 883
Painted Bird, The (Kosinski), 889
Paksy-Kiss, Tibor, 1477
Pakula, Alan, 488
Palairet, Sir Michael, 456
Palästina-Amt (ZVfD), 1736–1737, 1738
Palatinate, 571, 573, 630
Palemonas, 826, 1118
Pale of Settlement (Russia), 68–69, 170, 1383, 1525
Palestine
    American Jewish Assembly homeland resolution, 36
    Arab leadership, 703–707
    Arab riots (1936, 1939), 716
    Austrian Jewish immigration, 128–131, 1567
    Balkan Jewish immigration plans, 1232
    Biltmore Resolution (1942), 40, 181, **216–217**
    Bulgarian immigration, 271
    Czech immigration, 228
    Danzig immigration, 346–347
    displaced persons, 377–378, 385–386
    Eichmann and forced Jewish emigration to, 426, 427
    emissaries to Cyprus detention camps, 332
    Haavara agreement, **639–640**
    Hungarian immigration, 689–690, 925
    immigration policies, 1641

    Jewish Brigade Group, 80, 168, 193, **745–747**
    Jewish-German exchanges, **457–459**
    Jewish leadership, 626–627
    Jewish prisoners of war, **1191–1192**
    Joint Distribution Committee aid, 1335
    Joint Rescue Committee, **756–757**
    Lithuanian ex-partisans, 819, 823–824
    musical activities, 1022
    parachutists, 146, 182, 1249–1250, 1344, 1370, 1372, 1447–1448, 1693, 1715, 1716
    partition, 217, 300, 1197, 1356
    Rescue Committee of the Jewish Agency in Turkey, **1259–1262**
    "Tehran Children," **1454–1455**
    underground, 1687
    World War II impact on, 1687–1688
    Yishuv (Jewish community), 180, 182, **1686–1694**
    Youth Aliya immigration movement, **1695–1696**
    Yugoslav immigration, 136–137, 138
    see also Aliya Bet; Arab-Israeli conflict; Bergson Group; Haavara agreement; Hagana; Homeland, Jewish; Israel, state of; Jewish Agency; Refugees; White Paper, British; Yishuv; Zionist movement; specific kibbutz and organization names
Palestine Symphony Orchestra. *See* Israeli Philharmonic Orchestra
Palfinger, Alexander, 1611
Palgi, Yoel, 1104
Palmah
    and Cyprus detention camps, 332
    Jewish parachutists, 1103, 1250
Palmiry Forest, 1, 1599
Palmnicken, 352
Palombo, David, 1684
Palten, Günther, 577
PALTREU (Palaestina Treuhandstelle zur Beratung Deutscher Juden), 639–640
Palyam (Hagana naval arm), 29
Pamiętnik Justyny (Draenger), 885
Pamiętnik z getta łódzkiego (Poznanski), 884
Pan American Conference (1938), 82–83
Pancke, Günther, 1224
Pan Crescent (ship), 30
Paneth, Jacob Elimelech, 356
Panike, Kurt, 1559
Pankiewicz, Tadeusz, 885
Pankok, Otto, 96

Pontremoli, Giuseppe, 1027
Popczuk, Michael, 1084
Popescu, Dumitru, 1291
Popescu, Ion, 1291
Popes. *See* Vatican; specific names
Popov, Ivan Vladimir, 268
Popovici, Traian, 287
Popper-Lynkeus, Josef, 1564
Popular Greek Liberation Army. *See* Ellenikos Laikos Apelethoritkos Stratos (Greece)
Popular Polish Army, 1154
Porat, Dina, 671
Port-de-Bouc, 460
Port Lyautey, 994
Portney, Jekuthiel, 273
Portugal
    consular aid to Jews, 1280, **1381–1382**
    HICEM, **657–658**
    Jewish refugees in, 34, 259, 1239, 1381–1382
Post, Johannes, 401
Potok, 1287
Potopaenu, Gheorghe, 1291
Potsdam Agreement (1945), 359, 464, 1154
Povski Bazarchik, 596
Povurski partisan group, 1119
POWs. *See* Prisoners of war
Pozdunski, Moshe, 374
Pożegnanie z Marią (Borowski), 885
Poznań (Posen), 196, 433, 617, 648–649, 682, 800, 811, 1633
Poznański, Jakub, 373, 884
Pozsony. *See* Bratislava
PPR. *See* Polish Workers' Party
Pracovná Skupina (Slovakia), 121, 241, 495–496, 770, 787, 815, 935, 1174, **1183–1185**, 1250, 1251, 1368, 1369–1370, 1555, 1556
    Europa Plan, **450–451**, 953, 1656, 1691
    leadership, 1639–1641
Prady. *See* Brawde
Prague, **1185–1187**
    deportation of Jews, 229–230
    emigration, 227, 426
    Judaica collection, 230
Prauss, Artur, 242–243
Prawda nieartystyczna (Grynberg), 886
Preiļi, 410
President Garfield (ship). *See Exodus 1947* (ship)
President's Advisory Committee on Political Refugees (U.S.), 955, 990, 1065, **1187–1188**, 1303
President's Commission on the Holocaust. *See* Holocaust Memorial Council, U.S.
Press
    Belgian Jewish underground, 167, 250–251
    displaced persons', 383

German antisemitic, 84, 1415, 1420–1421
German Jewish, 200, 282, 563, 566, 569, 574, 1088
Greek antisemitic, 1325
Lithuanian Jewish underground, 1349
Nazi party, 999
Polish, 1032, 1457, 1599
Polish ghetto underground, 403, 1166, 1267, 1615, 1617, 1724
Soviet Yiddish-language newspaper, 464–465
U.S. coverage of Holocaust, **41–42**
Viennese Jewish, 1566
Warsaw ghetto underground, 1615, 1617
Yiddish underground, 891, 892
youth movement, 402, 403
Zionist, 199, 254, 1644, 1736
Pressburg. *See* Bratislava
Pressburger, Alexander, 1343
Presser, Jacob, 1056
Pretzsch, 220, 435–436
Preuss, Hugo, 559
Preuss, Lawrence, 1542
Preussischer Landsverband Jüdischer Gemeinden, 196, 447
Préveza, 614
Preysing, Konrad von, 1137
Preziosi, Giovanni, 1216
Prill, G., 623
Primo de Rivera, José Antonio, 477, 1395
Prints Ruveni (Bergelson), 894
Prisoner orderlies. *See Kapos*
Prisoners. *See* Concentration camps; Extermination camps; Forced labor; Internment camps; Political prisoners; Prisoners of war
Prisoners of war, **1188–1195**
    Allied, British war crimes trial on treatment of, 1497
    British, 433
    camp uprisings, 1270–1271
    Einsatzgruppen treatment of, 438–439
    as forced labor in Germany, 497–498
    French, escapees in Slovak national uprising, 1371
    international agreements on treatment of, 1228–1229
    Japanese treatment of, 1673
    Nazis' policies for, 671–1672
    Polish, Katyn massacre, 790–791
Prisoners of war, Jewish, **1188–1192**
    in Allied armies, **1188–1189**
    card index of, 397
    death march, 350
    escapes by, 3, 14, 1121
    Lublin-Lipowa massacre, 370, 919–920
    Nazi treatment of Soviet, 1189, **1190–1191**, 1241

Palestinian, **1191–1192**
war crimes case, 1502
Prisoners of war, Soviet
572, **1192–1195**, 1231 *ill.*
    in Aktion Reinhard extermination program, 15
    cremation by Germans, 13
    death marches, 350
    deportations to Chełmno, 286
    in extermination camps, 174–175, 462, 463
    gassings, 461, 540, 542
    German collaboration, 1098–1099, 1578–1580
    Hilfswillige, 659–660
    in Klooga camp, 806, 807
    Komissarbefehl (Nazi massacre policy), 311, 312, 342, 795, **814**, 1189, **1190–1191**, 1194, 1386, 1671, 1688–1689
    in Majdanek, 939
    in Mauthausen, 946, 950
    in Neuengamme, 1057
    Operation Zeppelin, 1330, 1331
    partisans, 411–412
    Pawiak Prison, 1123
    Poniatowa camp, **1181–1183**
    sabotage by, 314
    in Sachsenhausen, 1321
    Sobibór uprising, **1123–1124**, 1377–1378
    Treblinka gas chamber operations, 1483
Prisons. *See* Montelupich Prison; Pawiak Prison
Program for Living Space (Germany). *See Lebensraum*
Program for World Conquest by the Jews (Krushevan), 1198
Propaganda, Jewish Antifascist Committee, 743–745
Propaganda, Nazi, **1195–1196**, 1415, 1420–1421
    antisemitic films, **484–484**, 1570
    antisemitic political, 561
    antisemitic signs and posters, 564–565 *ill.*
    anti-Soviet, 1580
    for Euthanasia Program, 1128
    French antisemitism promotion, 714–715
    for German youth, 679
    Goebbels's role, 591–592
    in Great Britain, 761–762
    in Hungary, 701
    SA, 1319, 1320
    Sprachregelung, **1398–1399**
    in Syria-Lebanon, 1444, 1445
    Theresienstadt as model Jewish community, 1463
    war crimes case, 1502
Propaganda, Zionist, on plight of European Jews, 190–191
Pro Patria partisan battalion, 1118
Property confiscation

Q

Quakers. *See* American Friends Service Committee; Society of Friends
Quisling, Vidkun, 1066, 1068, **1203–1204**, 1513

R

Rab, **1205–1206**, 1721
  Jewish battalion, 327 *ill.*
Rabat, 993, 994, 995
Rabbis' Plan. *See* Europa Plan
Rabin, Iosif, 894
Rabinowicz, Adolph, 1104
Rabka, 831
Race and Resettlement Main Office (Germany). *See* Rasse- und Siedlungshauptamt
Rachkovski, Pyotr Ivanovich, 1198
Racial hygiene. *See* Eugenics
Racibórz. *See* Ratibor
Racism, **1206–1217**
  Anne Frank Foundation to counter, 524
  Arierparagraph, 83
  as basis for antisemitism, 62–63, 65, 69–72, 282–283, 560, 563
  as basis for Nazi legislation, 861, 1419
  "blood and soil" ideology, 348
  as core of Nazism, 391–392, 572, 1040, 1304
  and crimes against humanity, 322
  fascism and, 132
  in Fascist Italy, 724
  Führerprinzip, 534
  Generalplan Ost application, 551–553
  genocide, **553–554**
  Himmler's policies, 661
  Hitler's theories, 676
  Lebensraum policy, **857–858**
  Mischlinge issue, **981–983**
  Nazi forced-labor policy, 499
  in Nazi legal system, 854–856
  and Nazi medical views, 958–959, 964–966, 1127–1132
  Nazi occupation policies, 1671
  Nazi office for racial matters, 1223–1224
  Nazi population resettlement program, 1243
  Nazi propaganda to promote, 1196
  in Nazi scientific thought, 861
  Nazi theories, 31, **48–51**
  in Nazi World War II policy, 1661
  Nuremberg Laws, 567, 589, 676, 912–913, 1076–1077
  papal denunciation of Nazism, 568, 1136

SS ideology, 1401, 1402
  sterilization program, **965–966**
  studies of Nazi, 811
  Subsequent Nuremberg Proceedings on issue, 1501–1503
  in United States, 57–58
  Warthegau regulations, 1633–1635
Raczkiewicz, Władysław, 1146, 1177, 1178, 1749
Raczymov, Henri, 879
Raczynski, Stefan, 829 *ill.*
Rada Główna Opiekuńcza (Poland), 140, 940, **1217–1218**
Rada Pomocy Żydom (Poland). *See* Zegota
Rădăuţi, 400, 401
Radechov, 248
Rademacher, Franz, 922, 936, **1218–1219**, 1342, 1459, 1592
Radin, rabbinic scholars' escape via East Asia, 1263–1265, 1557
Radio Bruxelles, 164
Radnoti, Miklós, 351
Radogoszcz Prison, 901, 902
Radok, Alfred, 485
Radom, **1219–1221**
  Aktion Reinhard extermination policies, 14–18
  Bund members' arrest in, 273
  deportations, 623–624, 1159, 1485
  forced-labor camps, 1171
  as Generalgouvernement district, **549–550**
  ghetto, 580, 1162
  HASAG forced labor, 646, 647
  Jewish partisan units, 1121
  Judenrat in, 1160
  Majdanek satellite camps, 939
  SS leadership, 793
  Zegota relief aid, 1730–1731
Radomir, 612
Radtke, A., 623
Raeder, Erich, 936, 1203, 1490, 1638 *ill.*
Raffelsberger, Walter, 128
Ragauskas-Butenas, Z., 1116
Ragovski, Zerakh. *See* Ragauskas-Butenas, Z.
Rahm, Karl, 1460
Railways, **1221–1223**
  Belgian-Jewish underground attack on, 167
  to Bełżec, 174, 175, 177–178
  to Chełmno, 284
  for deportations, 367–368, 1658
  as extermination camp transport, 15, 16–17, 109, 113–114
  forced-labor camps adjoining, 1094
  Iaşi Jews' suffocation, 710 *ill.*, 711
  Nazi administration, 538–539
  to Sobibór, 1376–1377
  Soviet prisoner-of-war transport conditions, 1193
  to Treblinka, 1482, 1484

Treblinka monument, 1018 *ill.*
  war crimes prosecution efforts, 1509
  Warsaw deportations, 1532, 1618
Rajsko, forced-labor camp, 109
Rákosi partisan brigade, 700
Rakow Forest, 1133
Rakvere, 449
Rallies, Nazi. *See Parteitage*
Rallis, Ioannis, 105, 612, 614
Rangell, Johann Wilhelm, 494
Ransoms. *See* "Blood for goods" plan (Hungary); Europa Plan
Rapaport, Nathan, 96, 1624–1625, 1631 *ill.*, 1684
Rape of Poland: Pattern of Soviet Aggression, The (Mikołajczyk), 974
Rapoport, David, 32, 1107
Rapp, Nahman, 893
Rascani, 942–943
Rasch, Emil Otto, 133, 436, **1223**
Rascher, Sigmund, 8, 342, 960, 962 *ill.*, 963, 966, 1131
Rashid Ali al-Gaylani. *See* Gaylani, Rashid Ali al-
Rasse- und Siedlungshauptamt, **1223–1224**, 1401
  leaders at Wannsee Conference, 1592
  war crimes trial, 1502
Rassinier, Paul, 684, 685
Ratajski, Cyril, 357
Rath, Ernst vom, 86, 528, 569, 628, 676, 836, 837, 838, 1024
Rathbone, Eleanor, 1548
Rathenau, Walther, 66, 559, **1224–1225**
Rathorn, prisoner-of-war camp, 1189
Ratibor, forced labor, 1094
Rations, ghetto, **583–584**
Ratnitsi Napreduka na Bulgarshtinata, 265
Ratzel, Friedrich, 857
Rauff, Walther, 541, 1018, **1225**, 1522
Rausch, Günther, 596
Rauschning, Hermann, 345, 617, 1199, **1225–1226**
Rauter, Hans Albin, 1046, 1048, 1049, 1052, 1054, 1056
Raveh, Yitzhak, 430
Ravensbrück, 8, 337, 650, **1226–1227**
  death march, 353
  establishment of, 310, 315
  forced labor, 370
  French Catholics in, 1363
  gas chambers, 541
  Gypsies in, 637
  Jewish-German exchange, 459
  Jews in, 163, 202, 725, 728
  Lidice women in, 871–872
  medical experiments, 960
  resistance movement prisoners, 1031
  sterilization experiments, 302, 965